UNDERSTANDING
CHILDREN

SECOND EDITION

UNDERSTANDING CHILDREN

JUDITH A. SCHICKEDANZ

Boston University

DAVID I. SCHICKEDANZ

*Greater Lawrence
Mental Health Center,
Lawrence, Massachusetts*

KAREN HANSEN

Bethesda, Maryland

PEGGY D. FORSYTH

*The Millersville University
of Pennsylvania*

MAYFIELD PUBLISHING COMPANY

Mountain View, California

London • Toronto

Library of Congress Cataloging-in-Publication Data

Understanding children / Judith A. Schickedanz . . . [et al.].
    p.   cm.
   Rev. ed. of: Understanding children / Judith A. Schickedanz, Karen
Hansen, Peggy D. Forsyth.
   Includes bibliographical references and index.
   ISBN 1-55934-171-8
   1. Child development. 2. Child psychology. 3. Adolescence.
I. Schickedanz, Judith A. II. Schickedanz, Judith A.,
Understanding children.
HQ767.9.U53   1992   92-26573
305.23′1—dc20   CIP

Infants and Toddlers
   ISBN 1-55934-244-7
Infancy through Preschool
   ISBN 1-55934-245-5
Infancy through School-Age
   ISBN 1-55934-246-3
School-Age through Adolescence
   ISBN 1-55934-247-1

Manufactured in the United States of America
10 9 8 7 6 5 4

Mayfield Publishing Company
1240 Villa Street
Mountain View, California 94041

Sponsoring editor, Franklin C. Graham; developmental editor, Kathleen Engelberg;
managing editor, Linda Toy; manuscript editor, Loralee Windsor; art director, Jeanne
M. Schreiber; text and cover designer, Anna George; cover art, Pablo Picasso, "Claude
Drawing," Oil on canvas, 1955. ARS N.Y./SPADEM; illustrators, Robin Mouat, Natalie
Hill, GTS; photo researcher, Melissa Kreischer; manufacturing manager, Martha Branch.
The text was set in 10/12 Palatino by Graphic Typesetting Service and printed on 45#
Somerset Glare Free Gloss by R. R. Donnelley & Sons.

Text and photo credits appear on a continuation of the copyright page, p. 672.

BRIEF CONTENTS

CONTENTS

p a r t   t w o

INFANTS AND TODDLERS

4   The Neonate

part   five

ADOLESCENTS   **561**

FOCUS BOXES

PREFACE

Like many other authors, I undertook the job of writing a textbook because I couldn't find a book that satisfied all my teaching needs. In some child development books, the organization or selection of topics didn't match my approach. In others, the writing wasn't as clear or interesting as I thought it should be. In still others, the view of children seemed too fragmented and remote, making it difficult for the student to see children as whole human beings. To make these books work for me and my students, I had to modify the organization or coverage to achieve the necessary coherence, or provide additional illustrations and examples to make the material come to life, or compensate for the fragmented impression the book conveyed. At last I resolved to write a book myself, one that would solve the teaching problems I had encountered over the years. The result was the first edition of *Understanding Children*. The success of the first edition suggests that the book addressed the needs of many teachers like myself. The second edition was written to continue to fulfill those same needs.

AIMS

The aims of the second edition of *Understanding Children* remain fundamentally the same as those of the first. One of my primary aims has been to present a balance of research findings, theory, and applications and to integrate these aspects of the study of child development. *Understanding Children* is designed primarily for students who will be living and working with children as teachers, parents, child care providers, nurses, counselors, administrators of children's programs, and practitioners in a variety of other settings. These students need to have comprehensive, accurate, up-to-date information about child development, but they also need to know the uses and implications of this information. Thus, the emphasis throughout is on the working applications of expert knowledge.

I also wanted to present information in an accessible, appealing way. *Understanding Children* is written in a friendly style that invites students to read, learn, and remember. Each chapter and most major topics are introduced with a vignette in which the essence of the information or issue about to be presented is captured in a real-life situation involving children and adults. Additionally, each of the first two chapters—Chapter 1, Methods of Studying Children, and Chapter 2, Theories of Child Development—is organized around a specific, practical problem that gives the material immediacy and relevance.

Perhaps my most important goal in writing *Understanding Children* has been to convey the unique world view of children. I've tried to make clear that children are not miniature adults but individuals with their own ways of thinking and of seeing the world. This important premise is emphasized in the introduction to the book, entitled Prologue: Why Study Children? I hope instructors will encourage students to read this introduction to gain a preliminary orientation to the book.

ORGANIZATION AND CONTENT

Students should be able to see children not as fragmented objects of scientific study but as whole human beings. The best way to convey this sense of wholeness, in my experience, is to present information about all aspects of development in each successive stage of childhood. Therefore, *Understanding Children* is organized chronologically, introducing students to children as they grow, learn, and change, from earliest infancy to the threshold of adulthood. The book begins with the foundations for the study of child development (Part One)—research methods, theories of child development, and the biology of genetics, prenatal development, and birth. The remaining parts of the book cover four chronological age-stages. Part Two addresses the development of the child between birth and age 3—infancy and toddlerhood. Parts Three, Four, and Five cover the development of the preschool child (aged 3 to 6), the school-age child (aged 6 to 12), and the adolescent (aged 13 to 19), respectively.

Within this chronological framework, material on the different domains of development is presented topically. Parts Two through Five contain four chapters each, covering physical development, cognitive development, language development, and social and emotional development. Each part ends with an applications section called Knowledge in Action, a feature unique to this book. This format—four chapters plus Knowledge in Action—provides a clear and consistent organizational scheme for each part.

Understanding Children provides comprehensive, in-depth coverage of a range of topics and issues in child development, always with an emphasis on the practical uses of knowledge. Many topics discussed in the first edition continue to receive thorough coverage in the second edition. Included are such topics as the role of values in the study of children; the effects of prenatal exposure to alcohol, cocaine, and other teratogens on the developing fetus; advances in prenatal assessment tools and the latest treatments for infertility; theories of infant and maternal attachment; sex-typing in infancy and childhood; the development of metacognitive abilities in school-age children; socialization processes and the learning of prosocial behavior; psychological effects of early and late maturing on adolescent girls and boys; cultural bias in intelligence testing; and many, many more.

SPECIAL FEATURES

The special features that distinguished the first edition of *Understanding Children* from other textbooks have proven very successful and have been retained in this edition. Primary among them are the Knowledge in Action sections at the ends of Parts Two through Five. Although all chapters integrate theory and practice, these sections put very practical material relating to the care and education of children at the disposal of instructors, but without the suggestion that they *must* use it. Knowledge in Action sections provide information on such topics as the varieties of preschool, after-school, and day care programs; methods of assessing children; ways to ensure children's health and safety; and the kinds of activities and playthings that are appropriate for children of different ages.

Separate chapters on language development in every age-stage (Parts Two through Five) highlight this important area in child development. Typically, child development books include language development in their chapters on cognitive development, or, if they do treat language separately, they treat only the acquisition of language in early childhood. *Understanding Children* contains separate chapters on language in every age-stage, providing comprehensive coverage of the development of both oral and written language in childhood and adolescence. Topics covered include toddlers' strategies for opening conversations; emergent literacy in preschoolers and ways to support it; approaches to teaching reading, including the whole language approach; teaching children whose first language is not English; and current thinking on dyslexia.

A separate chapter on the neonate at the beginning of Part Two reflects the wealth of information and research findings available on this earliest period of adjustment in the child's life. Included are discussions of the effects of obstetrical drugs on newborns, learning in young infants, carrying as a method of soothing babies, and learning to live with the newborn.

Focus boxes throughout the text highlight current topics and issues in five different areas—research, health, safety, public policy, and special education—and add depth to discussions without interrupting the ongoing narrative. A few titles will suggest the range of topics covered: Social Referencing in Infants; How Does Day Care Affect Parent-Child Attachment?; Making Playgrounds Safe; Young Gifted Children; Does Early Antisocial Behavior Fade Away?; Children and AIDS; Dangers of Anabolic Steroids; and Consequences of Teenage Pregnancy.

CHANGES TO THIS EDITION

For this edition, the entire book has been carefully reviewed, revised, and updated. We have incorporated the latest research on important topics, new information on emerging issues, and material reflecting current thinking in the field. A brief summary will give a sense of these changes.

The second edition of *Understanding Children* makes greater use of the systems approach as a way of organizing and integrating the complex processes involved in child development. The systems approach is explained in Chapter 2, Theories of Child Development, and used as a framework for discussing numerous topics throughout the book.

This focus on systems leads to a greater emphasis on the interconnections among different developmental domains and on the bidirectional relations between the individual and the many contexts of development. The role of these dynamic interactions is explored in such areas as language learning, attachment formation, socialization, identity formation, self-esteem, self-control, perceived competence and self-efficacy, aggressiveness, and moral behavior.

In response to requests from users and reviewers of the first edition, the second edition includes more detailed discussions of Erikson's conceptualizations for each age-stage as well as a refocusing of the concepts of Piaget. Additionally, links among theories are explored as a way to help the student see broad patterns and acquire an integrated view of child development.

Also in response to users' and reviewers' suggestions, new material on child abuse has been added to the second edition. The Infant-Toddler Knowledge in Action section now contains a Safety Focus box on child abuse and neglect, and the Preschool Knowledge in Action section contains a discussion of child sexual abuse.

Many other topics have received new or expanded coverage, including the following:

- social cognitive theory
- early cognitive development and its relationship to reaching, grasping, and other forms of early motor development
- infant temperament and its role in the attachment relationship
- children's theory of mind
- metacognitive abilities
- Sternberg's triarchic theory of intelligence
- the heritability of intelligence
- academic achievement and school success from a systems perspective
- math achievement in American, Japanese, and Chinese children
- children's perceived competence and self-efficacy beliefs and the role of these beliefs in social and cognitive development
- the relationship between moral development and moral behavior, with an emphasis on social control and self-control
- class and racial variations in gender socialization in American society
- adolescent identity
- parenting styles and children's behavior
- adolescents' theory of mind
- adolescent suicide
- what schools can do about gangs

In this edition, two chapters have been refocused. Chapter 1, Methods of Studying Children, has been reorganized to give greater clarity to the discussion of methods. The chapter now describes three major research issues, four research methods, and three developmental research designs. Chapter 12, Social and Emotional Development in Preschool Children, has been reorganized to emphasize social learning theory and socialization processes rather than behavioral learning theory processes.

The one-page charts of developmental milestones for each age-stage that appeared at the end of the Knowledge in Action sections in the first edition have been moved to the beginning of those sections in this edition. Here, students can use them as summaries of achievements in the four developmental domains before they consider the working applications of that knowledge. Additionally, the Research Focus box on divorce and children has been moved from Chapter 20, Social and Emotional Development in Adolescents, to Chapter 12, Social and Emotional Development in Preschool Children, so that the topic can be considered for younger as well as older children.

In addition to these changes in the text, the photo program has been completely reviewed and revised. We have retained the best photographs from the first edition and added many new ones, almost all of them in color. The photos in *Understanding Children* not only provide beautiful and dramatic images of childhood but also reflect the growing diversity of American society.

LEARNING AIDS

The learning aids incorporated in the first edition of *Understanding Children* have proven useful in helping students understand, organize, and remember material, and we have therefore retained them in the second edition.

- Each chapter begins with a vignette that shows how a principle or issue discussed in the chapter translates into children's words, behavior, or beliefs. The vignette is followed by a brief introduction outlining the topics covered in the chapter.
- Key terms appear in bold type throughut each chapter and are carefully defined in context. The terms are listed at the end of the chapter for review and are included along with their definitions in a comprehensive glossary at the end of the book.
- Two different kinds of summaries appear at the end of each chapter. One is a brief overview of the chapter, drawn in broad strokes and making connections backward and forward in the child's life. The other is a longer chapter review, outlining the main points of the chapter.
- Annotated Suggestions for Further Reading also appear at the end of every chapter, extending the boundaries of the material for the student. Several new titles have been added to these listings for the second edition.
- Each part opens with an overview and includes a chart of developmental milestones for that age-stage.
- Numerous tables, charts, drawings, and photographs provide graphic illustration of the principles of child development. The captions inform and teach rather than simply label or identify.

ANCILLARY PACKAGE

A complete package of supplemental support material is available with *Understanding Children* to enhance both teaching and learning and to facilitate the application of knowledge to practical situations. The **Instructor's Manual** includes learning objectives, chapter summaries, key terms, suggestions for lecture topics, and demonstration projects. It also lists sources for free or inexpensive materials, additional reference resources, and films and videos. A new test bank, described below, appears in printed form in the Instructor's Manual.

Two exceptional sets of **videos** are available to adopters of *Understanding Children,* both from highly praised television series. The first set includes six half-hour segments from the Annenberg/CPB series *Discovering Psychology,* narrated by Philip Zimbardo. The second set contains segments from the University of Michigan/WQED-Pittsburgh series *Seasons of Life.* Each segment from these two outstanding series contains footage from classic experiments, interviews with key researchers, and discussions of current concepts and issues in child development. A description of each program, keyed to the textbook, is included in the Instructor's Manual.

Instructors may wish to have their students use the ***Study Guide to Accompany Understanding Children,*** available optionally with the textbook or packaged with the textbook at an additional discount. It includes learning objectives, chapter outlines, and chapter summaries as well as student projects and practice tests. Each practice test has multiple choice, true/false, matching, and short answer questions.

The second edition of *Understanding Children* is accompanied by an entirely new **test bank.** The multiple choice items were developed at the University of Florida Educational Foundations Program under the direction of Dr. David Miller and Tammie Meninger. The remaining questions were provided by the senior authors of the text, David Schickedanz and myself.

The easy-to-use Brownstone test generation system provides all test items on computer disk for IBM-compatible and Apple computers. For the first time, a version is also available for the Macintosh. Instructors can select, add, or edit questions, randomize test sets, and print tests for individual classes. Also included in the system is the "gradebook," which enables the instructor to keep detailed performance records for individual students and for the class as a whole; maintain student averages; graph each student's progress; and set the desired grade distribution, maximum score, and weight for every test.

A set of 51 overhead **transparencies** provides supplementary information that is not found in the text or that has been modified for lecture and discussion purposes.

ACKNOWLEDGMENTS

Many people have contributed to the development of the second edition of *Understanding Children.* Foremost among these are my coauthors and especially David Schickedanz, who joined the team for this edition.

I'm very grateful to the child development experts who gave such detailed critiques and offered so many useful suggestions in their reviews of the manuscript. The names of these academic reviewers are listed separately following this preface. The entire project has been greatly enriched by their suggestions, although any flaws or errors in the book are the responsibility of the authors.

Special thanks are due to the staff of Mayfield Publishing Company. Frank Graham, the sponsoring editor, showed great patience as we put together a new edition. He was always willing to consider new ideas and find ways to make them work. Kate Engelberg, the developmental editor, also deserves special thanks. She brought a quality of writing to the text that I could never have achieved alone. Linda Toy, production director, kept everything moving along on schedule with her expert managerial skills. She led the production team that created this beautiful book.

Finally, I once again owe a very big debt of gratitude to my family—David, my husband and coauthor, and Adam, my son.

Judith A. Schickedanz

REVIEWERS OF *UNDERSTANDING CHILDREN*

The following academic reviewers made an invaluable contribution to this project with their insightful critiques of the manuscript. I'm deeply grateful for their many helpful suggestions.

REVIEWERS OF THE SECOND EDITION

Nancy Hamblen Acuff
Human Development and Learning
East Tennessee State University

Sharon Antonelli
Child and Family Studies
San Jose City College

George R. Bieger
Professional Studies in Education
Indiana University of Pennsylvania

Bonnidell Clouse
Educational and School Psychology
Indiana State University

Beth Doll
School Psychology Program, School of Education
University of Colorado at Denver

Patrick Drumm
Psychological Sciences
Indiana University-Purdue University at Fort Wayne

Dianne Eyer
Early Childhood Education
Canada College

Saul Feinman
Child and Family Studies
University of Wyoming

Janet Gonzalez-Mena
Early Childhood and Development
Napa Valley College

Elizabeth A. Hasson
Childhood Studies
West Chester University of Pennsylvania

Karen S. Holbrook
Psychology
Frostburg State University

Michael Horvath
Teacher Education
Bradley University

Ethel L. Jenkins
Social Sciences
Florida Community College at Jacksonville

Dene G. Klinzing
Individual and Family Studies
University of Delaware

Ann Marie Leonard
Early and Middle Education
James Madison University

Rosalia L. McCann
Child Development
Gavilan Community College

Mary Ann McLaughlin
Education
Clarion University of Pennsylvania

Grace G. Nunn
Elementary and Junior High Education
Eastern Illinois University

Barbara Reynolds
Consumer and Family Studies
College of the Sequoias

Martha K. Ross
Early and Middle Education
James Madison University

Gary L. Shilmoeller
Human Development
University of Maine

Nancy J. Wanamaker
Child Development/Family Relations
University of Idaho

REVIEWERS OF THE FIRST EDITION

Nancy Hamblen Acuff
Human Development and Learning
East Tennessee State University

Linda Annis
Educational Psychology
Ball State University

Barry Arbuckle
Child Development and Family Studies
University of North Carolina at Greensboro

Patricia Barker
Humanities and Social Sciences
Schenectady County Community College

Fredalene Bowers
Home Economics/Education
Indiana University of Pennsylvania

Sandy Bucknell
Child Development
Modesto Community College

Annette Chavez
Education
Northern Kentucky University

Nancy Cobb
Psychology
California State University at Los Angeles

Janet Gonzalez-Mena
Early Childhood Education
Napa Valley College

Bernard S. Gorman
Psychology
Nassau Community College

Gloria Guzman
Child Development
Rancho Santiago College

Elizabeth A. Hasson
Childhood Studies
West Chester University of Pennsylvania

Eileen Gallagher Haugh
Education
St. Mary's College

Donald Holmlund
Psychology
Marin College

Sheila Jeyfous
Psychology
Indiana University

Betty Johnson
Education
Shelby State Community College

Elaine M. Justice
Psychology
Old Dominion University

Daniel Kee
Psychology
California State University at Fullerton

Dwayne Keller
Family Studies
University of Connecticut

Murray Krantz
Home and Family Life
Florida State University

Eugene W. Krebs
Family Studies and Home Economics
California State University at Fresno

Marylin Lisowski
Education and Junior High Education
Eastern Illinois University

Gloria G. Lyon
Child Development
San Diego City College

Barbara Macci
Early Childhood Education
Imperial Valley College

Patricia Major
Teacher Education
St. Thomas Aquinas College

Mary Ann McLaughlin
Education
Clarion University of Pennsylvania

Thomas Moeschl
Behavioral Sciences
Broward Community College

Philip J. Mohan
Psychology
University of Idaho

Annabelle Nelson-Burford
Human Development
Prescott College

Delores Nieratka
Psychology
Mercy College of Detroit

Grace G. Nunn
Elementary and Junior High Education
Eastern Illinois University

Cheryl Roberts
Early Childhood Education
Riverside City College

Helen Ross
Family Studies
San Diego State University

Bruce Stam
Early Childhood Education
Chemeketa Community College

Margaret Thornburg
Psychology
Henry Ford Community College

Mark Whitney
Family Studies
San Diego State University

Patricia Worden
Psychology
California State University at Fullerton

UNDERSTANDING CHILDREN

PROLOGUE:
WHY STUDY CHILDREN?

As you read about children in the pages that follow, you may think of a child you know—a niece or nephew, a young cousin, even your own child if you're already a parent. Or you may think of yourself when you were a child, calling on your memories and the stories your parents have told you. You may know this child—even the child you once were—quite well or not so well. You may have daily contact with children or never see them at all.

No matter what your experience with children, you have one thing in common with all other adults: You will never again directly experience the "magic time" of childhood. Once we become adults, we can no longer see the world through children's eyes. We trade that vision for a more rational understanding of how things work, an understanding that allows us to function competently in the world.

When we were children, we were guided and cared for by our families and teachers. Now the responsibility for guiding the next generation of children to healthy adulthood passes into our hands. And even though we were once children ourselves, we don't understand many of the things children say and do. They charm us—and bewilder us. They seem to live in a world apart, a world different from the one we experience. Their minds don't work the same way ours do. Even when we think we've explained things to them, we discover they have their own beliefs . . .

> . . . that after people die, they can "get alive" again
>
> . . . that when you get tired of having baby brothers around, you can return them to the hospital where they were "boughted"
>
> . . . that blankets and stuffed bears can have their own thoughts and feelings

3

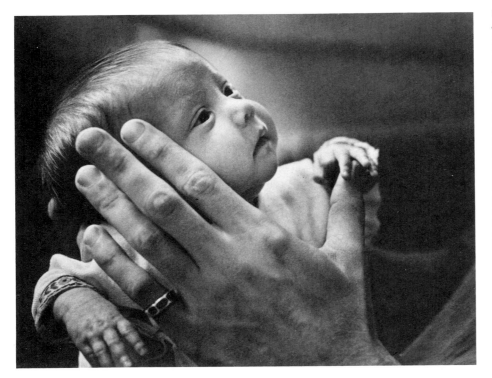

FIGURE 1
Although they're tiny and
seemingly helpless, babies are
born with many traits and
preferences that increase their
chances for survival. This premature baby's steady gaze and
attraction to the human face
and voice help him establish
eye contact with adults and
engage their attention, subtly
enhancing their inclination to
love and protect him. Over
the years, responsibility for
this child's care will be shared
by many people, including his
parents, relatives, and teachers. A working knowledge of
child development principles
will help them provide the
best conditions for his growth.

. . . that dreams are "made by the night" when the lights go out

. . . that children can be the secret but true reason for their parents' divorce

When we hear ideas like these, we realize how profoundly different children's experience of the world is from ours. We also realize that before we can take responsibility for them or provide the best conditions for their growth, we have to have some understanding of them. Our actions on their behalf have to be based on knowledge. Knowledge and understanding of children are what this book is designed to provide.

HOW WE APPROACH THE STUDY OF CHILDREN

Of course, children aren't like cars on an assembly line to be analyzed and put together piece by piece. They're whole people, living in the world, bringing themselves completely to their experiences. But this very complexity makes it difficult, at first, for the student to understand children in a whole way.

We have to begin the study of child development by considering its different aspects separately. In this book the study of children is divided into various domains—physical, cognitive, language, social-emotional. It's convenient to treat the various aspects of development this way, but we should never lose sight of the fact that children function as whole people.

We also approach the study of children from the point of view of chronological development, and we organize our material in "age-stages," from infancy to adolescence. Because we can see changes that set children apart at any point in time from their earlier and later selves, we can talk about how children at one age-stage differ from children at another age-stage. But we also stress continuity in development, the accumulation of experiences that makes a child what she is today and what she will be tomorrow. We look at any single behavior or characteristic as both a result of previous developments and a predictor of subsequent developments.

In addition, we look at the many factors that interact to make children what they are, not the least of which are the unique characteristics that each one brings into the world. But a child's uniqueness is shaped by the many contexts in which the child lives—family, school, community, country, world. Each context leaves its mark and must be taken into account. Today we are more aware than ever of the complex reciprocal interactions between the child and her environment. The threads of a child's life are woven from all these elements into a fabric not easily—or even appropriately—taken apart for closer analysis.

This complexity in human development means that there are limits to our knowledge. Although we have theories, research studies, and a vast amount of information about child development, some questions haven't been answered definitively in ways that help us know how to act. There are many questions that can't even be studied experimentally.

For example, children who watch a great deal of television tend to be poor readers. Does heavy television viewing cause low reading achievement? We can't be sure. To find out, we would have to enlist large numbers of children and ask them to watch many hours of television every day for a fairly long period of time—perhaps five hours a day for a year. Very few parents would allow their children to participate in such a study, and researchers who propose such an experiment believing that the experience would have a harmful effect would be acting unethically. Left with naturally occurring groups of children in real situations, we don't know if low reading achievement is caused by the television viewing or if some third factor causes both the low achievement and the heavy TV use. And we don't know if turning off the television would improve reading achievement or have no effect. Our knowledge is incomplete.

MAKING CONNECTIONS: THE PRACTICAL ASPECTS OF UNDERSTANDING CHILDREN

Even when research has provided clear-cut information about issues in child development, there's sometimes a gap between the research and the everyday world of parents and teachers. Some of our daily interactions with children raise questions that either haven't been investigated by researchers or haven't been answered in ways that are useful. The connection between scientific information and the everyday situation seems to be missing.

Understanding Children helps to make these connections. From the huge body of information about children—all important and relevant in one way or another—we have selected material that we judged to be particularly relevant to the practitioner, the person who actually cares for or teaches children. We have then explicitly discussed the implications of this knowledge, the way it relates to interaction with real children. Vignettes involving individual chil-

dren—both real children and composites of children we have known—illustrate and bring to life the principles of development discussed in each chapter.

Our focus throughout is on this practical side of information, but because of the need for a firm theoretical and research base in the chapters on physical, cognitive, language, and social-emotional development, coverage of applications and implications is limited in those chapters. To provide a balance, we include for each age-stage a section called Knowledge in Action. These sections provide practical information on such topics as living with children of different ages, ensuring their health and safety, and providing them with the most appropriate toys and playthings.

WHY WE CAN'T ACCOUNT FOR EVERYTHING: THE ROLE OF VALUES

When we study children, we begin by watching them. We notice how they look, what they do and say, how they respond to what we do and say. We wonder what makes them the way they are. We find ourselves worrying, too, about whether they're the way they "should" be. And sometimes we ask how this "should" is defined and who has established it as the right way. When we ask these questions, we're no longer talking about research alone—we're talking about values.

Whether they're explicitly stated or subtly implied, values are an ever-present element in the study of child development. All research reported, all topics covered, all actions recommended are based on values—ideas and beliefs

FIGURE 3
These caregivers at a day care center know that hearing stories and books read aloud is an enjoyable activity for young children. They probably also know that hearing and responding to stories is an extremely important early literacy experience, since children who are read to are more successful at learning to read when they enter school. Information like this, which comes from research findings in child development, helps adults plan the most effective and beneficial programs for the children in their care.

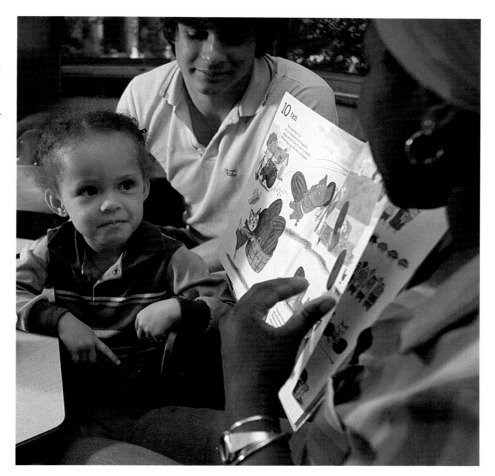

about what constitutes the "good" parent or teacher, the "good" society, the "best" child. Sometimes we don't agree with the values implied in research studies. We find ourselves making decisions about children that don't seem to follow from findings about child development. Our choices reflect our own histories and ideals as well as the information and theories we've learned. When we live and work with children, we have to take into account these personal factors too.

ABOUT UNDERSTANDING CHILDREN

We begin our study of child development with "foundations." Part One contains chapters on research methods; theories of child development and the values associated with them; and the biology of genetics, prenatal development, and birth.

Part Two covers the child between birth and age 3—infancy and toddlerhood. It begins with a separate chapter on the newborn, or neonate, who is very different from the older infant. The chapters that follow address the various functional domains of the infant and the toddler—physical development,

FIGURE 4
In every society and every family, certain traits and behaviors are promoted over others. Different groups embrace different—but equally useful—goals and directions for human development. These preferences shape children, like this young Asian American girl, in innumerable ways, encouraging them, for example, to be quiet or talkative, cooperative or competitive, individualistic or family-oriented. As American society becomes more culturally and ethnically diverse, we can expect to see more of these value-based differences among children.

FIGURE 5
Caught in the spell of a master storyteller, a young girl momentarily reveals the quality of wonder that children bring to their experience of the world. Perhaps our ultimate goal in dealing with children should be to inspire more moments like this.

cognitive development, language development, and social-emotional development. Part Two closes with Infant and Toddler Knowledge in Action, focusing on matters of daily concern.

The same format is followed in Parts Three, Four, and Five, covering the development of the preschool child (aged 3 to 6), the school-age child (aged 6 to 12), and the adolescent (aged 13 to 19). Summaries showing the highlights of development are provided at the end of each part to help you make sense of the information and get an overview of the process of development.

Despite limitations on our knowledge, the study of child development provides information of enormous importance to everyone who lives or works with children. It gives us a framework, a road map, with which to understand, guide, and support children on their journey through childhood—a journey on which it is our privilege and pleasure to assist them.

We wish you well in your study of this important topic and in your use of *Understanding Children.* We know that this book will help you understand children, and we suspect that it may increase your interest in children. We also hope that it will make your life and work with children filled with more wonder and less worry than they might have been had we never had a chance to meet across the pages that follow.

RESEARCH, THEORY, AND BIOLOGY

The study of child development begins not with the moment the child is born or even with the moment the child is conceived. A solid grounding in child development begins with the basics of how we get our knowledge and information about children—how research on children's behavior is conducted. It includes the ideas and principles—the theories—that we use to explain children's behavior and structure our information about them. Finally, it requires an understanding of all the things children bring into the world with them— their genetic inheritance and their formative experiences before birth. Only with these foundations in place does the study of children really make sense.

c h a p t e r 1

METHODS OF STUDYING CHILDREN

What would you think if you opened the newspaper one day and read about a research study claiming that differences in IQ between black children and white children had a genetic basis? Would you accept it at face value? Or would you wonder what kind of research could lead to such a conclusion? Would you read the article carefully to see if you could evaluate the research methods used? Would you think about the implications of a study like this for schools, families, and communities?

Such a study *did* appear not too many years ago. A research psychologist reported that the IQs of black children from poverty backgrounds declined as the children progressed through elementary school. He claimed that this "cumulative deficit in intelligence," which wasn't apparent in white children, was due to genetic differences between blacks and whites. When other researchers looked at his study, they found that his data were accurately reported but that his conclusions weren't warranted. He had used a research design that didn't support this interpretation.

Later in this chapter we look more closely at exactly why the conclusions from this study were flawed. Here, we wish to emphasize how vitally important accurate research methods are to our knowledge about children. If this study hadn't been critically examined, some inappropriate, and even damaging, actions might have been taken, based on its conclusions.

Rigorous research thinking provides the foundation for the study of child development. As pointed out in the Prologue, we must have some understanding of children before we can be responsible for them or take action on their behalf. Part of our understanding can come from personal experience or common sense, but this knowledge must be combined with knowledge from research. As a parent, teacher, or caregiver—and as an informed citizen—you will find it important to be able to understand and evaluate studies that report research concerning children. In addition, children are likely to benefit from your being able to research questions about them.

What is research in child development? The term *research* may evoke images of laboratories where children are asked to do certain things while researchers watch and record what they do. Or perhaps the term makes you think of statistical data displayed in tables and charts. Although these images do capture some aspects of research in child development, they aren't the whole picture. More than anything else, research is a careful and systematic investigation aimed at discovering the answer to a question. No matter what methods or settings or experimental designs they use, researchers must be extremely careful about how they arrive at their conclusions if their work is to benefit children rather than harm them.

This chapter discusses various research procedures and considers both their advantages and disadvantages. It also discusses the difficulties that researchers inevitably encounter in their work. Finally it explores the ethical obligations researchers must assume, especially when their research involves children. But before addressing these topics, let's consider a situation in which a research study has been conducted and its conclusions are being presented to the public. In this story we see how even a fairly simple study must conform to scientific standards if its conclusions are to be valid. We also see how research methods come into play in everyday life.

THINKING LIKE A RESEARCHER: A KINDERGARTEN LITERACY PROGRAM

An evening meeting has been arranged by a school district to introduce parents to a new instructional program. The district did a study, although professional researchers weren't in charge of it, and now is recommending that certain actions be taken, based on the results. In response, parents are doing some researchlike thinking.

Notice particularly the questions these parents ask about the study.

SCHOOL DISTRICT SUPERINTENDENT: *We're here tonight to tell you about a new program that will affect your children in next year's kindergarten classes. This program has been developed and pilot-tested by Cathy Pierce in her kindergarten classroom during the past year. We've just completed testing the children in her classroom, and they've done extremely well. In fact, the scores for this group of end-of-the-year kindergartners are similar to what children usually attain only after three-quarters of first grade. We think the program Mrs. Pierce has developed is very good, and we're ready to introduce it into other kindergartens in the school district.*

Let me tell you just a little about the program, and then I'll be happy to answer your questions.

The program involves the use of "big-print books" for story reading. The teacher reads a big-print book to the children each day. The format of these books is very large, as you can see from the one I have here to show you. The print is large too, so that all the children in the group can see the print when the teacher holds it up. The teacher reads the story the first time through, and then she encourages the children to read along with her as she reads it again. Often she reads it even a third time, or she asks the children to find certain words that appear in the text.

FIGURE 1-1
How should reading be taught? In one approach, the emphasis is on surrounding children with books and writing materials, filling their environment with print, and showing them what spoken words look like on the printed page, as this woman is doing with a group of preschoolers. In another approach, the emphasis is on more explicit and structured teaching. Which is the more effective approach? An accurate answer to this question depends on carefully thought-out research studies.

We have about 25 different Big Books. The stories have a lot of rhymes and repetition, which makes them easy for children to learn and remember. The teacher points to the print while she's reading, which helps children know where each word appears. The books are left out in the classroom during activity times so children can read them themselves if they want to.

The program encourages children to read books and to think of themselves as readers. It also teaches them to integrate different cues when they read—the words, the pictures, the sense of the story. When children learn to read by focusing on isolated phonics skills, which was our old system, they can get the idea that reading is a matter of "looking, sounding, and saying." We want them to get the idea that reading involves thinking, looking, sounding, and saying. Of course, children do need to have the phonics skills, such as knowing which sounds specific letters of the alphabet typically represent, but we know now that reading involves much more than phonics.

Besides the Big Books, we immerse the children in what we call functional environmental print. This means that they see print and use it in meaningful ways every day in the classroom. Their names appear on their artwork, on job charts, and on attendance sheets. Opportunities for practice in reading and writing are integrated into the daily program, replacing the workbook and phonics drill periods. In sum, the program helps kindergartners think of reading and writing as a normal part of their everyday lives. We think it's a better approach to reading, and the test results from Mrs. Pierce's class bear us out.

Well, I've talked long enough. Since this program will affect your children next year, I'm sure you have some questions.

MR. TAYLOR: *You said you did some testing. What kind of tests did you use?*

SUPERINTENDENT: *We used several different tests to see if the children were acquiring the skills good readers are known to use. One test involves reading a child a short story with every fifth word deleted. The child fills in the word as the teacher pauses. This tells us if the child is thinking about the story and using clues from the context to decide what word would fit.*

Another test involves asking a child to read back a simple story the teacher has just read and to point to the words while reading. This test tells us if children know that print is read from left to right and from top to bottom and if they know that one printed word represents one spoken word. We also did some phonics tests, such as letter recognition, because those are important skills too. We used a balanced set of tests because there are quite a few different understandings involved in reading.

MRS. SMITH: *Who did the testing? Did the school psychologist or the reading specialist test the children?*

SUPERINTENDENT: *No, Mrs. Pierce did all the testing. It would have been too time consuming for the psychologist or reading specialist. It would have been harder for the children, too, since they don't know them. Mrs. Pierce tested a few children a day over the course of a month.*

MRS. SMITH: *Did anyone observe Mrs. Pierce do the testing?*

SUPERINTENDENT: *Not that I know of. Of course, her teaching aide was in the classroom, but I don't believe anyone actually observed the testing.*

MR. TAYLOR: *Were children in other kindergartens also tested, to see what they knew?*

SUPERINTENDENT: *No, they weren't. We usually test children after the first three months of first grade, not in kindergarten.*

MR. TAYLOR: *So you really don't know how well they might have done on the same tests, even if they didn't have this new program?*

SUPERINTENDENT: *That's right.*

MRS. PALMER: *Isn't the school where Mrs. Pierce teaches located in a very affluent area of the school district, where the educational level of the parents is quite high?*

SUPERINTENDENT: *Yes, I think that's an accurate statement.*

MRS. PALMER: *Well, wouldn't these children be expected to do better on tests anyway, regardless of their kindergarten program? Maybe these children would score as well as first graders no matter what program they had.*

SUPERINTENDENT: *Yes, but Mrs. Pierce feels that this group of children made more progress than previous groups that she's had from the same neighborhood. She thinks the program made the difference.*

MRS. WINTER: *Well, even if the program was effective with this group, and even if it was the program that made the difference, how do you know it will work with children from less affluent homes? Maybe other children need a different kind of program, something more structured, one that really teaches the alphabet and phonics skills.*

SUPERINTENDENT: *We don't think so. We think this program provides a better, broader foundation for reading, no matter who the children are.*

MRS. WINTER: *Well, I don't think you can assume that just because the program worked with some children, it will work with all children. If you use the program throughout the whole school district, you'll need to keep a close check on children's progress.*

Also, I wonder about the testing conditions. I wonder if Mrs. Pierce coaxed the children at all as she tested them. Although I'm sure her character is wonderful, I do know, because I used to be a teacher, how difficult it is to resist helping children out.

Teachers become used to teaching. If a child makes
"Are you sure? Why don't you think about that a li̇ *ake, it's very easy to say,*
gives the right answer, you think, "Oh, she knew that *?" Then, when the child*
first answer, which was wrong." *'ll just ignore the*

SUPERINTENDENT: *Well, you certainly are asking all the right* *made some good points. Of course, to be able to answer you* *would have been necessary to run a pilot program in several c* *d you've* *included a control classroom that didn't use the program. We w* *etely, it* *hire outside testers. All this would have cost money, and I'm not* *have* *been allocated. So we did the best we could.*

We had formed a group two years ago to evaluate language arts ins *kindergarten, and this was what they recommended. Mrs. Pierce voluntee* *implement the recommendations in her classroom and work out the progra* *have every reason to believe the new program is better than the old one, and* *would like your support in implementing it.*

MRS. COHEN: *You know, I'm sitting here listening to all this talk about teaching read-*
ing in kindergarten, and I'm wondering what ever happened to finger painting,
nature walks, building with blocks, and all the other activities I thought kindergarten
was for. Why not let the first grade teacher worry about teaching reading? Kinder-
gartners should just be playing and learning how to get along with other children.

SUPERINTENDENT: *I understand your concern, and I'm glad you brought up this point.*
I want to emphasize that the Big Books program does not take up the whole day, and
in fact the teacher actually has more time for other activities when she's using this
program. In the old program, the teacher felt she had to set aside a fairly large part of
the day for instruction in the so-called reading readiness skills. In the new program,
she still reads storybooks, but other reading and writing practice is integrated into
ongoing activities. Children have more time to spend on play activities, but playing
includes chances to read and write. So we're actually headed more in the direction
you describe than we were before.

ANALYZING THE STUDY:
THE MAJOR RESEARCH ISSUES

In this school meeting we can see some of the major issues all researchers have to face, whether they want to do practical research with immediate applications (as when a teacher systematically observes his students) or basic research (as when a scientist tests a theory and publicly distributes the results). These are issues of (1) validity and reliability of measurement—whether a study has measured what it claims to; (2) external validity—whether the results of a study can be generalized to other groups; and (3) internal validity—whether an experiment has established a true cause-effect relationship. Let's consider each of these in turn.

Validity and Reliability of Measurement

In any study researchers have to select variables to measure as a test of their study's effectiveness. A **variable** is a category or general class of things that can take on different values or forms. In the case of the kindergarten program, the variable Cathy Pierce selected to judge the success of the program was the

used a typical test, on which scores could range
values of this variable could vary from 0 to 100.

children's test scoring at an important issue when he asked what kinds of
from 0 to 100 re to measure reading ability. He was wondering whether
Mr. Tay_le—the test scores—really measured the children's ability
ted to be sure Ms. Pierce wasn't teaching irrelevant skills just
tests hen do well on an irrelevant test. Mr. Taylor's question addressed
th e most fundamental issue researchers have to consider in planning
Is the measurement technique a valid measure of the behavior being
d? A test's **validity** is defined as the soundness with which it measures
at it is intended to measure.

When Cathy Pierce wanted to evaluate the kindergartners' reading skills,
she couldn't test them on their ability to read in a mature, conventional way.
Most of them simply couldn't do that. So she tested them on skills that are
thought to be related to reading ability, such as alphabet recognition and
understanding of print conventions. That is, she used what some might call a
test of prereading skills.

Researchers working with children often have to measure variables that
predict or are related to the behavior they really want to study. When predictor
variables are measured instead of the final behavior, researchers must be sure
that a connection between the two has been demonstrated.

There are many cases in which little or no relationship has been found
between predictor variables and final behavior. For example, for many years
people thought that reading ability was related to physical and visual-motor
skills, such as the abilities to walk a balance beam and to copy shapes. Many
kindergarten programs incorporated activities that would give children practice in these skills. The children did improve their physical and visual-motor
skills, but it turned out that these skills are unrelated to reading ability (Vellutino, 1987). Reading ability appears to be related to other skills—skills
related to experience with oral and written language.

The school superintendent said that good readers use the skills on which
the kindergarten children were tested. If this is so, there is some **validity** to
the tests that the school used. The tests were measuring skills that have been
shown to be related to reading ability. When we use a valid measure, we know
we're measuring the skill we're interested in, not some other, unrelated skill.

Predictive validity—the ability of a measure to predict later manifestations
of the behavior of interest (such as when a test of prereading skills predicts
conventional reading ability)—is one indication that a measure is valid.
Another indication is **construct validity**—the degree to which the measure is
related to other measures, such as IQ, that are also thought to be associated
with the behavior of interest (reading ability). Of course, we have more confidence in the validity of a measure if it also has **face validity**, that is, it appears
on the face of it to be related to the behavior of interest. For example, knowing
the letters of the alphabet has more face validity as a measure of reading ability than walking a balance beam does.

Validity increases if a measure is **reliable** (consistent or stable) when repea
edly measured. If Jennifer tests above average when Cathy Pierce tests her a
clearly below average when the school psychologist tests her, the test is ur
liable. And since it is unreliable, it is also not valid—these different scores
not both be good measures of Jennifer's reading ability.

BOX 1-1   An Observation with Conclusions

S arrives at school. He is glad to be at school. He doesn't miss his mother. He seems tired at the beginning of the day. After a while, he decides to play with blocks. He seems not to care about building something with blocks with a girl who is playing there, and he builds a road alone. But he seems to want to build with a boy, and when a boy comes close to the area, he invites him to play. S is very possessive of his road and the toy vehicles used with it. (record continues)

An important way for researchers to increase the reliability and validity of their studies is to be sure that their data are objective or well defined, which means recording the specifics of what is actually observed rather than opinions, conclusions, or judgments about behavior. Observers should provide "raw data" only, without trying to explain the meaning of a child's behavior. Examples of observations recorded with conclusions are given in Box 1-1. We read phrases like "seems tired," "doesn't seem to care," and "is very possessive." Yet we can't tell how these conclusions were reached because we aren't given any details of behavior.

In the example without conclusions, shown in Box 1-2, we see exactly what went on. Times are carefully recorded, and conclusions are not mixed with observations. Possible conclusions are listed separately (Box 1-3).

Although most researchers have learned to divorce their observations from their conclusions, they may have more difficulty identifying the influence of their theories and even their personal interests on their observations, as Mrs. Smith and Mrs. Winter pointed out. Researchers typically have a vested interest in what they're testing. If, as in Cathy Pierce's case, they develop a program or a treatment, of course they hope it will be effective. When the results of a program or treatment are measured, it's a good idea to have an objective third

BOX 1-2   An Observation without Conclusions

9:10 S arrived at school at 9:05. S's mother came with him into the classroom. S went to his cubby, took off coat, hung it up on hook. Smiled and waved goodbye to mother, who said "Have a good day."

9:15 Stood with back toward cubby. Rubbed eyes with right fist. Looked out into room—first in one direction, then in another. Yawned. Walked over to block area where girl was already playing. S entered area. Began taking a block from the top shelf. "You can't take my blocks," the girl said. "I won't," responded S. "I can use these." (gestured toward shelf).

9:20 S placed a long block on the floor away from the girl's building. S obtained another block, same as the first one, bent over, and placed one end of it next to the end of the first block. "I'm making a road," he said as he looked at the girl and then glanced at her building. "Don't make it go this way," she said (points toward her blocks). "I won't," S said. "It's going to be a long road that way." (points in direction away from girl's blocks)

9:25 A boy entered the block area. "Hi M____," said S. "Want to help me build this road? Then we'll drive on it." "Yeah," the boy said. He began to take blocks from the shelf and place them end to end with S's road. After adding five blocks, he took a truck off the shelf and began to push it along the top of the block road.

9:30 "Hey," said S. "I wanted the truck. You have to use the car. This is my road!"

(record continues)

BOX 1-3   Possible Conclusions about a Child's Behavior

1. The child does not select play areas based on sex of other children playing in the area.
2. The child initiates contacts with other children.
3. The child readily plays with other children.
4. The child shares materials with other children although he protects what is his.
5. The child uses words to communicate wishes to other children.
6. The child offers suggestions for solving problems.

party collect the data. It's even a good idea for this person to be kept "**blind**," or totally ignorant about which children received the treatment and which ones didn't. This helps eliminate the possibility of **research bias**—the tendency to want the results to turn out a certain way.

External Validity and Generalization

In the school example, Mrs. Winter raised another good point when she said, even if the program was effective with this group, and even if it was the program that made the difference, how do you know it will work with children

FIGURE 1-2
When children are tested under standardized conditions, there is a higher probability that the results will be reliable—repeatable from one testing situation to another—and a lower probability that researcher bias has affected the outcome. These fourth graders' scores are probably a reliable reflection of how much they know in comparison with each other and with children tested under similar conditions.

FIGURE 1-3
Researchers studying children could obtain some interesting information by observing or testing these four 5-year-old boys, but they couldn't generalize their findings to 5-year-old girls or to 10-year-old boys. Such a study would lack *external validity* because its sample wouldn't be representative of the general population of children.

from less affluent homes? Maybe other children need a different ki
gram, something more structured, one that really teaches the alphabe
phonics skills. In an ideal world, researchers would study each and every child and teacher to determine the effect of a particular program or treatment. In the real world, of course, it's impossible for researchers to do this. Instead they study a few people (a **sample**) whom they hope are representative of the larger population. But they have to be sure that what they learn from a study of one group can be generalized to the larger population. If the results of the study can be legitimately generalized to the entire population of interest, the study is said to have **external validity.**

If researchers studied only rural children, for example, they wouldn't be justified in generalizing their findings to urban and suburban children. If they studied only boys, they couldn't apply their findings equally to girls. And if they studied children from affluent homes, their findings might not be true for children from less affluent homes. Although all children are alike in many ways, they also differ depending on their age, where they live, what their parents do for a living, and so on.

The school superintendent didn't mention the lack of generalizability of the results of Cathy Pierce's study when he proposed that the program be implemented throughout the district on the basis of the test results in her kindergarten. Perhaps he didn't think about it, or perhaps he was anxious to get the program into all the classrooms. Whatever his thinking, he would have been on firmer ground if he had implemented the program in two pilot classrooms, located in different parts of the district. He would also have had more credibility at the parent meeting if he had stated these limitations at the outset and explained why he thought the program should be implemented despite the problems of generalizability.

The parents might have made another point about sampling and generalizability. Ms. Pierce is an experienced teacher who volunteered to pilot the new program. She may not be representative of all the teachers in the district. Maybe she's an exceptional teacher—brighter, more experienced and energetic, more inclined to take risks. Maybe her children's good test scores

own characteristics as a teacher as they did from
gram. If this is the case, children taught by other
well, regardless of the program. The study would
teachers selected at random had tried the new probe sure they were representative of all the teachers in

resulted as much fr
characteristics of
teachers would
have been
gram. T
the

22

ften difficult or impossible to select people randomly in sit-
In some school districts, for example, teachers' contracts pre-
ators from dictating unilaterally what they must teach. Without
of all the teachers, the superintendent couldn't assign them to the
ig program for the sake of a research study.

l Validity and Causation

. Palmer put her finger on an even more problematic issue when she sug-
sted that the children in Cathy Pierce's class might have done well in any
program. She implied that some factor other than the program—perhaps
home environment or native intelligence—was entirely responsible for their
good test results. That is, she suggested that even within the sample "studied"
(Ms. Pierce's present kindergarten, her previous kindergarten, and the first
grades), the superintendent's conclusion that the new program improved performance was not warranted. In order for researchers to claim to have demonstrated a cause-effect relationship, they have to make sure they've eliminated all possible causes except one. But Mrs. Palmer wondered quite
legitimately if it was the new program that really caused the children's good
test performance. Maybe they were advanced children who already knew
most of the content of the program before they entered kindergarten, and the
kindergarten and even first grade just repeated what they had already learned
at home.

The superintendent didn't mention any **pretesting**—testing done before the
program started—that would have indicated what prior knowledge the children had. With the resulting **baseline data** (data gathered before a treatment
is applied), Cathy Pierce could have provided evidence both that her children
were initially equivalent to other children and that something her kindergartners experienced that year did indeed enhance their performance.

To be sure that an experimental treatment causes a certain effect—for example, that a new reading program enhances reading ability—researchers have
to compare a group that receives that treatment with a group that does not
receive it, and these two groups have to be otherwise equal. If there are pretreatment differences between the groups, such as age or economic background, one of those pretreatment differences may contribute to any differences in final test results. The researchers will not clearly demonstrate the
cause of the final differences in reading between the groups.

If the groups of children sampled are equal to each other except for the
experimental treatment, the researchers will have soundly demonstrated that
the final results of the experiment are due to the treatment. The experiment
can be said to be internally valid or to have **internal validity.** Internal validity—the soundness of an experiment—is entirely determined by whether the
groups of children to be compared are equal in all significant respects except
for the experimental treatment.

Experimental group   Control group

FIGURE 1-4
If a population of children is randomly divided into two groups, a scientific experiment can be conducted using one as the experimental group and the other as the control group. Because the two groups are comparable at the outset, researchers can be certain that any differences between them at the end of the study are the result of the experimental treatment itself.

The group that does not receive the experimental treatment is called the **control group.** It "controls for" (or equates) all other variables that could explain the final difference in reading ability. Randomly assigning children is the best way to get two initially comparable groups—putting their names in a hat, mixing them up, drawing them out, and placing the children alternately in one group or the other. When we do this before beginning a program, we create the conditions for an **experimental study.** But when we take naturally occurring groups that might differ initially in some ways, we have conditions only for a **correlational study.** In an experimental study we can attribute results to the effects of the treatment or program. In a correlational study we can't be sure that any differences existing at the end of a program are due to the program. The differences, or the conditions causing the differences, might have been there from the start.

Mr. Taylor brought up this issue when he asked if children in any other kindergartens had been tested. He was looking for some kind of control or comparison group. Of course, if the children weren't randomly assigned to the kindergarten classes to begin with, it could be that Cathy Pierce simply had a more advanced class when the experiment began.

Besides ruling out preexisting differences, there is another reason for having both a control group and an experimental group in a study like this one. It may be that some event outside the school that year affected the children's reading ability. Perhaps the local library began a reading contest and awarded prizes to children for every book they read or had read to them. Or maybe a new educational television program started, or a series of articles for parents appeared in the local newspaper. Any of these events might cause children's reading scores to be higher than expected at the end of the year. But in these cases, we would see improvement in both the control group and the experimental group. We would know that something other than the reading program was causing *all* the children's test scores to go up.

THE MAJOR RESEARCH METHODS

Now that we have examined the major issues that researchers have to keep in mind when conducting studies in child development, let's consider the different methods they can use to test their theories and gain information about children. Each research method provides different kinds of information, and each is appropriate under different circumstances.

The Case Study

In a case study the researcher focuses on only one of something—a child, a teacher, a school. The kindergarten program described at the beginning of the chapter is an example of a case study (if one omits the rather questionable comparison of the kindergarten data with the imprecise "data" from the previous kindergarten class and the first grade). The traditional case study, in which one child is studied in her natural environment, is the oldest method of child study. As we saw with the kindergarten program, a limitation of the case study is that its results can't be generalized to other situations. The information it provides is about one case and one case only.

Of course, researchers wouldn't use a method at all if it wasn't helpful in some way, and the case study has some outstanding advantages. Probably the most important one is that it allows us to study something in great detail. When we study one child we can collect much more data, given the same amount of time, money, and human resources, than when we study 100 children.

One researcher used the case study method to study the development of literacy in her son between his second and third birthdays (Granucci, 1986). She taped nightly bedtime storytelling sessions. She kept track of the books he owned and the books he chose to have read to him. She kept a log noting the toys he had and what he played with. She wrote down the questions he asked about print, and she kept all his scribblings. She did this day in, day out, for one year, and by his third birthday she had many file boxes full of data. With this information, she was able to put together a complete picture of one 2-year-old's literacy development during this span of time.

This researcher obviously couldn't have studied a large number of children in this detail. A team of researchers might be able to, but it would be very costly. When we study more children, we usually settle for more superficial information.

Despite its limitations, then, the case study can provide detailed information about a child's behavior. This rich detail helps us understand how complex and multifaceted human behavior is. Case studies often give us ideas about the developmental sequence of many abilities and behaviors—how one ability emerges after another in the growing child—although they don't tell

FIGURE 1-5
Parents are in a good position to conduct case studies of their own children. This boy's parents might be interested in studying his fine motor skills as they develop over the course of a year, or changes in his literary tastes as he matures, or the effectiveness of the ''star chart'' on the wall behind him.

us if what we've learned about this one situation is characteristic of others. Finally, the ideas generated by case studies often provide hypotheses to be examined with other research methods.

Descriptive Studies

Descriptive studies are appropriate when a researcher wants to gather information about children without determining precisely whether there is a cause-and-effect relationship between variables. Descriptive studies of a random sample of children allow the researcher to generalize the results to the larger population from which the sample was taken.

Descriptive studies can involve large or small numbers of children, many or few observers collecting data, natural or contrived situations, and narrowly or loosely defined categories of behavior. All these variations determine how much the results can be generalized to other children and how objective and reliable the data are.

There are three commonly used kinds of descriptive studies—specimen records, behavior checklists and event sampling, and time sampling. Let's briefly examine each one.

SPECIMEN RECORDS. Sometimes observers try to record everything a child does in a short period of time. The result is called a specimen record. This technique was extremely difficult before audio and video technology gave the researcher the tools with which to observe a moment in a child's life over and over again. The specimen record is used mainly to get a detailed picture of some aspect of a child's everyday behavior.

BEHAVIOR CHECKLISTS AND EVENT SAMPLING. Sometimes observers start out with a list of carefully defined behaviors that they're going to watch for and count. The behavior checklist is a **closed method** of observation unlike the specimen record, which we call an **open observation method** (Wright, 1960). It also doesn't provide the rich detail that specimen records do. On the other hand, the behavior checklist makes it easier to observe children accurately, and the resulting data are more precise and reliable. These checklists are used for keeping track of all types of specific behavior, such as actions related to aggression, friendliness, or attention seeking. In research studies, baseline data on a variable of interest can be obtained by using a checklist. Following the treatment comparative data can be obtained by using the same checklist.

Event sampling is a descriptive technique in which an observer notes only one, well-defined type of behavior. Narrowing the range of behaviors to be observed means that very precise, accurate recording can be done. One researcher used this method to study children's quarrels (Dawe, 1934). He observed children during free play in a nursery school, watching for quarrels to occur. When they did, he moved closer to note the details. Because he carefully defined what he meant by a quarrel, other researchers could collect data at other nursery schools and compare them to his data in a meaningful way.

TIME SAMPLING. Time sampling is a technique in which regular observations are made on a specific schedule. Observations may be made over a fairly long period of time to ensure that a child's full range of behavior is seen, or observations of individual children may be made for specific lengths of time within one observation period. A researcher may observe one child for five minutes, then another for five minutes, and so on. In this way, the researcher observes each child in a variety of settings, rather than one child on the playground and another during snack time, which would make it difficult to compare their behavior.

One researcher used time sampling to see what kinds of play children were involved in (Parten, 1932). She defined four categories of play: (1) solitary play—children played alone; (2) parallel play—children played alongside other children; (3) associative play—children played with other children but without subordinating their own interests to the group; and (4) cooperative play—children played as a group. She set up a schedule allowing for one-minute observations of each child every day for several days, and she varied the schedule systematically so that each child was observed at a different time during the free-play period on different days. The results of a careful data-collection strategy like this are likely to be very reliable.

Descriptive studies give us a broad, rich picture of how children act. Because there's no intervention by the researcher, and often no direct contact at all, ethical issues—concerns about the effect of the study on the child—are kept to a minimum. On the other hand, descriptive studies do not readily allow us to draw conclusions about the causes of children's behavior.

FIGURE 1-6
When children are observed in a natural setting, the findings can be used as the basis for a descriptive study. A researcher observing these children might use the technique known as event sampling to note every incident of a particular behavior—sharing, for example—that occurs among them, or she might use a behavior checklist to record incidences of sharing, helping, quarreling, or any number of other behaviors of interest.

Correlational Studies

Correlational studies may draw their data from descriptive studies, from interviews, or from questionnaires. Correlational studies measure two or more variables. As previously mentioned, a variable is a class or category that can take on various values or forms. If changes in one variable are associated with changes in the other variable, we say that the two variables are correlated. If both variables change in the same direction, either increasing or decreasing in value, they are said to be **positively correlated**. If they both change, but in opposite directions, one increasing and the other decreasing, they are said to be **negatively correlated**. If one variable does not change systematically with changes in the other variable, the two variables are uncorrelated.

But even when variables are correlated, we can't assume that one causes the other. Height and weight are positively correlated, but we can't say that an increase in height causes an increase in weight. A third variable—growth hormone—causes increases both in height and weight.

A correlational study can tell us whether changes in one variable are related to changes in another, but a simple correlational study can't tell us *why* the changes are related. In our kindergarten example, we really didn't know if the achievement of the kindergarten children was due to the new program or something else—something about the children, the teacher, or the community. The danger of correlational studies is that they may be interpreted to mean that causation exists when it doesn't.

Studies involving naturally occurring groups, rather than specially constituted ones, are correlational studies. For example, if aggressive behavior is measured in groups of children who watch more or less violent television at home, we can't assume a causal relationship between the two factors. If it turns out that children who watch violent TV shows are more aggressive, we wouldn't be justified in saying that the TV viewing caused the aggressive behavior. Perhaps children who are already aggressive like to watch televised violence more than children who aren't aggressive. Or perhaps the parents of aggressive children allow them to watch more violent shows and also spank or punish their children more than parents of less aggressive children do. It could be that different parental behavior in general rather than television viewing in particular accounts for the difference in aggressive behavior.

Similarly, if we take some action with naturally occurring groups, we can't be sure that any differences found between the groups afterward were caused by our action. If we show a violent cartoon to children from one community and a prosocial program—one that demonstrates caring, sharing, and coop-

FIGURE 1-7
Does watching violent TV shows make children more aggressive, or do aggressive children choose more violent TV shows, or do parents who buy their children toy guns and let them watch violent TV shows cause them to be more aggressive? Correlations have been established between aggression in children and the viewing of television violence, but a causal relationship is much more difficult to prove.

erative behavior—to children from another community, we might find differences afterward in their aggressive behavior. But we wouldn't know if these differences were due to the films or if they existed before we ever undertook the study.

The advantage of correlational studies is that we're saved the time and effort of administering a treatment to specially constituted groups when no prior relationship between two variables has ever been observed. If we can show that two variables are correlated, it makes sense to pursue the possibility that they're causally related. If no correlation has ever been demonstrated, it's often a waste of time and money to do experimental studies, which are more complicated and costly.

Correlational studies are appropriate in another situation as well. Sometimes a treatment may actually be harmful, and we can't knowingly inflict it on subjects in an experiment. But if we consider an adverse condition that occurs naturally, we can ethically study it to see what its effects may be or what other conditions may be associated with it.

Experimental Studies

When we want to see if there is a causal relationship between two variables, we conduct an experimental study. Experimental studies have two major characteristics. The first is that a variable is always manipulated, so that one group receives more of it and another receives less. The variable that the researcher manipulates—changes or varies in the course of the study—is called the **independent variable.** The behavior that the researcher observes to see if it changes when the independent variable is changed is called the **dependent variable.**

The second major characteristic of an experimental study is that the groups receiving the different forms or amounts of the independent variable are always comparable before the study starts. Again, the best way to ensure that the groups are comparable is to assign large numbers of individuals randomly to different groups. We can then be fairly certain that children with similar backgrounds or characteristics are distributed among the groups, not bunched up in one group or another. We will know that differences found between groups after the study are the result of what was done in the experiment itself, or that the experiment has internal validity. Since case studies and descriptive and correlational studies usually require little more than validity of measurement, the term *internal validity* is not commonly applied to them. It applies only where a cause-effect relationship is truly demonstrated.

Most experimental studies are conducted in a laboratory setting. For example, in a study of the effects of viewing violent TV cartoons on children's behavior, groups of children might be brought into a special room to view films. One group might be shown a violent cartoon, a second might be shown a prosocial film, and a third might be shown a neutral film. Filmed violence is the independent variable that's being manipulated—a high level of violence is shown to one group, a low level to another.

The children's aggressive behavior after watching the various films is the dependent variable. If children who saw violent cartoons are observed to play more aggressively in the lab than children who watched some other kind of film, we can assume a causal link between watching filmed aggression and aggressive behavior.

FIGURE 1-8
Experimental studies often are conducted under carefully controlled conditions in a laboratory setting. If a researcher randomly assigns children to two groups, gives practice on specific types of tasks to one group but not to the other, and then finds that the treatment group (practice group) completes a test task in half the time that it takes the control group, the researcher can be fairly certain that the training caused the treatment group's performance to improve.

Not all experimental studies are conducted solely in the laboratory. The children who saw the different films in the lab could also be observed later in the classroom or playground. Although the dependent variable is now being measured in a naturalistic setting, the study is still experimental. A variable has been manipulated, and the groups were comparable at the beginning of the study, due to random assignment. These are the crucial characteristics of an experimental study that allow us to make statements about causation.

The disadvantage of the experimental method is that it's not always practical or ethical. Then we fall back on correlational methods. Sometimes, too, experimental studies distort events, so that we see a causal relationship in the lab that wouldn't hold true in real-life situations, when other factors are involved. We can overcome this drawback by observing the behavior in both lab and naturalistic settings.

We don't use the experimental method when we don't have much information about variables that might be affecting a behavior we're interested in. In these situations, it makes more sense first to ferret out some possible causes by using correlational methods and then to conduct follow-up studies using experimental methods.

THE MAJOR DEVELOPMENTAL RESEARCH DESIGNS: CROSS-SECTIONAL AND LONGITUDINAL

Regardless of the research *method*—case study, descriptive, correlational, or experimental—chosen for a study, researchers interested in developmental issues may also choose one of two basic research *designs*. The **cross-sectional design** uses groups of children of different ages—perhaps groups of 2-year-olds, 6-year-olds, and 10-year-olds. The **longitudinal design**, on the other hand, starts with a group of children of a specific age—perhaps 2-year-olds—

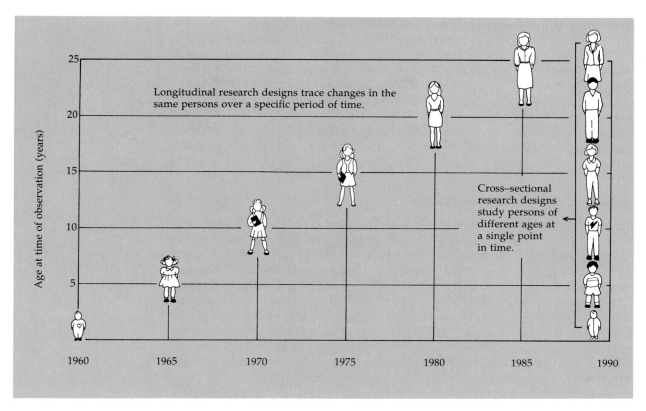

Age at time of observation (years)

Longitudinal research designs trace changes in the same persons over a specific period of time.

Cross–sectional research designs study persons of different ages at a single point in time.

25

20

15

10

5

1960   1965   1970   1975   1980   1985   1990

FIGURE 1-9
In experiments with longitudinal designs, the same subjects are followed over a number of years, allowing researchers to focus carefully on the process of development. In experiments with cross-sectional designs, subjects of different ages are studied at the same time, allowing researchers to work more efficiently and reducing the likelihood of certain kinds of research errors. A third type of research design, the sequential, combines the advantages of both designs.

and then follows them across the age-span of interest—perhaps until they're 10 years old (Figure 1-9). Each design has its advantages and its disadvantages, and we'll consider both below.

Advantages of the Cross-Sectional Design

The cross-sectional design allows studies to be completed more quickly than the longitudinal design does, because we don't have to wait for the children to reach the upper age of interest. When we use a cross-sectional design, we simply study children of different ages at the same time. The cross-sectional design also lessens the possibility of biased sampling, which is a problem in the longitudinal design. **Biased sampling** means that the children in the study are not representative of the population to which the researcher hopes to generalize the study's results. Biased sampling can occur when certain types of parents refuse to be included in longitudinal studies. This is because parents who allow their children to participate in longitudinal studies may be different from parents who refuse to participate. They have to make a long-term commitment to the research and agree to many observations of their children over a long period of time. They may be better educated, more interested in having their children participate in research, or more socially active. If so, their children won't be typical, and the research results can't be generalized to other children.

Another factor that may make longitudinal samples nonrepresentative is the likelihood that some children will withdraw over the course of the study. Their families may move, or their circumstances may change in some way that prevents them from continuing. This makes the group under study different from what it was in the beginning. Therefore, if the group of children in the study shows a difference in behavior between, say, age 6 and age 8, we can't know if this is an age difference—a difference due to development—or a difference due to the different composition of the groups of children who were included in the study at ages 6 and 8. We don't run into this kind of problem with the cross-sectional design.

Advantages of the Longitudinal Design

The longitudinal design allows us to observe changes in one child's behavior over time, which the cross-sectional design does not. The advantage of the longitudinal design can be seen in studies of the preadolescent growth spurt. Growth at this time is typically very fast, truly a spurt. However, if measurements from a cross-sectional study were plotted on a graph, the growth spurt would appear as a smooth curve rather than an abrupt peak. This is because the timing of the growth spurt varies from individual to individual—some experience it at 11, others at 14. There is a gradual increase in height in the general population of children spanning the entire period from 10½ to 15. This smooth curve tells us how 11-year-olds as a group differ from 14-year-olds, but it doesn't describe the growth experience of an individual.

Group averages like these may be all that are needed by clothes designers, but a parent or a physician also needs to know if an individual child's growth spurt is normal. The smooth curve may seem to suggest that children should experience gradual, continuous growth. Only longitudinal data show that actual abrupt, individual changes are normal for this age.

Another disadvantage of cross-sectional designs is that sometimes we can't tell whether differences between age groups are the results of developmental changes or of the different experiences the groups have had. This was the problem with the study that reported the "cumulative deficit in intelligence" among black children, mentioned at the beginning of this chapter. Psychologist Arthur Jensen reported that the IQs of black children got lower as they progressed through elementary school (1974, 1977). Because he didn't find the same kind of decline among white children, he attributed this decline to genetic differences in mental development curves between blacks and whites. However, his studies were flawed. He interpreted his data as if they were obtained from the same subjects studied over a long period of time rather than from different subjects studied at the same time.

Perhaps the 6-year-olds in the study were in better educational programs than the 12-year-olds were when they were 6. Perhaps educational TV or Project Head Start gave the 6-year-olds an advantage the 12-year-olds didn't have. If so, the older children's IQs at 6 might not have tested as high as those of the 6-year-olds in the study. If we assume that educational opportunity is gradually improving, we might expect that IQ would appear to decline with age: The older the children, the poorer their early opportunities. One researcher suggests that what seems to be a change related to age may really be a change related to personal history or conditions (Kamin, 1978).

FIGURE 1-10
The cohort of young adults who attended natural child-birth classes (and reunions) in the 1980's has a unique set of experiences and values in common that distinguishes them from other cohorts. Their parents' cohort, for example, probably had a very different experience of child-birth in the 1950s. Their children—these babies—form another cohort, one that will come of age in the twenty-first century. We can only guess what experiences will shape their lives.

A generation or a group of the same age (like the 12-year-olds in Jensen's study) is called a **cohort**. When differences among cohorts are a result of the common history and experiences unique to each age group, these differences are known as **cohort effects** (Schaie, 1965). The main problem with the cross-sectional design is that it confounds (confuses) age effects with cohort effects. We don't know whether differences we've measured are due to developmental changes from one age to another or to the unique experiences of the different age groups. In his study, Jensen is said to have confounded age with educational history.

Combining the Two Designs

We've seen that both the cross-sectional and the longitudinal designs have advantages and limitations. Sometimes researchers combine the best features of each in what we call a **sequential design.** Using this design they can study changes in physical aggression, for example, between, say, 8 and 16, and also follow individuals for a fairly long period of time. They test groups of 8-year-olds, 10-year-olds, 12-year-olds, and 14-year-olds (cross-sectional design feature) and then test them again two years later when they are 10, 12, 14, and 16 years, respectively (longitudinal design feature). This design yields data about development during a span of eight years, yet it only takes two years to complete. It provides information about changes in individual children from one age to the next and also controls somewhat for cohort or history effects.

SELECTING A SUITABLE RESEARCH METHOD

We've looked at a number of research methods and designs, and we've seen that no single one is clearly superior to the others under all circumstances. When people are doing research in child development, how do they decide which method is best for their purposes? The answer depends on three factors—the research question, the ethical considerations associated with the study, and the circumstances of the person doing the investigating.

The Research Question

What kind of questions do we want to answer about children? Do we want to know what children are like or what they do? We could get this information from a descriptive study. Do we want to know what behaviors are likely to be associated with each other? We could find out from a correlational study. Or do we want to know what causes a specific behavior? Then we would have to conduct an experimental study.

These different methods allow us to make different kinds of statements about children—descriptive, correlational, or causal—after we've collected and analyzed data in a research study. We always have to be careful to make only the kind of statement allowed by our research method. (Examples of each kind of statement are given in Box 1-4.)

Ethical Considerations

Some questions can't be investigated in the manner that would yield the most conclusive results because doing so might harm the research subjects. We couldn't study the effect of protein in infants' diets on their growth by depriving a group of infants of protein, for example. Instead, we could compare the growth of infants in naturally occurring groups that have more or less protein in their diets. Our results in this case would be correlational. If we did find a

---

BOX 1-4 Examples of Descriptive, Correlational, and Causal Statements

Which of the following statements do you think are descriptive? correlational? causal?

1. On the average, babies weigh about 7 pounds at birth.
2. The incidence of Down's syndrome in children increases as maternal age increases.
3. Older children tend to have more diseases than infants.
4. When the drug thalidomide is given to pregnant women early in pregnancy, it prevents the formation of arms and legs in the fetus.
5. Girls mature physically faster than boys.
6. Boy toddlers own more vehicle toys than girl toddlers do.
7. Prematurity is a risk factor for problems in attachment.
8. Aggressive behavior can be reduced if children watch prosocial TV programs rather than violent ones.

  Descriptive: 1
  Correlational: 2, 3, 5, 6, 7
  Causal: 4, 8

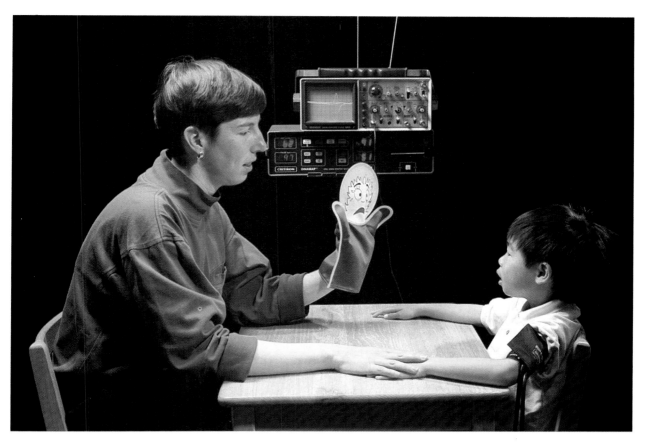

FIGURE 1-11
Research with children must be guided by ethical considerations. In this experiment, conducted as part of a University of California, San Francisco, health project, researchers studied children's emotional reactivity as measured by changes in their heart rate in response to various puppets. The researcher is attentive to the child's responses and provides reassurance. If he had become unduly frightened, the experiment would not have continued.

relationship between growth and protein, we couldn't be sure it was a causal relationship. We wouldn't know whether differences in growth were due to differences in protein or to some other differences in the naturally occurring groups. But these are the limits imposed on research by ethical considerations.

The ethics of research, especially research involving children, has been a concern to many groups over the years, including the American Psychological Association, U.S. governmental agencies, and the Society for Research in Child Development. These groups have developed a code of ethics for research with children, which includes the following guidelines:

1. Investigators may not use any research operations that may harm a child physically or psychologically.
2. Investigators must obtain **informed consent** from the parent or legal guardian of the child before the child can be a subject in a study. This means that the study must be explained completely and accurately to the parent or guardian in language he or she can understand.
3. Investigators cannot obtain consent by promising that the research will benefit the child.
4. Investigators may not force an unwilling child to participate in a study. The child has rights that supersede the investigator's.

5. Investigators should keep confidential all information obtained about the child.
6. When the experimental treatment is believed to benefit children, the control group should be offered the same or similar beneficial treatment. This applies even if it substantially increases the cost of the study.

These guidelines are relevant mainly to research that involves some kind of treatment, interaction, intervention, or manipulation of variables—the kind of action typical in experimental studies. Correlational and descriptive studies, which tend to involve the observation of children in natural settings, are much less likely to run into ethical problems or to meet resistance from parents. Regardless of the research question we're asking or the kinds of results we would like to get, ethical considerations have top priority when we're choosing a research method.

The Investigator's Circumstances

The third factor involved in choosing a research method is the circumstances of the investigator and his or her role in the child's life. A teacher, for example, is in an excellent position to observe children in a natural setting, so if a teacher were going to do a research study, he or she might do a case study or a descriptive study. On the other hand, teachers are not in a very good position to use the experimental method. As we saw in the kindergarten example, they would probably find it difficult to set up experimental and control groups in the classroom and to manipulate variables in a careful, rigorous way.

Let's consider the case of a teacher who notices that his students aren't reading as well as he thinks they should be. He might think of several possible reasons for this problem: (1) The reading books might be uninteresting or unattractive to the children; (2) the children might find reading irrelevant or meaningless because it's not tied to their daily lives; (3) the children might be tired during reading time because it comes right after physical education. To test the three hypotheses in an experimental study, the teacher would first have to divide the class into two groups, a control group and an experimental group. Then he would have to vary each of the three conditions systematically to see if a change in any of them caused a change in reading achievement.

Conducting such a study would be a long and tedious process. How long would the teacher have to use books he judges "very interesting" before he could legitimately expect to see an improvement in reading ability? How would he judge the interest level in the first place? Where would the more interesting books come from if the school budget for books has been spent on the books the class already has? How could the teacher prevent a child in the experimental group from letting a friend in the control group read the more interesting book at home? How would the teacher explain to parents that the books couldn't be changed for six months because of the research study, no matter how poorly some children were doing?

Obviously the teacher is in no position to conduct such a study. If he thinks some change will improve his classroom, he is obligated to make that change as soon as possible and then observe the results as best he can. He might try having reading time first thing in the morning when the children are fresh, or he might try letting the children pick their own books from the school library or he might explore ways to integrate reading and journal writing. When he finds that the children's reading ability has improved, he won't be able to say with assurance that the change he made caused the improvement. Only an experimental study would allow him to make that claim. But because he looked at the problem in a critical way, made careful observations, came up with reasonable hypotheses, and tested his hypotheses in a systematic way, he used what he could of a research method. And probably he's found a practical solution to his problem.

TYING THINGS TOGETHER

Now that you have some idea of what's involved in research, you probably understand why it's so difficult to conduct flawless research with children. You probably also understand why, despite the vast number of studies that have been done on various aspects of child development, our knowledge is still limited. You can see why, for example, after numerous studies, debate seems to continue over the effects of a mother's smoking on her unborn child. These studies have been correlational, not experimental. No matter how brilliantly conceived the hypothesis or how carefully executed the research, every study has limitations imposed by financial constraints or the reality of dealing with human subjects.

Even when knowledge is extensive and data about a particular behavior are conclusive, our ability to take action or make changes has limitations as well. Because people have different values, they have different ideas about the way children ought to be. We know, for example, that the amount and quality of parental talk to babies is related to the babies' language development. But it would be pointless to try to persuade a parent to talk more to a baby if the parent thought a quiet child was an ideal child. We know there's an association between watching violent TV shows and behaving aggressively, but that's not going to make parents who value rough-and-tough behavior in their child start to monitor TV viewing. Values are a product of one's philosophy, religion, culture, and personal experience; value questions can't be addressed by research studies alone.

Despite these limitations, research is invaluable as a source of knowledge and information about children. And an understanding of research methods is essential to anyone with a critical interest in the study of child development. Without that understanding, you wouldn't know what was wrong with the study of black and white children's IQs. You wouldn't know how valid the study of the kindergarten reading program was. You wouldn't be as knowledgeable and thoughtful as you could be when observing your own child or classroom group.

When you read about the many different aspects of child development in the chapters ahead, you'll often refer mentally to the material discussed in this chapter. Research methods, designs, and issues are the underlying foundation for the study of child development.

FIGURE 1-12
Breastfeeding is considered
preferable to bottle feeding
because breast milk contains
important antibodies and is
perfectly suited to the baby's
nutritional needs and digestive
capacities. Even so, some
women choose bottle feeding
because of personal or cultural
values. As these two women
demonstrate, both feeding
methods are compatible with
a loving mother-child
relationship.

OVERVIEW

Our knowledge of children is based on research, but people who live and work with children will find the research useless unless they're able to understand and evaluate the studies. Teachers, parents, and caregivers have to know what research issues might be involved, what kinds of studies might be conducted under different circumstances, and how the results of different studies can be interpreted. They also have to understand why, despite innumerable studies, our knowledge about children is still limited. Perhaps most importantly, they have to be willing to think in critical ways when they encounter research findings in child development. Just as researchers have to be careful about how they design their studies, practitioners have to be careful about how they interpret and apply research conclusions to the children in their care.

CHAPTER REVIEW

THE MAJOR RESEARCH ISSUES

- Researchers have to make sure they've selected variables to test that are valid measures of the final behavior they're studying.
- To obtain reliable results—results that can be duplicated by others—measures should be as objective and well-defined as possible. Raw data should not contain opinions, conclusions, or theoretical statements. Testing or measurement should be conducted by objective third parties who are "blind" regarding which children have received which treatment.
- Researchers have to make sure that the results they obtain from studying a few people can be generalized to other groups of people. They can ensure their study's external validity—its generalizability—by beginning with a representative sample of the population in question.
- Researchers have to make sure they eliminate other possible causes of the behavior they're studying before they claim to have established a cause-effect relationship. They can ensure their experiment's internal validity—the soundness of attributing the results of the experiment to the independent variable—by doing pretesting to gather baseline data or, preferably, by randomly assigning children to experimental and control groups.
- If these conditions are met, researchers can conduct an experimental study, whose results will indicate a cause-effect relationship. If researchers work with naturally occurring groups, they can conduct a correlational study, whose results don't indicate causality directly.

THE MAJOR RESEARCH METHODS

- Major methods of child study are the case study, the descriptive study, the correlational study, and the experimental study.
- In the case study the researcher studies only one person or situation, but in great detail. Since any one person or situation is unique, the results of the case study are not generalizable.
- Descriptive studies provide information about how people act. Descriptive studies include specimen records, behavior checklists and event samples, and time samples. Descriptive studies give a broad, rich picture of children's behavior without establishing causation.
- Correlational studies measure two variables of interest. If the variables consistently change in the same direction, they're said to be positively correlated; if they change in opposite directions, they're said to be negatively correlated. Data for correlational studies can come from descriptive studies, questionnaires, or interviews. Simple correlational studies do not firmly establish cause-effect relationships.
- In experimental studies, the researcher manipulates an independent variable by applying more of the treatment to one group than to another, control group. Experimental studies allow researchers to make statements about causes of changes in the dependent variable.

THE MAJOR RESEARCH DESIGNS

- The two basic research designs are the cross-sectional and the longitudinal. In the cross-sectional design researchers study groups of children of different ages at the same point in time. In the longitudinal design, researchers follow the same group of children over a certain period of time.
- Cross-sectional studies can be completed more quickly than longitudinal studies. They are also less likely to be affected by biased sampling, which occurs when groups that were originally comparable change over time.
- Longitudinal studies allow researchers to observe changes in one child over a fairly long period of time. They also eliminate the possibility that cohort effects will be confounded with age effects—that is, that differences between groups will be attributed to developmental changes when they're really the result of different experiences.
- The sequential design combines the best features of the two designs, yielding data about a long span of development in a relatively short period of time.

SELECTING A SUITABLE RESEARCH METHOD

- Researchers decide on a research method by considering three factors—the research question, the ethical considerations, and the circumstances of the researcher.
- Experimental studies are suitable if researchers want to discover causes of behavior. Correlational studies are suitable if they want to know what behaviors are associated with other behaviors. And descriptive studies are appropriate if they want to know what children do.
- Ethical considerations have highest priority when a research method is being chosen. Experimental studies are much more likely to raise ethical problems than correlational or descriptive studies, because experiments usually involve some intervention in the child's life.
- In choosing a research method, researchers also have to take into consideration their own role in the lives of the children they wish to study.
- Our knowledge about children is incomplete, but even when we have indisputable data, people's values play a part in what they do with research results. Despite these limitations, research is an invaluable source of information and knowledge about children; it provides the foundation for the study of child development.

KEY TERMS

variable	researcher bias	correlational study	cross-sectional design
validity	external validity	closed method	longitudinal design
predictive validity	pretesting	open observation method	biased sampling
construct validity	baseline data	positively correlated	cohort/cohort effects
face validity	internal validity	negatively correlated	sequential design
reliable	control group	independent variable	informed consent
blind study	experimental study	dependent variable	

SUGGESTIONS FOR FURTHER READING

Beatty, J. J. (1986). *Observing development of the young child.* Columbus, OH: Charles E. Merrill.
Provides checklists for use in observing many aspects of a young child's development, including social play, prosocial behavior, large and small motor development, and language. Very useful for the preschool teacher.

Bissex, G. L. (1980). *GNYS at work: A child learns to write and read.* Cambridge, MA: Harvard University Press.
A good example of a case study, written by a parent. Provides a portrait of the child's literacy development from age 5 to 9.

Cozby, P. C., Worden, P. E., and Kee, D. W. (1989). *Research methods in human development.* Mountain View, CA: Mayfield.
An overview of research techniques for the undergraduate who wants to use research wisely. Written especially for those in applied fields, such as teaching, social work, or counseling.

Vasta, R. (1979). *Studying children: An introduction to research methods.* San Francisco: W. H. Freeman.
A very informative little paperback. Not too technical, but very meaty. Excellent examples and illustrations.

THEORIES OF CHILD DEVELOPMENT

We sometimes hear people make the comment, "That's just theoretical." They usually mean that a statement is unproven, unrelated to real situations, or just someone's guesswork. It is true that theories often don't hold up when tested. But that doesn't mean that people shouldn't try to formulate them. In fact, it's difficult to imagine facing the world without theories of one kind or another. A **theory** is a set of systematically organized assumptions about why something happens or works the way it does. All of us, whether we consider ourselves scientists or not, approach the world with some basic assumptions about the causes of events around us. It's one of the ways we organize and make sense of the world.

Theories of child development are sets of assumptions about why children act the way they do, as well as why and how they change over time. Good theories of child development are useful in a number of ways. They help us organize information, which otherwise might be just a confusing collection of facts or observations. They help us analyze this information in terms of general principles and long-term processes. The help us formulate explanations for it. And they will generate new ideas and questions that can lead to further discoveries.

In this chapter we discuss four traditional child development theories—maturational, psychoanalytic, learning, and cognitive developmental. But before we look at the ideas embodied in these theories, let's consider the experience of a parent seeking advice about her child. In her story we'll see how theories organize the way people think about the world and guide their actions. We'll also get a sense of how the major child development theories translate into advice about real children.

THEORIES IN PRACTICE: ONE PARENT'S EXPERIENCE

Justin's mom, Peggy, was at her wits' end. Justin had become toilet trained during the day when he was 3, but now, a full year later, he still wasn't dry through the night. Peggy waited patiently for his diapers to be dry in the morning—a signal that he didn't need to wear them to bed—but they never were. In fact, things seemed to be getting worse. Some mornings, his pajamas and sheets were even soaked.

Then Peggy noticed that the largest size disposable diaper was starting to be tight on him. She began to worry—not just that she wouldn't be able to find big enough diapers for him but that he wasn't developing normally. If diapers weren't even made for 4-year-olds, why did her son still need them at night?

Finally, Peggy decided to get some advice. She made an appointment with her regular pediatrician, Dr. Blair, a doctor she considered very competent. Dr. Blair listened to Peggy's story and then advised her that Justin just wasn't ready for nighttime dryness. When Justin's body and brain were mature enough, Dr. Blair said, the problem would probably "take care of itself." He explained that Justin's ability to be dry was biologically determined by his genetic timetable and that different children could be expected to mature at different rates.

Dr. Blair even took a detailed history of Peggy and John, Justin's dad, to find out when they, as children, had been able to stay dry at night. Neither Peggy nor John could remember any particular problems with bed-wetting, although they couldn't say for sure what their early history had been. "These things sometimes run in families," said Dr. Blair. "You know, 'like father, like son.'" He told Peggy and John to "give it another six months" and then make another appointment if there had been no improvement.

Peggy didn't really want to wait six months. She was tired of the wet beds and not convinced Justin would become dry by himself. She called a local clinic for a referral and got the name of another pediatrician, Dr. Frazer. When she told Dr. Frazer about Justin's problem and expressed her frustration, he assured her that Justin probably wasn't wetting his bed on purpose. He asked if there had been any unusual events in the household within the last year, or if anything else could be upsetting Justin.

Peggy explained that Justin's grandmother, who had spent a lot of time at their house, had moved out of state about six months earlier to live in a retirement village. Justin didn't seem to miss her very much, Peggy told Dr. Frazer. "He goes to nursery school now," she said. "I think he's been too busy to miss her. It's his 20-month-old sister who seems to miss her the most. She stands by the telephone and says 'G'ma, G'ma'—I think because we used to call their grandma quite often to invite her over to our house."

Dr. Frazer noted that there had been three significant events in Justin's life within the fairly recent past—the birth of a baby sister, the start of nursery school, and his grandmother's move out of state. "The bed-wetting could be a symptom of any of these changes," Dr. Frazer explained. "Try talking with him about these events to see if one of them is troubling him. In the meantime, don't press him too hard about the toilet training. He might develop guilty or shameful feelings if you do. This might lead to 'fixation' in this stage of development and possibly to compulsive behavior later in life, such as not being able to go to sleep at night without three or four trips to the bathroom." Dr. Frazer suggested that Peggy give the problem another four to six months. If it hadn't improved by then, they might want to consider some sessions of play therapy.

Peggy was disturbed by Dr. Frazer's advice. She certainly didn't want to make toilet training traumatic for Justin or create any emotional problems that he would have to

FIGURE 2-1
Besides her complexion and facial characteristics, what else has this child inherited from her mother? Some child development theorists would say, a great deal of what she is and will become.

deal with later in life. She decided to stop trying to do anything about it for the time being. She resolved to stop worrying, too. But then her sister came to visit with her two children, and Peggy found out that her nieces had both been dry at night soon after the age of 3. Peggy's sister advised her to resolve the problem before it became "chronic." She knew of a doctor in Peggy's area who had been quite successful at treating bed-wetting, and Peggy made an appointment with her.

Dr. Rizzoli talked very confidently about her experience with night training. She was most enthusiastic about what she called a "bell and pad." This was a device that went on the child's bed at night. When the child urinated and wet the pad, an electric circuit closed. This caused a bell to ring, and the bell woke the child. After a few nights, the sensation of bladder fullness alone would awaken the child, who would then be able to go to the bathroom before wetting the bed.

Dr. Rizzoli also told Peggy how to begin what she called a behavior modification program. This was a systematic plan for changing behavior through rewards. She suggested that Justin be given a small treat or surprise each morning that he had a dry bed. To help "shape" this behavior, Dr. Rizzoli went on, Peggy and John could train Justin to hold his urine for longer and longer periods. They could wake him up to go to the bathroom at midnight for a few nights, then at 1 A.M., then at 2, and so on, until he could go through the whole night.

Peggy was glad to get some concrete advice at last. Yet she hesitated—she'd never heard of any of the things Dr. Rizzoli talked about, and no one she knew had ever had

FIGURE 2-2
Behavior modification programs are based on the idea that rewards (such as gold stars) can be used to increase the occurrence of desirable behaviors. This idea seems to be effective for this "Super Worker" except when it comes to combing her hair.

to go to such lengths to toilet train their children. She knew that John, who always seemed to believe that things would work out by themselves, would never go along with anything as elaborate as the bell and pad. When she heard another mother talking in the park about what she had done about bed-wetting, she couldn't help but join in the conversation. This mother said that her son had wet his bed until he was 8, and a wonderful doctor had helped them understand why. Naturally, Peggy got the doctor's name.

Dr. Graham stressed the importance of Justin's ability to understand what was involved in being dry at night and his interest in trying to change his behavior. She asked Peggy about Justin's language development and his understanding of some basic concepts, such as why clouds move and where dreams come from. She asked Peggy if she thought Justin understood the whole toilet-training process and the extra work created when sheets and pajamas had to be washed each day. Dr. Graham suggested that Peggy and John have Justin tested with a developmental scale of some sort to determine how egocentric he was in his thinking about the social world. Peggy said she'd call Dr. Graham if she decided to make an appointment for the test.

Peggy went home and thought about everything she'd been told. She had taken notes on what each doctor said, and as she reviewed them she was struck by how differently each doctor approached the problem. For something as common as bed-wetting, she mused, you'd think all these professionals would know what to do. You'd think there would be one tried-and-true solution. Why does what one doctor said contradict what another one said? And what should I do with all this advice? It looks like John and I will have to put our heads together and sort out what seems appropriate for Justin by ourselves.

Peggy may have received contradictory advice, but the pediatricians she saw weren't trying to make her life difficult. The advice each one gave her was, no doubt, good advice, from that physician's point of view. What none of them told her was that their advice was based on a *specific* point of view. Surely all the physicians knew about the bell and pad, yet only one recommended it. And all of them knew that bed-wetting correlates negatively with age—that is, bed-wetting decreases as age increases. Yet only one advised Peggy to wait for the problem to take care of itself as Justin got older.

The way that these physicians sift, sort, pay attention to, and select information is guided by their theoretical orientations, the way they think about the causes of behavior. As we explain the four major child development theories in the discussion that follows, you will be able to see the theoretical "camp" of each of the pediatricians Peggy consulted.

MATURATIONAL THEORY

Peggy's regular pediatrician, Dr. Blair, suggested that individual variations in behavior, like the age at which a child becomes dry at night, are the result of an inherited genetic timetable. This is why he tried to determine if Justin's parents had had bed-wetting problems as children and recommended that they just give Justin time. Dr. Blair believes in the maturational theory of child development.

Origins of Maturational Theory

Maturational theory was born in the late nineteenth century from the work of Charles Darwin on evolution (1859) and of his cousin Francis Galton on intelligence. Galton found that people who are genetically similar have comparable abilities, and he concluded that intellectual abilities are inherited and fixed at birth. Galton's conclusions, of course, were based on correlational data, and, as we saw in Chapter 1, correlational data can't be used to demonstrate cause-effect relationships. Members of the same family may have intellectual similarities not because of similar genes but because of a similar home environment. But Galton's discoveries spurred interest in the biological or genetic basis of behavior, the underlying idea of maturational theory.

According to maturational theory, the individual may be influenced by heredity either at birth, when certain genetically fixed characteristics are present, or later on, when genetically determined traits appear according to an inherited timetable. One example of a characteristic that is (usually) determined by this developmental timetable is the age at which puberty begins. Another is final adult height. Another, according to Justin's pediatrician, Dr. Blair, is the age at which the bladder can be controlled during the night.

Maturation is the process of biological change and development during which new behaviors steadily emerge one after another. Maturational theory suggests that, within a broad range of normal conditions, the appearance of a particular behavior depends on time, not on experience or environment.

Maturational Theory in the Twentieth Century

The most prominent American advocate of maturational theory in the late nineteenth and early twentieth centuries was psychologist G. Stanley Hall (1844–1924). Hall was the first president of the American Psychological Association and the founder of the first scientific psychological journal, *The Journal*

FIGURE 2-3
G. Stanley Hall (seated, center) established the first formal laboratory of experimental psychology in the United States, but he was also interested in more introspective approaches to psychology, including the work of Sigmund Freud (seated, left). In 1909 he invited Freud to come to Clark University to give a series of lectures on psychoanalysis. Hall apparently found no contradiction between maturational and psychoanalytic theory, since he claimed that Freud's work was his chief inspiration for the next 15 years.

of Genetic Psychology. He expounded a biological view of human behavior with an emphasis on stages of development unfolding in a predetermined way.

One of Hall's most famous students was Arnold Gesell, a physician whose work was influential in the 1920s and 1930s. Gesell observed and described the ages at which different behaviors emerged, such as walking and talking. Like other maturational theorists, he believed that these skills developed in accordance with the individual child's inner timetable, regardless of learning or experience. Learning could occur only after the individual was biologically ready.

Readiness, also called **neurological ripening,** was a major idea put forth by Gesell. Until the nervous system was mature enough for a particular skill or behavior, the child was not considered ready for it. In the 1930s, for example, it was suggested that children not be exposed to any type of reading instruction until they had reached a mental age of 6.5 years, as measured by intelligence tests (Morphett & Washburne, 1931). This landmark, 6.5 years, was thought to be determined by the biological maturation of the nervous system. No one seriously considered the idea that we believe to be true today—that *both* readiness for reading *and* intelligence as measured by intelligence tests might be influenced by other, nonbiological factors, such as a child's experience with language.

Another well-known student of Hall's was Stanford University professor Lewis Terman. Terman's primary interest was intelligence testing, and he wrote an English translation of the test constructed by the Frenchmen Binet and Simon (1905). This test became known as the Stanford-Binet Intelligence Test (Terman, 1916). It measured a person's intelligence, which was reported as an "intelligence quotient," or IQ. Terman believed that intelligence was basically a genetically fixed characteristic. Although children learned more the older they became, Terman thought their ability to learn—their IQ—was stable. Later in this book we will see that this assumption is open to question.

Several observers have remarked that child psychology in the first half of the 20th century consisted merely of gathering data to establish **norms**—age-related standards or patterns of behavior that apply to large groups—without

FIGURE 2-4
Arnold Gesell devoted his career to studying the orderly emergence of behavior patterns in infants and children, such as the locomotor progression of rolling over, sitting up, crawling, pulling up, walking with support, standing alone, and walking alone. The founder of the Gesell Institute of Child Development at Yale University, he popularized the idea that children can't learn or develop new behaviors until they reach the appropriate level of physical and neurological readiness.

the guidance of a theory. However, to a maturational theorist, establishing norms *is* part of a developmental theory, one in which maturation determines when behaviors will occur. Gathering data about the emergence of intellectual abilities, for example, was viewed as gathering data about the maturation of the nervous system. And maturation was the undisputed explanation of the times for the development of intellectual abilities. Intellectual and physical development were the main interests of maturational theorists.

Today few psychologists believe that abilities are fixed by genes for life without any influence from the environment. But some people, including some psychologists, parents, teachers, and pediatricians, have ideas that lean in this direction. They believe that inherited characteristics and maturation play a critical role in development and that learning and external conditions aren't very important. Dr. Blair, Justin's pediatrician, holds this point of view about bed-wetting. In fact, we hear statements every day about child development that have a maturational basis—see Box 2-1 for some examples.

PSYCHOANALYTIC THEORY

The second pediatrician Peggy visited, Dr. Frazer, was concerned about the emotional and social aspects of toilet training. He warned Peggy not to push Justin too much because a traumatic experience could leave him with emotional scars. Dr. Frazer's advice was molded by psychoanalytic theory, a view that originated with Sigmund Freud. We discuss Freud's work below, and then we discuss the work of Erik Erikson, who developed his own theory, which he did not divorce from traditional psychoanalytic ideas.

Sigmund Freud

In the early part of the 20th century, while maturational theorists were looking at intellectual and physical development, Austrian physician Sigmund Freud (1856–1939) was studying social and personality development. Like the maturationists, Freud recognized the importance of biology, but he also stressed the interaction of biology with the environment. Freud was interested in neurology and in nervous disorders such as tics and various types of hysteria. He learned that patients' nervous symptoms improved when the patients were encouraged to talk about them, and he developed a treatment based on this technique. This was the beginning of psychoanalysis, a therapy Freud referred to as "the talking cure."

BOX 2-1   **Common Statements Based on a Maturational View of Child Development**

- "We don't accept children for kindergarten until they're at least 5 years old."
- "Children aren't ready for reading until at least first grade."
- "Don't worry if your 2-year-old isn't toilet trained yet. When he's ready, he'll practically train himself."
- "Oh, she'll grow out of it. Just leave her alone."
- "They are born that way."

FIGURE 2-5
Sigmund Freud found his heir
in his youngest daughter,
Anna, shown here in 1913
when she was 18 and he was
57. The only one of his six
children to follow in his footsteps, Anna Freud went on to
become a noted child psycho-
therapist in London.

FREUD'S NOTION OF INSTINCT. In his work Freud focused on the biological component of the personality, which he called instinct. Freud used this term differently than other theorists, who use it to refer to an innate behavior in animals. Freud defined **instinct** as a mental representation of a body state or
need, such as hunger or sexual arousal (Freud, 1925). An understanding of
Freud's idea of instinct is the key to his entire theory.

According to Freud, all actions are motivated by the desire to maximize
instinctual or need gratification while minimizing punishment, guilt, and anxiety (Maddi, 1976). These motivations are what drive behavior. Because these
needs are basically biological or physical, Freud's theory is a biological theory
first of all. But environment is important too, because personality development
depends on how the biologically based needs are met.

THE PARTS OF THE PERSONALITY. Freud suggested that the psyche or personality
has three parts, the id, the ego, and the superego. The **id** is the inherited and
unconscious source of instincts. It constantly propels the individual to relieve
tension or excitation in the body—that is, to satisfy needs. The life of the
young child is dominated by the id and characterized by the tendency to gratify selfish instincts.

The **ego**—the reality-oriented part of the personality—tries to direct the id
to find satisfaction in appropriate ways, ways that won't be punished. The

TABLE 2-1 Freudian Defense Mechanisms

Defense	Definition	Example
Repression	Blocking out an unacceptable thought or feeling	A child feels he would like to get rid of his father so he can have his mother all to himself, but he keeps the thought from reaching his conscious mind.
Projection	Attributing an unacceptable thought or feeling to someone else; externalizing an internal experience	A child who dislikes a teacher feels that the teacher dislikes her.
Reaction formation	Doing the opposite of what one feels like doing to avoid experiencing an unacceptable impulse or feeling	A child who feels unsure of himself bullies other children and bosses them around.
Displacement	Transferring feelings from one event or person to a less threatening one	A child who is angry at her parents scolds her doll.
Acting out	Expressing an unconscious impulse directly rather than experiencing the emotion that accompanies it	A child sees his best friend playing with someone else and knocks down their block construction to avoid feeling jealous.
Intellectualization	Transforming thoughts about emotional conflicts into inaccurate, quasi-intellectual terms	A teenager rationalizes deep hostility toward her brother with a variety of extensive complaints.
Sublimation	Redirecting energy associated with an unacceptable feeling into a socially acceptable activity	A teenager feeling strong sexual urges focuses intensely on practicing the piano.

rules for nonpunished behavior in a particular society are taught to the child by her parents, and these rules become part of the personality, too. They make up the part called the **superego,** which itself begins to provide anxiety and guilt to punish the child's consideration of forbidden behavior. The superego guides the ego as the ego directs the id in finding gratifications that will not be punished. At times the superego blocks gratification altogether. When the superego effectively blocks direct instinctual gratification, the ego allows partial gratification by means of ego defense mechanisms (Table 2-1).

STAGES OF DEVELOPMENT IN FREUDIAN THEORY. The instincts responsible for the child's conflicts with the punishing world change "location" as the child moves from one stage of development to the next. Freud identified these stages as oral, anal, phallic, latency, and genital. Each one is associated with the particular zone of the body Freud thought was the source of troublesome instinctual energy for that period of life; that is, as the child matures physically, the instincts that are most likely to get the child into trouble change.

In the oral stage, lasting from birth to about 1 year of age, the mouth is the center of activity, the location of most satisfying (or frustrating) experiences. In the anal stage, which lasts from about the end of the first year to the end of the third, the anal region is the center of instinctual activity that comes in conflict with parental values. During this period, the child's developing sphincter control encourages the parents to attempt toilet training. The child, however, has an urge for immediate gratification of the instincts associated with defecation, so there is a conflict between child and parents. In the phallic stage, which lasts until about age 5, the genitals are the new source of prohibited instinctual activity. These early stages were considered by Freud to be especially important for personality development.

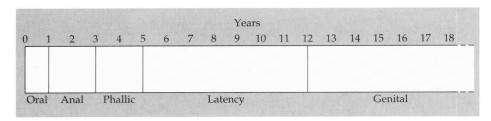

FIGURE 2-6
Stages of development in
Freudian theory. Early psycho-
analysts believed that if
instinctual energy became
blocked in any one stage,
characteristics of that stage
would become embedded in
the individual's personality. For
example, someone who was
fixated at the anal stage, when
toilet training is an important
issue, might be stingy, compulsive, punctual, and unable
to let go of possessions or
relationships.

The latency stage lasts from age 5 or 6 until adolescence. During this stage, no new instincts or activities emerge to create problems. In adolescence, the genital stage begins, and mature love of others and socialized adult behavior become possible. Desires may still conflict with social rules, but the ego and superego keep the id in check.

If instincts are not overgratified or undergratified by the parents, the child progresses naturally from one stage to the next, acquiring the defense mechanisms associated with each stage for keeping the id under control. These defense mechanisms largely determine the behavior we see. If the instincts are overgratified or undergratified at any point, however, the individual can become fixated at that stage. Some instinctual energy remains blocked in a previous zone rather than moving on to the next. As an adult, the individual continues to exhibit needs, defenses, and behavior more typical of individuals at an earlier stage. For example, an adult who overeats may be fixated at the oral stage. In our earlier illustration, Dr. Frazer, the second pediatrician Peggy consulted, was concerned that Justin might become fixated at the anal stage if his instinctual needs were undergratified at this point.

THE MEANING OF FREUDIAN THEORY FOR CHILD-REARING PRACTICES. Although Freud's theory asserted that fixation could result from either overgratification or undergratification, Freud lived in a formalized, repressive society with rigid rules about child rearing. It was much more likely in this setting that instincts would be undergratified than overgratified. Application of his theory, there-fore, usually meant a loosening of rules to prevent fixation at any one stage. Although there has been very little research that clearly supports Freud's ideas, Freudian theory has been a tremendously influential force in twentieth-century thought. We often hear teachers and parents make statements that show they accept Freud's ideas (see Box 2-2).

BOX 2-2   Common Statements Based on a Psychoanalytic View of Child Development

- "It's better to feed a baby on demand than on a rigid schedule."
- "Children who suck their thumbs weren't allowed to suck the bottle or breast long enough when they were babies."
- "Nursery schools should have a punching bag so that children who tend to quarrel with other children can release their emotions in a constructive way."
- "Don't interfere with children's dramatic play; it's important that they work out their emotional conflicts."

FIGURE 2-7
Erik Erikson proposed that development proceeds through a series of stages, each with a crisis to be overcome, before identity is finally achieved. Many people in early childhood care and education programs find Erikson's theory particularly relevant to their work.

Erik Erikson

Active in the 1940s, 1950s, and 1960s, Erik Erikson never actually broke from the psychoanalytic view of personality development, but his focus was different from Freud's. Freud focused on the instincts, especially sex, as the driving force behind actions; Erikson focused more on how society affects the ego (an **ego psychoanalytic** emphasis). Freud's emphasis was on the unconscious; Erikson's was more on the conscious (ignoring the id and the ego's unconscious defense mechanisms) and how the conscious interacts with the outside world.

ERIKSON'S PSYCHOSOCIAL THEORY OF DEVELOPMENT. Erikson proposed that the major crisis at each developmental stage originates in the complex demands of society on the individual, rather than simply in parental reactions to the child's bodily needs, as Freud believed. Erikson developed this idea because he recognized that healthy adaptation to reality differs greatly from one society to another, something that wouldn't be true if parental reactions to human biology were the primary factor determining personality. He also saw that society's demands on a person change as the person grows and that these demands can influence the course of development. Erikson's theory has been called a psycho*social* theory of development to reflect Erikson's emphasis on the individual's adaptation to social situations and demands in contrast to Freud's psycho*sexual* view.

ERIKSON'S STAGES OF DEVELOPMENT. In Erikson's theory there are eight stages of development, extending throughout the life span. Each stage is characterized by a major crisis or turning point, a time of increased vulnerability as well as increased potential for psychological growth. In Stage 1, which lasts from birth to about 18 months, the psychosocial conflict or crisis is between trust and mistrust. Depending on how the parent responds to the baby's needs, such as hunger, the baby will decide that he or she is either "all right" or "not all right." The appropriate resolution of this stage is the development of trust, but not complete trust, because that would lead to behavior that wasn't truly adaptive. This kind of appropriate resolution applies to each stage.

In Stage 2, which lasts from about 18 months to about 3½ years of age, the conflict is between autonomy on the one hand and shame and doubt on the other. If the child is allowed to move around, touch objects, and explore, and if toilet training is not severe, the child develops a sense of being a separate person, able to make choices and capable of some control over the world. In our illustration, Dr. Frazer considered Justin to be in this stage. He implied that Justin needed to develop a sense of autonomy by learning to stay dry without experiencing shame or doubt. Erikson's other stages are summarized in Table 2-2.

LEARNING THEORY

The third pediatrician Peggy saw, Dr. Rizzoli, didn't talk about Justin's emotional or intellectual development. Instead, she gave Peggy very concrete advice about what she could do to change Justin's bed-wetting behavior. Her

TABLE 2-2   Erikson's Eight Stages of Development

Psychosocial Conflict (Crisis)	Pivotal Events	Age	What a Person Learns When Development Proceeds Successfully
Trust vs. mistrust	Caregiver response to physical needs of infant, especially in feeding	Birth to 18 months	I am all right.
Autonomy vs. shame or doubt	Toilet-training, locomotion, exploration, and touching of objects in environment	18 months to 3½ years	I can make choices.
Initiative vs. guilt	Curiosity resulting from increased language, motor, and cognitive skills	3½ to 6 years	I can do and I can make.
Industry vs. inferiority	School tasks such as learning to read	6 to 12 years	I can join with others in doing and making things.
Identity vs. identity confusion or diffusion	Learning one's vocational and professional orientation	Adolescence	I can be to others what I am to myself.
Intimacy vs. isolation	Love relationship	Young adult	I can risk offering myself to another.
Generativity vs. stagnation	Parenting, nurturing others, civic responsibility	Mature adult	I am concerned for others.
Integrity vs. despair	Reflection on one's life	Older adult	I can accept my life.

SOURCE: Adapted from material in Erikson, E. H., Identity, youth and crisis. New York: W. W. Norton, 1968.

emphasis was completely on the external or environmental aspects of the situation. She indicated that behavior is learned, especially through praise and reward. Dr. Rizzoli's advice reflects a learning view.

In contrast to psychoanalytic theorists, who focus on inner personality developments over time, learning theorists tend to pay less attention to inner changes. They focus instead on observable, external behavior and how specific environments affect it. Psychoanalytic theory proposes that biologically based events set personality development in motion. Learning theory, on the other hand, generally ignores biological aspects of development (assuming a typical, intact individual) and proposes that developmental changes occur as a result

FIGURE 2-8
According to Erikson, a toddler who is allowed to explore, experiment, and try things for herself without being criticized for mistakes will develop a sense of being a separate, autonomous person. Similarly, older children who succeed in school will develop feelings of competence and achievement. Adults can help by understanding the tasks children face at different ages and responding appropriately.

of learning experiences. Learning is defined as a relatively permanent change in behavior as a result of experience.

Origins of Learning Theory

Learning theory originated in studies with animals, and variations of it have been known by different names over the years, including S-R theory, behavior theory, behavioral theory, and behaviorism. As we saw above, the name "learning theory," refers to the focus on how a new behavior can be acquired. (In Justin's case, the new, learned behavior would be waking when his bladder is full.) The name "S-R theory" refers to the connection between a stimulus ("S") in the environment and a response ("R") on the part of the organism. The name "behaviorism" reflects the belief that psychological theories should be based only on observable behavior and should not include references to inner states, such as thoughts, feelings, desires, anxieties, and so on. We explain these various aspects of learning theory as we summarize the history of its development.

CLASSICAL CONDITIONING. The roots of learning theory can be found in the work of the Russian physiologist Ivan Pavlov (1849–1936). Pavlov showed that under certain circumstances an animal can learn a new physiological response to a stimulus in the environment. These circumstances involve the pairing of the stimulus with another stimulus that produces a particular response naturally. After repeated pairings, the new stimulus produces the same response as the original stimulus. The response to the new stimulus is "conditional" on the previous pairing of the two stimuli. This type of learning is known as **classical conditioning.** Pavlov called the stimulus that produces the response naturally the **unconditioned stimulus** (often abbreviated UCS) and the new stimulus that is paired with it (often presented slightly before it) the **conditioned stimulus** (CS).

Pavlov's most famous illustration of classical conditioning involved teaching a dog to salivate at the sound of a bell. He rang a bell (the conditioned stimulus) at the same time that he gave the dog some food (the unconditioned stimulus), which naturally caused the dog to salivate (the **unconditioned response,** or UCR). After several of these learning situations, the sound of the bell alone caused the dog to salivate somehow (the **conditioned response,** or CR).

The bell and pad recommended by Dr. Rizzoli is based on the principles of classical conditioning. In this case, the bell is the unconditioned stimulus that leads naturally to waking up, which is the unconditioned response. When the sensation of bladder fullness, the conditioned stimulus, is repeatedly paired with the bell, eventually the sensation alone leads to waking up. Waking up now becomes a conditioned response. In diagram form, it would look like this:

Bell ringing (UCS)......... leads to........ Waking up (UCR)
    paired with
Bladder fullness (CS)... leads to..... Waking up (CR)

We often see apparent examples of classical conditioning in child development. Placing a nipple in a baby's mouth naturally elicits sucking. After the

FIGURE 2-9
Russian scientist Ivan Pavlov demonstrated that animals could acquire new reflexes through a process of conditioning. He conditioned dogs to salivate in response to a variety of signals, including a bell, a metronome, a light, and a rotating disk. His ideas and experiments formed the basis of the theory that behavior is the result of learning experiences. For his ground-breaking work, Pavlov was awarded the Nobel prize in physiology in 1904.

baby repeatedly sees the nipple just before it's placed in his mouth, the sight of the nipple alone may cause him to start sucking. In this case, the sensation of the nipple in the mouth is the unconditioned stimulus that elicits sucking, the unconditioned response. The sight of the nipple is the conditioned stimulus that also comes to elicit sucking, which in this situation is a conditioned response.

After the initial conditioning, the unconditioned stimulus must be paired at least occasionally with the conditioned stimulus to "reinforce" the conditioned response. In other words, if the baby continued to see the nipple but didn't experience its being placed in his mouth, he would gradually stop sucking at the sight of the nipple. Another phenomenon associated with classical conditioning is that responses to conditioned stimuli may generalize to other, similar stimuli. In this example, the baby might start sucking at the sight of a pacifier or a nipple-shaped toy.

Another idea related to classical conditioning is that of secondary versus primary rewards. **Primary rewards** reduce the physiological tensions or needs of hunger, thirst, sex, and pain. **Secondary rewards** come to have rewarding qualities by being associated with primary rewards. For example, a mother's smile may become a reward after being paired with food and other primary rewards. Although early behaviorists used terminology like *physiological needs* and *needs reduction,* they never viewed biological states as all-important for personality development as Freud did.

INSTRUMENTAL CONDITIONING. Pavlov studied how behavior was influenced by stimuli that occurred *before* the behavior. An American psychologist, Edward Thorndike (1874–1949), was interested in how behavior was affected by events that occurred *after* the behavior. He showed that he could increase or decrease the frequency of a voluntary behavior if he followed it consistently with a reward or a punishment. This type of conditioning is known as **instrumental conditioning,** and it provides the basis for **behavior modification** programs. When Dr. Rizzoli advised Peggy to reward Justin each morning he had a dry bed, she was assuming that the frequency of this desired behavior would be affected by rewards contingent on the behavior. This means that the reward would follow *only* when the behavior, or a close approximation of it, actually occurred. If Peggy gave Justin a similar gift when he didn't have a dry bed— if she simply gave him a gift each morning—she would defeat the purpose of the program.

THE SCIENCE OF BEHAVIOR. Another American psychologist, John B. Watson (1878–1958), was sharply critical of the introspective methods of studying human behavior used by other psychologists. He thought there were bound to be inaccuracies in people's own reports of their reactions to various stimuli, and these procedures couldn't be used with children or animals, the subjects in whom he was most interested. Above all, Watson wanted psychology to be a science of behavior, which he called **behaviorism.** He believed that valid data could be obtained only from the observation of behavior, those things that people actually say or do. Because of his revolutionary influence, Watson is known as the "father of behaviorism."

FIGURE 2-10
B. F. Skinner, shown here as a young man at Harvard in 1933, elaborated the ideas of John B. Watson into a broad theory of animal and human behavior. Skinner believed that people's actions—even such complex actions as speaking a language—could be explained as learned behaviors, acquired through the processes of positive and negative reinforcement.

B. F. Skinner

The most influential radical behaviorist was B. F. Skinner (1904–1990). Skinner's brand of behaviorism completely rejected such concepts as drives that are in some sense inside the organism and therefore unobservable. Instead, it attempted to explain behavior only in terms of what can be observed.

Skinner replaced the concept of reward with the concept of **reinforcement.** A reinforcer is defined as any observable stimulus that increases the frequency of a response when it's presented contingent on the response—that is, when it follows the response. Skinner called this process of increasing the frequency of a behavior by adding a reinforcing stimulus **operant conditioning**. (Thorndike had referred to the same type of learning as instrumental conditioning.)

Some reinforcers are **positive**—they consist of something added to the environment following a response. If a child asks politely for a cookie, for example, and her parent gives her one, the child is positively reinforced for being polite.

If the child begs and whines for the cookie and gets one, she's positively rein-forced for begging and whining. The cookie is the positive reinforcer that increases the likelihood that the behavior—whether polite or whiny—will occur again.

Other reinforcers are **negative**—they consist of removing something from the environment following a response. Let's consider the case of the child and the cookie again but from the parent's point of view. If the child is whining and the parent gives her a cookie, the whining stops. Something offensive has been removed from the parent's environment. If the parent then gives cookies more frequently to stop the whining, we say that the parent's cookie-giving behavior has been negatively reinforced by the child. Both positive and neg-ative reinforcers increase the likelihood that certain responses will occur again, the former by adding something, the latter by removing something.

One of Skinner's interests was how new behaviors are acquired. He and his followers became well known for teaching a new behavior by taking an exist-ing, similar behavior and reinforcing it to bring it closer and closer to the desired behavior. This process of reinforcing successive approximations until the desired behavior appears is known as **shaping.** For example, if researchers wanted a pigeon to walk with its head held very high, they give it grain first when it held its head slightly higher than average, then considerably above average, then stretched very high. Eventually the pigeon carried its head high most or all of the time.

In our illustration, Dr. Rizzoli suggested that Justin's parents wake him up during the night to have him go to the bathroom and that they wake him up later and later as time went on. Thus, they could reinforce Justin for morning dryness from the beginning, even though his initial behavior only approxi-mated unassisted morning dryness. Thereafter, they would require closer and closer approximations of unassisted bladder control before providing the reinforcement.

Social Learning Theory

Comparatively recently, some theorists concerned with human learning, nota-bly Julian Rotter and Albert Bandura, have been much more willing to talk about cognition (thinking) and have begun elaborating descriptions of cog-nitive processes (Rotter, Liverant, & Crowne, 1961; Bandura, 1973, 1977). Their ideas have for many years been labeled **social learning theory.** Bandura ini-tially emphasized that many behaviors are learned not gradually through shaping but quickly through observation and imitation of others. It's unlikely, for example, that many of us could learn to drive a car through shaping, which depends so heavily on trial and error. We might not live through the first les-son. Instead we learn through cognitive processes related to modeling (imi-tating the general form of behaviors observed in others) and verbal instruction.

As social learning theory has progressed, it has become more and more cog-nitive. Walter Mischel (1976) suggested that an individual's behavior in a par-ticular situation is determined not by the situation alone but by a whole com-plex of inner qualities that the individual brings to the situation. This includes abilities, values, expectations, interpretations, and plans. These essentially cog-nitive qualities are not directly observable. Mischel noted that the same stim-ulus or situation—for example, a classroom test—elicits different responses

FIGURE 2-11
Social learning theorists point out that human beings learn many behaviors through verbal instruction, observation, and imitation. Helping to wash the family car is a form of play for this toddler, but he's also learning certain behaviors and skills, as well as certain underlying attitudes and values, as he helps out.

from different individuals, depending on the qualities and interpretations they apply to it. Whereas the radical behaviorist would assert that the stimulus controls the response in a strict way, the social learning theorist allows room for individual variation in the stimulus-response pattern.

Recently Bandura has extended his theory into the realm of cognitive theory so far as to label it "social cognitive theory" (1986, 1989). Rather than conceiving of the individual as determined strictly by the learning history his environment has dealt him, Bandura has substituted a person who in large measure determines his own destiny by choosing his future environment as well as other goals he wishes to pursue. He reflects on and regulates his own thoughts, feelings, and actions to achieve those goals. The degree to which he is effective in thinking, motivating himself, and feeling positively about his goal-directed actions is in fact largely determined by his own **self-efficacy belief**—that is, the belief that he can actively control the events that affect his life rather than having to passively accept whatever the environment provides. So social learning theory accepts a number of the principles of behavioral psychology, such as the effects of reinforcement and other aspects of the environment on behavior, but it supplements these principles with ideas about cognition in a human being who can actively change his environment.

Examples of common statements based on learning theory are given in Box 2-3.

BOX 2-3   Common Statements Based on a Learning View of Child Development

- "You may watch television after you finish your homework."
- "In our math program children learn just one small step at a time. Success is guaranteed and children want to keep working with the materials."
- "When you finish your reading and math assignments, you may paint, play with blocks, or choose a learning game."
- "Ignore children when they're behaving badly; praise them when they're behaving well."
- "You'll spoil the baby if you pick him up when he cries."
- "Children who answer correctly will receive a gold star on their papers."
- "The baby stops crying as soon as she hears my footsteps. I guess she knows that she'll be fed soon."
- "If children see you hitting, they learn to hit."

COGNITIVE-DEVELOPMENTAL THEORY: JEAN PIAGET

The last pediatrician Peggy saw, Dr. Graham, asked if Justin understood what was expected of him and if he seemed to be interested in changing his behavior. This doctor probed Justin's general knowledge and understanding of the world. She wanted to evaluate his level of cognitive development, apparently to determine if he was capable of understanding his behavior and how it affected others. If he didn't have these understandings, a method like rewarding his behavior would be of little use or might even have a negative impact, according to Dr. Graham. If he did have these understandings, then his mother could make use of them to help him become dry at night.

Interest in cognition as a factor in determining behavior grew rapidly in the 1950s, even before the beginning of social learning theory. Theorists and researchers from a number of traditions, including learning theory and psychoanalytic theory, noted that exploration and learning often occurred best in situations unrelated to the satisfaction of commonly recognized reinforcers or primary rewards (those having to do with the satisfaction of physiological needs). One researcher found that monkeys would learn a task when it was followed by an opportunity to look at something outside their cages (Butler, 1953). An earlier researcher had found similar behavior in rats, who would cross an electrified grid to get to a maze filled with new objects (Nissen, 1930). Some theorists suggested that there might be a drive to play, explore, effectively manipulate, and become competent in mastering the environment (White, 1959), but others looked for a different explanation. The study of cognition seemed to be a fruitful area to investigate for an explanation of exploration.

At about the same time, information-processing theorists (Newell, Shaw & Simon, 1958; Miller, Galanter & Pribram, 1960) began using a computer analogy to describe cognitive phenomena, such as selective attention, information gathering, and problem solving. Information-processing theory is described in more detail in later chapters on cognitive development, since it addresses issues of particular relevance then.

However, since the 1930s Swiss biologist-turned-psychologist Jean Piaget (1896–1980) had been studying the development of cognition. Piaget was par-

FIGURE 2-12
Jean Piaget devoted his life to the study of children's intellectual development. He was interested in their ideas on every subject, from the rules of games as an index of their moral development to the origin of dreams as a clue to their understanding of thinking.

ticularly interested in what knowledge is and how people acquire it, and he approached the question of adult knowledge by investigating children's knowledge. He asked two basic questions: Why do children and adults think differently in similar situations? What causes human knowledge to change over time?

In his studies Piaget found that children have different levels of understanding at different ages. Their responses to a situation are determined not just by the situation alone but by how they understand the situation. This is the crux of the cognitive-developmental theory.

Piaget's Explanation of Knowledge Acquisition

Piaget's explanation for the changes in a person's knowledge over time is quite complex. He saw knowledge as constructed or created gradually as maturing individuals interact with their environment. Children are thus seen as being active in their own development. By contrast, in traditional maturational theory, you will recall, the child is at the mercy of the genes that determine the rate of maturation. When the child is physically ready for learning—when neural ripening has occurred for a certain area of development—the child can acquire knowledge quite easily from the environment.

Learning theorists also believe that knowledge is external, but they think it can be acquired through experience and reinforcement. Piaget, on the other hand, does not think of knowledge as something that exists independently in the external world and that a person can simply acquire. Knowledge is a creation resulting from the interaction of the developing person and the environment.

PROCESSES BY WHICH KNOWLEDGE IS ACQUIRED. Piaget proposed two processes to explain how knowledge is created and changed over time. **Assimilation** is the process of taking in information about the environment and incorporating it into an existing knowledge structure, or, as Piaget calls it, a **scheme**. A 2-year-old who is familiar with dogs, for example, can be said to have a dog scheme, which may cover medium-sized, four-legged animals found in people's houses. The first time the child sees a cat, she may call it a dog, because that's the most appropriate scheme she has. Gradually, as she sees more cats and notices how they're different from dogs, she develops two schemes, one for cats and one for dogs. This process of changing knowledge structures is known as **accommodation.**

Our schemes are always inadequate to handle all our experiences (Piaget, 1963), so assimilation tends to distort information from the environment to make it fit available schemes. Eventually these distortions are corrected as we change schemes to accommodate the new information. In this way our schemes come to conform more closely to the world around us. The 2-year-old changes her dog scheme to exclude animals that meow and climb trees, and she develops a cat scheme that includes these characteristics. Eventually her schemes will accurately reflect all the characteristics of both types of animal.

Piaget uses the term **equilibration** to refer to the process by which assimilation and accommodation attempt to balance each other. When children first start to learn about the world, it takes a long time for assimilated information to be accommodated. But as thinking becomes more complex, and as the person develops more and more schemes, accommodation occurs more quickly.

PIAGET'S STAGES OF DEVELOPMENT. Assimilation and accommodation lead not just to more knowledge but to reorganizations of knowledge, to different ways of thinking. The points at which reorganization takes place mark the beginnings of different stages. Each stage is characterized by a unique way of thinking. The four stages proposed by Piaget are summarized in Table 2-3, and we discuss each stage in considerable detail in later chapters.

Piaget and Motivation for Knowledge Acquisition

Piaget's theories have been enormously influential in many areas of child development. One implication of his ideas is that children will prefer moderately novel events because these are the events that are most likely to be accommodated (Hunt, 1965). Completely familiar events may be uninteresting

TABLE 2-3 Piaget's Stages of Cognitive Development

Stage	Description
Sensorimotor (0–18 months)	Knowledge is acquired and structured through sensory perception and motor activity. Schemes involve action rather than symbols.
Preoperational (2–6 years)	Knowledge is acquired and structured through symbols, such as words, but schemes are intuitive rather than logical.
Concrete operational (7–12 years)	Knowledge is acquired and structured symbolically and logically, but schemes are limited to concrete and present objects and events.
Formal operational (12 years and older)	Knowledge is acquired and structured symbolically and logically, and hypothetical/deductive ("if-then") thinking can be used to generate all the possibilities in a particular situation.

to the child because they require no change in scheme. But completely unfamiliar events may be incomprehensible to the child because the child has no scheme into which to assimilate them.

Piaget's ideas provide a theoretical basis for the notion of **intrinsic motivation,** or motivation that comes from cognitive processes (Hunt, 1965). In other words, a child may initiate actions without being motivated by hunger, thirst, sex, or pain and without being rewarded or punished. Children will act simply to understand. When they're interested in something, they're indicating both that they understand it in some sense and that they're trying to understand it in a better way. Because children's schemes differ from adults', children's interests also differ from adults'.

The cognitive-developmental theory is evident in many child-rearing and educational practices and beliefs. Some examples are listed in Box 2-4.

A BROADER SCOPE: THE SYSTEMS APPROACH

All of the theories described above differ from the others in significant ways, including their scope. *Scope* refers to the issues and areas addressed by the theories, or what they try to explain and what they don't. A detailed comparison of the scope of the theories is beyond the scope of *this* book, but two aspects of such a comparison are relevant here because they relate to a new and more general approach to theorizing.

BOX 2-4 Common Statements Based on a Cognitive-Developmental View of Child Development

- "Children learn best when they're interested in what they're doing."
- "Children are active learners."
- "When children answer questions incorrectly, ask them why they answered as they did before deciding how to help them arrive at the correct answer."
- "Children seek stimulation."
- "Don't put all of the new toys out in the classroom at once; add new ones gradually to renew interest."

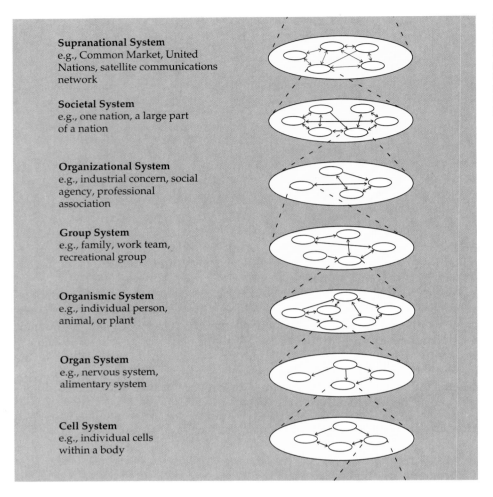

Supranational System
e.g., Common Market, United Nations, satellite communications network

Societal System
e.g., one nation, a large part of a nation

Organizational System
e.g., industrial concern, social agency, professional association

Group System
e.g., family, work team, recreational group

Organismic System
e.g., individual person, animal, or plant

Organ System
e.g., nervous system, alimentary system

Cell System
e.g., individual cells within a body

FIGURE 2-13
One model of levels of living systems. The systems approach suggests that human development occurs as a function of ongoing, mutual interactions among many systems. (From Sundberg, Tyler & Taplin, 1973, 104).

First of all, the theories can differ in the domain of behavior they try to explain and predict. Maturational theory focuses mainly on physical abilities and intellectual development. Psychoanalytic theory focuses on emotional and personality development. Learning theory focuses primarily on social and intellectual development. And cognitive-developmental theory deals primarily with the child's developing intellectual understanding of the world.

A second difference between the theories is the extent to which they take into account the interacting **systems** that affect behavior. Systems are all around us; a human cell is a system, as is the nervous system or the human body itself. A school or a community is also a system. Systems are groups of elements that have similar rules for relating to each other. These rules and relationships differ from the rules for relating to elements outside the system. Each system has a boundary separating things "inside" from things "outside." Furthermore, systems tend to exist in hierarchies; that is, each system has smaller subsystems within it and is at the same time an element of larger systems beyond itself. For example, a body cell (such as a muscle cell) is a system

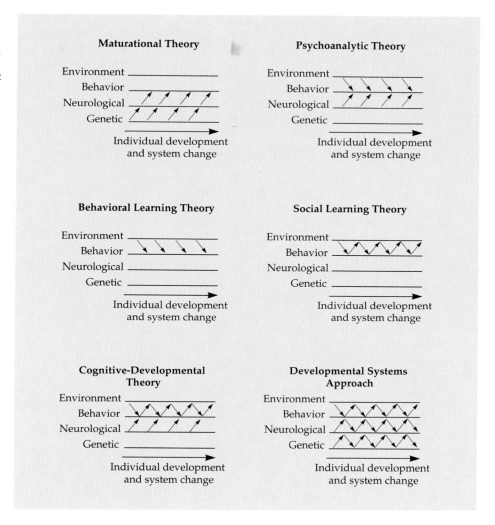

within an organ (such as the heart), which is a system within a group of body organs (the cardiovascular system), which is a system within a particular human being. One important, early model (Miller, 1971) of living systems is shown in Figure 2-13.

How can we understand and describe the systems and system interactions addressed by the four major theories of child development? To answer this question, let's identify four very general systems or levels of influence: genetic/cellular, neurological, child/behavior, and environment (see Figure 2-14). Maturational theory proposes that behavior is primarily a result of neurological maturation. Individual differences are seen as the result of genetic effects on neurological development. Behavioral learning theory spends little time describing anything other than environmental influences on behavior, although social learning theory has begun to address the effect of the individual on the environment.

Classical psychoanalytic theory describes behavior as determined by the stage of development an individual reaches as a result of need gratification. The environment provides responses that may undergratify or overgratify the needs, which appear as neurological maturation proceeds. Cognitive-developmental theory suggests in a general way that intellectual behavior is determined by the feedback the individual gets from small changes he produces in his environment. So Piaget claims there is an interaction between two systems, the individual's behavior and his environment. Cognitive-developmental theory also acknowledges that neurological development must have an effect on behavior, although it doesn't describe the precise nature of neurological influences on behavior.

Because all these theories have limitations in what they can address or explain, theorists in recent years have turned to a **developmental systems approach** as a framework for a more complete developmental theory. The major premise of this approach is that all systems influence all other systems. A complete theory should take into account this reciprocal or mutual interaction that occurs among all levels of the hierarchy of living systems and that goes on continually over time (Gottlieb, 1991). A single system influences both the systems within it and the system of which it is a part. Another way of saying this is that influences (or effects) go both to the level above ("bottom-up" influences) and to the level below ("top-down" influences). Those levels in turn act on the original system and on the levels above or below them. An extremely simplified illustration of the developmental systems approach is shown in the last panel of Figure 2-14.

Because the systems approach seems to capture much of the complexity of human relationships and human development, it has been used by a number of different theorists in child development, who have identified systems they think particularly relevant. Other names for the systems approach include "ecological" (Bronfenbrenner, 1977, 1979, 1989), "developmental contextual" (Lerner, 1986), "transactional" (Dewey & Bentley, 1949), and "interactive" (Magnuson, 1988).

Let's consider a few examples of "bottom-up" and "top-down" interactions among systems in human development. A person's genes influence the development of her nervous system, which influences her behavior, which in turn influences the environment around her—all cases of bottom-up influence. But it's also known that environmental stimulation can cause nerve cells to undergo greater growth and development, an instance of top-down influence (Greenough & Juraska, 1979). Another instance of top-down influence is the effect of environmental factors like light, length of day, and nutrition on hormones (Gorbman et al., 1983). The hormones circulate in the blood and make their way into the nucleus of the cell, where they activate genetic material, which results in the production of protein, which in turn affects body processes. So even genetic activity takes place in a context; genes by themselves do not produce physical structures or traits (Gottlieb, 1991). Rather, physical traits are the result of the interaction between genes and other systems above and below the genetic level.

The fact that heredity and environment are so interconnected over time makes it difficult, if not impossible, to answer the question *for any given individual,* How much of development is determined by heredity and how much is determined by environment? The developmental systems approach suggests that the best we can do with the **"nature versus nurture" issue** is to explain how biological and environmental systems interact to influence that individual's development. The effects of nature and nurture interact in such a way in development that they become inextricably intertwined. (For some kinds of behavior in some populations, the nature-nurture question is still a reasonable one to ask, as discussed further in Chapter 14, Cognitive Development in School-Age Children.) And because of this interaction, it's also impossible to give an either-or answer to another important question in child development, Does the child actively shape her environment or is she shaped by it? The answer is both.

THEORY, RESEARCH, AND VALUES: WHY THE CONTRADICTIONS EXIST

No matter which theoretical approach a researcher takes, that set of ideas will profoundly affect how he or she sees the world. Theoretical orientation influences the kinds of questions researchers ask and the kind of work they do to answer their questions. A researcher whose orientation is essentially maturational, for example, might collect data about the average age at which a particular behavior appears. A researcher with a psychoanalytic orientation might collect information about significant experiences occurring during childhood and then try to establish a relationship to problems during adulthood. A researcher with a behavioral orientation might keep track of the kinds of responses that parents make toward their child's misbehavior. A cognitively oriented researcher might record children's answers to questions about the way things work. Of course, data collected can be explained in different ways, and theoretical orientation guides what a researcher makes of the data.

Why is it that one person will view behaviors as basically driven by internal factors and another will see them as driven by external factors? Why is one person interested in the long-term emotional effects of a treatment and another interested only in how successfully it changes behavior? Theoretical orientations are shaped by several factors, including prevailing social and cultural ideas, the influence of respected teachers and authority figures, religious and philosophical beliefs, and personal inclinations and experience.

We expect scientists to base their theoretical views on objective analysis of evidence rather than on subjective beliefs, but it may not be possible for any human being to do this. There probably is no such thing as a purely "objective" analysis, given that all analyses are undertaken from some theoretical point of view. "We see what we know"—what we think we see is shaped by what we know or expect to be there. (See Wittgenstein, 1963, for a discussion of this intriguing idea.)

In a wonderful contemporary book about the solar system, *Coming of Age in the Milky Way,* Timothy Ferris describes the work of early philosophers and scientists attempting to explain celestial events. Many of them fit "facts" about the planets and stars to their ideas or models of the solar system, rather than allowing the "facts" to shape their models. It took a revolutionary thinker like

FIGURE 2-15
When we observe and study children, what questions will we ask? What answers do we hope to find? The way we organize our ideas and perceptions about the world will strongly influence the conclusions we reach.

Copernicus to get the "facts" straight, even though others had observed the same data for many, many years. Theories shaped the heavens in powerful ways for the people of an earlier age, just as theories shape the world for us today.

OVERVIEW

Data and theories interact in complex and subtle ways. We need theories to organize and make sense of the world, but how we perceive the world is influenced by our theories. Theories of child development provide a framework for the infinite variety of interpretations we can make of a child's behavior. Without them, we would lack the signposts and guiding principles that broaden our understanding and give meaning to our observations. At the same time, by their very nature, theories limit the aspects of children's behavior that we see or pay attention to; a single theory is always only one way of viewing a child's experience. When we understand this limitation, we can use the theories of child development in ways that increase our understanding without narrowing our perspectives.

CHAPTER REVIEW

- Four major child development theories are maturational, psychoanalytic, learning, and cognitive-developmental. A newer, developmental systems approach

attempts to provide a fra̶
explanation of developmen̶

̶ore complete

MATURATIONAL THEORY

- Maturational theorists believe that particular behaviors emerge at predetermined times, depending on the individual's inherited biological timetable, and that the timing is unaffected by environment or experience.
- Based on the work of Darwin and Galton, maturational theory dates from the nineteenth century and was expounded in the United States in the early twentieth century by G. Stanley Hall.
- Working in the 1920s and 1930s, maturational theorist Arnold Gesell described the regular emergence of dif-

ferent behaviors in children and ex̶
terms of readiness, or neurological ri̶
less of experience.
- Lewis Terman was responsible for the Sta̶
intelligence test, which measured a perso.
gence quotient, or IQ. Maturationists believ̶
is fixed at birth.
- Maturational theorists gather data to establish norms. The main focuses of their research are physical and intellectual development.

PSYCHOANALYTIC THEORY

- Developed by Sigmund Freud in the late 19th and early twentieth centuries, psychoanalytic theory is concerned mainly with personality development.
- Freud focused on the biological aspect of the personality, which he called instinct. He believed the body was driven by desires, particularly sexual desires, which were represented by mental images. The way people behaved was a result of their attempts to gratify these desires.
- Behavior is shaped, according to psychoanalytic theory, by the interactions of the id, seeking gratification; the superego, setting limits; and the ego, directing the id to find satisfaction in acceptable ways. The ego keeps the id in check by means of defense mechanisms, such as repression and sublimation.
- The instincts that drive the child change from one

period of life to the next. Freud identified five stages of development—oral, anal, phallic, latency, and genital. Children progress smoothly from one stage to another provided they don't become fixated, or stuck, in one stage by over- or undergratification.
- Erik Erikson focused not on instinct as the driving force behind actions but on the interaction of the ego and society. He suggested that conflicts arise at different stages of development because of societal demands on the individual.
- Erikson proposed eight stages of development, spanning not just childhood but the entire lifetime. Each stage is marked by a major crisis, the resolution to which either hampers the individual's growth or allows the person to move on psychologically to the next stage.

LEARNING THEORY

- Behaviorists focus on observable behavior and how it is affected by the environment. Behavior theory is also known as learning theory, S-R theory, and behaviorism.
Russian physiologist Ivan Pavlov demonstrated that animals can learn a new physical response to an environmental stimulus through a process known as clas-

sical conditioning. His most famous experiment involved conditioning a dog to salivate at the sound of a bell.
- American psychologist Edward Thorndike showed that he could increase or decrease the number of times a response occurred if he followed it with a reward or a punishment. This type of learning, known as instru-

70

...ides the basis for behavior

...own as the "father of behavior-
...argued that objective observation
...elf-report as the method of studying
...muli.

- John...wn modern exponent of behaviorism,
  ...ner, redefined rewards as reinforcers and
  ...ental conditioning as operant conditioning.
- ...er demonstrated that new behaviors could be
  ...ght by reinforcing closer and closer approximations of a desired behavior until the behavior itself
appears, a process known as shaping.
- Social learning theorists are willing to discuss conscious mental processes and inner experiences. They
  have pointed out that people learn things through
  observation and imitation as well as through reinforcement and shaping. They see the individual as
  actively choosing and changing his environment, setting his own goals, and reflecting on and regulating
  his own behavior. He is most likely to do this if he has
  a strong belief in his own self-efficacy.

COGNITIVE-DEVELOPMENTAL THEORY: JEAN PIAGET

- The idea that behavior and learning could be
  explained by something other than the satisfaction of
  drives or the reinforcement of responses to stimuli led
  theorists to begin investigating cognitive factors. The
  work of Jean Piaget tied in with these interests.
- Piaget discovered that children have different levels of
  understanding at different ages, which accounts for
  the fact that they don't think the same way adults do.
  He also found that responses to the environment
  depend not just on the situation but on how the individual understands the situation.
- According to Piaget, knowledge is constructed gradually through interactions with the environment. The
  child takes in information from the environment and
  incorporates it into an existing knowledge structure,
or scheme. This process is known as assimilation.
Since schemes are inadequate to handle all new information, the child gradually adjusts the schemes to
make better sense of the information. This process is
known as accommodation. Equilibration is the process
by which assimilation and accommodation are kept in
balance.
- Piaget proposed four stages of cognitive development,
  each characterized by a different, unique way of
  thinking: sensorimotor, preoperational, concrete operational, and formal operational.
- Piaget's findings suggest that children learn best
  when confronted with moderately novel events and
  that the desire to understand is a powerful motivating
  force behind children's behavior.

THE DEVELOPMENTAL SYSTEMS APPROACH

- Systems theory has attempted to provide a framework
  for a more comprehensive approach to theorizing
  about human development. The developing individual is conceptualized as a system, which is one member of a suprasystem, such as a family. This suprasystem is, in turn, a unit within a still larger system.
- A system is defined as a group of elements whose
relationships or rules of functioning differ from
relationships and rules found in other systems
reciprocal relationship with other systems in the
archy makes it extremely difficult to tease out th
ative effects of heredity and environmer
development.

THEORY, RESEARCH, AND VALUES

- Theoretical orientation influences how researchers see
  the world, what questions they ask, and how they
  pursue answers.
- Given the complexity of both the world and the ways
we can understand it, it's probably imposs
a purely "objective" opinion about th
human behavior.

KEY TERMS

theory
maturation
readiness
neurological ripening
norms
instinct
id
ego
superego
ego psychoanalytic

classical conditioning
unconditioned stimulus
conditioned stimulus
unconditioned response
conditioned response
primary rewards
secondary rewards
instrumental
　conditioning

behavior modification
behaviorism
reinforcement
operant conditioning
positive reinforcement
negative reinforcement
shaping
social learning theory
self-efficacy belief

assimilation
scheme
accommodation
equilibration
intrinsic motivation
systems
developmental systems
　approach

SUGGESTIONS FOR FURTHER READING

Baroody, A. (1987). *Children's mathematical thinking*. New York: Teachers College Press.

This book opens with a discussion of two views of development, the cognitive view and the learning view. Other chapters highlight corresponding differences in approaches to curriculum and to evaluation and remediation of children's difficulties in learning mathematics. The book provides a concrete example of how different theories lead to different observations and actions.

Ferris, T. (1988). *Coming of age in the Milky Way*. New York: Morrow.

This book tells the story of how human beings have come to their current understanding of the universe. Throughout history, human models have often matched theories more closely than they matched data. From ancient astronomers to present day astrophysicists, scientists "see what they know." This book provides interesting reading for the lay astronomer or philosopher of science.

Goodfield, J. (1981). *An imagined world*. New York: Harper & Row.

This story of a medical scientist investigating lymphocytes beautifully illustrates how we see what our the-

ory leads us to expect. This scientist saw things differently from other researchers because she went to her microscope with a different theory about lymphocytes. Well-written and engrossing.

Lerner, R. M. (1991). Changing organism-context relations as the basic process of development: A developmental contextual perspective. *Developmental Psychology, 27*(1), 27–32.

This article gives a comprehensive and detailed overview of systems theory.

Maier, H. (1978). *Three theories of child development*. (3d ed.). New York: Harper & Row.

This book discusses and compares three theories: the cognitive theory of Piaget, the behavioral theory of Sears, and the psychoanalytic theory of Erikson. It also discusses application of the theories to the helping process.

Nuland, S. B. (1988). *Doctors: The biography of medicine*. New York: Knopf.

This history of medicine and physicians provides many examples of how people's views—their theories—shape what they see and do. Readable and fascinating.

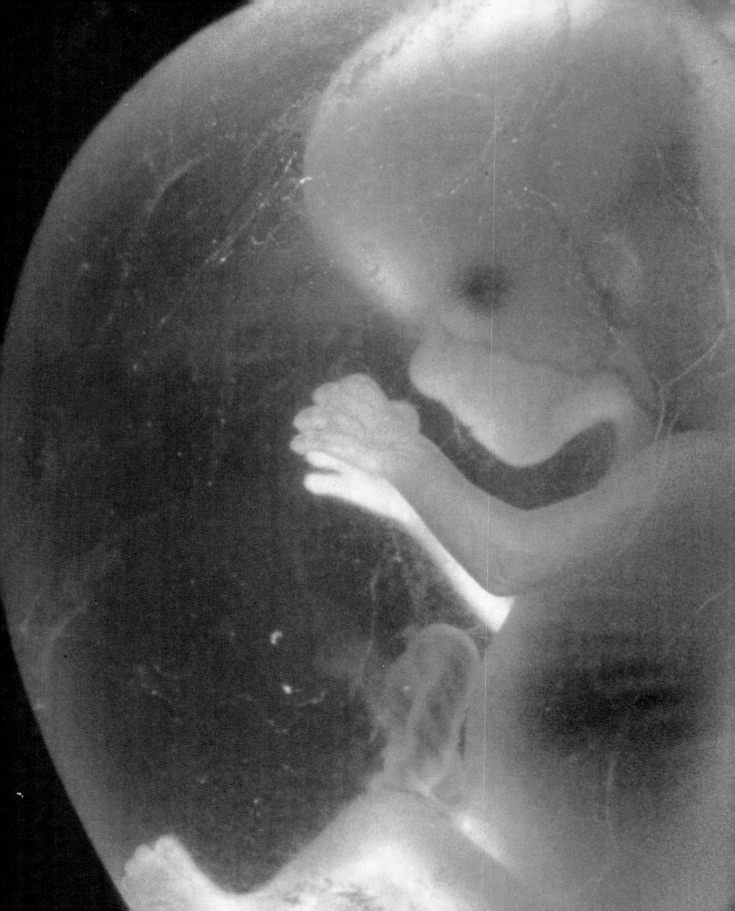

c h a p t e r 3

GENETICS, PRENATAL DEVELOPMENT, AND BIRTH

Lindsay woke from an afternoon nap with a start. The phone was ringing, but she couldn't bring herself to answer it. It was four and a half weeks since her amniocentesis, and any phone call could be the one from her obstetrician with the results. She let the answering machine take the call. Then, her heart pounding, she listened to the tape. She recognized her doctor's voice at once.

"Hello, Lindsay," he said. "This is Dr. Cortez. I know you're eager to hear the results of your amniocentesis, so I'll leave a message for you on your machine. Everything appears to be fine this time. And—it's a girl. Congratulations! I'll see you next week for your regular checkup."

Lindsay let out a shout of joy. Five years earlier, she had had a baby who was not fine. Samuel had seemed all right at birth, but when he was 8 months old, she noticed some worrisome changes. Instead of getting stronger and more mobile, he seemed to be getting floppier and weaker. He couldn't sit up as well as he could a month earlier, and he no longer seemed to be able to hold on to his toys. He stopped trying to crawl and pull himself up in his crib. Tests revealed that he was a victim of Tay-Sachs disease, a degenerative disorder of the nervous system. He went through a harrowing deterioration and died at the age of 22 months.

Lindsay's genetic counselor told her that although she and her husband were healthy, they were both carriers of Tay-Sachs disease. Any child they conceived would have a one in four chance of having the disease. For a long time they debated whether they should try to have any more children of their own. At last they decided to try again, this time making sure they had an amniocentesis to determine if the baby was healthy. They hadn't really thought beyond the amniocentesis, but they did know they wanted that information as soon as possible. After that, they'd consider their options.

Lindsay felt euphoric as she dialed her husband to tell him the good news. At last she could allow herself to think about this baby. For the first time in months she would be able to relax.

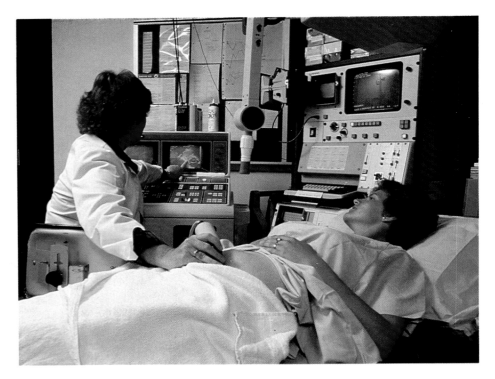

FIGURE 3-1
Ultrasound is just one of the technologies used today to monitor pregnancy and prenatal development. It can reveal important information about the fetus—its position in the womb, its size and gestational age, the presence of certain anatomical problems, and, if the genitals are visible, its sex. For expectant parents like this woman, ultrasound also offers dramatic and exciting proof that the baby does indeed exist!

FIGURE 3-2
Scientists learned what substance was responsible for genetic inheritance when they unraveled the structure of deoxyribonucleic acid (DNA). The DNA molecule consists of two strands connected in a twisting, ladderlike spiral known as a double helix. When the DNA molecule replicates, the two complementary sides of the double helix separate, and each strand makes an exact copy of its complement, resulting in two identical molecules. The double helix structure is clear in this computer model of DNA.

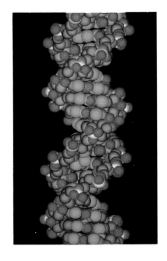

Lindsay's story isn't unusual today, but 25 years ago it would have been unthinkable. Advances in technology and knowledge have revolutionized pregnancy and birth for countless couples. Consider these new practices and trends:

- Couples thinking of starting a family can consult a genetic counselor to find out if they're likely to transmit a hereditary disease or abnormality to their child.
- Couples can choose when and if to have a child by using any of a number of birth control methods, rather than leaving the size of their family up to chance.
- Infertile couples can try a variety of conception methods, including artificial insemination and in vitro fertilization.
- Women can determine whether they're pregnant within 20 to 30 days of conception by using a urine test.
- Pregnant women can find out the sex of their baby and whether certain physical problems or genetic abnormalities are present through the use of ultrasound, amniocentesis, and chorionic villus sampling.
- Pregnant women are advised to eat well, get adequate exercise and rest, abstain from alcohol, cigarettes, and other drugs, and reduce the amount of stress in their lives.
- Women who attend prepared childbirth classes can actively participate in the birth process with reduced use of pain-relieving drugs.
- A majority of women are breastfeeding their babies.
- Fathers can be present at births, even when cesarean sections are performed.

- The emotional aspects of childbirth are being taken seriously by health care professionals. Some women are having their babies in alternative birth centers or at home. Challenged by prospective parents, hospitals are changing many of their traditional practices to promote the emotional well-being of both mothers and babies.

In this chapter we discuss genetics, prenatal development, and birth. Each of these areas has a direct impact on what kind of child a baby will eventually become. Each of these areas, too, has undergone profound changes in recent years, as a result of research discoveries, new technologies, and changing attitudes and social policies. Now more than ever we have a greater opportunity—and a greater responsibility—to see that all children get as fair a chance as possible, right from the start.

GENETICS: THE BASIS OF BIOLOGICAL INHERITANCE

FIGURE 3-3
Chromosomes are contained in the nucleus of the cell, which appears as a dark mass in this illustration of a human cell (top). The two twisting strands and the ladderlike bars connecting them are shown in the artist's model of part of a DNA molecule, shown at the bottom.

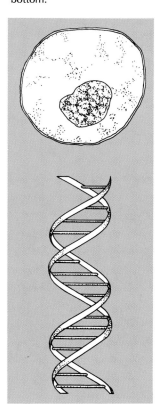

You don't have to look very far to see the incredible variation that exists within our human species. People differ in body size and build; skin color; eye, nose, and head shape; hair texture and color; and many other visible traits. Within the organism, beyond our observing eye, are other variations, such as blood type, hormone levels, intelligence, and predisposition to contract or resist cancer or other diseases.

What accounts for all these differences? What makes every human being a unique individual, unlike any other person who has ever lived or will ever live on the planet? The answer to these questions, or at least a large part of it, is genetic inheritance. Genetic inheritance doesn't *determine* everything a person is and becomes, but it does *influence* everything a person is and becomes. How much the person is affected by genetic inheritance—as opposed to environmental influences—is a long-standing question in the study of child development, as discussed in Chapter 2. We sometimes refer to this **nature-nurture controversy** in subsequent chapters when we discuss the effects of genetic inheritance on various aspects of development. To appreciate the controversy, and to understand an important part of development, you must know the basics of genetics.

Genes and Chromosomes

Genetics is the study of how biological traits are transmitted from one generation to the next. All of these traits—sex, eye color, final adult height, left- or right-handedness, and thousands of other characteristics—are encoded in **genes.** Every gene is a sequence of nucleic acids (DNA), which encodes the information needed to produce a protein, the basic building block of the cell. Genes are contained on **chromosomes,** extremely long strands of DNA coiled up in the nucleus of each cell. Chromosomes are long enough to be visible when we view a dyed cell under a powerful microscope.

Chromosomes occur in pairs, and every normal human body cell contains 23 of these pairs. The genes on one chromosome have counterparts on the other chromosome in the pair. The pairs of genes interact to determine which characteristics a person will inherit. Some genes are **recessive**—the informa-

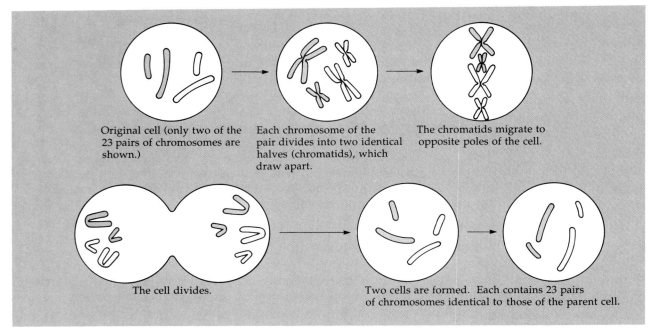

Original cell (only two of the 23 pairs of chromosomes are shown.)

Each chromosome of the pair divides into two identical halves (chromatids), which draw apart.

The chromatids migrate to opposite poles of the cell.

The cell divides.

Two cells are formed. Each contains 23 pairs of chromosomes identical to those of the parent cell.

FIGURE 3-4
Body cells replicate by mitosis. One cell divides, producing two new cells that are genetically identical to the original cell. This is the process by which bone, muscle, skin, and other cells of the body grow and repair themselves.

tion they carry won't be translated into a particular biological trait unless they're paired with another recessive gene. Blue eye color is an example of a recessive trait. To have blue eyes, a person has to have inherited a recessive gene for eye color from each parent.

Other genes are **dominant**—they override their gene partner so that their characteristic is always expressed. Brown eye color is dominant. A person with brown eyes may have inherited the recessive gene for blue eyes from one parent, but the dominant gene inherited from the other parent overrode that recessive gene. Some characteristics, such as hair color, are controlled by a single gene pair. Many others, such as intelligence, seem to be influenced by the actions of many pairs of genes.

Cell Division and Conception

Each of us has thousands of genes, and each of us has, in every cell, a unique set of genes that makes us distinct individuals. This unique set is produced at the moment of conception from the combining of two cells, an egg contributed by the mother and a sperm contributed by the father. Eggs, or ova (singular, ovum), and sperm—known as **germ cells** because they're involved in reproduction—are different from all other cells in the body, which are known as **somatic cells.**

Germ cells differ from body cells in the way they divide. For example, when we grow new skin cells or hair cells, a parent cell (or original cell) divides to produce two new cells, each containing the same 23 pairs of chromosomes as the parent. Each new cell, with its 46 chromosomes, is identical to the parent cell. This type of cell division, in which the original cell is exactly duplicated, is called **mitosis** (Figure 3-4).

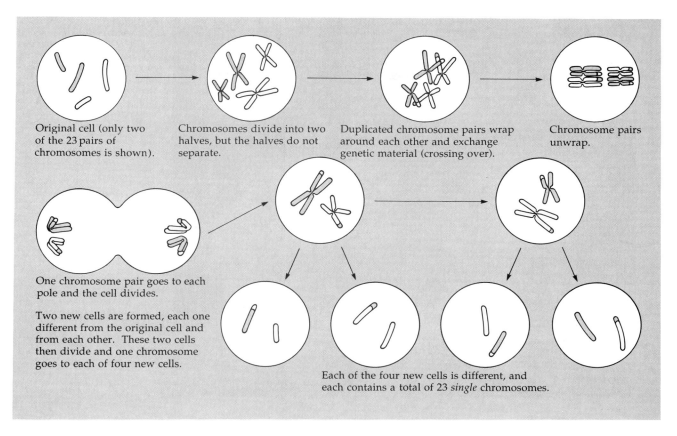

Original cell (only two of the 23 pairs of chromosomes is shown).

Chromosomes divide into two halves, but the halves do not separate.

Duplicated chromosome pairs wrap around each other and exchange genetic material (crossing over).

Chromosome pairs unwrap.

One chromosome pair goes to each pole and the cell divides.

Two new cells are formed, each one different from the original cell and from each other. These two cells then divide and one chromosome goes to each of four new cells.

Each of the four new cells is different, and each contains a total of 23 *single* chromosomes.

FIGURE 3-5
Germ cells replicate by meiosis, a process that results in cells with two important features: They contain 23 single chromosomes rather than 23 pairs of chromosomes, and they're genetically different from the original cell rather than identical to it. With these characteristics, eggs and sperm can combine to create a genetically new human being.

Germ cells, however, are designed to combine with other germ cells to produce an altogether new cell. If each germ cell brought 46 chromosomes to conception, the resulting organism would have 92 chromosomes. Obviously, this isn't what happens. Germ cells are prepared for conception by a different kind of cell division, called **meiosis.** In this kind of cell division, the number of chromosomes in the cell is reduced by half (Figure 3-5).

Meiosis provides the biological mechanism for the mixing and combining of characteristics that make every individual unique. During the crossing-over step shown in Figure 3-5, chromosome pairs in the parent cell wrap around each other and exchange genetic material. When they unwrap and the cell divides, the new cells contain genes that make them different from the parent cell and from each other. This accounts for the differences we see between parents and children and between siblings. Crossing over makes the possibilities for unique combinations virtually limitless (Pai, 1974).

Determination of Sex

One of the 23 pairs of chromosomes determines whether a fetus will be female or male. Females have a matching set of sex chromosomes, called XX (from the way they look under an electron microscope). Males have one X chromosome and one Y chromosome. After meiosis, eggs always contain an X

FIGURE 3-6
The wonders of human genetics are responsible for families in which individuals resemble each other and yet remain unique. The genetic relationship among the adult siblings in this family is clear from their remarkably similar eyes, noses, and mouths.

chromosome; sperm may contain an X or a Y chromosome. If the sperm contributes an X chromosome to the new organism at conception, the baby will be a girl. If it contributes a Y chromosome, the baby will be a boy (Figure 3-7). The sex of the child, then, is always determined by the father.

You might expect that exactly half the babies conceived would be females and half would be males, but this isn't the case. Actually, about 120 males are conceived for every 100 females. By birth, the ratio has dropped to 105 males for every 100 females. The reason for this is that the sex chromosomes carry many genes other than the ones that determine sex. If one of these genes is defective on an X chromosome in a female, a corresponding healthy gene on the other X chromosome can often compensate for it. A female would have to inherit two defective chromosomes to express the defect and suffer adverse effects from it.

If a male has a defective gene on the X chromosome, on the other hand, there may not be a corresponding healthy gene on the Y chromosome, which is smaller and is thought to carry fewer genes. The male would be more likely to express an abnormality encoded on the X chromosome. As a result, a higher mortality rate exists for male organisms, and more of them have to be conceived if a roughly equal number are to be born.

Characteristics encoded by genes that are carried on the sex chromosomes are known as **sex-linked characteristics.** Many of these characteristics are encoded by recessive genes carried on the X chromosome. They can be expressed in males because males don't have a second X chromosome with a

FIGURE 3-7
Sex determination. The process of meiosis produces germ cells (eggs and sperm) with just one sex chromosome. If a sperm with an X chromosome fertilizes the egg, the child will be a girl. If a sperm with a Y chromosome fertilizes the egg, the child will be a boy.

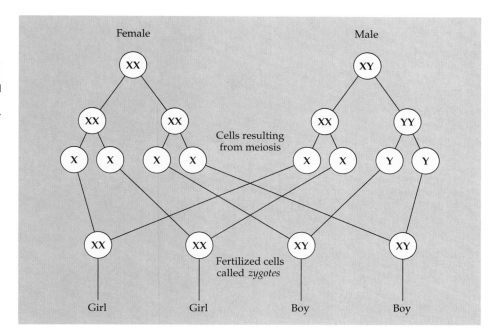

matching dominant gene to override them. Hemophilia and some forms of color-blindness are examples of sex-linked traits that normally occur only in males.

Multiple Births

The usual course of events at conception is that one egg and one sperm unite to produce one fertilized ovum, known as a **zygote**. But sometimes a woman's ovary releases two or more eggs during monthly ovulation. If both eggs are fertilized, two babies will develop. These twins will be no more alike than siblings born at different times, because each came from a different fertilized egg. Twins who develop this way are called **fraternal,** and may be two girls, two boys, or a boy and a girl.

Multiple births are sometimes caused by fertility drugs. Women whose body chemistry prevents them from ovulating (releasing an egg during each monthly cycle) may take these drugs when they want to become pregnant. Fertility drugs trigger ovulation, but sometimes they overstimulate the ovaries, and several ova are released. If all the ova are fertilized, the woman may find she's carrying twins, triplets, or even more fetuses. As many as six or seven babies have been born to women who have taken fertility drugs.

Twins can also originate from the division of a zygote by mitosis into two cells that then separate and develop independently. Because mitosis involves the exact replication of the genetic material in the original cell, these babies will be **identical** twins. These twins are alike in every way and are, naturally, the same sex (Figure 3-8). Identical triplets can develop if the original zygote separates by mitosis twice in a row (producing four identical cells), and then one cell dies.

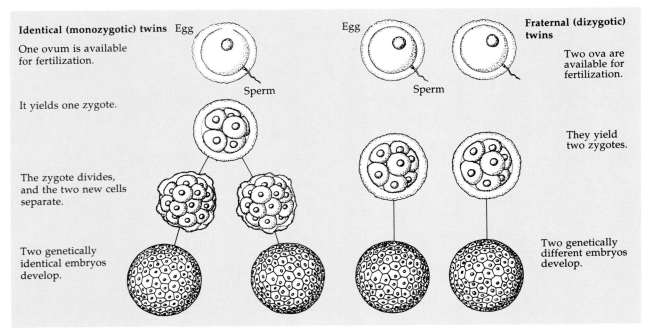

Identical (monozygotic) twins

One ovum is available for fertilization.

It yields one zygote.

The zygote divides, and the two new cells separate.

Two genetically identical embryos develop.

Fraternal (dizygotic) twins

Two ova are available for fertilization.

They yield two zygotes.

Two genetically different embryos develop.

Egg   Sperm   Egg   Sperm

FIGURE 3-8
Identical twins are produced when a fertilized egg divides and forms two cells, each containing the same genetic material. Fraternal twins result when two different eggs are fertilized at the same time and develop side by side in the womb. Their genetic material is as different as that of any two siblings born at different times.

Twins are born about once in every 89 births, and of these, about one-third are identical twins. Triple births occur about once in every 7,000 births. Quadruplets are very rare, occurring only once in about 400,000 births (Gedda, 1961). The incidence of multiple births varies among different population groups. For example, they are more frequent among Nigerians and quite rare in Chinese and Japanese populations (Stern, 1973). Multiple births are also positively correlated with maternal age: as the mother's age increases, so does the probability of a multiple birth.

PRENATAL DEVELOPMENT: LIFE IN THE WOMB

We think of birth as the beginning of a person's life, but a great deal has already happened to that person by the time birth occurs. The basic biological blueprint was laid down at conception, when the ovum was fertilized by a sperm. As we've just seen, the individual's unique genetic make-up was established at that moment. Now the individual begins the 9-month-long period of growth and unfolding that we refer to as **prenatal development**. During this period, development proceeds in a genetically determined pattern common to all human beings, but it is critically influenced by interactions within the context of the mother's body. A number of systems have worked together over time to form this new human being—systems related to human evolution, current social practices, and the parents' histories and choices, for example. The baby we see for the first time at birth is the end product of this long process.

The last 25 years have seen an explosion of knowledge about prenatal development. Embryologists can now tell us exactly when the heart, lungs, and other organs are formed, when the eyes open, when the fetus can cry and suck its thumb in the womb. Research scientists can tell us how the fetus is

FIGURE 3-9
Fraternal twins, like the girls on the left, can be told apart even when they choose to wear the same Mickey Mouse skirts. Identical twins, like the girls on the right, are nearly impossible for their friends and parents to distinguish, even when they wear different shirts.

affected by environmental factors, such as alcohol, cigarettes, and drugs, including such diverse substances as tetracycline, Valium, retin-A, and cocaine. Epidemiologists understand a wide range of genetic and developmental problems, and genetic counselors provide information and advice to parents whose babies may have genetic disorders.

Early Ideas about Prenatal Development

Although our knowledge about prenatal development is far from complete, we do have answers to some questions that have intrigued and puzzled people for thousands of years. Aristotle, for example, wrote that the male semen provided the "form" of the embryo and the female provided the material to which form is given (Needham, 1959). Modern genetics informs us, of course, that both parents contribute equally to the genetic make-up—the "form"—of the child.

Aristotle also raised a question that was fiercely debated for centuries: Does the embryo exist preformed from the beginning, perfect in every feature, and merely increase in size during the prenatal period? Or does it develop in successive stages? Aristotle favored the developmental, or **epigenic,** theory, but some scientists claimed they could actually see tiny, preformed embryos in the sperm or egg (Figure 3-10), and they argued against the epigenic view. It wasn't until the late 1700s and early 1800s that preformationism was finally laid to rest. Research on the chick embryo revealed easily observable stages of development, thus confirming the epigenic view.

Periods of Prenatal Development

How, then, does prenatal development proceed? Prior to conception, of course, certain physiological events occur that set the stage. Every month an egg is prepared in one of the woman's ovaries and released sometime between the 9th and 16th days of her menstrual cycle. The egg is drawn into the open end of the **oviduct,** or **fallopian tube,** and moved down the tube to the uterus. If it doesn't encounter a sperm, or if fertilization doesn't occur despite the presence of sperm, the egg is flushed out of the body at the end of the monthly cycle, which is usually about 28 days long.

The sperm, of course, have been produced in the man's testes and ejaculated from his penis into the woman's vagina during sexual intercourse, except in cases of artificial insemination or in vitro fertilization. Millions of sperm begin the long journey through the uterus and up the fallopian tubes, but only a few make it to the end, and only one will be allowed to penetrate the surface of the egg. (Many conditions can prevent fertilization from taking place; see Research Focus—Infertility for a discussion of causes and treatments of infertility.) If the egg is fertilized, prenatal development begins, lasting 38 weeks for the full-term infant. We usually divide prenatal development, also known as **gestation,** into three periods, each of which has a different focus of activity.

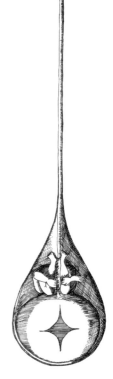

FIGURE 3-10
Early microscopes allowed scientists to view individual sperm cells for the first time, and some people proposed that a completely formed human being was curled up inside each sperm. This seventeenth-century drawing shows such a creature, known as a homunculus, or "little man." Others thought the homunculus was contained in the egg. According to these views, the child was really created by only one parent; the role of the other parent was simply to provide the environment for growth or to stimulate growth.

THE PERIOD OF THE OVUM: CONCEPTION TO WEEK 2. The first period of prenatal development, called the **period of the ovum,** begins in one of the oviducts (see Figure 3-11). It is here that fertilization occurs, when a sperm penetrates the egg. The fertilized cell, or zygote, begins to undergo cell division as it continues moving toward the uterus. In about three days, the cluster of 20 to 30 cells enters the uterine cavity, where it organizes itself into a hollow ball. In one area of this single layer of cells is a group of larger cells, called the **embryoblast,** which will develop into the embryo itself. The rest of the layer, the **trophoblast,** will develop into structures such as the placenta and chorion, which nourish and support the developing embryo. About six or seven days after fertilization, the embryo attaches itself to the uterine wall, and four or five days after that, it becomes embedded there.

Sometimes the developing embryo attaches itself to the wall of the oviduct instead of making its way to the uterus. Pregnancies that develop in an oviduct are called **ectopic pregnancies**. These pregnancies are dangerous because an embryo developing here can only grow so far before the oviduct bursts. If the embryo isn't removed surgically, the mother can die from internal bleeding. In fact, ectopic pregnancies are the leading cause of maternal death in the United States (Dorfman, 1983). An early prenatal exam can reveal whether the embryo is growing properly in the uterus.

Under normal circumstances, the embryo is firmly implanted in the uterine wall by the end of the second week. It's only about the size of the period at

FIGURE 3-11
The complex processes of ovulation, fertilization, cell division in the oviduct, and implantation of the embryo in the wall of the uterus take less than two weeks. When a woman becomes pregnant, the first sign is usually the missed menstrual period at the end of her monthly cycle, two weeks after ovulation.

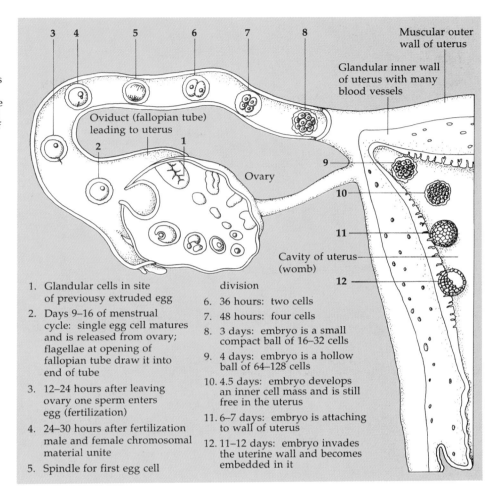

1. Glandular cells in site of previousy extruded egg
2. Days 9–16 of menstrual cycle: single egg cell matures and is released from ovary; flagellae at opening of fallopian tube draw it into end of tube
3. 12–24 hours after leaving ovary one sperm enters egg (fertilization)
4. 24–30 hours after fertilization male and female chromosomal material unite
5. Spindle for first egg cell division
6. 36 hours: two cells
7. 48 hours: four cells
8. 3 days: embryo is a small compact ball of 16–32 cells
9. 4 days: embryo is a hollow ball of 64–128 cells
10. 4.5 days: embryo develops an inner cell mass and is still free in the uterus
11. 6–7 days: embryo is attaching to wall of uterus
12. 11–12 days: embryo invades the uterine wall and becomes embedded in it

the end of this sentence, but it's already begun to form the remarkable system by which it will draw nourishment and oxygen from the mother for the next 36 weeks. The course of prenatal development is shown in Figure 3-12.

THE PERIOD OF THE EMBRYO: WEEK 2 TO WEEK 9. The second period of prenatal development, called the **period of the embryo**, lasts from the second week to the end of the eighth week. This period is a time of extremely rapid differentiation and change. All the major body structures are formed during this time, including the heart, the brain, the liver, the lungs, and the ovaries and testes. Some organs begin to function—the heart starts to beat, the liver begins to make blood cells, and the testes produce sex hormones. The eyes, nose, ears, tooth buds, and jaw form; arms and legs appear; and eyelids seal the eyes shut.

Because body structures are forming during this period, the developing organism is most vulnerable to damage from environmental influences such as drugs, infections, and irradiation. (Later in this chapter we discuss the outside agents that can damage the embryo, along with their effects.) Despite the

RESEARCH FOCUS

Infertility

There have always been couples who wanted to have children but couldn't. And there have always been ways of trying to bring about conception, ranging from herbal remedies to ritual practices to ingenious sexual positions. Today, we approach the problem of infertility—the inability to conceive a baby—more scientifically but with no less compelling interest. Infertility is a major trauma for the many people—20 percent of all couples in the United States—who are unable to have the children they want. Women have a higher risk of infertility after the age of 30; perhaps 15 percent of women between 30 and 35 may not be able to bear a child.

Treatment for infertility enables about half of the couples who seek help to have a child. But in many other cases, there isn't anything physicians can do; sometimes they can't even pinpoint the problem. In these cases, all our scientific knowledge and modern medical technology are no more useful than the folk medicine of a previous era.

IDENTIFYING THE CAUSE OF INFERTILITY

After a couple has been trying to conceive for a year, they may turn to an infertility specialist. An initial physical exam and a battery of lab tests may reveal a problem that can be corrected. A variety of conditions can cause infertility. In women these conditions include a failure to ovulate, endometriosis (a condition in which abnormal tissue in the pelvic cavity prevents conception), endocrine imbalances, and scarred fallopian tubes. Some women have physical abnormalities, such as an oddly shaped uterus, that make it more difficult for them to carry a pregnancy to term. In men infertility can be caused by too few sperm or sperm that don't swim properly. These problems are often traced to a case of mumps in early adulthood, untreated gonorrhea, or endocrine imbalances.

About 15 to 20 percent of all pregnancies end in miscarriage, and repeated miscarriage is another form of infertility. Miscarriage often occurs in the first days or weeks of pregnancy because of a serious fetal abnormality, sometimes without the woman ever knowing she was pregnant. Many women have miscarriages of this type and later experience successful pregnancies. But occasionally, one parent will have a chromosomal abnormality that causes repeated miscarriages. Hormone imbalances also may be linked to repeated miscarriages.

Miscarriage in the fifth or six month of pregnancy may be due to abnormalities in the cervix, a condition known as cervical incompetence, or in the uterus. Recent evidence has linked late miscarriages with certain kinds of infections; many women who have these infections are subsequently treated with antibiotics and go on to have successful pregnancies.

TREATMENT OF INFERTILITY

Some kinds of infertility can be treated; others cannot. Surgery can sometimes repair oviducts, clear up endometriosis, and correct problems in anatomy. Fertility drugs can help a woman ovulate, although they carry the risk of causing multiple births. Male infertility can be treated by collecting the father's sperm, concentrating it, and artificially inseminating the mother.

More advanced treatment techniques include in vitro fertilization, the use of frozen embryos, and laser surgery, which can sometimes be used in men to reverse a vasectomy (a sterilization method in which the small ducts that carry semen from the testes are severed) or in women to repair oviducts. Infertility is an area of great interest right now, so new treatments are rapidly emerging. But, as with so many forms of modern technology, new problems arise at the same

---

critically important developments that occur during this second period, the embryo at the end of the eighth week is only about $1\frac{1}{2}$ inches long and weighs less than $\frac{1}{10}$ of an ounce.

THE PERIOD OF THE FETUS: WEEK 9 TO BIRTH. The third and final period of prenatal development, called the **period of the fetus,** lasts from the ninth week until birth. During this period, structural development continues to completion. Hands, fingers, feet, and toes are formed; bones develop; neural cells multiply; and hair and nails appear. All body systems begin to function; even the lungs make breathing movements, moving fluids in and out. Beginning in the fifth month, the expectant mother can feel the baby's movements. Most of the fetus's growth—its increase in weight and length—takes place during this third-period, especially in the ninth month. By the end of the thirty-eighth week, the average baby weighs a little over 7 pounds and is about 20 inches long.

During this third period, the external male and female genitalia begin to develop. Although the genes inherited at conception determine whether the

time that old problems are solved. Two of the more controversial techniques are in vitro fertilization and surrogate motherhood.

In Vitro Fertilization
In this procedure, eggs are extracted from the mother and mixed with the father's sperm in the laboratory. (Babies born this way are commonly called "test tube babies.") One or more of the embryos that result is then implanted in the mother's uterus.

Although this procedure is often successful, it is very tedious and expensive. Not all embryos grow and thrive in the lab, and not all implantations become successful pregnancies. Any unused embryos that do thrive are often frozen and stored for the couple to use later. This aspect of in vitro fertilization has led to moral and legal debates. For example, a case in Australia involved the legal status of frozen embryos as heirs to the estate of their parents, who were killed in a plane crash before the embryos could be implanted. Another debate has focused on the moral implications of allowing research to be conducted on frozen embryos.

Surrogate Motherhood
The practice of surrogate motherhood is the most controversial of all approaches to infertility. It involves a contract between a fertile woman who agrees to carry a fetus and an infertile woman whose husband provides the sperm. The surrogate mother is impregnated by the father's sperm through artificial insemination, agrees to carry the child for the couple, and names the couple as legal guardians of the child who will be born. In return, she's paid for her services.

Some people question the morality of paying a woman to carry a baby. They see surrogate motherhood as an arrangement essentially to "sell" a baby, and they fear the psycho-

logical consequences for children who learn their biological mothers "sold" them. They also point to the possibility that a woman will change her mind after she has the baby and be unwilling to fulfill the contract she's signed.

In 1986 the public witnessed the very difficult dilemma created by surrogate motherhood, when Mary Beth Whitehead of New Jersey refused to give up a baby to the couple who had contracted with her for the child. She said that she hadn't realized how she would feel about giving the baby up, and she argued that she had the right to keep the baby because she was the real mother. She also tried to return the couple's money to them, but they refused to accept it. After a lengthy battle, the court awarded the baby to the couple and granted the surrogate mother limited visitation rights. Ms. Whitehead appealed the decision, and it may be that a ruling about the legality of surrogate motherhood will eventually come out of this case. It remains to be seen what, if any, psychological consequences there will be for the baby.

THE TRAUMA OF INFERTILITY
Infertility is a painful experience, and treatment for infertility can be a nightmare. Ovulation is monitored, sperm samples are collected and analyzed, intercourse practices are studied, and surgery may be performed. A couple may feel vulnerable and out of control; their sex life may become an unpleasant routine of more interest to their physician than to themselves; and they may lose perspective on the rest of their lives. Solutions that seem radical to outsiders, such as in vitro fertilization or surrogate motherhood, become acceptable options, if the couple can afford them. Many others remain childless or turn to adoption. Support groups for infertile couples can provide help in this difficult situation. Although many advances have been made, there are still very few easy answers to infertility.

baby will be a boy or a girl, both sexes initially develop as females. In the sixth week after conception, the male embryo releases male hormones known as androgens, which trigger the development of the male genitalia. On rare occasions, this hormone isn't released, and the child who develops is physically a female but genetically a male.

Various parts of the body grow at different rates during prenatal development. At first, the head region grows very quickly compared to the trunk and legs. Later, the lower parts of the body grow faster and begin to catch up. For example, at two weeks, 65 percent of the embryo's total body length is head, and 35 percent is trunk. At eight weeks, 44 percent is head, 36 percent is trunk, and 20 percent is legs. At birth, 25 percent of body length is accounted for by the head, with the trunk accounting for 42 percent and the legs for 33 percent. The head remains more fully developed than the other parts of the body throughout the entire prenatal period. Babies and young children appear "top-heavy" compared to older children and adults, whose heads account for only about 10 percent of their total height. This head-first pattern of development

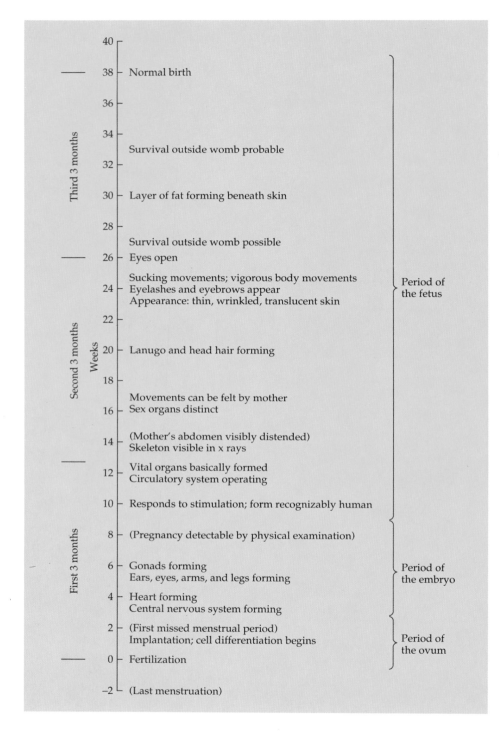

FIGURE 3-12
Chronology of milestones in prenatal development. The baby's anatomy is almost completely formed during the first three months of prenatal life, although the fetus is only a few inches long at the end of the first trimester. During the second trimester, the fetal heartbeat can be heard with a stethoscope, and the mother feels vigorous kicking and turning in her abdomen. The largest weight gain occurs during the last few months of prenatal development.

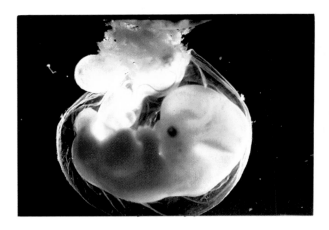

FIGURE 3-13

Scenes from prenatal life. By the sixth week (top left), the embryo is about an inch long. It has simple internal organs, including a heart that's pumping blood through the body. The arms and legs have formed, and the eyes have just appeared. By the fourth month (top right), the fetus is growing rapidly and obtains large amounts of food and oxygen from the placenta. About 10 inches long and weighing about 6 ounces, it can kick, turn its head, frown, and suck. By the seventh month (right), the fetus weighs about 3 pounds and has grown to about 15 inches. Although its lungs aren't completely developed and it still needs to acquire a layer of fat, the fetus can now survive if born prematurely.

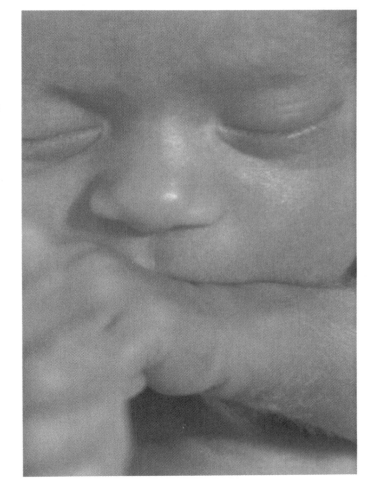

continues after birth, and is discussed further in Chapter 4 on the neonate (newborn).

Prematurity

The normal gestation period is 38 weeks, but premature babies born as early as 24 to 25 weeks have survived, although this is rare. The earlier they're born, the more medical problems they're likely to have. Premature babies are typically thin, because fat tissue isn't developed under the skin until the thirtieth to thirty-fourth week. Their low body weight makes them more sensitive to cold and more susceptible to dehydration than full-term babies.

More critical to their survival is the unfinished state of their lungs. The terminal air sacs in the lungs, called alveoli, don't develop until about week 32, and surfactant, a substance in the lungs necessary for gas exchange, isn't present until after week 34. Babies born before this period of gestation aren't equipped to breathe properly. Despite formidable problems, premature babies are being saved at earlier and earlier dates as a result of modern medical technology and advanced neonatal care. The problems and treatments of premature babies are discussed further in Chapter 4.

The process of prenatal development culminates in the birth of the baby, usually full-term and perfectly healthy. Birth—the beginning moment of a person's life—is also the climax for which the baby has been prepared during the nine long months in the womb.

BIRTH: TRANSITION TO LIFE IN THE OUTER WORLD

The journey down the birth canal out of the mother's body is the biggest transition any of us ever makes. It marks the end of life in physical union with the mother—a state in which food, oxygen, and hormones are obtained from her body—and the beginning of life as a separate individual. As you might expect, birth is a complex process, during which many remarkable changes occur that enable the baby to take up this new, physiologically independent existence.

The Physical Process of Birth

The birth process occurs in three stages (see Figure 3-14). Labor starts when hormonal changes in both the baby and the mother cause strong, rhythmic uterine contractions to begin. These contractions exert pressure on the cervix, the neck of the uterus, causing it gradually to pull back and open, or dilate. They also put pressure on the baby so that it descends into the mother's pelvis (in first babies, this descent usually occurs well before labor even begins). This first stage is the longest part of the birth process.

When the cervix is completely dilated, the second stage of birth, referred to as expulsion, begins. The baby slowly moves down, through the bones of the pelvic ring, past the tight, muscular cervix, and into the vagina, which stretches open from the pressure. The baby's back bends, the head turns to fit through the narrowest parts of the passageway, and the soft bones of the

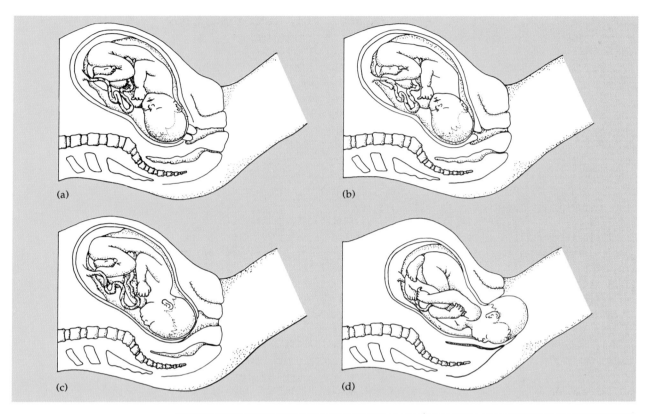

(a)   (b)

(c)   (d)

FIGURE 3-14

The birth process. Before labor begins, the full-term fetus rests comfortably in the uterus, typically in a head-down position (a). In the first stage of labor, uterine contractions pull the cervix open and push the baby downward (b). In the second stage of labor, the baby is pushed further down (c) and out of the mother's body (d). The baby's head turns toward the mother's back during the birth process and is completely turned as it emerges, or crowns.

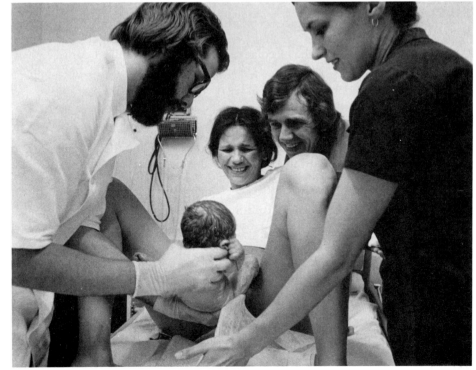

FIGURE 3-15

Her long labor ends; the baby's life begins.

baby's skull actually move together and overlap as it's squeezed through the pelvis. The baby's head finally emerges from the vagina, followed quickly by the rest of the body. A new human being appears in the world!

When the cervix is opening during the first stage, the woman having an unmedicated birth is encouraged to relax as much as possible, despite the contractions, and allow labor to proceed without tensing up her muscles. When the baby is being expelled during the second stage, the woman can "bear down" with the contractions to help push the baby out. When the top of the baby's head appears at the vaginal opening, the baby is said to be **crowning.** Since the head is the largest part of the baby's body and wider than the shoulders, the body usually just slips out after the head emerges.

The third stage of birth, known as afterbirth, is the delivery of the placenta. This usually occurs within 10 to 20 minutes of the baby's birth and is accomplished with a few strong uterine contractions. The whole birth process takes an average of about 12 hours for first babies and about 7 hours for subsequent babies. Averages can be misleading, of course. The first stage alone can take anywhere from 8 to 20 hours for a first baby and 3 to 8 hours for a second baby (Ingalls & Salerno, 1975). A variety of conditions can result in birth by cesarean section, the delivery of the baby through an incision in the mother's abdominal wall. This procedure is explained and discussed in Health Focus— The Increase in Cesarean Births.

Important physiological changes occur when the baby is born. As the infant is squeezed through the pelvis, cervix, and vagina, the fluid in the lungs is forced out by the pressure on the baby's chest. Once this pressure is released as the baby emerges from the vagina, the chest expands and the lungs fill with air for the first time. This process ensures that the baby starts breathing immediately after birth.

Other physiological changes occur at birth as well. Special blood vessels that were used during the prenatal period close off, no longer needed now that the lungs are part of the circulatory system; the umbilical cord seals off, even if it's not tied or cut; and changes in the composition of the baby's blood make the baby more suited for life outside the womb.

Emotional Aspects of Birth

The emotional impact of a baby's birth is almost unequalled in the human experience. Confronted with the mystery of the creation of life, moved by profound feelings for the tiny, helpless, but perfect new being, most adults are awed and elated by the birth of a baby. The baby, of course, has had a tumultuous experience too. It seems natural to take the emotional side of childbirth as seriously as the physiological one, but this view hasn't always been acceptable.

THE EVOLUTION OF HOSPITAL CHILDBIRTH PRACTICES. Until about a hundred years ago, birth was treated as a natural event in a woman's life, usually experienced at home with the help of a midwife and some other attendants. Mortality for both infants and mothers was high. As progress was made in medical knowledge and techniques, physicians attempted to lower this mortality rate by increasing medical intervention in the birth process. The use of drugs, forceps,

HEALTH FOCUS

The Increase in Cesarean Births

Cesarean sections have been performed for thousands of years—the procedure is named after Julius Caesar (100 BC–4 BC), who was delivered through an incision in his mother's abdomen—but they were usually performed at the cost of the mother's life. Unsanitary conditions meant the mother was doomed to massive infection, if she didn't bleed to death first. Cesarean sections became a true alternative birth method after antiseptic procedures were developed late in the 19th century.

WHY PERFORM A CESAREAN?

Cesarean sections are performed when a baby can't be delivered vaginally. Sometimes a mother's pelvis isn't big enough for the baby's head to pass through during birth. Sometimes the baby is in a feet-down or buttocks-down position in the uterus rather than in the usual head-down position, or even lying sideways across the uterus, all of which make vaginal birth difficult. In some cases the placenta is over the cervix rather than higher in the uterus (Guttmacher, 1973), and vaginal delivery would damage the baby's support system before birth. Mothers with diabetes, high blood pressure, kidney or heart disease, or toxemia (toxins in the blood, a condition that sometimes occurs late in pregnancy) often deliver their babies by cesarean section to reduce the stress on their bodies.

Sometimes a woman is unable to sustain labor. Contractions slow down or stop, and the cervix shows no progressing dilation. After 24 hours, physicians usually perform a cesarean section. This reduces the risk of infection to the newborn, which can be high once the protective membranes have ruptured at the beginning of labor. In the past, cesareans were also performed when women had previously had cesarean births. Physicians believed that the pressure of labor and vaginal delivery on the uterine wall would rupture the old incision. This has not proven to be true, and many women now have vaginal births after cesarean births (Rosen & Dickinson, 1990).

Cesarean sections are major surgery and carry some risk themselves, although much less than 15 or 20 years ago. Bet-ter antibiotics and refined understanding and use of anesthesia make the procedure relatively safe. Women now are often given a local anesthetic and remain conscious during the whole operation. The father can be in the operating room if the mother is given a local anesthetic.

WHY HAS THE NUMBER OF CESAREANS INCREASED?

Between 1965 and 1980 cesarean deliveries increased from 5 percent to 15 percent of all births in the United States (O'Driscoll & Foley, 1983). By 1987 the nationwide cesarean rate was reported to be 24 percent, with even higher rates in some states ("Caesareans up," 1987). The hospitals with very high cesarean rates are usually university hospitals, where many more high-risk pregnancies are handled than in the average community hospital.

One reason for higher cesarean rates is that hospitals now have more sophisticated techniques for detecting fetal distress. Fetal monitoring, for example, can reveal a slowed fetal heart rate due to inadequate oxygen during labor, possibly leading to a decision for cesarean section. Advocates of increased reliance on cesareans claim that the procedure makes birth safer for mothers and babies in a situation where prolonged, stressful labor is the alternative. They point to reduced maternal and neonatal mortality rates and the better health of newborns (fewer babies are born with brain damage from labor and delivery trauma) (Bodner et al., 1986).

Critics of the increased reliance on cesarean deliveries, including many physicians and surgeons, believe that cesareans are often performed unnecessarily and that labor isn't well managed by medical personnel in this country. They claim that not all relevant staff members, for example, can accurately interpret signs of fetal distress. They suggest that cesarean sections are frequently performed more for the convenience of the physician than for the mother's or baby's health. Until physicians can document the need for a cesarean in each and every case, and until the public becomes more aware of the benefits of this procedure for some mothers and babies, this debate is likely to continue.

and surgical techniques removed birth from the realm of natural events and placed it in the hands of specialists.

By the 1940s birth was treated as a medical emergency requiring lengthy hospitalization. In earlier practices the emotional aspects of birth were simply an integral part of the whole experience; they weren't considered separable from it. Now the emotional aspects of the experience were ignored as hospitals zealously pursued efficient, safe births. Women were routinely separated from their husbands during labor and birth, given no information about what was happening to them, and sedated during delivery. Immediately after birth, the mother was sent to her room and the baby was whisked away to the nursery. The father had no direct contact with his baby during the hospital stay—he could only look at the baby through the nursery window. The mother had no contact with her other children, who weren't allowed in her room. The baby was brought to the mother at scheduled feeding times and then returned to the nursery, where the hospital staff cared for all the newborns together. After two weeks in the hospital, the mother was sent home with a baby she hardly knew.

RESISTANCE TO HOSPITAL PRACTICES. In the early 1970s, many people began to question and resist this approach to birth. Parents were becoming aware of birth practices in other countries and making their dissatisfaction known to physicians and hospitals. In addition, medical research was beginning to show that routine heavy sedation during birth might be harmful to the baby, the mother, or both. Some researchers found that the presence of fathers greatly improved the comfort and emotional well-being of mothers in labor. Other studies suggested that early separation might interfere with later social interaction between mothers and babies.

Social practices changed too. Breast-feeding became the preferred feeding method, and hospitals had to allow more mother-infant contact to accommodate the demand feeding schedule required by nursing infants. It became apparent that older siblings adjusted better to a new brother or sister if they were prepared for the baby's arrival and if they could see their mother while she was in the hospital. And skyrocketing hospital costs made long stays prohibitively expensive for routine births. All these findings and social trends contributed to the changes in childbirth practices that have occurred since the early 1970s.

Current Childbirth Practices

Almost all the hospital childbirth practices just detailed have been modified in the last 20 years. Let's look more closely at what the typical childbirth experience is like today.

PREPARED CHILDBIRTH. Women are no longer routinely sedated during childbirth. The current view is that the less medication used, the better. Usually general anesthesia isn't administered even for cesarean sections. Instead of relying on drugs, many women learn techniques in childbirth preparation classes that help them deal with the discomfort and rigors of labor and delivery.

One method of prepared childbirth was developed by Dr. Grantly Dick-Read. Dick-Read believed that the pain experienced by women during birth was the result of learned fears and anxieties that interfered, through tension, with the naturally painless process of birth. To dispel these fears, childbirth educators teach parents the details of the birth process as well as physical and respiratory relaxation techniques. Dick-Read's method strongly discourages the use of pain-relieving drugs.

Another popular approach to prepared childbirth was developed by Dr. Ferdinand Lamaze. Unlike Dick-Read, Lamaze acknowledged that childbirth involves some inherent pain. But if a woman is concentrating on other activities, such as breathing, her brain will be unreceptive to the pain signals sent out by the uterus (Miller & Brooten, 1977). The Lamaze method teaches breathing techniques designed to occupy the brain and prevent pain messages from getting through to it. Like the Dick-Read method, it also teaches parents about

FIGURE 3-16
These seventeenth-century woodcuts show a variety of positions in which babies may present themselves at birth. They were probably based on midwives' experiences and used to teach new midwives what to expect. Today, many of these presentations would lead quickly to a decision to perform a cesarean section.

the birth process, on the assumption that ignorance breeds fear and knowledge dispels it.

The Lamaze method advocates minimal use of pain-relieving drugs. This policy ensures that both mother and baby are alert during the birth, and it reduces the risk to the baby. However, the limited use of drugs isn't discouraged, because the mother's comfort is an important part of prepared childbirth.

A third method of childbirth preparation is known as the Bradley Method (Barnes & Hassid, 1985). This method stresses relaxation, but teaches no specific method of relaxation. Instead, women learn several techniques, including massage, relaxation exercises, and breathing control, so that they will be able to choose what works best for them. Women are encouraged to practice all of the techniques they learn in childbirth classes, which meet in small groups for 10 to 12 sessions.

Most hospitals tend to instruct parents in a combination of Lamaze and other relaxation techniques. Childbirth classes are now almost a routine part of the prenatal experience for both mothers and fathers. The father typically acts as a coach, supporting the mother emotionally and helping her with her breathing. He might also be ready with various comforts, such as wet washcloths or ice chips to suck on. He remains with the mother throughout labor and delivery, even when a cesarean section is performed. A labor nurse or midwife attends the labor as well. The physician may be present during labor or may arrive just in time for the delivery.

Many hospitals have birthing rooms they can use as alternatives to traditional delivery rooms for births. These are special rooms, often designed to provide the comforts of a bedroom, where the mother can stay for the entire birth process. Traditionally, women went through labor in a "labor room" and then were moved to the more sterile delivery room when they were ready to

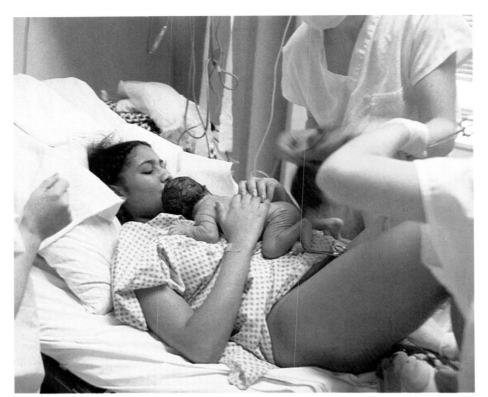

FIGURE 3-17
Current childbirth practices provide benefits to babies, mothers, and families. Attachment between mother and child begins immediately after birth as the baby is placed on the mother's body (top left). Newborns stay with their mothers after birth and room in with them during their hospital stay; they can begin to nurse right away (bottom left). Fathers are involved in the birth and care of the newborn, beginning a relationship with the newest family member (top right). Siblings can meet the baby in the hospital, see their mom, and be reassured about what this new experience is going to mean for them (bottom right).

give birth. But being moved at that critical moment in the birth process is extremely disruptive when a woman is trying to concentrate on staying relaxed and in control of her breathing. In a birthing room, no interruption is necessary.

CONTACT BETWEEN MOTHER AND BABY. One of the most dramatic changes in childbirth practices is in the amount of time hospitals allow babies to stay with their parents. Babies are no longer rushed off to the nursery right after they're born. They spend time with the mother and usually the father immediately following birth. They're taken to the nursery to be weighed and examined, and then they're often returned to the mother for rooming-in. **Rooming-in** is the practice of leaving the baby with the mother in her room for as much or as little time as she desires.

Fathers are encouraged to hold and care for the newborn. Many hospitals offer classes on infant care and fathering to new parents during the mother's hospital stay. Fathers can usually visit at any time. Siblings can visit too, but usually only during regular visiting hours. Some hospitals allow the newborn to remain in the room when brothers or sisters are visiting. The older children get a chance to meet the new member of the family, but more important is the chance to see and talk to mom.

Even if they haven't had rooming in, mothers have more contact with their babies than they used to simply because they don't stay in the hospital very long. A two- or three-day stay is typical following a vaginal delivery. Some hospitals release mothers within a few hours of the birth if all is going well. For a cesarean section, a hospital stay of five to seven days is now considered normal, as opposed to the traditional two weeks.

HOME BIRTHS AND OTHER ALTERNATIVES. Despite the dramatic changes hospitals have made in their childbirth practices, some parents have opted to have their babies at home or in alternative birth centers, attended by a midwife or a physician. Here, the surroundings are comfortable, the atmosphere is casual, and the company is familiar. Friends, family members, and children can be present at the birth if the parents wish.

Physicians, midwives, and other personnel who participate in alternative births usually have some medical back-up planned in case of emergency. For example, birth centers may have a car available at all times for immediate transport to the nearest hospital. They also carefully screen out high-risk cases to ensure that mothers and babies who are likely to have problems go through labor and delivery where they'll have the medical resources they may need. Despite precautions, births that take place at home and in other alternative settings outside hospitals are not without risk, as some advocates have implied.

Benefits of New Childbirth Practices

There is some debate about the actual advantages of these changes in childbirth practices. No one questions the benefits of reducing medication during birth, which allows mothers to play an active role in birth and both mothers and babies to be more alert. The involvement of fathers in labor and delivery is also considered an improvement, with psychological and emotional benefits

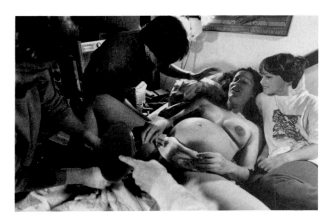 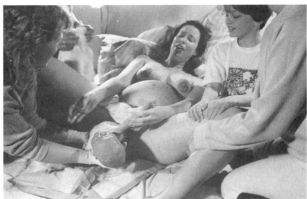

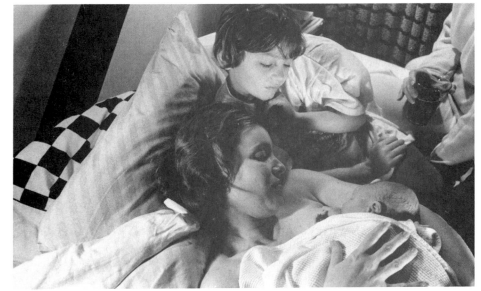

FIGURE 3-18
When babies are born at home, women have their childbirth experience in a comfortable setting surrounded by people of their own choosing. This woman wanted her older child with her when she had the baby. They both watched in a hand-held mirror as the baby crowned, and they witnessed the moment of birth together. Later, they contemplated the new person who had joined their lives.

for both parents. There are also definite financial advantages to shorter hospital stays.

But there are some misgivings over the increase in home births, which tend to be less safe than hospital births. Some people have questioned the importance given to early contact between mothers and babies. During the 1970s and 1980s, a tremendous emphasis was placed on uninterrupted contact as a requirement for attachment and "bonding," as the formation of an early emotional tie between mother and child is called. Research suggested that bonding had to occur immediately after birth or the baby might never form a proper attachment, and this idea was embraced by almost everyone involved in childbirth.

More recent research has contradicted these findings. We now know that bonding can occur even if mother and baby are separated after birth. Premature babies and babies with physical problems at birth are usually placed in neonatal care units, and women who have had general anesthesia are unable to interact with their babies immediately after birth. Attachment still forms between these mothers and babies, and early separation seems to have no permanent detrimental effects. There is no research evidence confirming fears that attachment will be disrupted by early separation (Goldberg, 1983). (We discuss attachment and bonding at length in Chapter 8 on the social and emotional development of infants and toddlers.)

Another problem arises when people adhere slavishly to new ideas and practices without allowing for unexpected complications or expressing their own preferences. Parents have sometimes been led to believe that their relationship with their child will be permanently impaired if they're separated following birth. Women have described feelings of failure and guilt for taking pain-relieving drugs during birth or for delivering the baby by cesarean section. The idea that there's only one "right" way to have a baby sets parents up for a disappointment that can be devastating. Actually, a variety of birth situations can have positive physical and psychological outcomes, especially if parents are encouraged to choose what feels comfortable to them.

The positive side of the new childbirth practices is that parents now have more choices. Mothers who choose rooming-in can have their babies with them virtually every minute of their hospital stay. But some mothers may not choose rooming-in, and this is acceptable too. They may have older children and many responsibilities to face at home. They need to use the hospital stay to rest and regain their strength. Still others may want to have their babies with them for short periods of time until they become confident that they can care for them. In most hospitals today, parents can decide for themselves what kind of childbirth experience they want to have, and this is an improvement no one disputes.

PROBLEMS IN EARLY DEVELOPMENT: WHEN THINGS GO WRONG

The end result of the long period of prenatal development and the transition period of birth usually is a full-term, healthy baby. Unfortunately a few babies aren't so lucky at the start. The origin of problems of newborns may be **prenatal**—meaning they originated before the seventh prenatal month—or **perinatal**—meaning they originated between the seventh month and a few minutes after birth (Kopp & Krakow, 1983).

Prenatal Problems

We saw at the beginning of this chapter how one family was affected by a problem in the prenatal development of their baby. Not all prenatal problems are as devastating as Tay-Sachs disease, but almost all create difficulties that the child, her family, and her community will have to deal with for her entire lifetime. Some of these problems result from genetic abnormalities, others from chromosomal errors, and still others from environmental factors. No matter what their origin, and no matter how they show up later in life, prenatal problems can never be erased from the child's make-up.

GENETIC PROBLEMS. As the name implies, genetic problems result from the inheritance of particular genes from the parents. Most common genetic problems are due to the inheritance of a pair of abnormal recessive genes. The proba-

FIGURE 3-19
The probability of inheriting a disease carried by recessive genes depends on whether one or both parents is a carrier.

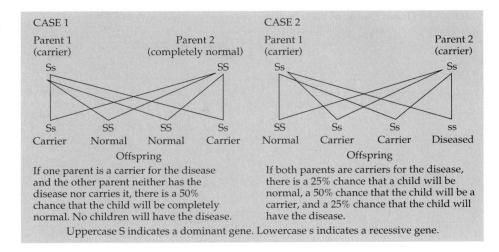

CASE 1

Parent 1 (carrier) Ss — Parent 2 (completely normal) SS

Ss Carrier — SS Normal — SS Normal — Ss Carrier

Offspring

If one parent is a carrier for the disease and the other parent neither has the disease nor carries it, there is a 50% chance that the child will be completely normal. No children will have the disease.

CASE 2

Parent 1 (carrier) Ss — Parent 2 (carrier) Ss

SS Normal — Ss Carrier — Ss Carrier — ss Diseased

Offspring

If both parents are carriers for the disease, there is a 25% chance that a child will be normal, a 50% chance that the child will be a carrier, and a 25% chance that the child will have the disease.

Uppercase S indicates a dominant gene. Lowercase s indicates a recessive gene.

FIGURE 3-20
A normal red blood cell looks like a doughnut—round and puffed up (top photo). A sickled red blood cell is elongated, flat, and curved (bottom photo). Sickled cells carry less oxygen and tend to clump together in blood vessels, clogging passageways. Children with this life-threatening genetic disorder tend to tire easily and have difficulty breathing because of insufficient oxygen.

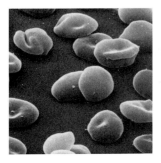

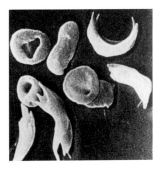

bility of inheriting a disease carried by two recessive genes is diagrammed in Figure 3-19.

Four of the most common genetic diseases are sickle-cell anemia, cystic fibrosis, phenylketonuria, and Tay-Sachs disease. Some genetic disorders occur disproportionately among certain groups, because recessive genes develop within a particular gene pool and tend to remain in it. For example, sickle-cell anemia, a disease of the red blood cells, occurs mainly in people of black African ancestry. Tay-Sachs disease, a fatal disorder of the central nervous system, primarily afflicts people of Eastern European Jewish ancestry. The probability of a child inheriting any of these four genetic diseases from carrier (outwardly healthy) parents is 25 percent. Descriptions of these diseases, along with the prognosis for children born with them, are given in Table 3-1.

Rh disease is a genetically related disorder, but it's not caused by abnormal recessive genes. The Rh factor is a protein found in the blood. If an Rh-positive father and an Rh-negative mother conceive an Rh-positive baby, the baby's blood will be incompatible with the mother's. If some of the baby's blood enters the mother's bloodstream during delivery, she will develop antibodies to it just as she would toward a virus. The first baby isn't affected, because at that time the antibodies aren't yet in the mother's bloodstream. But subsequent Rh-positive babies will suffer. The antibodies in the mother's blood, passing through the placenta, will destroy the fetus's red blood cells, which carry oxygen throughout the fetus's body. Jaundice, anemia, and other problems, sometimes leading to mental retardation or death, can result (Snyder, Schonfeld, & Offerman, 1945).

Fortunately, a serum now exists, called Rh immune globulin, that destroys Rh-positive cells as they enter the mother's body. It prevents the development of antibodies if it's administered to an Rh-negative mother within a few hours after she's given birth to an Rh-positive baby (Clarke, 1968; Zimmerman, 1973). Before this vaccine was developed in the 1960s, about 40,000 babies were affected each year by complications due to Rh incompatibility. Today, the condition is almost nonexistent.

CHROMOSOMAL PROBLEMS. Other prenatal problems occur when errors are made in the egg or sperm cell during meiosis. Sometimes, complete chromosomes

TABLE 3-1   Diseases Caused by the Inheritance of Two Abnormal Recessive Genes

Disease	Incidence	Description of the Disease and Consequences	Prognosis for Children Who Are Afflicted	Population at Risk
Sickle-cell anemia	1 in 625 live births among African Americans (Muir, 1983)	The abnormal hemoglobin in red blood cells sickles (changes shape) during periods of stress caused by such factors as infections or low oxygen. Sickled cells stick together and impair blood flow to organs. Children may be irritable, have swollen abdomens and a yellowish cast to their eyes.	Many children who are victims of this disease do not survive into adulthood.	The recessive gene is carried by a disproportionate number of people with African ancestry.
Cystic fibrosis	1 in every 2,000 live births, 1,500–2,000 per year	Essential enzymes of the pancreas are deficient. Thick mucus develops in the lungs and intestinal tract. Sweat contains a higher than normal concentration of sodium and chloride. Absorption of food is impaired. Susceptibility to respiratory infections is greatly increased, because salt and water are removed from lungs too fast (Clark, Hager & Gosnell, 1986).	Many victims die in early childhood, although antibiotic and enzyme therapies are effective in prolonging life into adolescence and early adulthood. Some cases remain relatively asymptomatic until early adulthood.	The disease is the most common of the serious recessive diseases afflicting Caucasians.
Phenylketonuria (PKU)	1 in 11,000–14,000 live births in U.S. (Muir, 1983; Cohen, Lilienfeld & Huang, 1978)	The enzyme needed to metabolize an amino acid (phenylalanine) into another (tryosine) is absent. Toxins accumulate in nerve tissue and destroy it. Mental retardation can result.	PKU can be detected early in infancy with a urine test. (All newborns are routinely screened in most states.) Foods high in phenylalanine are restricted so that toxins are not formed.	
Tay-Sachs	1 in 1,000 live births for Ashkenazi Jews (National March of Dimes, 1973)	Victims cannot metabolize fat properly. The brain and other nerve tissue deteriorates as a result. Children have motor weakness initially, followed by blindness, seizures, and death.	The condition is lethal. Death usually occurs by age 3 or 4.	The recessive genes causing this disease are carried primarily by Jews with Eastern European ancestry.

don't separate and go to different cells as intended. Other times, pieces of chromosomes break off, leaving extra genetic material in one cell and a shortage in another. Obviously, children with errors in their chromosomes will have serious problems.

The most common chromosomally related abnormality is **Down's syndrome**, which occurs about once in every 600 births. Down's syndrome is caused by an error in the number 21 chromosome, usually the presence of three chromosomes at this location instead of the normal two (Lilienfield, 1969; Kerkay, Zsako & Kaplan, 1971). Two of those chromosomes came from a defective ovum with an extra chromosome and one came from a normal sperm. Children with Down's syndrome are mentally retarded and have a characteristic physical appearance.

Down's syndrome occurs more frequently in mothers who are either under 20 or over 35. The risk of having a Down's syndrome baby increases from 1

FIGURE 3-22
This premature, cocaine-affected baby is off to a poor start in life. He's likely to be an unresponsive, extremely irritable baby, and when he's strong enough to leave the hospital, he may go home to a drug-addicted mother. The long-term outcome for cocaine-affected babies is something we won't know for years to come.

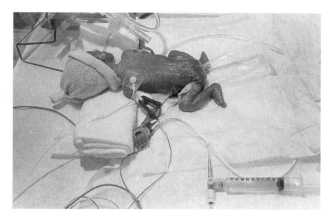

in 885 at age 30 to 1 in 50 at age 40 (Pai, 1974). Why this is so is not entirely clear, but hormonal regulation may be more erratic at the lower and upper ranges of the female reproductive lifetime.

Other chromosomal abnormalities create developmental problems. Klinefelter's syndrome is a disorder that results when a male receives an extra X chromosome. Males with this chromosomal error are mentally retarded and develop some female characteristics at puberty (Johnson et al., 1970). Girls with an extra X chromosome have problems with verbal skills and short-term memory (Rovet & Netley, 1983). In another syndrome in which the short arm of the number 10 chromosome is partially deleted, the child has unusual facial features, a very short neck, and psychomotor delays (Elstner et al., 1984).

PROBLEMS DUE TO ENVIRONMENTAL FACTORS. In 1964–1965 an epidemic of rubella (German measles) swept through the United States, and nearly 50,000 children died in utero or were born with birth defects as a result. A few years earlier, hundreds of European mothers who had taken the tranquilizer thalidomide gave birth to babies without arms or legs (Lenz, 1966). These are just two of the many environmental factors that can adversely affect prenatal development. As mentioned earlier, **teratogens** (agents that cause birth defects) inflict the most damage early in pregnancy, when basic body structures are rapidly forming.

Because of the increase in drug abuse in recent years, researchers have been focusing more intensively on the teratogenic effects of narcotics and other drugs. There are preliminary indications that about one in ten infants may be exposed to illicit drugs during pregnancy (Committee on Substance Abuse, 1990). Studies of pregnant women in urban areas indicate that the incidence in this population is between 13 and 15 percent (Chasnoff, Landress & Barrett, 1990).

EXPOSURE TO COCAINE

Among babies who have been exposed to harmful substances prenatally, there has been an alarming increase in the number of babies exposed to cocaine. These babies have a lower average birth weight than other babies (Zuckerman et al., 1989). They also have a smaller average head circumference, a difference that has been reported to persist through at least the second year of life (Chas-

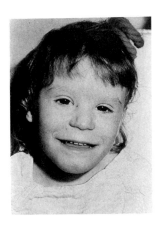

FIGURE 3-23
A child born with fetal alcohol syndrome has a typical appearance and impaired mental functioning. This condition is just becoming widely recognized, and women are now advised to abstain completely from alcohol during pregnancy.

noff & Griffin, 1989). In addition, they are more likely to be born prematurely or to be stillborn (born dead) (Little et al., 1989; Zuckerman et al., 1989). They're extremely irritable, too, and tend to be ultrasensitive to noise and touch. As a result they don't seem to be able to respond or relate to people the way normal babies do, and they're very difficult to comfort or console. These characteristics affect their social and emotional development, because it's difficult for parents to interact with them. As we see in later chapters, positive social interaction is crucial for appropriate language and cognitive development, so many areas of functioning are ultimately affected.

Other serious problems have been observed in cocaine-exposed children. However, so many other negative prenatal factors may be involved in this population that it's difficult to sort out the exact cause-effect relationship between prenatal cocaine exposure and later developmental difficulties. For example, cocaine users tend to be less well nourished than other mothers (Frank et al., 1988), and they may receive little or no prenatal care. Furthermore, babies born to cocaine-abusing mothers may be neglected or may live in impoverished or dangerous environments. Any of these factors, alone or in combination, can cause serious problems in a child's development.

EXPOSURE TO ALCOHOL

Although cocaine is currently in the spotlight as a teratogen, more babies are probably born every year who have been affected prenatally by a legal substance—alcohol. High levels of alcohol consumption during pregnancy are consistently associated not only with spontaneous abortions and stillbirths but also, in live babies, with mental retardation, lower-than-average birth weight, microcephaly (abnormal smallness of the head), and unusual facial features (Streissguth, 1979; Streissguth et al., 1989). Babies with this pattern of characteristics are said to suffer from **fetal alcohol syndrome** (FAS) (Zuckerman & Hingson, 1990). Although occasional or moderate drinking was earlier thought to have no negative effects on the fetus, many researchers now doubt there's any safe level of alcohol consumption, and they recommend total abstinence during pregnancy.

EXPOSURE TO CIGARETTE SMOKING

Cigarette smoking has also been studied intensively in recent years, since smoking has been associated with several adverse conditions in newborns, including low birth weight and possible congenital malformation. Compounds found in cigarette smoke have been related directly with a teratogenic effect in pregnant animals (Seidman, Ever-Hadani & Gale, 1990). The direct effects of nicotine in the human mother's bloodstream have also been observed in the fetus. For example, both breathing and movement patterns become more rapid and agitated in the fetus when the mother's nicotine level is high (Erikson et al., 1983).

Some research has been directed at determining whether children whose mothers smoked during pregnancy had any long-term social or cognitive disabilities. No evidence of this has been found, at least in middle-class samples (Lefkowitz, 1981). But cigarette smoking does pose a health hazard to children. Infants whose parents smoke are twice as likely to develop pneumonia or bronchitis during their first year as are infants whose parents don't smoke (Greenwood, 1979). This higher risk is probably due to exposure to smoke after birth rather than to any prenatal influence.

TABLE 3-2   Environmental Factors Associated with Impairments during Prenatal Development

Agent or Condition	Effects
Rubella (German measles)	Blindness; deafness; heart abnormalities; stillbirth
Cytomegalovirus (CMV)	Microcephaly (smaller than normal head); motor disabilities; hearing loss
Syphilis	Mental retardation; physical deformities; in utero death and miscarriage
AIDS virus	Death, often within two years of birth
Addictive drugs	Low birthweight; possible addiction of infant to the drug; hypersensitivity to stimuli; higher risk for stroke and respiratory distress
Smoking	Prematurity; low birthweight and length
Alcohol	Mental retardation; growth retardation; increased spontaneous abortion rate; microcephaly; structural abnormalities in the face; lowered IQ
Irradiation	Physical deformities; mental retardation
Inadequate diet	Reduction in brain growth; smaller than average birthweight; decrease in birth length; rickets
Tetracycline	Discoloration
Streptomycin	Eighth cranial nerve damage (hearing loss)
Quinine	Deafness
Barbiturates	Congenital malformations
DES (diethylstilbestrol)	Increased incidence of vaginal cancer in adolescent female offspring; impaired reproductive performance in same population
Valium	Cleft lip and palate
Accutane (13-cis-retinoic acid, a new drug used to treat acne)	Small or absent ears; small jaws; hydrocephaly; heart defects
Endocrine disorders	Cretinism; microcephaly
Maternal age under 18	Prematurity; stillbirth; increased incidence of Down's syndrome
Maternal age over 35	Increased incidence of Down's syndrome
Malnutrition	Lower birthweight; abnormal reflexes and irritability; altered brain growth
Environmental chemicals (e.g., benzene, formaldehyde, PCBs)	Chromosome damage; spontaneous abortions; low birthweight

SOURCES: Berger & Goldstein, 1980; Brown, 1979; Cohen, 1984; Dobbing, 1984; Greenburg, Pelliteri & Barton, 1957; Herbst, 1972; Herbst, Scully & Robboy, 1975; Joos et al., 1983; Lenz, 1966; Meredith, 1975; Naeye, 1983; Naeye, Blanc & Paul, 1973; Plummer, 1952; Siegel, Fuerst & Guinee, 1971; Snyder, Schonfeld & Offerman, 1945; Streissguth, Barr & Martin, 1983; Walters, 1975; Zeskind & Ramey, 1978.

As mentioned in Chapter 1, most of the evidence that cigarette smoking affects prenatal development is correlational. Much of the evidence comes from studies of children born with particular problems. Researchers try to discover common habits among the mothers of these children to see if they're different from the general population in some way. When they do find a correlation, such as the one between cigarette smoking and low birthweight, they haven't actually proved causation. The commonalities discovered among the mothers may not be the cause of the problem; something else may be. Perhaps more anxious mothers smoke cigarettes, for example. Anxiety might cause both smoking and low birthweight.

Researchers can't perform the experimental studies necessary to prove causation because it would be unethical. In their correlational studies, they do try to control for every other possible factor so that smoking seems to be the *likely* cause. In any event, since no evidence exists that smoking is beneficial to the fetus, many women take the safest course and stop smoking during pregnancy.

Other agents and conditions known to affect prenatal development are listed in Table 3-2. As mentioned earlier, most of them are dangerous early in pregnancy. German measles may affect eyes, ears, and brain during the first three months of pregnancy but do no harm later. Thalidomide taken early in pregnancy prevented the formation of arms and legs in fetuses, but taken later, when the limbs were already formed, it caused no damage. Some drugs, like alcohol, cause structural damage early and stunted growth later (Rosett et al., 1983).

Perinatal Problems

Perinatal problems are those that stem from some event or condition that occurs in the last two months of prenatal development, when the baby is basically structurally complete, during the birth process, or in the moments immediately following birth. Here we look at the three major perinatal problems.

INSUFFICIENT GROWTH. One of the major tasks of the last two months of prenatal development is growth. Of the 7 pounds the average baby weighs at birth, about 3 are gained in the eighth and ninth months. Sometimes late in pregnancy, the placenta becomes unable to provide the nourishment the fetus needs to reach its full size and weight. Sometimes a problem in the fetus itself prevents it from properly using the nourishment provided by the placenta. The fetus doesn't gain as much weight in the last few months as it should and is smaller than expected at birth. Sometimes other problems are present as well. Babies who are born small even though they're full term are referred to as **small-for-date** babies.

LACK OF OXYGEN. The main danger to the baby during birth and immediately afterward is oxygen deprivation, or **anoxia**. The baby may not get enough oxygen if the umbilical cord is compressed during delivery, if breathing doesn't start immediately after birth, or if breathing is impaired by respiratory distress in the first days or weeks of life. Respiratory distress usually results from premature birth.

Anoxia affects the lower centers of the brain most severely, where motor functioning is controlled (see Figure 3-24 for a diagram of the brain). Anoxia during or just before birth can cause cerebral palsy, a disorder of the motor system (Paneth, 1986). Children with cerebral palsy have problems speaking and controlling their muscles.

INFECTIONS. Any infection of the mother's reproductive tract can be contracted by the baby during birth or even before birth. The four most serious infections are syphilis, gonorrhea, herpes simplex virus, and AIDS. Syphilis can infect

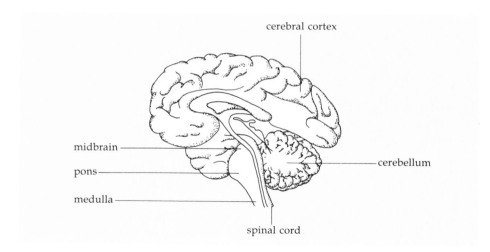

and kill the fetus during the prenatal period. If the baby is born alive, it will have syphilis. Penicillin given to the mother during pregnancy will cure the disease in both mother and fetus.

Gonorrhea can infect the baby during delivery and cause blindness. It can be present in the mother without any symptoms, so the danger to the baby may not be apparent. Because of this uncertainty, laws have been passed requiring that all newborns be treated with silver nitrate drops in their eyes soon after birth. Silver nitrate destroys the gonorrheal bacteria.

Herpes simplex virus can also be transmitted to the baby during delivery if the mother's infection is in the active phase. If this is the case, the baby is delivered by cesarean section to keep it from contacting the virus in the birth canal. Herpes can damage the baby's eyes and brain, and no cure has yet been discovered for the infection. (In adults the virus causes open sores on the skin or mucous membranes but no organ damage.)

Currently, the most serious infection affecting newborns is acquired immune deficiency syndrome (AIDS). This fatal disorder of the immune system, first identified in the United States in the early 1980s, is transmitted in blood and semen. The human immunodeficiency virus (HIV), which causes AIDS, can be passed to a fetus by an HIV-infected mother, because viruses from her body can cross the placenta into the developing child.

A population that has been at high risk for this fatal disease consists of children whose mothers are IV (intravenous) drug abusers or sexual partners of IV drug abusers. IV drug abusers often acquire the disease by sharing dirty needles with someone who already has the virus. Because drug addiction and the poverty associated with it are more common among blacks and Hispanics in the United States, a high proportion of the women infected by dirty needles are black and Hispanic, and black and Hispanic babies are at higher risk than non-Hispanic white babies for becoming HIV-infected (Johnson, 1988).

Like other aspects of child development, prenatal and perinatal problems have a social dimension as well as a biological one. Our discussion shows this to be true: Some babies are reaping the benefits of the most advanced scientific research and receiving medical treatment costing hundreds of thousands of dollars. Other babies are being thrown away to drug addiction and AIDS on the threshold of life. No treatment will ever give them the same chances that normal babies have. Only education, prevention, and wide-ranging social changes will solve these devastating problems for future generations.

PRENATAL DIAGNOSIS AND GENETIC COUNSELING

Like Lindsay, the woman we met at the beginning of this chapter, many couples now know well before birth whether their baby has a genetic or chromosomal defect. Modern technology has given us the tools and knowledge to assess prenatal development quite accurately, but accompanying these advances have come moral and ethical dilemmas that never existed before. As we pointed out in Chapter 1, scientific research can provide knowledge and techniques, but it can't provide the wisdom to use them the best way. Human beings still have to make hard choices—and make them earlier than ever—about what kind of children they want to have.

Prenatal Assessment Techniques

Several techniques are now used to examine fetuses and detect prenatal problems. **Ultrasound** is a technique in which sound waves are bounced off the fetus's body and converted into a visual image of the fetus on a TV monitor. It can reveal the number of fetuses in the womb, the position of the fetus, and certain problems in anatomy such as cleft palate.

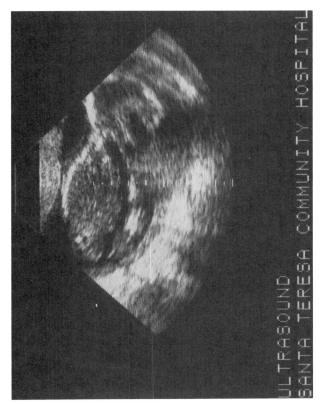

FIGURE 3-25
A sonogram (ultrasound image) of a 16-week-old fetus. Shown in an upright position, the fetus is facing toward the right and slightly away from the viewer. The back of the head and the back are highlighted on the left side of the image; the top of the head, forehead, and cheek can be seen on the right; and the ear is visible in the middle of the head. Amniocentesis revealed that this fetus was a healthy female.

RESEARCH FOCUS

Prenatal Assessment Techniques

Physicians and parents have rushed to take advantage of pre-natal assessment techniques as they've been developed. One of the first to be commonly used was ultrasound. In this technique, very high frequency sound waves, far beyond the hearing capacity of the human ear (thus the name *ultra-sound*), are bounced off the fetus in the uterus. Sound waves are deflected or absorbed at different rates, depending on the density of the object they strike. For example, they bounce off bone but are absorbed by soft tissue, water, or blood. These differences can be converted into electrical signals, which can in turn be converted into a visual image (Garrett & Robinson, 1970).

In prenatal diagnosis using ultrasound, a technician passes a hand-held transducer over the mother's abdomen. The transducer emits pulses of ultrasound. The deflected ultra-sound waves are converted into an image of the fetus on a TV monitor. The image reveals several things about the fetus—position in the womb, size and gestational age, and whether anatomical problems are present. For example, the image will reveal an abnormally large head, an improperly formed spine, or a heart with certain defects. The newest ul-trasound techniques also reveal less gross problems, such as a cleft lip or palate (Seeds & Cefalo, 1983).

Ultrasound appears to be a very safe procedure. Data have failed to confirm any harmful effects on patients or their fetuses. The benefits to patients exposed to prudent use of diagnostic ultrasound outweigh any slight possibility of risk (Reece et al., 1990).

Where ultrasound gives a picture of the fetus, amniocen-tesis provides a genetic profile. In this procedure, a techni-cian extracts a sample of amniotic fluid from the mother's uterus through a needle inserted into her abdomen. The fetal cells in the fluid are cultured in a lab for several weeks, and then their genetic, chromosomal, and biochemical make-up is analyzed. If a problem is apparent, the parents can decide whether to continue or to terminate the pregnancy.

Amniocentesis can reveal a variety of genetic and chromo-somal abnormalities, including Down's syndrome, Tay-Sachs disease, and sickle-cell anemia. Many hospitals routinely ad-vise all mothers over age 35 to have an amniocentesis be-cause of their higher probability of passing on a genetic dis-

order. The procedure can also be used to determine the fetus's maturity. For example, if a physician wants to deliver a baby as soon as possible because the mother's health is en-dangered by the pregnancy, amniocentesis can reveal if the fetus's lungs are mature enough for the baby to survive out-side the uterus (Kogon et al., 1986).

Amniocentesis is a relatively safe procedure (Chayen, 1978; Kelley & Gilman, 1983). It's even safer if ultrasound is used to determine the position of the fetus so the needle isn't stuck into the unborn infant or the placenta (Mennuti et al., 1983). The main drawback of amniocentesis is timing. It can't be performed until the fetus is at least 14 to 16 weeks old, because until then there isn't enough amniotic fluid to permit extraction. Then the cells have to be cultured for an additional three to five weeks before they can be analyzed. By the time the results are available, the woman is in her twentieth or twenty-first week of pregnancy—her fifth month. If she chooses to have an abortion, a saline procedure has to be used. A suction abortion, which is safer, can no longer be performed at this late date.

A relatively new technique, known as chorionic villus sampling (or chorionic biopsy), is under investigation as an alternative to amniocentesis. In this procedure, a tube is in-serted into the uterus and a small amount of chorionic tissue is extracted. Tissue from the chorion, part of the fetal support system in the uterus, is genetically identical to the fetus itself, because both originated from the zygote. Any genetic or chromosomal abnormality in the chorionic cells indicates an abnormality in the fetus too.

Chorionic sampling can be performed as early as the ninth or tenth week of pregnancy, a full month earlier than amniocentesis (Martin et al., 1986; Saltus, 1987). Results are available within one to seven days. This procedure is still being investigated, however. Potential problems include ma-ternal bleeding, infection, and premature rupture of the mem-branes (Martin et al., 1986). If these safety issues can be re-solved, chorionic sampling will be preferable to amniocentesis, because parents will be able to receive infor-mation about their child six weeks earlier than they can now (Hogge, Schonberg & Golbus, 1986).

Amniocentesis involves the extraction of some amniotic fluid from the uterus through a needle inserted into the mother's abdomen. The fluid sur-rounding the fetus contains fetal cells with the same genetic and chromosomal make-up as the fetus itself. From analyzing the fluid, technicians can detect a variety of abnormalities, including Down's syndrome, Tay-Sachs disease, and sickle-cell anemia. These techniques and another new technique, **chorionic vil-lus sampling,** are discussed in detail in Research Focus—Prenatal Assessment Techniques.

Ethical and Social Issues Related to Prenatal Assessment

When a fetus is assessed, the obvious implication is that the pregnancy may be terminated if a defect is found. This isn't always what happens, of course. Some parents use the information to prepare themselves to accept and care for

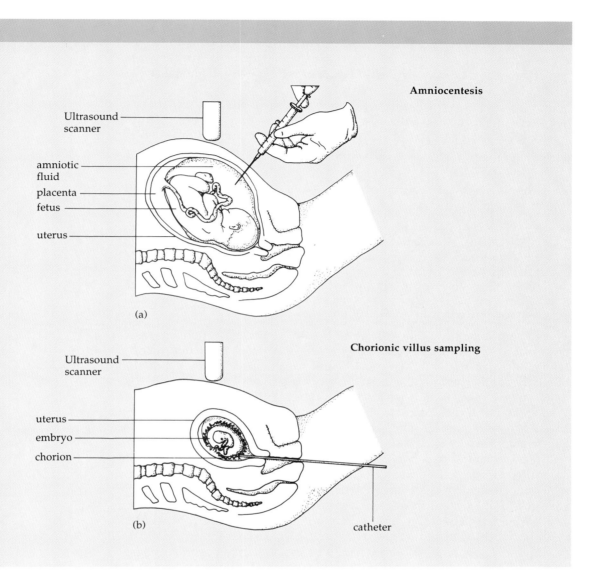

Amniocentesis

Ultrasound scanner

amniotic fluid

placenta

fetus

uterus

(a)

Chorionic villus sampling

Ultrasound scanner

uterus

embryo

chorion

(b)   catheter

a child with a disability. Many parents go into prenatal testing without having decided what they'll do if the results are negative. They're hoping, naturally, that there won't be any decision to make. But, in general, parents who wouldn't terminate a pregnancy under any circumstances don't seek prenatal assessment. That's why the choice to have an amniocentesis, for example, implies that parents might also choose to terminate the pregnancy.

The difficult decisions associated with prenatal assessment have wide-ranging moral, social, and political implications for both the parents and the larger society. Consider just some of the questions related to this issue:

• Which genetic disorders are likely to cause severe enough problems to warrant termination of a pregnancy?
• Can a civilized society decide that individuals below a certain level of development are incapable of living a worthwhile life?

- If so, what level of development is sufficient to ensure a worthwhile life? Worthwhile in what terms and from whose point of view? Who decides?
- Should more research be devoted to treatment methods for people born with genetic disorders, or should such births be prevented altogether? Who decides?
- If research on treatment methods is to be pursued, which disorders should receive top priority? If a disorder that occurs more frequently in a particular ethnic or racial group is given higher priority than another disorder, what are the social and political consequences of this choice?

The ethical aspects of prenatal diagnosis have been summed up as follows (Campbell, 1984, p. 1634):

> Some . . . see this enhanced information as a clear moral gain, allowing the avoid-ance of suffering, the weeding out of conditions which natural selection would in any case discard, the earlier termination of pregnancies where the outcome for the fetus is inevitably fatal, and the continuation of those clearly established as normal. Others, however, fear the reappearance of a eugenic philosophy which regards all less than perfect human beings as inferior and promotes what would be better described as 'ante-natal' euthanasia.

Although some people are concerned that the technology of prenatal assess-ment will be put in the service of eugenics—the "science" of improving the human race genetically through such policies as prenatal "mercy killing"—the opposite side of the coin is an issue too. Some parents will choose *not* to ter-minate a pregnancy even when a serious problem is detected (Campbell, 1984). Who should bear the economic burden for the care of a severely handicapped child born after prenatal diagnosis revealed the problem? The parents? The government? Where should the money come from?

Money, of course, is a critical element in all these questions. In the future, according to one researcher, we may see a "zero-sum system" adopted, in which medical budgets are closed (Bloom, 1984). The total amount of money allocated for medical purposes each year would be limited to a particular sum, and within that limit different medical services would compete with each other for funds. If more money were spent on intensive care for extremely ill neonates, for example, less money would be spent on immunization programs for all children. Or if more money were spent on all pediatric services, less money would be spent on care for the middle-aged or elderly (such as heart by-pass or transplant surgery, kidney dialysis, breast mammography, nursing home care, and so on.)

If recent history is any guide, children's services won't compete very suc-cessfully against services for the rapidly growing elderly population. And if the total amount allocated to medical care is increased, some other area has to be reduced. What will it be? Defense? Education? Social Security? And who will make *that* decision?

Changing Attitudes toward Children

There's one other implication of using prenatal assessment techniques—a change in attitude toward the children that are born. In earlier times (up to about 1970!), parents were largely the victims of fate, and there wasn't much they could do about it. If they had a normal child, they thanked their lucky stars, and if they had a disabled child, they grieved and managed the best they could. Now parents have more control over the health of their babies, and they increasingly expect, as a right, to give birth to perfect babies. If they don't, some parents are likely to sue the obstetrician who failed to mention some risk or recommend some test.

FIGURE 3-26
Do parents have the right to perfect children? Do children have the right to a healthy start in life? Our society faces many difficult issues involving children as we move toward the twenty-first century.

This attitude can also be seen later when the child gets to school. Many parents have the same high expectations for learning and achievement that they had for a healthy baby. If something does go wrong, they may believe that the knowledge exists to solve every problem, which is not always the case. Since many parents today are having only a few carefully planned children, they may invest all their hopes and dreams in one or two small human beings.

Unrealistic expectations like these make life hard for everyone. Children are pressured, parents are tense, and teachers and pediatricians face demands they can't meet. Despite great advances, there are still very real limits to scientific knowledge and technology, and these have to be accepted. Perfect children just can't be guaranteed.

OVERVIEW

Child development begins well before birth. In a sense, it begins even before conception if we take into account the parents' history, their health and habits, and the genetic material they may pass on to their children. Our knowledge about all these aspects of child development has increased so rapidly in the last 25 years, and technological advances have been so dramatic, that pregnancy and birth are radically different experiences today than they were a generation ago. But these advances have introduced new ethical and social dilemmas, and greater opportunities have brought greater responsibilities. The challenge of the future will be to use our sophisticated knowledge to protect and nurture every child from the start of life.

CHAPTER REVIEW

GENETICS: THE BASIS OF BIOLOGICAL INHERITANCE

- Every person on earth is unique, largely because of individual genetic inheritance. But how much people are affected by their genetic make-up, as opposed to their experiences, is a matter of debate, a question referred to as the nature-nurture controversy.
- Biological traits are transmitted from one generation to the next on genes (sequences of DNA), which are carried on chromosomes. Human body cells contain 23 pairs of chromosomes.
- A dominant gene always expresses its own characteristic; a recessive gene expresses its characteristic only when it's paired with another recessive gene.
- A child's genes come from two cells, one contributed by the father and the other contributed by the mother. Germ cells (ova and sperm) differ from body cells in the way they divide. Germ cell division, called meiosis, results in a new cell that contains only 23 single chromosomes.

- Individual genetic differences are the result of the crossing over that occurs during meiosis.
- The sex of a child is determined by the sex chromosomes it inherits. A female inherits an X chromosome from each parent; a male inherits an X from his mother and a Y from his father. Sex-linked characteristics are traits encoded by recessive genes on the X chromosome that can be expressed in males because there isn't a second X chromosome to override them.
- Fraternal twins occur when two different eggs are fertilized. Identical twins occur when a single fertilized egg divides after conception.
- Multiple births often occur when a woman has taken fertility drugs, which stimulate the ovaries to release more than one egg. Multiple births are linked to maternal age; they also occur more frequently in certain populations.

PRENATAL DEVELOPMENT

- In the past, many people thought the embryo was completely formed when implanted and simply increased in size until birth. Others advocated an epigenic, or developmental, theory of prenatal development.
- For couples who can't conceive a child, many treatments are available, including surgery, fertility drugs, and more radical approaches such as in vitro fertilization and surrogate motherhood. Sometimes infertility can't be treated.
- Once a child is conceived, it develops over a 38-week period, which we usually divide into three stages.
- The period of the ovum, from conception to week 2, begins in one of the fallopian tubes and ends when the embryo becomes firmly implanted in the uterine wall. If the embryo becomes implanted in the wall of the fallopian tube, the result is an ectopic pregnancy, which must be ended surgically.
- The period of the embryo, from the second to the eighth week, is the time when all the major body structures are formed. The organism is especially susceptible to environmental influences during this time.
- The period of the fetus, from the ninth week to birth, is a time of growth and further development. The body systems begin to function, and the external genitalia develop.
- Different parts of the body grow at different rates, but the head is more fully developed throughout the entire prenatal period.
- Babies born as early as the twenty-fourth or twenty-fifth week of gestation have survived, but all premature babies face formidable problems.

BIRTH

- The birth process occurs in three stages. During the first and longest stage of labor, the cervix dilates and the baby moves down into the mother's pelvis. During the second stage, the baby moves down through the birth canal and out of the mother's body. The third and final stage is the expulsion of the placenta.
- A variety of conditions can result in birth by cesarean section, delivery of the baby through an incision in the abdominal wall. The rate of cesarean deliveries has increased to almost 25 percent in this country, a rate many people consider far too high.
- Prior to the early 1970s, birth was treated as a medical emergency. Women were heavily sedated and gave birth in hospital delivery rooms. Babies were taken to a nursery after delivery and brought to the mothers only at scheduled feeding times. The father and any siblings had little or no contact with the baby during the hospital stay.
- In the early 1970s parents, physicians, midwives, and childbirth educators began to lobby for more parental involvement in the birth process and for the use of less medication during labor. Research findings and changing social practices, such as an increase in breast-feeding, also contributed to changes in childbirth practices.
- Today many parents take childbirth education classes in which they learn special breathing and relaxation techniques to use during labor, reducing the need for pain-relieving drugs. Women are often assisted by their husbands or partners, and they may labor and deliver in special birthing rooms if their deliveries are uncomplicated.
- If the baby is full term and healthy, the mother can usually keep the baby with her immediately afer birth. Rooming-in is available in most hospitals, and fathers and siblings have contact with the new baby before it comes home.
- Mothers stay in the hospital for two or three days following a normal, uncomplicated delivery, and women who have had a cesarean section stay from five to seven days.
- Some women who have normal, low-risk pregnancies choose to give birth at home or in alternative birth centers. They may be assisted by a midwife or physician. Home births have both advantages and certain risks.
- The main benefit of the new childbirth practices is the reduced use of medication. There are also psychological and emotional benefits to giving birth in a relaxed setting and having the father involved during the birth.
- Early contact between mother and baby is important, but studies have shown that mothers who couldn't have contact with their babies immediately after birth have no trouble establishing a strong emotional attachment once they do have contact.

PROBLEMS IN EARLY DEVELOPMENT

- Problems that originate before the seventh month of development are called prenatal; problems that originate between the seventh month and a few minutes after birth are called perinatal.
- Prenatal problems can be genetic, chromosomal, or environmental.
- Most genetic problems result when the child inherits an abnormal recessive gene from both parents. The most common genetic diseases are sickle-cell anemia, cystic fibrosis, phenylketonuria, and Tay-Sachs disease.
- Rh disease is a genetically related disorder that occurs when an Rh-negative mother gives birth to an Rh-positive baby. A serum now controls the disease.
- Chromosomal problems occur when errors are made during meiosis. The most common chromosomal abnormality is Down's syndrome, which is more common in mothers under age 20 and over age 35.

- Environmental problems occur when a fetus is exposed to teratogens, including viruses, prescription and illegal drugs, alcohol, and environmental chemicals.
- The three major perinatal problems are insufficient growth, insufficient oxygen, and infections.
- Insufficient growth occurs when the placenta fails to nourish the fetus adequately, resulting in a small-for-date baby.
- If a baby receives insufficient oxygen during or just after birth, the lower centers of the brain may be affected, causing cerebral palsy.
- Infections can be passed from the mother to the baby during or before birth. The four most serious infections are syphilis, gonorrhea, herpes simplex virus, and AIDS.

PRENATAL DIAGNOSIS AND GENETIC COUNSELING

- Advanced techniques for detecting prenatal problems include ultrasound, which gives a picture of the fetus, and amniocentesis and chorionic villus sampling, both of which provide a genetic profile.
- These new techniques have created ethical and political questions, such as how to decide when a prenatal problem is severe enough to warrant termination of a pregnancy.

- Prenatal assessment techniques have also affected parents' attitudes, in some cases leading to unrealistically high expectations that modern technology can create perfect children. New knowledge can enhance the chances of having healthy babies, but it can't guarantee them.

KEY TERMS

nature-nurture controversy	sex-linked characteristics	period of the ovum	perinatal
genes	zygote	embryoblast	Down's syndrome
chromosomes	fraternal twins	trophoblast	teratogens
recessive gene	identical twins	ectopic pregnancy	fetal alcohol syndrome
dominant gene	prenatal development	period of the embryo	small-for-date baby
germ cells	epigenic theory	period of the fetus	anoxia
somatic cells	oviduct	crowning	ultrasound
mitosis	fallopian tube	rooming-in	amniocentesis
meiosis	gestation	prenatal	chorionic villus sampling

SUGGESTIONS FOR FURTHER READING

Brigitte, J. (1980). *Birth in four cultures*. Montreal, Canada: Eden Press.
  A very interesting and readable book written by an anthropologist. Brings a cultural perspective to the birthing process.

Dorris, M. (1989). *The broken cord*. New York: Harper & Row.
  This compelling book is the story of a child (now grown up) who suffers from fetal alcohol syndrome. Written by his adoptive father, it not only reviews the

current research on FAS but also gives a clear picture of the kind of devastating brain damage associated with maternal alcohol abuse during pregnancy.

Institute of Medicine (1985). *Preventing low birthweight: Summary.* Washington, DC: National Academy Press. Presents an overview of the problem and what is known about its causes. Discusses policy steps that should be taken to help reduce the number of babies born with low birthweight.

Lane, D., & Stratford, B. (1985). *Current approaches to Down's syndrome.* New York: Praeger. This book provides detailed information about many aspects of Down's syndrome, including typical physical characteristics and problems and educational programs. Includes research on language, motor, and play behavior.

Pollock, L. (1987). *A lasting relationship: Parents and children over three centuries.* London: University Press of New England. This book uses diaries, memoirs, autobiographies, and letters to provide a portrait of children from the early 1600s to the mid-1800s. The first section covers views of pregnancy and childbirth. Fascinating reading.

INFANTS AND TODDLERS

A child is born; a new life has begun. Prenatal development now complete, the baby appears in the world with many qualities determined and many more still to be shaped. In the next few years the child will encounter an infinite variety of new sensations and experiences, and inner and outer influences will work together to create a complex, unique human being. The importance of these early years must not be underestimated. By the time they're 3 or 4 years old, children are launched on a course that often shapes their lives. Much of what they will be in life is set in motion now. Perhaps more than any other period of childhood, infancy and toddlerhood require our best efforts to understand, protect, and nurture.

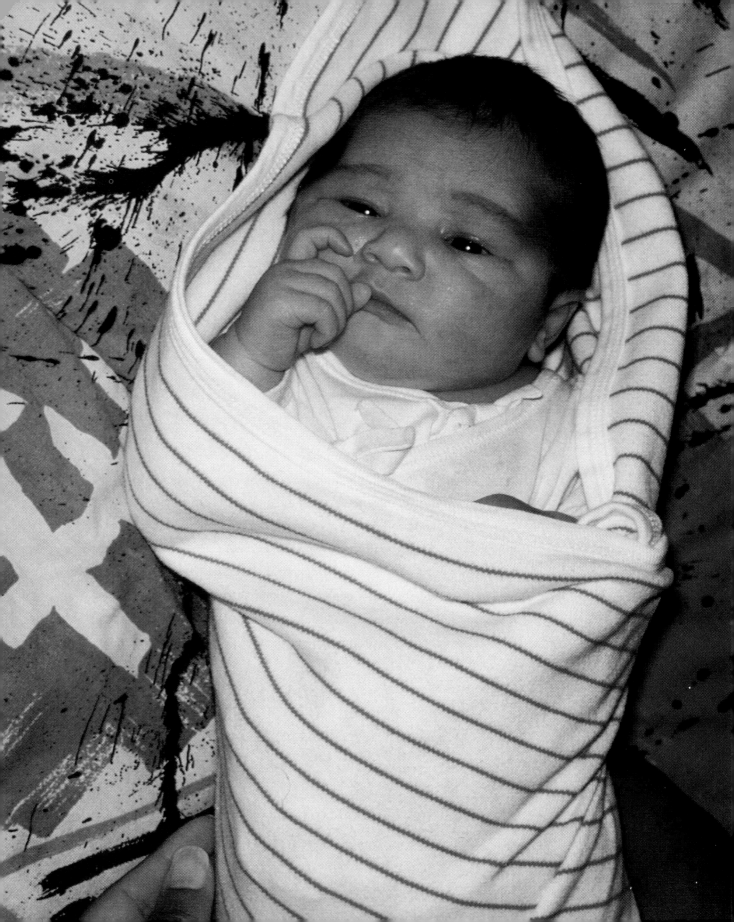

chapter 4

THE NEONATE

Lew Harding was finally coming back down to earth. His adrenaline had been pumping ever since his wife had gone into labor some time the previous night. He'd gotten her to the hospital, helped her relax and breathe through contractions for eight hours, and watched her give birth to their first child just 15 minutes ago. He had been stunned by the intensity of Susan's experience and deeply moved when the baby was born. Now he was just beginning to relax. The baby was lying on Susan's stomach under heated blankets, and he and Susan were gently rubbing the baby's back.

But as he watched his little son, Lew began to experience another feeling—worry, turning rapidly to alarm. The baby in front of him looked not at all like the baby he had imagined so many times or like the pictures in the books. Patrick's skin was bright red, chafed and creased at the wrists and elbows, and covered with a white coating that looked like old soap. His black hair was matted against his head, and there also seemed to be a coating of fine black hair all over his body. His eyes were swollen shut, his nose was flat, one of his ears was pasted forward on his cheek, his chin was nonexistent, and his head was pointy!

Lew looked up quickly to ask someone if the baby was all right. A nurse met his eyes and smiled. "Congratulations, Mr. Harding," she said. "Your son is perfect!"

Lew turned quickly back to his new family. Now, as he gazed at Patrick, he began to wonder why he'd been worried. The longer he looked, the more beautiful his son became.

If you've never witnessed a birth, you might also be surprised by the way Patrick looks. The round, rosy face you might imagine as that of a newborn is actually the face of a baby 4 or 5 months old. Patrick's appearance is quite different. He retains many features, now unnecessary, that suited him very well in his warm, dark, wet life in the womb. He also bears the marks of his long, hard journey from the uterus to the outside world. It takes some time—

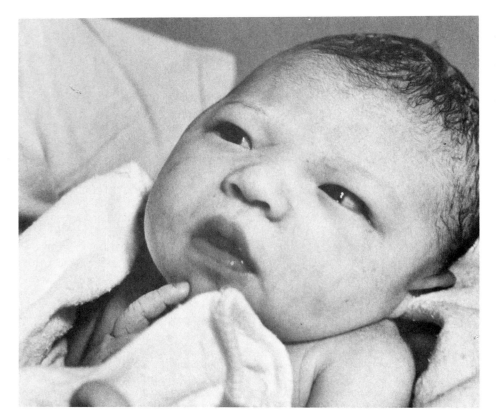

FIGURE 4-1
Just 10 minutes old, this neonate has the misshapen head and swollen eyes that result from a normal vaginal birth. One of the many wonders of birth is that parents delight in their newborn's appearance.

anywhere from a few days to a few weeks—for newborns to adjust to life in their new surroundings. During this time, the newborn is known as a **neonate,** and the period of adjustment is known as the **neonatal period.**

Neonates have a lot to do in their first few weeks of life outside the womb. They have many physiological adjustments to make, a social life to begin, and the wide world to observe. This chapter focuses on what neonates are like and what changes they go through in this early period. It also considers the very different experience of the premature baby. Finally it discusses the practical concerns doctors and parents have during the earliest period of the baby's life.

PHYSICAL CHARACTERISTICS

Appearance

Why does Patrick look the way he does? There's a reason for everything about his appearance. The white, greasy covering on his skin, called **vernix caseosa,** is accumulated sebum, a secretion from glands surrounding the hair follicles in his skin. Vernix forms a protective barrier between his skin and the fluid in his mother's womb. It also provides lubrication during the birth process and protects his skin from infection once he's born.

Patrick's misshapen head is a result of the squeezing that occurred as he passed through his mother's pelvis during birth. As explained in Chapter 3, the bones in the newborn's skull aren't completely formed and can be squeezed together, or **molded,** even to the point of overlapping. Molding permits the baby to have a larger, more mature brain at birth. Even if Patrick's head were an inch larger before molding than his mother's pelvis, his head could still fit through. The open spaces, or **fontanelles,** in the incompletely developed skull are covered with a tight web of skin and tissue that protects the brain from injury (Figure 4-2). The two diamond-shaped "soft spots" on the head will close sometime during the first two years of life as the bones harden and grow together.

Patrick's eyes are probably swollen shut from the pressure exerted on his face during birth. His ear and nose also are temporarily flattened. The puffiness in his face and eyes is caused by the accumulation of fluids when he was in a head-down position before birth. Additional puffiness is created when the silver nitrate drops are put in his eyes after birth to protect him from gonorrhea, which he could have contracted during delivery if his mother had been infected.

Patrick's skin is a deep reddish hue because his capillaries show through his thin skin. As he gains weight and builds up a thicker layer of fat under his skin, the intense redness will fade away. Patrick's appearance will change in some other ways as well in the next few weeks. His head will gradually assume a normal rounded shape, the puffiness will disappear from his eyelids, and the fine hair on his body, known as **lanugo,** will fall out. Still, he will be recognizable as a newborn because of other more enduring physical characteristics, which we consider next.

Body Proportions

When the nurse held Patrick before placing him on his mother's stomach, she made sure she supported his neck with her hand. If she didn't, Patrick's head would fall backward, and he wouldn't be able to bring it up again. This is not just because his neck muscles are weak (Prechtl, 1982); it's also because his head is very large and heavy compared to the rest of his body. As mentioned in Chapter 3, the head grows faster than other parts of the body during the

FIGURE 4-2
The fontanelles, or soft spots, in a young baby's skull will close as the bones grow and fuse. The process is usually complete by the time the child is 2 years old.

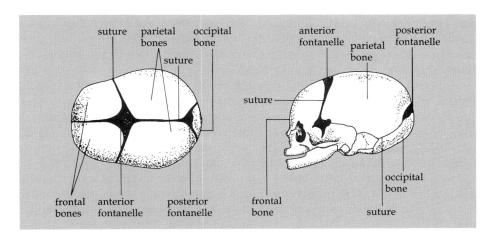

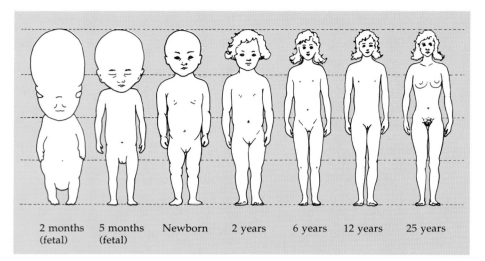

2 months 5 months Newborn 2 years 6 years 12 years 25 years
(fetal)   (fetal)

FIGURE 4-3
Body proportions change radically as children develop and mature. The head accounts for as much as 50 percent of body length prenatally and for about 25 percent at birth. After the first year, other parts of the body—trunk and legs—grow faster than the head. By adulthood, the head accounts for about 10 percent of overall body length.

prenatal period. The head of an adult is about one-tenth of the adult's height, but the head of a newborn is almost one-fourth its total body length (Figure 4-3).

Just as the top of the newborn's body is more fully developed than the lower portion, the top of the newborn's head also is more fully developed than the lower portion. Patrick's jawbones are underdeveloped, he has practically no chin, and his neck is very short. His head sits almost directly on top of his very narrow shoulders. As he grows, his facial features and body proportions will gradually evolve into those of the older baby and child.

Physiology: Feeding and Digestion

Patrick will be so sleepy at first that it may be hard for his mother to keep him from repeatedly falling asleep while she's nursing him. When he does nurse, he may gag frequently on mucus in his throat. However, his mother doesn't have to worry about his eating much in his first few days of life. He was born with stores of **glycogen,** a starch that his body can easily transform into sugar when he needs energy. He also has reserves of extra fat and fluids. The ability of newborns to survive for up to a week without food was demonstrated a few years ago when babies were found alive in the rubble of a hospital leveled by an earthquake in Mexico.

Although he's been nurtured through his mother's body for nine months, Patrick is able to eat food and absorb nutrients at birth. His digestive system produces enough enzymes to digest and absorb both proteins and sugars. He may be less able to absorb saturated fats efficiently, however (Katz & Hamilton, 1974). Since cow's milk is higher in fat than human milk, it's not as perfectly suited to babies as their mothers' milk.

It's convenient that Patrick won't start eating in earnest right away, because his mother won't start producing milk for one to three days after his birth. Since late in her pregnancy, however, she has been producing **colostrum,** a thin, yellowish liquid high in protein and low in fat—perfectly suited to

Patrick's nutritional needs and digestive capacities. Colostrum also contains **immunoglobulins,** antibodies for specific foreign agents that protect the young infant from infectious diseases. Mothers' milk continues to contain antibodies, and breast-fed babies are more resistant than formula-fed babies to gastrointestinal infections, as well as to infections such as pneumonia and meningitis, especially during the first six months of life. In addition, breast-fed babies have a reduced risk of developing chronic diseases, such as some allergic skin disorders and autoimmune diseases of the digestive tract (Cunningham, Jelliffe & Jelliffe, 1991). Since premature babies are more vulnerable to disease than full-term babies, some experts have urged that all premature babies receive human milk (Goldman & Smith, 1973).

One of the first things the nurse will do after Patrick's parents have held him for a while is weigh and measure him. If he's average, he'll weigh about 7½ pounds and measure about 20 inches long. But in his first few days, he'll actually lose some weight—up to 10 percent of his birth weight would not be unusual—because his body is using up some of the stored glycogen, throwing off fluids, and excreting feces. Bottle-fed babies, who are fed on their first day, start gaining weight sooner than breast-fed babies, who have to wait for their mothers' milk to flow. Premature babies gain weight more slowly because they can't eat very much at a feeding.

Although all newborns have a limited capacity at each feeding, they make up for it by eating frequently, usually every 2½ to 4 hours. In infants under 5 months of age, studies have found the average number of feedings per day to be about seven, with less space between feedings during the day than during the night (Michelsson, Rinne, & Paajanen, 1989). Smaller babies may eat less but a little more often. Of course, this means that newborns need to be fed at

FIGURE 4-4
The perfect food . . . a perfect fit. At birth, the mother is producing colostrum, a source of important antibodies that protect the newborn from infectious diseases. Within a few days, she starts producing milk.

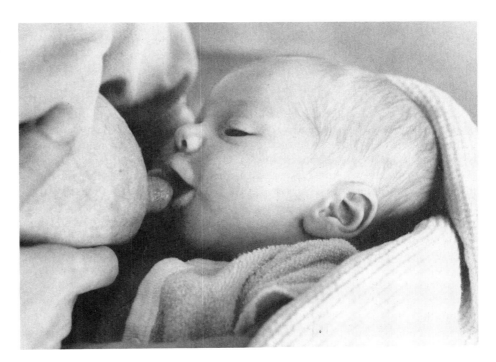

night, and someone has to get up to feed them. Although some babies sleep through the night right from the start, most need one or more night feedings for a few months or more.

At various times in the past, parents have been advised to keep their babies on strict feeding schedules in the belief that regularity was best for babies and parents alike and that being responsive to the baby's feeding demands would spoil the baby. Today most parents respond to the baby instead of following a rigid schedule; they establish a schedule by gradually lengthening the time between feedings.

Respiration and Circulation

When Patrick took his first breath, his lungs filled with air and he let out a healthy cry. But later, as he settles down into his first long sleep period, his breathing will become more irregular—rapid and shallow, punctuated by long, deep breaths. Sometimes he may stop breathing altogether for a few seconds, a normal and apparently harmless occurrence known as **apnea.** He will also cough and sneeze a lot because of the mucus in his nose and throat.

It's not surprising that it takes some time for Patrick's breathing to become regulated. Before birth he got his oxygen from his mother, through the placenta. His blood didn't even pass through his lungs when he was a fetus but bypassed them through a vessel called the **ductus arteriosus.** Immediately after birth, this vessel closed as air filled his lungs, and from that point on, he obtained his own oxygen from the air (Wennberg, Woodrum, & Hodson, 1973).

This change in source of oxygen causes a problem for some newborns. Because oxygen obtained directly from the air is richer, the baby needs fewer red blood cells to carry the oxygen through his body. The baby's body therefore destroys some unneeded red blood cells. This is a process that occurs naturally to some extent at all times. The destruction of the red blood cells produces a by-product called **bilirubin,** which is metabolized in the liver. The newborn's body can't handle the bilirubin very efficiently, and sometimes the liver can't produce enough of the enzyme that converts the bilirubin into a form that can be excreted. Then the baby's bilirubin level goes up, causing **hyperbilirubinemia,** a yellowing of the skin commonly known as *jaundice.*

Within a few days, most newborns are able to produce enough of the enzyme to break down the bilirubin, and the jaundice disappears. But some babies who have moderate jaundice and a rising bilirubin level are treated with special lights, a treatment known as **phototherapy** (Slater & Brewer, 1984). Phototherapy helps convert bilirubin accumulated in the skin into a more water-soluble form that can be excreted by the liver without further metabolism. The level of bilirubin goes down more quickly than it would without the lights (Cashore & Stern, 1982). Currently, a new technique is being explored to treat hyperbilirubinemia. It involves the use of an enzyme that slows the body's breakdown of red blood cells. This gives the baby's body more time to clear the blood of bilirubin as it builds up (Kappas et al., 1988). Jaundice is dangerous because the baby's blood can become overloaded with bilirubin and allow it to pass into the brain. When bilirubin gets into the brain, it enters brain cells—a condition known as **kernicterus**—and causes brain damage (Cashore & Stern, 1982).

FIGURE 4-5
Babies can't regulate their body temperatures for several weeks after birth, so they need to be kept warm. Swaddling babies in blankets keeps them warm and soothes them by restraining their arms and legs. This Algonquin Indian baby in Quebec, Canada, is swaddled in a traditional cradle board.

Other conditions increase the risk of serious hyperbilirubinemia and jaundice in the newborn, including Rh incompatibility, which was discussed in Chapter 3, the use of general anesthesia during labor and delivery, and bruising during birth. When general anesthesia is used, the drugs enter the baby's bloodstream and have to be metabolized by the baby's body. The processing of the drugs in the liver competes with the processing of the bilirubin. When the baby is bruised during birth, blood and fluid leak into tissues and blood cells are broken down. This increases the number of red blood cells the baby's body has to dispose of, thus raising the level of bilirubin.

Temperature Regulation

The temperature of the room in which Patrick was born was approximately 80 degrees. Even so, the nurse covered him with a warm blanket as soon as he was born. Then his mother held him closely against her body, and his father rubbed his back. Although it wasn't necessarily their purpose, this helped keep him warm too. Patrick needed all this warmth because newborns aren't able to maintain a normal body temperature by themselves until they're about 8 or 9 weeks old.

We don't know exactly why newborns have trouble keeping warm. Some researchers think the temperature-regulating mechanism in the brain is immature or that it works differently than the adult mechanism. Others note that the ratio of the baby's body surface to its mass is so high that heat escapes rapidly from the surface. Still others point out that the baby's body has very little fat under the skin to provide insulation (Mestayan & Varga, 1960; Perl-

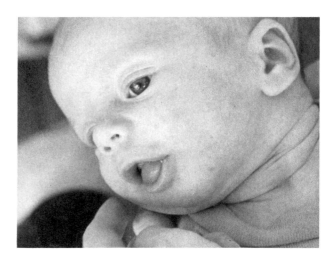

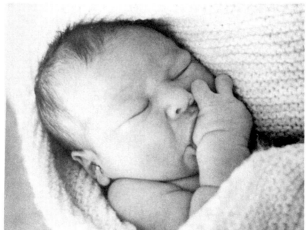

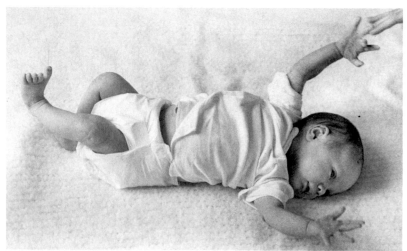

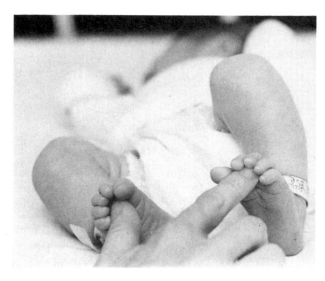

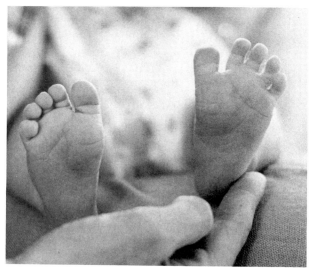

◄ **FIGURE 4-6**
Some newborn reflexes have obvious survival value, such as rooting (top left) and sucking (top right), both of which help the baby obtain nourishment. The purpose of other reflexes isn't as clear—the tonic neck reflex (center left), the Moro, or startle, reflex (center right), the toe grasp (bottom left), and the Babinski reflex (bottom right).

stein et al., 1974; Sinclair, 1975). Whatever the cause, we do know that babies have to be kept warm. When they're taken out of the bath, they should be quickly wrapped in a towel to prevent cooling from evaporation, and when they're taken outside in cold weather, even briefly, they should be dressed in a hat and coat.

It's hard to tell when babies are too hot or too cold because they don't shiver or perspire the way adults do (Klaus & Fanaroff, 1973). Parents have to keep track of what the temperature is and judge the baby's comfort to some extent by what they themselves are wearing. If a parent thinks a baby may be too cold, holding the baby is an excellent course of action with several benefits. It enhances temperature regulation (Phillips, 1974; Rovee-Collier & Lipsitt, 1982); it soothes a baby who's upset and whose crying is using up energy needed to maintain growth; and it enhances social interaction and learning, as discussed more fully later in this chapter.

MOTOR CAPABILITIES

Reflexive Behavior

Patrick appeared to be quite helpless at birth, but actually he has some inborn motor responses, or **reflexes,** that help him survive. If his mother touched or stroked his cheek, his head would turn toward her hand and his lips and tongue would move. This **rooting reflex** gets him in a good position to get mother's nipple into his mouth. The sensation of the nipple in his mouth triggers the **sucking reflex,** a complex behavior involving a combination of pressure and suction. Patrick also has a **gag reflex** that helps him clear mucus from his throat, and he sneezes and coughs reflexively.

If Patrick were placed face down on a surface and his nose and mouth became obstructed, he would be able to engage in a series of reflexive actions that would prevent him from suffocating. He would raise and turn his head, raise his shoulders, and extend and flex his arms and legs in movements that resemble crawling. This reflex makes it possible to put a newborn like Patrick on his stomach in bed without danger of his smothering in bedclothes. The existence of this and other reflexes indicates that even newborns can protect themselves to a certain extent (Brazelton, 1969). This "crawling" reflex can get the baby into trouble too, however. Parents who believe their baby is too young to move may leave the baby unattended on a bed. If the baby's face is repeatedly obstructed and the baby reflexively "crawls" each time, he can end up tumbling off the bed.

Newborns have other reflexes as well. The function of these reflexes isn't as apparent, but they do indicate the state of the baby's neurological well-being. If these reflexes are present, the baby's nervous system is presumed to be intact and working properly. One of these is the **tonic neck reflex.** If the doctor were to test Patrick for this reflex, she would lay him on his back and turn his head to one side. Patrick would stretch out his arm and leg on the side he's facing and flex the arm and leg on the other side.

A loud sound or a sudden dropping back of Patrick's head would elicit the **Moro,** or startle, **reflex.** He would throw out his arms, fan out his fingers, extend his neck, let out a cry, and then bring his arms back to "embrace" or clasp his chest (Dargassies, 1966). The Moro reflex is triggered when internal

TABLE 4-1   Examples of Infant Reflexes

Reflex	Description	Developmental Course
Blinking	If a light is shone in the baby's eyes, she closes them.	Permanent
Rooting	If the baby's cheek is touched or stroked, she turns her head toward the stroked cheek and moves her lips and tongue to suck.	Gone by 4 months
Sucking	When a nipple or other object is placed in the baby's mouth, she sucks on it using both pressure and suction.	Voluntary by 2 months
Gagging, coughing, sneezing	When mucus or other material blocks the baby's air passages, she clears them automatically.	Permanent
"Crawling"	When the baby is placed face down in such a way that her nose and mouth are obstructed, she raises and turns her head and shoulders and alternately extends and flexes her arms and legs.	Voluntary maneuvers take over by 3–4 months
Tonic neck	If the baby is laid on her back and her head is turned to one side, she stretches out her arm and leg on the side that she is facing and flexes her other arm and leg.	Gone by 4 months
Moro	If the baby is startled by a loud noise or by her head dropping back suddenly, she throws out her arms, fans her fingers, extends her neck, cries, and then brings her arms back to her chest and closes her fingers as if clasping something.	Weak by 5 months, gone by 8 months
Babinski	When the baby's foot is stroked from the heel to the toe, her toes fan out.	Gone by 12 months
Grasping	When the palms of the baby's hands are stroked or pressed, she closes her fingers around the object in a strong grasp. When her feet are pressed just below the toe, she curls her toes down.	Gone by 12 months, beginning to weaken by 3 months
Stepping	If the baby is held upright so one foot just touches a surface, she makes stepping motions as if walking.	Gone by 3 months

receptors sense movement in the neck muscles. Babies sometimes startle themselves during crying episodes and become even more frantic.

If the doctor stroked the outer edge of the soles of Patrick's feet, she would elicit the **Babinski reflex**—his toes would fan out. If she stroked or put pressure on the palms of his hands, she would elicit the **grasping reflex.** This **palmar grasp** is so strong that the doctor could lift Patrick from his back if he were lying on a flat surface. She could also elicit a toe grasp if she pressed on the bottom of Patrick's feet just below the toes.

The purpose of these reflexes isn't clear, but they were probably useful at some time during human evolutionary history. They diminish during the first few months of life as the brain matures. The lower brain centers (midbrain, pons, medulla, and cerebellum) come under the control of the higher brain center, the cerebral cortex, which inhibits reflex action. (For a diagram of the brain, refer to Figure 3-24 in Chapter 3.) It's hard to elicit a startle reflex by 6 months of age, for example, and by 8 or 9 months it's usually impossible. The Babinski reflex is usually gone by 4 months. If reflexes persist beyond the time when they typically disappear, it may indicate that the brain isn't functioning normally. (See Table 4-1 for descriptions and developmental courses of selected reflexes.) One of the early signs of cerebral palsy, for example, is the persistence of the tonic neck reflex, the Moro reflex, and the palmar reflexes (Barabas & Taft, 1986).

Voluntary Movements

Although Patrick has a variety of reflexes, he doesn't have much control over his voluntary movements. During the last few weeks in the womb, his muscles developed a considerable amount of muscle tone, or **tonus,** the continuous tension normal in muscles at rest (Dargassies, 1966). In the fetal position, his legs were crossed at the ankles and bent at the knees so they touched his abdomen. His arms were bent at the elbows and raised up, and his fists were clenched.

After birth, his movements are like the gradual unwinding of a tightly wound spring. His arms and legs jerk and flail, and he has trouble getting his fingers or hand to his mouth. As he gains control over his muscle activity, he becomes more successful at reaching his target with less excess motion.

BEHAVIORAL STATES

Newborns are typically awake and alert when they're born, but after about an hour they fall into a long, deep sleep (Wolff, 1965; Stratton, 1982). They might remain asleep for a day or more, possibly to give their body a chance to adjust to all the changes they're going through (Brazelton, 1961). After this sleep, their behavior will be organized into recurring patterns of wakefulness and sleep called **behavioral states.** At some times they'll be alert, at other times they'll be in one kind of sleep or another, and at still other times they'll be crying.

Researchers define behavioral states by looking at specific variables, which usually include eye movements, position of eyelids (open or closed), regularity of breathing, brain wave patterns, and motor activity (Prechtl & O'Brien, 1982). Various schemes have been devised to classify and assess babies' behavioral states, but the one shown in Table 4-2 is useful because it labels the states with descriptive terms, including regular sleep, irregular sleep, drowsiness, alert inactivity, waking activity, and crying (Wolff, 1966). During the alert inactive state, the baby is calm, bright-eyed, attentive, and particularly receptive to stimuli from the environment. After the first few days, the baby spends more and more time in the alert inactive state.

Regularities in Behavioral States and Variations among Infants

Behavioral states are organized and cyclical; they don't occur randomly (Prechtl & O'Brien, 1982). In other words, we can predict which state will follow the baby's present state. For example, alert inactivity often follows waking activity, and drowsiness often follows crying. Even though they follow the same pattern, however, all babies don't spend the same amount of time in the various states. Some babies cry more than others, some sleep more than others, and some are more alert than others. We don't know exactly why this is, but

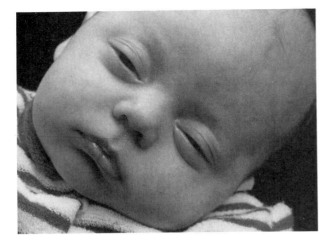

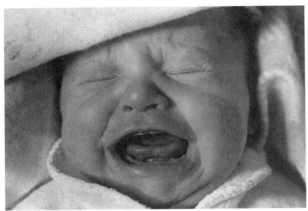

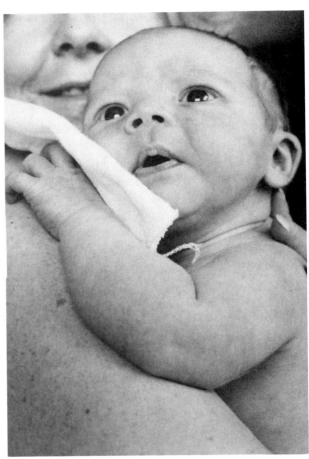

FIGURE 4-7
Researchers identify babies' behavioral states by observing a variety of different characteristics, including skin color, muscle tone, rate of breathing, and vocalization, but even the casual observer can identify drowsiness, crying, and alert inactivity. In the alert inactive state, the baby can observe, learn, and interact with adults.

genetic factors may account for some of the differences. Method of delivery may also be a factor. Babies whose mothers were anesthetized during the birth tend to be less active and alert, at least for the first few days. (For further discussion, see Research Focus—Effects of Obstetrical Drugs on Newborns.)

Child-rearing practices may also influence the baby's states. For example, swaddling (wrapping the baby tightly in a blanket) keeps babies from losing control of their arms and legs and startling (Brazelton, 1969; Friedman, Jacobs & Werthmann, 1981). Hospital nurses usually wrap babies tightly because they know it keeps them calmer. Parents, of course, quickly unwrap the blankets because they want to look at the baby. But they also hold the baby, which restrains the arms and legs and keeps the baby calmer.

Behavioral States, Attachment, and Learning

Whatever the individual baby's pattern, it does have an influence on the mother-child relationship. As suggested by the systems approach to development, the baby affects the mother as much as the mother affects the baby (Bell, 1971; Crockenberg, 1981). An extremely irritable baby or a baby who doesn't respond very strongly can have a negative effect on the mother, just as a baby who is responsive and calm can have a positive effect.

TABLE 4-2 Behavioral States in the Newborn

State	Motor Activity	Muscle Tone	Skin	Eyes	Face	Respiration	Vocalization
Regular sleep	No movement of limbs and trunk; startle reflexes present	Relaxed	Pink, but pale	Closed; no movement	Relaxed	Regular; breaths 36 per minute	
Irregular sleep	Movement of trunk and limbs between periods of rest	Moderate degree of tension	Flushed during activity	Closed, but movements present	Grimaces such as smiles and frowns	Irregular rhythm; 48 breaths per minute	
Drowsiness	More movement than during regular sleep but less than during irregular sleep	Moderate degree of tension		Eyes open and close; dull, glazed, and unfocused		Generally regular	Occasional high-pitched squeal
Alert inactivity	Inactive	Moderate degree of tension		Eyes are open, bright, shining, attentive; eyes move together in horizontal and vertical plane		Faster than during regular sleep	
Waking activity	Activity occurs in spurts	Higher degree of tension	Flushed during activity	Eyes are open but not bright and shining		Irregular	Moans, grunts, whining, but no sustained crying
Crying	Very active	Considerable tension	Flushed bright red	May be open or closed; tears in some babies	Grimaces	Fast and irregular	Crying

SOURCE: Wolff, P. (1966). The causes, controls, and organizations of behavior in the newborn. Psychological Issues, 5 (Whole No. 17), 1–105.

In Chapter 8 on the social and emotional development of infants and toddlers, we discuss in greater detail the importance of the mother-child relationship and the factors that influence it. Here, we mention just that a positive, nurturing relationship probably keeps the baby calmer and better able to take advantage of sights and sounds in the environment. Holding the baby up to the shoulder, for example, often stops crying and induces the alert inactive state, in which the baby is most likely to observe the surroundings (Korner & Grobstein, 1966; Hunziker & Barr, 1986). Thus, babies' behavioral states affect both the kinds of relationships they develop with their mothers and the kinds of opportunities they have for learning in their early months.

SENSORY ABILITIES

Vision

Patrick's eyes were open when he was born, and he seemed to be looking around the room. When his eyes came to rest on his mother's face, she smiled broadly at him in response. She wasn't sure how much he could see, but she

RESEARCH FOCUS

Effects of Obstetrical Drugs on Newborns

Until the mid-19th century, women delivered their babies without drugs or medication to relieve the pain of labor and delivery (Butarescu, 1978). Then in 1847, Scottish physician James Y. Simpson introduced the use of chloroform as an anesthetic for his obstetrical patients. Many people were outraged, because, they claimed, the Bible decreed that childbirth should be painful. But in 1853, Queen Victoria delivered a son under chloroform, and from then on the use of obstetrical drugs grew steadily.

Today, we know that drugs given to the mother quickly cross the placenta and enter the fetus (Ploman & Persson, 1957; Marx, 1961; Bonica, 1967; Morishima et al., 1966). We also know something about how drugs affect the newborn. This information, along with greater interest in prepared childbirth, has led to a decrease in the use of drugs during childbirth. Women are taking less medication than was common in previous years, and many women are having completely unmedicated births.

What are the effects of obstetrical drugs on newborn babies? First and most obviously, drugs make babies groggy at birth. Babies born to nonmedicated mothers are generally alert at birth, and they remain in the alert inactive state longer than babies of medicated mothers before falling asleep (Desmond et al., 1963). Babies born to medicated mothers suck less vigorously and for shorter periods of time than babies born to nonmedicated mothers. These differences have been found to last for one to four days (Brazelton, 1970; Kron, Stern, & Goddard, 1966; Richards & Bernal, 1972).

Babies born to medicated mothers also habituate more slowly to sounds, are less able to track objects with their eyes, exhibit less control of their behavioral states (Murray et al., 1981), and have poorer muscle tone and slower reflexes (Conway & Brackbill, 1970; Aleksandrowicz & Aleksandro-

wicz, 1974). Some differences are noticeable for as long as a month after birth. In fact, some effects don't peak until the 28th day after birth and presumably persist for an unknown period of time after that.

According to one study, the clearest difference between babies from medicated and nonmedicated births is in **consolability**, the ease with which a baby stops crying when talked to or held (Brackbill et al., 1974). Nonmedicated babies are cuddlier and more readily consoled. These characteristics, along with the length of time the baby is alert and attentive after birth, have the potential to influence the parent-child relationship in important ways.

Critics have faulted the research methods used in some of these studies (Federman & Yang, 1976), and effects of drugs lasting longer than one month haven't been demonstrated by any studies. But mothers' subjective experiences of their babies play a role in infant development just as physical condition does. And in some studies nonmedicated mothers have reported their babies to be more social, more rewarding, and "easier" than medicated babies have been reported to be. As one researcher points out, "Although direct biochemical drug effects may wear off in the first days . . . the mother's early impressions may remain to influence how rewarding she finds her baby and the manner in which she responds to her baby's initiatives . . ." (Murray et al., 1981).

As with all aspects of child development, no single event—whether it's separation immediately after birth, an extended hospital stay, or a groggy baby—determines the long-term outcome for a parent-child relationship. But if there's an accumulation of such events, particularly when parents are considered "at risk" for having problems interacting with the baby, the scales may be tipped toward future difficulties.

thought he was looking right at her. And she was right—although his vision wasn't as good as an adult's, he could see her face quite well.

As recently as 30 or 40 years ago, parents were told their newborns couldn't see, but now we know this is absolutely untrue. If an object is held in front of a baby until the baby's eyes fix on it, and then the object is moved, the baby will gaze at the object and track it. That is, the baby's eyes, or head and eyes, will move to keep the object in view (Salapatek, 1968; Brazelton, 1973a). By about 1 month of age, babies also have binocular fixation; that is, they can look at an object with both eyes simultaneously (Slater & Findlay, 1975). Whether babies this age actually see a fused visual image—that is, one image instead of two—has been a question pursued by some researchers. Apparently, fusion of visual images is not present until about 4 months of age (Fox et al., 1980).

Newborns' vision is limited in two other areas, as well—acuity and accommodation. **Acuity** refers to the resolving power of the eye, the sharpness of vision. It is measured in older children and adults with an eye chart. Babies don't have the same visual acuity as adults (20/20) until about 12 months of age (Fantz, Ordy & Udelf, 1962; Banks and Salapatek, 1983). **Accommodation** refers to the ability to change the shape of the lens to bring objects at varying distances into focus. Babies' eyes can accommodate as well as adults' eyes by

FIGURE 4-8
This premature newborn is being held at just about the right distance to form the best visual image of Mom's face.

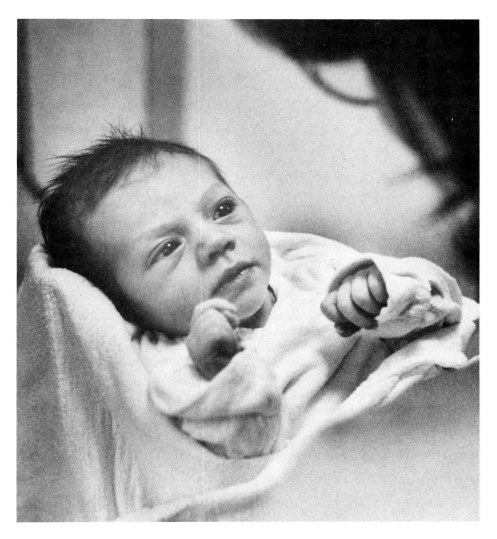

about 2 months of age (Banks, 1980). Until then, they can focus clearly only on objects that are about 7 to 8 inches from their faces (Haynes, White & Held, 1965). Not coincidentally, this is about the distance to the mother's face when the baby is nursing.

Hearing

Patrick could hear quite well at birth, too. In fact, it's likely that he heard a lot before birth, both the sounds of his mother's body and the muffled sounds of the world outside. Some women report that their babies jump or kick in the womb in response to a loud noise, and some mothers believe that their newborns recognize their voices.

If someone rings a bell or shakes a rattle, newborns turn toward the sound and look alert, as if searching for its source (Brazelton, 1969; Muir & Field, 1979). They are also able to distinguish between high and low sounds and loud and soft ones (Hirschman & Katkin, 1974). Researchers have learned these things about newborn hearing by using a process involving **habituation.** First, they expose the baby to a sound to which the baby responds. Then they repeat the sound several times until the baby stops responding to it. Now the baby is habituated to the sound. Finally, they introduce a different sound. If the baby becomes alert again, they know that the baby senses the difference between the two sounds.

Habituation can be explained by assuming that the baby is building a store of information—a "mental model"—about a stimulus (Cohen & Gelber, 1975). When the model is refined enough to match the stimulus itself, the baby stops paying attention to the stimulus. When a new stimulus is introduced, it no longer matches the model, and the baby starts building a new model. This activity requires more attention.

Taste and Smell

Was Patrick born with a "sweet tooth"? Yes, it seems he was. Newborns have been shown to prefer a sweet fluid to fluids with other tastes, and they even prefer sugar water to plain water (Desor, Maller & Andrews, 1975). This means that Patrick is well adapted to his mother's milk, since human milk is higher in sugar than cow's milk and tastes quite sweet.

Newborns have also shown their relative dislike for sour, bitter, and salty tastes by sucking less when offered fluids with those tastes (Lipsitt, 1977). They also indicate their dislike of certain smells, such as ammonia, by grimacing and turning their heads away. Habituation studies have been used to determine that babies are able to distinguish different odors right from birth (Lipsett, Engen & Kaye, 1963). Because they have a well-developed sense of smell, babies quickly learn to recognize the smell of their own mothers' milk and bodies (Cernoch & Porter, 1985).

Pain

A less pleasant sensation to contemplate is pain. Newborns do experience pain, such as from a pinprick in the heel for the PKU test that is administered routinely after birth. Baby boys experience pain during circumcision, and some doctors give the baby a shot of novocaine to anesthetize the penis before this procedure, although the shot itself is painful. As neonates grow older and their nervous systems become more developed, their sensitivity to pain increases (Lipsitt & Levy, 1959).

Visual Perception

We know that Patrick could see at birth, but that doesn't tell us what he saw or how he perceived the world. Does he have a particular way of organizing visual stimuli? Does he see things the way an adult does? Does he have preferences? The answers to all these questions is yes. Visual perception is discussed in detail in Chapter 5 on the physical development of infants and toddlers, but here we briefly discuss newborns' perception.

SIZE CONSTANCY. One important dimension of visual perception is the knowledge that an object remains the same size whether it's close to the viewer or farther away. When an object is viewed, light from the object passes through the lens of the eye and falls on the retina at the back of the eye. An object that is close creates a larger image on the retina than the same object seen farther away. Seeing an object as unchanging in actual size no matter what the size of the image it creates on the retina (retinal size) is known as **size constancy.** Size constancy is an extremely important requirement for the stability of our visual world.

Recent studies have confirmed that size constancy is present at birth (Granrud, 1987; Slater, Matock & Brown, 1990). In one study a group of newborns was shown a sphere of constant actual size (6 cm) at varying distances, and another group was shown three spheres varying in actual size (3, 6, and 12 cm) at distances that would result in the same retinal sizes that the first group saw (Granrud, 1987). The group seeing the constant-sized sphere showed a significant decrease in the amount of time they looked at the sphere each time it was shown. This visual habituation indicated that they correctly perceived the sphere as the same actual size each time, despite the fact that it created a smaller retinal image as it moved farther away. The group seeing the variable-sized spheres (though they formed retinal sizes similar to those seen by the group viewing the constant-sized sphere) did not habituate to the spheres, indicating that they correctly perceived them as varying in actual size. Since newborns correctly perceive (1) the same-sized object varying in distance as constant in actual size and (2) a variable-sized object projecting the same retinal sizes as in (1) as changing in actual size, they were shown to have size constancy.

PREFERENCE FOR PATTERN AND CONTRAST. Researchers approached the question of newborn perception by observing how long they look at different stimuli. Psychologist R. L. Fantz (1963) was the first to demonstrate that babies can notice the difference between patterned and unpatterned visual displays. He showed babies six different stimuli, three patterned (a face, concentric circles, and a piece of newspaper) and three unpatterned (white, yellow, and red). The babies—aged 10 hours to 5 days—looked at the patterned displays longer than the unpatterned ones; of the patterned displays, they liked the face best (Figure 4-9).

Other studies have shown that babies prefer contrast. These studies featured displays with large differences in brightness between background and foreground. It was found that babies fix their gaze on the edge of figures and are particularly interested in the area where black and white meet (Salapatek & Kessen, 1966).

VISUAL PERCEPTION AND THE NATURE-NURTURE ISSUE. If babies exhibit visual preferences at 10 hours, we know that these preferences are innate. There's no way they could have learned to like patterns and contrasts through experience. How this preference works as an adaptation for survival is quite remarkable. Babies are drawn to people's eyes when they see a face because of their preference for patterns and contrasts. Parents are quick to return their newborn's gaze and often interpret the baby's attention as a sign of recognition. This is one of the earliest ways the attachment between parents and baby begins to grow. Of course, nothing works to ensure the survival of the baby so much as a strong attachment with a caring adult, just as nothing endangers the baby as a lack of attachment does.

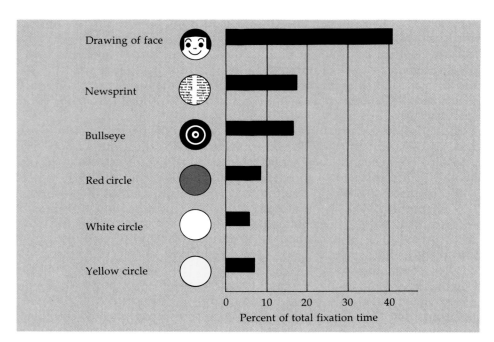

FIGURE 4-9
Using these visual displays, R. L. Fantz found that newborns preferred to look at patterns rather than solid colors and that of all the patterns, they preferred to look at the most complex—the smiling human face. We can't know exactly how they perceive the face, but we can say that this inborn preference plays a role in helping them establish attachments with adults.

LEARNING

Newborns have been eagerly studied for many years by researchers and theorists in child development. As in the perception studies just discussed, newborns are prime candidates for investigations of various aspects of the "nature-nurture" controversy—questions of whether preferences and reactions are innate or learned—because they haven't yet experienced many environmental influences. Since human behavior is the result of complex interactions among the child and her biological and environmental systems, these studies provide us with important information about the state of all these systems before the child is exposed directly to the environment beyond the uterus.

Studies of the relatively simple behavior of newborns helps developmentalists understand how behavior is organized and how this organization changes with time and experience. For example, a preference for visual contrast is present at birth, but visual preferences several months later will reflect not only the innate preference but also the experiences—the specific visual patterns—to which the baby has been exposed. The baby's behavior has been reorganized by experience.

Behavioral Studies of Newborn Learning

Learning is another area of interest to researchers. What can newborns learn? How do they learn it? Does newborn learning provide evidence for one or another of the major child development theories? Many behaviorists have tried to show that newborns can learn things through classical conditioning. If you recall from Chapter 2, this technique involves the pairing of a new stimulus with another stimulus that automatically elicits a certain response. After repeated pairings, the new stimulus alone elicits the response.

Researchers have paired the ringing of a bell or gentle forehead stroking with giving a baby sugar water or a nipple. If the baby could be classically conditioned, the bell or stroking alone would later elicit sucking after repeated pairings. Although classical conditioning is difficult with newborns because they don't stay awake and alert for very long periods of time, researchers have been able to elicit sucking with stimuli like bells and stroking (Rovee-Collier & Lipsitt, 1982; Blass, Ganchrow & Steiner, 1984).

Other researchers have tried to show that babies can learn through instrumental conditioning, the technique in which a response is followed with reinforcement. This kind of learning seems to be easier for newborns (Sameroff, 1972; Millar, 1974). In one study, researchers gave newborns a nipple when they turned their heads as part of the rooting reflex. They found that the babies turned their heads more often as a result (Siqueland & Lipsitt, 1966; Papousek, 1967).

Other studies have shown that babies change their sucking response, depending on whether a nipple provides food (Rovee-Collier & Lipsitt, 1982). If the nipple is attached to a bottle of milk or sugar water, babies squeeze the nipple with their tongues and cheeks *and* suck on it. If the nipple is attached to a pacifier, they just squeeze it. Experiments like this show that babies can respond to the environment in intelligent ways and learn from experience. Further questions about infant learning have been raised and addressed by other studies; some of these are discussed in Research Focus—Learning in Young Infants.

Piaget's Approach to Newborn Learning

Piaget, too, was interested in what newborns could learn, although he didn't approach learning from a behavioral point of view. He believed that babies continually modify their behavior on the basis of experience and thus respond differently to different kinds of situations. He noted, for example, that different objects are sucked in different ways: some things are sucked, some are spit out, some are sucked at one time and not another. This rudimentary "thinking" leads to more complex behavior, although babies' intelligence is based on sensorimotor experiences for the first two years of life. In other words, babies know about the world only through their physical and sensory interactions with objects. They can't represent what they know symbolically with words. (Sensorimotor intelligence is discussed in detail in Chapter 6 on the cognitive development of infants and toddlers). Whether we feel more comfortable with a behavioral or a cognitive-developmental point of view, we can see that babies are able to learn right from the start.

THE PREMATURE BABY

Tina stared in disbelief at her second child, born prematurely and lying in an incubator. Tubes connected Elizabeth to air and food—and life. She was so tiny she would fit in a large man's hand, and her bones showed clearly under her skin. Her eyes were shut; no flicker of awareness crossed her wizened face. She looked like some strange creature only distantly related to a newborn baby.

Tina's first child had been so healthy, so alert, that it never occurred to her she might give birth prematurely this time. The doctors told Tina that she and her husband might

RESEARCH FOCUS

Learning in Young Infants

Many studies have confirmed that infants can learn from both classical and operant conditioning methods, but some research has touched on more interesting issues. What motivation lies behind learning? What deeper lessons do infants learn from our responses to their efforts? What can we do to improve infants' ability to learn? These are some of the questions that have been raised by research on infant learning.

In one experiment, for example, researchers were interested in establishing learning in babies by using operant conditioning. To do this, they turned on a light when the baby turned her head 30 degrees to the right of midline (Papousek & Bernstein, 1969). Young infants learned how to make the light go on by turning their heads, and their head turning increased when they learned this behavior. But, surprisingly, head turning declined soon after they mastered the task.

The researchers then decided to present the light only after more complex head turning, such as a turn to the right followed by a turn to the left. When infants found that the usual head turning failed to turn on the light as it had before, they began a flurry of head turning, apparently trying to find out how to get the light to come on again. But once they had succeeded in turning on the light several times in a row with the more complex pattern, head turning again declined.

These results suggest that babies are motivated to learn by opportunities to solve problems, not simply by primary reinforcement such as food or stimulation. Although this experiment is from the behavioral tradition, its findings bear out some of Piaget's ideas. Children want to learn things just because they're interesting. It follows that we can motivate them more by making learning interesting than by rewarding them with candy or gold stars.

Another study showed that individual learning experiences build on one another and that babies can use prior learning experiences to learn something new (Papousek, 1967). In this experiment, a bell sounding meant that head turns to one side would be reinforced, and a buzzer sounding meant that head turns to the other side would be reinforced. Every day, a few trials of this task were given to two groups of infants the same age. One group had previously mastered a similar discrimination task, but the other group hadn't. The group without prior training took twice as many trials to learn the task as the group with prior training. The earlier learning experience made it easier for the infants to learn a new discrimination.

Babies may be learning something more important than the mechanics of a particular situation when their actions cause changes in the environment. They may be learning that they can make interesting things happen in the world. Babies whose actions don't produce results may learn "helplessness" instead (Maier, Seligman & Solomon, 1969). Two correlational studies have supported this idea. In one, researchers observed mothers and their 5-month-old babies at home and correlated their observations with the infants' test scores on an assessment instrument known as the Bayley Scales of Infant Development (discussed in Knowledge in Action: Infants and Toddlers, following Chapter 8) (Yarrow, Rubenstein & Pedersen, 1971; 1975). They found that babies whose mothers responded promptly to their crying had higher scores on three clusters of items—goal orientation, reaching and grasping, and effective action on the environment. Learning that their crying got results may have helped these babies understand that they could make things happen. A second study found that babies whose mothers responded quickly when they were hungry and who were sensitive to their needs during feeding had higher scores on IQ tests (Ainsworth & Bell, 1973).

Because both of these studies were correlational, we can't be certain about the relationship between responsive parenting and infant development. But experimental studies have demonstrated that when babies receive feedback contingent on their actions in one task, they're better able to learn a second, unrelated task (Finkelstein & Ramey, 1977; Ramey & Finkelstein, 1978). In another experimental study, monkeys whose feeding was contingent on what they did were observed to explore more, cling to each other less, and emerge more quickly from a cage to play in a playroom than monkeys whose feeding wasn't related to their own actions (Mineka, Gunnar & Champoux, 1986).

We can't conduct experimental studies with human infants to see if responsive parenting improves their ability to learn, but we can draw some conclusions from the correlational and experimental evidence that we do have. It seems that the responsiveness of the environment may provide some of the baby's most important lessons. Babies whose efforts produce results learn "I can"; babies who get no response learn "I can't."

be able to hold Elizabeth and help feed her within a week, although she would be attached to the respirator for at least three weeks and in the hospital for five weeks more after that.

As Tina looked at her daughter, she felt a numbing emptiness. She wanted to hold her right now and awaken the feelings she had felt toward her son when he was born. It was going to be a long eight weeks.

Elizabeth wasn't as lucky as Patrick. Instead of spending 37 to 40 weeks in the womb, as nature intended, she was born after only 30 weeks. Premature babies—those born before the thirty-seventh week of gestation—account for almost 7 percent of all births, and the percentage is rising. Modern medical technology has made survival possible for babies born earlier and earlier. The problems facing such babies and their families are formidable. Some people question the wisdom and morality of saving these tiny babies, at tremendous cost, only to have some of them face a lifetime of disabling medical problems. However, others strongly disagree (Grögaard et al., 1990). Some of the physical problems of premature babies are considered here, along with the long-term consequences of prematurity.

Small-for-date babies are also smaller than average but for different reasons. These babies are full term but weigh less than 5½ pounds, or 2500 grams. Their small size may be due to a variety of factors, but two of the chief causes are poor maternal nutrition during pregnancy and abnormalities of the placenta that prevent it from providing proper nourishment to the fetus (Lubchenco, Delivotia-Papodopoulos & Searle, 1972). Small-for-date babies are vulnerable to complications, or "at risk," during the neonatal period and later as well, but their problems aren't the same as those of premature babies. Many small-for-date babies—and some premature babies—recover completely from their early problems.

Physical Problems of Premature Babies

Because they're not fully developed, premature babies are vulnerable both during birth and postnatally. They're particularly susceptible to **hypothermia,** a dangerous drop in body temperature, and they must be kept in incubators, where the temperature can be carefully controlled.

A major problem for premature babies is the danger of brain hemorrhages, especially in those born earlier than the thirty-second week of gestation. The arterial system in the brain is not yet completely formed by this time, and certain stress conditions can cause an artery to burst (Tarby & Volpe, 1982). Severe hemorrhages result in death 50 percent of the time; mild to moderate hemorrhages result in death up to 15 percent of the time. Babies who do survive brain hemorrhages may suffer brain damage.

Premature babies are also likely to have respiratory problems. About 15 percent suffer from a serious breathing disorder known as **hyaline membrane disease.** If you recall from Chapter 3, lung development begins early in the prenatal period, but the alveoli, or air sacs, at the very ends of the branches of the lungs aren't completely formed until late in the prenatal period. The alveoli produce **surfactant,** a substance that keeps the lungs from collapsing when the breath is expelled. Premature babies lack surfactant (Kogon et al., 1986), so their lungs tend to collapse when they breathe and they can't get enough oxygen. Hyaline membrane disease is a potentially fatal disease. The younger the baby, the more serious the condition is likely to be, since surfactant isn't produced until the thirty-fourth to thirty-eighth weeks of prenatal life (Hallman & Gluck, 1982). In recent years, efforts have been made to supply surfactant to premature infants' lungs soon after birth or when respiratory distress sets in. This treatment has had good results in reducing respiratory distress in premature infants (Dunn et al., 1991; Merrit et al., 1991; Long et al., 1991).

Because babies with respiratory distress syndrome (RDS) can't get enough oxygen from the air, they're treated with concentrated oxygen. When this treatment was begun in the 1940s and 1950s, doctors didn't realize that high levels of oxygen could damage the blood vessels in the eye and cause **retrolental fibroplasia blindness** (RLF blindness). The lives of many premature babies were saved but at the cost of their eyesight.

Today doctors monitor oxygen levels in the baby's system very carefully to make sure the baby isn't getting too much, and RLF blindness has been greatly reduced. But when very premature babies need oxygen for a long period of time, it's still hard to prevent blindness. There is some evidence that excessive oxygen isn't the only factor involved. For example, premature babies' low level of antioxidants, such as vitamin E, may prevent them from using and binding oxygen the way normal babies can. There may be other factors at work as well, and research is underway to tackle this problem anew (Lucey & Dangman, 1984). Given the ever-increasing number of premature babies who survive, there's a critical need to understand and effectively treat both hyaline membrane disease and RFL blindness.

Long-Term Effects of Prematurity

It's clear that a premature baby like Elizabeth isn't off to the best start. But what's likely to happen to her later? Will she catch up physically? Will she have emotional problems as a result of being separated from her parents at birth for medical treatment? Will she develop learning problems or have trouble in school?

Children who were born prematurely do catch up to their genetically intended size as they grow. And premature babies are not destined to have disrupted attachment relationships with their mothers because of separation at birth, as mentioned in Chapter 3 and discussed in detail in Chapter 8. Newer hospital policies that allow contact between premature babies and their parents are helping families build strong relationships and avoid later emotional problems (Scafidi et al., 1990; Watt, 1990).

Many studies have followed premature babies to see if and how their later development is related to their earlier condition. Studies have found a link between premature birth and risk of showing a learning disability at school age (Field, Demsey & Shuman, 1983; Siegel, 1983). Other studies have found a link to hyperactivity in very low birthweight children (McCormick, Gortmaker & Sobol, 1990). However, most babies born prematurely show no learning difficulties at age 8, although their rate of learning difficulties as a group has been reported to be about 25 percent higher than that of their full-term peers (Cohen & Parmelee, 1988; Leonard et al., 1990; Pfeiffer & Aylward, 1990).

Another study looked at "social competence" and behavior problems among premature children when the children were 7 and 8 years old (Ross, Lipper & Auld, 1990). The study considered such variables as participation in sports and activities, number of friends, and school performance. Premature children, both boys and girls, had significantly lower social competence scores than the normative groups. Premature boys also had significantly higher scores on behaviors associated with conduct disorders, particularly in the lower income groups. Lack of family stability was the best predictor of behavior problems in the premature group.

This study, along with a number of others, points strongly toward one conclusion. In the words of one researcher who reviewed several studies of the

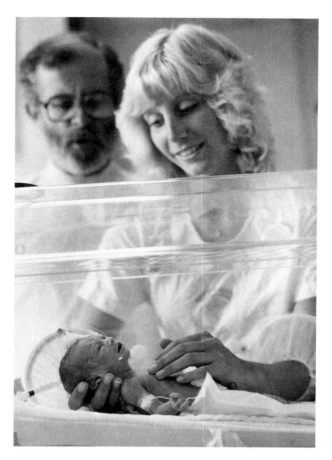

FIGURE 4-10
In the past, premature babies were deprived of normal human contact because its importance to their growth and well-being wasn't recognized. Special efforts are now made to ensure contact between mother and baby, with all its physical and emotional benefits for both of them.

long-term effects of prematurity, "the single most potent factor influencing developmental outcome turns out to be the cultural environment of the child, as expressed in socioeconomic status and parental educational level" (Sameroff, 1981, p. 392). According to another researcher, "social influences and family factors have a much more profound influence on a child's subsequent development than any of the biological factors that result in a child being born even extremely light-for-date" (Hawdon et al., 1990, p. 951). In other words, social factors like the mother's educational level and parenting skill—rather than the baby's physical condition at birth—are the best predictors of long-term outcome for premature babies (Cohen & Parmelee, 1983).

Prematurity in and of itself, then, doesn't lead inevitably to later difficulties, although premature babies *as a group* are more likely to encounter problems (Taub, Goldstein & Caputo, 1977; Drillien, Thomson & Burgayne, 1980; Cohen & Parmelee, 1983). If we compared one hundred 5-year-olds who had been premature with one hundred 5-year-olds who had been full term, we would find that more preterm children had problems. But we wouldn't be able to predict *which* of the preterm babies would do poorly by considering only the physical aspects of prematurity. Recent research indicates that even brain hemorrhage doesn't lead inevitably to severely impaired functioning (Sostek et al., 1987).

THE NEWBORN IN THE WORLD

As you can see, quite a lot of information is available about newborns. But how does all this knowledge actually help physicians and parents protect and nurture a baby? And how can parents use the knowledge available from research when they begin life at home with their baby? These are the questions addressed in this final section on the neonate—knowledge in action.

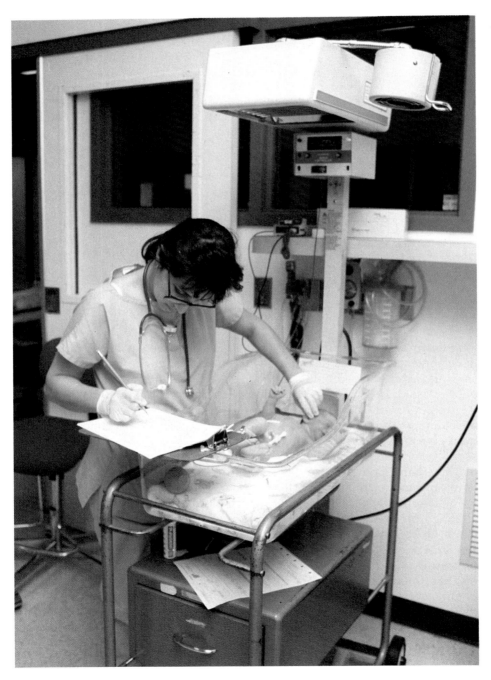

FIGURE 4-11
This physician is examining the newborn as part of an overall assessment. She measures his heart rate and observes his breathing, skin color, muscle tone, and responsiveness to stimulation. If he's pink and generally vigorous, he'll probably get a 10 on the Apgar scale.

Assessing the Newborn

Most newborns are like Patrick—healthy in every way. Some are like Elizabeth—premature and obviously in need of immediate medical attention. Still others have problems that may not be readily apparent but that require intervention. To make sure the needs of all newborns are met, doctors and researchers have developed various methods of assessment, or assessment instruments, as they are called. These instruments help doctors evaluate the newborn's physical well-being, and they also provide information of interest to researchers. For example, studies like those described previously involving premature babies looked at whether babies' conditions at birth, as measured by assessment instruments, predicted future development.

ASSESSMENT INSTRUMENTS. The **Apgar scale** (named for the physician who invented it) measures the newborn's physical well-being in the delivery room at one minute and at five minutes after birth. The baby is scored from 0 to 2 for heart rate, respiratory effort, muscle tone, reflex irritability, and color (see Table 4-3). The five scores are added up to give a total score ranging from 0 to 10. The higher the score, the better the baby's condition (Apgar, 1953).

Another assessment instrument can be used to assess the baby's neurological condition. The best known of these is the **Neurological Examination of the Full-Term Newborn Infant,** developed in 1964 by Prechtl and Beintema and revised in 1977 by Prechtl. This test, often referred to as the Prechtl, is used to evaluate babies within ten days of birth and has two parts: (1) an observation period during which spontaneous movement and posture are noted, and (2) an examination period during which reflexes and other motor behavior are checked. As mentioned earlier, the presence or absence of the various reflexes provides information on the baby's neurological functioning.

TABLE 4-3 The Apgar Scale

Sign	*Criterion**	*Score*
Heart rate (beats/minute)	100 or more	2
	Less than 100	1
	Not detectable	0
Respiratory effort	Lusty crying and breathing	2
	Any shallowness, irregularity	1
	Not breathing	0
Reflex irritability	Vigorous response to stimulation (e.g., sneezing or coughing to stimulation of nostrils), urination, defecation	2
	Weak response	1
	No response	0
Muscle tone	Resilient, limbs spontaneously flexed and resistant to applied force	2
	Limpness, lack of resistance	1
	Complete flaccidity	0
Skin color	Pink all over	2
	Partially pink	1
	Bluish or yellowish	0

*Observations made at 60 seconds after birth.

SOURCE: Apgar, V., Holaday, D. A., James, L. S., Weisbrot, I. M., & Berrien, C. (1958). Evaluation of the newborn infant—second report. Journal of the American Medical Association, 168, 1985–1988.

A third kind of assessment instrument is used to obtain behavioral information, although it typically assesses neurological well-being too. The most comprehensive of these is the **Brazelton Neonatal Behavioral Assessment Scale** (Brazelton, 1973a). This test is given on the third day of life and, ideally, on several subsequent days as well. It provides information about the baby's general neurological condition, capacity for self-organization, and reactions to a caregiver.

Specific items on the BNBAS involve the baby's behavioral state, the major reflexes, and habituation to repeated visual, auditory, and tactile stimuli. It also assesses the baby's orientation to the human face and voice, activity level, and muscle tone (Brazelton, 1973a; Jacobson et al., 1984). For example, one part of the test involves ringing a bell loudly overhead when the baby is awake and lying on a flat surface. The baby will usually startle the first time the bell is rung. The tester then rings the bell again. This time the baby startles but typically not as much as the first time. The baby habituates to the sound of the bell, so that after a few rings there is little or no reaction. To score the baby, the tester notes how many presentations occurred before the baby stopped reacting. The longer it takes for the reaction to stop, the poorer the rating. A long time may indicate that the baby has difficulty in processing information and learning.

Brazelton stresses the importance of taking the baby's behavioral state into account when giving this test. Results obtained when a baby is drowsy or crying wouldn't be comparable to results obtained when another baby is in an inactive alert state, which is the ideal state for testing. If a baby starts to cry, the tester must stop testing and hold the baby or provide some other comfort. If the baby becomes less irritable, the testing can continue; otherwise it has to stop, at least for the time being.

Specific assessment instruments have also been devised to diagnose hearing loss in newborns. The **Crib-O-Gram** and the **Brain Stem Evoked Response** test the baby's brain waves on special apparatus to see if sounds are registering in their brains (Downs, 1978; Stein et al., 1983; Murray, 1988). Babies are also observed to see if they respond to sounds.

ASSESSMENT ADEQUACY. What do physicians learn from these early tests? In general, they're able to detect both life-threatening conditions and risks for later problems. When potential problems are identified, steps can sometimes be taken to provide more support for development in the baby's environment.

Unfortunately it's often difficult to know which behaviors actually predict future problems. Neurological exams like the one developed by Prechtl simply measure reflexes, noting whether or not they occur. Newer tests, like the Brazelton, measure babies' reflexes as well as other characteristics, including their ability to inhibit response after a stimulus is repeated several times, to escape a stimulus, to quiet or console themselves, and to orient toward or seek out stimulation. The Brazelton scale is a better predictor of later functioning than basic neurological exams. This may be in part because the behaviors it measures are important to mother-child interactions, which continue to influence development for years. (See Chapter 8 for further discussion of this topic.)

Some of the other assessment instruments have additional problems. The Apgar is criticized because it measures only the most general aspects of physical well-being and reveals only the most obvious difficulties. Timing is a problem too. The Apgar is administered at one and five minutes after birth, but studies indicate that a baby's functioning two hours after birth may be radically different from what it was immediately after birth (Desmond et al., 1963). The later score may be a better predictor of future behavior. And again, the baby's behavioral state can influence the results of a test, but many tests don't take this into account.

It may be that different instruments are just appropriate for different purposes. The Apgar gives a quick assessment of physical condition immediately after birth. Neurological exams like Prechtl's reveal clinically important neurological problems during the neonatal period. The Brazelton scale may be most useful for predicting long-term problems related to difficult parent-child interaction (Prechtl, 1982). As long as their appropriate uses and limitations are kept in mind, all of these assessment instruments can provide useful and important information about newborns.

Living with the Newborn

We've seen what Patrick and Elizabeth are like as newborns and how they're treated and evaluated at birth. But what will it be like when their parents take them home? What is it like to live with a newborn? Newborns spend most of their time sleeping at first. During their brief waking periods, they'll eat and have an opportunity to look around and get acquainted with their new families. In our culture, they'll also spend a fair amount of time crying. This is the behavior that will probably be most difficult for their parents to deal with. (For a discussion of infant crying, see Research Focus—How Much Does a Baby Have to Cry?).

SOOTHING THE NEWBORN. Parents of older babies often say they can tell why their baby is crying. Does this mean that babies actually cry differently for different reasons? Apparently it does. One study of infant crying distinguished three kinds of cries: the basic, or hungry, cry; the angry cry; and the pain cry (Wolff, 1966; 1969). A baby who is startled or who is being overstimulated, for example, might give an angry cry. A baby with colic (gastrointestinal pain) would give the pain cry.

All the mothers in this study responded immediately to the pain cry and were worried or alarmed by it. All the mothers responded to angry cries too, but they weren't worried about this kind of cry. The basic or hungry cry usually got a quick response from first-time mothers, but experienced mothers sometimes waited a while before responding.

The important questions for parents or others who care for babies, of course, is what to do to quiet a crying baby. It depends on what the baby is crying about. Hunger cries can be stopped by feeding the baby, although holding the baby or putting a pacifier in the baby's mouth might stop the crying for a short time. (An angry cry may follow soon if some food doesn't supplement the pacifier! This is inappropriate "stimulation.") A crying baby who is undressed and flailing about can often be soothed by swaddling or by being held closely so the limbs stay in control. A pacifier can also soothe a baby and inhibit diffuse motor activity, which can leave a baby upset and awake (Wolff, 1966).

Many times babies are dry, fed, and being held, but they continue to cry. It's difficult to know what's causing the crying or what to do to stop it. At

RESEARCH FOCUS

How Much Does a Baby Have to Cry?

All babies cry, but how much crying is "normal"? In the United States, babies cry more and more until they're 6 weeks old, and then their crying gradually decreases. American babies also cry more in the afternoon and evening. Most people in our country expect babies to cry a certain amount; they consider it normal.

It occurred to one pair of researchers that the amount of crying considered "normal" might vary from culture to culture (Hunziker & Barr, 1986). In areas as diverse as southern Mexico and urban Zambia (Africa), for example, babies seem to cry considerably less, according to cross-cultural studies. The researchers hypothesized that these babies cried less because they were carried extensively, usually by their mothers, and that increasing the amount of time babies were carried would change the typical crying pattern found in the United States. Here, parents usually pick up their babies *after* they start crying, but there isn't a great deal of carrying of babies who aren't crying.

Hunziker and Barr set out to test this hypothesis. They recruited a number of mother-infant pairs and assigned them randomly to one of two groups: a control group with no increased carrying and a treatment group with increased carrying. The mothers in the treatment group were asked to carry their babies at least three hours a day and not just in response to crying. The extra carrying was to be spread throughout the day and was to be in addition to the time they normally held the baby during feeding. Infant carriers were provided for the treatment group. The researchers collected baseline data from both groups, so that initial rates of crying for all babies were known.

The babies in the control group increased their crying until the characteristic 6-week peak. The babies in the supplemental carrying group, however, never increased their crying, and the 6-week peak never occurred. Crying began to decrease after the third week of life, which was the week the supplemental carrying began. In addition, although babies in both groups cried the most in the late afternoon and early evening, the carried babies cried significantly less than the control group babies. They cried 54 percent less than the control group babies during the sixth week and 47 percent less during the eighth week.

Hunziker and Barr suggested that increased carrying "provided postural change, repetitiveness, constancy and/or rhythmicity, close proximity between mother and infant, and involvement of many sensory modalities" (p. 645). They also suggested that the increased carrying may have given mothers more information about their babies, which made them more skillful at understanding what was wrong and at soothing their babies when they did cry. Finally, since holding induces the inactive alert state, babies may have been less fussy because they were interested in observing their surroundings.

The researchers concluded that the amount of infant crying considered normal in the United States is "only normal in the sense of being typical for infant caregiving practices in our society" (p. 646). They recommend that parents soothe

their crying infants, or prevent excessive crying, by increasing carrying. However, babies with established patterns of colic—considerable crying, often concentrated during a specific time of day—do not seem to be helped by increased carrying (Barr et al., 1991).

One way parents can increase carrying is by keeping the baby in an infant carrier. Carriers of all kinds have become popular in recent years. For very young infants, these carriers are typically designed as pouchlike sacks that the parent straps onto the front of his or her own body. Parents have their hands free while they're holding the baby, and the baby experiences the security and warmth of the parent's body, as well as more carrying time. Recent research suggests that carrying in soft baby carriers not only reduces crying but also increases the rate of secure attachment in low socioeconomic status mothers (Anisfeld et al., 1990).

Infant carrying is a traditional practice in many cultures, as demonstrated by these Yoruba Tribe women from West Nigeria (above, left), a Bulong Minority woman from Yunnan Province, China (above, right), and an Inuit woman in Canada's Northwest Territory (left). This kind of carrying is convenient for mothers and gives them information about their babies' states. For babies, it provides the security of constant physical contact with their mothers and reduces crying. American parents (opposite page) have discovered the benefits of this traditional pratice, both for themselves and for their infants.

this point, parents have to become more ingenious. Sometimes recordings of a heart beating or of the sounds of the womb will soothe the baby. The noise of a rattle or a bright light placed in the baby's visual field will also inhibit crying, but only briefly in the very young baby. Parents may try rocking the baby in a rocking chair, pushing her in a stroller, or even taking her out for a ride in the car.

The type of activity that makes a baby stop crying begins to change after about the second week of life (Wolff, 1965). Up to this point, direct physical activities, such as feeding, swaddling, or giving a pacifier, work best. Psychological interventions, such as talking or offering the baby a bright object, don't work as well. By the end of the second week, however, babies are more interested in the environment, and sights and sounds often make them stop crying and become alert. There seems to be an intricate interplay between mental stimulation and the baby's emotional state.

At all ages, the most effective way to stop crying is to pick the baby up (Korner & Grobstein, 1966; Korner & Thoman, 1972). When babies are picked up, they not only stop crying but also become alert and begin to look around. Although this alert inactive state is usually quite infrequent in young babies, it is induced by picking them up. (See Research Focus—How Much Does a Baby Have to Cry? for another approach to handling crying.) How the parent responds to and soothes a crying baby affects not just the baby's emotional state but the baby's early learning as well. Since babies are most receptive to stimulation in the alert inactive state, parents who pick up their crying babies give them a chance to observe and learn about their world. There is even some evidence that crying reduces the flow of blood to the brain, a finding that underscores the importance of soothing a crying baby (Brazy, 1988).

LIVING WITH LITTLE SLEEP. One of the biggest adjustments new parents often must make is a reduction in their sleep. Young babies generally sleep 15 hours a day, on average (Bamford et al., 1990), but their sleeping schedules don't always match those of their parents. In one study, about 40 percent of babies under 9 months of age woke up at least twice between 11 P.M. and 6 A.M. By 9 months of age, 30 percent of the infants were still waking up twice or more between 11 P.M. and 6 A.M. (Michelsson, Rinne & Paajanen, 1990).

Parenting practices no doubt influence to some extent how much an infant wakes up during the night and how long the infant stays awake, but individual characteristics of infants probably play a role as well. Parents for whom nighttime sleep interruption is a major problem can consult their pediatrician, who is probably familiar with various strategies for helping the infant over 6 months of age to establish more continuous nighttime sleep patterns.

ADJUSTING TO INDIVIDUAL DIFFERENCES. Despite research findings, it's not easy to know exactly how to begin a healthy relationship with a newborn. Research evidence and everyday observation indicate that newborns differ, right from birth. Some babies simply cry more than others or respond more readily to soothing or stimulation (Brazelton, 1969; Korner, 1971). These individual characteristics have important influences on parent-child relationships and on infant learning. A baby who is difficult to soothe, for example, can make a parent feel incompetent, anxious, frustrated, and worn out, and a passive parent who expected a calm baby may have trouble coping with a lively one.

These feelings can affect the parent's approach to the baby, which may in turn affect the baby's responses. But most parents do adapt and learn ways to interact that work with their baby, as in the following example (Brazelton, 1969, p. 21):

> Daniel was hard to rouse from his deep sleep. He was wheeled into Mrs. Kay, breathing deeply and noisily, moving little. . . . Then, as if with a start, he shot from sleeping to an unapproachable state of screaming. He cried with a loud, piercing bellow that continued until he was quieted. Quieting him demanded a vigorous approach on the part of Mrs. Kay. . . .
>
> He could not be quieted with her crooning, with quiet rocking and cuddling, or with a bottle alone. His crying could only be broken into by a combination of tight swaddling of his extremities, plus vigorous rocking, plus the bottle nipple held in his mouth at his soft palate until he stopped crying to breathe and felt it there.
>
> His mother felt foolish and unhappy about the means that were necessary to quiet him, but she found they were successful, and after the second day of these maneuvers, she found that he could even be played with and enjoyed after one of his feedings.

FIGURE 4-12
How will these proud parents shape their newborn daughter, and how will she change them? Development proceeds as a constant interaction between the child, with her unique characteristics, and the elements in her environment, especially her parents, who have their own characteristics, histories, and capabilities.

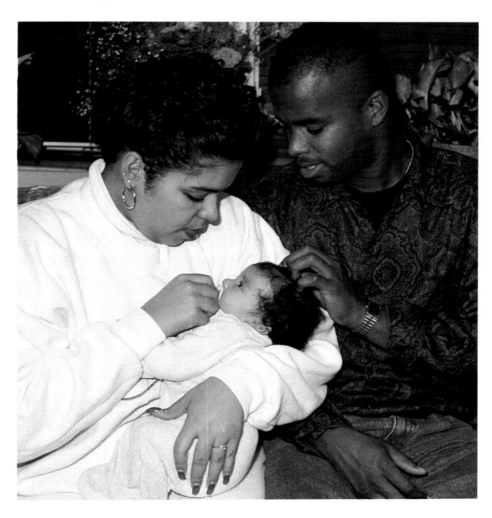

Although Daniel was difficult and not the kind of baby Mrs. Kay expected, she was able to adjust to her new son. It's the parents' ability to adapt to the baby, rather than any particular characteristics of the baby, that best predicts the long-term course of the baby's emotional and intellectual development (Belsky, 1984; Sroufe, 1983). Although babies differ in temperament right from the start—and "difficult" babies are at higher risk for later problems because they require nearly ideal parenting—no specific temperament or trait predisposes a baby inevitably to future difficulties. Parents most effectively support their baby's development by accepting and responding sensitively to whatever kind of person their newborn turns out to be.

A number of systems interact to optimize the child's relationships and development, an interaction we discuss in detail in Chapter 8. The child, the parent, and the family system—encouraged by a broader support system—can all contribute to a positive initial relationship. Ideally the child communicates his needs to family members through behavior that they can interpret; parents who are motivated to meet the child's needs, and who believe that they can do so, sensitively interpret the baby's signals; and larger systems provide the support parents need to act in ways that consistently communicate to the child that his needs will be met. Given sensitive and appropriate support, the child carries these positive effects into his later interactions with other family members and with larger systems as well.

OVERVIEW

The neonate is clearly different from the fetus, but she's also different from the older infant. Her first days and weeks are a period of transition between one mode of existence and another. The body systems that functioned in conjunction with the mother's body now begin to support life on their own. The physical characteristics appropriate for prenatal existence evolve into traits suitable for life outside the womb. The baby's senses awaken to the sights, sounds, tastes, smells, and feel of the world around her. Perhaps most importantly, she becomes a partner in a relationship with someone who cares for her. In this relationship, if all goes well, she will develop a strong emotional attachment that will nurture her throughout her childhood and influence her for her entire life.

CHAPTER REVIEW

PHYSICAL CHARACTERISTICS

- A white greasy coating called vernix caseosa protects the neonate's skin before, during, and after birth.
- Two diamond-shaped fontanelles allow the bones of the skull to squeeze together, or mold, as the baby passes through the mother's pelvis.
- Newborns' eyes and faces are often swollen and puffy from the accumulation of fluids and from silver nitrate drops in the eyes. Their skin is bright red because they have so little subcutaneous fat.

- The newborn's head is very large in proportion to his body, and the top of his head is more developed than his chin, jaw, and neck.
- Newborns are able to absorb nutrients right from birth. Mothers produce colostrum, an antibody-containing liquid perfectly suited to the newborn's needs. Breast milk, high in protein and low in fat, is the ideal food for infants.

- The average neonate weighs 7½ pounds and measures 20 inches long.
- Newborns require frequent, small feedings, and most need night feedings for a few months or more.
- The neonate's breathing is characterized by rapid, shallow breaths interrupted by periods of long, deep breathing and even brief periods of apnea.
- The respiratory system takes time to adjust to breathing oxygen-rich air, and a by-product called bilirubin often accumulates in the blood. The liver has difficulty metabolizing and excreting the bilirubin, and the baby often develops hyperbilirubinemia, or jaundice, which sometimes requires treatment by phototherapy to protect against brain damage.
- Newborns can't maintain their own body temperatures until they're about 2 months old, and care has to be taken to keep them warm.

MOTOR CAPABILITIES

- Babies are born with innate responses known as reflexes that help them survive.
- Newborns have a rooting reflex, which allows them to find the nipple, and a sucking reflex, which allows them to suckle and ingest food. The gag reflex prevents them from choking on mucus or extra milk.
- A "crawling" reflex prevents newborns from suffocating if their mouths and noses become obstructed. It can also result in enough movement to topple them off a bed if they're left unattended.
- Other reflexes include the tonic neck reflex; the Moro, or startle, reflex; the Babinski reflex; and the grasping reflexes. As the baby matures, reflexes gradually disappear; their presence or absence at different times is a good indicator of the infant's neurological functioning.
- Newborns have little control over voluntary responses.

BEHAVIORAL STATES

- When newborns awaken from their first long sleep after birth, their behavior is characterized by recurring periods of wakefulness and sleep known as behavioral states.
- Typical behavioral states include regular sleep, irregular sleep, drowsiness, alert inactivity, waking activity, and crying. These states are cyclical; they don't occur randomly.
- Infants' overall behavioral patterns, including how long they spend in each state, are probably influenced by heredity and by their parents' responses to them.

Their patterns, in turn, affect the parent-child relationship. A baby who spends a lot of time crying is more difficult to care for and requires more creative parenting.
- The initial parent-child interaction is affected by obstetrical drugs. Pain-relieving drugs given to mothers in labor quickly cross the placenta and enter the fetus. Newborns of medicated mothers tend to be less alert, less responsive, and less consolable than the newborns of nonmedicated mothers.

SENSORY ABILITIES

- Newborns can see right from birth, focusing best on objects about 7 or 8 inches from their face. They are capable of tracking a moving object.
- Babies have binocular fixation by about 1 month, and see fused visual images by about 4 months. Their visual acuity is as good as an adult's by about 12 months, and their eyes can accommodate as well as an adult's by about 2 months.
- Babies can hear at birth and even in the womb. They respond to new sounds and then gradually become accustomed to everyday noises, incorporating them into their repertoire. Researchers use this process of habituation to conduct studies on their hearing and other senses.
- Newborns prefer sweet tastes over sour, bitter, and salty tastes. They can distinguish odors right from birth and soon learn to know the smell of their mother's milk.
- Newborns feel physical pain; their sensitivity to pain increases as they mature.
- Babies have size constancy from birth. They also like to look at patterns, especially the pattern of faces, as well as areas of contrast. These preferences are innate and support the development of parent-child attachment.

LEARNING

- Newborns have been shown to be capable of learning through both classical conditioning and instrumental conditioning.
- Piaget believed that babies are continually learning about their environment and modifying their behavior based on what they experience.

- Research indicates that babies are motivated to learn by opportunities to solve problems. These opportunities may have long-term implications for whether they learn that they're powerful or helpless in their interactions with the world.

THE PREMATURE BABY

- Babies are considered premature if they're born before the thirty-seventh week of gestation. About 7 percent of all babies are born prematurely, and more and more premature babies are surviving due to advances in medical technology.
- Premature babies, prone to hypothermia, have to be kept in incubators. They're also at risk for brain hemorrhages because the arterial system of the brain isn't completely developed.
- About 15 percent of all premature babies develop hyaline membrane disease, a serious lung disorder caused by undeveloped alveoli and a lack of surfactant.

- When premature babies with respiratory distress are treated with oxygen, the levels have to be carefully monitored to prevent retrolental fibroplasia blindness.
- There are long-term differences in development between premature and full-term infants as groups, but it's difficult to predict the outcome for any individual premature child.
- The strongest factor affecting the outcome for a premature baby appears to be the social and emotional environment provided by her family as she grows rather than her physical condition at birth.

THE NEWBORN IN THE WORLD

- Babies are assessed at birth to see if they require any medical or developmental intervention.
- The Apgar scale is used to assess the baby's physical condition.
- The Neurological Examination of the Full-Term Newborn Infant is used to evaluate the baby's neurological condition.
- The Brazelton Neonatal Behavioral Assessment Scale provides information about the baby's neurological condition and behavioral patterns.
- All the neonatal assessment instruments have their limitations, but they do provide important information about newborns.

- Babies cry differently, depending on whether they're hungry, angry, or in pain.
- Prior to the end of the second week, direct physical intervention soothes a crying baby most effectively. Later, the baby may be soothed by different sights and sounds.
- The most effective way to stop crying at all ages is to pick up the baby, thus inducing the alert inactive state. Carrying the baby in an infant carrier also seems to reduce crying.
- Newborns have different personalities right from the start, but no specific temperament or trait destines a baby to future social or emotional problems.

KEY TERMS

neonate	apnea	gag reflex	binocular fixation
neonatal period	ductus arteriosus	tonic neck reflex	fused visual image
vernix caseosa	bilirubin	Moro reflex	acuity
molded	hyperbilirubinemia	Babinski reflex	accommodation
fontanelles	phototherapy	grasping reflex	habituation
lanugo	kernicterus	palmar grasp	size constancy
glycogen	reflexes	tonus	hypothermia
colostrum	rooting reflex	behavioral states	hyaline membrane disease
immunoglobulins	sucking reflex	consolability	surfactant

retrolental fibroplasia	**Neurological Examination**	**Brazelton Neonatal**	**Crib-O-Gram**
blindness	**of the Full-Term**	**Behavioral Assessment**	**Brain Stem Evoked**
Apgar scale	**Newborn Infant**	**Scale**	**Response**

SUGGESTIONS FOR FURTHER READING

Brazelton, T. B. (1969). *Infants and mothers.* New York: Dell.

This book discusses the entire first year of life, but the first four chapters focus on the neonate. Good discussion of individual differences among infants, with stress on the need to adapt to the individual baby.

Goldberg, S., & Devitto, B. A. (1983). *Born too soon: Preterm birth and early development.* San Francisco: W. H. Freeman.

Contains good descriptions of premature infants and discusses ways to interact with premature infants.

Gottfried, A. W., & Gaiter, J. L. (Eds.). (1985). *Infant stress under intensive care.* Baltimore: University Park Press. This book contains much interesting information about the physical setup and operation of neonatal intensive care units. The ethical dilemmas involved in caring for very ill infants are discusssed. Technical in spots, but useful.

PHYSICAL DEVELOPMENT IN INFANTS AND TODDLERS

"Dr. Marquez will see Sabina now, Mrs. Austen," the pediatric nurse called from the open door, and Ursula began picking up her baby paraphernalia and putting it into the diaper bag she carried with her everywhere.

"Put the puzzle back on the table, Sarah," she said to her 15-month-old. "It's time for Sabina to see the doctor." As Ursula gathered her things, Sarah picked up the two remaining puzzle pieces from the floor and placed them on the frame of the puzzle she had been trying to put together. Then she leaned forward on her hands to raise herself from her sitting position. Once up on her feet, she squatted down, with knees bent, to pick up the puzzle with both hands. She carried it to the low toy table in the corner of the waiting room.

Ursula, meanwhile, had made her way to the door leading to the examination rooms and was holding it open for Sarah with the side of her body. She held 6-week-old Sabina in an upright position against her shoulder, supporting the back of her head with her other hand. Sarah toddled quickly to her mother and reached up to take hold of the diaper bag strap, which hung from Ursula's shoulder. She'd learned in the past six weeks that her mother didn't have a free hand for her to hold when she was carrying Sabina up against her shoulder, so she latched on to the strap or to her mother's skirt or leg.

In the examination room, Ursula placed Sabina on the table and began to undress her. Sarah stepped up on a small stool beside the table to get a better look. She put her finger in her sister's hand, and Sabina's fingers closed tightly around it. She probably would have held on to Sarah's finger for some time if Ursula hadn't had to get the sleeve of her sleeper over her hand.

Sabina didn't seem to like being undressed. She began to cry. Her hands were squeezed into tight fists, and her arms waved in jerky arcs. Ursula leaned over to try to talk her out of her distress. Sarah stepped down from the stool and walked over to the large medical scale, which she stepped up on. Beside it was a sturdy wooden chair, and

FIGURE 5-1
Right now, these infants are relatively immobile, but that will change quickly. Every month brings impressive advances in the first years, when the growth rate is the highest it will ever be in the child's life.

Sarah decided to climb onto it next. She reached across the seat, taking hold of the far side with her hands and then pulling herself up and across it. When she had pulled her legs up far enough, she bent her knees under herself and sat up on them. Then she turned toward the back of the chair, put her hands on its top, and stood up. She was reaching up to get hold of a blood pressure cuff that was mounted on the wall behind the chair when her mother caught sight of what she was doing.

 "Sarah! Get down from there!" she called. "That's not a toy. And you might fall!"

 Sarah turned around to face her mother, but she didn't sit down. Ursula scooped Sabina up from the table and walked over to the chair. Taking Sarah's hand with her free hand, she said, "Sit down right now." Sarah bent her knees to lower herself down onto the chair seat. "This is not a place to play. You may sit and watch, but you can't touch things. Here, find one of your books in the bag." As Sarah began to search in the diaper bag, Dr. Marquez came through the door.

 "Well, hello, Sarah," she said. "Did you get up on that big chair all by yourself?"

 "I'm afraid so," Ursula replied, with just a touch of dismay in her voice.

Ursula had her children so close together that she has two infants to care for at the same time. Although we call both these girls infants, they are very different in appearance and abilities. The changes that take place in babies in their first few years of life are truly phenomenal, and physical changes are probably the most astonishing. A person who hasn't seen a baby in a few weeks or months will probably remark, "Look how she's grown!" A person who hasn't seen a baby for a year or so since birth might not even recognize the child.

In this chapter we discuss the dramatic growth and the changes, both inward and outward, that occur during infancy and toddlerhood. We also focus on the exciting new motor skills that allow infants and toddlers to reach and grasp and eventually to move around with ever-increasing agility and speed. Finally, we discuss the achievement that comes at the end of toddlerhood and that separates toddlers from preschoolers in so many people's minds—toilet training.

HOW DO THEY GROW?

Increases in Weight and Length

FIGURE 5-2
Height and weight for boys and girls from birth through 36 months of age. Children of the same age naturally vary in size. The graphs show heights and weights for children who are average (fiftieth percentile). Between birth and 9 or 10 months, the slope of the line is quite steep, reflecting the rapid rate of growth during this time. After 1 year of age, the slope flattens out. If prenatal growth were shown, the slope of that line would be even steeper than that for the first nine months after birth.

The most obvious difference between the two girls in the examination room is that Sarah, at 15 months of age, is so much bigger than Sabina, who is only 6 weeks old. If you picked them up, you might guess that Sarah weighed two or three times what Sabina weighed. You would be right—babies usually double their birth weight in their first six months and triple it by their first birthday. This means an increase in weight from about 7 to about 21 pounds.

In their second year, weight increases by about a third, with the average 2-year-old weighing about 28 pounds. Although the baby has continued to grow, the rate of growth has not been as fast. In the third year the growth rate slows down even more; the average 3-year-old weighs about 32 pounds. The growth charts shown in Figure 5-2 illustrate these changes graphically. Notice that the curves are very steep the first year and flatten out somewhat after that.

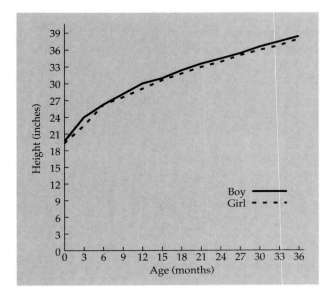

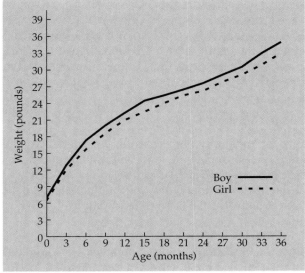

Babies' increase in length parallels their increase in weight—they grow quite a lot in their first year and then less in the following years. The typical baby grows from about 20 inches at birth to 25½ inches at 6 months, to 28½ inches at a year, to 33 inches at 2 years (Lowrey, 1978).

VARIATIONS IN GROWTH. Although it's useful to refer to typical increases in weight and length, some infants and toddlers grow more than average or less than average. This kind of variation can be due to several different factors, including heredity and nutrition. If a fetus is cramped in the womb, or if the mother's nutrition is inadequate during pregnancy, a baby may not grow as much as it can during the prenatal period. If nutrition is adequate after birth, such a baby may catch up by growing much faster than average in the first months of life. This situation often occurs when a baby has a small mother and a large father (Tanner, 1970). Crowding of the large fetus in the uterus triggers a mechanism that slows prenatal growth, but after birth the child continues toward his genetically determined potential. Other factors can also influence growth in the postnatal period, such as the quality of food available and the infant's ability to adapt to feeding.

PREDICTING ADULT HEIGHT FROM TODDLER DIMENSIONS. We can say with a fair amount of certainty that a 2-year-old girl who is 33 inches tall will be 66.33 inches tall, or 5 feet 6 inches, as an adult. Toddler dimensions provide a reliable index of adult height, and multipliers have been determined for these calculations (Garn, 1966). For boys, the multiplier is 2.06; for girls, it's 2.01. Thus, if a 2-year-old boy is 35 inches tall, we would predict his adult height to be 72.1 inches, or 6 feet. The multiplier is smaller for girls than for boys because girls have a faster rate of physical maturation. A 2-year-old girl is already closer to her adult height than a boy the same age would be.

EFFECTS OF GROWTH RATE ON APPETITE. Very young infants seem to be hungry all the time, crying to be fed every three or four hours. Toddlers, on the other hand, pick at their food, and their parents sometimes worry that they're not getting enough nutrients. This difference in appetite is a normal reflection of the slackening growth rate by 2 years. Toddlers are growing at a much more leisurely pace than young infants, and they aren't so hungry. Toddlers would often rather play with their food than eat it. Parents do well to serve small portions of nutritious food to their young children and to accept their smaller appetites with a relaxed attitude.

Tissue Growth

Size isn't the only physical difference between younger and older infants. Toddlers are stronger and have more stamina; their appearance and body proportions are radically different from those of younger infants; and they can move in ways that younger infants can't. All these physical characteristics reflect neurological changes and patterns of tissue growth in the first years of life.

BODY FAT. Subcutaneous fat, the layer of fat just below the skin, begins to form in the fetus about six weeks before birth. Premature babies don't have the benefit of this layer, as mentioned in earlier chapters, so they look unusually scrawny at birth. Subcutaneous fat accumulates rapidly in the first nine months of life and then more slowly after that, making the baby look rounded and filled out.

In the past, especially before antibiotics were discovered, many babies contracted infectious diseases that led to emaciation and death. The more fat reserves babies had, the better they were able to survive these diseases. People wanted babies to be fat because they thought fat infants were healthier.

Then, for a while, experts were concerned that very fat babies were more likely to grow up to be fat adults. It was suggested that the number of fat cells in a person's body was determined by how much the person ate in the first year of life (Winick, 1974). But subsequent research has shown that the cell-number hypothesis of obesity isn't very accurate and that most fat babies don't become fat adults (Dobbing, 1984). Today, there's not as much concern about very fat babies as there was a few years ago. On the other hand, there's no advantage to be gained from overfeeding a baby.

MUSCLE AND BONE. No new muscle cells are formed after birth, but during infancy changes do occur in muscle fibers already present. One change is that the proportion of water in the fibers decreases and salts and proteins increase. This gives the baby greater strength and stamina.

Bones are changing too. At birth, babies have soft bones composed mostly of cartilage. Minerals are gradually deposited through the process of **ossification,** and the cartilage turns to bone. As the bones in the baby's skull harden and fuse, the fontanelles gradually close. The large fontanelle at the top of the head usually closes completely by about 2 years (Wennberg, Woodrum & Hodson, 1973). As bones grow and become stronger, the support structure of the body changes, and the child eventually is able to learn to walk. Bone growth continues throughout childhood and adolescence (Stoner, 1978), making it essential that children have adequate minerals, especially calcium, in their diet. (For a discussion of the development of the teeth, see Health Focus—Teething and the Care of Teeth.)

Because some bones and bone parts ossify before others in a regular pattern, ossification provides an index of children's physical maturity. The extent of ossification can be determined by X-rays, since the ossified areas are denser and show up on the X-ray film. Maturity studies using this technique have confirmed that girls mature physically faster than boys. At birth girls are ahead of boys in skeletal maturity by about four weeks. By age 5 or 6, the gap has widened to a year (Tanner, 1970). Today, the X-ray technique is not used to do maturity research, because X-rays are known to be dangerous.

THE BRAIN. At 15 months, Sarah is well into the "brain growth spurt," which extends from the last three months of prenatal life through the first year and a half of postnatal life. During this time, more than half of the adult brain weight is achieved (Dobbing, 1984). By 5 years of age, the brain is almost at full adult weight (Tanner, 1978a). (See Table 5-1 for a breakdown of this weight gain.)

Brain cells begin to develop early in the prenatal period (Figure 5-3). **Neurons,** or nerve cells, which make up about 10 percent of the brain, develop between the second and fifth months of prenatal life (Dobbing, 1984). **Dendrites** and **axons,** the fibrous extensions from these cells, continue to grow after the child is born. These fibers carry impulses to and from the cells.

HEALTH FOCUS

Teething and the Care of Teeth

"Ouch!" squealed Cathy one afternoon as she nursed 7-month-old Evan. "That hurt!" She slipped her finger into the side of his mouth to break the suction and ran her finger along his slippery bottom gum. Right in the middle she felt the hard edges of his first two teeth.

"You're getting teeth!" she exclaimed. "I didn't even notice!" Evan smiled up at her. "Well, I'm happy about your teeth," she went on, "but no more biting!"

Whether it's accompanied by pain and fretting or by no signs of discomfort at all, teething begins at about 7 or 8 months of age. By their first birthday, children have four teeth on the top gum and two on the bottom. By 1½ they usually add six more, and by age 3 they have their full set of 20 deciduous, or baby, teeth.

First molars don't come in until 10 months, second molars not until 20 months at the earliest, so babies have to be fed minced or chopped meat and cooked vegetables. Not until they have their full set of teeth, between 2½ and 3 years, can they really chew meat very well.

EFFECTS OF DIET AND FLUORIDE ON TOOTH DECAY

Even young babies can get dental caries—over 8 percent of children between 18 and 23 months have them, and by 3 years, almost half of all children have them (Miller & Rosenstein, 1982). The development of caries is influenced by diet and by fluoride in the drinking water. Sugar in sticky form, such as in chewy candy, cake frosting, and chewing gum with sugar, is the most pernicious form of sugar, as opposed to nonsticky forms found in fruit juice, milk, ice cream, and so on (Herrmann & Roberts, 1987). Bathing the teeth in sugar, by sucking lollipops, for example, is particularly conducive to tooth decay. When babies fall asleep sucking a bottle of milk or juice, they're likely to have "nursing bottle" caries, a particular pattern of cavities in those teeth most directly exposed to the flow of liquid from the bottle (Crall, 1986).

Water fluoridation reduces tooth decay by as much as 50 to 70 percent (Shelton, Ferratti & Dent, 1982), and fluoride drops or tablets have the same effect where the water isn't fluoridated (Herrmann & Roberts, 1987). Frequent brushing—at least twice a day—also helps to fight tooth decay. Parents should begin cleaning their babies' teeth as soon as they erupt, at first with a wash cloth, then with a soft toothbrush.

TOOTH BRUSHING AND VISITS TO THE DENTIST

Toddlers can learn to brush their own teeth, although they don't have the coordination or skill to do a very good job. A

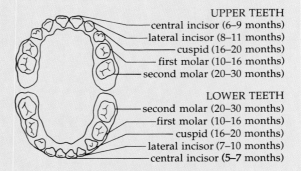

UPPER TEETH
central incisor (6–9 months)
lateral incisor (8–11 months)
cuspid (16–20 months)
first molar (10–16 months)
second molar (20–30 months)

LOWER TEETH
second molar (20–30 months)
first molar (10–16 months)
cuspid (16–20 months)
lateral incisor (7–10 months)
central incisor (5–7 months)

Teeth erupt in a regular pattern, often beginning with the two central incisors in the lower gum. The 20 baby teeth are usually in place by the time the child is 3 years old.

parental supervising technique that ensures clean teeth without interfering with the child's budding confidence is saying, "You did a good job with that one, and that one, and that one," while checking (and quickly rebrushing) each tooth.

Dentists often recommend that parents bring children in for a visit at about the age of 3. Children can look at the dentist's tools and get a demonstration of how the chair goes up and down. The dentist looks at the teeth, perhaps touches each one with a dental tool, and records the teeth on a dental chart. With a particularly cooperative child, the dentist might be able to do some quick scraping of plaque. With children who are more hesitant, the dentist might be able to give a fluoride treatment, which consists of having the child bite down on some toothpastelike material that contains fluoride.

EFFECT OF THUMB SUCKING ON THE TEETH

Parents often worry that thumb or finger sucking will harm the alignment of a child's teeth. These habits do affect the alignment of the baby teeth, pushing the upper front teeth forward and the lower front teeth back. But if the habit stops by the age of 5 or 6, the teeth self-correct (Schneider & Peterson, 1982). Parents therefore don't need to worry about thumb or finger sucking in the toddler or take any drastic action to stop it. Of course, parents who provide an emotionally secure and intellectually stimulating environment for the toddler's play and development will be laying the foundation for the day when thumb and finger sucking will disappear.

TABLE 5-1 Growth of the Brain

Age	Percentage of Weight of Adult Brain
Birth	25
6 months	30
12 months	60
20 months	75
5 years	90

FIGURE 5-3
Prenatal brain development. The human brain is highly developed at birth, with the most rapid growth, especially of the cerebral cortex, having taken place in the last trimester of pregnancy. If a woman has an inadequate diet during pregnancy, it may be reflected in her child's mental abilities.

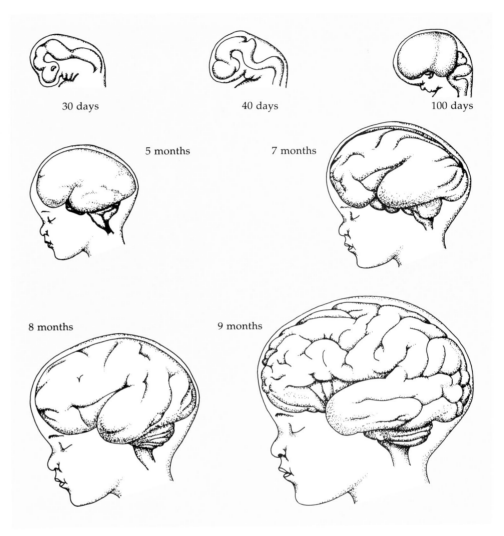

The rest of the brain consists of **glial cells**, which begin to appear about three months before birth and continue to multiply for several years after birth. These cells support the nerve cells and may have some nutritional and regulatory functions as well (Thompson, 1967). They also produce **myelin**, a fatty substance that forms a sheath around nerve fibers and greatly increases the speed with which impulses are transmitted. **Myelination** of some parts of the brain begins before birth, but most is completed postnatally. Myelination of certain parts of the brain isn't complete until several years after birth (Konner, 1982).

IMPLICATIONS OF BRAIN GROWTH PATTERNS. The brain, then, begins to develop early in fetal life and continues developing for several years after birth. What are the implications of this long development period? Probably the most important is that good nutrition must be maintained throughout this entire period to ensure proper brain development. It's particularly important that pregnant women have adequate diets during periods when fetal brain cells are growing rapidly. The mother's diet is not as important to the formation of the neurons

PUBLIC POLICY FOCUS

The WIC Program

Children's health is a matter of such consequence to the larger society that many different government assistance programs have been established over the years to support good health and nutrition in children. One of the most successful of these is the Special Supplemental Food Program for Women, Infants, and Children, commonly known as the WIC program. As the only nutrition program that provides both food and health services, the WIC program is unique (Egan, 1977). It serves pregnant women, nursing mothers, infants, and children under the age of 5 who meet low-income guidelines and who are judged to be at risk for health and nutrition problems.

Established in 1972, the program provides a specified amount of food to the participants each month. Only certain foods are made available, including iron-fortified infant formulas, iron-fortified cereal, fruit or vegetable juices high in vitamin C, milk, cheese, and eggs. These foods were selected because iron-deficiency anemia, insufficient vitamin C, and low protein intake are common among the at-risk population. They also provide the nutrients necessary for healthy prenatal development, rapid growth during infancy and early childhood, and protection against disease (Select Committee on Hunger, 1988).

Between 1973 and 1976, the WIC program was associated with several health improvements (Egan, 1977, p. 237):

- Infants in the program gained weight and grew more quickly than similar infants not enrolled in the program.
- Fewer infants had anemia, and the mean blood hemoglobin concentration of infants in the program increased.
- Women gained more weight during pregnancy than similar women who weren't in the program.
- Newborns weighed more at birth than similar newborns not in the program.
- Participants took greater advantage of health services than they had prior to enrolling in the program.

Research has shown that enrollment in the WIC program improves the intake of essential nutrients in populations of women at risk for deficient diets (Farrior & Ruwe, 1987). Program enrollment also increases length of gestation and birthweight (Batten, Hirschman & Thomas, 1990).

Like all publicly funded programs, the WIC program is reviewed periodically and is subject to the political and social views of changing administrations. But because of its success, the program would probably be one of the last nutrition programs to be cut back or discontinued. It appears to be an effective way to prevent nutritional problems when they're most likely to lead to serious impairment of physical and mental growth.

early in pregnancy as it is to the formation of the nerve fibers and glial cells in the later months of pregnancy (Dobbing, 1984). A good diet is also important for many metabolic processes in the brain. These processes are controlled by enzymes, and if the nutrients needed for the production of these enzymes aren't available, brain function can be impaired. Studies of the effects of nutrition on learning have found impaired learning ability in malnourished children (Grantham-McGregor, Schonfield & Powell, 1984; Sigman, et al. 1989). (For a discussion of a government program designed to prevent nutritional problems in infants, see Public Policy Focus—The WIC Program.)

Factors in the environment other than nutrition also affect brain development. A stimulating environment can produce growth of brain cells and increased brain functioning (Greenough, Black & Wallace, 1987). Studies with rats have shown that environmental factors have a direct impact on the weight of the brain cortex, the chemistry of the brain, and problem-solving abilities (Rosenzweig, 1984). Stimulation apparently has similar, or even greater, effect on human babies. Babies who have been malnourished, for example, but who were later brought up in stimulating environments often seem to develop normally (Winick, Meyer & Harris, 1975). And studies of both nutritional status and intellectual stimulation have found independent effects for both variables (Sigman et al., 1989). Even when the brain presumably has been affected in some physical way by malnutrition, a rich, caring environment seems able to compensate for disturbances, or at least makes it difficult to identify specific, detrimental effects of the malnutrition. As with other aspects of development, many factors, including both nutrition and stimulation, interact to form the intellect (Dobbing, 1984, 1987; Galler, 1987; Johnston et al., 1987). Unfortu-

FIGURE 5-4
Brain cells continue to increase in size and number during the first year of life and beyond, as can be seen in these drawings made from photomicrographs. Both nutrition and sensory stimulation must be adequate during this important time to ensure proper growth and development of the brain. (From Conel, 1939–1963.)

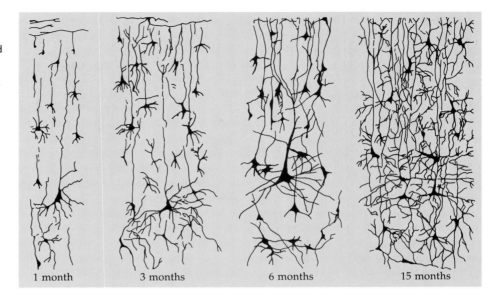

1 month   3 months   6 months   15 months

nately, children who are malnourished are often the same ones who also receive less than optimal stimulation.

All parts of the brain don't mature at the same time. Lower brain structures, such as the midbrain, the pons, and the medulla, develop earlier than higher structures such as the cerebral cortex. These lower structures control functions such as reflexes and balance. Within the cerebral cortex different parts of specific areas, such as the motor area, mature at varying rates (Tanner, 1978a). This is why babies master various physical skills in a specific sequence. They can hold their heads up before they can sit up, for example, and they can sit up before they can walk.

FIGURE 5-5
Too much stimulation, or just the right amount? Judging by the baby's happy face, these parents know how to adjust their actions to their child's desires and needs. Appropriate stimulation supports children's emotional development; it is also essential for the physical development of the brain.

Changes in Body Proportions and Shape

The shape and proportions of a toddler's body are quite different from those of a young infant's body. The head is the fastest growing part of the body early in development both prenatally and postnatally, but then this growth slows down. At other times, the legs and trunk grow very fast. As with the brain, different parts of the baby's body grow at different rates. The various kinds of body tissues grow at different rates too, giving the child a different appearance at different ages.

A toddler's head is still larger in proportion to her body than an older child's or an adult's, but she's not nearly so top-heavy as a young infant. Toddlers have also lost some of the "baby fat" that accumulates during the first nine months, and their bodies have more muscle and bone. By age 3, they look considerably leaner than they did at age 1.

Toddlers continue to be chubby around the middle, however, because the trunk grows slowly during infancy and early toddlerhood. At the same time, the internal organs grow quite a lot. The organs push out and the underdeveloped abdominal muscles can't hold them in. Toddlers keep their swaybacked silhouette until they're 3½ or 4 years old. By then their trunks have grown enough to provide more room for their organs.

Children start walking when they're 12 or 13 months old, but they walk with short steps and a wobbly gait. They can keep their balance only by plac-

FIGURE 5-6
The toddler is easily recognized by his characteristic body shape. As his trunk grows and his abdominal muscles become stronger, he'll be able to tuck that tummy in.

FIGURE 5-7
This 2-month-old has become strong enough to lift her head when she's on her stomach, her first big motor achievement and one that reflects the cephalocaudal trend in development.

FIGURE 5-7
This 2-month-old has become strong enough to lift her head when she's on her stomach, her first big motor achievement and one that reflects the cephalocaudal trend in development.

ing their feet very far apart. This is the accommodation babies and toddlers make to compensate for their big heads. As the trunk and legs stretch out during the preschool years, the child's center of gravity moves ever lower, and balance improves. The toddler's characteristic stance and walk gradually evolve into the surer, more graceful movements of the preschooler.

DEVELOPMENT OF MOTOR ABILITIES

We saw at the beginning of the chapter that a 15-month-old like Sarah can walk, step up, climb onto furniture, pick up puzzle pieces, and engage in a number of other useful actions. A 6-week-old like Sabina is limited to waving her arms in the air and a few other gestures. What are the developments that give Sarah her comparatively impressive motor skills?

During infancy, great advances in physical abilities occur. Motor development proceeds in two directions: (1) from the center of the body out to the arms, hands, and fingers and (2) from the top of the body downward. Development in the outward direction is known as **proximodistal** (literally, "near" to "far") development; this trend leads to ever-increasing skill in using the hands. Development in the downward direction is known as **cephalocaudal** (literally, "head" to "tail") development; this trend eventually leads to using the legs to stand and walk.

Fine Motor Development: Reaching and Grasping

Although newborn babies do show some tendency to direct arm movements toward objects (Hofsten, 1982), they are not at all skilled in executing reach and grasp motions. Only gradually do their abilities improve. By about 2½ months, they reach for objects by swiping at them, and by about 4½ months, they can reach for and grasp an object, but only if object and hand are in the visual field. If the infant can see the object but not her hand, or can see her hand but not the object, she will not reach for the object. Not until about 5 months of age does a baby reach for an object when her hand isn't in view.

At first, a baby grasps an object awkwardly by surrounding it with her fingers and pressing it into the palm of her hand. Later she uses her thumb to help hold the object. By about 9 months, she's able to grasp small objects by using just her thumb and index or forefinger. This is known as a **pincer grasp** (Figure 5-8).

To use a pincer grasp, babies have to be able to separate the forefinger from the other four fingers. Once they can do this, they can also point to objects in the environment. This skill is useful for language development. The child can point to an object and make a sound using a rising intonation, meaning, "What is that?" (Language development in infancy is discussed in detail in Chapter 7.)

By the time babies are 1 year old, they're playing with blocks and attempting to build towers. Not until they're 15 months old, however, will they be able to place blocks precisely where they want them. This is because they haven't mastered the skill of letting go. A 6-month-old finds it impossible to control letting go because the palmar grasp hasn't yet disappeared. This reflex is gone completely by 1 year, and between 1 year and 18 months the child learns to let go of objects voluntarily.

FIGURE 5-8
Between 9 and 12 months the baby perfects her pincer grasp, which allows her to pick up small objects (and, most likely, put them in her mouth).

TABLE 5-2   Types of Manual Manipulation Found in Infants

Rotation (second month)	Twists of the wrists cause a held object to take on different angles.
Translation (third month)	Objects are moved closer or farther away from the infant.
Vibration (fourth month)	Objects are shaken or waved.
Bilateral Hold (fifth month)	Both hands are employed to hold or explore different objects.
Two-Handed Hold (fifth month)	One object is held with both hands.
Hand-to-Hand Transfer (sixth month)	One object is passed from one hand to the other.
Coordinated Action with One Object (sixth month)	The object is held by one hand, while the other hand performs some action on it (e.g., fingering, patting, pulling apart).
Coordinated Action with Two Objects (eighth month)	Two objects, one held in each hand, are related to each other (e.g., one object is tapped by the other).
Deformations (eighth month)	The hands are used to alter the shape or size of objects (e.g., by crushing or ripping).
Instrumental Sequential Actions (ninth month)	The two hands perform different acts, in a sequence, to accomplish a goal. For example, one object is held up while something under it is removed by the other hand.

SOURCE: Rachel Karniol (1989). The role of manual manipulative stages in the infant's acquisition of perceived control over objects. Developmental Review, 9, 205–233.

With this difficulty behind them, babies gain immensely in coordination, strength, and steadiness. They're able to build sturdy towers by the time they're 2 years old. They're also able to snap pop-beads together, make marks on paper with some control, and work simple puzzles with two to four pieces. They're even able to string large beads if the end of the string is stiff enough to pass completely through a bead.

The ability to manipulate objects with her hands tremendously increases the information and knowledge gained by an infant, thus providing extremely important support for cognitive development. Even before they develop independent reach and grasp ability, infants explore objects that adults place in their hands. (Their grasp reflex allows them to hold objects.) Recent studies show that exploration of objects held by 2-month-old infants consists largely of oral contact. But by 4 months of age, infants begin to inspect a held object visually before moving it to their mouths, and then they move it back and forth between the visual field and the mouth. In addition, at about 4 months of age, infants finger objects; that is, while one hand holds or supports the object, the fingers of the other hand explore the object (Karniol, 1989). This research suggests that the hands play an important role in object manipulation and exploration and thus contribute considerably to infant learning. With increased ability to use the hands, particularly the ability to reach and grasp objects for oneself, possibilities for exploration and manipulation obviously increase. (See Table 5-2 for a summary of the manual manipulations infants apply to objects.)

Factors Affecting Reaching and Grasping Development

When we discuss landmarks like the disappearance of the palmar grasp and the emergence of the pincer grasp, you may think that motor development is completely a matter of maturation. And, if you recall from Chapter 2, the proponents of the maturation theory of development took much of their evidence from the realm of physical development. However, we know now that although motor development is *largely* under the control of maturation, experience plays a role as well (Konner, 1982). Studies of blind babies have given us some of this knowledge, and additional information has come from studies in which the environments of sighted babies were modified.

STUDIES OF REACHING AND GRASPING IN BLIND BABIES. Blind babies attempt to reach and grasp early in life when they hear a sound. But the sound doesn't tell the baby how far away the object is, and more often than not the baby fails to touch the object. Soon the baby stops reaching (Bower, 1977). In her studies of blind babies, psychologist Selma Fraiberg (1975) found that the ability to reach for an object on the basis of sound alone requires a higher level of conceptual development than reaching for an object on the basis of sight *and* sound. Sound alone doesn't convey the sense that something is an object and can be grasped. Blind babies have to acquire this concept, as the following observations from Fraiberg's studies show (Fraiberg, 1975, p. 48):

> For a perilously long time in the first year of life the blind baby behaves as if the musical toy in his hand is one object and the sound of the musical toy "out there" is another object . . .

FIGURE 5-9
The 15-month-old can play with blocks more easily than she could just a few months ago. With her growing manual control, she can pick blocks up and put them down where she wants them.

Fraiberg created an environment that would help these blind babies acquire the concepts they needed to continue developing their motor skills:

> Toys that united tactile and sound qualities were sought out by us and the parents to encourage a sound-touch identity for objects. . . . Through the devices of a special play table and a playpen we created "an interesting space" in which a search or sweep of the hand would guarantee an encounter and interesting discovery. . . . Even the motor patterns for reaching may not appear in a blind baby who has no incentive to reach.
>
> Then, one day . . . the sound of the bell would motivate the hands. A grasping-ungrasping motion would appear. . . . There was not yet reach, but we knew the idea was emerging. A few days later, a few weeks later . . . without vision, a baby would discover that the sound that we call "a bell" and the bell which he could not experience in his hand were "out there" in space.

Since blind babies don't have the same physical equipment as sighted babies, the environment has to be adapted to their abilities to ensure their development. Fraiberg's studies help us realize that the development of motor skills is not simply a matter of maturation. The stimulation and feedback babies get from the environment is a crucial factor, even in physical development.

STUDIES OF REACHING AND GRASPING IN MODIFIED ENVIRONMENTS. Further evidence for the role of experience in motor development comes from a study done by psychologist Burton White (1971). Working with infants just a few months old,

White added visual stimulation to their environments. He gave them multi-colored sheets on their mattresses, additional time on their stomachs (a good position from which to view the world), and large stabiles (stationary mobiles) above their cribs.

One group of infants received the stabile during their second, third, and fourth months. A second group received an attractive pacifier centered on a disk at both sides of the crib during their second month and the stabile during their third and fourth months. A control group didn't receive any additional stimulation.

Babies in both experimental groups began reaching and grasping with the hand out of view at about 130 days of age (4½ months), a month earlier than the norm. Babies in the control group didn't reach and grasp until about 170 days of age (5½ months), which is right in line with the norm. Again we see that the environment has an effect on what might seem to be a purely biological development.

An important side effect of this study was that the babies who received the stabile in their second month cried at first more than any other group. The stabile may have been too stimulating—too novel or frightening—for them. If a baby expresses extreme surprise or fear, or if he frequently looks away from stimulation, it is probably too novel. If he gazes continuously, the level of stimulation is probably just about right.

Locomotor Development: Up and About

A baby's first unassisted steps are usually celebrated as the major achievement of infancy, coming, as they do, at the end of the first year. Walking is an important milestone of infancy, but it's preceded by an equally impressive—and orderly—series of developments. Before they can walk, babies have to be able to stand. Before they can stand, they have to know how to sit; and to sit, they have to be able to hold their heads up. The cephalocaudal trend in development means that the head, neck, trunk, and leg muscles come under control in a head-to-tail order. The cephalocaudal development of **locomotor skills** (skills used in moving from place to place) is shown in two classic illustrations done by researchers working in the 1930s. Figure 5-10 shows the development of creeping (Ames, 1937), and Figure 5-11 shows the development of walking (Shirley, 1933). Today babies seem to reach these milestones earlier than they did in the 1930s, perhaps because of better nutrition or more opportunities to move around on the floor. The order in which they achieve them, however, remains the same.

A baby who has just started walking has to give her full attention to remaining upright and taking a few steps. As she gains experience, she begins to move faster and with more abandon and ease. The difference between these two levels of skill can be seen in children's abilities to use two different kinds of toys. A baby just starting to walk can use a push toy; a more experienced walker can also use a pull toy.

Factors Affecting Locomotor Development

Like the fine motor skills, the locomotor skills emerge according to a built-in biological timetable. And like the fine motor skills, they emerge normally only with appropriate stimulation and feedback from the environment. Evidence

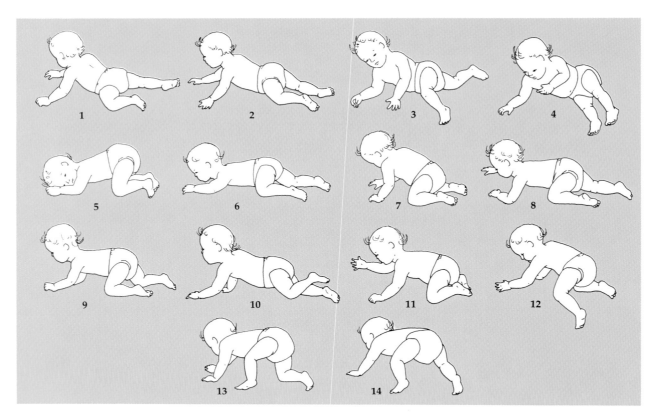

FIGURE 5-10
The development of creeping.
One milestone of locomotor
development is broken down
here into 14 steps. The baby's
persistence pays off first with
crawling (step 9) and then
with creeping on the hands
and feet (step 14).

for this relationship comes from some of the same sources as the evidence about the development of reaching and grasping.

STUDIES OF LOCOMOTOR DEVELOPMENT IN BLIND BABIES. Fraiberg's work with blind babies provides information about locomotor development as well as fine motor development, illustrating how heredity and experience are intertwined (Fraiberg, 1975, p. 48):

> In normal development when control of the trunk is achieved in a stable sitting posture, there is a smooth transition to bridging and creeping. In our sample, most of our babies achieved stability in sit well within the range for sighted babies. Then, something that should appear on the developmental timetable did not appear. The baby did not creep!

> The sighted child will reach for the out-of-reach toy which propels him forward. It is the visual incentive that initiates the creeping pattern. At every point where vision would normally intervene to promote a new phase in locomotor development we had to help the blind baby find an adaptive solution. The prone position, for example, is not an "interesting" position for the blind baby. . . . The blind baby, without . . . incentives, may resist the prone position. We build in "interest" in prone through speaking to the baby, through dangle toys or other devices.

> Practicing pulling to stand and cruising will be more "interesting" in the familiar space of a playpen with favorite toys offering sound-touch incentives. And one day, sometime between 13 and 19 months, the blind baby steps out into the vast black space to his mother's voice across the room and the news is telegraphed to us that he is walking!

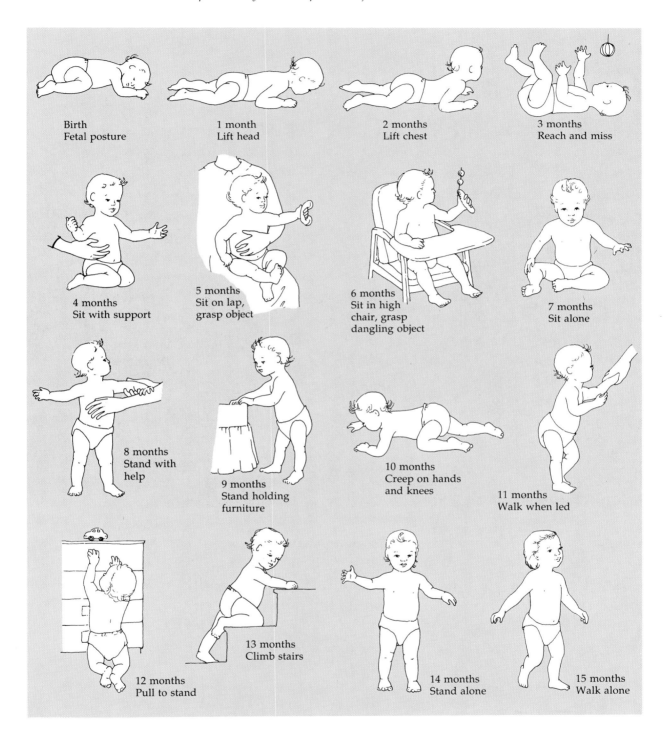

Birth
Fetal posture

1 month
Lift head

2 months
Lift chest

3 months
Reach and miss

4 months
Sit with support

5 months
Sit on lap,
grasp object

6 months
Sit in high
chair, grasp
dangling object

7 months
Sit alone

8 months
Stand with
help

9 months
Stand holding
furniture

10 months
Creep on hands
and knees

11 months
Walk when led

12 months
Pull to stand

13 months
Climb stairs

14 months
Stand alone

15 months
Walk alone

FIGURE 5-11
Milestones of locomotor development. The cephalocaudal trend in development can readily be
seen in this chart. As the baby's brain and muscles mature, her achievements center on progressively lower parts of the body, leading eventually to walking.

FIGURE 5-12
Upright and on the move—walking adds a new dimension to the baby's world. Most children reach this major developmental milestone at about 12 months of age.

STUDIES OF LOCOMOTOR DEVELOPMENT IN INSTITUTIONAL SETTINGS. Many studies have shown that babies' motor skills are delayed when they're raised in non-stimulating environments, especially in institutional situations. A well-known study by psychologist Wayne Dennis (1960) focused on orphans in three institutions in Iran. In one institution, which Dennis labeled Institution I, 600 children under the age of 3 lived with one attendant to care for every eight children. Babies who couldn't yet sit up spent their time lying on their backs in their cribs. They were never propped up or given toys. They were even fed in their cribs with bottles propped up on pillows.

When babies managed to pull themselves into a sitting position, they were placed on the floor while they were awake, but still they were given no toys. Not surprisingly, only 42 percent of the children between 1 and 2 years could sit up, and none could walk. In fact, only 8 percent of the children between 2 and 3 years could walk. When they turned 3, most of these children went to Institution II, where conditions were just as bad. Only 15 percent of the children between 3 and 4 years at Institution II could walk.

Institution III had been opened as a model of improved child care. The babies with the most retarded development at Institution I had been transferred to Institution III very early in infancy. Here there was one attendant for every four babies. Babies were held when they were fed, placed on their stomachs or in a sitting position in their cribs, put in playpens when they were 4 months old, and given toys. At Institution III, 90 percent of the children could sit alone by 2 years of age (as compared with 42 percent at Institution I), and 15 percent could walk (none could walk at Institution I). By age 3, all children could walk alone (compared to 8 percent at Institution I). Dennis attributed this more normal development to the better child care at Institution III, especially the practices of placing the babies prone in bed and on the floor. In this position, babies can push up and learn to sit up, roll over, and crawl.

Studies have shown that retarded motor development in early infancy can be overcome later if the baby is placed in better conditions (Dennis, 1960; Kagan, Kearsley & Zelazo, 1978). But Dennis's institutional study demonstrates conclusively that child care practices do have an effect on motor development. In our society most parents provide the environment and experiences that foster rapid motor development. This leads us to believe that normal motor development occurs spontaneously and inevitably. This isn't true; children's development depends in part on the conditions we provide for them.

Motor Development: Maturation or Experience?

Some earlier studies seemed to demonstrate that motor skills would emerge on schedule no matter what experiences a child had. In a classic experiment on maturation and learning, maturational theorists Arnold Gesell and Henry Thompson (1929) compared the stair-climbing skill of children with and without stair-climbing experience. They used identical twins in their experiment so that differences in behavior couldn't be attributed to genetic or biological differences. They gave one twin daily practice climbing stairs for six weeks, beginning at 46 weeks of age. By the fourth week of practice, this twin could climb the stairs alone, and at the end of six weeks, at 52 weeks of age, he could climb them in just 26 seconds.

FIGURE 5-13
The child raised in an unstimulating environment suffers in many ways. She's likely to have motor delays from lack of opportunities for practice, mental deficiencies from impaired brain development, and emotional disturbances from inadequate emotional attachment. Awareness of the importance of stimulation has led to many changes in institutional practices, reducing the number of situations like this one.

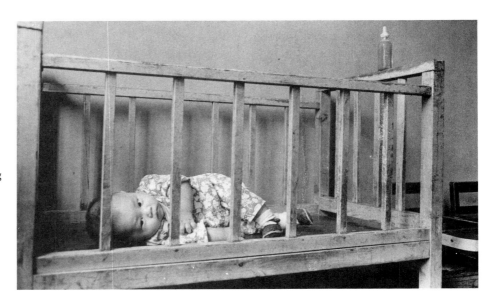

FIGURE 5-14
This 14-month-old can manage a big step not only because his bones and muscles have reached a certain size and strength but because he's had ample opportunities to crawl, pull up, stand, and walk. Maturation is the crucial factor—he couldn't have taken this step at 10 months—but experience influences the timing of motor developments.

The other twin had never climbed stairs. The researchers introduced him to stairs at 53 weeks of age, and on his first attempt he climbed them in 46 seconds. Two weeks later, at 55 weeks, he could climb them in just 10 seconds. In other words, without any experience of stairs at all, he equaled or surpassed his brother's performance at a particular age.

The conclusion researchers drew from this and similar studies was that maturation alone was responsible for motor development. What these researchers didn't take into account was that the ability to climb stairs might be influenced not just by practice in climbing stairs but by practice in other motor skills as well. The twin who hadn't had any practice climbing stairs *had* had just as much practice crawling, creeping, and walking as his brother. The researchers demonstrated that learning a behavior doesn't require a specific experience, but they didn't prove that the behavior will occur without any experiences at all (Bower, 1974). Again, although maturation plays a primary role, experience does influence the development of motor skills. (For a discussion of a question that hasn't received as much attention, see Research Focus—Effects of Motor Development on Other Areas of Development.)

DEVELOPMENT OF BLADDER AND BOWEL CONTROL

Sarah and Sabina, the sisters we met at the beginning of the chapter, are different in many ways, but in one way they're alike: They're both in diapers. Sarah won't be able to be toilet trained for another 15 to 20 months, at age 2½ or 3, although she may begin to show an interest in it by the time she's 2½.

FIGURE 5-15
If toilet training is begun before the child has the physical maturity to control her bladder and bowel functions, a very difficult struggle may ensue. Interest in using the toilet or potty is a good sign that a child is becoming ready for toilet training.

RESEARCH FOCUS

Effects of Motor Development on Other Areas of Development

Quite a lot of research has been devoted to investigating the factors—both inborn and environmental—that influence motor development. As we've seen in this chapter, experimenters have manipulated the environment in many ingenious ways to see how changes affect motor skills. Not nearly so much research has been designed to test how the development of motor skills affects other areas of development. But it seems clear that greater mobility and agility must have a profound impact on the rest of the child's life. The information that we do have suggests that motor development does affect other aspects of development in important ways.

In some early animal studies, researchers found that kittens who were prevented from walking had impaired visual development (Held & Hein, 1963). Other studies showed that locomotion was a critical step in providing the feedback necessary for normal social development in some species (Schneirla, 1957; Schneirla & Rosenblatt, 1961; Schneirla, Rosenblatt & Tobach, 1963).

Human studies have indicated that infants' avoidance of drop-offs, as demonstrated in the visual-cliff experiments (see Chapter 6) (Gibson & Walk, 1960), is learned quickly after infants have some experience crawling (Campos et al., 1978). Infants' spatial knowledge probably increases after they begin moving around independently because they experience so many different spatial orientations (Acredolo, 1978). And, as every parent surely knows, babies who move around independently change the terms of their interactions and relationships with adults (Bowlby, 1969b; Green, Gustafson & West, 1980). These studies suggest that cognitive, perceptual, and social development are all affected by advances in motor skills.

A study designed specifically to probe the effects of locomotion on other behavior involved the use of mechanical walkers (Gustafson, 1984). Babies who weren't yet crawling independently were placed in a walker in a laboratory equipped with several wall posters, a popular "activity center" toy mounted on the back of a chair, and toys in a pan on a shelf. Babies were observed to see how much they traveled around the room; what they looked at and for how long; what objects they manipulated and how they manipulated them; and how much they vocalized, smiled, gestured, or fussed.

Babies traveled much more in the walkers than they did when they weren't in them. They entered more areas of the playroom and approached the activity center and the adults more often (their parents were present as well as a research assistant). They looked more at the people and at nontoy aspects of the room, such as the wall posters, when in the walkers. They also smiled more and directed more vocalizations toward adults.

A second group of infants was also investigated. These were babies who were already crawling independently. For this group, placement in the walker didn't lead to as many changes in behavior. However, there were some differences between their behavior when out of the walkers and the be-

Motor developments rearrange both the baby's experiences and the parents' lifestyle.

havior of the noncrawlers when the noncrawlers were in the walkers. Out of the walkers, the babies who could crawl spent more time close to adults, manipulating them physically. They crawled into adults' laps and played with their faces, hair, and jewelry. The babies in the walkers couldn't get as close to the adults, so they spent more time manipulating features of the room.

This researcher suggests that the ability to move around independently affects babies' social interactions, language development, and cognitive and perceptual development. But he cautions against parental attempts to speed up normal motor development to accelerate development in other areas. There is no evidence to suggest any long-term advantages to such attempts. The implication from this research is simply that locomotion, when it occurs, will result in a major reorganization of infant experiences and behavior. Unless motor development is delayed excessively by poor environmental conditions, we can assume that this reorganization will occur for all individual children in their own good time.

Just as children gain control of the muscles of the upper and lower body in a certain order, they also achieve control over the **sphincters**—the smooth, circular muscles of the bladder and bowel—at a certain time in an overall pattern. Control of these muscles comes after control of the lower trunk and legs.

In young infants, the sphincter of the rectum or bladder relaxes reflexively, permitting the contents to escape. As infants mature physically and neurologically, they learn to inhibit these reflexive actions. This requires an awareness of the sensations associated with a full rectum or bladder, which depends on the maturation of the cerebral cortex. The cephalocaudal order of development applies not just to the motor area of the cerebral cortex; it also applies to the sensory area. Sensory development of the leg area in the brain is not fully achieved until age 2 or even a little later (Tanner, 1978b).

Bowel control comes first, often beginning late in the second year. Control of the bladder comes later, first during the day and then also during the night. Boys achieve control later than girls because they're less mature physically. Girls may be toilet trained by age 2½; boys may not be ready until age 3. It usually takes several months for children to gain control of these functions. Sometimes it takes even longer, especially if parents misjudge physical readiness and start too soon or try to push the child. It may take several years for some children to gain complete night control. And all children occasionally have relapses (for example, when they're sick, tired, absorbed in play, or "off-schedule" on a family trip).

Toilet training is a subject that's been considered exhaustively by doctors, theorists, and other child care experts. Many techniques and approaches—often with conflicting advice—have been devised for parents and other caregivers. Toilet training is discussed further in Knowledge in Action: Infants and Toddlers, following Chapter 8.

OVERVIEW

Young infants are relatively weak and helpless, but in their first weeks and months of life they grow and develop faster than they ever will again. In the first six months, they double their birth weight; develop more fat, stronger muscles, and harder bones; and begin to acquire fine motor and locomotor skills. In the second half of the first year, they acquire a few teeth; start to move out and about, and finally, around the time of their first birthday, begin to walk. In their second and third years, they spend a good part of every day practicing their new motor skills. By the end of the third year, we have to look hard to find a hint of the infant's face or body in the rambunctious toddler, who is taller, leaner, stronger, and eager to tackle the preschool play yard.

CHAPTER REVIEW

GROWTH

- Babies triple their birth weight by their first birthday and then grow more slowly in their second and third years. Length also increases rapidly at first and then proceeds at a slower rate.

- Variations in growth among different babies can result from either genetic or nutritional factors. Babies whose growth was limited in the prenatal period will catch up to their genetic potential after they're born, given adequate nutrition.

- As the growth rate slows down, toddlers' appetites diminish, and they're able to eat less.
- Body tissue grows and changes in a particular pattern. Subcutaneous fat accumulates rapidly in the first nine months, giving babies their rounded look; muscle fibers lose water and gain in salt and protein, making them stronger; and soft, cartilagenous bones begin to ossify, providing the support structure needed for walking. The fontanelles on the top of the head are fully closed by the time children are about 2 years old.
- Teething begins at about 7 months, and babies have their full set of 20 deciduous teeth by the time they're 3 years old. A lifetime of healthy teeth can begin in toddlerhood with proper brushing, a good diet, fluoride treatments, and regular trips to the dentist.
- The brain is about one-quarter of its adult weight at birth. The "brain growth spurt," when more than half the adult brain weight is achieved, takes place between the last three months of prenatal life and the first year and a half of postnatal life. The brain reaches almost its full adult weight by the time the child is 5 years old.
- Adequate nutrition, both prenatally and postnatally, is crucial to proper brain growth and functioning, as is environmental stimulation during infancy.
- Different parts of the brain mature at different times, causing physical abilities to appear at different times but in a specific sequence.
- The proportion of fat to muscle and bone decreases in the second and third years of life, giving toddlers a leaner look. But because of rapid growth and undeveloped abdominal muscles, they keep their protruding tummies and swaybacked silhouettes until they're about 4.
- Toddlers are still top heavy, although not as much as infants. Their body proportions cause them to walk with quick, short steps—their characteristic "toddle."

MOTOR DEVELOPMENT

- Motor development proceeds in two directions: (1) from the center of the body out to the fingers, known as proximodistal development, and (2) from the top of the body downward, known as cephalocaudal development.
- Proximodistal development results in reaching and grasping with the hands and fingers. At first, babies swipe at objects; later they reach if they can see both the object and their hand; by about 5 months, they reach even if they can't see their hand. Once babies acquire the pincer grasp (at about 9 months) they can pick up tiny objects, and after they lose the palmar reflex, they can voluntarily let objects go (between 12 and 18 months).
- Although the emergence of reaching and grasping is largely controlled by maturation, experience plays a part as well. Research has shown that babies develop these skills earlier if there are stimulating objects in the environment that they want to grasp.
- When babies have mastered standing up and controlling their leg muscles, they can learn to walk. They reach developmental milestones somewhat earlier than babies did years ago, but the order in which the locomotor skills are achieved remains the same.
- Like fine motor development, locomotor development is largely controlled by biological maturation but is also influenced by environmental factors. Stimulation and opportunities to move around are necessary for normal motor development. Delayed motor development in early infancy can be overcome if the environment is improved.
- Research has shown that the development of motor skills affects other areas of babies' development and experience, including their social interactions, language development, and cognitive and perceptual development. But researchers caution against trying to speed up motor development, since it occurs for all children, given adequate stimulation, in their own time.

BLADDER AND BOWEL CONTROL

- Toddlers can become toilet trained only after a certain level of neurological and motor development has been reached. They also have to gain control of the sphincter muscles of the bladder and bowel.
- Bowel control is usually achieved before bladder control. Girls are typically ready earlier, about age 2½, than boys, who aren't ready until about age 3. Night control isn't achieved until after daytime control, sometimes several years later.
- If the child is ready, toilet training takes several months, although there are many accidents and relapses. For some children it takes much longer.

KEY TERMS

ossification   axons   myelination   ƿ
neurons   glial cells   proximodistal trend l*sp*
dendrites   myelin   cephalocaudal trend s*kills*

SUGGESTIONS FOR FURTHER READING

Caplan, F. (1978). *The first 12 months of life*. New York: Bantam.
  Extensive discussion of physical development during infancy.
Cratty, B. J. (1986) *Perceptual and motor development in infants and children* (3d ed.). Englewood Cliffs, Prentice-Hall.
  Includes detailed information about early brain

growth, how brain developme
capability, the reflexes found in
tors that affect movement develo
Tanner, J. M. (1978). *Fetus into man: ʔt conception to maturity*. Cambridge, versity Press.
  Provides a thorough discussion of ƿ all stages of life.

COGNITIVE DEVELOPMENT IN INFANTS AND TODDLERS

Adam, 24 months old, sits in his high chair, waiting for his lunch. His mom has given him a blue felt-tip marker and a white piece of paper to occupy him until his lunch is ready, and he eagerly puts marker to paper. He begins by making a patch of circular marks in the upper left portion of the paper. He pauses to inspect it for a moment and then creates another patch to its right. A second pause for inspection is followed by a third circular creation, placed practically on top of the first one. Then he begins to draw horizontal lines, from left to right. The first line begins in the right-hand circular patch, another begins above that patch, and another is placed at the very top of the upper left portion of the paper. He makes several more horizontal lines lower on the paper.

Next, a different sort of experiment—vertical lines. Adam adds two, slowly and deliberately, on the left side of the paper. Then he draws one line straight through the middle of the first circular patch and another line diagonally down from the patch. Finally, he adds a series of "combination" lines. One starts as a vertical line, drawn from the top, but then turns and makes its way horizontally to the right before looping around to make a tiny, irregular circle. It continues horizontally, then around, to create a larger circle, and still doesn't stop. It continues upward, then bends to the right horizontally. Adam adds several more lines now that combine the separate vertical, horizontal, diagonal, and circular lines that he used when he first began to draw. At last, apparently finished, he sits back and looks with satisfaction at his creation.

From Adam's apparently random scribbling, shown in Figure 6-1, we can tell quite a lot about his cognitive development. First, he didn't make a line or shape just once; he repeated them several times. He also seemed to be varying his movements in a systematic way, as if experimenting to see what differences he could create. After he had made different types of lines separately—horizontal, vertical, diagonal, and circular—he joined them into complex lines and then experimented with several combinations.

FIGURE 6-1
Adam's experiments with a
felt-tip marker give us clues
about his intellectual
development.

Adam's behavior is typical of a child in a certain stage of cognitive development. Regardless of the materials themselves, whether paper and pen, a
spoon, a musical toy, or a toy containing tiny beads that scatter when shaken,
the 18- to 24-month-old takes a predictable approach. He experiments and
watches; then he repeats what he's discovered. A drawing that looks like a
meaningless scribble to the unknowing eye can turn out to be a fairly sophisticated "thinking" piece. The same is true of other materials. A spoon isn't just
thrown from the high chair: first, it's dropped; then, it's tossed straight out;
finally, it's flipped in the air. The child-scientist is at work.

It's not easy to interpret or understand cognitive development in children,
and it's particularly challenging in infants and toddlers, who can't tell us what
they know or think. Probably the best known approach to cognitive development in children is that of Jean Piaget, whose theories we described in
Chapter 2. In this chapter, we discuss his theory and study of the intelligence
of the infant and toddler.

Another fruitful approach to infant cognitive development is the study of
visual perception in babies. This research gives us a somewhat different,
though equally fascinating, picture of the baby as a very active intellectual
being. We can also study thinking and knowing in children by observing their
play—an open book in which we can read what's going on in their minds. In

this chapter, we begin with a discussion of visual perception, then move on to Piaget, and finally consider play. Together, these three approaches give us a comprehensive view of infant and toddler cognitive development.

VISUAL PERCEPTION

People have long been interested in how babies see the world and how they process visual images. Do babies see our faces? Are they born with depth perception? Can they organize the world into meaningful pictures, or is it a blur of colors and shapes? Many studies have addressed these and other questions, and we discuss some of these studies here.

Preferences for Certain Patterns

We saw in Chapter 4 that even newborns have definite preferences when they gaze at objects. They like to look at patterned displays rather than nonpatterned ones; they like circles and ovals, such as the shape of the face; and they like areas of high contrast, such as edges where black and white meet.

HOW PREFERENCES EVOLVE. As babies get older, they prefer patterns that are increasingly "complex." ("Complexity" is defined differently by different researchers, as we discuss below.) For example, babies prefer patterns with more elements. Checkerboard patterns, like those shown in Figure 6-3, are often used in studies to see how babies' visual preferences change as they get older.

In one such study, checkerboard patterns of 4, 64, and 576 squares were shown to groups of babies aged 3 weeks, 8 weeks, and 14 weeks (Brennan,

FIGURE 6-2
These 2-year-olds are learning about their world and what they can do to it through experimentation. Observing their play gives us important information about infant and toddler thinking.

 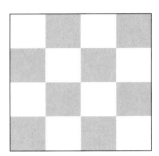 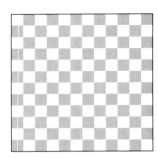

SOURCE: Hershenson, M. (1964). *Visual discrimination in the human newborn.* Journal of Comparative Physiological Psychology, 58, 270–76.

FIGURE 6-3
Examples of stimuli used in infant perception complexity studies. Researchers found that younger babies preferred the checkerboard with the fewest squares, and older babies liked checkerboards that were increasingly complex. But we can't tell exactly what it is about the increasingly complex patterns that makes the older babies prefer them.

Ames & Moore, 1966). Since young babies can't focus very well, the researchers thought the youngest babies might see the 576-square pattern only as a patch of gray. They added a fourth pattern, a plain gray square, to see if the babies looked at it for the same length of time as the 576. If looking time was the same, it could be assumed that they didn't perceive the most complex pattern as a pattern.

The researchers found that the 3-week-old infants could definitely see the most complex pattern, but it wasn't their favorite. They liked the least complex pattern best, followed by the intermediate pattern. The 8-week-olds liked the intermediate pattern best, and the 14-week-olds preferred the most complex pattern. Clearly, preferences for different patterns change with age. As babies get older, they prefer to look at patterns with more and more elements.

THE PROBLEM OF DEFINING "COMPLEXITY." Despite many studies like this, researchers do not agree on what it is about a particular pattern that makes babies of different ages like or dislike it. The definition of "complex" is one of the problems. Is complexity a matter of the number of elements? The number of angles? The arrangement of elements or angles? Is a regular, symmetrical pattern more or less complex than an asymmetrical pattern with the same number of elements? No one can agree.

For any given stimulus—checkerboards, alternating black and white lines, angles, and so on—researchers can determine what is preferred by younger babies versus older babies. But calling a stimulus more or less complex isn't enough to explain the reasons for babies' choices (Banks & Salapatek, 1983). For example, if we increase the squares in a checkerboard, we increase not just the number of elements but also the amount of contrast in the pattern. We don't know which quality the baby actually prefers. That's why researchers hesitate to say simply that older babies prefer increasingly complex patterns.

Luckily for babies and parents, this problem doesn't affect child care practices very much. In our society, babies have a lot to see in their environment, and they can choose what they want to look at. Most babies' cognitive development is just fine, although they're giving some researchers a very difficult puzzle to sort out.

Changes in Scanning Behavior

Another aspect of infant perception is scanning behavior, that is, how babies move their eyes across a pattern and settle their gaze on one part of it or another (Figure 6-4). Investigations have revealed that scanning behavior changes as babies get older. Bronson (1990a) has recently suggested that scanning appears to change in part because very young infants may center the image of an attracting stimulus on some unusual location on the retina—not near the middle of the retina as older babies do—and so only *appear* not to be fixating on the stimulus. Regardless of whether this controversial theory (Hainline, Harris & Krinsky, 1990) is correct, newborns appear to fixate on one feature of a stimulus at most, such as one angle of a triangle. Older babies, about 2 or 3 months old, scan several parts of the figure (Rovee-Collier, Earley & Stafford, 1989; Bronson, 1990b).

Similarly, if a dot or a line is inserted inside the outline of a triangle or a square, 1-month-olds fixate on the outline and ignore anything in the middle of the figure. But 2-month-olds fixate on the dot or line inside the figure (Salapatek, 1975). When the complex stimulus of the face is used, the same behavior occurs. The 1-month-old looks at the outline or border of the face, such as the hairline (Haith, Bergman & Moore, 1977). The 2-month-old looks within the face to the eyes. This development coincides nicely with the onset of smiling, discussed in Chapter 8. The baby clearly looks at the parents' eyes and simultaneously smiles; the parents feel that the baby recognizes them and returns their affection. This feeling enhances the development of attachment (also discussed in Chapter 8)—an excellent survival strategy!

Changes in Preferred Faces

We can extend what we know about babies' scanning behavior to explain their preferences for faces. When newborns and 1-month-olds are shown pictures of faces with normal features and with scrambled features as in Figure 6-5, they don't indicate that they like normal faces any better than scrambled ones. Considering how they appear to fixate at the edges of figures, it's not surprising that they don't show a preference for the normal arrangement of facial

FIGURE 6-4
Babies' visual scanning behavior changes as they get older. At 1 month, babies appear to look mainly at the borders of a figure, or the outside edges of a face. By 2 months, they're looking inside the figure and, if it's a face, especially at the eyes.

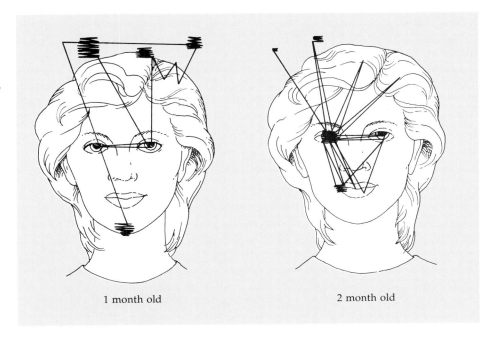

1 month old   2 month old

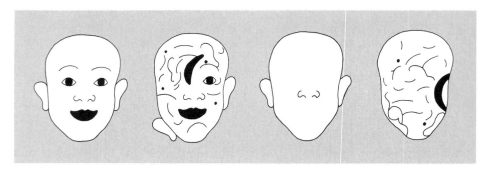

FIGURE 6-5
Only babies about 3 or 4 months old prefer the normal face to the scrambled ones. Older babies seem to be intrigued by the unusual faces, and very young babies don't show any preference at all.

features. They probably haven't formed a very stable idea of what a face should look like.

By 3 or 4 months of age, babies show a definite preference for the normal face over a partially scrambled or totally scrambled face. They clearly scan and analyze the internal features. Then again at about 1 year, babies look longer at a scrambled face than a normal face. Perhaps they're attracted by the novelty of the arrangement of features, or they may be comparing it to what they know about normal faces and trying to figure it out (Haaf & Bell, 1967; Wilcox, 1969).

Do Infants Have Depth Perception?

Another question about what babies see and know is whether they have depth perception, that is, the ability to tell how far away something is or to understand a drop from one plane to another. A classic study, involving a "visual cliff," revealed that babies can perceive a drop-off in surface level (Gibson & Walk, 1960). In this study, babies 6 to 14 months old were placed on a special surface that appeared "shallow" on one side and "deep" on the other (Figure 6-6). The deep side was covered with glass so babies could crawl across it just as they had crawled across the shallow side. Their mothers stood on the far side and encouraged them to crawl across to them. The babies in this study would not crawl across the deep side even after they felt the glass on top of the drop.

Gibson concluded that depth perception is innate and that fear of cliffs is innate as well. Other researchers have suggested that although depth perception might very well be innate, fear of cliffs is more likely to be learned quickly from experience once the infant begins to crawl about (Campos et al., 1978). Further study is needed to determine which of these views is correct.

Perception as a Clue to Infant Thinking

Studies of infant perception have also led to discoveries about how babies think. Some researchers wondered if babies could form **concepts,** which are ideas about general sets of characteristics that apply across many different individual cases. For example, a child who understands the concept "dog" will be able to recognize several different kinds of dogs as members of the category "dog." Babies can't tell us if they recognize dogs as dogs, of course, so we have to infer that understanding from their responses.

To see if babies form concepts, researchers used the principle of habituation. As you recall, babies stop responding to a stimulus after a certain number of repetitions, indicating they've become habituated to it. In this study babies were shown several different instances of a given category, such as the same adult face in different orientations (profile, full face, three-quarter face, and so on) (Cohen & Strauss, 1979). Once the babies were habituated to that face, two new stimuli were shown, one that could be part of the same category and one that couldn't. If babies recognize a new stimulus as a member of the same category, they should remain habituated, that is, show no increase in looking time. But a totally new stimulus that's not a member of the category should elicit longer looking time.

Studies like this indicate that babies can indeed form concepts. Babies who are 30 weeks old recognize a new orientation of a face as an example of the same face they've been viewing. They recognize a totally different face as not a member of this face category by becoming more alert and looking at it longer (Cohen & Strauss, 1979). Other researchers are trying to determine just what elements babies are noticing when they form notions about categories and concepts (Sherman, 1985; Younger, 1985). These assertions about what babies know and how their thinking develops lead us to our discussion of Piaget, who approached these questions from a different point of view.

FIGURE 6-6
The visual cliff experiment was designed to determine whether depth perception is innate, but it has been used to learn about other aspects of child development as well. For example, researchers have studied infants' ability to read emotions in other people's faces by observing how they respond to their mother's expression as they approach the "deep" side. If mothers appear pleased, babies are more likely to cross; if they appear angry or afraid, babies are less likely to cross.

Deep side Shallow side

Glass over pattern surface

Floor pattern seen through glass

SENSORIMOTOR INTELLIGENCE: PIAGET'S STUDIES OF INFANTS AND TODDLERS

Piaget's theory and research span the entire childhood period. Through careful observations, ingenious experiments, and tireless questioning and listening, Piaget built a theory of how children think and acquire knowledge. As mentioned briefly in Chapter 2, he believed that cognitive development progresses through a series of stages. During each of these stages, there are certain ways that information is obtained from the world and certain ways that knowledge is organized. In other words, each stage is characterized by a particular way of thinking.

Piaget labeled the period of infant intelligence the **sensorimotor period.** He chose this name because behavior during this period consists of simple coordinations between what babies sense and how they react physically. Babies don't think the way older children or adults do. They don't gain knowledge or insight by sitting back and contemplating what might happen. They act, look, taste, smell, hear, and feel. Through these strategies—acting and sensing—babies build intelligence during the sensorimotor period.

Dimensions of Infant Intelligence

Piaget proposed that within the sensorimotor period, which extends from birth to about 2 years of age, babies pass through six levels, or substages. He observed and described several different aspects or dimensions of infant intelligence. For each of these dimensions, he described the developments that occur during the various substages. Three of the dimensions Piaget described are discussed here. The first is one he called "means for achieving desired environmental events"; the second is imitation; and the third is object permanence. These dimensions are described in detail to explain Piaget's work and give its flavor. Some of the objections that other researchers have raised to Piaget's work are also discussed.

MEANS FOR ACHIEVING DESIRED ENVIRONMENTAL EVENTS. As the name suggests, this dimension of intelligence involves figuring out ways to make things happen. Another name for it might be problem solving. During the six stages of this dimension, babies become progressively more skilled at influencing the environment.

- *Stage 1: Reflexes (birth to about 1 month—all ages are approximate).* At this stage, babies' behavior is dominated by the use and progressive organization of the reflexes. The baby has the reflex to suck, for example, and a nipple or finger inserted in the mouth elicits the sucking response and maintains it. It doesn't take long for babies to learn that sucking provides food. If they're hungry and get a pacifier instead of a nipple, they'll quickly stop sucking. They've begun to "think," based on their prior experience with things inserted in their mouth. What they think in turn affects what they do.
- *Stage 2: Primary Circular Reactions (1 to 4 months).* A circular reaction occurs when something a baby does leads accidentally to an interesting result. The baby tries to achieve the result again by repeating the original action, which again leads to the interesting result, which again makes the baby repeat the

action, and so on. This reaction is called circular because an action-event-action sequence is repeated over an extended period of time. The sequence is called *primary* because it involves only the baby's own body, not any objects in the environment.

A primary circular reaction may involve actions that were once reflexive, but it develops beyond this primitive level. Thumb sucking is a good example of this kind of reaction, as described by Piaget and his colleague Barbel Inhelder (Piaget, 1969, pp. 7–8):

> Fortuitous or accidental thumb sucking may occur as early as the first day. The more advanced sucking is systematic and dependent on a coordination of movements of arms, hand, and mouth.... It is quite clear that this is a genuine case of acquisition in a broad sense, since there exists no reflex or instinct for sucking one's thumb.

Another primary circular reaction occurs when a baby touches his tongue to his lips, notices the sensation, touches them again, notices it again, and so on. Cooing, too, is an example of this type of reaction. The baby makes a sound, hears or feels it, makes it again, and so on.

- *Stage 3: Secondary Circular Reactions (4 to 8 months).* These circular reactions are called "secondary" because they involve objects in the environment, not just the baby's body. In the following example, Piaget had attached a hanging toy to a string and tied the string to the baby's arm (Piaget, 1952, p. 161):

> [At 3 months] I attached a string to the left arm after six days of experiments with the right. The first shake is given by chance: fright, curiosity, etc. Then, at once, there is coordinated circular reaction: this time the right arm is outstretched and barely mobile while the left swings ...

FIGURE 6-8
The discovery that banging his feet on his mattress produces some interesting changes in the environment leads this 5-month-old to continue banging his feet and observing the changes—a secondary circular reaction.

The baby notices that when he moves his arm, the toy moves, so he moves his arm again to make the toy move again.

A common secondary circular reaction occurs when a baby shakes his crib to make a mobile move. He accidentally makes the mobile move the first time, notices it, and then tries to make it move again. In the process, he discovers that banging his legs or feet on the mattress makes the mobile move. He bangs his feet, watches, bangs his feet, watches. The reaction is circular—it involves an action-event-action sequence. But unlike the primary circular reaction, this reaction involves something beyond the baby's own body.

• *Stage 4: Coordination of Secondary Circular Reactions (8 to 12 months).* In this stage, Piaget saw what he considered the first acts of true intelligence. The baby in this stage can intentionally perform an action with a goal in mind. In primary and secondary circular reactions, the first action occurs accidentally. The thumb gets into the mouth, the tongue touches the lips, the mobile moves—all by accident. The baby notices and tries to make it happen again.

But now the baby conceives of the action, the goal, in his own mind. He then pursues this goal with some familiar means. The action the baby takes to reach the goal isn't new, but the idea to do it is. In the following example, Piaget placed a piece of paper on the hood of his son's bassinet. Laurent had already had experience with a string attached to the hood, and he used the string to get the paper (Piaget, 1952, p. 214):

> Laurent, at 6 months and one day, tries to grasp a big piece of paper that I offer him and finally place on the hood of his bassinet (and on the string connecting the hood with the handle of the bassinet). Laurent begins by stretching out his hand, then as soon as the object is placed, he reacts as he always does in the presence of distant objectives; he shakes himself, waves his arms, etc. . . . After

having behaved thus for a moment, he seems to look for the string hanging from the hood, then pulls it harder and harder while staring at the paper. At the moment when this is ready to fall off the hood, Laurent lets go the string and reaches toward the objective, of which he immediately takes possession. Several sequential attempts have yielded the same result.

In this case, the paper didn't come down accidentally the first time. After several unsuccessful attempts to reach the paper, Laurent sized up the situation and *thought* of a way to achieve his goal. He took hold of the string, pulled it, and knocked the paper down. His thinking consisted of "schemes," or ways of behaving, that were already in his repertoire.

Laurent coordinated two familiar actions to get hold of the paper—pulling the string and picking up the paper. The object of his efforts was in the environment rather than part of his own body, and these two factors account for the name Piaget gave this stage—coordination of secondary circular reactions.

We often see this kind of action in 8- to 12-month-olds. For example, we'll see a baby crawl to an object (first action) and then grasp it (second action) when it's within reach. Or, if a baby wants a toy that's blocked by some other object, we might see the baby push the object away (first action) and then pick up the toy (second action). In both these cases, the babies think of putting together two actions to achieve a goal.

- *Stage 5: Tertiary Circular Reactions (12 to 18 months).* In this stage, babies seem to be less interested in achieving their goal than they were just a few months earlier. Now they're interested in experimenting with ways to achieve it. In the course of these experiments, they often invent or discover new ways to act on the world, as Laurent did in the following example (Piaget, 1952, p. 283):

  > I place my watch on a big red cushion (of a uniform color and without a fringe) and place the cushion directly in front of the child. Laurent tries to reach the watch directly and not succeeding, he grabs the cushion which he draws toward him as before. But then, instead of letting go of the support at once, as he has hitherto done, in order to try again to grasp the objective, he recommences with obvious interest, to move the cushion while looking at the watch. Everything takes place as though he noticed for the first time the relationship for its own sake and studied it as such. He thus easily succeeds in grasping the watch.

Adam, the boy we met at the beginning of this chapter, was in this stage of cognitive development. He was more interested in experimenting, discovering, and repeating actions than in drawing a particular picture. Another kind of Stage 5 behavior involves the dropping experiments most parents recognize (Piaget, 1952, p. 269):

> Laurent is lying on his back but nevertheless resumes his experiments of the day before. He grasps in succession a celluloid swan, a box, etc., stretches out his arm and lets them fall. He distinctly varies the positions of the fall. Sometimes he stretches out his arm vertically, sometimes he holds it obliquely, in front of or behind his eyes, etc. When the object falls in a new position (for example on his pillow), he lets it fall two or three times more on the same place, as though to study the spatial relation; then he modifies the situation. At a certain moment the swan falls near his mouth: now, he does not suck it (even though this object habitually serves this purpose), but drops it three more times while merely making the gesture of opening his mouth.

Younger babies also drop spoons from highchair trays, but they don't experiment with trajectories. They simply pick the spoon up, let it fall, and listen for the crash. They'll repeat this sequence for as long as someone is willing to pick up the spoon. But it's not until Stage 5 that babies experiment with how they drop the spoon.

- *Stage 6: Invention of New Means through Mental Combinations (18 to 24 months).* This stage marks the end of the sensorimotor period and the beginning of the period in which the child uses mental representation to solve problems. If the child wants something but doesn't have a way to get it, he invents a way to get it. And the child invents this way not by physical means as in the past, such as trial and error or groping, but by "insight." It's not the idea of the goal that marks this stage as different from previous ones—that was the achievement of Stage 4 thinking; it's the fact that the child creates the means to achieve the goal by thinking, rather than by actions, that makes this stage different. Consider Laurent in the following example (Piaget, 1954, p. 335):

Laurent is seated before a table and I place a bread crust in front of him, out of reach. Also, to the right of the child I place a stick about 25 cm long. At first Laurent tries to grasp the bread without paying attention to the instrument, and then he gives up. I then put the stick between him and the bread; it does not touch the objective but nevertheless carries with it an undeniable visual suggestion. Laurent again looks at the bread, without moving, looks very briefly at the stick, then suddenly grasps it and directs it toward the bread. But he grasped it toward the middle and not at one of its ends so that it is too short to attain the objective. Laurent then puts it down and resumes stretching out his hand toward the bread. Then, without spending much time on this movement, he takes up the stick again, this time at one of its ends (chance or intention?) and draws the bread to him. He begins by simply touching it, as though contact of the stick with the objective were sufficient to set the latter in motion, but after one or two seconds at most he pushes the crust with real intention. He displaces it gently to the right, then draws it to him without difficulty. Two successive attempts yield the same result.

When Laurent picked up the stick the second time, he seemed to adjust the position of his hand by insight. He seemed to know in his mind that this position would be more effective than the way he held it previously. He also didn't need to grope at the bread with several different actions. After seeing that just making contact had no effect, he immediately moved the stick in a more effective way.

In Laurent's adjustments of action, we can see the budding ability to think—to judge and anticipate, to select an action that will have a desired result. Children at this stage no longer have to respond to accidents in the environment to make things happen. They have a kind of knowledge and intelligence that allows them to take much more control of their world. For example, in playing with a shape box (a toy with holes of different shapes and pieces that fit in each one), they can inspect the individual pieces and decide where they go. They no longer have to solve the puzzle by trial and error, trying a piece in every hole until they find the one where it fits.

This new ability to relate things to other things and to imagine actions in the mind results in more efficient behavior, because action can now be guided

FIGURE 6-9
Toward the end of the sensorimotor period, children begin to solve problems less by trial and error and more by thinking. An 18-month-old would attempt to do a puzzle by forcing pieces together at random. A 2½-year-old, like this boy, looks, compares, and chooses pieces that appear to match.

by thought. A Stage 6 child who is drawing on paper with a marker copies forms from the environment. Instead of experimenting, he thinks about how to move the marker before he begins, discovering movements that create interesting lines and then repeating them. Although the drawings of a Stage 6 child may not be accurate from an adult point of view, they're guided much more by thought than ever before.

FIGURE 6-10
A 1-year-old can imitate her mother's whooping noises quite quickly and accurately, but if she doesn't imitate and learn this behavior right now, she won't be able to imitate it an hour later. This child is probably in the stage Piaget called tertiary circular reactions.

IMITATION Another dimension Piaget investigated was **imitation,** the acquisition of a new behavior by copying it from someone else. The newborn isn't capable of imitation, according to Piaget, but in Stage 2 (primary circular reactions, 1 to 4 months), the first glimmerings of imitation appear. Piaget called this behavior **pseudoimitation** (literally, "false imitation"), because it has two requirements that aren't necessary in real imitation. A Stage 2 baby will repeat an action made by an adult on two conditions: first, the action must be something the baby can already do, and second, the baby must have recently performed the action.

Pseudoimitation occurs, for example, when an adult interrupts or joins in with a baby's vocal play. The baby says "aah," the adult says "aah," the baby says "aah" again, and they continue as if taking turns. But because it's really the adult who's doing the imitating, Piaget didn't consider this type of behavior real imitation.

In Stage 3 (secondary circular reactions, 4 to 8 months), babies can imitate a specific behavior they've never performed before, but it must involve familiar schemes. They can put an old action to a new use. For example, if a baby is banging on her high chair tray with a spoon and her mother responds by banging on the bottom of a pot with a spoon, the baby would be able to bang on the pot if her mother gave it to her. The baby already knew how to bang. She quickly learned how to bang on a pot after she saw her mother do it.

In Stage 4 (coordination of secondary circular reactions, 8 to 12 months), imitation increases. New actions can be imitated if they resemble actions the baby already knows how to perform. For example, at this age a baby can learn to wave good-bye. It might be a novel behavior, but it resembles a lot of the motions she already makes with her hands and arms. Even so, she has to see several demonstrations of the motion and make several attempts to copy it before she'll have it down. In Stage 5 (tertiary circular reactions, 12 to 18 months), babies can imitate more novel actions, and they learn them more quickly.

In the first five stages, children imitate actions only immediately after they've seen them. In Stage 6 (18 to 24 months), they become capable of **deferred imitation,** as Jacqueline does in the following example (Piaget, 1954, p. 63):

> Jacqueline had a visit from a little boy... whom she used to see from time to time, and who, in the course of the afternoon got into a terrible temper. He screamed as he tried to get out of a playpen and pushed it backward, stamping his feet. Jacqueline stood watching him in amazement, never having witnessed such a scene before. The next day, she herself screamed in her playpen and tried to move it, stamping her foot lightly several times in succession.

Now babies begin to imitate everything they see and hear. Parents have to start being careful about what they say or do in front of their children at this age, because the child is likely to be capable of repeating it at any time, in any place.

OBJECT PERMANENCE. A third dimension of infant intelligence investigated by Piaget is **object permanence.** This is the knowledge that objects exist even when we can't see them. As adults, we know that something we see on two different occasions existed somewhere, unseen by us, in the meantime. A typical 6-month-old doesn't make this same assumption. If a 6-month-old watches a favorite toy being covered up with a cloth, she won't pick up the cloth to get the toy—out of sight, out of mind. But a typical 1-year-old will search for the hidden toy. The 1-year-old has object permanence; the 6-month-old doesn't. Let's follow the development of object permanence through the six stages:

FIGURE 6-11
A 9-month-old baby will search under a cloth for a completely hidden toy, indicating that she knows it exists even when she can't see it. But her grasp of object permanence is still somewhat tenuous, and she can easily lose track of exactly where an object has been placed.

- *Stage 1.* Newborns will follow a moving object continuously with their eyes over a short arc in an attempt to keep it in view. But if it goes out of sight, they don't keep searching for it. We assume there's no object permanence at all at this age.

- *Stage 2.* Babies 1 to 4 months old will continue to stare at the place where an object disappeared as it left the field of vision. For example, if we slowly move a red ball back and forth in front of a 3-month-old's face, the baby will move her head and eyes to follow it. But if we move the ball all the way around behind the baby, her eyes will linger for a moment at the spot where she last saw the ball before it disappeared. Then she will look away. The baby's lingering glance suggests some notion that the ball still exists, but this awareness is fairly fleeting.

- *Stage 3.* Babies 4 to 8 months old begin to reach and grasp for objects in the environment, and they will search for a partially hidden object. If we partially cover a baby bottle with a cloth so that only the bottom of the bottle shows, the baby will search for the bottle. But a Stage 3 baby won't search for a completely hidden object, and Piaget took this to mean that objects have not yet become permanent for the baby in this stage.

- *Stage 4.* Babies 8 to 12 months old first begin to search for completely hidden objects placed under a screen. But even at this stage, the baby's notions of object permanence are uncertain. Piaget found that if he hid a toy under one screen, then took it out in full view of the watching baby and hid it under a second screen, the baby would look for it under the first screen. Even though the baby saw him hide it under the second screen last, she seemed to retain the first image more strongly. This mistake is known as the **perseveration error.**

- *Stage 5.* The 12- to 18-month-old baby has very strong notions of object permanence. Piaget found that even if he used three screens, hiding the toy first under one, then under another, then under the third, the baby would go right to the last screen where she saw the toy disappear. But some situations still confuse the Stage 5 child. If the screens themselves are moved around, along with the hidden toy, the baby looks under the screen that's in the position where the toy was originally left. Not finding it there, she simply gives up the search.

  The child in this stage is also confused if the tester hides the toy in his hand or in a box before he places it under the screen. The child sees only the hand or the box pass under the screen; she doesn't see the toy placed there. If the first screen she tries doesn't reveal the toy, she gives up. The technique of concealing the object in something else before placing it under the screen is known as **hidden or invisible displacement.**

- *Stage 6.* The 18- to 24-month-old baby isn't fooled by switching screens or by hidden displacement. If she doesn't get the right screen the first time, she flips up the others until she finds the toy, as if to say, "It's got to be here somewhere!" Apparently, her new ability to imagine actions in her head allows her to understand the unseen path of the toy. She now has a strong and durable concept of object permanence.

Other Interpretations of Piaget's Tasks

Other researchers have had different perceptions of the situations Piaget put babies in and the tasks he asked them to do. Their different views have led to a certain amount of controversy over Piaget's interpretations and conclusions. None of these researchers disputes how babies respond to Piaget's tasks. When they repeat his experiments, the results are exactly the same. The controversy is over the tasks themselves and how to interpret babies' responses to them. Many researchers believe babies have the notion of object permanence, for example, long before Piaget thought they did. Different kinds of tests and tasks indicate that this may be true.

MODIFYING THE OBJECT PERMANENCE TASKS. One researcher, who had doubts about the timing of object permanence, tried hiding the toy *behind* a screen rather than *under* it, as Piaget usually did (Brown, cited in Bower, 1974). He found that a Stage 3 baby (aged 4 to 8 months) would search for an out-of-sight toy that was behind a screen but not for one that was under a screen. Apparently, the difficulty is not so much that these babies think unseen objects don't exist but that they can't figure out how two objects can be in the same place at the same time. Babies this age don't yet understand the concept "under." When the screen is placed on top of the toy, they see that the screen itself now clearly occupies the space. They're stumped about where the toy could possibly be, and they don't lift the screen to look under it. These babies do have the concept "behind." When the toy is placed behind the screen, they search for it even though it's completely hidden. This behavior indicates that Stage 3 babies know an object still exists even when it's hidden in *some* ways.

TESTING OBJECT PERMANENCE WITH HABITUATION TECHNIQUES. Another group of researchers changed the traditional task even more dramatically (Baillargeon, Spelke & Wasserman, 1985; Baillargeon, 1987). They wanted to test for object permanence without relying on the baby's ability to search for the object. They devised quite an ingenious apparatus to do this:

> . . . a box was placed on a surface behind a wooden screen. The screen initially lay flat, so that the box was clearly visible. The screen was then raised, in the manner of a drawbridge, thus hiding the box from view. Infants were shown two test events: a possible event and an impossible event. In the possible event, the screen moved until it reached the occluded box, stopped, and then returned to its initial position. . . . In the impossible event, the screen moved until it reached the occluded box—and then kept on going as though the box were no longer there! The screen completed a full 180-degree arc before it reversed direction and returned to its initial position, revealing the box standing intact in the same location as before.

If the babies expected the box to be there even when they couldn't see it, they would be surprised to see the screen continue moving into the space supposedly filled by the box. If they didn't expect the box to be there—out of sight, out of mind—they wouldn't be surprised (Figure 6-12).

The researchers measured surprise with a habituation technique. They showed the babies the screen moving all the way back and forth until the babies became habituated to it and no longer paid attention. If the babies paid more attention to the moving screen after they saw the box put in place, it would indicate surprise. And surprise would indicate that they understood how strange it was—in fact, impossible—for the screen to be able to move into the space filled by the box. Surprise would reveal that they had object permanence.

The 5-month-old babies in this experiment did pay more attention to the impossible event. They assumed the box was still there when they couldn't see it, and they were surprised to see the screen move past the upright posi-

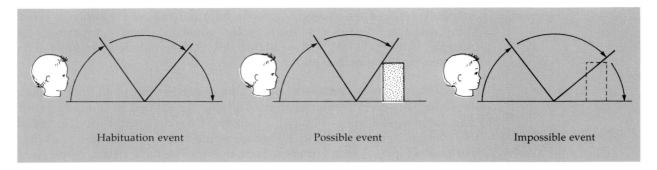

Habituation event   Possible event   Impossible event

tion. This study suggests that babies just entering Stage 3 (age 4 to 8 months) do have object permanence, even though Piaget thought it didn't begin to develop until Stage 4 (age 8 to 12 months).

These researchers believe that Piaget asked the wrong question. They think the problem is "not to establish whether young infants believe objects are permanent" but to "determine what they know about the displacements and transformations of objects, and how they attain and represent this knowledge" (Baillargeon, Spelke & Wasserman, 1985, p. 206). In other words, the issue is what babies know about how objects can be moved and changed rather than whether they know objects always continue to exist when they can't see them.

FIGURE 6-12
In Baillargeon's experiment (1987), babies didn't have to look for a hidden object to demonstrate their grasp of object permanence. They only had to show surprise at an "impossible event"—a screen moving through a space where they had previously seen a box standing. Baillargeon found that babies showed surprise at a considerably younger age than the age at which babies search for a completely hidden object in Piaget's tasks.

The Enduring Value of Piaget's Work

Although Piaget's theoretical interpretations and behavioral timetables have been questioned, his data on the order in which behavior develops have held up. Table 6-1 shows the relationships among the three dimensions of sensorimotor development discussed in this chapter. A child may not reach a particular stage at the same time in all three dimensions (Uzgiris, 1973). For example, a child may be in Stage 4 in his object permanence skills, such as uncovering a hidden object, before he reaches Stage 3 in imitation skills, such as imitating familiar sounds (Schickedanz, 1976). Within any one dimension, however, very few babies show behavior of a higher stage before they show behavior of a lower stage (Brainerd, 1978). For example, no baby would be able to solve a problem by insight before he could solve it by trial and error. In this aspect of cognitive development, no one has been able to challenge Piaget's findings.

COGNITIVE DEVELOPMENT AND PLAY

Piaget observed that at about 2 years of age a new way of thinking, which he called **representational thinking,** begins to emerge. Children are able to think about the world even when they aren't experiencing it directly, and they start to use symbols to represent things. Nowhere do we see a more enthusiastic celebration of this new ability than in pretend play.

Mark and Samantha are playing with toys on the living room rug. In his chubby hand, 10-month-old Mark clutches a red plastic ring from a set of stacking rings. Nearby, Samantha, age 3½, holds her baby doll in her arms and feeds it with a toy bottle.

TABLE 6-1   Summary of Three Dimensions of Sensorimotor Development

Stage	Development of Means to Achieve Desired Environmental Events	Imitation	Object Permanence
1. Reflexes Birth–1 month	Elaboration of reflexes		Follows object with eyes over short arcs
2. Primary circular reactions 1–4 months	Use of means to produce interesting effects involving own body	Pseudoimitation	Glance lingers where an object disappears
3. Secondary circular reactions 4–8 months	Use of means to produce interesting effects involving objects in environment	Imitation of familiar schemes	Uncovers partially hidden object
4. Coordination of secondary circular reactions 8–12 months	Novel coordinations of familiar schemes	Imitation of somewhat novel schemes	Uncovers hidden object but shows perseveration error
5. Tertiary circular reactions 12–18 months	Progressive modification of familiar schemes to produce novel schemes as means to an end; groping	Imitation of novel schemes	Uncovers hidden object but shows switching error
6. Invention of new means through mental combinations 18–24 months	Insight without groping	Deferred imitation	Uncovers object hidden through invisible displacement

Mark looks at his red ring, passes it from one hand to the other, chews on it briefly, and taps it on the floor. Samantha looks up at Mark and then down at her doll. She carefully places the doll on the floor and reaches over to take the ring out of Mark's hand. In exchange, she offers him the orange ring from the stack. He releases the red ring and accepts the orange one without making a fuss. Samantha picks up her doll again and says, "Here's a bracelet, baby. I just buyed it for you at the store."

Mark and Samantha were playing next to each other, but their minds were miles apart. To Mark, the red ring was an object to explore: What does it look like? How does it feel and taste? What kind of sound does it make when tapped on the floor? These are the burning questions for a 10-month-old.

Samantha, on the other hand, was interested not in what the object was but what she could pretend it was. Her thoughts went beyond reality into a world created by her imagination, where objects can be what you make of them. The red ring could become a very special object, a bracelet fashioned by her mind, bought on a trip to an imaginary store. Flights of fancy like this are the hallmark of pretend play, the remarkable intellectual feat of the toddler.

The Significance of Pretend Play

The ability to engage in pretend play, or **pretense** as it's sometimes called, marks a revolution in the child's way of thinking. The child now has the ability to use one thing to stand for another. We also see this capacity for **symbolic representation** in the emergence of language at about the same time. The child becomes able to use words to stand for things. Both pretend play and words start to emerge around the first birthday or soon after.

The toddler—the child between 18 and 36 months of age—brings pretend play into full bloom, but the roots of pretense extend back somewhat into infancy, as we will see. We also look ahead a bit to the preschool years to see how pretend play becomes **sociodramatic**—filled with roles and acted out in combination with other players. For the toddler, however, pretend play is rarely coordinated with the play of a real-life partner. It seems that the combination of pretense and social interaction is far too complicated for the toddler to manage.

Analyzing Pretend Play

Pretend play emerges at about 1 year and continues as the child grows. But a 2-year-old doesn't pretend the same way a 4-year-old does. Pretend play changes dramatically as the child's understanding and cognitive abilities develop. People who have observed and described children's play have often noted three different kinds of changes, or trends, that occur. They've called these trends decentration, decontextualization, and integration.

DECENTRATION. Decentration has to do with the child's role in the pretend play. As he gets older, he slowly becomes able to remove himself from center stage and to take on the role of other, imaginary characters. For example, when Samantha was 1 year old, she often pretended to feed herself or to be asleep. When babies do this, they may smile or giggle, which helps their parents know they're pretending (Bretherton, 1984). One distinguishing feature of this pretense is that it involves no one but the child herself. Another feature is that the content of the play—what the child pretends—comes from her daily life (Fein, 1981; McCune-Nicolich, 1981; Fenson, 1984).

FIGURE 6-13
The youngest toddlers, like this 15-month-old, can play at pouring and drinking only if the pretend objects look very much like the real objects they represent. More far-fetched substitutions stretch the toddler's imagination beyond its limits.

When Samantha got a little older, she began to feed her doll rather than herself and put the doll rather than herself to bed. Children between about 15 and 21 months of age begin to include others as the recipients of their playful actions (Fenson & Ramsey, 1980; Fein, 1981). The other player, however, remains passive. The doll doesn't "come alive" or act on its own (Bretherton, 1984). The child doesn't make the doll talk, arrange its arms and legs as if it were moving, or give it a will of its own. The child does things *to* the doll. At about the same time, the child starts to include objects in her play, such as a cup for stirring imaginary food (Fenson & Ramsey, 1980).

When she was about 2 years old, Samantha began to put a spoon in her doll's hand and make it look as if it was feeding itself. At this age, children begin to make their dolls come alive (Fenson & Ramsey, 1980). They give them a cup or a comb and pretend they're drinking or combing their hair. They no longer just do things to the doll; they make the doll do things to itself. The child has removed herself somewhat from center stage, thus the name for this trend, *decentration*. Children seem to animate their dolls first by making them talk—in some cases, as early as 20 months—and later by making them move (Fenson, 1984).

At the same time, children begin to assume the roles of others in their play (Bretherton, 1984). They do this in two ways: They include activities that don't come from their own real-life activities, and they pretend to be other people. At this point, we might have seen Samantha "reading" a newspaper and heard her say, "Mommy read paper." In other words, "I'm pretending to be a mommy who's reading the paper."

Later still, Samantha went "camping out" in her room with her dolls. She set up a play tent with a blanket and put the dolls in it. One doll served hot cocoa with marshmallows to the other in a plastic cup, and then they went to sleep in sleeping bags in the tent. When Samantha's dad came into her room, Samantha wanted to serve him pretend cocoa too. At this higher level of decentration, the child is able to create two roles, either for herself and a doll, for two dolls, or for herself and another person. To do this, she has to be able to stand back a bit and consider one role in relation to another. This ability appears between 24 and 30 months of age (Bretherton, 1984; Miller & Garvey, 1984).

Between ages 3 and 6, children become much more skilled at playing out pretend roles. They can give roles to an increasing number of dolls or figures (Watson & Fischer, 1977), and they can coordinate their role with an increasing number of real players. Pretend play becomes more and more elaborate up to the age of 6, when it begins to diminish.

DECONTEXTUALIZATION. When Samantha pretended to feed herself at 1 year, she used a real cup for this pretend action. Very young pretenders, aged 12 to 20 months, need real objects, or at least realistic replicas of these objects, to support their pretend play (Fein, 1975; Fenson, 1984). They can't pretend a cube or a leaf is a cup, for example.

By 20 to 24 months of age, most children have begun to substitute one object for another (Fein, 1975; Ungerer et al., 1981). This phenomenon is known as **decontextualization**—increasingly taking objects out of their original context and pretending they're something they're not. At first, substitutions are limited. The child may be able to use a stick to pretend to feed a realistic doll, but she may not be able to pretend both that a block is a doll and that a stick

FIGURE 6-14
At 2½ years of age, this child can easily assume the role of a mother in her pretend play, dressing and undressing her lifelike baby doll. She is also capable of pretend play that integrates several different kinds of actions, such as removing the doll's clothes, bathing it, dressing it in pajamas, and putting it to bed.

is a spoon. When too many transformations, or changes from reality, are required, it puts a damper on the play of the youngest pretenders. Children under age 3 can accept a substitution only if plenty of other things in the play situation are realistic (Fein, 1975).

Substitution also depends on how much an available object resembles the object needed in the pretend play. Children under 26 months will substitute one object for another if it looks like the needed object (Fenson, 1984). Children from 26 to 34 months old are most likely to use substitute objects, and they use them freely, no matter how unlikely the substitute seems to be (Ungerer et al., 1981). Older children choose less defined, more ambiguous substitute objects for their play. For example, a 4-year-old would probably resist using a plastic golf club as a fishing pole, because a golf club has a very specific function for him. But he could use a rolled-up newspaper as a fishing pole; this object has no clearly defined or contradictory use in his life. This research finding suggests that older preschoolers' pretend play can be enhanced when they have access to "raw" materials such as blocks, paper tubes (from paper towels, toilet paper, or gift wrapping), an assortment of paper, and a supply of tape.

The creation of imaginary objects is another aspect of pretend play that appears in older toddlers and continues during the preschool years. It occurs first when other objects support the presence of the imaginary objects (Fenson, 1984). When Samantha went camping out, for example, she pretended there

FIGURE 6-15
By 3 years of age, children can readily substitute one object for another in their pretend play. The pervasive imaginary gun can be nearly anything that comes to hand—a stick, a stone, a crayon, even a shoe or a lunchbox.

was hot cocoa with marshmallows in the cups. The cups obviously supported the idea of hot cocoa. Later, children invent imaginary objects without support from the rest of the situation (Fenson, 1984). For example, a child might look across the room and say, "Now you sit over there, doggy." Or a child might knock on a pretend door to enter a particular area of a nursery school play room. In these cases the imaginary objects are created "out of thin air."

INTEGRATION. When Samantha was playing in the living room, she was involved in several actions: holding her doll, feeding it, and giving it a brace-let. Younger children can't manage so many actions; they use only one, per-haps feeding or combing hair, applying the action to themselves or to a doll. As pretend play develops, children invent several actions and put them

TABLE 6-2   Stages of Pretend Play

Age	Symbolic Level	Examples
10–12 months	*Presymbolic scheme:* The child shows understanding of the object and uses it meaningfully. However, there is no pretending. What is done with an object is dictated by its characteristics, not by the child's imagination.	Child picks up lid to a cooking pot, looks at it, and puts it on the pot.
12–14 months	*Auto-symbolic scheme:* The child begins to pretend. Activities are self-centered in that actions (1) are from the child's own daily actions, and (2) are directed toward the child's own body. This level includes the meaningful object use from the previous level, along with a pretending—playful—quality.	Child pretends to drink from a cup. Child pretends to sleep.
15–21 months	*Single-scheme symbolic games:* The child now extends pretend play beyond himself or herself in two ways. 1. The child applies pretend action to others. 2. The child begins to use actions that are not part of his or her typical repertoire.	Child pretends to feed a doll or his or her mother. Child pretends to read a book to a doll. Child makes a toy dog go "woof-woof."
19–24 months 24 months and beyond*	*Combinatorial symbolic games:* The child now begins to combine action sequences. These can be of two types: 1. Single-scheme combinations relate one action to a number of recipients. 2. Multischeme combinations involve different actions related to one another in a sequence.	Child drinks from a cup and then gives a doll a drink from a cup. Child feeds doll, puts doll to bed. Child gives doll a bath, dresses doll, then feeds doll.

*Beginning at about 24 months, object substitution—decontextualization—begins to take place; a block might be used as a cup, for example.

SOURCE: Adapted from McCune-Nicolich, L. (1977). Beyond sensorimotor intelligence: Assessment of symbolic maturity through analysis of pretend play. Merrill Palmer Quarterly, 23 (2), 89–99.

together. These combinations and sequences change as children get older (McCune-Nicolich, 1981; Fenson, 1984). **Integration of play** refers to the child's ability to combine actions in increasingly complex sequences.

Younger children, aged 15 to 24 months, are most likely to use **single-scheme combinations.** This kind of action sequence involves one action applied to several things. The child might pretend to feed a doll and then pretend to feed his mother.

Children over 24 months begin to put more than one action together in sequence; these action sequences are called **multischeme combinations** (Fenson & Ramsay, 1980; McCune-Nicolich & Fenson, 1984). Now the child applies a series of different actions to the same object. This is what Samantha was doing in the living room—holding her doll, feeding it, giving it a bracelet. As children get older, they can combine more and more actions.

Another aspect of children's play that observers have noted is **theme**—the content of the play. The child's actions can relate to one theme or to more than one theme. A multischeme combination relating to the theme "putting baby to bed" might consist of rocking the doll; putting the doll into bed; covering the doll with a blanket; and kissing the doll good-night. A multischeme combination on the theme "feeding the baby" might consist of putting the doll in the high chair; putting a bib on the doll; offering the doll some food from a spoon; reheating the doll's food in a pan because it was too cold; and feeding the doll again.

If the child feeds the doll and then puts the doll to bed, he has combined two themes, each of which involved a multischeme combination. This kind of complex play involving two themes isn't really possible for children until they're about 2½ or 3 years old (Bretherton, 1984). Extensive action sequences combining three or more themes aren't observed until children are age 3 or older.

Developmental Stages of Pretend Play

We've seen that children's pretend play begins during the second year of life and develops in terms of three dimensions: decentration, decontextualization, and integration. One researcher has analyzed the changes that occur in each of these three areas and organized them into a summary of the developmental stages of pretend play (Nicolich, 1977). She suggests that there are several stages, or symbolic levels, of pretend play during early childhood. These stages are shown in Table 6-2.

The toddler's cognitive achievements show up in more areas than pretend play. But we focus here on this one achievement because it's such a dramatic one. It also illustrates more than any other change the impact of the child's ability to use symbolic representation. After all, symbolic representation (or mental representation, in Piaget's terms) is the cognitive ability lacking in the infant. This is why Piaget referred to the period of infant intelligence as the "sensorimotor period."

As children's capacity for representational thinking emerges and increases, their thinking and acting take on many new qualities, as seen in the changes that occur in their pretend play. Other aspects of early representational thinking are apparent late in the toddler years and in the preschool years. These are covered when we discuss cognitive and language development in preschool children. But whether we consider pretend play, Piagetian stages of development, or changes in perception and concept formation, it is apparent that the transformations in thinking and understanding that occur in the first few years of life provide a solid foundation for a lifetime of intellectual growth.

OVERVIEW

Human beings are born with tremendous potential to learn, but it takes many years—virtually all of childhood—for this intellectual potential to be fully realized. Children spend their earliest years rapidly expanding their knowledge and developing their problem-solving skills. Their visual preferences and behaviors change in significant ways, their sensorimotor intelligence builds through several stages, and their pretend play evolves from the 1-year-old's first pretense to the 4-year-old's elaborate symbolic play. If all goes well, the unfolding of cognitive abilities that begins in infancy continues into later childhood and beyond, establishing the pattern for a lifetime of learning.

CHAPTER REVIEW

VISUAL PERCEPTION

- Babies like to look at patterns and areas of contrast, and as they get older, they prefer to look at increasingly "complex" patterns, although researchers don't agree on how to define that complexity.
- Newborns fixate on one feature of a visual display, but by 2 months, babies scan from one point to another. At 1 month, babies look at the outline of a figure, but at 2 months they look at whatever is inside the figure.

- Babies' preferences for faces change too. When given a choice between normal and scrambled faces, newborns and 1-month-olds show no preference. Babies 3 and 4 months old prefer the normal face, but 1-year-olds prefer the scrambled face.
- We still don't know the extent of babies' depth perception at birth, although they do show a fear of heights once they begin to crawl.
- On the basis of habituation studies, researchers conclude that babies are able to form concepts.

SENSORIMOTOR INTELLIGENCE

- Piaget suggested that infants build intelligence and learn about the world during their first two years by sensing and acting.
- According to Piaget, infants pass through six substages of development during the sensorimotor period, as follows: Stage 1: reflexes (birth to 1 month); Stage 2: primary circular reactions (1 to 4 months); Stage 3: secondary circular reactions (4 to 8 months); Stage 4: coordination of secondary circular reactions (8 to 12 months); Stage 5: tertiary circular reactions (12 to 18 months); and Stage 6: invention of new means through mental combinations (18 to 24 months).
- Piaget described several dimensions of infant intelligence, including means for achieving desired environmental events, imitation, and object permanence.
- The dimension of intelligence referred to as means for achieving desired environmental events involves solving problems or learning to make things happen.
- Another dimension of infant intelligence, imitation,

involves learning a new skill by copying it from someone else.
- Object permanence refers to the ability to remember that an object still exists even when it can't be seen. Babies begin to demonstrate object permanence during Stage 4, although they tend to think an object is located in the first place they saw it hidden, a mistake known as a perseveration error.
- Researchers sometimes use the technique of hidden or invisible displacement to test object permanence, but this technique doesn't fool the Stage 6 child.
- Some researchers believe that babies have object permanence well before Piaget said they do. They suggest that infants have trouble locating objects because their spatial and temporal concepts aren't yet well defined.
- Although the timing of some of Piaget's stages may be debatable, his description of the order in which cognitive skills emerge has stood the test of time.

COGNITIVE DEVELOPMENT AND PLAY

- The capacity for symbolic representation—using objects or words to stand for something else—emerges at about 1 year of age. Pretend play is the hallmark of the toddler years.
- Changes take place in children's pretend play as their cognitive skills increase. These changes have been referred to as decentration, decontextualization, and integration.
- Decentration refers to the child's gradual removal of herself from center stage in her play.
- Decontextualization refers to the child's increasing

ability to take an object out of context and pretend it's something it's not.
- Integration refers to the child's ability to combine actions in increasingly complex sequences.
- Multischeme combinations involving more than one theme (the content of the play) are seen in the play of older toddlers and preschoolers.
- Pretend play illustrates the child's growing ability to use symbolic representation, the ability lacking in the infant.

KEY TERMS

concept
sensorimotor period
imitation
pseudoimitation
deferred imitation

object permanence
perseveration error
hidden or invisible
   displacement
representational thinking

pretense
symbolic representation
sociodramatic play
decentration
decontextualization

integration of play
single-scheme
   combination
multischeme combination
theme

SUGGESTIONS FOR FURTHER READING

Gottfried, A. W., & Brown, C. C. (Eds.) (1986). *Play interactions: The contribution of play materials and parental involvement to children's development.* Salisbury, NC: Lexington Press.

Includes chapters on mother-child interaction, affect and play, and the roles of physical and social environments. This book will interest the student who is serious about understanding play.

Piaget, J. (1952). *The origins of intelligence in children.* (Margaret Cook, Trans.) New York: International Universities Press.

The original Piagetian discussion of sensorimotor intelligence. Slow reading for those who aren't accustomed to reading Piaget.

Rubin, K. H., Fein, G. G., & Vandenberg, B. (1983). *Play.* In P. H. Mussen (Ed.), *Handbook of child psychology.* (Vol. 4, 4th ed.). New York: Wiley.

This chapter provides a thorough review of children's play.

Sawyers, J. K., & Rogers, C. S. (1988). *Helping young children develop through play.* Washington, DC: National Association for the Education of Young Children.

A very practical book written to help caregivers provide for children's play.

c h a p t e r 7

LANGUAGE DEVELOPMENT IN INFANTS AND TODDLERS

"Dat?" Morgan asks, as she points up to the sky.

"That's an airplane," her father tells her. "It's making a loud noise, isn't it?"

"'Pane? 'Pane?" Morgan says, as she continues to follow the airplane with her eyes.

"Yes, that's an airplane. It's a very noisy one, isn't it?"

"Vroom, vroom," Morgan answers back.

"That's right. The plane is going 'vroom, vroom,' like a car . . . like you do when you play with your cars."

"'Pane . . . vroom . . . vroom."

"Uh-huh. The plane is going vroom, vroom, just like your cars."

Morgan, who is 17 months old, is just beginning to talk. She can say a few recognizable words, and she can vary her intonation to indicate if she is asking a question or making a statement. Quite recently, she has begun to join two or three words to form a very primitive sentence: "Pane . . . vroom . . . vroom." Morgan's father is used to hearing her talk and can interpret what she says. Their shared history also helps him understand what Morgan means when she says something like "vroom, vroom." He knows that she makes this sound in a very loud voice when she plays with her toy cars and that after he mentioned the airplane's noise, Morgan was trying to tell him that the plane's noise reminded her of the car noise.

Learning to talk is one of children's most remarkable accomplishments during the first few years of life. Newborn babies are able to communicate by crying and gazing, but they can't use words. But 12 months later, a word or two spills out of the mouth of almost every baby. Just a year after that, at the age of 2, most toddlers are using rudimentary sentences. This chapter discusses infants' and toddlers' language development milestones—the different ways they understand and produce speech before they can do either one exactly the way adults do. This discussion is rounded out with an examination of several explanations, or theories, of language development.

MILESTONES IN LANGUAGE PRODUCTION

There are two sides to children's language behavior: **productive speech,** or the speech they produce, and **receptive speech,** or the speech they understand. We'll take each side in turn, starting with language production, as we describe language behavior from birth up to about 2½ years of age.

Vocal Behavior during the First Year

Vocal behavior during the first year of life is called **prelinguistic** because it contains no actual words. The relationship between this early speech and later speech is still not known. It includes crying and cooing, babbling, and intonation variations.

CRYING AND COOING. The first vocalization is uttered at birth when the infant cries. Other, noncrying, vocalizations appear soon after birth. They seem to emerge at first out of "fake crying"—the type of crying that parents commonly call "fussing." This cry is not the high-pitched, screeching sort of cry that babies use when they're terribly mad, hungry, or in pain. It's lower in pitch

FIGURE 7-1
At 4 months of age, this baby pleases both herself and her mother with her cooing, open vocalizations. The mother's enjoyment encourages the baby to say more.

FIGURE 7-2

During the second half of the first year, babies practice both vowel and consonant speech sounds by babbling, often accompanying their speech with gestures. This 8-month-old is also learning that what he says is of great interest to the important people in his life.

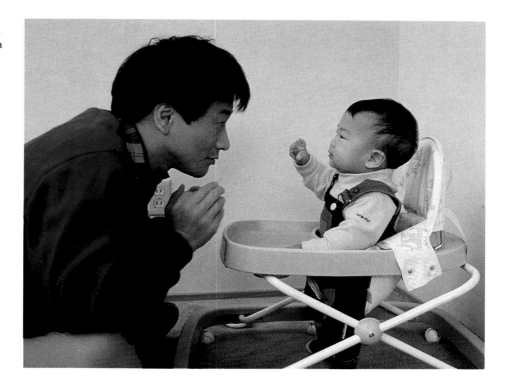

and quieter, with more drawn-out, moaning sounds (Wolff, 1969). Once the baby makes these sounds accidentally while fussing, he apparently reproduces the individual sounds in the circular pattern described in the discussion of Piaget's primary circular reactions in Chapter 6.

This first type of noncrying vocalization is called *cooing*. Initially, coos consist mostly of "open" sounds, or vowels (Cruttenden, 1970; Menyuk, 1977), such as "aaaah" and "oooooo." The few consonantlike sounds that appear in early cooing are produced primarily by stopping air with the very back of the throat (/k/ as in *k*ite; /g/ as in *g*oat) or with the lips (/w/, /p/) (Cruttenden, 1970).

BABBLING AND INTONATION PATTERNS. By 4 or 5 months of age, infants begin to include a larger number of both vowel and consonant sounds in their cooings. Then at 8 months of age, they begin to combine these sounds into consonant-vowel strings such as "mamamama" or "dadadadada." Vocal behavior consisting of this type of syllable combination is called **babbling.** For several months, infants produce long strings of babble. Then, at about 10 or 12 months of age—about the time that most infants say their first real word—they shorten their babbles to one or two repetitions of the syllable. For example, the infant says "da-da" rather than "dadadada" (Menyuk, 1977). These word-like forms are sometimes called **protowords** (Kamhi, 1986).

Infants also begin to vary the intonation of their vocalizations during the second half of their first year. For example, they sometimes babble with a raised or lowered pitch. These intonation patterns correspond to the signals older children and adults use for asking a question versus making a statement. Variations in intonation increase during the infant's second year (Bruner, 1975a; Tonkova-Yampolskaya, 1969, cited in Rosenblith & Sims-Knight, 1985). Pointing, accompanied by a babble with a questioning intonation is a fairly common behavior in children 10 to 14 months old (Lemish & Rice, 1986).

FIGURE 7-3
A baby says her first word at about 12 months, often to name some familiar object in the environment. This mother has probably supported her daughter's language development by pointing to pictures in books and talking about them. Now her daughter is beginning to do the same thing.

RESEARCH FOCUS

Children's First Words

Christina loved the cheese her mother often gave her for lunch. Her first word was "cheese," although she didn't say it very clearly. Sometimes she would say "cheese" as soon as she was put in her high chair for meals. Other times she would go to the refrigerator door and say, "cheese, cheese."

When Tod started talking, his first word was "light." He usually said it when a light was turned on in the room. "Water" was Nicholas's first word. During the hot summer when he was 11 months old, Nicholas often visited his grandmother, who watered her garden with a hose. He "helped" with this chore and played with the hose for hours on end, filling and refilling buckets and pans with water. When he was inside the house, Nicholas often went to the door, reached for the doorknob, and said, "Water, water."

What do Christina's, Tod's, and Nicholas's first words have in common? A study conducted by Katherine Nelson (1973), a language researcher, may provide an answer to this question. She recorded the first words used by 18 children between 1 and 2 years of age and found they could be categorized into five groups:

1. Nominals (nouns), or words used to refer to things. Subgroups within this category include specific nominals (proper nouns)—words used to refer to one example of a category ("Mommy," "Spot")—and general nominals (common nouns)—words used to refer to all members of a category ("doggie," "key," "milk").
2. Action words, or words that describe, demand, or convey action or that express or demand attention ("bye-bye," "up," "hi").
3. Modifiers, or words that refer to properties or qualities of things or events ("pretty," "hot," "all gone," "more").
4. Personal-social words, or words expressing affec-

tive states or social relationships ("please," "ouch," "want," "thank you").
5. Grammatical function words ("what," "where," "is," "for").

Nelson found that for the 18 children she studied, more than half of their first 50 words were general nominals. And, of these, most were names of things that the children acted on in some way. Nelson suggests that children ignore things that simply exist, such as tables, carpets, grass, and sidewalks. They notice and learn the names of things that do something or that they do something to. Christina's "cheese," Tod's "light," and Nicholas's "water" are consistent with this idea—they can all be acted on.

Why should action matter? It may be because action produces change, change produces novelty, and novelty—the discrepancy between what a child already knows and what actually happens—catches the child's attention. When a baby hears the sound of the cuckoo clock, she may stop what she's doing to look at it. Her mother or father may follow her gaze and say, "Clock? Did you hear the clock? Do you see the clock?" The baby hears the name for the object that's attracted her attention and learns to associate the object with the name.

Parents do seem to follow their baby's line of regard—the direction the baby is looking—from as early as the baby's fourth month (Scaife & Bruner, 1975). This tendency helps ensure that parents and baby are paying attention to the same thing and that the baby associates the names with the appropriate object. It also explains why children's first words are so often the names of things that act or can be acted on: These are the things that catch children's attention.

Vocal Behavior during the Second Year

Morgan's speech is well beyond the babbling stage. Children start to use specific utterances to refer to objects and express intentions soon after their first birthday. At this point, speech is used meaningfully and is considered to be linguistic rather than prelinguistic.

FIRST WORDS. Babies usually say their first real word at about 12 months of age (Huttenlocher et al., 1991). First words often approximate adult sound patterns, as when "boo" is used to refer to boots and "ku" is used to refer to cookies. But sometimes, children use a totally different sound sequence from the one used by adults to refer to an object or action, such as "ga-ga" to refer to a blanket (Winitz & Irwin, 1958; Carter, 1975). It's not the child's use of a conventional sound sequence that defines an utterance as a word; it's the child's consistent use of a particular sound sequence to refer to a specific object or action. If a child always calls his blanket "ga-ga," then he is using "ga-ga" as a real word (see Research Focus—Children's First Words).

As young children learn words, they often use them differently than adults do. Sometimes they **underextend** the meaning of a word, not using it as broadly as an adult might. At other times they **overextend** the meaning of a word, using it more broadly than is common. For example, a child might use the word *shoes* only to refer to mommy's shoes because it was in this context that she first learned the word. In this case, she's underextended the word's meaning. Or a child might call a horse a dog, because it has four legs and hair like a dog. In this case, the child has overextended the word's meaning. Much of what occurs in language learning during the early years involves expanding and contracting the meaning of known words to make them more accurate with respect to their actual meanings. Considerable growth in this area probably depends on increased skill in children's ability to differentiate things that are closely related. Children appear first to form global ideas or categories of things (or schemes, in Piagetian terminology). For example, they consider dogs and horses as more similar than dogs and birds, and cars and motorcycles as more similar than cars and airplanes (Mandler, Bauer & McDonough, 1991). It's not surprising then that they sometimes refer to horses as "doggies" or call motorcycles "cars." At about 2½ years of age, children begin to make finer contrasts between similar items (Mandler, Bauer & McDonough, 1991), and at this point overextensions usually begin to diminish.

LANGUAGE PRACTICE. The appearance of words doesn't mean that a baby stops babbling. Word development and babbling interact with each other in early language behavior. Researchers have even suggested that children produce two kinds of speech during the first-words period: meaningful speech using "real" words and babbling speech using a combination of meaningful words

FIGURE 7-4
Because his dad reads to him, this baby will babble using two different intonations. Some of his babbling will sound like conversation, and some will sound like a person reading a book.

and nonmeaningful sounds. Children use the meaningful speech to talk to people. They use the babbling speech to practice speech sounds and words that will soon show up in their "talking" speech (Elbers & Ton, 1985).

Soon after the first-words stage, at about 14 to 18 months, another kind of practice appears as well. This type of practice involves the intonation patterns of sentences, also known as the **suprasegmental features of language.** (*Suprasegmental* literally means "above the parts" and refers to the overall sound pattern of language.) The child is now practicing the sound of people talking in her language. The content of her sentences is nonsense; she's using babble, not words. Still, this **expressive jargon**, as it's called, sounds remarkably like "real" talk because it captures the overall rhythm and flow of actual speech.

Two kinds of expressive jargon can be distinguished among infants whom adults have talked with and read to: **conversational babble** and **book babble**. Each kind appears in the appropriate social context. When the child is "talking" to herself, with another person, or with a doll or stuffed animal, she uses conversational babble. But when she's "reading" a book, she uses book babble, which has unique suprasegmental features (Schickedanz, 1986).

HOLOPHRASES. Once infants or toddlers can vary intonation, they can express several different intentions even though they can utter only a word or two. For example, if a baby says "milk" with a rising intonation, she might mean "Is that milk?" or "Can I have milk?" A falling intonation might mean "That is milk," or "Give me some milk." A single word that expresses a more complex thought or sentence is called a **holophrase**.

A fairly common holophrase in 14- to 18-month-olds is "Dat?", which Morgan used when she spotted the airplane in the sky. This holophrase, meaning "What is that?" often appears suddenly after the child gains the insight that things have names. The child typically points to an object when uttering "Dat?" Given a willing adult partner, this naming game can go on for quite a long time and often results in rapid acquisition of words (Nelson, 1973; Kamhi, 1986).

The use of holophrases depends very much on adult partners who can interpret what the baby means. We saw that Morgan's father paid close attention to both the immediate situation and Morgan's intonation. He also referred to his knowledge of her past use of sounds and language.

MULTIWORD UTTERANCES: TODDLERS' TELEGRAPHIC SPEECH. Children usually begin to combine words into primitive sentences when they are between 18 and 24 months of age. They begin to say things such as "Doll cry," "Jamie go," "Daddy car," "No eat," or "Mommy up." Although the number of words they include in their sentences is limited, toddlers can communicate quite a few meanings and relationships with these two- and three-word utterances. For example, they can indicate where something is, who it belongs to, what someone is doing, and what they want or don't want to do (Schlesinger, 1974; Bloom, Lightbown & Hood, 1975). These and other meanings expressed by toddlers in the two-word stage are given in Table 7-1.

Despite the fairly extensive variety of relations that children can express with their two- and three-word utterances, these utterances still are not completely formed. When adults interpret what a toddler says, they often need to "read" the extralinguistic context—the situation "outside" or "beyond" the

TABLE 7-1   Meanings Expressed by Toddlers in the Two-Word Stage

CATEGORY OF MEANING	EXAMPLE
Identification	That plane See man
Location	Kitty here Bottle [on] chair
Recurrence	More juice Tickle again
Nonexistence	Nomore cookie Milk allgone
Negation	No bed
Possession	Sarah book
Agent, action, object	Mommy throw Throw ball
Attribution	Big clown Go truck
Question	Where bottle? What that?

Adapted from A first language, *R. Brown, 1973, Cambridge: Harvard University Press.*

FIGURE 7-5
The "telegraphic" speech of 2-year-olds can often be understood only in context. This dad may have to interpret his daughter's utterances by relying on the extralinguistic context and on his knowledge of his child.

language—to know exactly what the toddler means. The burden of determining what the child means is considerably less during this stage than it is during the prelinguistic and holophrase stages of language development, when children use either no actual words or only one at a time. When language is confined to just one word, as many as 50 percent of the children's communications are unclear to mothers (Golinkoff, 1986). Toddler talk, with its two- and three-word constructions, is easier to understand, but statements still can't stand on their own without cues from the situation.

Toddlers' speech has been called **telegraphic**, because children this age omit words that are not essential to their meaning. Toddlers change an adult sentence like "Mommy is going to the grocery store" to "Mommy go store." Adults do this when they send a telegram and have to pay for every word. The person who receives the telegram has to fill in the missing words to understand the message. When toddlers talk in their two- and three-word sentences, adults have to interpret their "telegrams." Parents often repeat the toddler's utterance and add words that are missing—responses known as expansions (Brown & Fraser, 1964). If a toddler says, "Mommy milk?" the mother might say, "Is this mommy's milk? Yes, it's mommy's milk." Adults respond in other ways too, and we discuss these later in this chapter.

MILESTONES IN LANGUAGE PERCEPTION

The other side of children's language behavior is the receptive side, the speech the baby perceives or understands. When do babies recognize the sound of human speech? When do they start to understand?

Speech Perception

PERCEPTION OF SPEECH SOUNDS AND INTONATIONS. Infants hear all kinds of sounds, not just the sound of speech; there's the hum of the air conditioner, the patter of rain, the creaking of the crib. But the human voice has special significance for the baby, especially when it is cast in the high-pitch register known as "motherese." For example, in one study, infants only 2 days old were found to prefer infant-directed (motherese) versus adult-directed speech (Cooper & Aslin, 1990).

Very young babies can also discriminate between various speech sounds, as indicated by habituation studies. Infants as young as 1 month old can differentiate the voiced and voiceless stop consonants /b/ and /p/ (Eimas et al., 1971; Eimas, 1974). They can also tell the difference between /d/ and /t/ and between /b/ and /g/ (Moffit, 1971; Trehub & Rabinovitch, 1972), and they differentiate pairs of vowels, whether they are presented in combination with consonants (/pa/, /pi/) or as vowels alone (/a/, /i/) (Trehub, 1973).

The fact that infants can hear differences between speech sounds at such an early age suggests that this language ability is innate. However, young infants can't detect all contrasts in sounds (Eilers, Wilson & Moore, 1977), and the ones they can detect may be influenced by their language experiences, such as the native language to which they're being exposed (Streeter, 1976). So, we really can't say for certain how much language ability is innate and how much is a result of experience on the basis of early ability to perceive speech sounds.

Infants also perceive or understand the suprasegmental features of language—the intonations—when they hear others talk. Infants as young as 8 months of age can differentiate between rising and falling intonation patterns, that is, between statements and questions (Kaplan & Kaplan, 1970). Infants as young as 6 months of age can also recognize melody contours across different frequency ranges—the equivalent of recognizing the same song sung in different keys (Trehub, Bull & Thorpe, 1984). Furthermore, 7-month-old infants can categorize sounds based on timbre, the quality of sound that allows us to differentiate a trumpet from a clarinet, for example, or a male voice from a female voice (Trehub, Endman & Thorpe, 1990).

Since babies recognize different sounds and intonations from an early age, it's not surprising that they recognize and respond to "baby talk" (often abbreviated BT), or motherese. Motherese involves speaking in a higher pitch than is typical in adult-to-adult speech, varying intonation more, and using shorter sentences. For example, a mother inquiring about her child's apparent distress might ask, "Does your tummy hurt?" rather than, "Do you have abdominal pain?" Similarly, a mother would probably say, "That's Mommy's," rather than "That's mine," so the child wouldn't have to figure out the referent of the pronoun "mine" (Mann & Boyce, 1982).

Many studies have confirmed the existence of baby talk and have demonstrated that babies not only can distinguish it from adult talk but also prefer to listen to it. When given the opportunity to choose between a tape of baby talk and a tape of adult talk by turning their heads to one side or the other, they choose to listen to baby talk (Fernald, 1985). One reason for this preference may be the exaggerated pitch variation characteristic of motherese.

LANGUAGE COMPREHENSION. Babies' and toddlers' language comprehension is typically more advanced and varied than their language production. They understand quite a few words when they can say only two or three (Goldin-Meadow, Seligman & Gelman, 1976). And they understand multiword utterances when their own productive language is at the holophrase stage. In one study, children who could produce only one-word utterances could respond to such requests as "Kiss Teddy," "Throw ball," and "Smell truck" (Sachs & Truswell, 1978).

In everyday situations, there are many multiword utterances that children in the holophrase stage seem to understand ("Wave bye-bye to grandma," "Give the book to mommy"). But the child receives many clues to their meaning from the context in which the sentences are said—grandma getting in her car and waving, mommy holding out her hand toward the book. It's doubtful that children would understand the meaning of all that's said to them in the absence of this contextual support.

SOCIAL ASPECTS OF LANGUAGE DEVELOPMENT: LEARNING TO BE A CONVERSATIONAL PARTNER

Language acquisition isn't just a matter of learning how to speak and understand words and sentences. Language is fundamentally a social activity, and learning how to hold a conversation is part of learning how to talk. There are rules, commonly accepted ways of interacting, that we follow when we carry

FIGURE 7-6
Toddlers understand much more than they themselves can say. This boy may be absorbing quite a lot about slider turtles from his dad, but he wouldn't yet be able to tell someone else what he learns about them. Perhaps the more important lesson for him right now is that language can be used to convey interesting information about the world.

on a conversation with someone else. For example, we use strategies for getting a conversation going and for taking turns. We also have ways of maintaining the topic of conversation and of signaling that we're changing the topic.

Between about 2 and 2½ years, toddlers begin to use specific strategies for opening conversations: (1) They talk about what their listener is doing, ask a question, or give a command; (2) they get the listener's attention by looking at him or her; (3) they stand relatively close to the listener; and (4) they use attention-getting gestures and verbalizations, such as "Hey!" or "Guess what?" (Mueller et al., 1977).

These strategies are remarkably similar to the approaches mothers take in communicating with their infants, beginning late in the first year. When they want to interact, for example, mothers first follow their infants' gaze to see what they are looking at. Then they provide labels for the object and comment about it (Collis & Schaffer, 1975; Collis, 1977). When babies are about 9 months old, mothers begin to point to call their babies' attention to things they're talking about (Murphy & Messer, 1977). At first, babies aren't very skillful at following their mothers' pointing, and mothers often try to bring objects closer to the child if they can. Mothers work hard to establish joint reference or joint attention with their babies when they want to communicate with them.

Book-reading routines provide an ideal situation for mothers and babies to practice establishing joint attention. One mother attracted her baby's attention with such verbalizations as "Look!" followed by a question like "What is that?" (Ninio & Bruner, 1978). The mother answered her own questions at first, because the baby wasn't yet able to talk. But as soon as the baby could talk, the mother paused and allowed the baby to respond.

By the time they're toddlers, children already have a long history of verbal interaction in which they've seen and practiced different kinds of attention-getting devices. Given mothers' typical strategies, it's no wonder that toddlers attempt to open conversations by such tactics as standing close, commenting on what the listener is doing, and saying "Hey!" and "Guess what?"

Once toddlers have someone's attention, they have to pursue the conversation, and this is harder to do. They know how to take turns, in the sense that they can avoid interruptions and simultaneous starts, but they don't know how to take the lead in maintaining a dialogue. What they say during their turn doesn't push the conversation forward. They respond to questions and comments, but they don't ask questions or link their comments to their partner's previous remarks (Kaye & Charney, 1980; Kaye, 1982b). It's the adult who takes this responsibility, leading the dialogue and making longer conversations possible.

THEORIES OF LANGUAGE DEVELOPMENT

We've seen quite a lot so far about what babies and toddlers can say and understand. But how is it that they learn language at all? Do human beings have an innate ability to understand the symbols and representations of the world contained in language? Are they born with the power to express themselves in words and sentences? Or do they simply learn "language behavior" from their parents the same way they learn to eat with a spoon or put on their socks? Like theories of other aspects of child development, theories of language development vary in the emphasis they place on internal versus external factors—the nature-nurture controversy. Learning theories claim that language is learned primarily from contact with the environment. Nativist theories claim that language comes primarily from within. We turn now to a closer look at the major theories of language development and the evidence that supports or undermines each one.

Learning Theory

Learning theory explains language development exclusively in terms of environmental factors. Following the lead of B. F. Skinner, learning theorists claim that children gradually learn how to speak and understand their language because they're reinforced for doing so.

Some aspects of language learning are obviously influenced by the environment. The language we learn as our mother tongue, for example, is the one we hear around us in our environment. Human beings don't have an innate language the way animals do—different species of birds, for example, sing different, genetically determined songs regardless of where they live (although even birds' songs are partially learned, it now seems). But what interests theorists is the very ability to learn a language—any language. They disagree about the extent to which humans have a specific neurological make-up that facilitates language learning. Learning theorists give less importance to these internal characteristics than they do to external factors when they explain language development.

The major learning mechanisms proposed by learning theorists are imitation, reinforcement, and punishment. They suggest that children learn to speak by imitating what they hear and repeating it in appropriate situations. When they do this, adults lavish praise and attention on them, which increases the likelihood that they'll do it again. When they use language incorrectly, adults' responses are not so reinforcing.

This explanation doesn't account for some things that actually happen in language development, however. Children generate words and sentences that adults never model for them. They say "mouses" instead of "mice," for example, and "What it is?" instead of "What is it?" These creative constructions can't be explained by direct imitation or other behaviorist mechanisms. To generate words and sentences never before uttered in their presence, children seem to induce grammatical rules from things they *have* heard. Learning theory doesn't have a way of explaining such inductive learning.

The other learning theory mechanisms of reinforcement and punishment don't seem to play a great part in language development either. Most parents don't explicitly approve correct pronunciation and grammar or disapprove incorrect forms. They look past the form to focus on what the child is trying to communicate. Grammatical errors are ignored, but errors of fact are pointed out as shown in the following example (Brown, Cazden, & Bellugi, 1969, pp. 57–58):

> In general, the parents fit propositions to the child's utterances, and then approve or not, according to the correspondence between propositions and reality. Thus "Her curl my hair" was approved because mother was, in fact, curling Eve's hair. However, Sarah's grammatically impeccable "There's the animal farmhouse" was disapproved because the building was a lighthouse, and Adam's "Walt Disney comes on, on Tuesday" was disapproved because Walt Disney comes on, on some other day.

More recent research has demonstrated that parents do provide some feedback to their children about how well they're speaking, and we discuss this research later in the chapter. Although these studies are offering some support for the learning theory position, it still appears to be inadequate as a complete explanation for language development.

Nativist Theory

Nativist theory stands at the opposite end of the nature-nurture continuum from learning theory. To a nativist, language development depends not on what is in the environment but on what is in the child. In this view, the child is endowed with an innate language acquisition device (LAD). This is a metaphor for a specific neurological structure that enables children to derive a grammar from the language they hear (McNeill, 1966).

Noam Chomsky launched this view of language development when he sharply criticized the learning theory views about language learning (Chomsky, 1959; 1965). Chomsky and other nativists made the observations just mentioned—that imitation doesn't explain children's creative utterances and that

FIGURE 7-7
According to Noam Chomsky, the human language faculty is a specific innate endowment, a "mental organ," that "grows" in the mind once it has been triggered by experience. Children are born knowing how to construct grammar, Chomsky claims, just as birds are born knowing how to fly. What they learn from experience is the specific language that will be their mother tongue. Chomsky's nativist view is diametrically opposed to the learning theory view, which asserts that children acquire language the same way they learn other behaviors, mainly through imitation and reinforcement.

parents don't explicitly approve or disapprove children's grammar. They also argued that the way parents provide language to children doesn't fulfill the behaviorist requirements for learning, which are simplicity and step-by-step sequencing of information. And parents often use less-than-perfect grammar themselves when talking to their children. Chomsky felt it was unlikely that children could learn a grammar according to behaviorist mechanisms, given the "sloppy" nature of parents' input. Therefore, he argued, children's knowledge of grammar must be innate, part of their species-specific endowment.

Support for the nativist view comes from information about the universal nature and orderly progression of language development in every culture (Slobin, 1982). No matter what the specific language, development follows certain paths and language forms appear in the same sequential order in virtually all children. In every different environment, children acquire a grammar for their mother tongue. These facts suggest that language ability is due to something within the child rather than something about the environment. Challenges to the strong nativist view of Chomsky and others have come from various sources. Following is a brief discussion of three of these theoretical challenges.

Challenges to a Strong Nativist Theory

THE COGNITIVE UNDERPINNINGS VIEW. Some cognitive theorists have questioned the notion of a special language acquisition device to account for language development. They believe that the basic cognitive schemes constructed during the sensorimotor period can provide the basis for language. They suggest that children's sensorimotor knowledge of ordered relations, such as the relationship between agent, object, and action, provides the basis for understanding grammar (Bruner, 1975a). Thus, according to this view, acting on the world during the first two years gives children a grasp of such grammatical propositions as "I shake the rattle" or "She rolls the ball." Because this view considers both maturation and experience vital to the acquisition of language, it falls somewhere in the middle of our theory continuum.

Critics of this view point out that even if these cognitive understandings are present, the exact expression of them varies from one language to another. The same meaning is coded by different sequences of subjects, objects, and verbs in different languages (Slobin, 1982). Even though cognitive development might provide the necessary basis for language learning, it appears that something additional is required for language-specific learning to occur.

THE CASE OF MOTHERESE. Another challenge to the strong nativist view has come from research on motherese. Contrary to what Chomsky and others thought, research has shown that motherese is not sloppy or ill formed. Rather, it consists of short, grammatically well-formed utterances, cast in a high pitch (Furrow & Nelson, 1986). Mothers seem to "fine-tune" their responses to their infants' utterances, making their input match the infant's current linguistic status (Rondal, 1985).

This simplified register may serve a teaching function (Kemler-Nelson et al., 1989), and the baby's experience of conversational give-and-take in motherese may play an important role in language development (Ginsberg & Kilbourne, 1988). In one recent study motherese was found to be especially prevalent in

FIGURE 7-8
Mothers often exaggerate their expressions when they use motherese with their babies. Although the role of motherese in teaching language isn't clear, the preference of babies for its sound is well documented.

the second half of the baby's first year, and the extent of motherese used at 9 months correlated with the extent of receptive language development at 18 months. The use of motherese was a better predictor of receptive language development at 18 months than either the baby's expressive communicative skills at 9 months or the general responsiveness and stimulation in the home (Murray, Johnson & Peters, 1990).

Although this research supports the claim that motherese plays a role in language development, it is not clear just what that role is. It may serve a communicative function but not a direct teaching function. In other words, motherese may get the baby's attention and permit more of the mother's message to be understood (Newport, Gleitman & Gleitman, 1977; Fernald, 1984) without teaching the baby anything about grammar. Knowledge of grammatical relations may still be due to innate predispositions (Wexler, 1982).

IMPLICIT FEEDBACK. A third challenge to a strong nativist view has come from research on the feedback that parents give their children about their speech. A major study that documented the absence of parents' disapproval for poor grammar (Brown & Hanlon, 1970) has recently been challenged by new research. This research has found that although parents don't provide explicit approval or disapproval of children's grammar, their implicit responses do vary, depending on whether the child's statement contains grammatical errors

FIGURE 7-9
It appears that language is acquired as a result of interactions between innate capabilities and environmental input. The children in this family hear language used all around them every day, and so they learn to use it too. But if they didn't have the inborn ability to acquire language, no amount of environmental support would elicit it from them.

(Demetras, Post & Snow, 1986). When a child's statement is grammatically correct, for example, parents tend to move on to another topic or statement. When a child's statement contains a grammatical error, parents frequently ask a clarifying question and repeat the child's statement with some modifications. Parents' responses thus often contain implicit feedback about grammar.

Critics point out that this negative feedback isn't consistent or specific and that it's hard to see how a child could learn from such vague and erratic responses. But other researchers have suggested that mothers may implicitly correct only those language structures they perceive the child to be mastering at that particular time. They may ignore more complicated errors until later in the child's development (Demetras, Post & Snow, 1986).

These three theoretical challenges have undermined the strong nativist view of language learning. There is currently a renewed interest in taking a closer look at how "input" factors affect language learning (Akhtar, Dunham & Dunham, 1991; Huttenlocher et al., 1991). According to some language theorists, the field is shifting away from extremes, "with nativist theories leaving room for learning, and nonnativistic theories leaving room for initial biases in the system. . . . The 1990s may herald a welcome shift toward noting the testable points of agreement in theories of acquisition, allowing a larger perspective in which different theories all explain a piece of the puzzle" (Golinkoff & Hirsh-

Pacek, 1990, pp. 82–84). Thus the direction in language theory parallels the current trend in child development theory as a whole that we discussed in Chapter 2: A move away from simple, either-or theories, to a systems approach, which accounts for complex interactions. As Golinkoff and Hirsh-Pacek (1990, p. 83) point out, "when young children hear an utterance, they are at one and the same time in a cognitive world that can be analyzed into causal components, in a social world where language is used to request action or share information, and in a linguistic world of subjects, predicates, nouns. . . ." The theoretical task is to understand how these many worlds combine with each infant's own world to produce a child who is a skilled language user.

OVERVIEW

Spoken language, that uniquely human achievement, emerges over the course of the first few years of life. Babies listen, attend to certain noises, show preferences for certain tones, and soon begin to produce the sounds of their native tongue. By the second half of their first year, they're babbling in the rising and falling intonations of questions and statements, and by the end of that year, they're forming words. A year later they're putting words together into sentences and beginning to initiate conversations. How do they do it? Is it a matter of learning to imitate the sounds they hear other human beings make and being rewarded for it? Or do they have a genetically inherited ability to derive grammar from the speech they hear, an ability that emerges according to a developmental timetable? Research hasn't yet provided a clear answer to this question, but what remains clear is that learning to talk—the linguistic hallmark of the infant-toddler period—is a formidable accomplishment.

CHAPTER REVIEW

MILESTONES IN LANGUAGE PRODUCTION

- Children's productive language behavior is the speech they produce. Their receptive language behavior is the speech they understand.
- Babies' vocalizations during the first year are called prelinguistic because they typically don't contain any words. Crying and cooing are forms of prelinguistic language.
- Babbling, a type of vocalization consisting of vowel-consonant strings, emerges at about 4 or 5 months. By about 10 or 12 months, babies shorten their babbling to one or two syllables that begin to sound like real words, called protowords. They also vary their intonation patterns, so their babbling resembles the inflections used in their language.
- Most babies say their first real word at about 12 months, and their speech is now considered linguistic.

- Young children often use words differently than adults do, underextending the meanings to refer to too few cases or overextending them to refer to too many cases. Their understanding and use of words change as they progress to new cognitive levels.
- Babies continue to babble after they can say words, perhaps using the real words to communicate and the babble to practice sounds.
- Between about 14 and 18 months, children practice the intonation patterns of sentences in their language, known as the suprasegmental features of speech. Babies who have been read to and talked to produce two kinds of this expressive jargon—conversational babble and book babble.
- Once children can vary intonations, they can use holophrases, which are single words that represent more

complex thoughts or sentences. Children using holophrases need an adult who can interpret their meaning.

• Between 18 and 24 months, children begin to combine words into primitive sentences. Toddlers' speech is referred to as telegraphic, because they leave out words that aren't crucial to their message. Adults have to interpret their statements, often by repeating them and filling in the missing words. Adults' responses to both holophrases and telegraphic speech aid in the child's language development.

MILESTONES IN LANGUAGE PERCEPTION

• Infants can perceive the difference between human speech and other sounds very early in life, but it's difficult to determine how much language ability is innate and how much is learned. Infants can also distinguish intonations when people talk.

• Babies' ability to recognize speech and intonation probably makes them receptive to the higher-pitched, lilting tones of motherese, or baby talk, a "dialect" that they seem to prefer.

• Babies and toddlers comprehend more language than they are able to speak. Their comprehension is assisted by context clues.

SOCIAL ASPECTS OF LANGUAGE DEVELOPMENT

• Toddlers use strategies for opening conversations that resemble mothers' approaches to communicating with their children. Mothers typically establish a common object of attention and then label the object. Toddlers stand close, comment on what the listener is doing, and say "Hey!" or "Guess what?"

• Toddlers aren't very skilled at the complex give-and-take necessary to carry on long conversations, and adults have to take the lead in dialogues.

THEORIES OF LANGUAGE DEVELOPMENT

• Learning theorists believe that babies acquire language through the learning mechanisms of imitation, reinforcement, and punishment. This theory doesn't account for certain grammatical errors children make that they've never heard modeled. Furthermore, most parents don't reinforce correct grammar; instead, they respond to the truth value of their children's utterances.

• Nativists believe that human beings are born with a specific neurological structure, or language acquisition device (LAD), that enables them to learn language. Championed by Noam Chomsky, this theory is supported by the universal nature of language development in every culture.

• One challenge to the strong nativist view comes from cognitive theorists who claim that the basic schemes constructed during the sensorimotor period provide the basis for language and that the notion of a special neurological device is unnecessary. They believe that once babies have knowledge about agents, objects, and actions, they can translate this knowledge into an understanding of grammatical forms like the sentence. This theory doesn't explain how children learn to express these understandings in the specific grammar of their native language.

• Another challenge to the strong nativist view comes from those who point to motherese as a way mothers teach babies language. However, the role of motherese in language development remains unclear.

• A third challenge to the strong nativist view comes from recent studies of parents' feedback to their children about their speech. Although parents don't explicitly correct their children's grammar, they do provide implicit feedback by "moving on" when grammar is correct and repeating or asking clarifying questions when grammar is incorrect. Children can be seen as learning language through these parental reinforcements.

• The complete explanation for language acquisition probably lies somewhere in the middle of the learning theory-nativist continuum, and complex systems theories will be needed to explain it.

KEY TERMS

productive speech
receptive speech
prelinguistic
babbling

protowords
underextend
overextend

suprasegmental features
 of language
expressive jargon

conversational babble
book babble
holophrase
telegraphic speech

SUGGESTIONS FOR FURTHER READING

Brown, R. (1973). *A first language.* Cambridge, MA: Harvard University Press.
 A classic work. Essential reading for all students who are seriously interested in learning about children's early language behavior. The book is technical but very understandable, even to those with minimal background in the subject.

Lee, D. (1986). *Language, children and society: An introduction to linguistics and language development.* New York: New York University Press.
 This is a book for the beginner, as its title implies. Of particular interest is the chapter on meaning, which focuses on how children learn language through social interaction with adults.

Lindfors, J. W. (1987). *Children's language and learning.* (2d ed.). Englewood Cliffs, NJ: Prentice-Hall.
 A comprehensive overview of language development at a beginning level. Language acquisition theories, as well as the details of language behavior during infancy and toddlerhood, are discussed.

Reilly, A. P., & Stark, R. E. (Eds.). (1980). The communication game. In *Pediatric Round Table: 4.* New York: Johnson & Johnson.
 Written for parents and practitioners in the medical and child care fields, this small book discusses normal language development as well as screening for language difficulties. Includes many short pieces contributed by researchers well known in their fields.

SOCIAL AND EMOTIONAL DEVELOPMENT IN INFANTS AND TODDLERS

It's the first day of play group! Excitement and confusion fill the brightly colored room as parents and 2-year-olds explore activities. Wooden puzzles dot the tabletops in one corner, and two boys head for them eagerly. Dumping the pieces out on the table makes a loud "ker-plop!" Then comes the hard part—putting the puzzles back together. After a few tries, Juan turns to his mom, who is sitting nearby watching him, and says, "Where this goes?" "Try it here," she suggests, pointing to an empty spot. He smiles as the piece slips in.

Daniel is also trying to reassemble his puzzle. He tries to force a piece into a spot, then throws it down and tries another, then a third. His mom picks up the first piece, hands it to Daniel, and says, "This will work. All you have to do is turn it around." But Daniel shouts, "No!" and pushes her hand out of the way. He selects a different piece and tests it in the same unyielding spot.

In a few minutes, Juan has his puzzle back together. He sits back to admire it, saying, "All done! I do again!" But Daniel has abandoned his puzzle, leaving the empty frame on the table and the pieces on the floor. He's in the block corner now, and his mother calls to him, "Daniel, come here! You're going to have to finish this puzzle. I'm not going to pick up this mess for you!" But Daniel doesn't look at her or answer; he keeps playing with the blocks.

By the end of the morning, Juan is tired and happy. He leaves hand in hand with his mother, chattering about the morning. But Daniel has worked himself into an angry frenzy. He darts out of the room ahead of his mother, ignoring her calls to wait or to say good-bye to the teacher. She chases after him, shouting, "Daniel, stop! Get back here right now, young man!"

When all the children are gone, the teacher turns back to the disordered room. Putting toys away, she muses, "I wonder if Daniel was having a bad day or if there's a problem in his relationship with his mother. They definitely seem to be at odds." Closing

*the door behind her as she leaves for the day, she thinks, "If he still seems to be this
angry after the first week, I'll talk to her to see how she perceives his behavior and how
long he's been this way. They may need some help learning more positive ways of interacting. Judging from past experience, I'd say there's a lot of work ahead for Daniel and
his mother, and for me too."*

The teacher might not have known what was making Daniel act this way,
but she suspected that something had gone wrong in his relationship with his
mother. It wouldn't be surprising if she were to discover, as she got to know
them, that the trouble started a long time ago, back in the early part of his
infancy. Perhaps Daniel and his mother had never quite gotten along with each
other, never quite "clicked." Perhaps instead of building a comfortable give-
and-take relationship, they had become locked in a struggle that eroded their
good will and wore them both down. We would say they had experienced a
problem in their attachment relationship.

Attachment is the strong emotional tie babies and their mothers (or other
primary caregivers) develop for each other. The quality of the attachment relationship is correlated with the child's tendency to become independent, confident, flexible, and positive, on the one hand, or withdrawn, rigid, easily frustrated, and negative, on the other hand. The attachment relationship also
influences the development of trust, which Erikson sees as the fundamental
task of infancy, and autonomy, the fundamental task of toddlerhood. This
chapter explores various aspects of attachment—how it forms, what each partner brings to the relationship, and what the connections are between attachment history and the child's later development. The chapter also addresses
several other topics. Moving from the relationship between infant and mother,
it explores infants' and toddlers' interactions with each other and their growing ability to play together. Like so many other features of development, the
child's social "style" with other children is strongly influenced by attachment
history.

The chapter also considers the development of empathy in young children—their ability to respond to others' distress. Finally, the chapter discusses
sex-typed behavior, particularly the role parents play in teaching their children
to act "like boys" or "like girls." Taken together, these topics provide a comprehensive picture of the emotional and social underpinnings that shape children's personalities and the way they interact with others as they grow.

ATTACHMENT

To begin to understand attachment, let's look again at the case of Daniel. Picture him not as an angry 2-year-old but as a newborn. He interacts with his
mother for many hours every day, and his attachment to her forms from these
interactions. The quality of this attachment becomes a crucial factor in his
social and emotional development. From the way he interacts with his mother,
he learns patterns of interacting with others. From the way he feels about her,
he learns ways of feeling about himself and others.

If his mother responds to him in ways that are comforting, satisfying, and
interesting, he develops feelings of confidence, enthusiasm, and trust. In Erikson's terms, he learns that he is "all right." If she does not respond in this way,

FIGURE 8-1
The attachment relationship has many faces. This child shows her attachment to her mother by seeking safety and comfort after receiving an inoculation. The mother shows her attachment by holding and soothing her daughter, providing comfort in a nurturant way.

he associates his initial expectations with feelings of disappointment, sadness, and anger. He fails to develop a sense of trust in her; he feels uneasy and dissatisfied; and he decides he is "not all right." Because he has not established a secure attachment to his mother as an infant, he may have difficulty separating from her as a toddler. It may be hard for him to begin to gain a sense of autonomy—a sense of himself as an independent person. Without a solid base from which to explore the world, he may be fearful and passive or angry and aggressive with other people. And because so much of learning hinges on social interaction, the same factors that cause disruptions in attachment may have an effect on his cognitive functioning as well. A child with a disrupted attachment is often unable to stick with tasks or to seek or accept help.

There are many theories about how and why an emotional tie develops between parent and child. In this chapter, we consider three of them—the psychoanalytic, the behavioral, and the ethological—and the evidence available that supports or challenges them. We discuss the first two theories together and then go on to the third, which is now the favored explanation. Next, we focus on details of the two sides of the attachment relationship, the infant's and the adult's. Finally, we explore how attachment history is related to other areas in the child's life.

Theories of Infant Attachment

THE PSYCHOANALYTIC AND BEHAVIORAL EXPLANATIONS. Both psychoanalytic and behavior theories propose that babies become attached to adults who satisfy their basic needs, especially hunger. Traditional Freudian psychoanalytic theory is based on this notion of **drive reduction.** According to this theory, inner needs (hunger, for example) create tension, which in turn generates a drive to reduce the tension. The individual seeks to reduce the drive by satisfying the need (by eating, for example). The adult who gratifies a baby's needs becomes associated with the pleasurable sensations that result. Psychoanalytic theory also assumes that each person has a limited amount of mental energy for attachments, so a baby becomes attached to only one person, preferably the mother. Later, the child comes to identify with the parent of the same sex, but only after having worked through conflicts associated with this first emotional tie with the mother. According to Freudian theory, a person's sexual identity is likely to be disrupted if early attachment is disrupted.

The first relationship with the mother is also assumed to be extremely important for personality development and as a model for later love relationships. The first attachment is seen as an enduring part of the psyche. According to Freud, the mother and father continue to be present in the individual's mind as objects of love, admiration, and fear long after the actual parent-child relationship is over.

Early behavioral theorists also explained attachment in terms of drive reduction: The adult who feeds a baby becomes a **secondary reinforcer.** If you recall from the discussion of behavior theory in Chapter 2, a secondary reinforcer is something or someone who takes on reinforcing properties as a result of having been associated with a primary reinforcer, which, in the case of hunger, is food. Babies become attached to their mothers because they associate them with being fed.

Unlike psychoanalytic theory, however, behavior theory has never used ideas like "mental energy" and thus has never claimed that the mother is the baby's only attachment figure. A baby might become attached to several adult caregivers if all of them are involved in feeding. In addition, in behavior theory the first attachment is not considered central to all others. In fact, behavior theory suggests that later relationships may depend as much on the circumstances surrounding them as on the first relationship with the mother.

THE ETHOLOGICAL EXPLANATION. The ethological explanation for attachment, first proposed by John Bowlby in 1969, claims that infants are **preprogrammed**— genetically "wired"—to form attachment to the adults who best ensure their survival. **Ethology** is the study of animal behavior, particularly the aspects of behavior having to do with ecology and evolution. The ethological explanation for attachment focuses on the ways young animals, including young humans, keep in touch with their mothers (Waters & Deane, 1982).

Originally an ego psychoanalyst, Bowlby became impressed with the theories of ethologists like Konrad Lorenz, perhaps best known for demonstrating **imprinting** in animals. Imprinting is an innate tendency to follow or attach to the first moving object seen during a critical early developmental period.

Human babies keep in touch with their mothers by sending signals, and mothers respond by reacting to the signals. Babies prefer adults who read their signals accurately and respond to them appropriately. Although signals often revolve around feeding, attachments are not necessarily based on this situation. Babies may develop strong attachments to adults who have never fed them or provided them with other basic physical care.

Bowlby suggests that the essence of secure attachment is a strong bond of affection between the adult and the baby and that the manifestation of this

FIGURE 8-2
According to the ethological explanation for attachment, babies become attached to adults who correctly read their signals, ensuring their safety and supporting their efforts to explore. This little girl is being kept safe—an adult holds her hand to prevent her from falling down—at the same time that she's being allowed to find out about her environment. A proponent of the ethological explanation would say that the conditions for a healthy attachment relationship are being provided by a sensitive adult.

affection is the adult's sensitivity to the baby's signals. Over time, the child's experiences with his mother (or other adult responsible for his care) lead him to form expectations about future social interactions. These expectations form the basis of his **internal working models** of his mother and himself. If his mother is generally responsive to his signals, he builds a model of her as responsive and trustworthy and of himself as competent and worthy of her responsiveness.

The ethological explanation accounts both for the way babies try to stay near their mothers and for the way they separate to explore. Babies must be able to explore if they are to learn about their environment and become independent, but they also need to be kept safe from danger. As the human species evolved, both babies and mothers needed to learn to send and read signals about feeding, danger, and so on if they were to survive. Those who learned the best were the ones who survived and passed on their genes to succeeding generations.

The ethological theory predicts that babies will become attached most strongly to the adults who respond the best to their signals. Although the theory is based on studies of animal behavior, it doesn't claim that babies have an innate attachment to their biological mothers. What it does suggest is that babies are born with certain capabilities for building relationships with adults. It also assumes that adults have to be able to respond to the subtle signals babies send if these relationships are to work.

FIGURE 8-3
In Harlow's experiments, monkeys obtained food from the wire mesh mother but spent much more time clinging to the terry cloth mother. These findings undermined the belief that feeding alone is the crucial factor in the formation of attachment.

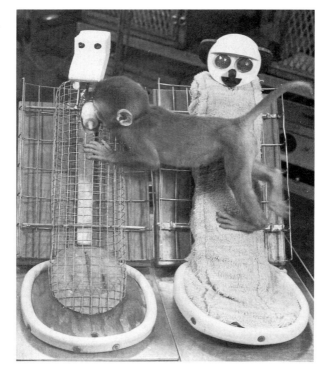

EVIDENCE FOR THE THEORIES. Research has not supported the drive reduction explanation for attachment that lies at the heart of both the psychoanalytic and behavior theories. It was struck down first when Harry Harlow, a psychologist at the University of Wisconsin, conducted studies with baby monkeys to determine why they became attached to a caregiver (Harlow, 1958). He used two types of surrogate (substitute) mothers, one made from a tube covered with terry cloth and the other made of wire mesh. The baby monkeys were fed from a bottle placed on the wire mesh surrogate; the cloth mother provided only "contact comfort." If the monkeys showed a preference for the surrogate who fed them, it would support the drive reduction explanation for attachment, because it would indicate that they developed an emotional tie to a caregiver who fed them. If they showed a preference for the cloth mother, it would not support this explanation.

As it turned out, the baby monkeys spent more time on the cloth mother, and when a frightening wind-up toy was placed in their cage, they ran to the cloth mother for protection. This experiment undermined the drive reduction and secondary reinforcement explanations for attachment, because they're both based on the satisfaction of hunger. (Harlow's experiment didn't rule out the possibility that there's a drive for contact, but ethological theories haven't focused on this possibility, because they tend to stress interconnecting needs and behaviors, not isolated ones.) Further evidence against the secondary reinforcement hypothesis came when a study reported that 30 percent of the infants in the study were attached to an adult other than the one who took care of them most of the time. Additionally, 22 percent of the infants were attached to someone who had never performed any basic caregiving activities for them at all, such as feeding or diapering (Schaffer & Emerson, 1964). More

FIGURE 8-4
Babies can become attached to adults other than the people who feed them or take care of them most of the time. Attachment depends more on sensitive responses to signals sent back and forth between the baby and the adult. This woman knows exactly how to interact sensitively with her great-grandson. She cradles him at just the right distance from her face, affectionately returning his friendly gaze.

recent cases have reported that foster children were attached to their biological parent, even though they were cared for almost exclusively by their foster parents (Gaensbauer & Harmon, 1982).

Right now, the best explanation we have for infant attachment is the ethological one—babies come into the world equipped to build relationships with people who will take care of them. They send signals to adults, and they build the strongest relationships with adults who respond most sensitively to these signals.

Several questions come to mind at this point in our discussion. First, how do we know when an infant has become attached to an adult? What does the baby do that indicates attachment? Second, what are the signals babies send to adults, and what are the so-called sensitive responses? Finally, what makes some adults respond sensitively and others insensitively? A discussion of these questions follows.

Infant Attachment Behavior

THE STRANGE SITUATION. How do we tell if a baby has become attached to a particular adult, and how can we judge the quality of the attachment? A standard method has been devised to study and describe attachment behavior in babies between 1 and 2 years of age. The so-called strange situation was developed by Mary Ainsworth and colleagues in 1969. It involves seven episodes and three participants—mother, baby, and stranger.

The experimental procedure begins with the mother and baby being introduced to the laboratory playroom. Then the mother and baby are left alone in the room, but the mother doesn't play with the baby (episode 1). Next, a

TABLE 8-1   Patterns of Attachment Observed in 12- to 18-Month-Olds in the Strange Situation

	Exploratory Behavior before Separation	Behavior during Separation	Reunion Behavior	Behavior with Stranger
Secure	Separates to explore toys; shares play with mother; friendly toward stranger when mother is present; touches "home base" periodically.	May cry; play is subdued for a while; usually recovers and is able to play.	If distressed during separation, contact ends distress; if not distressed, greets mother warmly; initiates interaction.	Somewhat friendly; may play with stranger after initial distress reaction.
Anxious/ambivalent (resistant)	Has difficulty separating to explore toys even when mother is present; wary of novel situations and people; stays close to mother and away from stranger.	Very distressed; hysterical crying does not quickly diminish.	Seeks comfort and rejects it; continues to cry or fuss; may be passive—no greeting made.	Wary of stranger; rejects stranger's offers to play.
Anxious/avoidant	Readily separates to explore toys; does not share play with parent; shows little preference for parent versus stranger.	Does not show distress; continues to play; interacts with the stranger.	Ignores mother—turns or moves away; avoidance is more extreme at the second reunion.	No avoidance of stranger.

SOURCE: Compiled from Ainsworth, M. D. S., & Wittig, B. A. (1969). Attachment and exploratory behavior of one-year-olds in a strange situation. In B. M. Foss (Ed.), Determinants of infant behavior *(Vol. 4). London: Methuen.*

stranger enters, talks with the mother a bit, and then focuses her attention on the baby (episode 2). The mother leaves, introducing episode 3, in which the baby is separated from the mother, leaving the stranger and the baby alone. Soon, the mother returns (episode 4); this is the first reunion. The mother talks to the baby and comforts the baby if he is distressed. (If the baby is very distressed at any point, the experiment is terminated.) Then the mother leaves again. Episode 5, the second separation, follows. This time the baby is left completely alone, and the stranger, not the mother, enters the room first after this separation (episode 6). Finally, the mother returns, and the stranger leaves (episode 7).

Several features of infant attachment become apparent in the strange situation. The researcher or observer can see to what extent the baby uses the mother as a secure base for exploration, how much the baby prefers the mother to the stranger, and how likely the baby is to consider the mother a haven of safety when frightened (Connell & Goldsmith, 1982). From observing many babies in the strange situation, researchers have identified and described three major patterns of response. These patterns, which indicate the quality of babies' attachment to their mothers, have been labeled **secure attachment, anxious/avoidant attachment,** and **anxious/ambivalent attachment.** (A fourth pattern, which is labeled disorganized/disoriented and includes disorganized elements of ambivalence and avoidance, has recently been proposed and is currently under investigation [Carlson et al., 1989]). Table 8-1 shows details of the behaviors associated with all three patterns.

In secure attachment, the baby separates from the mother to explore the toys in the playroom but periodically touches base with her. When she leaves, the baby is moderately distressed and either cries or plays in a more subdued way. When she returns, the baby greets her warmly.

In the anxious/avoidant attachment, the baby readily separates from the mother to explore the toys and doesn't seem to prefer the mother to the stranger. When the mother leaves, the baby shows no concern, and when she returns, the baby ignores or avoids her.

In anxious/ambivalent (also called resistant) attachment, the baby stays close to the mother and doesn't explore the toys. When the mother leaves, the baby reacts with great distress; when she returns, the baby seeks her and rejects her at the same time (that is, the reaction is ambivalent).

What do these different patterns of attachment tell us? As the labels imply, one of the patterns is considered optimal or normal, and two are considered deviant. Each pattern seems to reflect different patterns of behavior by the parents. When parents respond sensitively to the baby's signals, the baby tends to become securely attached. When parents respond inappropriately, or not at all, the baby tends to form an anxious attachment of one kind or the other. A discussion of parent's responses follow, but first let's take a closer look at how babies signal their needs to their parents.

THE INFANT'S EARLY SIGNALS. Some of the newborn's signals are subtle, but others aren't subtle at all. Probably the least subtle and most powerful signal is crying. Adults find infant crying unpleasant, and they usually move quickly to do something about it. As mentioned in Chapter 4, many parents can tell from listening to the crying whether their baby is hungry, angry, or in pain. Their judgments are based on how suddenly the crying starts, how loud and high-pitched it is, and how long it lasts (Wolff, 1969). Considering the context of the crying as well—when the baby was last fed, for example—the parent decides what's causing the crying and begins to do something about it.

Most parents respond to a crying baby by picking her up and holding or rocking her. This not only soothes her (Korner & Thoman, 1972; Hunziker & Barr, 1986) but also tends to induce the alert inactive state, which was discussed in Chapter 4. She opens her eyes and searches with them, often fixating on her parent's eyes if the parent is looking at her. If you recall, babies like to look at patterns like the one provided by the face and eyes (Brazelton, 1973a; Als, 1977).

The baby now uses another very powerful signal—gazing. This steady, intent attention to another's face indicates that the baby wants to engage in a social interaction. The parent will probably gaze back at the baby and smile or speak; the baby may smile or coo in return. Parents like this eye contact—it makes them feel that the baby is enjoying their company. They'll often gaze back at the baby as long as the baby gazes at them (Robson, 1967). Gazing between parent and baby can go on for much longer than is typical between adults. Even when they're not engaged in gazing, adults like to look at babies' faces because they find them "cute" (Lamb, 1982).

Babies signal their wish to reduce stimulation or end the interaction by looking away. Gaze aversion is an expression that often indicates disgust (Izard & Dougherty, 1982). Sensitive parents do something different when the baby looks away. Of course, starting to cry again is another way the baby says, "That's enough."

Besides crying and gazing, babies have other inborn ways to make adults pay attention to them and interact with them on their terms. When they're eating, for example, babies suck in rhythmical bursts and then pause. Mothers often jiggle babies during the pauses, and in the first few weeks, they learn that short jiggles make the baby start sucking again. This biologically based sucking pattern, with its alternating bursts and pauses, keeps the mother actively involved in the feeding. She sees that her attention is important to the feeding process, and she watches the baby's face closely. The baby often gazes back at her, and this, too, keeps her attention. When the baby is done eating, the mother may wish to continue this pleasing interaction in some other situation, such as playing. The turn-taking nature of the feeding interaction may help mothers learn to observe their babies closely and adjust their responses to the babies' behavior (Kaye, 1982a).

As the newborn matures, another powerful signal emerges—the **social smile.** It begins to appear on the baby's previously expressionless face by about 2 months of age. (See Research Focus—The Developmental Course of Smiling.) One day, often after some searching of the mother's or father's face, the baby's eyes light up and her face breaks into a smile. News that "the baby smiled today" is thrilling for parents, who may need a boost at this point in their sometimes thankless daily routine with the newborn. This smile is their reward; it makes them feel that there is truly a relationship between them and their baby (Robson, 1967). Smiling is the baby's way of saying that all is well with the interaction that's going on at that moment. When the smile starts to fade and the baby sobers, something is going amiss. Smiling and sobering, gazing and gaze aversion are the signals with which the baby regulates her interactions with her parents in the early months.

This may not seem like much in comparison with the virtually infinite variety of signals older children and adults use to communicate, but it's enough for the sensitive parent. How do these signals and cues work in action? Consider the following examples of parent-infant interactions (Stern, 1977, pp. 3,

FIGURE 8-5
Infants gaze more intently and for longer periods of time than adults do, unless the adults happen to be falling in love with each other.

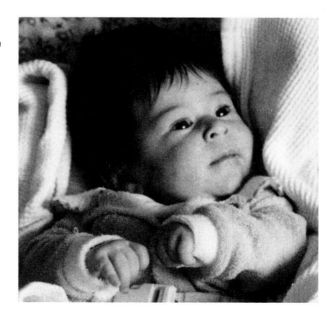

RESEARCH FOCUS

The Developmental Course of Smiling

Newborns are often seen smiling in their sleep, but these spontaneous smiles are triggered by changes in their internal sleep states and are known as **endogenous smiles** (Emde & Gaensbauer, 1981). Between 6 and 8 weeks of age, the *social smile* appears—a smile given in response to something outside the baby. The baby smiles more and more frequently over the next few months (Wolff, 1969; Anisfeld, 1982; Konner, 1982).

At first, the social smile is indiscriminate: The baby smiles at familiar and unfamiliar adults alike, as long as they make some friendly gesture, such as gazing, smiling, or talking. Then from 2 to 4 months of age, babies begin to react more positively to familiar figures than to unfamiliar ones (Mizukami et al., 1990). The baby begins to search the faces of unfamiliar people and to sober a bit toward them (Emde, Gaensbauer & Harmon, 1976; Kurzweil, 1988). By 6 to 8 months of age, the baby's reaction may be so intense that he cries if a stranger approaches (Konner, 1982; Lamb, 1982). The baby's smile is now a very selective social smile, reserved only for familiar people. Unfamiliar people are likely to make the baby cry. When a baby reacts this way to a stranger (usually between 6 and 18 months of age), he's showing **stranger anxiety.**

What makes a baby smile? Does the baby learn to smile by seeing smiles, or is the impulse to smile innate? It seems that it's the latter. Evidence comes from a study of smiling in premature babies. Researchers hypothesized that smiling is an innate capability, programmed to emerge at a certain point in the baby's development, and they calculated this point in weeks from conception rather than weeks from birth. They suggested that babies born 8 weeks prematurely would smile not at 6 weeks, when full-term babies smile, but at 12 to 14 weeks, when their developmental age would match that of 6-week-olds. This is exactly what they found (Anisfeld, 1982). Further support for a biological view of smiling comes from research showing that social smiling begins at about the same time that certain portions of the brain develop. (See Konner, 1982, for an excellent discussion of this topic.)

It turns out, then, that one of the baby's most powerful social signals isn't especially social in origin. But the baby's intention isn't what's important at this point. What matters is how the parent perceives and responds to the signal—and parents read the smile as a friendly social gesture. Commenting on the parent's point of view, one researcher writes (Kaye, 1982, p. 196), "fantasies are not to be disparaged. Fantasies, are, in fact, part of the evolved apparatus with which parents are provided (the evolution in this case being cultural, not only genetic), so that they treat the infant as a person from the start. . . . Parents capitalize on certain aspects of the newborn organism that, so far as we can tell, evolved for that very purpose, so as to involve the infant in social frames." In other words, smiling is another behavior that may have evolved to help ensure the survival of the baby—and the species.

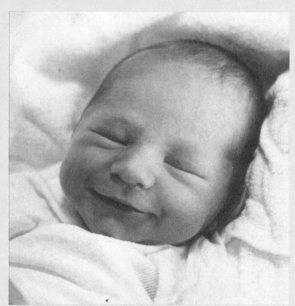

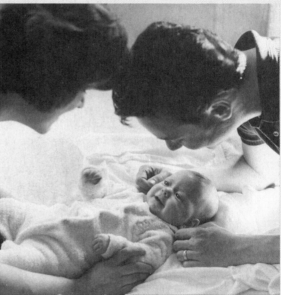

The newborn smiles mysteriously to herself (top); the older baby smiles at her parents (bottom).

110–111): In the first example, the mother adjusts what she does to the level desired by the baby. The baby, too, is skillful: When the mother reduces stimulation below the level he wants, he smiles more broadly to get her to raise it again. In the second example, the mother misreads the baby's signals or chooses to ignore them. She continues with strong stimulation even after the infant breaks her gaze to signal she wishes to stop or slow down.

EXAMPLE 1:

While talking and looking at me the mother turned her head and gazed at the infant's face. He was gazing at the ceiling, but out of the corner of his eye he saw her head turn toward him and turned to gaze back at her. This had happened before, but now he broke rhythm and stopped sucking. He let go of the nipple and the suction around it broke as he eased into the faintest suggestion of a smile. The mother abruptly stopped talking and, as she watched his face begin to transform, her eyes opened a little wider and her eyebrows raised a bit. His eyes locked on to hers, and together they held motionless for an instant. The infant did not return to sucking and his mother held frozen her slight expression of anticipation. This silent and almost motionless instant continued to hang until the mother suddenly shattered it by saying "Hey!" and simultaneously opening her eyes wider, raising her eyebrows further, and throwing her head up and toward the infant. Almost simultaneously, the baby's eyes widened. His head tilted up and, as his smile broadened, the nipple fell out of his mouth. Now she said, "Well, hello! . . . hello . . . heeelloooo!", so that her pitch rose and the "hellos" became longer and more stressed on each successive repetition. With each phrase the baby expressed more pleasure, and his body resonated almost like a balloon being pumped up, filling a little more with each breath. The mother then paused and her face relaxed. They watched each other expectantly for a moment. The shared excitement between them ebbed, but before it faded completely, the baby suddenly took an initiative and intervened to rescue it. His head lurched forward, his hands jerked up, and a fuller smile blossomed. His mother was jolted into motion. She moved forward, mouth open and eyes alight, and said "Oooooh . . . ya wanna play do ya . . . yeah? . . . I didn't know if you were still hungry . . . no . . . noooooo . . . no I didn't . . ." And off they went.

EXAMPLE 2:

The dance they had worked out by the time I met them went something like this. Whenever a moment of mutual gaze occurred, the mother went immediately into high-gear stimulating behaviors, producing a profusion of fully displayed, high-intensity, facial and vocal infant-elicited social behavior. Jenny invariably broke gaze rapidly. Her mother never interpreted this temporary face and gaze aversion as a cue to lower her level of behavior . . . Instead, she would swing her head around following Jenny's . . . She would reinitiate the same level of stimulation with a new arrangement of facial and vocal combinations. Jenny again turned away . . . Again, instead of holding back, the mother continued to chase Jenny . . . She moved closer, in an apparent attempt to break through and establish contact. She also escalated the level of her stimulation even more by adding touching and tickling to the unabated flow of vocal and facial behaviors. . . .

With Jenny's head now pinned in the corner, the baby's next recourse was to rapidly swing her face from one side to the other right past her mother's face. When her face crossed the mother's face, in the face-face zone, Jenny closed her eyes to avoid any mutual visual contact and only reopened them after the head aversion was established on the other side. All of these behaviors on Jenny's part were performed with a sober face or at times a grimace.

These examples show that babies can be real partners in even the earliest social interactions, regulating their parents' actions and responses with their repertoire of signals. The examples also show that having the repertoire doesn't necessarily guarantee the best interaction. Parents must be able to read and respond to the signals. What happens to the relationship when parents are insensitive to their baby? This is the question we look at next.

THE RELATIONSHIP BETWEEN INFANT ATTACHMENT AND PARENT BEHAVIOR. The parent's overall pattern of behavior toward the baby determines the kind of attachment the baby will develop for the parent. We saw earlier, in discussing the strange situation, that some babies are securely attached to their mothers and others are anxiously attached. We now know that babies become securely attached when their parents give them responsive feedback. This means that they (1) pay attention to the baby's signals; (2) interpret the signals accurately; (3) give appropriate feedback; and (4) respond contingently, that is, they respond promptly enough for the baby to feel that his signals caused the response (Ainsworth et al., 1978). Responsive parents also cooperate with the baby's ongoing activity rather than intruding or interfering. Mothers of securely attached babies "are more responsive to their infant's cries, hold their babies more tenderly and carefully, pace the interaction contingently during face-to-face interaction, and exhibit greater sensitivity in initiating and terminating feeding" (Crockenberg, 1981, p. 857). Researchers continue to find a link between responsive parenting and secure attachment (Isabella & Belsky, 1991).

Parents of anxiously attached babies act quite differently. They may ignore the baby's signals, or they may respond but in inappropriate ways. For example, a mother may take the opportunity to read the newspaper every time she feeds the baby, holding him loosely and not noticing his gaze. A father may consistently ignore the baby's hungry cries in the middle of the night to get some extra sleep. A parent might bounce a baby vigorously when the baby prefers to be cuddled or end a feeding when the baby only wants to rest or, as we saw in Example 2, continue to stimulate the baby when the baby wishes to stop.

More serious problems in attachment occur when a parent's behavior is more disturbed. For example, some mothers dislike physical contact with their babies or treat them in an angry or threatening way (Bretherton et al., 1986). Some mothers have "restricted affect," meaning that they express fewer emotions than other mothers, especially positive, joyful ones (Ainsworth et al., 1978; Main, 1981). Some mothers even mock their babies' behavior, speak sarcastically to them, handle them roughly, and "stare them down." Babies treated this way are likely to have severe problems in their emotional and social development.

One researcher has suggested that sensitivity in parenting has two dimensions: responding versus not responding, and responding appropriately versus responding inappropriately (Lamb, 1982). The first dimension probably affects the baby's sense of power and effectiveness in the world. Babies whose parents respond to their signals learn that what they do matters. Children whose parents are insensitive to their signals may come to exhibit "learned helplessness," the sense that they have little effect on the world.

Babies whose parents don't respond contingently or consistently seem to show the ambivalent (or resistant) pattern of anxious attachment (Isabella &

FIGURE 8-6
Sometimes problems occur in the attachment relationship when a parent is too intrusive or controlling with the child. This mother has helped her daughter write her name, but the child might have preferred to scribble or color with the crayon.

Belsky, 1991). The response they receive may be appropriate, when it comes, but they're not sure when it's going to be given or if it will come at all. Because they can't be sure the parent will give the desired comfort, they seek it but then resist it, as if both anticipating disappointment and testing for consistency.

The second dimension of sensitivity in parenting—responding appropriately versus responding inappropriately—in combination with contingent responding may affect the development of the child's trust in others. Babies whose parents respond to them appropriately learn to expect that people will react to them in desired ways. Babies whose parents respond inappropriately, by being intrusive, for example, may tend to show the avoidant pattern of attachment (Isabella & Belsky, 1991). They stop sending signals and may even try to avoid the parent, perhaps as a protection against getting an inappropriate response. Children showing the resistant pattern of attachment seem to involve their mothers in power struggles almost as a goal (Sroufé, 1981); avoidant children, on the other hand, seem to want to get away from the mother's sphere of influence.

Unfortunately the dimension of responding appropriately versus inappropriately has been difficult to examine because of problems of measurement and definition. That is, many repeated observations are necessary for observers to identify mothers with traits of punitiveness and irritability (Schaefer,

1989), since these are traits that mothers try to hide. Any intrusiveness appears to be shown not only by mothers who generally are overstimulating but also by those who appear to be going overboard during the observation sessions to look like "good mothers" (Bohlin et al., 1989). In spite of these problems, the dimensions of responding appropriately versus inappropriately and of responding versus not responding offer promising ways of exploring further patterns of interaction and attachment.

At this point we don't fully understand the links between specific maternal behavior and the two anxious patterns of attachment. But we do know that the quality of parenting in the early months is vitally important to the child's long-term development and future happiness; therefore we need to be alert to situations in which a parent and child seem headed for trouble.

ATTACHMENT REACTIONS: STRANGER ANXIETY AND SEPARATION DISTRESS. During the second half of the first year—between 6 and 12 months—babies add a whole new set of actions to their repertoire: They begin to move around. They learn to cling, creep, crawl, and finally walk. Now they don't have to wait for their parents to come to them or just watch them as they move away. They can follow them around. At about the same time, babies start to discriminate sharply between familiar and unfamiliar adults (as described in Research Focus—The Developmental Course of Smiling). When approached by someone they don't know, they sober and may even cry, a response known as **stranger anxiety**. Babies also become capable of gaining information about new people and situations by **social referencing**, as described in Research Focus—"How Do You Feel about Her, Mom?" Social Referencing in Infants.

By late in the first year, somewhere between 8 and 10 months of age, babies start to be able to express on their faces emotions such as joy, surprise, and anger (Hiatt, Campos & Emde, 1979; Stenberg, Campos & Emde, 1983). Now they can put together facial expressions, sounds, and motion to produce the full-blown attachment reactions that parents (and babysitters) know so well. When they see their parents after a separation, they greet them with joy and stretch out their arms or crawl to them. When they're separated from their parents, or when they're concerned that a separation may be coming, they show **separation distress**—they sober, cry, and cling or try to follow. (Knowledge in Action: Infants and Toddlers discusses the implications of this development for parents placing their infants in day care.) The older infant and the toddler show attachment by walking or running to keep in contact with the parent. With the acquisition of language, the child adds words to the protest: "Mommy! Daddy! Stay here! I go!" These kinds of scenes are practically the hallmark of the toddler years, when separation distress is at its height.

In sum, then, babies come into the world well equipped to interact with adults and to regulate those interactions. But the "amazing newborn" has an amazing parent as well. "Left to their own devices," says one child development specialist, "infants' intrinsic amazingness would not amount to much" (Kaye 1982b, p. 196). The parent is the crucial element in the relationship. The baby's signals—gazing, smiling, crying, and sobering—get the parent going, and then the give-and-take of the interaction keeps them both going, if all proceeds smoothly. But what ensures that things get going on the parent's side? And what happens if they don't? These questions are discussed next.

FIGURE 8-7
Stranger anxiety—acute fear of anyone unknown who approaches too closely—reaches its height between the middle of the first year and the middle of the second. Many tears can be avoided if parents wait another year or two for a photo of their child with Santa.

Theories of Attachment: The Parent's Side

Newborns turn life upside down. They wake every few hours to be fed, leaving their parents sleepless and irritable. They sometimes may cry many hours a day, challenging the patience and ingenuity of even the most resourceful adult. Old family patterns break down and new ones emerge as the baby takes

RESEARCH FOCUS

"How Do You Feel about Her, Mom?" Social Referencing in Infants

Ten-month-old Anthony is playing with brightly colored plastic rings on the living room floor when the doorbell rings. His mother gets up from the sofa to answer it. She has been expecting a visit from a new neighbor. When this virtual stranger enters the room, she stops for a moment to chat with Anthony. "Well, hello there, big boy," she says, as she kneels down on the floor. "What are you doing?"

Anthony, meanwhile, has stopped playing and clutches the yellow ring in his hand. He looks toward his mother, who sits down once again on the sofa. She smiles at Anthony and says, "Say hi to Mary Beth, Anthony. Say, 'Hiiii, Mary Beth.'"

Anthony looks at this new person, Mary Beth; he looks hard, as if concentrating on figuring out who she is or what she's going to do. Then he casts a glance back toward Mom, who is still smiling as she talks now with Mary Beth about how old Anthony is. Anthony looks back toward Mary Beth, as if led there by the direction of his mother's gaze. Anthony slowly raises the hand that holds the ring, and then he extends it toward Mary Beth. "Oh, what a pretty yellow ring!" Mary Beth exclaims. "Does it go on this post?" Mary Beth reaches for the post as she asks and tilts it toward the ring that Anthony holds out to her. Anthony looks up at Mary Beth for a moment and glances at his mom once more. Then he slips the ring over the end of the post, and his face breaks into a smile.

WHAT IS SOCIAL REFERENCING?

Anthony used his mother's facial expressions to gain information about a new situation. Anthony didn't know Mary Beth, and he wasn't quite sure how to respond to her. Should he be friendly, or should he retreat to his mother's arms? Anthony's strategy of using information about how another person feels about a third event—in this case, Mary Beth—is called *social referencing* (Clyman et al., 1986). It involves scanning the face of a familiar and trusted person to pick up information about a new situation. From that person's emotional reaction to the situation, the child can form his response. Babies 8 or 9 months of age and older often use this strategy. As they get older, they get better at interpreting and using the information their parent provides, and they are more likely to look to the parent before touching unfamiliar toys, for example (Walden & Baxter, 1989; Walden & Ogden, 1988).

STUDIES OF SOCIAL REFERENCING

Social referencing has been documented in many studies of how babies react to situations when their mothers change their facial expressions. In one study mothers were asked to pose different expressions as their babies were presented with a new toy (Klinnert, 1981). When mothers looked happy or joyful, their babies were more likely to accept the toy. Babies react similarly to fathers' signals (Hirshberg & Svejda, 1990). Babies' reactions to strangers have also been shown to be related to their mothers' facial expressions (Boccia & Campos, 1983; Feinman & Lewis, 1983). In still another situation, mothers' facial expressions were observed to influence babies' willingness to cross over the "visual cliff." (If you recall from Chapter 4, this is a laboratory apparatus, originally designed for the study of infant depth perception, in which a drop in surface level is covered with a transparent sheet of glass or plastic). When babies get close to the part of the surface where the cliff appears, they hesitate. Often they look up at their mothers for clues about this novel situation. In studies of social referencing, researchers asked different mothers to show such emotions as interest, anger, or fear as their babies approached the cliff. The results were clear: When mothers looked pleased or interested, babies were much more likely to cross the cliff than when mothers looked angry or afraid.

BABIES' ABILITY TO READ FACIAL EXPRESSIONS

When babies engage in social referencing, it indicates that they recognize and can respond to the facial expressions that reflect various emotional states. Babies start discriminating facial expressions by the time they're 4 or 5 months old, but they probably don't attach appropriate, or any, meanings to different expressions (Appel & Campos, 1977). Somewhat later, between 6 and 9 months of age, they begin to respond differently to different expressions, which indicates they understand some of the meanings attached to the expressions. A baby might cry, for example, on seeing an angry face or smile on seeing a joyful one. At this point, they start to be able to communicate with someone else, via emotional expressions, about an uncertain third event (Campos et al., 1983).

her place in the household. All of this is stressful for parents. But they're helped through the difficult parts of parenting by their own feelings of attachment to their baby. When parental feelings of attachment are lacking, it's more likely that the parent will respond to these stresses with child abuse or neglect (Crittenden & Ainsworth, 1989; Spieker & Booth, 1988).

Like infant attachment, maternal attachment has been a subject of great interest in the study of child development. What causes maternal attachment to form? Three explanations for its development have been proposed: the biological explanation; the parental history explanation; and the social system explanation. Each of these is discussed below.

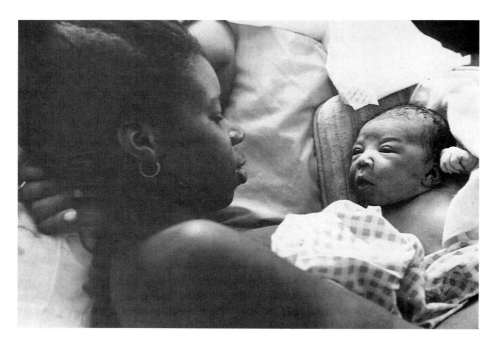

FIGURE 8-8
Proponents of the biological explanation for maternal attachment believe that the moments after birth are a critical period for bonding between mother and baby. Although these moments _are_ special, as this mother and baby show, the evidence indicates that attachment develops over a longer period of time and depends on factors other than contact during a critical period.

THE BIOLOGICAL EXPLANATION. The biological explanation, also known as the critical period explanation, claims that maternal attachment is based on hormones. The theory is that hormones released at the end of pregnancy or soon after birth "prime" the mother to bond with her baby. **Bonding** is the dramatic and immediate emotional tie that mothers feel toward their newborn babies, according to the proponents of this explanation (Klaus & Kennel, 1976). According to the biological explanation, it is triggered in the hormonally primed mother by contact with her baby within a **critical period** immediately after birth, when the hormones are at their highest level. If the mother bonds with the baby during this early period, her love will continue to grow, and she will be able to provide the responsive care needed to ensure the baby's attachment to her.

The biological theory of maternal attachment originated in research on lower animals. Studies of sheep, goats, and rats showed that mothering was disrupted when the young were separated from their mothers immediately after birth, even for only one or two hours (Collias, 1956; Hersher, Moore & Richmond, 1958). Mothering wasn't disrupted, or the disruption wasn't as serious, when some contact was allowed before mothers and young were separated. The identification of a critical period for maternal attachment emerged from these studies.

Other studies investigated maternal behavior in rats. Researchers found a higher level of maternal behavior in pregnant rats than in nonpregnant rats, and when blood plasma from pregnant rats was injected into nonpregnant rats, these rats also exhibited maternal behavior (Rosenblatt, 1965). This research established a hormonal basis for maternal behavior in rats.

General interest existed in investigating whether the findings from animal studies could be applied to humans. One research group in particular wanted to know if there was a causal relationship between severe disruption in maternal attachment—the kind that results in child abuse—and separation at birth.

Physicians who cared for premature newborns in the neonatal intensive care unit of a large city hospital noticed that an unusually high number of these children returned to the emergency room as child abuse victims. They wondered if the mothers of these babies had been unable to bond with them because they were separated during a critical period for bonding.

In pioneering studies to test the critical period theory in humans, these physicians and their colleagues (Klaus et al., 1972; Klaus & Kennell, 1976), as well as other groups of researchers, manipulated the amount of contact between mothers and their newborns in hospitals. Some mothers were kept on traditional schedules, which involved contact mainly at regular feeding times; others were given contact immediately after birth and for increased periods of time in the days that followed (Leifer et al., 1972; Hales et al., 1977; Carlsson et al., 1978; Rode et al., 1981).

Results from these studies were mixed. Some studies found that attachment seemed stronger in the mothers who had more contact, but other studies found no long-term differences. In general, the studies did not provide strong evidence for a critical period during which bonding must take place. Hormones probably play a more important role in animal behavior than they do in human relationships. Maternal attachment in humans seems to depend not on one critical event but on many different factors occurring over a period of time. Early contact between mother and baby is probably beneficial to the relationship, but the evidence indicates that it's not essential to the formation of attachment (Goldberg, 1982; Svejda, Pannabecker & Emde, 1982).

THE PARENTAL HISTORY EXPLANATION. Other theorists and researchers have suggested that maternal attachment is closely related to the mother's history—her earlier experiences in life. A mother's ability to form a close, nurturing tie with a baby is seen as a function of her personality and of the way she was cared for when she was a child. This explanation comes from observations and studies of disrupted attachment, such as in cases of neglect and abuse, rather than from observations of healthy mother-child relationships. Mothers who have no positive attachment to their children are seen as lacking in parenting skills, knowledge about children, or the ability to act responsibly because of their own immaturity. Sometimes these mothers have psychological problems or personality disorders. Attachment theorists often suggest that these parents have acquired internal working models that represent others as untrustworthy and themselves as ineffective.

In support of the parental history position, it can be said that abusive parents as a group are more likely to have been poorly parented than nonabusive parents (Oliver & Taylor, 1971; Green, Gaines & Sangrund, 1974). Additionally, mothers who suffer from psychosis or major depression may well have difficulty being effective parents (Field, Healy & LeBlanc, 1989; Musick, Clark & Cohler, 1981). And it generally has been confirmed that past childhood relationships, at least the reconstructed memories of those relationships, influence how individuals parent their own children (Ricks, 1985; Simons et al., 1991).

However, parent's childhood histories don't completely explain maternal attachment behavior. The majority of abused children apparently do not become abusive parents (Kaufman & Zigler, 1989). And although some abusive and unresponsive mothers do have personality disorders, other mothers who fail to develop an attachment to their babies don't appear to suffer from such obvious problems. Parental history and personality characteristics may

FIGURE 8-9
When maternal attachment fails, children are placed at tremendous risk. This child was found in a shopping cart outside a supermarket after he was abandoned by his mother on a cold winter night. Although no simple theory explains attachment and no easy solutions are possible when things go wrong, our society attempts to protect and help the children of these troubled relationships.

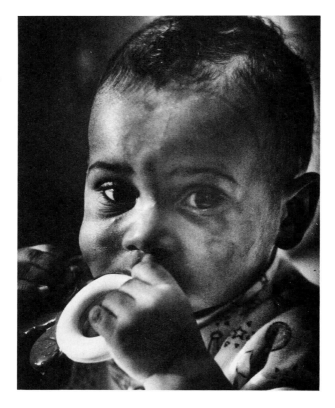

provide part of the explanation for maternal attachment, but they don't account for it completely (Parke & Lewis, 1981).

THE DEVELOPMENTAL SYSTEMS EXPLANATION. As in other areas of child development research, researchers working in the area of attachment are increasingly formulating systems explanations for events. They have proposed a model, known as the interaction/social system explanation, suggesting that maternal attachment is a function of several interacting factors: (1) characteristics of the mother (such as personality traits and psychological well-being); (2) characteristics of the baby (such as health, degree of development at birth, and activity level; (3) characteristics of the family (such as number of children, role of the father in child care, and economic resources); and (4) social supports beyond the immediate family (such as extended family, friends, and medical resources) (Belsky, 1984; Rauh, Wasserman & Brunelli, 1990; Cooley & Unger, 1991).

These factors are thought to interact bidirectionally—that is, in both directions, or reciprocally—to determine the kind of attachment the mother forms and the extent of her ability to nurture attachment in the baby. For example, correlational evidence indicates that a baby can affect his mother's responsiveness and the mother's responsiveness in turn can affect the quality of the baby's attachment. One study found that babies classified as highly irritable in the first two weeks of life were less sociable with their mothers at 1 year of age and tended to be anxiously attached, whereas nonirritable babies were more sociable and tended to be securely attached (van den Boom, 1989).

Some theorists believe the baby's initial temperament directly affects his later sociability and attachment (e.g., Kagan & Snidman, 1991), but others believe temperament influences attachment mainly by the effect it has on the parent's responsiveness (e.g., Belsky & Vondra, 1989). In the study of irritable and nonirritable babies, for example, researchers found that the baby's level of irritability was related to the mother's later attentiveness (van den Boom, 1989). Mothers of irritable babies interacted progressively less with them as the first year went on, while mothers of nonirritable babies interacted progressively more over the course of the first year.

When babies do have a negative temperament, however, parents can still overcome attachment difficulties, given appropriate resources. In another part of the study of irritable babies, some mothers of irritable babies were visited by a worker 6 to 9 months after birth and given assistance in relating to their children. The worker encouraged the mother to pay attention to the baby's signals, interpret them correctly, choose an appropriate response, and then act on it. The worker also encouraged the mother to imitate the baby, repeat vocalizations, be silent when the baby looked away, and soothe the baby when he cried. This intervention was clearly effective. Mothers became more responsive and babies became more sociable, more exploratory, and less irritable than control babies, who were initially as irritable. At 1 year of age, 68 percent of the program babies were securely attached, but only 28 percent of the control babies were.

These results are consistent with the position of attachment theorists, as well as students of other infant-parent interactions (e.g., Uzgiris, 1990, regarding imitation) who believe that parents take the lead in social interchanges during the baby's first few months. Although it's not clear exactly what direct role infant temperament plays in attachment formation, it is clear that it's an important factor in cases in which mothers find it hard to adapt to irritable or difficult babies.

To see how a number of factors interact to determine the kind of attachment that develops between a mother and her infant, let's consider the case of the premature baby.

Premature babies overall are more difficult to parent than full-term babies. They signal their needs less clearly, avert their gaze more often, and smile less (Brown & Bateman, 1978; Crnic et al., 1983). Adults find their cries more unpleasant and their faces less attractive or cute (Frodi & Lamb, 1978). All these characteristics mean that the premature baby can't contribute as much to a relationship as the full-term baby. But if the premature baby is born to a mother with some parenting skills, a healthy personality, a stable relationship, a supportive extended family, a network of friends, and a secure economic situation, the baby's initial deficiencies probably won't stand in the way of the mother's forming an attachment (Belsky & Vondra, 1989).

If an extremely robust and "easy" baby is born into a situation that's not ideal or to a mother who's barely able to keep an interaction going, the baby might be able to contribute enough to make the relationship work. But when a difficult baby is born into difficult circumstances, there probably will be trouble ahead (Vaughn et al., 1979; Crockenberg, 1981). Any baby with a difficult temperament may be "at risk for developing attachment problems," because such a baby needs parenting under ideal circumstances, which not all mothers can provide. When a relationship does seem to exist between early tempera-

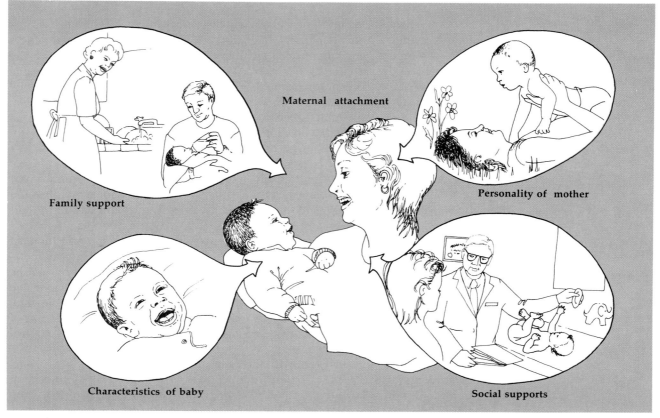

FIGURE 8-10
The social system theory of
maternal attachment suggests
that four different factors
affect the quality of the
mother-child relationship.

ment and later poor attachment, it's probably because a difficult baby challenged an overtaxed mother (Sroufe, Fox & Pancake, 1983).

The interaction/social system explanation for maternal attachment focuses on the complex interweaving of many factors, both those that create stress and those that provide support. The balancing of these elements seems to "buffer" parenting, because if one part of the system is weak, another part can compensate for it. However, if something must go wrong in the system and only one part can be intact, it will be best if the intact part is the parent. The most vulnerable situation occurs when the only strong part of the system is the baby (Belsky, 1984). The interaction of systems is explored further in the discussions of child abuse in later chapters.

The interaction/social system model is currently the favored explanation for maternal attachment. In its complexity, it reflects what we see in real families, where nothing happens in a vacuum or in isolation. It also makes sense from an ethological point of view. If we think of maternal attachment in terms of its role in preserving the species, we realize that nothing that important would be left to only one or two determining factors.

Implications of Early Attachment

Now that we've viewed attachment from both the baby's side and the parents' side, we need to consider how early attachment affects the child's emotional and social development. If a baby is found to be anxiously attached in the strange situation at 1 year, what kind of child might she be at 2 years? What will she be like later in life? Many studies have shown that the quality of early attachment is correlated with the child's later social and cognitive development. Attachment theorists suggest that the child's internal working model of others as untrustworthy and herself as ineffective consistently undermines later opportunities to learn that others are trustworthy and she can be effective. It has also been suggested that early attachment history is correlated with later social and intellectual behavior because parents who were inconsistent in their responsiveness to signals will also be inconsistent in setting limits and in other aspects of socializing the child. Such later socialization processes are discussed in more detail in Chapter 12.

Table 8-2 gives a sampling of some of the studies that have reported on the later behavior of children whose attachment was evaluated in infancy. Keep in mind, however, that not all studies have found a strong link between attachment history and later development (Fagot & Kavanagh, 1990).

As the table shows, children who were securely attached as infants tend to grow into toddlers and preschoolers with a trusting attitude, a friendly interest in other people, and a confident approach to problems. Children who were anxiously attached as infants, on the other hand, have a much harder time getting along in the world. Like Daniel, whom we met at the beginning of the chapter, they tend to become difficult children who are avoidant, distrustful, and aggressive with people. They evoke reactions from others that keep them in negative relationships and that prevent them from developing more positive social behavior and possibly more trustful models of others. According to one researcher, "not all anxiously attached children later show acting-out behavior problems, but a young child manifesting such problems in an extreme form is likely to have a history of avoidant or resistant attachment relationships" (Sroufe, 1981, p. 15). Taken together, these studies paint a rather bleak picture for children whose early attachments are anxious. If other factors or events trouble these children's lives (divorce, poverty, accidents, and so on), the picture may become even more bleak.

The question, of course, is what can be done to help these children. The first line of defense is prevention. Neonatal intensive care units in hospitals, for example, are making valiant efforts to involve parents in the care of even the smallest premature babies. This involvement helps parents learn to read their babies' signals and gain confidence in caring for them.

Hospital staff and other professionals can identify parents who may be at risk for parenting difficulties, even if their baby is full-term. These parents can be offered counseling, parent support groups, or home visits by a nurse or social worker. Older children in the family can be provided with day care or other programs to relieve the demands on the mother while she's dealing with a new baby. Extra support and help during the first few months can help a mother and baby get off to a good start. Additional programs are available for parents who are known to be at very high risk for parenting difficulties. One such program, designed for mothers with mental illness, is described in Knowledge in Action: Infants and Toddlers.

Even parents having no special problems and a typical baby need support in parenting, especially with a first child. Parenting classes and other support services are now offered by community agencies, local school districts, and private groups. Legislation for parental leave from jobs, which has recently been discussed at the federal level, is intended to ensure that parents have every chance to establish strong relationships with their children.

TABLE 8-2   **Later Behaviors of Children Whose Attachment Was Assessed in Infancy**

Behavior of Children Who Were Securely Attached as Infants	Behavior of Children Who Were Anxiously Attached as Infants	Current Age	Study
When separated from mothers, cried less and played more than anxiously attached peers.	Cried more, played less.	1½	Jacobson & Willie, 1984
More likely to engage in play session with stranger; IQ, language, and social relations intercorrelated and related to stimulating and positive maternal behavior.	Less likely to play with stranger.	2	Clarke-Stewart, Vanderstoep & Killian, 1979
Engaged in more pretend and imaginative play; accepted mothers' suggestions in problem solving; showed more enthusiasm and persistence in problem solving.	Engaged in less symbolic play; ignored mothers' problem-solving suggestions.	2	Matas, Arend & Sroufe, 1978
Approached problems with enthusiasm; were more persistent; used mothers to help them.	More likely to throw tantrums, act aggressively, ignore mothers' suggestions.	2	Sroufe, 1982
More likely to engage in purposeful behavior, be more involved in activities, and get along well with peers.	More likely to be aggressive with peers, to be on the fringes of activities, and to use materials in destructive rather than purposeful ways.	3½	Sroufe, 1982
More flexible in handling feelings and impulses; more independent in helping selves and managing social relations; more compliant; more empathic.	More likely to create problem behaviors and exhibit aberrant behavior.	3	Sroufe, 1981
Appropriately independent: sought contact with teacher when ill or hurt or when they needed help, but otherwise functioned autonomously.	Showed emotional dependence that interfered with autonomous functioning; needed teacher's constant attention and support.	3	Sroufe, Fox & Pancake, 1983
	Toddlers in day care setting who were abused as infants showed anxious attachment; they were more aggressive, more inhibited in approach to adults, and more resistant to friendly overtures than peers who were not abused.	2–3	George & Main, 1981
At lower risk of becoming bullies or the victims of bullies at school during the preschool years.	High risk for becoming a bully or a victim of a bully at school during the preschool years.	4–5	Troy & Sroufe, 1987
At lower risk for developing attention-deficit disorder with hyperactivity in kindergarten.	At increased risk for developing attention-deficit with hyperactivity in kindergarten.		Jacobvitz & Sroufe, 1987

When preventive measures haven't been available or effective and a toddler or preschooler with a history of anxious attachment has obvious difficulty relating to others, then help can be given directly to the child as well as to the parents (George & Main, 1981). Sometimes these interventions take the form of home visits by trained social workers or psychologists who can help a mother learn to respond to her baby's signals and provide developmentally appropriate learning activities (Lieberman, Weston & Pawl, 1991).

A way to help children with behavior disorders directly is the therapeutic preschool. Specially trained staff are necessary because the behavior of these children is hard to understand and manage. The following excerpt is an example of the kind of changes that can occur under the right circumstances (Sroufe, 1981, pp. 23–24):

E.L. is a good example of this reachability of young disturbed children. His malicious, antisocial behavior, his apparent pleasure at other's distress, and his fearless contesting of wills with the teacher had all the marks of incipient sociopathy. His elaborate deviousness and his swaggering style seemed to confirm that he was beyond reach. But in fact, of course, no 4-year-old can "pull off" being a sociopath. And beneath the swagger was a desperately needy child . . . The teachers quickly learned to see opportunities for closeness with E.L. and explicitly disconfirmed his feelings of low self-worth by not rejecting him. As often as possible, the teachers prevented E.L. from engaging in hostile behavior. And when it was necessary to separate E.L. from other children, which was often the case early in the term, a teacher would stay with him. Having difficulty confirming his image of himself as bad, and being totally unable to confirm the belief that he was unworthy, E.L. had little choice but to change his behavior. He formed a strong attachment to the male teacher and made remarkable progress toward learning to meet his basic needs for closeness. . . . The "veneer of toughness" E.L. was building would have, of course, been much "thicker" in later years . . . But I have no doubt that in the preschool years the vast majority of these troubled children could be helped in a fundamental way toward healthier development. One unfortunate implication of our data is, however, that without help these children are likely to carry forward patterns of maladaptation into later childhood and even adulthood.

THE EMERGENCE OF PROSOCIAL BEHAVIOR

One of the characteristics we sometimes observe in securely attached children is **empathy**, the ability to understand how another person is feeling. Babies at first are purely self-centered. They're unable to realize that others have their own points of view and their own emotions. When children start to show empathy, we know that certain social understandings are beginning to dawn on them.

We see empathy when a child hugs or pats a friend who's crying. This type of behavior involves at least three things: (1) the ability to perceive the distress, (2) some idea of what might be causing the distress and what might be done to help, and (3) the willingness and emotional wherewithal to go to someone's aid. Researchers have been interested in when children start to notice that someone is sad or hurt, what they do once they notice, and what kinds of differences in capacity for empathy exist from one individual to another.

One study reported that 12-month-olds responded to another's distress about half the time, although their response consisted of crying, frowning, or looking toward their mothers (Radke-Yarrow, Zahn-Waxler & Chapman, 1983). They couldn't take any action, but they clearly noticed the distress and were aroused by it. By 18 months, children began to try to do something for the distressed person, such as touching or patting. By 2 years, children sometimes offered an object, said something supportive, or went to get help. If their first efforts didn't work, they tried something else. By 2 to 2½ years, children could communicate verbally about emotions and knew how to provide comfort with words, such as, "Baby crying. Kiss. Make it better," "I love Mommy. I want to hold Mommy," and "No cry, Mom. It will be all right" (Bretherton et al., 1986, p. 536).

Although children are capable of empathic responses before the age of 2, whether they actually respond is a different matter. Children aged 2 to 4 at day care centers have shown surprisingly low rates of response to other chil-

dren's distress. This may be because they expect the teachers to take care of the crying child, which they usually do. But when they do respond, most of their actions appear to be prosocial and include approaching, commenting, mediating, or consoling (see Table 8-3).

But there are wide differences in children's responses to others' distress. While some children respond prosocially, others have been observed to leave the scene where a child is crying or even attack the crying child (Radke-Yarrow, Zahn-Wexler & Chapman, 1983). Varying responses among different children may reflect how much the child's own needs were being met at the moment, the reaction the child has received to prosocial gestures in the past, and the general level of nurturing among the adults serving as models for the child. (For a discussion of the effects of models on preschoolers' prosocial development, see Chapter 12).

Perhaps more important to children's development of empathy is their own attachment history. If a parent has been responsive to a child's distress, the child will tend to be more competent in responding to the distress of someone else (Roberts & Strayer, 1987). If the parent has been relatively nonnurturing, the child will tend to be unresponsive to others' distress (Crockenberg, 1985).

All in all, we can say that prosocial response to others' distress *begins* in the late toddler period. The seeds of empathic understanding are present in chil-

FIGURE 8-11
An important element in prosocial behavior is empathy. These girls are capable of sharing their feelings, which encourages cooperating, sharing toys, and taking turns in order to play a game. It's likely that they would also be capable of helping and comforting each other if the need arose.

TABLE 8-3   Responses of Children to Peer Crying at One Day Care Center

Category	Definition
Stare	Child stands near crying child and watches but takes no action and remains silent.
Approach	Child walks over to child and observes silently.
Comment	Child talks about the episode with another child or gives the teacher information about the child who is crying.
Mediate	Child tries to remove the source of pain or conflict or takes the crier to the teacher.
Console	Child offers physical or verbal comfort by patting or hugging the crier, offering an object, or apologizing when the child has caused the distress.
Ignore	Child appears unaware of or ignores crying, even when close by.

SOURCE: Compiled from Phinney, J. S., Feshback, N. D., & Farver, J. (1986). Preschool children's response to peer crying. Early Childhood Research Quarterly, 1(3), 211. Adapted by permission.

dren well before they're 2 years old. Such understanding continues to develop throughout childhood and beyond.

BABY TO BABY: PEER INTERACTION AMONG INFANTS AND TODDLERS

Rebecca, a bouncy 16-month-old, arrives in the pediatrician's office in her mother's arms. Her mother finds a chair in the crowded waiting room and sits down with Rebecca on her lap. She reaches into her purse and takes out a small stuffed rabbit, which she places in front of Rebecca. But Rebecca doesn't grab it. In fact, she doesn't seem to know it's there. She's turned around, looking behind her, at a baby sitting on another mother's lap across the room. Rebecca's mother taps her softly on the head with the stuffed rabbit to get her attention. Rebecca turns around, sees the rabbit, and takes hold of it. But she doesn't play with it. Instead, she immediately turns around again to look at the same baby she was staring at before. Then she waves her rabbit-filled fist up and down as she squeals a greeting to her peer. The other baby looks serious for a moment, and then her face breaks into a smile too. She slaps her hands against her lap and gives out a friendly squeal in answer to Rebecca's greeting.

Babies notice and interact not just with adults but with other babies as well. Like Rebecca, they're curious and interested in what their peers might be like. But since they're not yet very skilled at social interactions—we've seen that infant-adult exchanges are kept going by the adult partner—babies' peer interactions are different from parent-child interactions. We look more closely now at this aspect of social and emotional development.

Signals, Responses, and Interaction

Babies start to watch other babies and send them social signals as early as 10 months of age. They might smile, laugh, or vocalize to them, more often than not from a distance. Or they might cry or fuss while watching another baby.

Occasionally, they might touch or strike another baby (Eckerman, Whatley & Kutz, 1975). Many times the interactions among infants and toddlers involve a toy. Toddlers often offer a toy to another child, reach for the toy the other child is playing with, or attempt to play with a toy while the other child is playing with it (Bronson, 1981).

Of course, real social interaction requires not just a signal but also a response, and infants and toddlers aren't very adept at responding. By far their most frequent response to a social gesture from another infant or toddler is to ignore it (Bronson, 1981). They also might look at the other child or passively grasp an offered toy. Sometimes they hit, poke, or pull hair. Responses that seem to reciprocate the social intention of the other child are fairly rare in the first or second year of life.

When a child of this age does respond to a social gesture, it's most often a single response with no further interaction following. Sometimes a second "contact burst" occurs between the same two children, involving a different toy or theme. Parallel play, in which two children play with similar toys near each other, is very rare at this age, as are "contact chains," in which children engage in a series of back-and-forth actions and reactions—true social interaction (Bronson, 1981).

What we see, then, is that children up to about 2 years of age don't yet have much ability to sustain social interaction with peers. Interactions do increase when children are brought together more than once and have a chance to become acquainted with each other (Rubenstein & Howes, 1976; Mueller & Brenner, 1977). They also sometimes get caught up in **social games,** activities

FIGURE 8-12
Toddlers have limited understanding of group activities and are easily distracted, so moments of shared fun tend to be fleeting. But for the moment at least, these young children are playing a game together and enjoying each other's company.

that involve taking turns, repetition, and imitation, along with lots of smiling and laughing (Fein & Rivkin, 1986). Consider this example, in which two 22-month-old boys discover the fascination of spinning a wheel on an overturned doll carriage (Fein, 1984, p. 97):

> David approaches the overturned doll carriage. After exploring the spokes of the wheel, he discovers that the wheel can be made to spin. Sam wanders over, watching David's motion on the wheel and the resulting spin. David looks up at Sam, grinning. The wheel is no longer spinning, and Sam timidly puts his hand on it, giving it a push. He laughs, looks at David, who is smiling broadly. As the spin slows down, David gives it a push, and when it slows again, looks at Sam who again makes it spin. The children continue to take turns, but soon they begin to overlap. After five turns, Sam moves the wheel continuously, studying its motion. David fingers the spokes, then wanders off to another toy.

Certain aspects of this interaction made it possible for the children to sustain several rounds of play. The actions were repetitive, and they involved interactions that parents often practice with their children, such as taking turns. Once the children established a **shared meaning**—an understanding about the content of the game (Brenner & Mueller, 1982)—they could coordinate and maintain the action. If pretend play had been involved, these children probably couldn't have managed it. Children between 2 and 3 years of age begin to be able to engage in pretend play (see Chapter 6), but play is fairly solitary until about age 3.

Peer Interaction and Attachment History

We know that children's attachment history has a powerful effect on their social and emotional development. How does it specifically affect their relationships with other children? By the time children are in elementary school, some of them are popular and preferred as playmates and others are disliked and rejected. (Popularity in middle childhood is discussed in greater detail in Chapter 16.) The ones who are popular are often children who have positive, friendly personalities and who don't engage in much aggressive, hostile, or harassing behavior. This kind of social "style" seems to be related to a child's attachment history.

Toddlers who were securely attached as infants seem to be more positive toward other children than toddlers with histories of anxious attachment (Pastor, 1981). They're friendlier and more cooperative, more outgoing, and more flexible in struggles over toys. Toddlers with secure attachment histories also seem more comfortable with symbolic play (Slade, 1987). They can pretend play for longer periods of time, and they spend more time planning and creating make-believe scenes. Their greater ability to plan may be related to a greater capacity to delay action and control their impulses. These are skills that serve children well later on. Older children who are popular seem to be good at sizing up ongoing play situations and accurately timing their bids to be included.

There also seems to be a connection between attachment history and the tendency to be a bully or a victim. A recent study of 4- and 5-year-olds found that victimizers, or bullies, had anxious/avoidant attachment histories at 12 and 18 months (Troy & Sroufe, 1987). Furthermore, most victims—children who are consistently passive in the face of aggression—had anxious/ambiv-

FIGURE 8-13
A momentary struggle or a pattern of bully-victim behavior? The early parent-child relationship has important implications for all the child's future interactions; behavior problems often stem from an anxious attachment relationship.

alent attachment histories. In fact, in all of the cases in which a child with an avoidant attachment history was paired with a child with an ambivalent attachment history, one victimized the other. Children with secure attachment histories tended not to be victims or victimizers—they didn't exploit or bully others, but they also didn't respond passively when others tried to bully them. We see again that the effects of early parent-child attachment reverberate throughout the child's life, long after infancy and toddlerhood are over. We might even say they become embedded in the personality. Clearly it's worth all our efforts to make sure the early attachment relationship is a good one.

SEX-TYPING IN INFANCY

Today, Benjamin is 4 weeks old. His mother puts him in his cradle for a nap and then sits down to write some thank-you notes for baby gifts. As she mentions each gift in the notes, it dawns on her that Benjamin received very different baby presents than his older sister received 3 years ago. Back then, there weren't any soft hammers or squeezable choo-choo trains, nor was there a sturdy metal dump truck to put away for later. And she couldn't recall a single item of clothing that had been blue. Everything was pink, white, or pale yellow. "Well," she thought, "the birth announcement did say, 'IT'S A BOY!'"

The first thing most parents ask about their baby is whether it's a boy or a girl (Itons-Peterson & Reddel, 1984). This information is proclaimed on the birth announcement along with other vital statistics like weight and length.

There's no question but that everyone is interested in the baby's gender, but does this information then influence how they act toward the baby? Do people treat boy babies differently from girl babies? And if they do, what are the consequences of this different treatment?

We've all seen 2- or 3-year-olds acting "like boys" or "like girls." At a nursery school, for example, we would probably see more boys than girls playing with trucks and cars, building with blocks, or chasing each other outdoors. We would probably see more girls than boys caring for dolls, having tea parties, or playing house.

Where do they learn to act this way? It's clear that many of these apparently sex-appropriate behaviors aren't "built into" the biological make-up of boys and girls but are acquired during childhood. The question is whether children learn these different behaviors because their parents—consciously or unconsciously—treat them differently right from the day they're born.

How Adults See Boy and Girl Babies

Adults do seem to have different perceptions and expectations of boy and girl babies. In some studies with actor babies (babies who were not the children of the adults being observed), adults were misled about the baby's sex and their reactions to the baby were observed. When a 6-month-old boy was presented as a girl to some women and as a boy to others, they played differently with him depending on how he had been labeled (Will, Self & Datan, 1976). The women who thought he was a girl offered him a doll rather than a train or a fish. The women who thought he was a boy offered the train. In another study, adults encouraged "boys" to walk, crawl, or engage in physical activity more than they encouraged "girls" (Smith & Lloyd, 1978).

Parents perceive their own babies differently too, based on whether they're boys or girls. When one group of parents rated their newborns on a questionnaire, they made clear distinctions between the sexes. Although the babies didn't differ in their newborn measurements or their Apgar scores, girls were judged to be weaker, prettier, softer, and more delicate, and boys were judged to be firmer, more alert, stronger, hardier, and better coordinated. Fathers' ratings showed even more differences for the sexes than mothers' ratings did (Rubin, Provenzano & Luria, 1974).

These studies confirm that adults do perceive and treat babies differently based on their sex, but some flaws are apparent in these experimental situations. When actor babies are involved, the brief interaction with a strange child might be expected to evoke a stereotypical reaction (Frisch, 1977). And when parents are new and inexperienced, they may be forced to rely on sex role stereotypes when answering questions about their newborns (Rubin, Provenzano & Luria, 1974). It's probably more important to know whether parents treat their own children in stereotypical ways over longer periods of time.

How Parents Treat Their Own Boy and Girl Babies

Many studies have found no differences in how parents treat their boy and girl babies, but other studies have turned up some differences. For example, fathers have been observed to play in more active, physical ways with their sons than with their daughters (Parke & Suomi, 1980; Power & Parke, 1982). Boys and girls have also been found to have different toys, most of them pre-

FIGURE 8-14
A football, a brisk day, warm sweats—what more could a boy want? By selecting a football as a toy, the parents of this 22-month-old tell him that outdoor physical play and rough-and-tumble games are acceptable behaviors for him. The perceptions and expectations of adults shape children's sex-typed behavior in subtle ways throughout childhood.

sumably bought by their parents (Fein et al., 1975). And mothers have been observed to respond differently to their sons' and daughters' emotions. When their infant girls showed pain, mothers matched their expressions with furrowed brows, but they almost totally ignored their infant boys' expression of pain. When their boys showed anger, on the other hand, mothers responded with expressions of concern and sympathy, but they met their girls' anger with a return of anger (Haviland, 1982). Although at this point we can only speculate about the effect of these reactions, it seems logical to conclude that they teach boys to hide their pain and show their anger and girls to show their pain and hide their anger—the stereotypes of "masculine" and "feminine" emotional expression.

The mixed results of these studies don't give us clear answers to our questions about the origin of the sex-typed behavior we see in children and adults. We can note that the studies that turned up no differences in how parents treat their boy and girl babies are the ones in which researchers were observing basic, daily caregiving and social interaction. The studies that did report differences focused on activities like playing and shopping for toys or clothes. It may be that the job of taking care of a baby is so demanding that it overrides all other considerations. Most parents are so busy that they treat their babies just as babies, not as girl babies or boy babies.

However, the few occasions when they do treat them differently may be important, such as when they respond to the expression of emotions. This is exactly the subtle kind of teaching and learning we would expect when we're dealing with something that seems so innate, so much a part of one's basic nature, as sex-typed behavior. Future research in many areas of child development, psychology, and biology will probably shed more light on how boys and girls come to adopt the behaviors that fit the sex roles accepted in their society.

OVERVIEW

When infancy and toddlerhood are over, a 3-year-old has emerged. Most of us think of this child as very, very young, and of course she is. But a lot has happened in those three years, a lot that will influence the child and those she touches in all the years to come. It isn't that what she is at this age is impossible to change in any way—it isn't. But change will come hard and will take great effort, if the course now set is to be altered. What is already there will need to be—and will demand to be—taken into account.

We would run into the most difficulty trying to alter the effects of a history of anxious attachment, although even this is not impossible. And apparently it is well worth the effort to try, given the wide-ranging implications of a child's attachment history. As we have seen, general stance toward life, personality characteristics related to trust and autonomy, patterns of peer interaction, responses to others' feelings, and general cognitive functioning are influenced by attachment history. It's safe to say that not a single other aspect of a child's experience will be able to exert such a profound influence on the child's life. And that's worth thinking—and doing—quite a lot about.

CHAPTER REVIEW

ATTACHMENT

- Attachment, the emotional tie between infant and mother (or other primary caregiver) is a crucial factor in the social and emotional development of the growing child.
- Early theories of attachment assumed that infants develop a preference for the adult who feeds them. Both psychoanalytic and early behavioral theories were based on notions of drive reduction and secondary reinforcement.
- Ethological explanations of attachment focus on the aspects of this behavior that would have enhanced chances of survival as the species evolved. They suggest that adults who are skilled in reading and responding appropriately to babies' signals are the ones most likely to foster healthy attachments and trust of others.
- Harlow's study of surrogate mothers among monkeys discredited the secondary reinforcement explanation of attachment. Ethologists have used this study as support for their view.
- Infant attachment is assessed in a standard laboratory procedure known as the "strange situation," which highlights the way infants use their mothers for both safety and exploration.
- Three basic patterns of attachment—one normal and two deviant—emerged from experiments involving the strange situation: secure, anxious/ambivalent, and anxious/avoidant. Securely attached infants use their mothers as a home base from which to explore and as a source of comfort when they're distressed. Infants exhibiting the anxious/avoidant pattern rarely interact with their mothers during play and show no distress when separated. Infants exhibiting the anxious/ambivalent pattern show extreme distress when separated from their mothers but don't accept comfort from them when they return.
- Crying, gazing, and averting the gaze are among the earliest social signals at the infant's disposal. Smiling emerges by 2 months of age, apparently as a result of maturational rather than social factors.
- The child usually exhibits "stranger anxiety"—wariness of unfamiliar adults—between 6 and 18 months of age.
- It has been suggested that the anxious/ambivalent pattern of attachment may result when parents fail to respond contingently to a baby's signals. The anxious/avoidant pattern may result when parents routinely respond inappropriately to a baby's signals.
- Social referencing—scanning the face of a familiar and trusted person to pick up information about a new sit-

uation—begins at about 9 months. Infants can discriminate facial expressions by the time they are 4 or 5 months old, but they don't know their meaning until they are between 6 and 9 months old.
- On the parent's side of attachment, the hormonal theory suggests that maternal attachment is a result of bonding with the baby in the first hours after birth. This theory has not been supported by research.
- A mother's history has an effect on her parenting behavior, but it's not the sole determining factor in the kind of attachment she forms with her baby.
- The currently accepted social system theory suggests that many factors interact with each other to influence attachment. Characteristics of the parent seem to have a stronger influence on parenting behavior than do characteristics of the baby or those of the environment. Temperament—the child's inborn characteristics—can influence the attachment relationship, but it's not necessarily a crucial factor.
- Children with anxious attachment histories are at a higher risk of becoming emotionally dependent, aggressive, noncompliant, easily frustrated in the face of challenging tasks, inattentive, and hyperactive.

THE EMERGENCE OF PROSOCIAL BEHAVIOR

- Signs of empathy—the understanding of another person's feelings—reflect the child's social and emotional development.
- At 12 months, babies tend to respond to the distress of others by showing distress themselves. By 18 months, they begin to focus on the distressed person and try to provide comfort. By 2 years, children share, help, and look concerned often enough to indicate that the seeds of empathy are present by this age.
- When parents have been nurturant and responsive to their child's distress, the child is better at responding to others' distress.

PEER INTERACTION AMONG INFANTS AND TODDLERS

- Children between 12 and 24 months of age have a repertoire of social signals that they can use with peers, but true social interaction is rare in this age group.
- Children under 3 years enjoy social games, which involve actions familiar to them from their games and play with adults.
- Pretend play is usually solitary prior to the age of 3.
- Social "style" seems to be related to attachment history. Toddlers with secure attachment histories are more positive toward peers than are toddlers with anxious attachment histories. They engage in more planning during pretend play, sustain their play episodes for longer periods of time, and tend to be neither bullies nor victims in later social interactions.

SEX-TYPING IN INFANCY

- Sex role development is the learning that results in children's acting "like boys" or "like girls."
- Adults perceive babies differently, depending on whether they're labeled boys or girls.
- When basic caregiving is examined, few, if any, gender-related differences in how parents treat their babies have come to light.
- An important area in which boys and girls do seem to be treated differently is emotional expression.

KEY TERMS

attachment	internal working models	social smile	bonding
drive reduction	secure attachment	endogenous smile	critical period
secondary reinforcer	anxious/avoidant	stranger anxiety	empathy
preprogrammed	attachment	social referencing	social games
ethology	anxious/ambivalent	separation distress	shared meaning
imprinting	attachment		

SUGGESTIONS FOR FURTHER READING

Belsky, J., & Nezworski, T. (Eds.). (1988). *Clinical implications of attachment.* Hillsdale, NJ: Lawrence Erlbaum. The articles in this book describe in detail how various systems interact to affect attachment quality as well as the relationship between early attachment quality and the child's later behavior.

Bowlby, J. (1988). *A secure base: Parent-child attachment and healthy human development.* New York: Basic Books. In the nine lectures in this book, Bowlby describes the implications of his attachment theory for clinical psychology and personality development.

Karen, R. (1990). Becoming attached. *The Atlantic Monthly,* February, 35–70. A very readable summary of attachment theory and research, including a brief discussion of disagreements between attachment and temperament theorists.

Kohnstamm, G., Bates, J., & Rothbart, M. (1989). *Temperament in childhood.* New York: John Wiley & Sons. An overview of the field of temperament in childhood, including its measurement, clinical implications, cultural differences, and relationship to biology and development.

Plomin, R., & Dunn, J., (Eds.). (1986). *The study of temperament.* Hillsdale, NJ: Lawrence Erlbaum. A number of chapters in this book treat different aspects of temperament—the presumably inborn personality characteristics of children.

Stern, D. (1977). *The first relationship: Infant and mother.* Cambridge, MA: Harvard University Press. A very readable book about the development of attachment; includes material on behaviors of the infant and the caregiver and things that can go wrong in mother-infant interactions.

MILESTONES IN INFANT AND TODDLER DEVELOPMENT

AGE	PHYSICAL	COGNITIVE	LANGUAGE	SOCIAL-EMOTIONAL
0–6 mos.	Holds head up when on stomach Rolls over from front to back Reaches for objects Exhibits many reflexes	Demonstrates primary circular reaction stage of sensorimotor intelligence Scans within a face Shows preference for contrast in visual displays Prefers looking at normal face	Cries and coos Recognizes human voice, prefers ''baby talk'' Can discriminate /d/ from /t/	Signals needs with crying and gazing Becomes attached to caregiver Smiles in sleep Smiles at people but indiscriminately
6–12 mos.	Demonstrates fewer reflexes Gets first tooth Sits up Develops pincer grasp Creeps, crawls Stands holding on	Demonstrates secondary circular reaction Demonstrates coordination of secondary circular reactions Imitates new behavior if scheme is familiar Searches for completely hidden object Looks longer at scrambled face	Repeats consonant-vowel syllables Varies intonation Says protowords Says first word	Smiles selectively Begins to use social referencing Shows stranger anxiety Responds to distress of other by showing distress, crying
12–18 mos.	Walks Climbs stairs	Demonstrates tertiary circular reactions Includes others as recipients of play behaviors	Uses holophrases Uses expressive jargon	Experiences peak of separation distress
18–24 mos.	Begins to run	Demonstrates invention of new means through mental combinations Finds hidden objects through invisible displacement Shows deferred imitation Activates toy or doll in pretend play	Uses telegraphic speech Understands multiword utterances	Demonstrates less separation distress Begins to show empathic responses to another's distress
24–36 mos.	Jumps Begins to ride a tricycle	Shows ability to substitute objects in pretend play Shows greater ability to substitute objects in pretend play Shows ability to integrate themes in play	Uses verbal strategies to start a conversation Uses less telegraphic speech	Begins to respond verbally to another's distress Includes others in pretend play

INFANTS AND TODDLERS

"Good morning! How are you doing today?"
"Good morning! I'm doing just fine! How about you?"
Jasmine and Monica exchange greetings as they leave their homes with their babies. Jasmine has a 6-month-old daughter, Jenna, and works full time for a large advertising agency. Her next-door neighbor, Monica, has a 9-month-old daughter, Ellie. Monica is a full-time, at-home mother right now, although she worked as a scientist in a major research center before Ellie was born.

Jasmine is headed for work, but first she'll take Jenna to the day care center that her advertising company owns and operates as an employee benefit. Monica is setting out for the early stimulation program her daughter attends three mornings a week. Ellie, retarded at birth, is enrolled in a special program intended to maximize her potential. Monica may leave Ellie with the program staff while she runs errands, or she may stay at the center to observe the staff as they work with her daughter. Once a week, the center holds an informal discussion session for parents and staff, and she often attends that. Monica relies heavily on the program for support in raising her daughter and for respite from the extra stress of having a child with developmental delays. Jasmine also relies heavily on Jenna's program for the day care that allows her to lead the life she's always dreamed of, as both a mother and a business executive.

Infant and toddler education and care programs can serve many different purposes. Some parents use them because their children have special needs. Others use them as a way to nurture their child's development and provide stimulation that's not otherwise available in the child's environment. Still others use them because they work full time or they're finishing their own education.

Regardless of a program's specific purpose, the overall goal of infant and toddler programs is to provide the best conditions for the development of their young clientele. How do the people who design these programs know what the best conditions are? They're guided by the kind of research discussed in earlier chapters of this book. Many programs have made the development of cognitive abilities and language skills a top priority. They include moderately novel stimulation in their activities to keep babies' interest and to promote learning. They're sensitive to the importance of responsive caregiving when they're with the children. These programs increasingly reflect the latest findings in child development research.

Infant and toddler education and care programs are only one "real-life" area in which child development research has important implications and applications. The previous chapters have discussed many kinds of research and described many facets of knowledge about children. This chapter describes knowledge in action—how that knowledge about children can be used. Knowledge gained from research makes it possible to plan appropriate education and care programs for children. It provides the tools to assess children for possible developmental problems. It guides and supports adults' efforts to keep children healthy and safe, to feed and toilet train them, and to provide them with appropriate toys and playthings. This Knowledge in Action section addresses these areas of applied knowledge.

INFANT AND TODDLER EDUCATION AND CARE PROGRAMS

Twenty years ago, only 25 percent of mothers with babies under 1 year of age were in the work force in this country. In 1988 the figure was at 53 percent (Hymes, 1989). Financial pressures, changing social conditions, new cultural ideals, and special needs all contribute to the ever-growing demand for out-of-the-home education and care for young children.

Over the years some programs have become prominent as models of outstanding care for both the average child like Jenna and the child with special needs like Ellie. Here, we discuss four such programs, which have focused on the following concerns: (1) how to provide appropriate day care; (2) how to prevent language and cognitive delays in children who live in conditions of poverty; (3) how to assist parents of children with disabilities; and (4) how to help parents whose personal problems put their children's emotional development at risk.

The four programs described here are aimed at children who are economically disadvantaged, who have cognitive or physical disabilities, or who are at risk for developmental delays and emotional difficulties because of a parent's severe mental problems. They've provided models for many of the care programs we see today, both for typical and for atypical children.

The Florida Parent Education Infant and Toddler Program

The Florida Parent Education Infant and Toddler program, begun in 1966 at the University of Florida, was designed to help children whose families were economically disadvantaged. Developed by Dr. Ira Gordon, the program emphasizes parent education. Parents are trained to teach their own babies, rather than taking the babies to a program where professional educators teach

FIGURE 1
Ideally, child care programs provide infants and toddlers with a safe, stimulating environment, responsive caregiving, and support for cognitive, social, and emotional development. From the child's point of view, however, the most important elements may be friends to play with and toys to enjoy.

them. This is a common feature when programs serve children who may be at risk for developing delays because of a family's economic situation. Focusing on the parents as the babies' primary teachers makes it more likely that the effects of the program will be carried over into the home and will continue after the child "graduates" from the program.

RESEARCH UNDERPINNINGS. Dr. Gordon relied heavily on Piaget's conception of sensorimotor intelligence when he developed the program. He devised activities for parents to engage in with their babies that would support the babies' cognitive growth. He especially wanted to help parents solve what has been called "the problem of the match" (Hunt, 1965)—the need to give children experiences that challenge them but that don't go beyond their level of skill and understanding.

Dr. Gordon also recognized that babies should learn that they can make things happen. In Chapter 8, we discussed what happens when babies don't get responses to their efforts—they develop "learned helplessness," the feeling that what they do has no effect on the world. Dr. Gordon designed activities that would help babies gain feelings of mastery, competence, and autonomy.

SAMPLE ACTIVITIES. Two sample activities from the Florida Parent Education program demonstrate how Dr. Gordon translated research findings into specific activities for babies and their parents. The first is called "Look Ma, No Hands." Here are the instructions (Gordon, 1970, p. 16):

> Baby will be delighted to learn he can make some things happen, even when he can't touch them.
>
> You can use either the cradle gym, or you can fasten a mobile to the crib, or you can tie some colorful pieces of cording or other fabrics to the top bar of the crib over the baby's feet, where he can see them.
>
> Bounce the crib mattress with your hand near his feet to make the objects move.
>
> Take one of his feet, and gently tap it on the mattress to set the objects in motion. He'll see that movements on the mattress cause an interesting action, and he can do it on his own, when he wants to.

FIGURE 2
Playing with a baby at the baby's own level fosters both cognitive and emotional development. This mother provides an appropriate toy and carefully observes her child's responses to it. This kind of attention is needed for sensitive interactions with an infant.

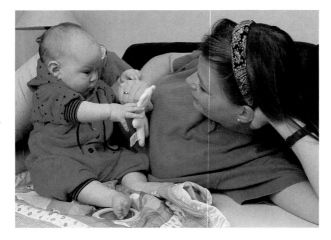

This activity enables babies to act on their environment and see the effects of their actions. You'll recognize the action and effect as an example of Piaget's sensorimotor Stage 3, secondary circular reactions.

The second activity is called "Hide and Seek." The instructions are as follows (Gordon, 1970, pp. 32–37):

> Begin with a simple game using a toy and some soft covering material, such as a blanket. Attract his attention to the toy and then partly hide it under the blanket so that baby can still see a part of it.
>
> Then say, "Where did it go?" "Find the toy."
>
> If he's puzzled and doesn't seem to know how to retrieve it, show him how. If he ignores the toy after it is hidden, play with it yourself in front of him, but don't demand his attention or any action. He will, on his own, get interested in what you are doing. Partly hide it again until he's able to get it himself.
>
> Play the same game, but hide the toy completely under the soft materials.
>
> Repeat this for fun a number of times and then leave the child with both toy and blanket . . .
>
> A third approach to hide-and-seek is to place one of his favorite objects in a box or other container where he can no longer see it. Be sure the container is easy to open. Ask him, "Can you get it now?" . . .
>
> Remember, don't tease, don't frustrate and don't force. Watch for the child "turning off."
>
> When he discovers the toy is in the container, he'll enjoy putting it in, closing the box, opening it, taking it out, and then he can be left to repeat this for his own continued learning and amusement.

This activity involves object permanence, another concept from Piaget's work. The instructions emphasize various aspects of parent-child interaction discussed in earlier chapters—verbalization while the parent interacts with the baby; careful observation of the baby's behavior; variation in the kind and level of stimulation given; and responsiveness to the baby's signals. All of these components contribute to a healthy, nurturing parent-child relationship. The relationship, in turn, supports the baby's cognitive development.

The Mother-Child Home Program

As the name implies, the Mother-Child Home Program is based in the home rather than at a center or school. This orientation reflects the program's philosophy that the parent is the child's first and most important teacher. Having the program at home gives the parent the opportunity to learn effective ways of interacting with the child. It also recognizes that children are often more receptive to learning experiences if they're introduced in a familiar setting by someone they know. This program, developed by Phyllis Levenstein in New York State, is also aimed at economically disadvantaged families.

PROGRAM ORGANIZATION AND ACTIVITIES. The Mother-Child Home Program is for toddlers. Parent and child enroll when the child is age 2, and they stay in the program until the child is age 4 (one year into the preschool period). The curriculum, or content of the program, focuses on language and conceptual development. Each week during the school year, a trained home visitor comes to the home with a toy or book that the child can keep. The home visitor reads the book or shows the child how to play with the toy, at the same time encouraging the parent to participate in the session.

The criteria for selecting the toys and books are listed in Tables 1 and 2, along with suggested toys and titles. These materials are called Verbal Interaction Stimulus Materials (VISM) because their primary purpose is to promote

FIGURE 3
A wooden puzzle gives this toddler practice with both his problem-solving abilities and his fine motor skills. Equally important is the positive interaction with his mother. This kind of activity is at the heart of the Mother-Child Home Program.

TABLE 1 Criteria for VISM Toys

Criteria	Names and Descriptions of Toys	Criteria Met by Toys
Verbal 1. Induces language 2. Permits language	*Block cart* Wooden wagon, colored blocks with holes, rods that fit into holes	All but 6, 15
Perceptual 3. Strong colors 4. Geometric forms 5. Space organization 6. Size differences 7. Sound differences 8. Tactile differences 9. Form matching	*Hammer and pegs* Pegs fixed into wooden bench can be pounded through to under side; bench can then be reversed *Mail box* Copy of corner mail box; colored wood beads are dropped through top holes into bin	All but 5, 6, 11, 13 All but 15
Motor 10. Specific skills 11. Fitting parts 12. Hitting 13. Pulling 14. Lifting 15. Diffuse motor discharge	*Transportation puzzle* Jigsaw puzzle, each piece a different vehicle *Two plush hand puppets* Animals, movable mouths *Circus puzzle* Jigsaw puzzle of circus tent, circus scene beneath	All but 7, 12, 13, 15 All but 5, 6, 9, 12, 15 All but 7, 12, 13, 15
Conceptual 16. Problem solving 17. Intelligible goal 18. Intrinsic reward 19. Imaginative uses 20. Social concepts 21. Sex neutrality 22. Ethnic neutrality *Other* 23. Low anxiety potential 24. Safety 25. Durability 26. Easy care for mother	*Cash register* Simple copy with cash drawer and bell activated by crank *House puzzle* Jigsaw puzzle of street and outside of house; inside of house and buried *utilities* shown under pieces (fewer pieces than same puzzle used with 3-year-olds)	All All but 7, 12, 13, 15

SOURCE: Levenstein, P. (1977). The mother-child home program. In M. C. Day and R. Parker (Eds.), The preschooler in action: Exploring early childhood programs (2nd ed) (pp. 28–49). Boston: Allyn & Bacon. Copyright © 1977 Phyllis Levenstein. Reprinted by permission of the author.

language development. The toys and books are classics, available today in toystores, bookstores, and libraries and present in most preschools.

PROGRAM RESULTS. Children enrolled in this program have gained long-term positive benefits. They do better in elementary school than similar children not enrolled in the program. We can pick out various aspects of the program that probably contribute to its success—the emphasis on the parent's participation in the child's play, the provision of appropriate toys and books, the focus on reading.

Another factor for success is probably the age of the children. Toddlers are energetic, busy, willful—even the most resourceful parents don't always know what constructive experiences to offer them. The program gives concrete ideas and models of positive interaction at an important time in children's lives. It begins in time to help set the stage for learning during the toddler and preschool years. The model provided by the Mother-Child Home Program is widely used today.

TABLE 2   Criteria for VISM Books

Criteria	Titles and Authors of Books by Subject Groups (in Order of Presentation)
1. Contents geared to children's age and interest; interesting to mothers; leads to verbalized associations; widens experience	**2- and 3-Year-Olds** Runhardt, D. *Pat the Bunny* Brown, M. W. *Good Night Moon* Rojankovsky, F. (Illus.) *The Tall Book of Mother Goose*
2. High literary standards	Keats, E. J. *The Snowy Day*
3. Language simple, rhythmic, with some repetition	Zion, G. *All Falling Down*
4. Reading level within ability of all mothers	Krauss, R. *The Carrot Seed*
5. Content, illustrations, and general format attractive to both sexes and any ethnic group	Keats, E. J. *Peter's Chair* Eastman, P. D. *Are You My Mother?* Keats, E. J. *Whistle for Willie*
6. Illustrations profuse, large, colorful, detailed, rich source of labeling and classification	**2-Year-Olds** Tresselt, A. *Rainy Drop Splash* Tresselt, A. *Wake Up Farm* Gag, W. *Millions of Cats*
7. Low anxiety potential	**3-Year-Olds**
8. Durability	Brown, M. W. *The Runaway Bunny* Seuss, Dr. *The Cat in the Hat* MacGregor, E. *Theodore Turtle*

SOURCE: Levenstein, P. (1977). The mother-child home program. In M. C. Day and R. Parker (Eds.), The preschooler in action: Exploring early childhood programs (2nd ed) (pp. 28–49). Boston: Allyn & Bacon. Copyright © 1977 Phyllis Levenstein. Reprinted by permission of the author.

The Marin County, California, Program for Atypical Infants

Sponsored as part of the community mental health services, this early intervention program was designed for babies with special needs. It serves physically handicapped and mentally retarded babies, emotionally disturbed babies, and babies who are at risk because of such factors as low birthweight or mental illness in their mother (Nielsen et al., 1975).

The program includes several subprograms. There are weekly home visits, group meetings for parents and children, and group meetings for children alone. Children enrolled in the last subprogram come to the center several mornings a week for a therapeutic day care program.

The program emphasizes development in many areas: sensorimotor, language, motor, and feeding. To support sensory development, for example, teachers provide various tactile experiences. Children can walk (or crawl) on carpeted and tiled areas of the floor and on grass and foam rubber as well. They're given various materials to feel—wet and dry sand, corn meal, warm and cool water. Babies are allowed to play with edible materials such as pudding, whipped cream, or mashed potatoes.

To encourage language awareness, teachers introduce new sounds for back-and-forth language play and associate words with actions and objects. To support motor development, they provide appropriate activities, depending on individual babies' handicaps—swinging one in a blanket or hammock, for example, and helping another explore a space. Teachers also help parents recognize the different signals their handicapped babies may give, and they encourage them not to give up when responses aren't typical.

Ellie attends a program similar to this one. As an atypical infant with moderate retardation, she has not yet begun to sit up independently or use her

FIGURE 4
Programs for children with disabilities are designed to serve their needs. Trained teachers or therapists often work with children individually on special equipment or in appropriate activities. This game provides practice in balance and coordination and enhances the child's sense of control and competence.

hands to explore the world in the active way that normally developing infants will. Her approach to the world is quite passive, both because she lacks the motor skills needed for active exploration and because her retardation makes her less curious and less capable of thinking of things to do.

One infant caregiver works directly with Ellie, trying to encourage her to respond to and act on the world. One morning, for example, Ellie's caregiver held a brightly colored rattle in front of her and shook it. The color of the rattle, as well as its sound, caught Ellie's attention. When she looked at it, the caregiver raised her hand so that she could take hold of the rattle. Then she moved the rattle toward Ellie's mouth so she could mouth it. After giving Ellie a few minutes to explore the rattle in this way, the caregiver moved it so that it was a little bit out of the direct range of Ellie's gaze. Then she shook the rattle again. Ellie turned her head and eyes to catch sight of the rattle, and the caregiver again raised Ellie's hand to the toy. All these maneuvers are designed to increase Ellie's repertoire of actions on objects and to raise her interest in attending to and exploring the world around her.

The Threshold Mothers' Project

This program, funded by the National Institute of Mental Health and developed by a psychiatric rehabilitation agency in Chicago, focuses on the children of mentally ill mothers. These children are more likely than other children to have attachment disruptions and cognitive impairments. The program has three facets: It treats the mothers alone, the babies alone, and the mothers and babies together (Musick, Clark & Cohler, 1981).

Mothers attend weekly therapy sessions, receive training in parenting, and take a child development course. Children attend a therapeutic nursery five mornings a week. Language and emotional development are the main concerns here. Once a week, each mother participates in the nursery program, where she can observe the positive interactions modeled by the staff.

Every few months, each mother-child **dyad** (pair) participates in a video-taping session. The staff analyzes the tapes with the mother, helping her understand her interactions with her child. These tapes can be used to sensitize the mother to her child's cues and help her respond more appropriately to the child's needs.

Day Care for Children without Special Needs

The four programs just described are designed for children with special needs of one kind or another. But what about the children like Jenna—ordinary children from ordinary families who need day care because their parents work? This is the fastest-growing population of children in need of educational programs today and the group most teachers of young children are likely to have in their programs. What are their needs, and what are their programs like?

Jenna's day care center has a large playroom for each age group. In Jenna's infant room, there are many toys, including colorful plastic balls; push and pull toys; a "climbing/crawling" area with ramps and tunnels; simple shape boxes; some picture books with cardboard pages; a low, unbreakable mirror; and numerous rattles and other manipulatives that babies can feel, look at, and mouth.

The infant caregivers spend their day playing with and talking to the infants, feeding them, and rocking or patting them to sleep. Each infant is assigned to one of the three caregivers for primary care, although all caregivers interact with all the babies. Because different babies are on different schedules, all these activities go on throughout the day. Not until the babies graduate to the toddler classroom is there a daily schedule for eating, playing, and napping that's more or less followed by all the children.

Finding suitable day care is a difficult problem for many working parents. More and more businesses are providing some help, either in the form of company-run centers like Jenna's or in the form of information and referral services to help parents locate appropriate care. Other companies provide day care vouchers—payments the parents can use toward day care services not associated with the company. Voucher programs typically pay only a portion of the day care costs and are adjusted to give more help to workers with lower salaries. Some employers give special consideration to parents whose children are sick and can't go to day care, allowing them time off or flexible hours (see Public Policy Focus—Sick Child Day Care).

Even though the demand for day care for children without special needs is a fact, there's considerable debate over its merits. Many people question the wisdom of separating infants from their mothers for long periods of time early in life. (For a discussion of the day care debate, see Research Focus—How Does Day Care Affect Parent-Child Attachment?) In our society, where care has traditionally been provided for infants and toddlers only when their families can't care for them (Grubb & Lazerson, 1982), some people find day care for babies living in so-called normal family situations unnecessary or inappropriate. Working parents respond that they must work to survive economically, that the role of full-time parent is too narrow and limiting, or that both parents are entitled to a career. Given the complexity of the issue, this debate is likely to continue for some time.

PUBLIC POLICY FOCUS

Sick Child Day Care

When children get sick, as they often do in the first few years of life, someone has to take care of them. This isn't a problem when a parent is available at home. But when parents are working and children normally go to day care centers, their illnesses pose a difficult problem for parents, day care regulators, and public health officials.

Several strategies have been suggested to solve this dilemma for working parents. Obviously, very sick children need and deserve to have their parents' attention, and work policies need to be flexible enough to handle such situations. But when children are just mildly sick—when they need a quieter day or a little more attention than is available in their usual day care setting—other arrangements may be possible. Some solutions that have been suggested include the following:

- *Special rooms within day care centers.* These rooms would keep sick children isolated from other children in the center and would be staffed by a specially trained person. Several children could be accommodated in the same room. This solution has the advantage of keeping sick children in their regular day care center.

- *At-home sick child services.* The child would stay at home but would be cared for by a visiting adult rather than by a parent. Although expensive, this solution would allow children to remain in their familiar home environment.
- *Special family or group care facilities for sick children.* Sick children would go to a special child care facility that served their day care center or day care home. These facilities would be attended only by sick children. This solution would be the most stressful for the child. No one likes to be taken care of in an unfamiliar place by unfamiliar people. A sick child is likely to find this arrangement especially intolerable (Fredericks & Kendrick, 1985).

Children are sensitive and vulnerable when they're sick, and a quiet, familiar environment helps them recover their sense of well-being. Although the suggestions listed here have some promise, none of them meets all the needs of the sick child. The best solution probably is for employers to allow parents to take time off or work flexible hours so they can stay at home and care for their sick children themselves.

INFANT AND TODDLER ASSESSMENT

One morning in July I was driving [the] children to their half-day nursery play session, and as I honked in front of Joshua's, his dad opened the back door to get a peek at Zach.

"Hi, you rascal," he said, sticking his head in right next to Zach in his car seat. Zach was awake, but he did not even look at John. . . . The car motor was running. I felt the uneasiness spread. . . .

In New York that summer to see my parents, the visit was fraught with tension. . . . Before we left New York, my father asked me when I was going to see the pediatrician. "Zach really doesn't hold his head up very well, Fernie. Ask the doctor about that the next time you go."

From Kupfer, F. (1982). Before and After Zachariah *(pp. 31–32).*

As it turned out, Zachariah had severe brain damage caused by a rare genetic disease. Zach's parents had him examined and evaluated many times, but it was months before they got any definitive word about the extent of his retardation or the prospects for his future. Assessing development—observing what a child can and can't do—is easy enough, but interpreting the observations is something else. It's often hard to decide exactly what a specific performance means, especially when it comes to predicting the child's development in the future.

How do we know when a baby isn't developing normally? There's a fair amount of normal variation among individual children for the emergence of behaviors such as holding up the head, smiling, sitting up, walking, talking, and so on. But when things don't happen within a certain range of time, as was the case with Zach, we're likely to want to assess the child. Assessment results can help in devising plans for children with problems so they can develop to their full potential.

In this section, we discuss four different assessment tools—tests designed to elicit specific behavior from children. The children's responses provide information about their current level of functioning. After we describe these tools, we discuss the issue of why assessment is easy and prediction is hard.

The Denver Developmental Screening Test

The Denver test is widely used to screen children for a broad range of developmental problems. It can be used with children ranging in age from a few weeks to 6 years. The test is divided into four areas of development. In the personal-social domain, testers observe appropriate-age behaviors such as smiling, playing pat-a-cake, or using a cup or spoon. In the fine-motor domain, they test for such behaviors as grasping a rattle, building a tower, or drawing a person. In the language domain, they test for vocalizing, turning toward a voice, imitating sounds, saying specific words, and so on. In the gross motor domain, they observe holding up the head, standing, walking, hopping on one foot, and so on.

A child's development is assessed in terms of norms—the average ages at which children can perform the specific behaviors on the assessment test. These norms have been established by studying hundreds of children. The scoring sheet provided with the Denver Test indicates the ages at which 50, 75, and 90 percent of children pass each item. A child who is delayed in passing clusters of items is judged to be in need of further evaluation to determine whether significant developmental problems are present.

FIGURE 5
For a 9-month-old, the fine-motor domain of the Denver Developmental Screening Test includes assessing the child's control and coordination in handling blocks. The Denver's activities are fun for the baby but carefully designed to reveal developmental delays.

RESEARCH FOCUS

How Does Day Care Affect Parent-Child Attachment?

It used to be that textbooks about child development hardly mentioned mother-child interaction. Freud's work in the early part of the twentieth century changed all that. Now we know that the mother-child relationship is crucial to all areas of development, and many people have wondered how appropriate full-time day care is for young infants. There isn't any question but that this practice runs counter to traditional doctrines of motherhood and domesticity in our society. Mothers have long been idealized as the keepers of a refuge against a cold outside world. Now women are shrugging off this role. They're going out into the world, and they're taking their babies with them (Lasch, 1977; Grubb & Lazerson, 1982). What effect do these new practices have on attachment?

HOW DOES DAY CARE AFFECT ATTACHMENT?

Researchers interested in how day care affects attachment posed the question, Is there a difference in attachment behavior between babies reared at home and babies in full-time day care? One of the first studies to document such a difference used the strange situation to assess attachment behavior in two groups of babies (Blehar, 1974). In this study, more of the children in the day care group than in the home-reared group were judged to be anxiously attached to their mothers.

Many studies followed (Brookhart & Hock, 1976; Doyle, 1975; Kagan, 1978). Overall, they showed no significant deleterious effects from the day care experience (Clarke-Stewart & Fein, 1983; Rutter, 1981). But studies continued; and in the early 1980s, two studies again found a difference in attachment in day care versus home-reared infants (Schwartz, 1983; Vaughn, Gove & Egeland, 1980). Day care infants showed a greater tendency to avoid their mothers upon reunion after separation. Several more recent studies also have found a slight increase in avoidance during reunion in infants placed in day care more than 20 hours per week during their first year (Belsky, 1988).

HOW STRONG IS THE EVIDENCE?
HOW SERIOUS IS THE PROBLEM?

These concerns do need to be put into perspective. In studies where increased avoidance has been found, 50 percent of the full-time day care infants did *not* show more avoidance toward their mothers upon reunion than home-reared infants.

Thus it seems that it's not the daily separation itself that produces the increased avoidance.

It also appears that increased avoidance is not correlated with the type of day care facility the child attends (Belsky, 1988). Increases in avoidant behavior have been found in high-quality, university-based programs, in family day care homes, and in day care centers. Apparently, something other than the care itself is responsible for the various effects. (An alternative explanation is that the quality or location of the day care experience *is* responsible for the different effects, but our current measures of quality aren't fine-tuned enough to pick up these differences.)

What accounts for the different attachment patterns found among day care infants? Some researchers point to what they call **family process variables**—the different attitudes, beliefs, and patterns of behavior in different families, such as the mother's attitude toward working or her assumptions about how her working affects her child. For example, one researcher suggests that a mother who feels guilty about working might try to pack more interaction into the short amount of time she has available to spend with her baby. This concentrated dose of stimulation might be more than the baby can tolerate, leading the baby to show avoidant behavior (Belsky, 1988). If this were the case, it wouldn't be the separation itself but the mother's attitude toward the separation that affects the infant's attachment behavior. Because not all working mothers feel guilty, and because infants differ in their ability to handle stimulation, the effects associated with full-time day care would show a fair amount of variability across infants.

Another fact from the research helps put the situation in perspective. Although more day care infants showed avoidance, the amount of avoidance observed in some studies wasn't enough to change the infants' overall attachment classifications. In other words, the day care infants had secure attachment patterns overall, although their behavior at reunion showed more avoidance than did the behavior of home-reared infants (Thompson, 1988).

At this point it's unclear why more avoidance is apparent in day care infants. Maybe their parents encourage them to be more independent, or maybe they're more accustomed to routine separations and reunions (Thompson, 1988). It's also

The Bayley Scales of Infant Development

The Bayley Scales are used to assess development in children from early infancy up to about 3 years. Devised by Dr. Nancy Bayley at the University of California at Berkeley, the scales have been revised several times since they were first used in the 1930s.

Children are tested on a motor scale and a mental scale. The motor scale includes items such as pulling up, creeping, walking, going up and down stairs, and balancing. The mental scale includes items that measure small motor skills, such as using the hands to build towers or to put pegs in pegboards. The mental scale also tests sensory abilities, such as the child's response to sound and light, and it measures language abilities and adaptability (Bayley, 1969).

unclear exactly what the differences mean. Avoidance in populations of day care infants may have a different meaning than it would in home-reared populations. Only follow-up studies done in the years ahead will clarify this.

WHAT SHOULD PARENTS AND DAY CARE CENTERS DO?

Right now, full-time day care for infants under 1 year of age is considered a slight **risk factor** for attachment disruption. It doesn't inevitably lead to attachment disruption, but it's associated with a greater probability of disruption than home rearing. Babies in part-time day care—less than 20 hours per week—don't show changes in attachment behavior, nor do babies who begin day care after 1 year of age.

Given the current research findings, parents should probably try to avoid full-time day care for infants under 1 year of age. At the same time, policymakers can take a number of steps to help. They can make sure women's jobs are still available after adequate maternity leave; they can support job-sharing and part-time work for mothers and fathers; and they can provide incentives for employers to set up child care in the workplace, enabling parents to see their children, however briefly, during their work day.

Day care workers and other professional caregivers can also help parents maintain close relationships with their children. They can encourage parents to linger in the morning to let the child see their interest in her day. Day care staff who view parental concern as an affront to their professional competence need to rethink their attitudes. Parents should probably show their children that they wish they could stay with them even though they know they must go, rather than leave abruptly as if they didn't care.

Day care staff and parents also need to work out effective ways to communicate with each other about the child. They have to share the information that helps explain the child's behavior. This kind of information is the basis for responsive caregiving, which underlies secure attachment.

When parents bring their baby in the morning, for example, they should tell the staff when the baby was last fed and changed, whether a new tooth is coming in or a new food was introduced, and so on. Then when the baby cries, the staff won't have to try everything before they find the cause

of the discomfort. At the end of the day, the staff can give similar information to the parents. This kind of open exchange enhances adult responsiveness to the baby both at day care and at home.

Nurturant caregivers like these women are an essential part of day care, but many people ask whether full-time day care, even under the best circumstances, is appropriate for young infants.

The Bayley Scales are widely used to assess children's initial level of development when they enter an early intervention program. Information from the test is used to plan a program for the individual child. The test can also be administered after children have been in programs to see how effective the programs are.

The Uzgiris-Hunt Ordinal Scales of Psychological Development

The Uzgiris-Hunt Ordinal Scales are narrower in focus than the Denver or the Bayley. They measure sensorimotor development in children from birth up to about age 2 or $2\frac{1}{2}$. This test is based on the work of Piaget and uses his conceptualizations of infant intelligence. There are several different subscales in the test, each measuring development in a specific sensorimotor area. For example, one scale assesses the child's development of means to achieve desired environmental events, which was discussed in Chapter 6 on cognitive development. Another measures development of object construction, and a third measures development of verbal imitation (Uzgiris & Hunt, 1975).

The Uzgiris-Hunt Scales are often used to evaluate the effectiveness of educational programs for infants. They can also be used to evaluate a child's current level of development. For example, a tester would be able to find out if a child was at Stage 3 or Stage 4 in a particular dimension of sensorimotor intelligence and plan the child's program accordingly.

Summary of Assessment Instruments

All of the assessment instruments provide norms—age references—that indicate the typical age range during which particular behaviors emerge in children. Results of assessments can indicate whether a child is developing normally, within the typical age range. The tests can also be used to evaluate the effects of specialized programs—to see, for example, if early intervention programs alleviate developmental delays in economically disadvantaged children or children with disabilities.

All these tests and more were probably administered to Zachariah. Yet his parents were unable to find out what, if anything, was wrong with him for many anxiety-filled months. Assessment instruments have very definite limitations, and we turn now to an explanation of what they are.

Issues in Assessment

The biggest problem with infant assessment is prediction. If we were to assess 100 babies at 1 year of age, ranking them in terms of developmental maturity, and then test them again at 5 years of age, we would find quite a few changes in ranking. Infant assessment simply doesn't predict later problems very well, which of course is what we often would like to know (Honzik, 1983).

One reason for this poor showing is that infant/toddler assessment relies heavily on motor and sensorimotor skills, which have low predictive value for later cognitive functioning. For example, in a recent study, motor development was found to be the poorest of the five variables used to predict later intellectual functioning (Largo et al., 1990). Other skills, such as language skills, are more closely tied to later intellectual development and school achievement. But these are the very skills that have not yet emerged in the young infant, which is why infant-toddler assessments typically rely on other developmental measures, such as motor skills (Bornstein & Sigman, 1986).

For example, neither a normal 1-year-old nor a 1-year-old with moderate mental retardation would have much language ability. A test given to both of them at this age might show very few differences between them. But at age 3, when the normal child's language has emerged and the retarded child's has not, an assessment would show significant differences. And the assessment at age 3 would reliably predict later differences in school achievement, because language is so crucial to school performance. We see, then, that infant/toddler assessment can't pick up variability in the very area that is most vital to later academic achievement (Harris, 1983).

A second problem with infant/toddler assessment instruments is that they're so heavily normed in terms of chronological age. In other words, they show the typical ages at which behaviors emerge in most children. What they don't account for is the very wide variation that occurs among perfectly normal children in the emergence of specific skills. Since we know this variation exists, we often can't say whether a child with developmental delays has a slow developmental timetable or whether the child has serious problems. This is no doubt what happened with Zachariah. The doctors who examined him saw that he was delayed, but they couldn't at first say why.

The younger a child is, the more difficult it is to say whether a problem exists. Consider walking as an example. The normal age range for the emergence of this behavior is 9 to 14 months. A child who hasn't walked by 13 months might worry her parents or doctor, because most children do walk by this age. But it would be hard to know the significance of this behavior at 13 months. If the child still isn't walking by 18 months, however, the meaning of her behavior at 13 months becomes clearer.

A related problem with assessment instruments is that they necessarily include items that are easy to score and exclude items that are hard to score. Behaviors like habituation time—time it takes for attention to an event to subside—and goal-directedness are more difficult to assess than are reaching and grasping or initial orientation to a stimulus, which are the items typically administered in infant tests.

Currently, infant/toddler assessment instruments predict best when the child's scores are very low (Largo et al., 1990). Of course, these are the very children whose problems are readily apparent to parents and experts alike, without the aid of a test. Other assessment approaches, such as judging information-processing abilities by habituation, hold some promise of better prediction of later mental functioning (Bornstein, 1989), but this approach is not widely used for clinical assessment. Until better assessment tools are available, results of assessments done during the infant and toddler years should be viewed with caution, especially if scores are only slightly below normal. At the same time, normal scores on a screening instrument should not lull caregivers into complacency when children *are* at risk due to poor environments or health problems, such as chronic ear infections. In a review of studies using the Denver Developmental Screening Test for prediction of later problems, 80 percent of children who eventually had problems in school had not been identified as children likely to have problems (Greer, Bauchner & Zuckerman, 1989).

LIVING WITH THE YOUNG CHILD

It was 2 o'clock in the morning, but instead of sleeping soundly in their bed, Frank and Donna McKinney were up with their 18-month-old daughter, Kimberly. Early in the evening, Kimberly had been cranky and had refused to eat her dinner. She had been listless and uninterested in playing. Frank and Donna chalked it up to fatigue, since they'd been out all evening at Donna's mother's house.

Kimberly had begun to cry at about 1 A.M., and Donna had gone to see what was the matter. When she reached down to smooth Kimberly's hair, Donna realized that she was very hot. She got the thermometer and took her temperature under her arm. It was an alarming 105 degrees. Calling to Frank to come help, Donna quickly took off Kimberly's sleeper to allow heat to escape from her body. Frank got the acetaminophen from the medicine cabinet and managed to get a dropperful of it into Kimberly's mouth.

Kimberly was crying hard now. Donna picked her up and carried her into the living room. Frank decided to get a damp washcloth to sponge Kimberly's body and try to cool her through evaporation. After 15 minutes, they thought she was getting cooler. The thermometer read 103. Frank stopped sponging, thinking that the acetaminophen was probably beginning to take effect. They considered calling the doctor but decided to wait a little longer. Within half an hour, Kimberly's temperature was down to 101, she had taken a drink of water, and she was beginning to doze off.

"I'll rock her for a while," Frank offered. "If her fever goes up again, we'll call the doctor. Why don't you get some sleep?"

"Okay," said Donna. "Can you stay home with her tomorrow morning and then work later in the afternoon? I could go to work early and then take the afternoon as half a sick day."

"I have to turn in a report in the morning. Can you drop it off for me?"

"Not if I want to get to work early myself. Maybe Bob could stop by on his way to your office and take it in."

"Good idea."

Donna went back to bed, but she couldn't fall asleep. She wasn't worried about Kimberly, who seemed to be getting better already. She was trying to figure out all the arrangements she'd have to make tomorrow to accommodate this unscheduled event—calls to her office, to Frank's office, to the day care center, to her pediatrician. Whenever Kimberly got sick, it threw a wrench into their busy, carefully choreographed life. Well, thought Donna, that's just how it is once you have a baby. I didn't know it then, but, ohhh, life used to be so simple.

Living with a young child *is* complicated. It requires patience, resourcefulness, and information about children. Individuals who live with infants and toddlers—whether parents or professional caregivers—have a number of practical, everyday concerns. They need to know how to comfort babies, how to keep them safe and healthy, and how to approach feeding and toilet training in toddlers.

We discussed ways to comfort a baby in Chapter 4, because that seems to be the primary concern during the early weeks of a baby's life. Here, we address the other issues—health, safety, and play.

Ensuring Health in the Infant and Toddler

Children are relatively healthy during their first two years of life. In fact, they have fewer illnesses at this time than at any other time during childhood. During the first six months, a baby has passive immunity gained from the mother in utero. Breast-fed infants gain added immunity, because breast milk carries the mother's antibodies. Infants' low illness rate is also due to their relatively low exposure to other children.

Once this exposure increases during the preschool years, children suffer from a rash of illnesses, ranging from the common cold to chicken pox. In fact, the highest incidence of illness in children occurs during the preschool years, when they're first exposed to many other children and haven't built up

RESEARCH FOCUS

Sudden Infant Death Syndrome

Probably nothing fills parents with more dread than the thought of finding their infant dead in his crib. This fear becomes reality in Sudden Infant Death Syndrome (SIDS). Two out of every 1,000 infants—about 8,000 infants in all—die of SIDS each year in the United States. Currently, this disease is the major killer of infants between 1 and 12 months of age (Merritt & Valdes-Dapena, 1984).

THE MYSTERY OF SIDS

SIDS usually strikes infants between 2 and 4 months of age, at night, while they are asleep. Most have no apparent illness. In fact, the mystery of the disease is that it suddenly strikes apparently healthy infants (Kelly & Shannon, 1982).

The cause of SIDS is still unknown, but researchers suspect that some kind of assaults on the brain stem—where breathing is controlled—during the prenatal or perinatal period may be responsible (Kelly & Shannon, 1982). There might have been slight oxygen deprivation, for example. Viral infections are also suspected in some cases (Williams, Uren & Bretherton, 1984), as is airway closing (Martinez, 1991).

Even though we don't know the cause of SIDS, we can say that some infants are more likely than others to be victims. Several risk factors have been identified, based on analysis of the characteristics of previous victims (Grether & Schulman, 1989; Guntheroth, Lohmann, and Spiers, 1990). Groups considered to be at risk for SIDS include the following:

- Infants born to mothers who are less than 20 years old
- Infants born to mothers who smoke cigarettes
- Infants born to mothers who abuse narcotic drugs
- Premature infants
- Small-for-date infants
- Infants who are twins or triplets
- Infants with a sibling who was a SIDS victim
- Male infants who have some of the above risk factors

APNEA MONITORING

High-risk infants may be monitored, at the hospital and at home, for sleep apnea (periods when breathing stops). Apnea is associated with some, although not all, cases of SIDS (Ariagno, 1984). Infants may be judged high risk because they had a sibling who was a SIDS victim, because they showed abnormal breathing patterns in the hospital nursery, or because their parents reported that they found them blue, pale,

and apparently not breathing at some point (Krongrad & O'Neill, 1986). The monitor is attached to the infant during sleep. If the infant stops breathing, an alarm sounds to alert the parent.

Parents of infants at risk for SIDS have tremendously high levels of anxiety about their child. They usually feel they have no choice but to use a monitor, and yet it doesn't completely relieve their fears. The equipment is expensive, so it places a financial burden on the family. An evening out of the house is hard to arrange, because babysitters have to know how to use the monitor and how to resuscitate a baby who has stopped breathing. Parents who are monitoring their baby need the understanding and support of their doctor and home monitor staff (Smith, 1984), as well as the help of their friends and relatives. One mother who had lost a child to SIDS described the monitoring experience with her second child (Silvio, 1984, p. 231):

> Jerry and I learned quickly the meaning of monitoring. We became the constant companions of our baby, Ashley. Monitoring meant that we were always within hearing range; it meant that routines such as going to get the mail or watering the flowers were not done while she was sleeping. In short, it meant a total adjustment in our lifestyle, not to mention the adjustment to our budget. The bottom line, though, was that the monitor could give us the chance to save her life if it became necessary, the chance we wish we had had with Adam. It gave us a feeling of security knowing that without keeping a constant eye on her, she was doing fine. I learned a great deal from my adjusted lifestyle. I learned to appreciate the constant companionship of Ashley and the rest of our family. I learned how to take a shower while listening for the alarm. I became quite skilled at vacuuming while keeping a constant eye on the remote alarm. I learned that monitoring can be very trying at times and that the value of a night out did not compare to the value of my child's life. I soon realized that adjusting to monitoring was much easier than adjusting to the loss of a child.

The tragedy of SIDS will go on until research tells us what causes it and how we can prevent it. Until then, apnea monitoring, although far from ideal, is our best hope for sparing families the trauma of infant death.

their own immunities. Sharing toys in preschools makes contagion more likely too.

When children under 2 years do get sick, the illness can be more serious than illnesses in older children, mainly because of their small body size. Infants have narrow air passages that easily become blocked from respiratory infections, and they dehydrate—lose water—rapidly when they vomit or have diarrhea. These conditions require careful monitoring and prompt medical attention in young infants. (For a discussion of another medical problem in infants, see Research Focus—Sudden Infant Death Syndrome.)

FIGURE 6
Children become sick more often as soon as they're exposed to other children on a regular basis. Special arrangements have to be made for sick children who normally attend day care or preschool. The sick child is fragile and needs to be in a quiet, familiar place to rest and get well. A thumb, a blanket, and a stuffed toy help too.

COMMON CHILDHOOD DISEASES. Childhood diseases are often grouped into four categories: respiratory (colds, bronchitis, tonsillitis, and so on), communicable (mumps, German measles, whooping cough, and so on), gastrointestinal (those that affect the stomach and intestines and cause vomiting and diarrhea), and accidents.

Children today are immunized against many communicable diseases. One shot, known as the DPT immunization, protects against diphtheria (an upper respiratory illness), tetanus (an infection causing contraction of facial muscles), and pertussis (an upper respiratory illness, commonly known as whooping cough). Another shot contains the vaccines against measles, mumps, and rubella (German measles). Children are also immunized against polio and hemophilus influenza B, the organism primarily responsible for meningitis. Immunizations are given during regular checkups at 2 months, 4 months, 6 months, 1 year, and 18 months (influenza type B). "Booster" shots are given at 18 months and again when the child is 5 years old.

THE DEBATE OVER IMMUNIZATION. Immunization is a surprisingly controversial issue. Public health officials are anxious for as many children as possible to be immunized to control the spread of disease. Although we refer to them as common, childhood diseases are serious and can cause permanent disabilities and death. In the late 1970s, the problem of unimmunized children in the schools became so serious that a federally funded program, the Childhood Immunization Initiative, was begun to increase the number of immunized children in the United States. At the time the program started, 40 percent of children under 5 years were not immunized. Within a few years, less than 10 percent of the children in this country had not been immunized (Bumpers, 1984). Since then, many states have passed laws requiring that children be

FIGURE 7
Regular physical checkups are important for infants and toddlers. They give the pediatrician the chance to answer parents' questions, spot any problems that may be developing, and immunize the child against such life-threatening diseases as polio and diphtheria. Toys, games, and friendly adults help the child develop positive associations with the visit.

immunized before they may be allowed to attend day care, preschool, or elementary school.

Despite the obvious benefits, many parents have resisted having their children immunized. Their primary concern has been the safety of the vaccine. In extremely rare cases, a child has contracted the disease itself from the vaccine. More often, children have reactions to vaccines, consisting of fever, headache, nausea, and other flulike symptoms, which occur as the body begins to develop antibodies toward the diseases the immunizations prevent. The reaction rate for the pertussis vaccine is particularly high, although most reactions aren't severe (Frenkel, 1986).

Physicians often respond to these concerns by asking parents to put them in perspective. They point out that the risk of dying in a traffic accident is 1 in 8,000; the risk of dying from pertussis itself, if the child has not been immunized and contracts the disease, is 1 in 1,000; and the risk of dying from a pertussis immunization is 1 in 2,000,000. Pediatricians do, however, follow guidelines for administering the pertussis vaccine to individual children. If a child has had a very strong reaction to the vaccine at 18 months, for example, the doctor will probably not give the booster shot at age 5.

Many other diseases can't be prevented by immunization, but they can be controlled through good hygiene. A full discussion of this topic is provided in Health Focus—Sickness at Day Care Centers.

Ensuring Health in the Older Toddler

People who live with toddlers face two major health-related challenges: feeding and toilet training. How these two aspects of child care are handled has long-range consequences for the child's well-being, so they're worth careful consideration.

HEALTH FOCUS

Sickness at Day Care Centers

Parents who take their babies to day care often worry that they'll catch colds and other contagious diseases there, and they're right to be concerned. Day care children do get sick more often than babies who stay at home. On the other hand, although respiratory infections are more frequent among infants and toddlers who attend day care than among those who remain at home, recent research suggests that day care children have fewer respiratory infections during their preschool and school-age years than children who didn't attend day care (Hurwitz et al., 1991). Apparently, their early day care exposure provides them with some immunity to respiratory infections. Nevertheless, both parents and day care centers can and should take steps to reduce the risk of illness for children.

SOME DAY CARE CENTERS HAVE MORE ILLNESS
Certain types of day care centers have higher rates of infectious diseases than others. One type is the center that serves non–toilet trained children under 2 years of age. At this age, children mouth everything, come in close contact with each other, and eat with their hands. Germs pass easily from one child to another.

Large day care centers also have more disease, simply because children come in contact with larger numbers of other children. Centers that allow drop-ins—children who can't attend their regular center because they're sick—have higher rates of infection as well. Finally, centers that employ immigrants from certain countries seem to have higher incidences of tuberculosis in their children. This problem can be controlled if day care centers insist on proof of negative tuberculin skin tests before they hire new employees.

WHAT KINDS OF DISEASES DO CHILDREN GET?
Even if parents don't use day care centers with these features, they can still expect their children to get sick. It's virtually impossible to protect children who attend day care centers from contagious diseases. Parents may see any of a wide range of illnesses, including respiratory infections, meningitis, hepatitis, gastrointestinal infections, and cytomegalovirus (CMV) infections.

People get respiratory infections—colds, bronchitis, pneumonia, and so on—from close contact with an infected person. The bacteria and viruses that cause these diseases are in the saliva and mucus secretions and are spread when people talk, cough, sneeze, or pass on germs with their hands. Tissues and towels used to wipe children's noses and hands can carry the germs.

Meningitis, an inflammation of the meninges, the membranes covering the brain and spinal cord, can cause brain damage and even death in children. It's caused by the bacteria hemophilus influenza B and, like the common cold, is spread through respiratory secretions.

Hepatitis is a viral infection of the liver. It's transmitted orally and through the feces. In some cases, hepatitis causes the skin to turn yellow, but many children don't have any symptoms. When this is the case, the disease can spread until many children and adults are infected (Smith, 1986). Close to 30 percent of all hepatitis type A outbreaks in the

FEEDING. Two trends affect the toddler's eating behavior: a decrease in appetite and an overwhelming urge to explore the world. Together, they create fairly messy and prolonged feeding times, during which remarkably little food is consumed. Adults often wonder if toddlers are getting enough nutrients—and if the dining room rug is going to survive.

We saw in Chapter 5 that toddlers' appetites decline because their growth rates slow down so drastically. They don't need or want large amounts of food. Adults can manage toddler feeding in a positive way by offering small portions of nutritious food at mealtimes and limiting between-meal snacks. Toddlers are likely to be more interested in attractively served foods and in foods that adults appear to be enjoying. But none of these tactics will work with children who simply aren't hungry. Toddlers' desire to explore food can be satisfied by offering "finger" foods, such as slices of apple or banana, small pieces of bread, or bits of dry cereal. Because these foods can be easily managed by the child, they also support the toddler's emerging sense of independence.

Parents who want to curtail extreme messiness can teach their children to handle only finger foods, for example. They can also teach them not to turn cups upside down. They can serve the toddler's food on nonbreakable dishes, use cups with lids, and feed the toddler over a washable floor. They can also be diligent about removing the child from the highchair promptly when she

United States can be traced to day care centers (Marwich & Simmons, 1984).

Gastrointestinal infections—often labeled "the flu" and characterized by vomiting and diarrhea—are also spread orally and through the feces. CMV infections are viral. Children with CMV infections usually don't have any symptoms, but the disease still has to be controlled. Pregnant women and women of child-bearing age who contract CMV are at risk for having babies with birth defects.

HOW CAN DAY CARE CENTERS CONTROL DISEASE?

Health experts have recommended the following procedures for controlling the spread of disease in day care centers:

- Day care staff should frequently *wash their hands* with soap. Hand washing is the most effective way to prevent infections. Workers should wash their hands when they arrive at the center; before eating, preparing, or serving food; and after diapering a child, wiping noses, or being outside. Children should wash their hands after using the toilet, before meals, and after playing outside. Hands shouldn't be washed in a sink where food is prepared.
- Workers should *change diapers carefully* as soon as they're soiled. The changing table should be covered with a disposable surface and used only for changing diapers. The table top should be cleaned and disinfected after each use. Diapers should be properly disposed of in plastic bags and put in a plastic-lined trash can with a lid. The diaper-changing table should be near a sink so caregivers can wash their hands immediately after changing a diaper.

- Day care staff should *wash and disinfect toys and equipment* daily. They should disinfect high chair trays after each use.
- Centers should *establish and stick to a sick child policy*. They should maintain a regular enrollment and not allow any drop-ins. Children with fever, diarrhea, or other signs of infection should not be allowed to attend the center. Children who become ill at the center should be isolated from the other children until a parent can take them home.
- Centers should require that all children between the ages of 2 and 5 be *vaccinated against hemophilus influenza B*, the virus that causes meningitis. Some doctors recommend this vaccination as early as 18 months for children in day care.
- Day care centers should make sure they *employ enough people*. When workers are extremely busy, they tend to forget about washing hands, cleaning the diapering area, and so on. Centers should also *avoid overcrowding among the children*, since this increases contact and the spread of germs. Day care *staff should be educated* about how diseases are transmitted and how they can be controlled. (The National Centers for Disease Control in Atlanta provides excellent training material.) Finally, all centers should have a pediatrician or nurse as a health consultant to provide training and advice when diseases do occur.
- Parents should *keep sick children home* from day care, despite the inconvenience and disruption in their working life. Some possible solutions to this dilemma are discussed in Public Policy Focus—Sick Child Day Care.

FIGURE 8
The toddler is too busy feeding himself to care about mealtime decorum. He's getting more than sustenance right now—he's learning that he has the ability to do things for himself. Messy meals are the small price his parents pay for his growing sense of autonomy.

indicates that she's done, since keeping her there with food on her tray only encourages her to play with it or throw it on the floor. Despite all precautions, however, toddlers are messy eaters. They often emerge from meals covered with food from their hair to their shoes. Again, adults are wise to accept a certain amount of mess from their curious toddlers.

TOILET TRAINING. A second major issue in the toddler years is toilet training. Between ages 1 and 2, most toddlers begin to be aware of how it feels when the bladder is full. This is the first stage of readiness for bladder control (Doleys & Dolce, 1982). But the bladder still releases urine reflexively in children this age. The child can't retain urine and can't anticipate the need to use the toilet. Children may indicate that they have a full bladder by dancing around or holding the genital area at this stage, and children who show these signs are often ready to get to the toilet and take appropriate action.

By about age 3, and sometimes earlier in girls, children become able to retain urine for a short period of time after sensing that the bladder is full. At this point, the child can consciously control the bladder muscles so urine isn't reflexively released. This is the second stage of readiness for bladder control. Now children can begin to anticipate the need to use the toilet, and parents or caregivers can help them get there in time.

This is the point at which parents usually teach their children to use the toilet, and many different approaches to toilet training have been proposed over the years. In the 1970s and 1980s, a social learning approach using reinforcement and modeling promised that children could be toilet trained "in less than a day." It's probably wise to modify any system to fit individual children, keeping in mind that praise and encouragement are the best teaching tools and that scolding and punishment are not only inhumane but counterproductive.

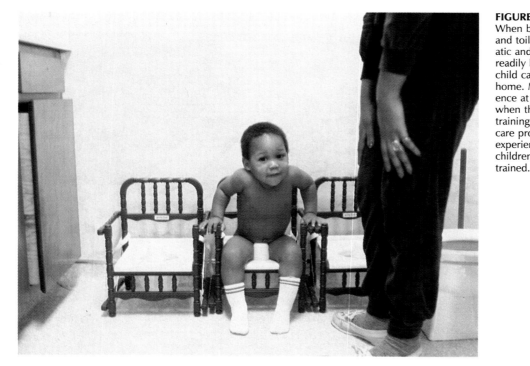

FIGURE 9
When bathrooms are clean and toilet training is systematic and humane, children can readily be toilet trained at their child care center as well as at home. Most parents experience at least one moment when they despair of ever training their child, but child care providers know from experience that virtually all children will eventually be trained.

Children stay dry at night after they've achieved daytime control, usually 6 to 12 months later. In one study of Dutch children, girls were wetting the bed twice a month between ages 4 and 5, but by age 5, they were wetting the bed significantly less. By contrast, about 15 percent of the boys were still wetting the bed about twice a month at age 5. Not until they were 8 years old did the boys' rate of bed-wetting fall to the girls' 5-year-old level (Verhulst et al., 1985). These differences are largely due to girls' faster physical development, which by age 5 is almost a full year ahead of boys'.

The inability to control bladder function during the night after the age of 4 is known as **enuresis**. According to various studies, 15 to 20 percent of 5-year-olds and 5 percent of 10-year-olds are still wetting the bed, with boys again having the harder time. There are several possible reasons for enuresis. Some children have deep-sleep patterns that prevent them from waking to go to the bathroom before it's too late. Others have a genetic predisposition toward immaturity in bladder control. Still others might not have received daytime training or might not have learned toileting behavior well enough (Doleys & Dolce, 1982). Older children who still wet their beds often feel embarrassed or ashamed, especially if they've received negative reactions from their friends or parents. Experts urge families to seek medical or psychological help to prevent these secondary consequences if they do have an enuretic child.

Children typically achieve bowel control several months before they achieve bladder control. This is mainly because the sensations are easier to detect and the expulsion of the waste is easier to control. But some children—one to two out of every one hundred 4-year-olds—have trouble gaining bowel control, a difficulty known as **encopresis**. This problem, again more common in boys than in girls, can have serious consequences and requires medical attention (Rappaport & Levine, 1986).

Teachers and other caregivers can help all the children in their care avoid toileting problems by letting them use the bathroom when they need to. Since children are usually very sensitive to the condition of bathrooms, adults can also help by keeping bathrooms fresh and clean.

Keeping Infants and Toddlers Safe

About 4,000 children under 4 years of age die each year in the United States from accidents (Caldwell, 1984). In addition, many others are seriously injured or have their later health and intellectual functioning seriously compromised by accidents or exposure to toxic substances, such as lead. To prevent tragedies, everyone living with infants and toddlers must make sure the environment is safe for young children (see Safety Focus—Burns in Young Children). Certain precautions can help keep children safe:

- Never leave a baby unattended on a bed, on a table, or in a crib with the side down. Even newborns can move reflexively and plunge over the edge.
- Place gates at the tops and bottoms of stairs and in doorways to areas that are off limits to children.
- Place barriers around stoves, floor grates, and radiators. Babies might be able to roll close enough to touch a hot surface but then not be able to move away.

SAFETY FOCUS

Burns in Young Children

Burns are a serious threat to infants and toddlers, ranking third (behind auto accidents and drowning) as a cause of death in children (McLaughlin & Crawford, 1985). About 1,300 children die of burns every year in the United States. House fires cause the most deaths, and hot water causes the most nonfatal burns.

How can children be protected from burns? Several simple precautions can help. Tap water set at 160 degrees Fahrenheit takes just two seconds to cause a third-degree burn (the most serious burn). Water set at 120 degrees Fahrenheit, by contrast, takes ten minutes to cause the same burn (Caldwell, 1984). Obviously, if hot water heaters are set no higher than 120 degrees Fahrenheit, many serious burns can be avoided. A simple device, easily installed by a plumber, can regulate the mix of hot and cold water that comes out of a faucet. Child care centers in many states are required to install such devices and to keep them set so that water temperature is within acceptable limits.

In the kitchen, many children are burned by spills of hot liquids such as coffee, tea, or cooking fat. The same danger exists in child care centers when caregivers carry hot cups of coffee into the children's play areas. A bump from a child can easily make some of the liquid spill onto a child who is underfoot.

A new type of kitchen scald has recently started to appear. When baby bottles are heated in microwave ovens, the liquid inside can become extremely hot without the outside of the bottle getting very hot at all. (The heat only gradually gets conducted to the outside container.) Adults should always test the contents of the bottle on their wrists before feeding the baby. Safer methods of heating bottles (such as setting them in a pan of hot water) should be used in day care centers, where distractions can easily cause workers to forget to test the temperature on their wrists.

Adults can protect children from kitchen scalds by keeping them out of food preparation areas. At home, gates can be put up in kitchen doors, or a child can be placed in a high chair with toys on the tray to get him out from underfoot where he could trip the adult.

If a child is burned by a hot liquid, an adult should pour cool water on the burn *immediately*. This cools the hot liquid and the affected tissues and prevents the burn from going still deeper. Adults should not take the time to remove a child's shirt or pants before holding the child under cold running tap water.

Burns from electrical current are another category of burn. They don't occur very frequently, but when they do, they're usually serious. They often occur when a child sucks on the end of an extension cord that has been left plugged into a wall socket (Crikelair & Dhaliwal, 1976). Obviously, extension cords should always be unplugged and put away when not in use. Adults should also use plastic plugs in unused wall sockets to prevent infants and toddlers from putting objects into the holes, another way they get electrical burns.

Chemical burns usually occur when children drink caustic substances such as lye or household bleach. The peak age for this injury is 24 months (Wasserman & Ginsburg, 1985). Doctors are now seeing chemical burns caused by the miniature batteries used in cameras, hearing aids, and camera flash attachments (McLaughlin & Crawford, 1985). Like everything else the infant or toddler comes across, these tiny batteries seem fair game for mouthing and swallowing. Good poison prevention procedures can prevent chemical burns. All dangerous substances should be kept behind locked doors or out of reach, with the toddler's ingenuity and persistence taken into account.

Adults can protect children from sunburn by limiting exposure to the sun, using sunscreen, and keeping the sun off children's faces with hats. Child care center playgrounds should be designed with areas of shade so that children can play outdoors without constant exposure to direct sunlight.

Adults can lower the danger of house fires by installing smoke alarms in their homes and by holding family fire drills to teach children what to do in case of fire. These same measures increase safety in day care centers. All states have fire codes that must be followed in buildings where groups of young children are housed. They often specify that children must be on the ground floor, where they have the easiest access to the outside. Additional procedures may be required where there are nonmobile infants. For example, special aprons with large, deep pockets have been designed for emergency evacuations. Caregivers can carry two babies in their arms and tuck more into the pockets of the aprons. Training and practice reduce the likelihood that children in any setting—home, day care center, or school—will be seriously injured in a fire.

- Don't use tablecloths on tables. Babies pull themselves up on tablecloths and can pull dishes and hot food down on themselves.
- Store medicine in locked cabinets or well out of a child's reach. Buy medications in the smallest available quantity, and keep purses out of reach.
- Strap infants and toddlers into government-tested car seats when driving them in cars. Never hold a child in your lap while a car is moving. In the event of an accident, holding onto a 10-pound infant in a car going 30 miles per hour requires the same strength needed to lift a 300-pound weight. If you're not wearing a seat belt and are holding an infant, your body will continue to move forward at the speed the car was moving before impact. The infant would be crushed between your body and the interior of the car (Robertson, 1985).

- Keep small objects out of reach of children under age 3, and don't give them raw carrots, nuts, popcorn, or hard candy. They can easily choke.
- Inspect toys carefully for small parts that could come loose and be put in the mouth. Many toys are now labeled if they have small parts and are unsuitable for children under age 3. Don't give them balloons, which they tend to bite and may choke on.
- Inspect hand-me-down furniture to make sure it's free of lead-based paint and other hazards, such as spaces where a young child's head could become stuck.
- Don't put babies to bed wearing jackets with drawstring hoods. The strings could strangle them.
- Don't use talcum powder, which contains a substance that damages the lungs.
- Keep cleaning solvents, laundry detergents, furniture polishes, and all other toxic substances in locked cabinets or in places inaccessible to infants and toddlers.
- Keep the number of the poison control center near your telephone.
- Keep a bottle of ipecac syrup on hand. Use it to induce vomiting in the event of accidental poisoning, but don't use it if caustic substances or petroleum products have been ingested.
- Use plastic covers over electrical outlets.

(For a discussion of the most serious challenge to children's safety, see Safety Focus—Child Abuse and Neglect.)

It's important that toddlers be able to explore their environment. They learn what the world is like by being active participants in it, and they achieve a sense of mastery by making things happen. Children's sense of themselves can

FIGURE 10
Toddlers approach the world without preconceived ideas about how things should work—an approach that often leaves them in precarious positions. The parents of adventurers like this 18-month-old have to be vigilant to keep their child safe.

SAFETY FOCUS

Child Abuse and Neglect

Stories and descriptions of child abuse have existed throughout history, but not until 1962, when Dr. C. Henry Kempe described the "battered child syndrome," did this devastating problem receive widespread official attention in the United States and Europe (Kempe et al., 1962). Laws were subsequently passed that required physicians and other professionals to report cases of suspected abuse to state authorities. These laws make it clear that the principle of physician-patient confidentiality does not apply in such cases.

INCIDENCE OF CHILD ABUSE

The number of reported abuse cases rose dramatically after the laws were passed. In California, for example, the number increased from 4,000 in 1968 to 40,000 in 1972. In Michigan the increase was from 741 to 30,000. The actual incidence of child abuse is extremely difficult to determine, not only because abusers try to hide the problem but also because medical, legal, and sociological authorities often disagree on the definitions of abuse and neglect. Until recently, cases of neglect were often lumped together with cases of abuse. The number of abuse and neglect reports confirmed each *year* by state child protective services is on the order of 2 per 100 children, although this may be a gross underestimate of the actual incidence of abuse and neglect. The first nationally representative survey of women in the United States about sexual abuse alone, *sometime* during their childhood, reports that 27 percent consider themselves to have been sexually abused (Finkelhor et al., 1990). (For a more detailed discussion of sexual abuse see Knowledge in Action: Preschool Children.)

INDICATIONS OF ABUSE

Professionals dealing with children have to be alert to indications of possible abuse. Children's reports of abuse should not be ignored. Nor should physical indications, such as bruises or welts on an infant, especially on the face, or corner fractions of long bones, caused by twisting or pulling. Behavioral indications include overly compliant and passive behaviors, particularly among high IQ children, and extremely rageful behaviors of the kind seen in very insecurely attached

babies. A significant lack of supervision in medical care, hygiene, shelter, nutrition, education, or general protection from harm probably indicates neglect. Most communities have child abuse hotlines through which parents and professionals can obtain information about how to identify an abused child, where to go for help, and how to ensure the child's safety.

BEHAVIORS OF ABUSED CHILDREN

Abused and neglected infants and toddlers tend to show high levels of both avoidance and resistance when reunited with caregivers. Whether they show more of one of these reactions than the other may depend on either temperamental characteristics or the particular combination of abuse and neglect (Youngblade & Belsky, 1990). Rather than smiling, vocalizing, or approaching the parent, an abused or neglected infant is likely to abort the parent's approach; look away; ignore, push, or kick the parent; or present a disorganized combination of these reactions. Such behaviors are probably tied not only to the immediate negative situation but, especially in older infants and toddlers, to the child's having learned internal working models of others as untrustworthy (Crittenden & Ainsworth, 1989; Sroufe, 1988). As a result of insecure attachment, maltreated toddlers are more likely than their peers to avoid or assault other children and caregivers, by responding to a distressed peer with aggression, for example (Youngblade & Belsky, 1990). The mistrust and feelings of worthlessness and helplessness that frequently result from abuse obviously interfere with the fundamental developmental tasks—learning trust and achieving autonomy—of the infant and toddler period (Erikson, 1968a).

CAUSES OF CHILD ABUSE

Efforts to understand and control the causes of child abuse continue. Many factors are involved, and one of the most comprehensive attempts to describe them is the systems or ecological approach of Jay Belsky (1980). This approach was a forerunner of the systems approach to attachment described in Chapter 8 (Zigler & Hall, 1989). Belsky drew on

be distorted when parents constantly have to say, "No! Don't touch!" They can become fearful and uncertain or, on the other hand, angry and defiant. Although it requires work and attention, it's far easier and less dangerous in the long run to adapt the environment to the child than to try to make the child fit into a hands-off home.

Toys for Infants and Toddlers

Living with a young child is by no means all worries. Playtime can be fun for both child and adult, and many toys are made that support play at the various skill levels of infancy and toddlerhood. We look at some of them here before we close with a few words about playing with young children.

TABLE Determinants of Abuse: Compensatory and Risk Factors

	Ontogenetic Level	Microsystem Level	Exosystem Level	Macrosystem Level
Compensatory Factors	High IQ Awareness of past abuse History of a positive relationship with one parent Special talents Physical attractiveness Good interpersonal skills	Healthy children Supportive spouse Economic security/ savings in the bank	Good social supports Few stressful events Strong, supportive religious affiliation Positive school experiences and peer relations as a child Therapeutic interventions	Culture that promotes a sense of shared responsibility in caring for the community's children Culture opposed to violence Economic prosperity
Risk Factors	History of abuse Low self-esteem Low IQ Poor interpersonal skills	Marital discord Children with behavior problems Premature or unhealthy children Single parent Poverty	Unemployment Isolation; poor social supports Poor peer relations as a child	Cultural acceptance of corporal punishment View of children as possessions Economic depression

From Kaufman & Zigler (1989, p. 139).

Bronfenbrenner's ecological approach to the study of child development (1977, 1979) to organize the risk factors contributing to abuse. As shown in the table above, Belsky organized these factors into four different levels. He used the term **ontogenetic** to refer to factors associated with characteristics of the caregiver. At the **microsystem** level are characteristics of the immediate setting, such as the family. At the **exosystem** level are characteristics of community institutions, and at the **macrosystem** level are the influences of the society or culture in which the family and community are embedded. The table shows factors that both increase and decrease the likelihood of abuse at each of the four levels.

TREATMENT

The treatment is as complex as the problem. The abusing parent is usually separated from the family as a first step. Treatment for potentially abusive parents often takes the form seen in the Threshold Mothers' Project (described earlier in this section). It consists of direct teaching about what can be expected of children at different ages and how to respond appropriately to the young child's signals (Lieberman, Weston & Paul, 1991). Psychotherapy for both parent and child often focuses on changing internal working models of relationships and on fostering responsive interactions within the family and other support systems (Nezworski, Tolan & Belsky, 1988).

TOYS FOR VERY YOUNG INFANTS, CRAWLERS, AND BEGINNING WALKERS. Most toys for babies are designed to provide sensory stimulation. Crib mobiles have become popular as research on babies' visual perception and sensorimotor intelligence has sifted down to the popular level. The best mobiles have designs on the bottoms of the figures (not just on the sides), so the baby (not just the parents) can see them. Babies will be most interested in them if they have sharp contrasts in color or design. Mobiles should be removed when babies can reach them, since most of them aren't made to be handled or mouthed. Babies also like to look at themselves and other interesting sights reflected in nonbreakable mirrors attached to the sides of their cribs.

Rattles are another popular toy for young infants. A 3-month-old will grasp a rattle (although she won't be able to let go of it voluntarily), look at it, put

FIGURE 11
The best toys and activities are those that are appropriate for a child's level of development. A 10-month-old can comfortably play by himself with an intriguing toy on the living room carpet, his head and chest raised and his upper body supported by one arm. Toddlers are happy playing with other children in the playground, though they may need an adult's help if a disagreement arises.

it in her mouth, feel it with her free hand, and shake it. She'll like the sound it makes and the puzzle of who or what is making the sound.

When babies start to crawl, they enjoy pushing a colorful ball in front of them. They like the changing colors or patterns and the moderately predictable path of movement. Another good push toy for crawlers is a nonbreakable mirror attached between two wheels. As the mirror moves, it reflects a variety of stimulating displays to catch the baby's attention.

Babies who have begun to walk can use musical push toys, such as the popular plastic lawn mower. These toys help the top-heavy toddler stay upright and balanced. Pull toys are for more experienced walkers.

TOYS AND BOOKS FOR TODDLERS. With their improving fine motor coordination, toddlers start to enjoy simple puzzles, boxes with shapes to sort and fit, stacking toys, small blocks, and crayons and paper. Dolls and stuffed animals give them something soft to hug, and old hats, purses, shoes, and clothes suggest roles to toddlers who are just beginning to play pretend games. Play dishes and pots and pans will be used too.

Even very young infants like the rhythm of nursery rhymes and children's songs. Older babies like looking at pictures of familiar objects in books and naming the objects. Books for babies are made of heavy cardboard, cloth, or plastic to withstand the mouthing, chewing, and sucking to which babies subject them.

By about age 2, children can enjoy actual stories, which the younger baby can't tolerate. Toddlers like stories about familiar events such as taking a bath, sitting on the potty, or getting ready for bed. Bedtime stories often become a ritual during the toddler period. As nursing or a bedtime bottle becomes a thing of the past, the bedtime story can take its place. This ritual can form the basis for a childhood of warm relationships and a lifetime of enjoyable reading.

SOCIAL PLAY. Perhaps the favorite play of babies of all ages is social play with adults. Babies love old favorites like "tickle the tummy," "ah-boo," and "peek-a-boo." Adults can keep the games interesting by varying the pace of the tickling or booing and their facial and vocal expressions. They should also be careful to watch for gaze aversion and sobering—signs that the baby has had enough stimulation and wants to stop the game.

Young toddlers like to be with other children, but they can't sustain interactions. Adults can help them be together happily by providing duplicate toys as well as equipment that can be used by several children at the same time, such as sandboxes, water tables, playhouses, rocking boats, and climbing structures. This kind of play equipment helps keep struggles over objects to a minimum and encourages parallel and joint play.

Adults have to supervise toddler play because toddlers aren't able to settle disagreements among themselves constructively. When toddlers want a toy another child is using, they're likely to grab it out of the other child's hands. It's helpful if an adult can offer an identical toy, but this isn't always possible. When it's not, adults have to take the time to explain to toddlers, "That's Laurie's toy—she doesn't want to share it right now," or "It's Maria's turn—you'll have to wait for your turn. Let's look for something else for you to do until she's finished." With help like this, toddlers can begin to learn how to play together in relative harmony.

OVERVIEW

Individuals who live and work with infants and toddlers have many important practical concerns. They may wonder about child care: What should a program provide in order to nurture and support a young infant? An older infant? A toddler? Given all we know about attachment relationships, is child care appropriate at all for young infants? They may wonder about assessment: Is it significant if a child doesn't walk by 14 months? If he doesn't talk by 24 months? Or they may have questions about health, safety, or play: If a child has a reaction to a vaccine, should she get the booster shot? If she's not toilet trained by age 3, is there cause for alarm? These are the kinds of questions and concerns that can be addressed by applying research findings to everyday life with children.

KNOWLEDGE IN ACTION REVIEW

INFANT AND TODDLER EDUCATION AND CARE PROGRAMS

- Over 50 percent of mothers with babies under 1 year of age are in the work force today.
- The Florida Parent Education Infant and Toddler Program supports the cognitive and emotional growth of children from economically disadvantaged families. Its activities are based on Piaget's stages of sensorimotor intelligence.
- The Mother-Child Home Program focuses on cognitive and language development. Home visitors bring books and toys to the home and help parents interact constructively with their children.
- The Marin County, California, Program for Atypical Infants serves babies with special needs, such as mental retardation or a physical disability, and includes a therapeutic day care program.

- The Threshold Mothers' Project focuses on the children of mentally ill mothers and includes activities that sensitize mothers to their babies' signals and teach them appropriate ways to respond.
- Parents of all children in day care face problems when their children are sick, and no truly satisfactory solutions have yet been devised. The best solution is probably for employers to allow parents to take time off when they have a sick child.
- Babies in full-time day care show more avoidance toward their mothers than babies raised at home. The meaning of this behavior isn't clear. Full-time day care for infants under 1 year of age is considered a risk factor for attachment disruption.

INFANT AND TODDLER ASSESSMENT

- The Denver Developmental Screening Test tests for problems in personal-social, fine motor, language, and gross motor development.
- The Bayley Scales of Infant Development assess children from early infancy to 3 years of age on both a motor and a mental scale.
- The Uzgiris-Hunt Ordinal Scales of Psychological Development measure sensorimotor development in children from birth to 2 or $2\frac{1}{2}$ years of age. This test is often used to evaluate infant educational programs.

- Assessment instruments indicate whether children are developing normally—within the norms—for their age, but they don't predict problems very well because later functioning depends heavily on language skills, which haven't emerged yet in infants. Infant assessment instruments also don't account for the wide variation among normal children, nor do they include items that are hard to measure and score.

LIVING WITH THE YOUNG CHILD

- Natural immunities and limited exposure to other children make the first two years of life relatively healthy ones, but illnesses in children under 2 years can be serious.
- Sudden Infant Death Syndrome is a mysterious disease that can strike infants while they're sleeping. When a child is judged to be at risk for SIDS, parents can use a device that monitors the child for sleep apnea.
- Once children are exposed to other children, they contract a variety of illnesses. The most common ones are respiratory infections, gastrointestinal viruses, and communicable diseases.
- Most children are immunized against diphtheria, pertussis, and tetanus (the DPT shot); measles, mumps, and rubella; polio; and bacterial meningitis.
- Public health officials want to make immunization universal, but many parents worry about the safety of vaccines. The benefits of immunization do outweigh the risks and side effects.
- Babies who attend day care centers get sick more often than babies who stay at home, and parents should select centers that follow strict sanitary and health procedures.
- Feeding and toilet training are two health-related challenges facing those who live and work with toddlers.
- Toddlers have small appetites and an urge to explore everything in their world. Their needs are best suited by small portions and foods and dishes that allow them the greatest independence.
- The first stage of readiness for toilet training occurs between 1 and 2 years of age, when the toddler becomes aware of the sensation of bladder fullness. At about age 3 (earlier in girls), the child can consciously control the bladder muscles so that urine isn't released reflexively.
- A popular social learning approach uses reinforcement and modeling to teach toileting behavior.

- Children stay dry at night after they achieve daytime control. The inability to control bladder function at night after the age of 4 is called enuresis.
- Children typically achieve bowel control several months before they achieve bladder control. Some children, usually boys, have encopresis (difficulty with bowel control), a condition that requires medical attention.
- Inquisitive, mobile, and motivated by a desire for independence, toddlers easily get into trouble and require constant supervision. Accidents are the leading cause of death among children aged 1 to 4.
- Burns are a serious threat to young children. Adults must protect them against burns from hot water, electrical current, chemicals, the sun, and house fires.
- Adults should "baby proof" children's environment rather than restrict their explorations of it.
- Abuse and neglect are devastating problems for the developing child, although their precise incidence is unknown. People working with children should learn to recognize the physical and behavioral indicators of abuse; most such professionals are required by law to report suspected cases to authorities. A number of factors are thought to interact and lead to abuse or protect against it. Intervention and psychotherapy programs can help abused children and abusing and neglectful adults who are motivated to change to learn better ways of interacting.
- Toys for young infants are designed to provide sensory stimulation. Crawling babies like toys they can push with their hands. Beginning walkers enjoy push toys that help them steady themselves as they walk.
- Toddlers enjoy toys that require fine motor coordination and items that can be used as props for their emerging pretend play.
- Young infants like looking at colorful picture books and hearing nursery rhymes. Older infants like books full of familiar objects they can name. Toddlers love actual stories about familiar events.

- The favorite play of all babies is social play with their parents or caregivers. Adults have to keep alert for signs of overstimulation.
- When young toddlers play together, adults can pro-vide duplicate toys and equipment that can be used by more than one child, and they can help toddlers understand and handle their interactions with other children.

KEY TERMS

dyad   enuresis
family process variables   encopresis
risk factor

SUGGESTIONS FOR FURTHER READING

Ammerman, R., & Hersen, M. (1990). *Children at risk: An evaluation of factors contributing to child abuse and neglect.* New York: Plenum Press.
A readable volume covering most important aspects of the psychology of child abuse and neglect.

Brazelton, T. B. (1984). *Neonatal behavioral assessment scale* (2d ed.). Philadelphia: J. B. Lippincott.
A complete discussion of the Brazelton scale for neonates.

Butler, D. (1979). *Cushla and her books.* Boston: The Horn Book.
A case study of a child born with a number of disabilities. The "intervention" described is home based and delivered by the child's parents. Gives an inside view of the challenges presented by disabled children and how experiences can sometimes be adapted to their advantage.

Godwin, A., & Schrag, L. (1988). *Setting up for infant care: Guidelines for centers and family day care homes.* Washington, DC: National Association for the Education of Young Children.
This little volume discusses the nitty-gritty of providing care for the youngest of children. Gives a good overview of what's involved.

Gonzales-Mena, J. (1993). *Multicultural Issues in Child Care.* Mountain View, CA: Mayfield.
This introduction to issues of cultural differences in caregiving stresses diversity as a source of strength. It promotes such goals as improving the match between caregivers and parents; developing an antibias curriculum; increasing caregiver sensitivity; identifying and avoiding stereotypes; and increasing appreciation of diversity. The focus is on working toward these objectives in the course of daily caregiving routines with infants and toddlers.

Gonzales-Mena, J., & Eyer, D. (1989). *Infants, toddlers, and caregiving.* Mountain View, CA: Mayfield.
This practical text focuses on the special relationship between the young child and the caregiver. It provides problem-solving strategies and caregiving principles.

Gunzenhauser, N. E., & Caldwell, B. M. (Eds.) (1986). Group care for young children. *Pediatric Round Table: 12.* Skillman, NJ: Johnson & Johnson.
This small volume contains chapters on the current use of child care, care for disabled children, special programs for children of women who are in prison, health in child care settings, and corporate support of child care. Provides a good overview of contemporary needs, issues, and programs in a very readable fashion.

Reynolds, E. (1990). *Guiding young children: A child-centered approach.* Mountain View, CA: Mayfield.
A practical guide for caregivers in day care and family care. The book describes how to set up and maintain a child-centered facility, how to relate to the child, and how to provide for the child's intellectual and physical growth and social-emotional security.

PRESCHOOL CHILDREN

Remarkable changes occur between the ages of 3 and 6. The 3-year-old, perhaps still in diapers, becomes the enthusiastic preschooler of $3\frac{1}{2}$ and 4 and then the more confident kindergartner of 5 and 6. Curious and exuberant, preschoolers are eager to find out what they can do and make happen in the world; Erikson identified the psychosocial challenge of this period as developing initiative. This quest is supported by improved physical and motor abilities; new ways of thinking, solving problems, and representing the world; and a growing awareness of a supportive social world. Over the course of the preschool years, magical thinking, with its confusion of real and pretend, gives way to a somewhat more rational comprehension of the world. Preschoolers' charming coined words and invented linguistic forms are replaced by nearly perfect grammar. And the awkward social gestures of the inexperienced playmate evolve into the complex social skills that underlie true friendships. All these advances help prepare the child for the great leap into formal schooling that will take place at the end of this period. In the meantime, these years are for experiencing life with all the senses open, learning about social relationships beyond the family, and discovering the self and the world through play.

PHYSICAL DEVELOPMENT IN PRESCHOOL CHILDREN

"Push us, push us," sang out a trio of girls on swings.

"I can't push all of you," called Monique, one of their teachers, as she came across the nursery school yard toward them. "Someone's going to have to pump."

"Oh, I know how to pump. My brother teached me," said one. She backed up against the swing and then plopped onto it as it swung forward. She thrust her short legs out in front of her awkwardly.

"That's right," said Monique. "Your legs go out as you go forward and back as you go back."

"I want to try," said one of the other girls. "Me, too," said the third. Monique watched as they struggled to coordinate their movements with the swings. "You're getting it," she called to them.

As they practiced, Monique kept an eye on other activities in the yard. Two children were climbing a jungle gym, and a third was hanging upside-down by her knees from the top bar, about 4 feet above the sandy ground. "Hang on tight, Alice," Monique called out. Nearby, a child was standing on top of a seesaw, trying to find the midpoint where it would balance. He shifted his weight back and forth, raising and lowering his arms like a windmill.

Monique looked over at the sandbox. Four children were digging canals and filling them with water from a hose. In some places, the canals were so wide they had put boards across them as bridges. They ran back and forth across the boards, or jumped over the canals, to repair their sandy aquaducts.

"It's one of those perfect mornings," thought Monique as she surveyed the busy scene. "I better enjoy it while it lasts."

Preschoolers *are* busy, both outdoors and indoors. The preschool years can very aptly be called the play years. Children spend a lot of time running, chasing, galloping, balancing, and climbing. Indoors, they paint, build, string

FIGURE 9-1
Preschoolers are more skilled physically and more confident than they were a year or so earlier. These boys are enjoying the challenges offered by a San Francisco playground.

beads, cut with scissors, do simple puzzles, and color with crayons. Both their large and small motor skills have improved immensely since they were toddlers. Let's take a closer look at their appearance and what they can do with their bodies.

APPEARANCE AND GROWTH

It's easy to see the difference in physical appearance between toddlers and preschoolers. Preschoolers have a different silhouette than toddlers. They're longer and leaner, and their heads aren't so large in proportion to their bodies. During the preschool years, children's legs and trunks continue to grow faster than their heads, producing this change in body proportions (see Figure 4-3 in Chapter 4). Preschoolers' stomachs don't protrude so much any more, either. The lengthening of the trunk and the increase in muscle tissue that occurs between ages 3 and 6 gradually provide the space and resistance the body needs to keep the large internal organs tucked in.

Although their appearance changes quite a lot, preschoolers don't actually grow very much—at least not compared to babies. The slowdown in growth rate that began during the toddler years continues in the preschool years. The growth rate now is the slowest it's been in the child's short life.

Of course, the child does gain weight and grow taller. Weight gain during the preschool period amounts to about 3 pounds per year (compared to 14 pounds gained between birth and 1 year), or 9 pounds in all. The average American child weighs 31 pounds entering the preschool period; 35 pounds at age 4; 38 pounds at age 5; and 43 pounds at age 6, the end of the preschool period (Figure 9-3).

Increases in height follow the same pattern. The child grows about $2\frac{1}{2}$ inches per year from the age of 3 until the age of 10 (Lowrey, 1978). Compared to the gains of 10 inches between birth and 1 year, $4\frac{1}{2}$ inches between 1 and 2 years, and $3\frac{1}{2}$ inches between 2 and 3 years, these increases are very moderate. At age 3, the average child is 37 inches tall. By age 6, the average child is 45 inches tall.

As we pointed out when discussing physical development in the toddler, slower growth means a smaller appetite. Preschool children usually don't eat very much, and sometimes they eat very little indeed. Children sometimes have a one- or two-month period of hearty eating followed by a period when they're not interested in food. These periods, exasperating as they can be for parents, correspond to bursts of faster and slower growth. Children are simply responding to the demands of their bodies.

As with toddlers, parents do well to accept the child's small appetite as normal. They should curtail nonnutritious, between-meal snacks and offer children wholesome foods when they see that they're eating less. If children have a choice of nourishing foods, their appetites can be the guide to how much they should eat.

FIGURE 9-2
Preschoolers have lost their baby fat and toddler tummies. Their longer legs and trunks give their bodies a more mature appearance.

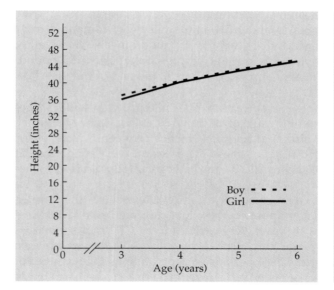

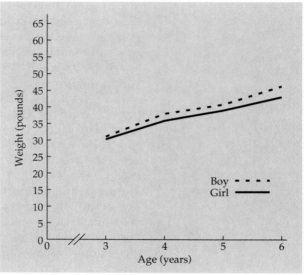

FIGURE 9-3
Height and weight for children 3 to 6 years of age. The graphs reflect height and weight for children who are average (fiftieth percentile). Growth is slower during the preschool years than it was during toddlerhood.

MOTOR DEVELOPMENT

How do preschoolers use their stronger, more coordinated bodies? And how can adults help them develop their motor skills in appropriate ways? We look more closely now at the development of preschoolers' fine and gross motor skills, as well as at the implications of these developments for parents and teachers.

Fine Motor Development

Toddlers learn how to use their hands and fingers to grasp, let go, wave, and point. But toddlers don't have much flexibility in the way they use or move their fingers. The major change in **prehension** (grasping) during the preschool years involves the increasing use of finger movements (Carlson & Cunningham, 1990). When movement of an object is controlled by the fingers rather than by the wrist or arm, the distance between the pivot (point of movement) and the object being moved is shorter. The movement can therefore be much more precise. As a result of increasing skill in finger movement, preschoolers can become adept at putting pegs in pegboards; cutting; stringing beads; and manipulating markers, crayons, and pencils.

The increasing use of finger movement also enables preschoolers to become more independent in dressing themselves. They can button large and easily accessible buttons, zip up and snap their trousers (if the snaps aren't too stiff), and pull on their socks and shoes and take them off. Connecting the two ends of a zipper on a jacket or coat presents quite a challenge to the young preschooler, but many 5-year-olds have mastered this task. Other aspects of getting dressed are beyond the abilities of preschoolers, and they'll ask for help with these—tying shoelaces, buttoning small buttons, wrapping and tying scarves, and snapping large, stiff snaps.

This improvement in fine motor skills corresponds nicely with preschoolers' desire to be independent and help themselves. If parents choose their clothes wisely, young preschoolers can begin to dress and toilet themselves. This means parents should avoid clothing with tiny buttons, difficult snaps, openings in the back, and strings to tie. (For a discussion of how parents and teachers can help children with disabilities achieve independence too, see Special Education Focus—Adapting the Environment to the Child with Disabilities.)

Gross Motor Development: Locomotor Skills

At the beginning of this chapter, a variety of motor activities that would be impossible for toddlers were mentioned—balancing on a seesaw, hanging upside-down from a climber, and jumping over canals in the sand. Preschoolers owe a great deal of their agility to their lower center of gravity. The **center of gravity**—the point in the body around which the weight is evenly distributed—is very high in the newborn, near the bottom of the breastbone. As children grow, their center of gravity moves down. By the time they're age 5 or 6, it's below the navel (Lowrey, 1978). This lower center of gravity provides a firmer foundation for balance and movement, allowing preschoolers to improve both their locomotor skills and their upper body and arm skills.

WALKING AND RUNNING. Preschoolers' days are full of movement, including twisting, turning, running, bouncing, and jumping. What are the specific skills they acquire during this period? As toddlers, they learned to walk, of course, and they started running between ages 2 and 3. They appeared to run before age 2, but in this early kind of running, the feet never actually left the ground at the same time. Between ages 2 and 3, they started moving quickly enough

FIGURE 9-4
Advancing fine motor control allows preschoolers to accomplish many tasks that would be impossible for toddlers. This intent preschool girl is able to prepare her own fishing pole.

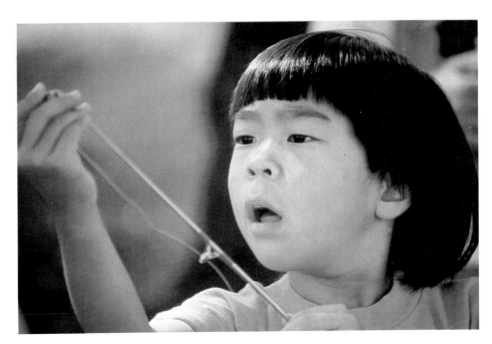

SPECIAL EDUCATION FOCUS

Adapting the Environment to the Child with Disabilities

Parents and teachers often have to restrain themselves from rushing to help young children who are struggling with buttons and zippers, forks and spoons, combs and toothbrushes. It's even harder for adults to watch the struggles of children with physical disabilities. Children work very hard to master the daily tasks of taking care of themselves, and children with disabilities, including those with impaired motor control or limited use of their arms or legs, are no exception. How can adults help these children attain the fullest possible measure of independence and self-sufficiency?

One thing parents can do is make sure their child's clothing is adapted to specific needs. It should fit properly, allow easy movement, be strong enough to withstand abrasion from braces or other mechanical aids, and have openings and fasteners the child can reach. A preschooler may be able to dress herself as well as her able-bodied age-mates if her shirt is fastened in the front with Velcro instead of buttons. She may be able to zip a zipper if a large ring, such as the kind used to hold papers together, is inserted through the tab at the end. And she may be able to get her coat on by herself if she sits down with the coat in her lap and flips it over her head. A child with delayed physical development will be top-heavy and will fall over if she tries to flip her jacket while standing.

Some simple adjustments in equipment and tools can also help the preschooler with disabilities do the same things the other nursery school children do. For example, a child who has poor wrist rotation (a common problem among children with Down's syndrome) may be able to pour her juice from a pitcher if the lid is attached so the spout is 90 degrees from the handle rather than opposite it. A child with poor balance or muscle tone may be able to use a toilet more confidently if there's a low stool in front of it where she can rest her feet. Children who have difficulty grasping objects can be given eating utensils and toothbrushes with extended or thickened handles (Schleifer, 1987).

Children with disabilities often have poorer coordination and slower reaction time than other children. They can benefit from practicing T-ball—batting a ball from a stationary holder rather than a ball that's moving. Movable playground equipment can be taken apart and the pieces placed flat on the ground. Children who couldn't otherwise use parts of play structures can practice walking across them when they're on the ground.

Teachers often have one or more mildly disabled children in their regular classrooms, and their presence can be a positive experience for all the children. Teachers can help them be part of the group by meeting their needs in many large and small ways. Of course, a great deal of special equipment and clothing is now made for children with disabilities, and many parents and teachers take advantage of it. A good source for information about these materials is the journal *The Exceptional Parent* (605 Commonwealth Avenue, Boston, MA 02215).

FIGURE 9-5
To swing sideways, a child has to shift his weight, coordinate two different pushing motions, and keep his balance at the same time. The preschooler loves to experiment with interesting new ways to use familiar equipment, whether it's a swing or his body.

FIGURE 9-6
Walking along the top of a playground stockade is a challenge for a preschooler because he's still developing his sense of balance and his large motor skills. This 4-year-old uses his arms to steady himself. As the motor areas of his brain develop and his center of gravity moves lower, his balance will improve.

for both feet to leave the ground for an instant. By age 3 they run, but they can't change direction while staying on the go, and they can't stop quickly. By age $4\frac{1}{2}$ or 5, preschoolers perfect these skills (Cratty, 1986).

Toddlers have to keep their legs spread wide apart to balance themselves as they walk. Young preschoolers begin to narrow the base on which they walk; they can place one foot in front of the other to walk a line drawn on the floor. By age 4, they can walk a curved line, which is even harder because they have to place one foot in front of the other and turn at the same time. Still more difficult is walking a balance beam (a board raised off the ground), which narrows the base of support even more. Children have to place one foot in front of the other and at the same time make adjustments in how their weight is distributed to each side. Preschoolers have a hard time walking a balance beam—they usually have to step off to the ground several times to regain their balance (Cratty, 1986).

JUMPING. The children digging canals in the sandbox were accomplished at jumping, another locomotor skill that preschoolers master. Before they're 2 years old, children jump from a low height by stepping off with one foot, keeping the other foot in contact with the higher surface. By age 2, they can jump with both feet suspended off the ground for a moment.

(a)

(b)

(c)

FIGURE 9-7
Movements involved in selected motor skills. The skillful execution of a broad jump (a) involves extending the arms at takeoff, lifting off at a forward angle, and landing with flexed knees and arms thrust forward. Many children can broad jump at 5 or 6 years of age. Hopping (b) involves making a springing push into the air on one foot. Most 4-year-olds can hop. Skipping (c) involves a combination of a skip and a hop on alternating feet. Most children can't skip until they are at least 6 years old.

By age 3, children are getting higher when they jump off a low height, but they "wing" their arms—throw them back behind them—and lean backward rather than forward. This makes for an awkward jump that tends to leave them off balance when they land. By age $4\frac{1}{2}$, they learn to move their arms forward and up at take-off for a two-footed jump, leaning forward as they go into the air. To leap over obstacles, they start by leading with one foot; later they can jump over things with both feet together. By age 5, most children have a whole repertoire of jumps they can perform. The movements involved in jumping and other locomotor skills are illustrated in Figure 9-8.

CLIMBING. Climbing is another playground skill that preschoolers master. They've been climbing stairs practically since they could walk, although as toddlers they went up stairs by climbing a step with one foot and then the other before attempting the next step. This kind of climbing is called **marked-time climbing.** By the beginning of the preschool period, children can walk up stairs by alternating feet. Walking down stairs is still a challenge, though, because of the different balance problem. Children usually don't alternate feet going down stairs until they're about 4 years old.

The same sequence of climbing skills is used on play equipment. Children use marked-time climbing to get up ladders, climbers, and jungle gyms before they climb with alternate feet. And they can get up before they can get down. At the beginning of the school year, preschool teachers have to watch for children who have climbed up bars by themselves but can't figure out how to get down. Teachers can usually talk them down, giving them verbal instructions about how to retrace their steps. Gradually preschoolers come to feel comfortable on climbing structures. The girl at the beginning of this chapter who was hanging upside-down from a climber was an older preschooler, probably about 5 years old.

COORDINATING MORE DIFFICULT MOVEMENTS. Other, more difficult activities seen in the nursery school play yard include hopping, skipping, and galloping. These locomotor skills require better balance and coordination than the more basic skills. Hopping, for example, narrows the base of support to one foot and requires good balance. By age $3\frac{1}{2}$, children can hop a few steps on one foot; by age 5, they can hop eight to ten steps. Rhythmic hopping—hopping on alternate feet—requires balance and coordination beyond the ability of most 5-year-olds.

Galloping and skipping are hard because they require coordination and shifts in balance. Galloping involves an uneven rhythmic movement with a lead foot, but since the legs don't alternate, coordination isn't as much of a problem. Most 4-year-olds can gallop. Skipping requires alternation of the feet and coordination of a step forward and a hop; it's a relatively difficult skill to learn. Most children can't skip until they're about 6 years old (Cratty, 1986). The development of the large motor skills during toddlerhood and the preschool years is summarized in Table 9-1.

Preschoolers are eager to try any physical activity they see other children doing. Most 3-year-olds can ride a tricycle; most 6-year-olds can ride a bicycle. Older preschoolers can maneuver a scooter quite well, but they have to wait until they're older to handle a skateboard. Older preschoolers can even begin to learn to roller-skate, ice-skate, kick a soccer ball, and ski.

SUPPORTING MOTOR DEVELOPMENT. As was the case with babies and toddlers, preschoolers' physical abilities and motor skills emerge according to a biological timetable. Their bodies grow, they develop more muscle tissue, and the motor areas of their brains continue to mature. They become capable of running, climbing, jumping, and skipping when their bodies and brains are ready. But, as with babies and toddlers, these developments are supported by stimulation from the environment and opportunities for practice. Preschoolers flourish when they have a place to stretch their bodies and their minds.

Many parents wonder if they should support their children's motor development even more by participating in some of the many movement and pre-gymnastics programs that have sprung up in recent years. In these programs, children walk on balance beams, crawl through tunnels, tumble on mats, roll on balls, climb ladders, and interact with other children. For older children, real gymnastics classes are available.

TABLE 9-1 Large Motor Skills

Age	Walking	Running	Jumping	Pedalling	Climbing	Throwing
8 months–1 year	Walks in a wide stance like a waddle				Climbs onto furniture and up stairs as an outgrowth of creeping	
1–2 years	Walks in a toddle and uses arms for balance (does not swing arms)	Moves rapidly in a hurried walk in contact with surface	Uses bouncing steps off bottom step of stairs with one foot		Tries climbing up anything climbable	Throws items such as food in a jerky sidearm movement
2–3 years	Walks upstairs two feet on a step	Runs stiffly; has difficulty turning corners and stopping quickly	Jumps off bottom step with both feet	Sits on riding toy and pushes with feet	Tries climbing to top of equipment, although cannot climb down	Throws ball by facing target and using both forearms to push; uses little or no footwork or body rotation
3–4 years	Walks with arms swinging: walks up stairs alternating feet; walks downstairs two feet on step; walks straight line	Runs more smoothly; has more control over starting and stopping	Springs up off floor with both feet in some cases; jumps over object leading with one foot	Pedals and steers tricycle	Climbs up and down ladders, jungle gyms, slides, and trees	Throws overhand with one arm; uses body rotation; does not lose balance
4–5 years	Walks up and down stairs alternating feet; walks circular line; skips with one foot; gallops; walks balance beam	Displays strong, speedy running; turns corners, starts and stops easily	Jumps up, down, and forward	Rides trike rapidly and smoothly	Climbs up and down ladders, jungle gyms, slides, and trees	Uses more mature overhand motions and control but throws from elbow
5–6 years	Walks as an adult, skips alternating feet	Shows mature running, seldom falls, displays increased speed and control	Jumps long, high, and far; jumps rope	Rides small bicycle	Displays mature climbing in adult manner	Steps forward on throwing arm side as throws

SOURCE: From Beaty, Janice J. 1986. Observing the development of the young child, p. 148. Columbus, OH: Merrill.

Although these programs provide a stimulating, cheerful environment, practice in locomotor activities, and opportunities for learning and social interaction, there's no evidence that they significantly improve children's motor skills. Most children develop their motor skills by using whatever they find at hand—at home, in their local playground, or in their nursery school play yard. (For a discussion of what to look for in a safe playground, see Public Policy Focus—Making Playgrounds Safe.) As long as there's space to run, a few things to climb on, and a soft place to fall, children attain a fair degree of skill at motor activities by the time they leave their preschool years. But if parent and child enjoy other activity opportunities—like pregymnastics—that's fine too.

FIGURE 9-8
Swinging on rings requires strength in the muscles of the arms, the upper body, the abdomen, and the legs. The child swings her lower body like a pendulum and moves from ring to ring by throwing her weight back and forth. This favorite activity of 5- and 6-year-olds also requires timing, coordination, and blister-resistant hands.

FIGURE 9-9
Gymnastic training can help young children gain flexibility and strength and learn specific skills, such as how to do a back bend or a cartwheel. But it doesn't speed up physical development or the acquisition of motor skills in very young children. Under normal circumstances, motor skills appear in sequence in all young children without special training or classes.

PUBLIC POLICY FOCUS

Making Playgrounds Safe

Skinned knees, scraped elbows, bruises, and bumps—these are the battle scars all children wear at one time or another as they work at developing their physical skills. Parents and teachers usually find that a few words of sympathy, along with a Band-Aid, some antiseptic wash or spray, or an ice cube wrapped in a wash cloth, are enough to ensure a speedy recovery. These occasions of being hurt and healed are actually an important part of the child's learning experience.

But sometimes children suffer more serious injuries at play, many of them the needless result of unsafe conditions at playgrounds. Approximately 150,000 children per year are seen in hospital emergency rooms for injuries sustained on playgrounds. Most injuries are caused by swings and swing sets. Climbing equipment comes in second, followed by slides and seesaws. Other injuries are caused by protruding bolts and sharp edges on play equipment and by play equipment that entraps a body part. The most serious injuries (and the most deaths) are caused by falls from a height (Greensher & Mofenson, 1985).

What should adults look for in a safe playground? The Consumer Products Safety Commission (1981) has proposed safety standards for playgrounds, although these standards haven't become mandatory. For surfaces under play equipment, the association rates concrete, asphalt, brick, and packed earth as very hazardous and unacceptable. Minimally acceptable are gravel, wood chips, 2-inch-thick gym mats, and 1⅜-inch-thick rubber mats. The only acceptably safe surface is sand to a depth of 8 to 10 inches.

A research lab also conducted tests to investigate the relative safety of various playground surface materials. They wanted to determine the heights from which a child could fall before the critical limit for receiving a concussion was ex-

ceeded, expressed as 50 G (G = gravity) (Reichelderfer, Overbach, & Greensher, 1979). As shown in the accompanying figure, a child would have to fall from over 11 feet to receive a concussion if the surface below were sand, but from less than a foot if the surface were concrete or asphalt.

The association suggests that safety zones surround play equipment like swings so that children don't run into the path of moving swings. Low bushes, railroad ties partially sunk in the sand, or some other border barrier should be used to mark the zones. They also recommend that structures built over a certain height have protective railings or be completely enclosed to prevent falls. Designers of playground equipment must remember that young children are thrilled to be 4 or 5 feet off the ground—10 or 12 feet is unnecessary.

Adults can also inspect equipment for exposed bolts, rough or rusty surfaces, or deteriorated parts. Broken glass, crushed soda cans, and other trash in sand or wood chips are particularly hazardous, and children should never go barefoot where these dangers are evident. Splinters from all wood chips are unpleasant; those from redwood chips quickly become inflamed.

Even when playgrounds are very safe, young children need supervision and guidance in using them. A safety zone around a swing won't do much good if children don't know they're not supposed to run through it. Children have to be taught not to climb over railings, not to roughhouse at the top of a slide, and not to ride tricycles off set paths. But when the equipment is safe, adults can concentrate on helping the children play safely.

What can adults do to make playgrounds safer for children? A demonstration project in New York State illustrates what's possible (Fisher, Harris, & VanGuren, 1980). The people who undertook this project inspected the playgrounds in

Gross Motor Development: Upper Body and Arm Skills

"OK, Darren, I'm going to throw it again. Get ready." Rick stands about 5 feet away from his son and gently tosses a soft ball to him.

Darren stands with his arms extended straight out in front of his body. As Rick throws the ball, he continues to look at his dad's face rather than looking at the ball, and as the ball approaches him, he turns his head to the side and squeezes his eyes shut.

"Ohhh, you missed! Throw it back." Darren runs to get the ball. He extends his arm up above his head and throws the ball onto the ground in front of him. Rick picks it up and gets ready to throw it again.

"OK, are you ready?" Darren smiles and nods. "Put your arms out in front of you. Now, this time, try to watch the ball, OK? Keep your eye on the ball." He tosses the ball. Darren watches Rick's face again as the ball approaches, and again turns his head away and shuts his eyes as it bounces softly against his chest.

"Ohhh, almost! Try again!"

Anyone who has played catch with a young child will recognize this scene. As long as the child is having fun and the adult understands his limitations,

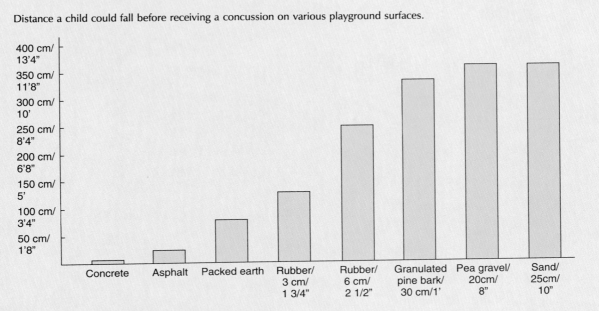

Distance a child could fall before receiving a concussion on various playground surfaces.

SOURCE: KOMPAN INC. 1985–1986 Catalogue, p. 75.

one community, gave seminars and provided literature about playground safety to community personnel, and dispensed information to the public through the local newspapers. As a result, the community made significant changes in the local playgrounds. They covered hard surfaces under play equipment with softer materials and reduced other hazards by 42 percent. Local hospitals subsequently reported that playground-related injuries had dropped by 22 percent. Clearly, training personnel and providing information to the public are important steps in improving safety in local playgrounds.

a ball game is a positive experience for a preschooler. But some ball skills are very difficult to master, and older children and adolescents are still learning and practicing them. Preschoolers have their hands full learning the rudiments of throwing and catching a ball.

THROWING A BALL. The groundwork for ball playing is laid even before the preschool period. Infants enjoy rolling a ball forward once they can sit up. In the second year of life, children start to throw or toss objects in the air from a sitting position during Stage 5 of the sensorimotor period (see Chapter 6). Older toddlers stand and toss a ball with both hands, shifting their weight very little as they let go of it.

Once a child like Darren starts using a one-handed strategy for throwing, we can observe a four-stage pattern of development (Williams, 1983). At first, he holds his body stiffly and throws the ball with a simple, fast arm extension. He doesn't rotate his body or "get behind the ball." In the next stage, he twists his shoulder a bit to follow his arm as it moves forward, but he doesn't shift his body weight or change his footing.

Stage 1

Stage 2

Stage 3

Stage 4

FIGURE 9-10
Throwing a ball isn't as easy as it looks. Skill develops over a number of years and progresses through the stages shown here.

In the third stage, he takes a step forward with the leg on the throwing-arm side of the body as he extends his arm and releases the ball. He rotates his shoulder slightly but doesn't turn his body much. Finally, he starts to rotate his body, first twisting it back as he pulls his arm back, then twisting it forward as he throws. As he rotates his body, his arm moves through quite a wide arc, increasing the ball's velocity. Illustrations of this developmental process are shown in Figure 9-10.

It takes anywhere from three to five years for a child to move from the first to the fourth stage in ball throwing. At age 3, a child is usually at the first stage; by age 6 to 8, the child has usually attained a rudimentary stage 4. Although school-age children and adolescents continue to develop their throwing skills, the basics are mastered during the preschool period.

CATCHING A BALL. Catching also develops in stages. It begins when babies sit and capture a ball that rolls between their legs. Young children find it easier to catch a large ball tossed straight at them than a smaller ball thrown up like a fly ball (Randt, 1985). Even so, they extend their arms stiffly to try to trap the ball with arms, hands, and body rather than reaching to grasp the ball with their hands. Like Darren, they're unable to follow the ball with their eyes and often turn their faces away in a protective gesture as the ball approaches.

Somewhat later, they start to watch the ball as it approaches and to use just their hands to grasp it. Later still, usually at about age 5, they place their feet wide apart on the ground in anticipation of needing to move to one side or the other to catch the ball. When they actually close their hands around the ball, they pull their arms back to cushion the force of the throw against their bodies (Cratty, 1986). Only older children and adolescents are able to execute such maneuvers as jumping and extending one gloved hand to catch a fly ball.

FIGURE 9-11
Maturation and experience both play a role in the development of physical dexterity and coordination. Although right now she closes her eyes and holds both arms stiffly out in front of her when she tries to catch a ball, this 4-year-old is building the skills that will help her, with time, become a good ball player.

REACTION TIME. In addition to the physical skills needed to catch a ball, children have to develop the mental agility to respond to the throw. The time it takes the child to respond is called **reaction time.** Reaction time consists of the time it takes for the child to assimilate the stimuli (such as the appearance of an oncoming ball), make judgments about the throw, and decide which movements to make to catch the ball and the time it takes the mental plan to reach the muscles (Cratty, 1986).

Even a ball thrown slowly from a short distance requires a judgment the instant it's in the air if the child is going to catch it (Whiting, 1969). As we saw, reaction time in a 3-year-old like Darren is very slow. It improves quite a lot between ages 3 and 5, but it still lags way behind the reaction time of older children and adults. A lot of older children's skill at throwing, catching, and batting can be attributed to their faster reaction time.

Like the locomotor skills, the upper body and arm skills of throwing and catching develop as the child grows. The center of gravity changes, muscle tissue increases and fat decreases, and the nervous system matures, producing better coordination and improved reaction time. All the child needs from the environment is a ball, a willing companion, and plenty of opportunities for practice.

OVERVIEW

The chubby toddler with her protruding tummy and waddling walk gives way now to the leaner, more coordinated preschooler who can run, climb, and jump with relative ease. The preschool yard is filled with children pedalling tricycles, pushing each other in wagons, scrambling up play structures, and pursuing imaginary bad guys and monsters. Preschoolers' improved large and fine motor control allows them to do many things for themselves that they couldn't do just a year earlier. With their greater desire for independence, this development suits them just fine. By the end of the preschool years they've gained so much in physical abilities and motor skills that they're ready to take on the elementary school physical education program.

CHAPTER REVIEW

APPEARANCE AND GROWTH

- Preschoolers are longer and thinner than they were as toddlers, and their heads are more in proportion to their bodies.
- They continue to grow at a slowed-down rate, gaining about 3 pounds and growing about $2\frac{1}{2}$ inches a year.
- Preschoolers often don't have very big appetites. They should be given a nutritious diet and not be pressured to eat.

MOTOR DEVELOPMENT

- Children gain more control of their fingers during the preschool years and use this ability in many fine motor activities, such as drawing, cutting, and stringing beads.
- They also gain the ability to dress themselves. Parents can support independence by providing manageable clothes as well as any necessary help and supervision. When children have disabilities, parents and caregiv-

ers may have to make certain adaptations in the environment to help them become independent.

- The preschooler's center of gravity has moved down to the abdomen, providing a more secure base for balance and locomotor activities.
- Preschool children are adept at running, jumping, and climbing. Movements requiring more coordination, such as galloping, hopping, and skipping, take them longer to master. Their balancing skills also improve during this period.
- Motor skills emerge as more muscle tissue develops and as the brain matures. These skills are nurtured by

a stimulating environment and opportunities to practice. Playgrounds are important places for preschoolers, although adults should make sure they're safe and free from hazards.

- Preschoolers begin to master the basics of throwing and catching a ball. By the age of 6, the typical child can get her body behind the ball to throw it and can maneuver to catch it. Children's reaction time also improves during the preschool years, so they're able to respond more quickly when catching or batting a ball.

KEY TERMS

prehension
center of gravity
marked-time climbing
reaction time

SUGGESTIONS FOR FURTHER READING

Cratty, B. J. (1986). *Perceptual and motor development in infants and children* (3d ed.). Englewood Cliffs, NJ: Prentice-Hall.
This highly readable classic provides a thorough discussion of physical growth and motor development. Chapters on hands, visual perception, and the effects of exercise provide interesting information.
Engstrom, G. (1971). *The significance of the young child's motor development.* Washington, DC: The National Association of Young Children.

This short booklet discusses the importance of motor development in the preschool child. Included are useful pictures of sequences of movements young children use in throwing a ball and jumping from a height.
Sinclair, C. B. (1973). *Movement of the young child: Ages two to six.* Columbus, OH: Merrill.
This book provides a thorough, but readable, overview of many physical skills that develop in young children.

c h a p t e r 10

COGNITIVE DEVELOPMENT IN PRESCHOOL CHILDREN

Margaret and her dad are playing a board game. Margaret, who is 4, rolls the dice.

"A five and a two," she says as the dice come to rest. Then she starts to count out the dots, pointing to each one with her finger, to find out how many spaces to move her token. "One, two, three, four, five, six, seven."

Next, Margaret's dad takes his turn. He rolls a four and a three. "Seven," he says, as he starts to make his move.

"Hey! You can't do that," Margaret protests. "You have to count the dots."

"Well, four dots and three dots are seven dots," her dad replies.

"No," Margaret insists. "You have to count to see."

Her dad complies, but since he thinks Margaret is questioning his ability to add, he starts with the four as a given. "Four," he says, pointing to one die. "Five, six, seven," he continues, pointing to the dots on the other die. "See? Four and three do equal seven."

"But you have to count that one, too," Margaret persists, pointing to the die with four dots.

"I do?" asks her dad. "Why?"

"To see how many it is," she explains, sounding a little exasperated.

"Oh, I see," her dad answers. "Okay. I thought we already knew that it was four."

"No, we didn't," Margaret says, as she watches to make sure her father counts all four dots.

"One, two, three, four, five, six, seven," her dad counts out loud. "Did I do it right that time?"

"Uh-huh. Now you can move."

Margaret's behavior is fairly typical of most preschoolers. On the one hand, her cognitive abilities seem quite sophisticated. She can recognize the pattern of five dots at a glance, and she can count accurately at least to seven. On the

other hand, she doesn't exploit the knowledge she has. She can say, "That's a four," at the same time that she says, "We have to count to see if it's four." Her knowledge about one situation doesn't extend to another situation.

Preschoolers have pieces of knowledge, but they don't have an overall framework into which they can fit the pieces. Their knowledge is fragmented and tied to certain contexts. Their thinking seems inflexible and illogical. They lack some of the basic assumptions on which adults base their understanding of the world.

Despite these limitations, preschoolers have made some important advances since they were toddlers. Their thinking is now **preoperational** rather than sensorimotor; that is, they can represent objects and events symbolically in ways that weren't possible before, even though they don't apply the logic that's characteristic of older children's thinking.

In this chapter, we examine the typical thinking of preschoolers. We see, for example, that they rely on appearances rather than on ideas, that they can focus on just one relationship at a time, and that they often see things primarily from one point of view—their own. We begin by looking at the cognitive skills and abilities that they have and the ones they don't have yet. We explore their difficulties with seemingly simple tasks such as judging whether quantity changes when spatial arrangement changes, creating an ordered series, classifying items into categories, understanding another person's physical perspective, and counting. We then consider children's thinking about thinking itself—about thoughts, dreams, ideas, false beliefs—and the mental abilities that make their thinking unique. From these discussions, we arrive at an overall picture of the child's cognitive development between ages 3 and 6.

UNDERSTANDING THE CONCEPT OF NUMBER

As with cognitive development at other ages, much of our knowledge about the abilities of preschoolers comes from the work of Piaget. Additional ideas and data come from researchers who questioned Piaget's methods and clarified his findings, researchers known as neo-Piagetians. Here we discuss Piaget's classic contributions before turning to some of the qualifications of Piaget's work and to more current research.

Perhaps the most famous of Piaget's experiments are his investigations of **conservation,** the idea that changes in arrangement or shape do not affect number or amount. No matter how we arrange ten blocks, for example, they will always be ten blocks. And no matter how we distribute a cup of water, it will always be one cup. When children understand that rearrangement of a substance or a group of objects doesn't affect its quantity, we say that they have conservation, meaning they can think in such a way as to arrive at a logical conclusion about what does and does not affect quantity. Piaget investigated several different areas of conservation, including conservation of number and conservation of continuous quantity, or mass.

Conservation of Number

In the classic Piagetian number conservation task, the experimenter arranges eight to ten objects in a row and asks the child to make a second row with just as many objects as the first row. Most 3-year-olds and even some young 4-year-olds are unable to do this task. They pay attention to the length of the row and make sure their row begins and ends just opposite the model, but they use either more or fewer objects than the model in constructing their row (Figure 10-2a). When the child performs this way, the experiment has gone as far as it can.

If, on the other hand, the child is able to create a second row equal to the first row by matching the objects one-to-one, the experimenter can proceed with the second part of the task. Now the experimenter changes the distribution in one of the rows so that it becomes either longer or shorter than the

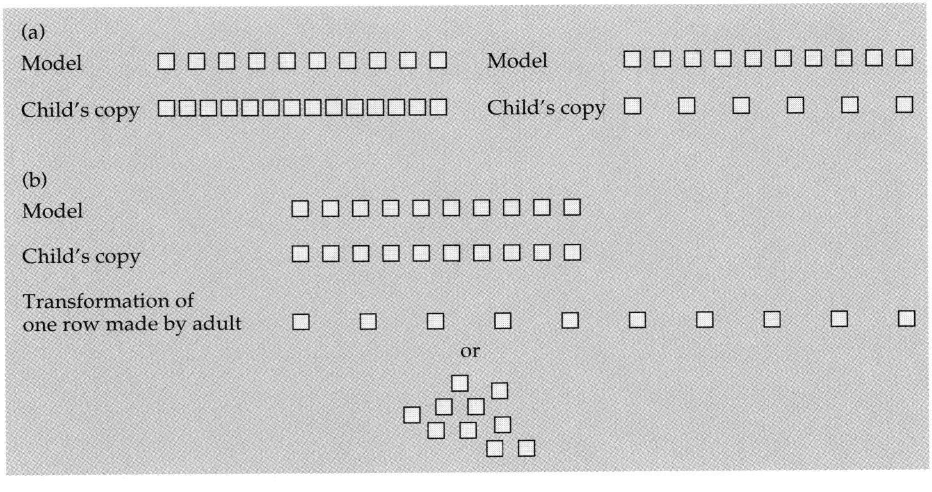

FIGURE 10-2
In the Piagetian conservation of number task, the experimenter asks the child to create a row with the same number of objects as the row created by the experimenter (a). If the child can do this (b), the experimenter rearranges the row and asks the child if it still has the same number of objects as before. Most preschoolers answer no, basing their response on appearances rather than logical thinking.

other (Figure 10-2b). The child is told to watch what the experimenter does, and afterward, the child is asked if the two rows still have the same number of objects or if one has more or less than the other.

Less advanced children say that the new row contains a different number of objects. Some children focus on the density of the rows; they say the shorter row contains more objects. Other children focus on the length of the rows, and they say the longer row has more objects. Most children between ages $4\frac{1}{2}$ and 6 deny that the two rows could have the same number after they've been rearranged.

By 6 years of age, most children say that the two rearranged rows still contain the same number of items. When asked why they think this is so, they usually give one of three explanations: (1) No item was taken away or added (that is, they explain it by **identity**); (2) the longer row has big gaps (they explain it by **compensation;**) or (3) the displaced row could be put back the way it was in the beginning (they explain it by **reversibility**). According to Piaget, any of these responses indicates that a child can conserve number. Children typically begin to respond to the conservation of number task in terms of logic—what they think about the rows—rather than in terms of perception—how the rows look—when they're about 6 or $6\frac{1}{2}$ years old.

Conservation of Continuous Quantity

Whereas the conservation of number involves individual objects or units, the conservation of continuous quantity involves mass. The Piagetian task with which this cognitive ability is investigated involves two large identical beakers (referred to here as beaker 1 and beaker 2) filled with colored water. The experimenter asks the child to look at them to be sure that they contain the same amount of liquid. The child can pour liquid from one to the other, if necessary, until they are exactly the same. When the child has agreed that the quantities in the two beakers are identical, the experimenter pours the water in beaker 2 into another beaker of a different shape or into several small containers (Figure 10-3). The experimenter then asks the child if beaker 1 contains the same amount of liquid as beaker 3 (if the beaker is used) or as the small cups (if cups are used).

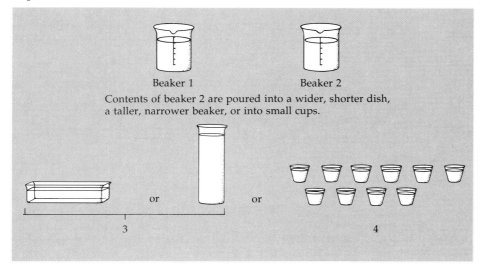

Beaker 1   Beaker 2

Contents of beaker 2 are poured into a wider, shorter dish, a taller, narrower beaker, or into small cups.

or   or

3   4

FIGURE 10-3
In the Piagetian conservation of continuous quantity task, the experimenter pours water from one beaker into a beaker of a different shape or into several cups. Most preschool children think the amount of water is different at the end of this procedure.

FIGURE 10-4
Does the tall beaker contain more liquid than the shorter one? Even when she pours it herself, this 5-year-old would probably answer yes. Preschoolers rely on the evidence of their senses rather than on logical thinking processes when it comes to understanding the world.

Three-year-olds and young 4-year-olds think that the liquid that has been transferred into a different container has also changed in quantity. Between ages $4\frac{1}{2}$ and 6, children sometimes say that the quantity of the transferred liquid is the same as before, especially when the liquid is now in a different-shaped beaker. But when the containers are very different, as they are when cups are used, these children revert to saying that the quantity has changed. It's not until children are 6 or 7 years old that they disregard what they see and instead rely on logic. They explain the apparent discrepancy by saying, "This container is wider, but it isn't as high," or "There are more little cups, but they don't hold very much," or "We could pour all these back into this one."

As you can see, preschoolers typically are unable to demonstrate conservation on the Piagetian conservation tasks. However, there is some debate about preschoolers' understandings: Some critics say that preschoolers are more competent than the Piagetian tasks reveal (Gelman & Gallistel, 1978). They've found that changing the tasks affects how children perform on them. To clarify the issue in this debate, we elaborate briefly on how Piaget explained preschoolers' difficulties on the conservation tasks.

Piaget's Explanation: Preoperational Thinking

Piaget described many aspects of children's cognitive development in terms of mental operations. Mental operations are specific processes of reasoning we go through in our minds. Thinking that a taller, thinner container of water is equal to a shorter, fatter container of water is an example of a mental operation—a logical comparison or multiplication, in this case. According to Piaget, preschoolers have certain limitations in their operational abilities that make it impossible for them to think about things in this logical way. For example, they tend to **center**—focus mentally—on only one aspect of a relationship at a time, to the exclusion of all other aspects, perhaps the tallness of one container of water and the shortness of a second container. What they cannot do is focus on both tallness and thinness versus shortness and fatness. The conservation tasks require that *two* relationships be compared and coordinated, and this is the thing that preschoolers typically can't do.

Another limitation of preschoolers' thinking is its **irreversibility**. After observing an action, preschoolers can't play it backward in their heads to reconstruct how things were originally. They focus more on states—how things look at the end of a particular action—than on transformations—how one state changes to another and is related to it. When a child watches the experimenter spread out a row of pennies so they're no longer directly opposite the pennies in another row, the child doesn't realize the action of spreading out the pennies could be reversed. If the child watches someone else put the pennies back, or if the child does it himself when asked, he will then say that the rows once again contain the same number of pennies. The child thinks only about pennies opposite each other or pennies not opposite each other. The transformation connecting these two states escapes him.

Piaget referred to the preschool child's thinking as preoperational; that is, it's not characterized by such operations as coordinating two aspects of a relationship (such as length and density of rows of pennies) or reversing an action to coordinate two different positions of the same objects (such as close together and spread out). The child who can conserve, on the other hand, is said to be thinking at a **concrete operational** level. A child at this level can apply logical thinking to a situation, as long as the data can all be seen and the situation is therefore concrete.

Children usually become capable of concrete operational thought by 7 years, the age at which many new mental functions appear and many new activities are introduced at school. This age has traditionally been recognized as marking the "dawn of rationality." By age 7, many children have figured out through logic that Santa Claus, the Tooth Fairy, and the Easter Bunny don't exist (probably). This is in contrast to the thinking of a 6-year-old who responded indignantly when told by a 9-year-old that "your mom and dad" perform all those duties. "Santa Claus *does* exist," she stormed. "I *know*, because how could your mom and dad get all the way to the North Pole?!"

Critiques of Piaget and Approaches to the Conservation Tasks by Neo-Piagetians

Piaget's discoveries about the limits of children's thinking have been generally accepted, but some people have questioned the ages at which he found various understandings in children. They believe, for example, that children really understand conservation earlier than Piaget's tasks indicated. They have looked carefully at the tasks to see if another explanation exists for the children's performance. Some critics suggest that the standard procedure used in administering the tasks was influencing children's expectations and leading them astray.

For example, the child is told to "watch closely while I do something." A statement like this may lead the child to believe that a significant change is being made, which isn't really the case. In children's everyday life, people rarely call their attention to something insignificant. When they're told to "watch carefully," it's usually because something important is going to happen. But in the task, quantity *doesn't* change. They may understand this, but they may take the experimenter's words as a cue that a trick of some kind is going on. If this is the case, the experiment is measuring not just their concept of number but also their social awareness—their knowledge that sometimes people try to fool other people.

One researcher decided to change the conservation task to reduce the likelihood that children were being influenced by false expectations (Donaldson, 1978). She used a stuffed animal named Naughty Teddy to intrude on the task and "mess up" one of the rows of cubes. The exasperated experimenter then invited the child to put Naughty Teddy back in his box, and she resumed the experiment, saying, "Now, where were we? Ah yes, is the number in this row the same as in this row?"

In Piaget's standard experiment with 4- to 6-year-olds, only 13 out of 80 children could conserve number, but in the Naughty Teddy experiment, 50 out of 80 did so. The researcher concluded that young children know more about the logic of number than Piaget's task suggests. If their expectations aren't biased by the experimenter's statements, we can discover more about their actual knowledge.

Other researchers agree with this assessment and have devised a variety of alterations on the standard test. In one study, children were asked about the equality of the rows only once, after the transformation, instead of both before and after. Children again demonstrated more understanding than in the standard test (Rose & Blank, 1974). Other researchers have reduced the number of objects used in the tasks and changed the task format (Gelman & Gallistel, 1978). Under these conditions, they found that preschool children do realize when quantities have been changed and when they've just been rearranged.

Still other critics have objected not so much to the way early parts of the task are presented as to Piaget's requirement that children be able to explain their answers. If they couldn't give one of the three reasons mentioned previously to explain why the two quantities were still the same, Piaget didn't believe they could conserve number. Critics suggest that this rigorous requirement brings in verbal and expressive abilities and obscures children's understanding of number (Brainerd, 1978).

How Much Do Preschoolers Really Understand?

Despite the validity of the critics' comments about the Piagetian tasks, Piaget did put his finger on a significant difference between the thinking of preschoolers and that of 6- or 7-year-olds. Younger children's thinking is not as logical, not as "connected," as older children's. Consider this incident:

4-year-old Andy was setting a table for snack time at his preschool. On one side of the table, he accidentally put an extra place setting, leaving a chair on the other side without a napkin and cup. "I don't have enough," he told the teacher.

"Well, we counted out six cups and six napkins, and there are six chairs at your table," answered the teacher, *"so it should work out."*

"But I don't have enough," Andy protested. *"Come look."*

The teacher saw the problem and picked up the extra cup and napkin that Andy had positioned between two chairs on one side of the table. *"Where do these go?"* he asked Andy.

Andy straightened the place settings, making sure there was one in front of each chair. *"Oh,"* he said, *"Those go here. Now we have enough."*

An older child would probably have viewed this situation differently. If he had counted out six napkins and six cups and had come up one place setting short, he might have thought, "I know I had enough. Where did I goof up?" After surveying the table, he might have said, "Oh, I see. I made a mistake over there." But Andy assumed the number of cups and napkins—not their arrangement—was the problem. Even after putting the place settings in the right place, he said, "Now we have enough," rather than "I made a mistake," as if the rearrangement itself had created a different number of items.

In their everyday behavior, whether setting tables or counting the dots on dice, preschoolers do demonstrate a limited understanding of number. Both Piaget and his critics have given us valid information about their mental competence in this area. Drawing on both sources, we conclude that preschoolers can often function at quite a high level if we're careful about how we organize the situation and if we're willing to give a helping hand.

UNDERSTANDING THE CONCEPTS OF SERIATION AND CLASSIFICATION

Some of the same kinds of limitations in thinking are obvious when we look at preschoolers' ability to create a series by placing different objects in order by size (a process called **seriation**). As with the concept of number, Piaget did the ground-breaking work, but others have added refinements to his conclusions.

Piaget's Standard Seriation Task

The seriation task involves arranging about ten sticks, all a little different in length, into a graduated series. This task is impossible for most 4-year-olds and young 5-year-olds. They might put the shorter sticks together in one pile and the longer ones together in a second pile (Figure 10-5a). Or they might focus only on the tops or only on the bottoms, creating a pseudoseries (Figure 10-5b).

The task is somewhat easier for 5- and 6-year-olds. They can make a series, but they get there through a process of trial and error. They still can't think of two aspects of each stick at the same time—its length in relation to the last one placed in the series and its length in relation to the rest of the sticks in the pile. They tend to select a stick that's longer than the last one but also longer than some of the remaining ones. Only when they pick up another stick and discover it's shorter than the last one do they discover their error and make an adjustment. Piaget called this approach **intuitive**—based on a vague

FIGURE 10-5
In the Piagetian seriation task, children are asked to arrange a number of sticks in order from smallest to largest. Preschoolers often create series like those shown here. Most children younger than 6 or 7 are unable to select the stick that comes next except through trial and error.

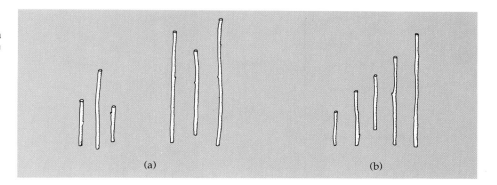

(a) (b)

notion of what's involved in seriating—and **empirical**—discovered as they go along.

Children aged 6 and 7 can solve the problem **operationally**. They select each successive stick correctly by thinking about how long or short it is in relation both to the sticks already used and to those that remain. They think, "The next one has to be longer than the last one but shorter than all the others." Unlike the preoperational child, who can only make one comparison and make it on the basis of how things look, the operational child can make two comparisons, using mental operations.

The Nesting Cup Task

Other information about children's ability to create a series comes from research that wasn't specifically designed to test Piaget's findings. Psychologist Judy DeLoache (DeLoache, Sugarman & Brown, 1985) was interested in how children correct their errors when they encounter a problem. She devised a study involving ten nesting cups (a series of graduated plastic cups that fit inside each other) of the kind parents frequently buy for babies and toddlers. She wanted to see how children between $1\frac{1}{2}$ and $3\frac{1}{2}$ years approach the task of getting all the cups to nest inside each other.

The youngest children in the study, those under $2\frac{1}{2}$ years, often responded with force when they couldn't insert one cup inside another. They pushed, banged, or used some other way to force the fit. They also sometimes put down one of the cups they held and tried another. The idea that the two they already held could be reversed didn't occur to them. A third strategy was also seen: Regardless of whether the child had already fit several cups together, once a problem was encountered, the child took the whole series apart and started over!

Older children, those between $2\frac{1}{2}$ and $3\frac{1}{2}$, were less likely to use brute force or to dismantle the series once they encountered a problem. Often, they simply reversed the two cups they had, putting the smaller one into the larger instead of the larger into the smaller. This maneuver suggests that they understood the size relationship of the two cups to each other. An even more sophisticated strategy involved insertion. This involved taking apart the stack of cups assembled so far until the point was reached at which the new cup could be inserted. Both of these approaches—reversing and inserting—involve reordering and are similar to the trial and error approaches of 5- and 6-year-olds in Piaget's seriation task.

FIGURE 10-6
Research findings differ on the age at which children have the cognitive ability to create an ordered series. Young pre-schoolers like this 3-year-old initially use trial and error to perform the seriation task represented by a ring and post toy.

Of the 40 children in the study, 18 actually created a correct series. Given the age of these children, the results are surprising. In the standard Piagetian task, children much older than this are just starting to be able to seriate.

The Two Tasks Compared

Why do we see this big discrepancy between the two tasks? The answer, again, seems to involve the variables of the testing situation. The nesting cups can't be placed incorrectly; it's physically impossible. But the sticks used in the Piagetian task can be put anywhere; they don't physically resist the child's mistake. Children have to notice an error on their own before they can rearrange the sticks. Some of the mistakes children make with the sticks may be due to a failure to notice things about the different sticks, not to an inability to make a series by operational processes. Furthermore, many children have experience with the cups, and they may already know that they have to pay close attention if they're going to get them all inside each other.

The nesting cups test highlights the big differences between preschoolers' abilities and those of toddlers. The Piagetian tasks were administered to preschool and older children, not to children under age 3. They make us focus on what preschoolers *can't* do rather than on what they can do. The nesting cups experiment helps us put preschool cognitive abilities in better perspective.

Classification

A third dimension of logical thinking that researchers have studied in children is the ability to classify—separating objects and grouping them in classes according to certain attributes. To see what's involved in this process, consider this task:

> On a table are a large red felt circle, a large blue felt circle, a large blue felt square, a little red felt square, a little blue felt square, a little red felt circle, a paper clip, an elastic band, and an eraser. Organize the materials.

First, you might separate the shapes from the objects. Then you might work within the class of shapes to create finer categories. You could put the red shapes together and the blue shapes together and then divide these groups further into circles and squares or big shapes and little shapes. Groupings like these can be represented schematically as shown in Figure 10-7. This process is known as hierarchical classification because subclasses are created within classes.

When we classify, we create categories, or classes, in our minds. Shapes become red shapes and blue shapes, or big shapes and little shapes, or circles and squares. A classification system is constructed and imposed on objects—it's not inherent in the objects themselves, although objects' attributes determine the classes we're able to construct.

Children under 4 years of age would have trouble classifying the shapes and objects in this task. They can group objects into collections but not into true classes, which are groups defined by a stable attribute (Inhelder & Piaget, 1969). They might start with one defining attribute in mind, such as color, and then switch to another one, such as shape. They would start with a red square, follow it with a red circle, and follow that with a blue circle. Preoperational children are guided less by thinking—by keeping an idea of an attribute in mind—than by what they see in front of them and have in their hands.

Sometimes young children "organize" these shapes and objects by making a picture with them (a house, a bridge, an airplane). They group them not according to any specific attribute but by what fits the picture they want to make. No defining "class" characteristic is selected at all.

Children between 5 and 7 years of age can make classes based on a single, defining attribute (Freund, Baker & Sonnenschein, 1990). They can put all the red shapes together, or all the squares together, without losing track of the attribute they're working with. They even organize subclasses within classes, such as red squares, blue squares, and yellow squares. But children this age have trouble thinking about **class inclusion**, about the fact that both red circles and red squares are members of the larger class, red. This difficulty is particularly noticeable if they're asked questions such as, "Would we have any red objects left if we lost all of the red circles?" To answer questions like this, children have to think about parts (red circles and red squares) in relation to the whole (all the red things). Children are unable to comprehend questions like this until they're 7 or 8 years old (Ginsburg & Opper, 1988).

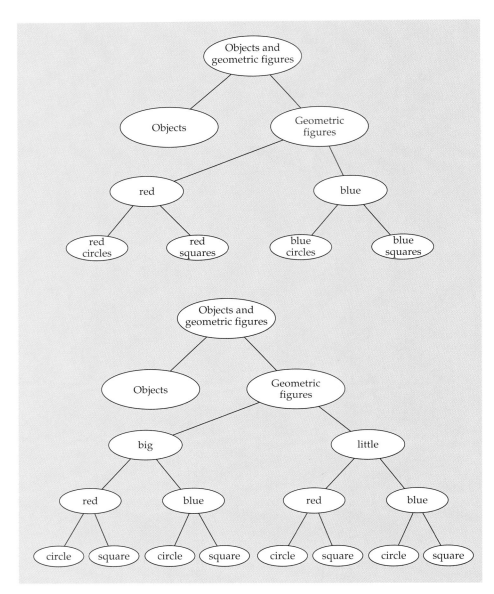

UNDERSTANDING PHYSICAL POINT OF VIEW

The last dimension of logical thinking that we consider here is the ability to understand that another person's physical perspective might be different from one's own and to figure out what that perspective might be (Piaget & Inhelder, 1967). The apparatus Piaget used in this task consists of a three-dimensional display of three mountains, which differ in height, color, and landscape features (Figure 10-9). The child is asked to walk around the display and to look at it from all vantage points. The child is then seated on one side of the display opposite a doll who faces it from the other side and asked to select the doll's view of the display from among a series of ten photographs.

FIGURE 10-8
These girls in an educational preschool program can select and match blocks by color, indicating that they have some sense of the attributes by which objects can be classified. Because of their preoperational thinking, however, their ability to keep an attribute in mind while sorting objects is somewhat limited.

The youngest children (4-year-olds) select photographs at random. By age 5, children usually select the photo showing the view they see. By age 6 or 7, children seem to realize that the doll can't see what they see, but they rarely pick out the correct photo. Not until the age of 9 or 10 do they reliably select the doll's actual view. From these results Piaget concluded that preschoolers are unable to take another's point of view.

This task, like some of the other Piagetian tasks, has been criticized by other researchers. Modifications in the task have shown preschoolers to be somewhat more competent than Piaget found. For example, when children are asked to rotate a model to show what the doll sees, they perform better than when they're asked to pick out a photo (Huttenlocher & Presson, 1973).

FIGURE 10-9
In Piaget's famous three-mountain experiment, a child is asked to select the view of the display that would be seen by a doll sitting across the table from the child. Preschoolers typically select their own view. Not until they're 9 or 10 years old are most children able to select the doll's point of view when Piaget's methods are used.

Aerial view

Children's performance on completely different tasks also indicates that even 2- and 3-year-olds have some awareness of different perspectives. For example, when asked to hide an object so that an adult could not see it, they made it invisible to an adult (by placing it behind a screen) while keeping it within their own view (Flavell, Shipstead & Croft, 1978).

Preschool children are certainly more aware of their own perspectives than of the perspectives of others, and in this sense we can say they're egocentric. But as with other abilities, Piaget may have underestimated their ability to see things from another's point of view.

ARITHMETICAL SKILLS AND UNDERSTANDINGS

Research on conservation, seriation and classification has given us insight into the limits of preschoolers' logical thinking. But these aren't the kinds of problems young children normally have to deal with as they play games or live their everyday lives. The cognitive tasks they're more likely to encounter involve counting or adding simple sums. The way they perform these tasks also reveals how their cognitive functioning differs from older children's.

Early Counting

Carla was counting the chairs set up around a small table to see if there were enough for herself and four other 3-year-olds. "One, two, three, four, five, six, seven," she counted, before her teacher interrupted. "Whoa there, Carla! I think you counted some of those chairs twice. Start again, and this time I'll keep my hand on the chair you began with. Then you'll know where to stop."

Counting isn't the simple skill it may at first appear to be. By definition, it involves enumerating units to arrive at a total number of units. It also involves giving a stable, consistent meaning to each of the conventional counting words (called **tags**). We might see toddlers and young preschoolers pointing to objects and reciting counting words, but this behavior doesn't mean they're really counting. The skills and understandings required for true counting are just being acquired by preschoolers. On their way to these achievements, they make a number of typical errors.

THREE KINDS OF COUNTING ERRORS. **Tagging errors** are among the first counting errors made by preschoolers. They often use unconventional tags ("one, two, three, four, a, b, c") or use conventional tags in nonstandard order ("one, two, three, six, eight, ten"). And even if they know the conventional number names in order, they are likely to make **coordination errors,** that is, failing to match their numerical recitation to the objects they're counting (Baroody, 1987). For example, they start saying number names before they touch or point to the first object, say them faster than they touch or point, or keep on saying them after all the objects have been accounted for. Preschoolers playing board games often make coordination errors. They move their playing piece down the board path at a different rate than they say the tags.

Carla made a counting error that's very common among preschoolers. She counted items more than once because she failed to notice which ones she'd already counted and which she hadn't. Sometimes children neglect to count some items because they skip over them. In either case, this **partitioning error** involves a failure to separate counted items accurately from uncounted items (Gelman & Gallistel, 1978).

AGES ASSOCIATED WITH COUNTING SKILLS. The ability to use the conventional tags for numbers has been tied to average ages. Many 3-year-olds know and use the first five tags and can recite them in order, (Saxe, Guberman & Gearhart, 1987), but after this they jump ahead: "One, two, three, four, five, seven, ten" (Gelman & Meck, 1983). Most 4-year-olds can recite the conventional tags up to about 15 (Saxe, Guberman & Gearhart, 1987), but they tend to make errors when they get to the teens: "twelve, fifteen, sixteen, thirteen, twenty." Because some of the teen numbers do not match their one-to-ten counterparts (we say "thirteen" rather than "threeteen," for example), the teen tags are hard to remember and use in the correct sequence (Baroody, 1987).

When 2-year-olds start to count a group of objects, they make a partitioning or coordination error almost immediately. Most 4-year-olds can count about five objects accurately before they begin to make errors (Gelman & Gallistel, 1978; Saxe, Guberman & Gearhart, 1987). Many 5-year-olds can count 20 objects accurately if the objects aren't in disarray (Baroody, 1987).

When objects are in disarray, and when there are a lot of them in a group, children have to order the objects mentally in some way to count them without making partitioning or coordination errors. Understanding the need to establish some order is probably tied to an increased understanding of the meaning of counting. Unless children realize that counting implies **hierarchical inclusion**—the idea that 1 is included in 2, 2 is included in 3, and so on—they're not likely to be careful about counting each object once and only once (Kamii, 1982).

Even 5-year-olds have trouble counting large groups of disorganized objects (Fuson, 1988). Objects arranged in a straight line are easier for children to count than objects arranged in a circle, because the beginning and end of the

FIGURE 10-10
Counting tree rings is an ambitious task for a 5-year-old. Even if he counts slowly and uses his finger to keep track of the rings he's already counted, it will be hard for him to avoid the common pre-school counting errors. And with a tree this old, he may not know or remember the names of all the numbers he'll need. In just a year or two, he'll be much more skillful at counting accurately.

group are clear. Movable items like cubes and buttons are also easier to count than immovable items like dots on the face of a die. They can be moved away from the group as they're counted, making them distinct from the items still to be counted. Like the teacher who helped Carla count by putting his hand on the first chair Carla counted, parents and preschool teachers can modify situations to help children learn to obtain more accurate counts.

Understanding Simple Arithmetical Relations

As mentioned previously, one of the understandings involved in counting is hierarchical inclusion. Older children and adults know that counting implies that 1 is included in 2, 2 in 3, and so on, and that this implies further that 3 is more than 2 and 2 is more than 1. Relationships as simple as "greater than" and "less than" are not self-evident to young children. Some 3-year-olds are just beginning to understand these relationships with small numbers and can tell you, for example, that 3 is more than 2 (Schaeffer, Eggleston & Scott, 1974).

By 4 years, children can make many accurate comparisons between numbers under 10 when asked which number of a pair is larger. The greater the difference between the two numbers—4 compared with 9, for example, rather than 8 compared with 9—the more accurate they are. By the time they're 5 years old, children are more accurate than they were at 4 years, especially with numbers that are only one number apart (Baroody, 1987).

UNDERSTANDING THINKING

We've looked now at several aspects of young children's cognitive abilities and skills. A topic we haven't discussed is what children think about thinking—about what thoughts are, where knowledge comes from, and so on. This domain of children's knowledge has recently been referred to as children's "theory of mind" (Astington, Harris & Olson, 1988).

Distinguishing Appearance from Reality

The Gilbert family were on their way to the Natural History Museum's latest exhibit, called "Return of the Dinosaurs." Sitting in the back seat, 5-year-old Jacob chattered away excitedly about the show.

"Boy, moving dinosaurs that look real! I can't wait. I hope they have a big tyrannosaurus rex, and a triceratops, and a pterodactyl . . ."

"I'm sure they'll have them all," said Arthur, his dad. "I'm curious about how they do this kind of thing with computers. It'll be interesting to see."

No one noticed that 3-year-old Noah was hunched up in the corner of the back seat, clutching his blanket and sucking his thumb. When they got to the museum, Helen, his mom, turned around and said in surprise, "Noah, what's wrong? Don't you feel OK?"

He looked at her miserably and said, "I don't want to see any old dinosaurs. I want to go home!"

"Oh, Noah, they're not real!" she said. "They're just pretend. There's no such thing as a dinosaur any more. They lived millions of years ago. These dinosaurs are made of metal, and motors make them move. They can't hurt you!"

Noah allowed himself to be pried out of the back seat, and he cheered up as he walked into the museum and saw an exhibit of baby chicks in an incubator. After he watched them for a while, he asked if they could go to the space capsule exhibit they'd seen the last time they came.

"No!" said Jacob. "Let's go see the dinosaurs!"

"Yes, let's see the dinosaur exhibit now," agreed Helen. But Noah started to whimper, and Arthur had to pick him up and carry him. When they got to the dinosaur exhibit, he looked around for a second and then hid his face against his dad's shoulder.

"Noah, look," said Arthur. "These dinosaurs are just big motors covered with paper and material. They look like real animals, but they aren't. They're pretend. Here, look."

But Noah wouldn't look. Instead, he started to sob.

"He's trembling all over," said Arthur in surprise. "He's really scared. I better take him out. We'll go to the space exhibit and meet you later."

Why is a 5-year-old able to enjoy an animated display like this and a 3-year-old frightened by it? The reason is that younger children simply can't distinguish appearance from reality the way older children can. They respond to what they see. A huge gray creature with sharp teeth and claws and a moving head *is* a dinosaur to a 3-year-old, and it *is* dangerous. In the same way, a person wearing a gorilla costume and mask *is* a gorilla to a 3-year-old—even if the child sees the person put the mask on! (This is why Halloween can be a truly terrifying experience for very young children.)

When do children begin to be able to distinguish appearance from reality? Some recent studies have confirmed that at age 3 there's very little ability to make this distinction. In one study 3-year-olds were shown various objects both as they really were and as they appeared behind colored filters (Flavell, Green & Flavell, 1986). One object was a toy seal that was partly covered with a filter; another was a glass of milk covered by a red filter; and another was a small white fish that swam behind a larger, blue, transparent fish. In a fourth task, children wore colored glasses.

Before the tasks were presented, the children were trained in making appearance-reality distinctions with puppets. They were shown a Charlie Brown puppet first dressed as himself and then dressed up in a ghost costume. When the puppet was disguised as a ghost, the children were told, "When you look at this with your eyes right now, it looks like a ghost. It looks like a ghost to your eyes, but it isn't. It's really and truly Charlie Brown. Sometimes things look one way to your eyes (costume is put on again) when they really and truly are a different way (costume is removed)" (Flavell, Green & Flavell, 1986, pp. 7–8). When the tasks were administered, the children were asked, "How does the object look to your eyes right now?" and "How does the object really and truly look?"

Only about half the children were able to answer the questions correctly, although the rate was higher when they were asked about the seal, whose real color was always partially visible. Because these tasks seemed so easy, the researchers tried the experiment again but gave the children more training first. The results remained the same. The researchers then included some older children in the experiment and found that 6- and 7-year-olds could make the appearance-reality distinctions quite easily.

These researchers also tested the 3-year-olds on their ability to distinguish between real and pretend objects. They showed them a real coffee mug and a

FIGURE 10-11
Preschoolers rely on appearances for their information about the world, and when appearances are strange or contradictory, they're bewildered. One problem seems to be that they can't think two thoughts about something at the same time. In this case, they may not be able to think of the superheroes Batman and Spiderman appearing on their street (as they see with their own eyes) at the same time that they think of them as two people wearing sneakers and costumes (as they also see and suspect).

FIGURE 10-12
Hands-on experience helps preschoolers distinguish "real" from "pretend." It takes many such experiences before children are willing or able to override the evidence of their senses.

real kitchen knife, for example, as well as a plastic (pretend) cucumber and a plastic ice-cream bar. While the child inspected each item, the researcher said, "Right now this looks like a real cucumber (coffee mug, ice-cream bar, and so on). Is it a pretend cucumber, or is it a real cucumber?"

The children did much better on these tasks than they did on the color appearance-reality tasks. Part of the children's success in identifying real and pretend cucumbers and ice-cream bars may have come from the fact that they inspected these objects and were familiar with them. Noah's difficulty in understanding that the dinosaurs were pretend may have been partially due to his refusal to get close enough to inform himself about them.

Distinguishing Other Aspects of Mind: Thinking about Thinking

Very young children also have difficulty making distinctions between two different thoughts and holding two different thoughts about the same object in mind. For example, in one study, children were shown a familiar candy box that they would expect to contain candy. But when it was opened, the children saw that it contained pencils instead. When asked what they had thought was in the box at first, before it had been opened to reveal its actual contents, 3-year-olds often reported that they had thought the box contained pencils. They seemed to be unable to focus on two different representations (thoughts) formed at different points in time—that they first thought the box contained candy and then thought that the box contained pencils. The 4-year-olds did much better at distinguishing their two different representations, and the 5-year-olds did better still (Gopnik & Astington, 1988). As in the conservation tasks, the younger child focuses on the two different end states—the appearance of the material at the end of the change—rather than on the transformation that links the two states.

The researchers also asked the children what another child, who hadn't seen the pencils, would think was in the box. This question was asked to probe children's understanding of "false beliefs," the idea that someone can have an incorrect belief about something, such as that a box contains candy when it actually contains pencils. When asked this question, the 4- and 5-year-olds showed a fairly good understanding of the possibility of false beliefs, but 3-year-olds did not (Gopnik & Astington, 1988). They responded that the other child would think there were pencils in the box. Apparently, 3-year-olds have a hard time realizing that other people might be ignorant of some fact that they themselves know, unless they are given extremely straightforward and specific questions that help them respond correctly (Lewis & Osborne, 1990).

This particular difficulty that 3-year-olds show in their thinking has been confirmed by some researchers (Juergen, Wimmer & Perner, 1986; Moses & Flavell, 1990). But others attribute these findings to the attention required of 3-year-olds in this lengthy task and to the linguistic complexity of the questions asked them (Chandler, Fritz & Hala, 1989). The debate about whether 3-year-olds have a functional "theory of mind" may continue, with one group of researchers requiring a kind of unimpeachable evidence and the second group being unable to provide such evidence, due to the attentional and linguistic limitations of the 3-year-old.

Very young children are also unaware of the source of their own knowledge. When they know something, they can't say whether they actually saw it with their own eyes, whether someone specifically told them about it, or whether someone gave them clues and they drew an inference about it (Gopnik & Graf, 1988). Overall they seem to be unaware of the source of thoughts. Instead they focus on the object represented by a thought.

A related difficulty is young children's inability to distinguish another person's visual perspective from their own, which we described earlier in this chapter. When asked how something, such as a doll, would look to someone in a different position, they describe how it looks to them. Children aged 4 and 5 in this experiment had much less difficulty than younger children distinguishing their own view from the view of the other person (Flavell et al., 1981).

The Limits and Growth of Understanding in Preschool Children

One common thread running through all the research findings about young children's abilities to think about thinking is that 3-year-olds just aren't capable of thinking about an object in two different ways at the same time. They form one representation about an object and answer all questions in terms of that one thought (Flavell, Green & Flavell, 1986). Older children and adults can have two representations of the same object, even though the object itself isn't two different things. For example, an object can't really be a rock and a sponge at the same time, but it can *appear* to be a rock even though it's a sponge. We can think these thoughts about a rocklike sponge; 3-year-olds can't.

There seem to be at least three different kinds of reality versus nonreality distinctions. Children of 2 and 3 have the most difficulty distinguishing reality from illusion (e.g., the rocklike sponge). They have less difficulty distinguishing reality from pretend. And they have very little difficulty distinguishing thoughts from physical substances. Regardless of their precise capabilities as 3-year-olds, children do become capable of more sophisticated ways of thinking as they mature and gain new experience. However, new research is suggesting that the preschool child is actually a more capable thinker than once thought.

Perhaps children begin to get their first sense of the distinction between thoughts about real things and nonreal things when they engage in pretend play, starting at about 1 year of age. Pretend play is a favorite activity of 3-year-olds, and experience gained from this kind of play could account for the vastly better performance of 4- and 5-year-olds on most tasks requiring them to consider two different representations of objects.

Children also play increasingly with other children from about the age of 3 on. This social interaction introduces them to the fact that different people can have different thoughts about the same object. "That's my magic carpet," one child says about a doll's blanket. "No, it's my tablecloth," says another, grabbing it from the first child. "We'll eat first, and then we'll go for a ride." Perhaps when they first encounter two different pretend thoughts about the same real object, children begin to become aware of the distinctions between thoughts and things thought about and between different thoughts about the same thing (Gopnik & Astington, 1988).

Whatever the reason, a remarkable transformation in thinking occurs between the ages of 3 and 5—one of the most important of all the many

FIGURE 10-13
Preoperational thinking lends the child's world its "magical" quality. Children believe in elves and fairies, witches and spells, and animals that talk and wear clothes. From an adult point of view, the earliest years are almost like a dream from which children awaken as the age of reason dawns at about age 7. But during these years they often surprise and delight us with their original ideas about how the world works.

changes that occur during these years. Without the ability to realize that thoughts are subjective and changeable, human beings would be unable to think the way they do—to reflect about their thinking, to correct their misperceptions and misunderstandings, to allow their ideas to change and evolve, to accept that other people may have different ideas than they do about the same thing, to understand many forms of art and music. We see a glimmer of such understanding in 3-year-olds. A year or two later, the foundations for these understandings are more complete. The school-age child and the adolescent will sharpen these abilities, but in a 5-year-old who knows that an animated dinosaur isn't real we see the dawning of the revolution in thinking that is to come.

OVERVIEW

The preschool years are the prime years for "magical thinking." Children are likely to have a doll or toy they consider "real," and impossibilities such as talking animals and flying reindeer aren't a problem for them. Their thinking, referred to as pre-operational, tends to be untouched by logic and is guided instead by appearances, by particular contexts and situations, and by certain limited cognitive abilities. These limitations shouldn't obscure the remarkable advances preschoolers have made from the sensorimotor thinking of toddlerhood, however, as well as the significant improvements they make during the preschool years. By the end of this period, they have some understanding of the differences between real and pretend, between fantasy and reality, and between their own thoughts and those of others.

CHAPTER REVIEW

UNDERSTANDING THE CONCEPT OF NUMBER

- One of the important areas of cognitive development investigated by Piaget was conservation, the understanding that a quantity doesn't change when arrangement or distribution changes.
- Piaget found that conservation of number doesn't emerge until children are about 6 or $6\frac{1}{2}$ years old. By this age, they realize that rearranging the objects in a group doesn't affect how many objects there are. Preschoolers, on the other hand, judge the group by its appearance.
- Conservation of continuous quantity also becomes established by age 6 or 7. Before this, children believe that the quantity of water in a beaker changes when it's poured into a beaker of a different size or shape.
- Piaget tested children in other areas of conservation, such as length, area, and weight, and found that these understandings are generally beyond the preschooler's abilities.
- Piaget referred to preschoolers' thinking as preoperational, meaning that they don't use the logical mental operations that older children and adults use to make sense of their experiences. Limitations in their operational thinking—such as their tendency to center (focus on only one aspect of a relationship at a time) and their inability to reverse transformations mentally—make it impossible for preschoolers to think logically.
- Some researchers who believed that children are able to conserve at an earlier age than Piaget found have modified his experiments to see just what they're testing. Their results indicate that many children do have conservation of number during the preschool years, but they can easily be confused, distracted, or misled by the experimenter.
- Despite these findings, a significant qualitative difference in thinking does exist between the preschool child and the school-age child, with the preschool child much less able to think logically.

UNDERSTANDING THE CONCEPTS OF SERIATION AND CLASSIFICATION

- Young preoperational children are unable to arrange objects in a graduated series, mainly because they can't focus on more than one characteristic of an object at one time. Older preschoolers form a series by using trial and error, an approach Piaget called intuitive and empirical. School-age children approach this task operationally.
- Different findings about children's ability to seriate comes from experiments with nesting cups. Research showed that $3\frac{1}{2}$-year-olds were able to construct a series through trial and error when the materials were familiar and supported their efforts.

CLASSIFICATION

- Separating and grouping objects into hierarchical classes is difficult for children under age 4. Between ages 5 and 7, children can classify objects based on a single attribute, but they still can't think in terms of class inclusion. Not until they're 7 or 8 years old do children really master classification.

ARITHMETICAL SKILLS AND UNDERSTANDINGS

- Counting and doing simple sums are the kinds of cognitive tasks preschoolers typically encounter.
- Preschoolers learn the number words, or tags, and begin to acquire the skills needed for true counting.
- Preschoolers typically make three kinds of counting errors—tagging errors (using unconventional tags or nonstandard order), partitioning errors (not separating objects counted from those not counted), and coordination errors (not saying the tags at the same time they point to the object counted).
- Until children understand that counting implies hierarchical inclusion, they have difficulty avoiding these errors. When objects are in disarray, they're also harder to count.
- Some 3-year-olds are just beginning to understand the concepts of "greater than" and "less than"; 4-year-olds are able to make more accurate number comparisons; and 5-year-olds are quite accurate.

UNDERSTANDING THINKING

- Children's thoughts and ideas about the nature of thinking are sometimes referred to as children's "theory of mind."
- At age 3, children have little ability to distinguish appearance from reality, although they do better if they can examine the real and pretend objects.
- Young preschoolers have difficulty distinguishing between two different thoughts (for example, what they thought about one thing at two different points in time). They also at times have difficulty with the concept of false beliefs, the idea that someone could have an incorrect belief about something. By age 4 or 5, children understand these ideas fairly well.
- Young preschoolers don't really understand where their own knowledge comes from, nor are they able to understand that the visual perspectives of others may differ from their own.
- Experience with pretend play probably helps children learn to distinguish between the real and the nonreal. Playing with other children also helps them realize that other people can have different thoughts than they do.
- Experience and neurological maturation together account for the better understanding of reality versus appearance that is apparent in 4- and 5-year-olds.

KEY TERMS

preoperational thinking	center	intuitive	tagging errors
conservation	irreversibility	empirical	coordination errors
identity	concrete operational	operational	partitioning error
compensation	thinking	class inclusion	hierarchical inclusion
reversibility	seriation	tags	

SUGGESTIONS FOR FURTHER READING

Donaldson, M. (1978). *Children's minds.* New York: Norton.
This researcher/author thinks the Piagetian tasks underestimate preschoolers' reasoning ability. This readable book presents some of the research that has been conducted to support this conclusion.

Gelman, R., & Gallistel, C. R. (1978). *The child's understanding of number.* Cambridge, MA: Harvard University Press.
Stresses the development of counting skills in preschool children. As such, the book is a contrast to Piaget's work and may be interesting to the student who wishes to take a broader look at children's cognitive development in relation to mathematics.

Ginsburg, H. P., & Opper, S. (1988). *Piaget's theory of intellectual development* (3d ed.) Englewood Cliffs, NJ: Prentice-Hall.
This readable book discusses Piaget's theory and stages of development. The book covers constructs such as conservation and seriation.

Kamii, C. (1985). *Young children reinvent arithmetic.* New York: Teachers College Press.
This author uses a Piagetian framework as a basis for developing a program of mathematics education.

Wellman, H. M. (1990). *The child's theory of mind.* Cambridge, MA: MIT Press.
This book discusses the child's theory of mind across the early childhood years.

LANGUAGE DEVELOPMENT IN PRESCHOOL CHILDREN

When 4-year-old Kate came home from nursery school one day, her dad asked what she had done at school. "Oh, nothing," she replied.

"Well, I know you did something," her dad continued. "You brought a painting home, so you must have painted today."

"No, I painted a picture the last day. Today, I didn't paint. I clayed with clay."

"Oh, I see. You played with clay today. What did you do after you played with the clay?"

"Mmmmmmmmm. Well, I think that is when Jessica teached me how to staple papers together for a book."

"You and Jessica were using a stapler?"

"Yes! You press it very hard—very, very hard—and the staples stick in the paper. Then, you pull the stapler away. The papers stay sticked together because the staple you put in there holds them."

"I hope you didn't stick your finger."

"No, we didn't."

"That's good. A staple in the finger hurts."

If we hadn't already known Kate's age, we could have pegged her as a preschooler quite easily, because her language is typical of children between the ages of 3 and 6. She no longer speaks the way a toddler does, but she doesn't yet speak as well as a school-age child either. In this chapter, we look at the characteristics of preschoolers' language and the origin of the peculiar kind of mistakes they make. We also examine the development of preschoolers' language comprehension. Finally we discuss emergent literacy—the beginning stages of written language development.

ORAL LANGUAGE DEVELOPMENT

Language Production: What Preschoolers Can Say

Kate's language is quite different from her language of just a year or two earlier. As a toddler, her statements were telegraphic—short and incomplete. She might have said, "Mommy sock," for example, to mean "This is Mommy's sock." Now, her sentences are grammatically complete and contain many more words and morphemes. A **morpheme** is the smallest unit of meaning in a language. It can be a word, or it can be a smaller group of letters that changes the meaning of a word, such as the word endings "ing" or "ed." Preschoolers learn many morphemes, and they learn them in a specific sequential order (see Research Focus—The Grammatical Morphemes Young Children Acquire for a list of some of these morphemes).

Despite these advances in language ability, however, Kate's speech is still imperfect. What marks it as essentially different from the speech of older children and adults is her use of words that she's coined herself.

ACQUIRING MORPHOLOGICAL RULES. Kate has learned **morphological rules**—the rules of word formation in her language. In fact, we can even say that she's overlearned them. Kate thinks that all English verbs, for example, are changed to the past tense by adding the morpheme "ed" to the end. She doesn't know that some verbs are irregular and that their past tense is formed by using a

---

RESEARCH FOCUS

The Grammatical Morphemes Young Children Acquire

Children's oral language emerges in a definite, predictable way. A child who now says, "Daddy go," will soon be saying, "Daddy going," and later, "Daddy is going." With each new utterance, the child has learned a new morpheme and made a linguistic leap. The following list includes 14 morphemes that young children learn to use, in the order in which they learn to use them (Brown, 1973).

Name of Morpheme	Example
Progressive (-ing)	Daddy going.
Locative (in)	Bat in room.
Locative (on)	Hat on head.
Regular plural (-s)	Boys there.
Irregular past	Ran home.
Possessive (-'s)	Adam's shoe.
Uncontractible copula*	Susan is here.
Articles (the, a)	The pail has a hole.
Regular past (-ed)	Daddy walked home.
Regular third person (-s)	He runs.
Irregular third person	He does that.
Uncontractible auxiliary	She is running.
Contractible copula	She's afraid.
Contractible auxiliary	She's running.

*That is, the child doesn't form contractions with the copula ("is").

RESEARCH FOCUS

The Words Children Invent

Preschoolers are notorious for their invented words. Once they catch on to a particular usage, they tend to generalize it to other cases they perceive to be similar. When we know the model they had in mind, we can see that their statements aren't so strange. One researcher made extensive studies of children's invented words in English, French, and German, and some usages she reported are given here (Clark, 1982, pp. 402–406). In the third column, we've added a model that could explain the child's choice.

All of these statements are based on the notion that nouns can also be used as verbs. Given the complexity of sorting out exceptions to general rules in English, it's no wonder that we still hear invented words in the language of 6- and 7-year-olds.

Situation	Invention	Model
Child was referring to cheese that had to be weighed.	"You have to scale it first."	"You have to drill it first."
Child was hitting a ball with a stick.	"I'm sticking it and that makes it go really fast."	"I'm batting it to make it go really fast."
Child was using tongs to remove spaghetti from a pan.	"I'm going to pliers this out."	"I'm going to hammer this out."
Mother was sweeping child's room.	"Don't broom my mess."	"Don't mop the floor."
Child was putting crackers in soup.	"I'm going to cracker my soup."	"I'm going to dye my hair."
Child was putting beads in play dough.	"I think I'll bead it."	"I think I'll salt it."
Child wanted chocolate syrup in milk.	"Will you chocolate my milk?"	"Will you salt my eggs?"

different word altogether. Because she's heard "walk" and "walked," she says "run" and "runned." Once children learn that most words can be changed in form according to certain rules, they **overgeneralize** the rules, applying them even when they're inappropriate. Kate will notice the exceptions to the rules as time goes on, and she'll begin to use them instead of her own invented words. But it will be another two or three years before the last traces of her tendency to overgeneralize will vanish altogether.

Preschool children overgeneralize rules not only for forming verb tenses but also for creating plurals, forming superlatives, and using nouns as verbs (Branigan & Stokes, 1976; Garvey, 1977). For example, most preschoolers refer to teeth as "tooths," to feet as "foots," and to mice as "mouses." Overgeneralizing from a statement like "Giving a hug is the nicest thing you can do," they say that jumping on the bed is the "funnest" thing you can do. And they say they "clayed" with the clay, because they assume this is similar to saying they hammered with the hammer or sawed with the saw. (Other examples of rule overgeneralization are listed in Research Focus—The Words Children Invent.)

Before children learn any morphological rules—when they're $2\frac{1}{2}$ years old, for example—they use the correct forms of the common irregular nouns and verbs (Brown, 1973), because they're imitating what they've heard. But as they learn rules and start to overgeneralize, they begin to make mistakes. Children typically learn the irregular past before the regular past (see Research Focus—The Grammatical Morphemes Young Children Acquire). Thus, at age $2\frac{1}{2}$, Kate repeated what she heard and said "ran" and "went"; by age 4, she's learned the morpheme "ed" for forming the regular past, so now she says "runned" and "goed." Later still, she will sort out the exceptions to the rule and once again say "ran" and "went." This is a good example of something we often see in development: New skills and abilities lead to errors or problems that didn't exist before. Kate's language emerged at a whole new level once she acquired some morphological rules; however, a new kind of mistake appeared too.

CREATING SENTENCES. Just as there are rules in our language for inflecting individual words, there are also rules for forming different kinds of sentences. When asking a question, for example, we invert the order of the subject and verb—we say, "Where is she going?" rather than "Where she is going?" It takes some time for children to master the rules of sentence construction. Their early sentences are different from adults', particularly their questions and negative statements. At first, they ask questions by changes in intonation ("Daddy work?"). Next they form questions by combining a "wh" word with a primitive sentence: "Where dolly?" "Where man?" As they get older, the structuring of their questions changes in a predictable pattern (Menyuk, 1969, p. 73):

1. Where goes the wheel?
2. Where the wheel goes?
3. Where the wheel go?
4. Where does the wheel goes?
5. Where does the wheel go?

Negative sentences are another challenge. At first, children just combine "no" with a word or short sentence: "No break." "No eat." Later, they start to include subjects and verbs: "I no eat." Eventually, at $3\frac{1}{2}$ to 4 years of age, they learn how to add and rearrange words within sentences: "I don't want to eat."

Another problem area for preschoolers is the use of comparative adjectives. At first, children double-mark words for comparison, using both the adjective and the adverb "more" (Gathercole, 1985): "I had my birthday yesterday, so now I'm more older than you are." Later, during the school years, children learn to drop the superfluous "more" from these sentences.

CORRECTING CHILDREN'S GRAMMAR. Kate's father didn't correct her grammar, although he did model the correct forms himself. Sometimes adults wonder if they should go further than this and correct children directly. The research indicates that adult efforts to get children to correct their speech aren't very successful. In the following examples, we can see how resistant children are to changing the language forms they've used (Gleason, 1967, cited in Cazden, 1972, pp. 4–5):

A child said, "My teacher holded the baby rabbits and we patted them."
I asked, "Did you say your teacher held the baby rabbits?"
She answered, "Yes."
I then asked, "What did you say she did?"
She answered, again, "She holded the baby rabbits and we patted them."
"Did you say she held them tightly?" I asked.
"No," she answered, "She holded them loosely."

In this second example, a more direct approach was used (McNeill, 1966, p. 69):

FIGURE 11-1
Children learn language from their parents in the course of everyday life. Research shows that parents seldom provide direct corrections of their preschoolers' grammatical errors, listening instead for the content of the child's speech. Being listened to uncritically probably enhances not only language development but cognitive and emotional development as well.

CHILD: *"Nobody don't like me."*
McNEILL: *"No, say 'Nobody likes me.'"*
CHILD: *"Nobody don't like me."*
    (eight repetitions of this dialogue)
McNEILL: *"No. Now listen carefully; say 'Nobody likes me.'"*
CHILD: *"Oh! Nobody don't likes me!"*

Most parents respond to their children's early grammatical errors the way Kate's dad did. They talk naturally with children, concentrating on getting their meaning and judging the truth of what they say. In the second example just given, in fact, one might wish that the researcher had paid more attention to what the child was saying instead of trying to correct his grammar. Parents' responses to sentences containing errors do differ somewhat from their responses to sentences that don't have errors, however, as was noted in Chapter 7. It's possible that this varying feedback serves a "correction" function, although we don't know that it does. In any event, children appear to correct their mistakes over time, even though most adults don't call mistakes to their attention in any direct way. The best type of "instruction" seems to consist of exposure to natural, meaningful language in which the correct use of rules is constantly demonstrated.

Language Comprehension: What Preschoolers Can Understand

Preschoolers' comprehension of spoken language has increased dramatically from toddlerhood. The average 3-year-old understands about 900 words—an impressive gain from the 100 or so understood by the average 18-month-old (Moskowitz, 1978). But some word meanings and some elements of **syntax** (sentence construction) still elude them. We look now at preschoolers' typical trouble spots in language comprehension.

UNDERSTANDING WORD ORDER. When we hear, "John hit the ball," we know that John is the subject and the ball is the object of his action, even though the sentence is reversible—it would make sense if interpreted as, "The ball hit John." At what age do children begin to understand the meaning of sentences despite word order?

Children on the brink of the preschool years understand only active sentences—those following the subject-verb-object word order. They find it impossible to understand passive sentences, such as "The ball was thrown by John." The response of 2-year-olds to passive sentences is correct only 50 percent of the time, which means that they're only guessing, just as we do when someone flips a coin and we call out "heads" or "tails" (Bever, 1970; deVilliers & deVilliers, 1973). It's not until late in the preschool period—at about 5 years of age—that children finally understand passive sentences. The exception is cases in which incorrect interpretation makes the sentence unlikely. For example, even a 3-year-old will correctly interpret the sentence "The baby was fed by her mother," because babies don't feed their mothers. In these cases, however, children are using their knowledge of events rather than their knowledge of language structure to determine the meaning of the sentence. Only when a sentence makes sense both ways, such as "The cat was chased by the dog," do we see that the younger preschooler doesn't understand the passive construction (Strohner & Nelson, 1974).

Preschoolers also overgeneralize from sentences using other verbs, such as "tell" (Chomsky, 1969). For example, in the sentence "Amy told Susan to be quiet," Susan is the one who is to be quiet. But in the sentence "Amy promised Susan to be quiet," it's now Amy who is to be quiet. Because of this difficulty, a preschooler may not be able to understand a sentence like "You promised Emily to share the blocks."

UNDERSTANDING LOCATIVE EXPRESSIONS. Locative expressions—words such as "in," "on," "under," and "beside"—provide information about where something is located. Young preschoolers are just beginning to master the meaning of these words as they're used in such phrases as "in the box," "on the sofa," and "beside the chair."

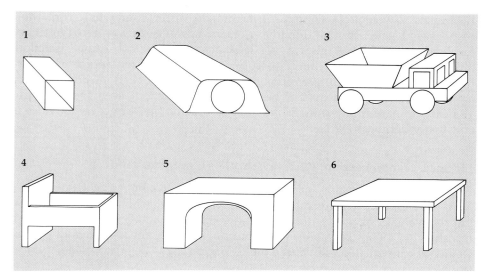

FIGURE 11-2
Objects used by Clark to test young children's understanding of locative expressions. The children in the study always placed something "in" a container, such as object 3 or 4, even when instructed to place something "under" it, demonstrating that they pay more attention to clues in the situation than to specific word meanings.

FIGURE 11-3
Young children learn language at first from action and context. In the course of demonstrating how to core and slice an apple, the caregiver at this day care center may have told the children to put the apple on a plate, put the slicer on top of the apple, hold the sides of the slicer, and carefully press down. The pre-schooler in the group may particularly benefit from hearing locative expressions used in context.

In one well-known study, the objects pictured in Figure 11-2 were shown to children so that only two relationships were possible at a time (Clark, 1978). Objects 1 and 2 allowed the relations "in" and "on"; 3 and 4 allowed "in" and "under"; and 5 and 6 allowed "on" and "under."

Children interpreted instructions differently, depending on which objects they were shown. If children saw any kind of container, such as objects 3 and 4, they always placed something in it, even when the instructions contained other locatives such as "on" or "under." Similarly, they interpreted any instruction to mean "on" when the object had a supporting surface, even if they were asked to place something under or in it.

Clark's study showed that children don't understand the meanings of any of these words until they're about $2\frac{1}{2}$ years old. Instead, they interpret sentences containing locative expressions in terms of what's available in the situation. When children do begin to understand the actual meanings of the words, they learn "in" first, followed by "on" and then "under."

Other locative expressions are even harder to learn. Children don't master the words "beside," "between," "front," and "back" until they're $4\frac{1}{2}$ or 5 years old, and when they do learn these terms, they learn them in the following order (Johnston & Slobin, 1979): beside; between; front (when the object itself has a front); back (when the object itself has a back); back (when the back depends on the position of the person in relation to the object); front (when the front depends on the position of the person in relation to the object).

Parents and teachers of preschoolers often find that children are puzzled by instructions involving locative expressions and need to be shown what is meant. For example, a preschool teacher who tells a child that the crayons are on a shelf between the paste jars and the scissors rack might find that the child approaches the shelf but doesn't direct her gaze to the right spot, even when the teacher repeats the instruction. A child who behaves this way probably doesn't understand the word "between." The teacher may need to approach the shelf and say, "Here are the crayons, right here (pointing at them) between (with emphasis) the scissors and the jars of paste." Or, if the teacher can't go to the shelf, she might say, "Find the jars of paste." Then she might add, "Now find the scissors." In the process of moving from one item to the other on the shelf, the child would discover the crayons. At this point, the teacher might comment, "Oh, good—you found the crayons, right there between the jars of paste and the scissors."

UNDERSTANDING OPPOSITES AND SIMILARITIES. The meaning of a word isn't always obvious to a child; in fact it may take repeated associations over the course of many years for children to realize exactly what a particular word means. The words "more" and "less" are a case in point. Children don't understand the use of the word "more" to refer to the greater of two amounts until they are about $3\frac{1}{2}$. They have a better understanding of "more" with countable objects such as pennies or blocks than with uncountable quantities such as clay or sand (Gathercole, 1985). By the age of $4\frac{1}{2}$, children's use of "more" is accurate with both countable items and mass quantities, although by age 5, they tend to prefer using "more" when they mean greater in number and "bigger" when they mean greater in amount or mass.

It takes children even longer to understand the word "less." When asked which of two quantities is less, children will sometimes point to the quantity that actually is more. Perhaps they know at first only that "less" also refers to quantity, and they use it interchangeably with the other quantity word they know. Only later—at about age $4\frac{1}{2}$—do they distinguish the two terms, using "more" to indicate the greater of two quantities and "less" to indicate the smaller. Preschoolers also tend to confuse other opposites, such as warm/cold and bigger/smaller.

If children have a hard time understanding words for opposites, they have an even harder time grasping words for things that are similar. This is probably because they fail to sort out features of objects or situations that indicate when they should use one term rather than the other. The greater the number of features there are to sort out—size, shape, color, content, function, and so on—the longer it seems to take children to see the difference.

For example, 3-year-olds use "glass" and "cup" almost interchangeably, regardless of whether the container is tall or short, has a handle or doesn't, or is made of glass, ceramic, or plastic (Nelson & Nelson, 1978). In labeling the container, they pay very little attention to context—whether it's filled with ice water or hot cocoa, for example. Children 4 and 5 years old, on the other hand, consider both physical form and context in deciding which word applies, using the word "glass" for taller containers filled with ice water, for example. By 6 to 8 years of age, children refer to containers that are twice as high as they are wide as "glass" regardless of what they hold. By age 10, children add the observation that shorter containers may be called "glass" when they hold

FIGURE 11-4
Children learn vocabulary, word meanings, and many other linguistic understandings from "real-world" experiences that involve all their senses. This preschooler is going to have a deep personal understanding of such words as "cow," "goat," and "petting zoo."

cold drinks. From this example, it is clear that children's understanding of word meanings continues to evolve well beyond the preschool years.

CONTEXT AND COMPREHENSION. In our discussion of language comprehension, we've mentioned several times that children read the context of language—the situation at hand—to obtain clues about the meanings of words and sentences. In fact, if young children were forced to rely only on words, they would understand very little. Early language learning is **context bound**, that is, language is understood not in terms of linguistic structures alone but also in terms of the extralinguistic context (Bates, 1979). Later, language becomes more **decontextualized**, that is, less dependent on immediate physical or social cues, although neither spoken nor written language can ever be understood completely out of context (Cazden, 1987). The shift is from concrete, face-to-face, immediate contexts to "contexts of the mind," from almost total reliance on the situation to an ability to understand on the basis of both linguistic structures and background knowledge (Ricard & Snow, 1990).

Because the younger preschool child's understanding of linguistic structures is limited, the child is still very dependent on context. But even the older preschool child, as well as the much older school-age child, is still building "contexts of the mind." Because of this, it's vitally important that children's experiences, especially preschoolers' experiences, be broad and concrete, based on a wide range of meaningful activities. Preschoolers need to experience not just how things look but also how they feel, move, taste, sound, and smell, to build that rich and lasting storehouse of information and knowledge crucial to an understanding of the spoken and written word.

WRITTEN LANGUAGE DEVELOPMENT

A teacher was reading Maurice Sendak's Where the Wild Things Are *to Matt and Amy, two 4-year-olds, in the library area of the preschool classroom. When he got to the pages with pictures but no print, Matt told him to turn past them, saying, "You can't read these—you have to turn to where the words start again."*

Amy objected. "No!" she said. "He has to read all of the pages."

"He can't read those pages," protested Matt. "They don't have any words on them."

"Yes, he can!" repeated Amy.

At this point, the teacher suggested that he talk about the pages with pictures but no words and then begin reading where the words start again. Matt and Amy accepted his compromise.

These two children are at different levels in their understanding of print. Amy doesn't think there's any difference between text and pictures at all. To her, a page with pictures but no print can be "read." Matt, in contrast, thinks that pictures and text serve different functions. The text tells the story and is read; the pictures illustrate or confirm the text. It's common for young preschool children to assume at first that the pictures in a book, not the print, are what you read (Ferreiro & Teberosky, 1979). As they gain experience, they gradually come to understand that reading involves getting meaning from print.

In the past people thought that preschoolers were incapable of understanding very much about written language. Now we know that they understand quite a lot about it. Because of this discovery, the term **emergent literacy** has replaced the term **reading readiness.** The latter term implied that children needed to learn many things before they could begin to have "real" reading experiences. The former term suggests that even very young children engage in "real" reading and writing activities. What changes as they get older is the way they read and write, not the basic nature of what they attempt to do (Teale & Sulzby, 1986).

In this section, we discuss some of the current knowledge about emergent literacy in preschoolers. We also discuss some of the different home experiences and activities that seem to foster the highest level of literacy development.

Understanding Print

When Jonathan, age 4, reads Eric Carle's *The Very Hungry Caterpillar* out loud to himself, he doesn't miss a word of what's actually printed in the text. He even sounds like a person who's reading a story. Jonathan has heard this story read many times, of course. Furthermore, the book has a **predictable text** (Rhodes, 1981)—a text with many repetitions—which makes it an easy book to learn and remember. Given a totally unfamiliar book, Jonathan probably would be at a loss. But in many ways he *is* reading the book, and although

FIGURE 11-5
In our society, many children are exposed to books almost from birth and have very sophisticated understandings about them by the time they reach the preschool years. These kindergartners may be enjoying the pictures of bones and skulls in their book, but they probably also know that the printed words contain much of the book's meaning.

he's not yet a beginning reader, he deserves to be called an emergent reader rather than a nonreader. This is an important early stage in the long process of learning how to read. A closer look at this process, which extends well into the school years, is provided in Research Focus—Children's Storybook Reading later in this chapter.

DISTINGUISHING WRITING FROM NONWRITING. Jonathan knows that some things he sees in *The Very Hungry Caterpillar* are words and some things are pictures.

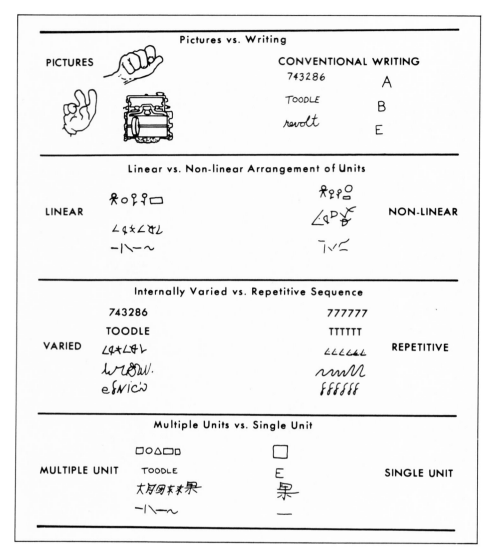

FIGURE 11-6
Displays used by Lavine
(1977) to see if children could
distinguish writing from nonwriting. Even 3-year-olds were
found to be highly print
aware.

Matt, too, knew that some pages in *Where the Wild Things Are* had pictures but no words on them. Recognizing writing and distinguishing it both from pictures and from other kinds of marks are some of the early literacy skills children acquire. How and when do they become capable of making these distinctions?

In a study designed to answer the question of how English-speaking preschoolers recognize writing, children ranging in age from 3 to $6\frac{1}{2}$ were shown various combinations of letters, numbers, pictures, and doodles printed on cards (Figure 11-6) (Lavine, 1977). Children were asked to sort the cards into two piles, one of writing and one of marks that weren't writing.

Even when children couldn't yet name letters or read words, they labeled as writing displays that had general features of writing. For example, in the displays shown in Figure 11-6, many 3-year-olds identified as writing the third, fourth, and fifth writing samples in the "Varied" group, but not the first and second writing samples in the "Repetitive" group. In other words, 3-year-olds often rejected samples with repeated characters even if they contained actual alphabet letters, but they accepted samples with a variety of characters even if the characters weren't letters of the alphabet. Apparently, children first identify writing in terms of overall characteristics, such as linearity (it's arranged in lines), multiplicity (it must be made up of a sequence of more than one character), and variety (no more than two identical characters can be placed together). Later, they look at the internal characters themselves and incorporate this information into their categorization scheme. For example, a 3-year-old is likely to reject writing samples such as iiiii or l but not a sample such as *@%lp&. A 5-year-old, on the other hand, would categorize the first display as writing but not the third, because the first is composed of characters used to make words. For the 5-year-old scrutiny of the internal characters would override gross characteristics of linearity, variety, and multiplicity. Five-year-olds also are much more likely than 3-year-olds to accept "I" as a word, because they know that even though most words have multiple characters, some don't.

FIGURING OUT HOW ALPHABET LETTERS CODE WORDS. Once children begin to notice and recognized writing, they may next try to figure out how printed words are related to what they say and hear. In English, each letter of the alphabet represents a **phoneme**—an individual speech sound—within a word (with the exception of some silent letters and letters that are combined to represent one sound, such as "th," "ch," and "ei"). There isn't any reason for children to assume that the English **orthography** (system of writing) works they way; in many other languages, it works differently.

In Chinese, for example, each character represents an idea, not a sound within a word. Students learning to write Chinese must memorize thousands of different characters (Taylor, 1981). In Japanese, characters represent syllables; this reduces the number of characters needed, since a single syllable can appear in many different words. But fewer characters still are needed for an alphabetically based system such as English, because it uses just a few characters, combined in different ways, to represent a small set of phonemes and create all the words in the language (Taylor, 1981).

In the course of trying to connect oral and written language, children often think that each letter represents a syllable. For example, a child named Adele might write her name as "AD," because she has divided it into two parts—A-Dele—and selected one letter to represent each part. A child trying to read a familiar storybook title might point to one letter for every syllable she hears:

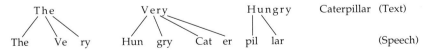

Similarly, a child dictating a story to an adult to write down might talk much faster than the adult can write, because the child assumes that each letter the adult writes down represents much more speech than actually is the case.

The young child's tendency to use this **syllabic hypothesis** when trying to match speech to print is understandable, given that syllables are much easier

FIGURE 11-7
When an adult records a preschooler's story, she may find
herself saying, "Just a minute—you're going too fast."
The child may think that every
letter the adult writes down
on the page represents a word
or syllable of speech.

to hear than phonemes (Ferreiro, 1986; Schickedanz, 1987). Apparently the peaks of acoustic energy that fall at syllable centers provide cues that make it easy for the listener to pick them out of the stream of speech (Liberman et al., 1974).

In time children give up the syllabic hypothesis. But what events cause them to discount it? There are several likely candidates. First, the mismatch between speech and print, such as when the child tries to read print in familiar book titles, probably causes the child to reconsider how print might work. In addition, because children such as Adele continue to see their own names written out in full, they probably begin to wonder what function is served by the "extra" letters. Finally, words coded syllabically will, on average, be much shorter than most words children see in their environment. Thus, children's syllabically coded words probably don't look right, especially to children who begin to notice more and more print in their environment.

Many children don't move smoothly from a syllabic, sound-based coding system to a phonemic-based system; other strategies they try are described in Research Focus: How Children Create Written Words. When children do begin to think about individual speech sounds in language, they've gained a new level of what we call **phonemic awareness.** Of course, children who respond

RESEARCH FOCUS

How Children Create Written Words

Many researchers have described strategies young children use to create written words (Ferreiro & Teberosky, 1979; Schickedanz, 1990). The strategies that have been identified can be found in the accompanying list.

What makes children give up one hypothesis for another? It is doubtful that these ideas simply unfold from within the child as a result of maturation. Instead their development probably depends on some combination of child characteristics and environmental conditions.

For example, a child's shift from the syllabic strategy to the visual rule strategy might depend on opportunities to see considerable print in the environment. The shift from the visual rule strategy to an authority-based strategy might depend on the availability of an adult, first to respond to questions about letter strings and second to answer spelling questions. The shift from an authority-based strategy to an independent, phonemic strategy might depend on the extent to which the adults who answered spelling questions segmented phonemes—sounded out each letter for the child—and thus made explicit the basis for letter selection.

Thus, it seems likely, as one researcher suggests, that shifts from one strategy to the next "occur because of active comparisons that the child engages in" (Clay, 1983, p. 263) and that adults are involved in getting children to make these comparisons. In sum, "development seems to depend on a series of adult-child transactions that take place within a print-rich environment where children have many opportunities to write and to interact with print" (Schickedanz, 1990, p. 12).

Further research is needed to help us understand exactly how children construct mature understandings of alphabet-based writing systems.

WORD CREATION STRATEGIES

Physical Relationship Strategy
With this strategy, the child tries to relate the number and appearance of marks to some physical aspect of the object or person represented. For example, a 3-year-old might use

SOURCE: Adapted from J. Schickedanz (1989), *The place of specific skills in preschool and kindergarten.* In D. S. Strickland and L. M. Morrow (eds.), *Emerging literacy.* Newark, DE: International Reading Association, p. 103.

three marks to write her name but many more marks to write her father's name, "because he's bigger."

Visual Design Strategy
The child accepts the arbitrary nature of words—the fact that they do not resemble their referents in any physical way. The child tries to write some words, usually her name, by copying from models. She assumes that each word has its own "design." There's no appreciation for the fact that a small set of letters can be used to make all words.

Syllabic Strategy
The child realizes there is a relationship between the oral and written versions of words. She segments spoken words in terms of beats or syllables and codes each syllable with one mark. The same letters reappear in different "words" the child creates.

Visual Rule Strategy
The child creates words by stringing letters together so that they look like words. She uses several rules: (1) Don't use too many letters. (2) Don't use too few letters. (3) Use a variety of letters, with no more than two of the same letter in succession. (4) Rearrange the same letters to make different words. The child often takes her letter string words to adults and asks, "What word is this?"

Authority-Based Strategy
This strategy often follows on the heels of the visual rule strategy, apparently because the child gets discouraged when most of her letter strings turn out not to be real words. The child asks adults for spellings or copies known words from environmental print or familiar books.

Early Phonemic Strategy
The child begins to generate spellings by segmenting and coding individual sounds within words. The result is "invented" spellings.

Transitional Phonemic Strategy
The child begins to realize that her sound-based spellings do not look like the same words she sees in the environment. The child often becomes dissatisfied with her own spellings and begins to ask again for spellings. This strategy is not common among preschoolers, although children who read early are often reluctant to create invented spellings.

differently to the words "bat" and "rat" have phonemic awareness; otherwise, they wouldn't be able to distinguish these words. However, children do not think consciously about phonemes when they make distinctions of this sort. But **phonemic segmentation,** that is, separating the individual sounds within words, requires high levels of conscious phonemic awareness (Yopp, 1988). This ability is a very good predictor of success in learning to read (Ball & Blachman, 1991; Dickinson & Snow, 1987; Share et al., 1984).

FIGURE 11-8
This girl knows that putting marker to paper produces results that please both her and her parents. Access to the tools of literacy gives children important early experiences with reading and writing. When access is limited at home, preschools can often make up the difference.

Children begin to write differently once they've gained the ability to segment words phonemically. Since they're starting to think about individual sounds in words, they use more than one letter to represent each syllable. For example, to write "Kate," they might use "KT" or "KAT." There's still much the child needs to learn about spelling, of course, but the ability to segment words phonemically is one of the major milestones of literacy development.

The age at which phonemic segmentation skills appear varies among different groups of children. It has been observed in children as young as $3\frac{1}{2}$ (Read, 1975), but it also has been found to be absent in 6-year-olds (Ferreiro & Teberosky, 1979). The timing seems to be related to the kind of opportunities children have to interact with written language. When there are many opportunities, phonemic segmentation skills appear earlier; when there are fewer opportunities, they appear later.

LEARNING TO RECOGNIZE LETTERS OF THE ALPHABET. Besides learning that letters represent phonemes, children also have to learn to recognize the individual letters of the alphabet. As adults we recognize the letters of our alphabet instantaneously. To appreciate the difficulty of this task, which we mastered so long ago, we only have to examine a writing sample from a language that uses an alphabet we're not familiar with, such as Greek or Cyrillic. Suddenly the letters are indistinguishable, and we don't know one from another.

Children face a similar challenge when they first begin to learn the letters of their own alphabet. How do they begin to sort the letters out? This process seems to involve the gradual differentiation of distinctive features. **Distinctive features** are the characteristics of a set of similar things (such as our alphabet) that make that set different from other sets (such as the Greek alphabet). At the same time, distinctive features are combined in different ways within the set to make individual units (in this case, the letters) different from each other.

The distinctive features of our alphabet are characteristics such as whether a line is straight or curved, whether curves are open or closed, and whether straight lines are diagonal, horizontal, or vertical (Gibson, 1969). For example, some letters are closed (D, O), and others are open (C, L); some letters have curved lines (C, S, O), and others have straight lines (L, E, T); and some straight-line letters contain diagonal lines (K, N, M), and others don't (L, E, T).

When children first begin to recognize letters of the alphabet, they often consider letters "the same" that share some distinctive features. For example, if you give children two sets of letters with instructions to put letters that are "the same" together, they might very well place "D" with "O" because both letters are closed figures containing curved lines. They might confuse "E" and "F" because both are made from straight horizontal and vertical lines. They might confuse "M" and "N" because both are made from straight diagonal and vertical lines. But they would rarely pair "O" with "L" or "M" with "O" because in both cases, the letters have no distinctive features in common.

Distinguishing letters from each other requires that the child pay attention not to how they're the same but to how they're different. This kind of learning probably runs counter to how children (and human beings in general) have to deal with much of their world. A lot of learning requires that we form categories of things that are similar. We can't cope with a world full of separate and unrelated things; we make the world more manageable by lumping similar things together and responding to them as a group.

FIGURE 11-9
This boy is practicing the alphabet by matching the letters in his hand with the letters on the pegboard. Because the letters of our alphabet share so many distinctive features, it's hard at first to sort them out. Z shares straight horizontal lines with E, F, L, and T and diagonal lines with M, N, V, W, and X.

FIGURE 11-10
Seeing high-interest words in context helps children learn how to recognize letters, associate sounds with them, and begin to understand what's involved in reading. Even words like "Bubblicious" can promote emergent literacy.

This is exactly how children first approach the alphabet letters. They note similarities and ignore differences. This allows them to discriminate among certain letters but not others. Gradually, with more exposure to alphabet letters and their different, distinctive sounds and uses, children begin to see each letter as different from all the others. When children grow up surrounded by **environmental print**—the written language they see all around them in stores, on the street, on "Sesame Street," and so on—it's not uncommon for them to know most of the upper-case alphabet letters by the time they're 4 or 5 years old. One distinctive feature that is especially difficult for children to sort out,

FIGURE 11-11
Which two cups would you pick as "identical"?

however, is orientation in space—whether a letter faces right or left, up or down. This feature is what makes the letters "W" and "M," "p" and "q," and "b" and "d" different. All of the other distinctive features of these letter pairs are identical. **Reversals,** or errors in a letter's orientation, are common in children's writing, even during the first grade. One reason children find this distinctive feature difficult to notice is that it contradicts all their previous experience with three-dimensional objects.

To understand the child's problem, imagine that you are going to a cupboard to get two identical coffee mugs. There are four mugs on the shelf (Figure 11-11): (1) a tall, brown, plastic mug sitting upside down with its handle to the left: (2) a short, brown, ceramic mug sitting upright with its handle to the right; (3) a second tall, brown, plastic mug sitting upright with its handle to the right, and (4) a second short, brown, ceramic mug sitting upside down with its handle to the left.

Chances are you would select mugs 1 and 3 or mugs 2 and 4 as a pair, completely ignoring whether the mugs were upside down or whether their handles were turned to the left or the right. This example shows that orientation is not used as a distinctive feature in distinguishing three-dimensional objects. When children first begin to look at print, all their previous experience has involved objects, and although they see that some letters are reversed versions of others, they assume that the differences don't matter any more than they did with the physical objects.

A child named Adam, who deliberately wrote his name both "frontwards" and "backwards," considered both versions to be his name, just as a chair is still a chair whether it's right side up or upside-down. At the same time, he recognized other kinds of errors—starting his name with two A's, for example—as mistakes. He didn't consider a mirror-image version of his name wrong—just "backwards"—until a year and a half after he recognized that other errors made his name wrong (Schickedanz, 1987).

Learning the letters of the alphabet and the sounds they represent used to be considered the only, or at least the most important, "prereading" skill that children had to acquire. Now we know that this is only one of many things an emergent reader and writer must learn. We also know that knowledge of letter names is not a "prereading" skill in the sense that the child can't engage in reading and writing activities until letter names are mastered. Children do engage in these activities long before they know any specific alphabet letters. They "read" stories in familiar storybooks (Sulzby, 1985), respond to labels and signs (Mason, 1980), and "scribble-write" messages (Clay, 1987) before they have much, if any, knowledge of letter names. Learning the letters is just one part of the long-term, complex process of learning to read.

Creating Print

To learn to write, children have to master many skills, both physical and cognitive. They also have to learn the conventions—established ways of doing things—of writing in our language. Two conventions that preschoolers usually confront are the formation of letters and the arrangement of print on a page.

LEARNING PRINT CONVENTIONS: HOW LETTERS ARE FORMED. Many children will write—represent a message with marks—long before they can form or even recognize most alphabet letters. The marks they use often include **scribble-**

FIGURE 11-12
Mirror writing is common among preschoolers and shouldn't be taken as a sign that a child has a learning disability. Children who write this way simply haven't acquired a strong sense of where to begin and which way to head when they start to write.

writing, or chains of zigzags or loops across a page, and **mock letters,** which resemble actual alphabet letters and indeed would make good candidates for a twenty-seventh or twenty-eighth letter of our alphabet, should we ever need one. Examples of both scribble-writing and mock letters are shown in Figure 11-13.

Children often mix scribble-writing, mock letters, and conventional letters as they learn to write, using one, then another, then the first again (Clay, 1987; Schickedanz, 1987). Many children who can write conventional letters turn to scribble-writing in certain situations, such as when creating a very long story. Temporarily reverting to an earlier, more comfortable strategy—in this case, scribble-writing—is not uncommon in childhood. We see the same thing when beginning walkers drop to their hands and knees to crawl when they want to get somewhere in a hurry.

LEARNING PRINT CONVENTIONS: HOW WORDS ARE ORGANIZED ON A PAGE. Another aspect of writing that children must learn is how print is organized on a page. Does it go from right to left, from left to right, or both, sweeping back and forth on alternate lines like a computer printer? And how is the page filled vertically? From top to bottom or from bottom to top?

There isn't any one absolute, right way to arrange print on a page. There are simply conventions in every language. Some languages, like Hebrew, are written from right to left; others, like Chinese, are written from top to bottom in columns. Still others, like English, use a left-to-right, top-to-bottom organization.

FIGURE 11-13
Examples of preconventional writing: (a) Continuous scribble-writing; (b and c) mock letters; (d) conventional letters with a few mock letters intermingled; (e) individual scribble marks.

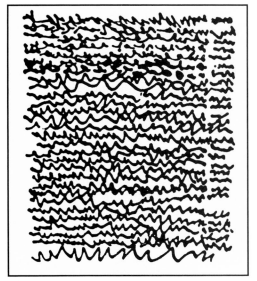

(a)

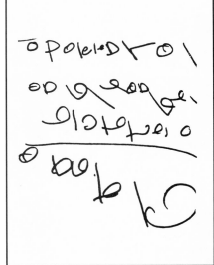

(b)

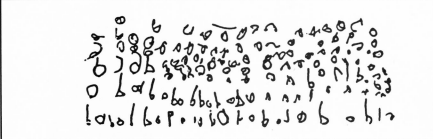

(c)

(d)

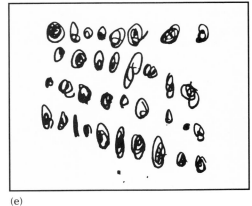

(e)

The writing done by young preschool children often appears quite disorganized, and it is. Most preschoolers don't know how print is placed on a page in our language. They also lack the concepts of space that would enable them to stick with specific conventions even if they knew them. For example, children often mix orientations when writing, perhaps writing the first few letters of their name from left to right across the top of a page and then turning the page to write more letters from left to right across the new top of the page. The finished product is written in several orientations, and the reader has to rotate the page to read it. Children who mix orientations this way often lack a spatial concept that Piaget called **projective space** (1967). A person who has projective spatial understandings knows that there are different points of view and can adopt a view and stick with it. Children who mix points of view in the same writing sample often don't know that there are specific points of view or that their writing contains contradictions (two sides of the paper treated as the top, for example). Mixed orientations can be seen in the writing samples in Figure 11-14.

Once children are able to adopt a point of view and stay with it consistently, they still have to realize that certain specific conventions are considered "right" in our language. One 5-year-old who had invited an adult to write a book with him asked the adult if they could write from left to right so they wouldn't be "confusing to each other." This child realized that internal consistency was a good idea, but he didn't realize that left-to-right organization is the accepted convention in our language. He thought the organization of

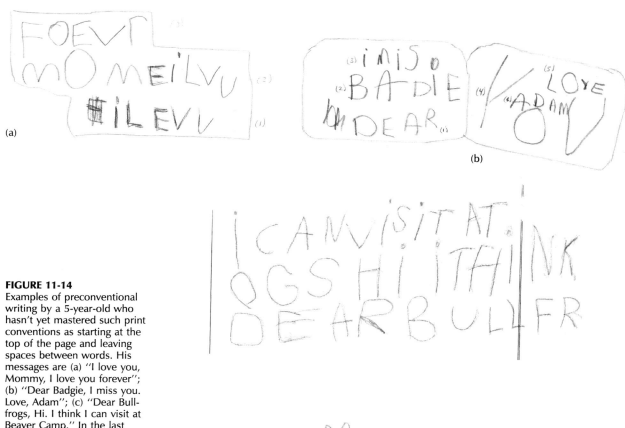

FIGURE 11-14
Examples of preconventional writing by a 5-year-old who hasn't yet mastered such print conventions as starting at the top of the page and leaving spaces between words. His messages are (a) "I love you, Mommy, I love you forever"; (b) "Dear Badgie, I miss you. Love, Adam"; (c) "Dear Bull-frogs, Hi. I think I can visit at Beaver Camp." In the last message he ran out of room, so he finished up on the other side of the paper with mirror writing.

FIGURE 11-15
Literate homes help children view themselves as readers and think of reading as an enjoyable, natural choice from an early age. These children have been told to keep their clothes clean while they wait for a party to begin—an ideal time for a book.

writing on the page was something you decided each time you sat down to write.

Another print convention involves strategies for marking where one word ends and the next begins. Dots, slashes, hyphens, and special letters have all been used in different languages to indicate word endings. In English, of course, we separate words with a space. Young children—preschoolers, kindergartners, and even early first graders—typically string their letters together without any spaces between words (Figure 11-14). Sometimes they invent their own ways to show where words end, such as slashes or dots. As with other literacy skills, in time they notice how other writers separate words, and they adopt the convention in their own writing.

The Social Context of Emergent Literacy Development

Everything in child development takes place in a context—in some kind of setting—and emergent literacy is no exception. The development of reading and writing skills occurs in the context of home, school, and community. Many studies have shown that high levels of written language development in preschoolers are associated with easy and frequent access to literacy activities (Durkin, 1966; Read, 1975; Ferreiro & Teberosky, 1979; Bissex, 1980; Schickedanz & Sullivan, 1984).

RESEARCH FOCUS

Children's Storybook Reading

Many parents and teachers know that preschool children often attempt to "read" storybooks that have been read to them. The pictures in storybooks guide children's early reading attempts. Only gradually do children begin to pay attention to the print, a shift that seems to be aided by repeated readings of the same stories (Morrow, 1988).

Some researchers have attempted to describe the various ways in which children reread familiar storybooks. The accompanying chart provides one researcher's description of the strategies children use to reread storybooks before the emergence of actual reading, starting with their most primitive attempts and ending with their most mature.

1. Attending to pictures but not telling a story	The child "reads" by looking at the pictures in the book, but the child's speech is only about the picture in view; the child does not create a story across several pages. For example, a child might label the pictures or comment on each one.
2. Attending to pictures and forming an oral story	The child "reads" by looking at the pictures in the book. The child weaves a story across pages, but the wording and intonation resemble storytelling more than story reading.
3. Attending to pictures, forming an oral and written story, mixed	The child "reads" by looking at the pictures in the book. The child's wording and intonation sound sometimes like conversation and sometimes like reading.
4. Attending to pictures and forming a written story	The child "reads" by looking at the pictures in the book. The child's wording and intonation sound consistently like reading. Sometimes the child paraphrases much of the actual story; at other times the child repeats the actual story verbatim.
5. Attending to print	The child looks at the print in the book. Several substages within this stage precede fluent reading.

SOURCE: Adapted from Sulzby, E. (1985). *Children's emergent reading of favorite storybooks: A developmental study.* Reading Research Quarterly, 20(4), 464; and Sulzby, E. (1991). *Assessment of emergent literacy: Storybook reading.* The Reading Teacher, 44(7), 498–500.

High on the list of important literacy experiences is storyreading. Children who are read to during their preschool years typically enjoy higher levels of success in learning to read in elementary school than their peers who have not been read to, and some even learn to read before they go to school (Durkin, 1966; Briggs & Elkind, 1977; Clark, 1976; Goldfield & Snow, 1984; Lartz & Mason, 1988; McCormick & Mason, 1989; Wells, 1985, 1986). Studies have helped us understand variations in the frequency with which preschool children are read to, adult styles of reading to young children, and how young children change their interactions with books as they hear more and more stories and hear the same stories repeated (Heath, 1983; Lartz & Mason, 1988; Morrow, 1988; Teale, 1986; Yaden, Smolkin & Conlin, 1989). All the evidence suggests that hearing and responding to stories read from books is probably the most important literacy experience a preschooler can have. (See Research Focus—Children's Storybook Reading for a discussion of how children's interactions with books change with experience.)

The research on literacy development has also documented what perhaps is obvious: Different homes provide different literacy experiences for children. In some homes, parents do more talking and explaining; they read and write more; and they provide more literacy activities and toys for their children (Heath, 1983; Teale, 1986). Parents also differ in style when interacting with children while talking or reading stories (Dickinson, 1989; Heath & Thomas, 1984; Snow & Ninio, 1986). These differences have profound implications for children's later success in school. The more schoollike the experiences and interactions, the better prepared the child will be for school, regardless of the child's innate learning ability.

Many attempts are being made to provide optimal literacy experiences for all preschool children. Some of these programs try to help parents learn to read effectively to their children and to increase the books children have in their homes (Edwards, 1989; McCormick & Mason, 1989). Other programs help parents improve their own reading skills, as well as share books with their children; still other programs are aimed at improving the literacy experiences children are provided in preschool programs such as Head Start (Dickinson, 1989; Paratore, 1991). Such efforts should help provide all preschool children with the literacy experiences that enable them to become successful in reading and writing when they go to elementary school.

Parental Behavior and Emergent Literacy Development

Since early literacy experiences do seem to influence children's literacy development, it is important to focus on what effective parents do. Contrary to what might be expected, parents whose children have reached high levels of literacy development before entering elementary school typically do not set out to teach their children to read and write. Parents obviously do give their children information about reading and writing, but it's not in the form of organized, teacher-directed lessons (Schickedanz et al., 1990). Instead, literacy experiences occur in meaningful contexts as the family lives its life, or they are selected with the specific child's interests and current abilities in mind (Anbar, 1986; Schickedanz & Sullivan, 1984). For example, a mother gives her son a piece of paper and a pencil to make his own scribbled shopping list or to write a letter to grandma while the mother writes hers. Or a parent hands a child a deposit slip from the checkbook to scribble on while taking care of business at the bank. Or parents establish storybook reading as a calming bedtime routine to prepare the child for going to sleep. It is this meaningful, functional aspect of early literacy experiences that many program designers are trying to incorporate into preschoolers' classroom and home experiences.

OVERVIEW

There isn't much guesswork involved in figuring out what preschoolers are saying. Unlike toddlers, who say only part of what they mean, preschoolers can "tell all." But they haven't perfected all language forms yet. They still have to sort out the complexities of syntax and the exceptions to all the rules that they've miraculously picked up. These tasks begin during the preschool years and are completed in the school years. Preschoolers rely heavily on physical and social contexts to understand language, and broad, rich experiences help them build inner "contexts of the mind." Preschoolers learn a great deal about written language as well, usually without the kind of specific lessons we typically associate with school. But early schoollike literacy experiences do give children an advantage later in learning to read. Providing these experiences to more children will be one of the challenges of the 1990s.

CHAPTER REVIEW

ORAL LANGUAGE DEVELOPMENT

- Preschoolers' speech is no longer telegraphic. Their sentences are longer and more complete than those of toddlers.
- Preschoolers overgeneralize morphological rules, producing the coined words and ingenious usages for which they're famous.
- Word order rules for formulating questions and negative sentences are gradually acquired by preschoolers.
- Children learn correct speech not from being corrected directly but from being exposed to correct usage in a natural, meaningful way.

- An understanding of passive sentences is not attained until about age 5.
- Understanding the locative expressions "in," "on," and "under" emerges at about age $2\frac{1}{2}$, but "beside," "between," "front," and "back" are not understood until age $4\frac{1}{2}$ or 5.
- It can take children many years to acquire some word meanings.
- Preschoolers use context to figure out what is being said; rich experiences help them build "contexts of the mind."

WRITTEN LANGUAGE DEVELOPMENT

- The term "emergent literacy" has replaced the term "reading readiness" to describe all the literacy activities children engage in before becoming conventional readers and writers.
- Children's reading strategies evolve over a long period of time. At first children often think that pictures in books are what one reads; only later do they realize that reading involves getting meaning from print.
- Learning that letters of the alphabet code phonemes rather than whole words or syllables is one thing that children must figure out about print.
- Children as young as 3 years old recognize general features of writing and can distinguish writing from nonwriting.
- Recognizing letters of the alphabet involves the gradual differentiation of distinctive features. One of the

hardest features for children to sort out is orientation in space, a difficulty that accounts for the frequency of letter reversals by young children.
- Scribble-writing, mock letters, mixed orientations, and lack of space between words can be seen in children's writing attempts before they master print conventions.
- High levels of written language development are associated with easy and frequent access to literacy activities and high levels of responsive, adult interaction during the preschool years. Children who have had many schoollike experiences tend to be more successful when they start school.
- Parents support literacy development with the many reading and writing experiences that occur naturally in the home every day.

KEY TERMS

morpheme	orthography
morphological rules	syllabic hypothesis
overgeneralize	phonemic awareness
syntax	phonemic segmentation
context bound	distinctive features
decontextualized	environmental print
emergent literacy	reversals
reading readiness	scribble-writing
predictable text	mock letters
phoneme	projective

SUGGESTIONS FOR FURTHER READING

Clay, M. (1987). *Writing begins at home*. Portsmouth, NH: Heinemann Educational Books.

This short book is full of samples of preschoolers' writing. It's an excellent introduction for anyone unfamiliar with young children's writing.

Lindfors, J. W. (1987). *Children's language and learning* (2d ed). Englewood Cliffs, NJ: Prentice-Hall.

This basic text provides an excellent survey of all areas of language development. Included in this second edition is information on written language development.

Muma, J. R. (1986). *Language acquisition: A functionalistic perspective*. Austin, TX: Pro-Ed.

This book reviews and summarizes considerable bodies of research and is for the student who is seriously interested in studying language acquisition.

Schickedanz, J. (1990). *Adam's righting revolutions: A case study of one child's writing development from age one to seven*. Portsmouth, NH: Heinemann Educational Books.

This book provides detailed descriptions of a young child's gradual understanding of the alphabetic nature of English orthography. Many writing samples illustrate the book.

Schickedanz, J. (1986). *More than the ABCs: The early stages of reading and writing*. Washington, DC: National Association for the Education of Young Children.

This short paperback provides an overview of research on emergent literacy and suggests ways that parents and teachers can support young children's curiosity about written language.

c h a p t e r 12

SOCIAL AND EMOTIONAL DEVELOPMENT IN PRESCHOOL CHILDREN

Two children were playing on an outdoor play structure at a birthday party. Laura, 4 years old, was swinging, and Aaron, 6, was climbing on a ladder nearby. They were talking and laughing in a friendly way. Suddenly, Martina, $3\frac{1}{2}$ and a classmate of Laura's at nursery school, burst out of the house and came running across the grass.

"I want to swing, I want to swing," she called out. As she got to the play structure, she gave Laura a shove and grabbed the swing away from her.

"I had it, Martina," Laura protested.

Martina held onto the swing and glared at Laura for a moment. Then she raised the swing behind her and let it go in Laura's direction. The swing hit Laura in the face, and she burst into tears. As she ran off, Martina jumped onto the swing.

"Martina," Aaron called from the ladder above the swing, "if you don't give Laura back the swing, I'm going to spit in your hair." Martina squinted up at him and hesitated. At the same time, a parent started across the grass toward the play structure with a tearful Laura in tow.

"Martina," she called out, "you'll need to wait for your turn to use the swing. Laura was using it."

As Martina scooted off the swing, the parent said, "Come with me. I want to talk to you. I saw you hit Laura with the swing. It gave her a bump on her head. Why did you do that?"

"Because I wanted the swing. I wanted her to leave so I could have it."

"You need to learn a better way to get a turn. What do you think you could do?"

Martina looked down at the ground without answering.

"Let's go back and talk to Laura. We're going to go tell her that you want a turn on the swing and ask her how much longer she thinks she's going to be using it."

With support and coaching from the parent, Martina was able to tell Laura that she wanted a turn and to ask how long she'd have to wait. Laura said that she didn't know how long it would be.

FIGURE 12-1
Even though their most important relationships are still with their parents and other family members, preschoolers find fun and friendships with their peers. Support and guidance from adults help preschoolers work out interpersonal difficulties in a positive way.

"Well, we'll be over in the sandbox while we wait," said the parent. "Come tell us when you're finished, in case we don't see you get off. And, remember, Martina needs a turn before the party is over."

"Okay," Laura agreed.

With their improved motor skills and cognitive abilities, preschoolers can engage in much more complex social exchanges than they could as toddlers. But very often they get themselves hopelessly entangled in social difficulties from which only adults can rescue them. Very young children have neither the skills nor the experience that are needed for smooth social interactions. They acquire many of these skills through socialization during the preschool period. **Socialization** is the process by which children learn the values and behaviors accepted in their society. Children have to learn how to act in social situations—how to share and be fair; how to express themselves and solve problems without hurting or depriving other children; and how to trust, enjoy, and care for people both inside and outside their families. While adults are teaching children all these things—or, in Erikson's words, helping them acquire a conscience—they also have to be careful not to "oversocialize" the children in ways that interfere with their budding sense of initiative. Erikson (1968a) insists that a successful resolution of the developmental crises of the preschool period comes with the child's growing conviction, undaunted by inappropriate guilt, that she can be what she imagines she wants to be.

Between ages 3 and 6, children make great strides in controlling their aggressive impulses, contributing to the welfare of others, and resisting doing what they know they shouldn't. How do they become socialized? And what are the best ways for adults to help children become responsible yet enthusiastic people, with an appropriate measure of self-control? These are the issues addressed in this chapter on the social and emotional development of preschool children.

SOCIALIZATION PROCESSES

Socialization results from learning, and many of our current approaches to socialization are based on learning theory, particularly social learning theory. The usefulness of such approaches is especially obvious in federally funded special education programs for retarded and behavior-disordered children, which are frequently available for the first time during the preschool years. These programs lean heavily on socialization techniques rooted in behavioral and social learning theory. As described in Chapter 2, social learning theory focuses on the processes of reinforcement and punishment; verbal instruction (telling children about expectations); extinction (ignoring inappropriate behavior); and modeling, or observational learning.

But these socialization processes don't operate in a vacuum. They are part of a child's history of relationships with adults, especially the critical attachment relationship with parents, as we saw in Chapter 8. The attachment relationship determines the child's orientation to adults and his feelings toward them. These, in turn, affect the extent to which the child imitates adult behavior, listens when they explain the reasons for an admonition, and feels dissatisfied with himself when he fails to meet their expectations. On the parents' side, the attachment relationship influences the extent to which parents are likely to teach appropriate social behavior. Parents who are consistent in

FIGURE 12-2
The most effective socialization is based on a high-quality attachment relationship. A child who has a secure relationship with his mother, as this boy appears to have, is likely to want to adopt the standards of behavior she sets for him.

RESEARCH FOCUS

Children and Divorce

For adults, divorce means the end of a marriage. For children, it means the end of everyday life as they know it. The disruption and stress of divorce are experienced profoundly by children, at least temporarily. And it's an experience with which more and more children are becoming familiar. In the United States, about half of all marriages now end in divorce, and about half of all children are expected to live in a household with just one parent during some portion of their childhood (Grusec & Lytton, 1988). The rate of divorce in the United States is the highest of any country in the world (Weitzman & Adair, 1988). How do children react to divorce, and what can parents do to protect them from long-term negative effects?

GENERAL EFFECTS OF DIVORCE

Both boys and girls of divorced parents show more behavior problems and lower academic achievement than their peers. But recent studies suggest that this was the case even before the divorce; it is not necessarily the divorce *per se* that leads to an academic or behavioral decline (Cherlin et al., 1991). In fact, where there is a great deal of conflict between parents, the divorce can actually be a relief for those concerned. Nevertheless, divorce always involves the separation of the child from one parent, and this separation requires a major adjustment.

In addition to this adjustment, the child might move, might have to get used to a lower standard of living, and might need to adapt to a mother's beginning to work full time. Young children often have to enter and adjust to day care. Because divorce is highly traumatic for the parents, most children also experience disruptions in parenting behavior (Emery, Hetherington & DiLalla, 1984; Grusec and Lytton, 1988).

STAGES OF REACTION TO DIVORCE

Children's adjustment to divorce goes on for some time, often two to three years. Their reactions a few years later are usually quite different from what they were in the beginning.

Three stages of adjustment have been identified by researchers Weitzman and Adair (1988). In the first, known as the *acute stage,* there is considerable trauma and disruption. This is the time when one parent leaves, when the child and one parent might move, and when parents are likely to be the most irritable, depressed, or anxious. Children typically show the most troubled behavior during the two-year acute stage. They might be aggressive, or they might regress, such as when an older child reverts to bedwetting. If the child is in school, there might be a decline in grades. Not all children react in these ways, of course; some children's academic achievement actually improves after a divorce.

The second stage is labeled the *transitional stage.* Changes still occur during this stage, but the child's life is much more predictable now, as is the behavior of the parents. The biggest adjustment the child might have to make is to the parent's new relationships with other adults or to a stepparent (Weitzman & Adair, 1988). The third stage is the *postdivorce stage.* By this time, everyone is accustomed to the dissolution of the previous family, and a sense of stability has emerged.

HOW DO CHILDREN OF DIFFERENT AGES REACT TO DIVORCE?

Not surprisingly, children's reactions to divorce vary depending on their age. Preschoolers typically show the most regression in their behavior and seem the most fearful about their

responding to their baby's signals tend to be consistent and clear in setting and maintaining limits for their older child (Sroufe, 1983; 1988).

With the development of a more cognitively oriented social learning theory (Bandura, 1977), agreement has been growing between attachment theorists and social learning theorists about the factors influencing children's behaviors and ways of relating to others. Both groups agree that these behaviors result from social experience. Both see the child as an active agent whose social experience shapes his expectations—his "internal working models" of himself and others—which in turn shape how he processes subsequent social experiences (Youngblade & Belsky, 1990). Even though attachment theorists emphasize bonds of affection and social learning theorists emphasize social skills, the two groups agree in their predictions about the development of the child's behavior. (An event that seriously affects the child's behavior, at least temporarily, is divorce. For a discussion of the disruptive effects of this experience, see Research Focus—Children and Divorce.)

Neither attachment theorists nor social learning theorists have extensively addressed two other factors—cognitive development and temperament—and yet these two factors clearly affect the ease with which adults are able to socialize and deal with the child. In this chapter, therefore, we also include a disown welfare. They may become concerned about being abandoned and overreact to routine separations. They also tend to blame themselves for the divorce more than older children do (Grusec & Lytton, 1988).

Young school-age children tend to have more overt, direct reactions than preschoolers. They may cry, or they may express feelings of rejection. They may feel and express more anger and less fear than preschoolers. These children usually feel less responsible for the divorce than preschoolers do, but they're more aware of issues of loyalty to one or the other parent. Even so, they usually don't side with one parent against the other. Older school-age children also react angrily to a divorce, often blaming one parent and siding with the other to resolve the loyalty issue (Grusec & Lytton, 1988).

Adolescents are buffered somewhat from the effects of divorce because they're already distancing themselves from their parents in the normal course of developing autonomy. Divorce does make adolescents feel anxious, though, especially about their own likelihood of success in marriage. They sometimes deal with issues of loyalty by rejecting both parents. In any case, they rarely align themselves with either parent (Grusec & Lytton, 1988). Perhaps they can understand the complexities of the situation better than the 9- or 10-year-old, who often does choose one parent over the other.

HOW CAN ADULTS EASE THE EFFECTS OF DIVORCE ON CHILDREN?

Children's adjustment to divorce, especially in the long run, has a lot to do with the amount of conflict between parents both before and after the divorce. If parents can keep conflict in check and work together in parenting, the child's long-term adjustment is greatly facilitated (Weitzman & Adair, 1988).

Children also do better if they are able to have consistent contact with the noncustodial parent (the parent who doesn't live with the child) (Grusec & Lytton, 1988). It doesn't seem to matter whether both parents have actual custody (***joint custody***) or whether one parent has custody and the other has visitation rights. The important predictors of long-term outcome are contact with the noncustodial parent and absence of parent conflict and anxiety (Kline et al., 1989). The family's financial situation and the degree of communication within the family, especially about the divorce itself, have also been found to affect the child's adjustment (Grusec & Lytton, 1988).

WHAT IS THE OUTCOME FOR CHILDREN OF DIVORCE?

Divorce alone is not a crucial factor in children's ultimate adjustment to life. More important is the amount of conflict the child sees and experiences in the family. Children from intact families with high levels of conflict fare worse than children from divorced families with low levels of conflict (Brown, 1980). It's not so much specific events or circumstances that shape the child's development, but *family process variables*—how the family functions.

Preschool and young school-age children react most negatively to divorce, probably because of their greater vulnerability and dependence on their parents. Regardless of age, many children make a good long-term adjustment to divorce. Stability isn't achieved, however, until at least two to three years after the initial breakup of the family.

cussion of the effects of cognitive development and biology on the social and emotional development of the preschooler.

Verbal Instruction

During a free play period in school one day, Joann and Amelia began chasing each other around a table. As they bumped into other children's activities and their laughter got louder and louder, their teacher came over to them. She took hold of both their hands and said, "Let's stop the running. You might hurt someone or fall down and hurt yourselves. Let's find something else to do. There's clay on the art table, or you could play in the block corner or read a book in the library area."

"Let's build with blocks," said Joann. "We can make cages for animals!"

"Okay," agreed Amelia.

"Good idea," said their teacher as they hurried off. "I want to see those cages when they're done."

Joann and Amelia's teacher used verbal instruction to involve them in some positive activity that was incompatible with running around the classroom. The teacher's concrete suggestions helped the girls find something else to do.

FIGURE 12-3
In many situations verbal instruction is the most effective method of socialization. Here, a day care teacher helps a preschooler learn new and more acceptable ways to behave by explaining the effect of her actions on others and telling her other ways she could have acted.

Studies have shown that once children are engaged in an activity, they're likely to increase their involvement with that activity in the future (Staub, 1979). In this case, now that they have experience with the blocks, Joann and Amelia are more likely to play with the blocks another day. Their teacher can make their block play even more interesting by providing additional props, such as animals to go in the cages.

In many situations, verbal instruction is the quickest and most effective method of socialization. It not only discourages inappropriate behavior but also teaches and encourages positive alternative behaviors. Verbal communication can also be used to lead children to see themselves in certain ways. A parent might say, "You're such a good helper. I don't know what I'd do without your help. It would take me forever to fold all this laundry by myself." Or a teacher might say, "You're such good listeners. I don't think I've ever seen such good listeners as you are today." Children often respond to this process of **positive attribution** by seeing themselves in these favorable terms and trying to live up to the image in the future (Miller, Brickman, & Bolen, 1975; Jensen & Moore, 1977).

Comments like these must be made appropriately, however—when children *are* helping or listening well (gauged in terms of their level of development, of course). Children usually know whether they're behaving well in terms of a standard, and if they're praised when they're not behaving well, they'll see no reason to improve.

Another kind of verbal communication can also influence children's behavior. **Exhortation** informs children of what they should do or what behavior is desirable. Two kinds of exhortation—power-assertive and inductive—were distinguished in one study (Smith et al., 1983). A parent using power-assertive exhortation makes an assertion about the expected behavior: "I'm going outside to get the newspaper. I want you to listen for the telephone while I'm gone." A parent using inductive exhortation relies on **induction** (reasoning):

"I would like to go outside to get the newspaper, but I won't be able to hear the telephone if it rings while I'm away."

In this study, children were given opportunities for prosocial behavior such as helping to move chairs, looking for a lost pen, and teaching someone how to make a picture. Children in the group receiving power-assertive exhortation were told to help. Children in the group receiving inductive exhortation were given a description of the need and of the effect of their behavior if they decided to help. None of the children suffered any consequences if they didn't help.

The researchers expected the inductive approach to be more effective than the power-assertive approach in getting children to help and share. They knew that a history of power-assertive parenting is usually associated with noncompliant behavior in children and that induction is associated with cooperation. The study showed, however, that the two types of verbalization were equally effective. Children in both groups cooperated and helped. The researchers explained this discrepancy by noting that parents who use power-assertive exhortations also often use punishment, such as spanking or denial of privileges, if children don't do what they tell them to do. It's probably the whole pattern of power-assertive disciplinary practices that makes their children less cooperative than other children (Dix, Ruble & Zambarabo, 1989).

What this study showed is that verbal instruction alone *can* be effective in getting children to behave in the ways adults want them to. But other studies have shown that verbal communications combined with other techniques, such as reinforcement and modeling, are typically more powerful than words alone.

Reinforcement, Punishment, and Extinction

One Saturday morning while playing in the family room, Susan, age 3, turned the knob of the TV and watched the screen as it lit up. Then she turned it off and on again. She was intrigued by the dot of light that appeared and spread across the screen. She turned the knob off and on again and again. In the next room, her dad heard what was going on and came in to investigate.

"Susan, where's your play dough?" he asked. "Weren't you going to make some cookies this morning out at the picnic table?"

Susan ran to get her play dough and pushed open the back door. Her dad went outside with her and helped her set up her place mat and cookie cutters. Then he settled into a nearby chair to continue his reading.

After a while he looked over and said, "Looks like Christmas cookies." He got up and went over to the table. "Can I have a bite?" He took an imaginary bite, and Susan laughed in delight. She continued playing with the play dough for the next hour, apparently having forgotten all about the TV knob.

A learning theorist would say that Susan's responses in this situation were reinforced. **Reinforcement** is defined as a consequence to a response that increases the probability that the response will occur again in the same situation or a similar one. The interesting light appearing on the screen reinforced Susan's turning of the TV knob; her father's attention reinforced her playing with the play dough.

Susan's dad showed thought and skill in his response to what she was doing. He didn't simply tell her to stop fiddling with the TV knob, for example. By redirecting her instead to an interesting alternative activity, one in which she was likely to stay engaged for some time, he helped her avoid becoming involved in other play activities that might create additional problems. The play dough activity was also one for which her father could easily provide positive reinforcement in the form of attention, even though he wanted to do some reading. Effective socialization depends in large part on the skill of adults in organizing situations and redirecting behavior so that they can give positive reinforcement.

Another parent might have slapped Susan's hand or sent her to her room to teach her not to play with the knob. If Susan's knob-turning behavior decreased after these kinds of actions, we would say that they were punishers for her behavior. **Punishment** is defined as a consequence that decreases the probability that the response will recur.

Learning theory distinguishes two different kinds of punishment. One kind adds stimuli to the environment, such as a slap on Susan's hand. The other kind removes stimuli from the environment, often those that were previously reinforcing the behavior. Sending Susan to her room, where she couldn't play with the TV or the other toys in the family room, would be an example of this kind of punishment.

Punishment of the second kind—in which reinforcement is removed—is referred to as **response cost** (Reese & Lipsitt, 1970). In other words the child's response costs the child positive reinforcement. When children are sent to their rooms at home, or when they're sent to sit somewhere by themselves at school, away from where reinforcing activities are taking place in their classroom, the procedure is called time out from positive reinforcement, or, more commonly, **time out.** Because children's normal environments at home or school have so many interesting activities and social interactions with other people, taking them out of these environments for misbehavior usually serves as a punishment.

A third way to reduce inappropriate behavior, besides reinforcement and punishment, is to arrange the environment so the child receives no reinforcement at all for the behavior. In Susan's case, her dad might have unplugged the TV. When she turned the knob, she wouldn't have seen any spreading light that would have made her want to repeat her action. When a behavior doesn't produce any interesting consequences, it often disappears. This process is called **extinction**. In the classroom, a teacher who ignores obnoxious behavior is attempting to use extinction.

CHOOSING AN APPROPRIATE METHOD. Although reinforcement, punishment, and extinction can all get results, one is considered the learning technique of choice—reinforcement. Both extinction and punishment have serious drawbacks. Extinction isn't used very often, because it's difficult for adults to ignore children's misbehavior. Some misbehavior can't be ignored because it hurts or endangers other people or the misbehaving child. And parents and teachers know that children often need practical ideas about what they *should* do instead of the thing they're doing that's getting them into trouble. Susan's dad sensed that she needed a suggestion about something else to do besides play with the TV knob. He directed her to an alternative, engaging activity that

FIGURE 12-4
Struggles over toys naturally arise when children play together. With young children, a caregiver might provide another toy or involve them in an alternative activity. If an older child consistently grabs toys from other children even after instruction, the caregiver might want to consider time out—removing the child from the reinforcing situation for a short time.

took her outside, away from the TV, where she wouldn't be tempted to turn the knob again.

Susan's dad may also have known that punishment has its drawbacks. One of them is that it can backfire and produce exactly the opposite effects of the desired ones. We've all witnessed scenes like the following:

> Kevin approaches the TV set and turns the dial. His father, Edward, looks up from his book and tells him, "No!" Kevin stops playing with the dial, and Edward returns to his book. Kevin again turns the TV dial, but Edward doesn't notice right away. Finally, Edward notices and intervenes again, once more telling Kevin, "No!" He returns to his book, and Kevin begins to play with some toys. Kevin then approaches the TV, turning to look at his dad. Edward looks back at

him. Kevin smiles broadly and turns the dial. Edward intervenes, says, "No!" again, picks Kevin up, and puts him down on the other side of the room. Kevin runs to the TV, laughing in delight, and turns it on. Edward by now is very angry and spanks Kevin hard.

In this situation, Edward's responses reinforced Kevin's behavior rather than punishing it—they increased his involvement with the TV rather than decreasing it. Kevin was pleased that he'd found a way of getting his dad's attention. The "class clown" often behaves this way. The teacher's attention reinforces the child's misbehavior, making it increase. A no-win situation quickly develops, with the teacher often escalating punishment to a harsher level, as when Edward spanked Kevin for playing with the TV dial. But escalation to physical punishment has definite problems.

DISADVANTAGES OF PHYSICAL PUNISHMENT. One problem with physical punishment is simply that we can't explain or teach very much to a crying child. The period of time following misbehavior is often a unique one for instruction, and learning during this period may generalize to other situations. We can use this time to help the child understand why the behavior was inappropriate or what

FIGURE 12-5
Physical punishment isn't an effective socialization technique. A child who is crying after a spanking often feels too much pain, anger, and resentment to process any messages his parents were trying to give him. The only lesson he may learn is not to get caught the next time.

a person should or could do in that particular situation. But if the child is upset or in pain, the opportunity for learning is wasted. An explanation might reduce the inappropriate behavior just as well as the physical punishment, especially if the child has never before received that instruction.

A second problem with punishment—and with time out—is that it may reduce exploration and initiative, especially if it comes without warning. A child in a new situation must be given the chance to find out what behaviors work and what behaviors are considered inappropriate. Consider the following example:

> Two preschoolers were each attempting to look in a small, round mirror they were both holding. They started tugging it back and forth.
> "Let *me* have it," shouted Katie.
> "*I* want it," Andy responded.
> Katie's mother came over and took the mirror. She put it on the table and showed them that if they stood back a little, they could both see themselves at the same time. The two children played happily together for the next several minutes as they both looked in the mirror.
> Later, Andy relayed the incident to his mother, who asked him why he hadn't shared the mirror with his friend in the first place. "Well, I didn't know *how* to do that before Katie's mom 'splained it to me," he said.

If Katie and Andy had been punished for quarreling with spanking, yelling, time out, or loss of use of the mirror, they may have learned that the only way to avoid punishment is to avoid new situations altogether. Children who are treated this way may become timid, hesitant, and fearful. Or they may develop only a limited repertoire of responses when they find themselves again in conflict situations over toys. When Katie's mom demonstrated a way for both children to use the toy, she may have not only helped them solve their current problem but also given them the idea that sometimes a way can be found to use a toy together. Obviously, children learn more when they don't avoid situations out of fear and when adults provide suggestions for alternative behavior.

A third problem with punishment is that it can create hostility and resentment, making the adult an **aversive stimulus** for the child. An aversive stimulus is something a person seeks to avoid. A punishing adult will become particularly aversive if the child thinks the punishment is harsh, unnecessary, or motivated by anger rather than concern for the child's well-being. If Katie and Andy had been spanked for quarreling, they may have had such feelings of hostility and resentment. After all, as Andy explained, they didn't know how to share the mirror until an adult provided an idea. The fact that they played cooperatively with the mirror after being shown how indicated that they hadn't really wanted to fight with each other. They were simply two young children without the means to solve a problem.

A very serious problem with punishment is that it can lead to child abuse. Some parents have reported that child abuse occurred in disciplinary situations that simply went too far (Gil, 1970). The principles of social learning apply to adults too—if physical punishment works, it can reinforce the parent for hitting. And if the punishment used is severe or is seen as coming from anger or hostility, so that the parent becomes an aversive stimulus, then any positive reinforcement the parent tries to initiate will have limited effect. Praise, for example, works only if the child likes the person who is giving it.

A vicious cycle can be set up this way. The parent begins to control less by using rewards and more by using punishment. But the level of punishment necessary to have an effect increases, because punishment too is enhanced when a child cares about the person who delivers it. In a nurturant parent-child relationship, for example, a small amount of punishment can go a very long way. But if the child is resentful and angry toward the adult, mild forms of punishment—which serve mostly to inform the child of how serious an adult is about some expectation—don't work. The angry and resentful child resists the parent's authority (Brehm, 1981). In these cases, physical punishment is often escalated. And because an angry and resentful child is often willing to absorb quite a lot of physical hurt rather than submit to the adult, the adult feels compelled to increase the hurt even more. The result is likely to be abusive.

Physical punishment is also dangerous because it provides the child with a model of aggressive behavior. A correlation between parents' use of physical punishment and children's aggressive behavior has been heavily documented

FIGURE 12-6
A parent who wishes to teach her child a lesson he'll remember uses induction (reasoning). This mother has a better chance of getting her message across than would a mother who spanked her misbehaving preschooler.

(Eron, Walder & Lefkowitz, 1971; Trickett & Kuczynski, 1986). We also know that parents who use aggressive parenting techniques have children who grow up to use similar techniques with *their* children (Simons et al., 1991). Since the evidence is correlational, we don't know which way the association works; that is, we don't know if more aggressive children lead parents to use more physical punishment or if more physical punishment produces more aggressive children. But we do know that a lot of aggression can be learned by imitation, and the assumption that physical punishment produces more aggressive children is consistent with these findings.

As suggested earlier, the most effective disciplinary strategy with children has been found to be induction—reasoning with them to inform them about how their misbehavior affects others and why they need to change their actions. Power-assertion techniques, including mild punishment, often have a role in induction because they can be effective at getting children to stop what they're doing and pay attention to what adults are saying to them. One researcher asserts that "too little power assertion or love withdrawal may result in children's ignoring the parent. Too much power assertion or love withdrawal produce fear, anxiety, or resentment in children, which may interfere with the effective processing of the induction" (Hoffman, 1984, p. 304).

Physical punishment, no matter how mild, always models aggressive behavior. For this reason, we believe it's wise to avoid it. But adults don't need to tolerate situations where their admonitions are ignored. Parents and teachers of young children often need to intervene physically in situations, such as when they must restrain a child who is kicking someone or when they must carry a child to a chair where they can review the child's misbehavior. And if induction is not effective, adults probably need to use loss of privileges or time out, especially if the child clearly has the ability to understand the situation and is felt to be capable of behaving as expected.

Observational Learning

Another socialization process by which children learn the ways of their society is **observational learning.** Everyone has seen children imitating the adults they know—their parents, teachers, neighbors, and people who work in their community. Their motivation to imitate others has been explained in various ways. Freud, for example, believed that imitation occurred because of children's identification with the parent of the same sex. During the phallic stage of psychosexual development, boys compete with their fathers for their mother's attention. This creates what Freud called the Oedipal conflict. The little boy even contemplates killing his father, but because this is too frightening, he decides instead to become like his father—to adopt many of his behaviors, attitudes, and beliefs. This is the process Freud labeled **identification.**

Social learning theorists don't argue with the fact that children imitate their same-sex parent. But they don't think we need constructs like the Oedipal conflict to explain it. They think children imitate behavior because of incentives—reinforcement and punishment—and because of the model's status or value. A parent who is nurturant and helps a child solve conflicts by serving as a source of good suggestions, for example, is likely to be held in high esteem by a child and to be considered a desirable model.

FIGURE 12-7
Observational learning accounts for much of the sex-typed behavior we see in children. These 5-year-olds discussing the merits of Wonder Woman have already identified some powerful models of female appearance and behavior in our society.

The social process by which one person demonstrates behavior that another imitates is called **modeling**. Many studies have shown that when children watch another person act a certain way and receive reinforcement for it, they're likely to imitate the person's actions (Bandura, 1977). Also, they're more likely to imitate a person whom they perceive as being similar to themselves, because they think it's possible to become like the model.

It doesn't require much imagination to realize that when girls see their mothers reinforced for looking pretty, they want to look pretty too. And when boys see their fathers reinforced for acting tough, they're motivated to act the same way. Today, our society is providing a much wider variety of models for children, so that girls have assertive, successful women to imitate and boys have articulate, nurturing men in their environment. But a tremendous amount of sexually identified behavior is deeply engrained, so adults still model traditional behaviors for children in many ways. This may be why we see girls and boys acting in stereotypical ways by the age of 3, as discussed in Chapter 8. Regardless of whether we explain imitation in psychoanalytical or social learning terms, the fact that children learn this way is beyond dispute.

Other Factors Influencing Socialization

How children behave in a particular situation depends on more things than how they've been socialized, including their attachment history. Another important factor is their level of cognitive development. A child who's been encouraged to help in the past, and whose previous helpful behavior has been reinforced, still might not help in a new situation. She may not understand that help is needed, or she may not know what kind of help she might offer.

This knowledge is a matter of cognitive development. As children get older, their level of **social cognition**—the ability to understand other people's problems and feelings—gets higher. With more understanding, it becomes easier for children to respond in socially appropriate ways. A higher level of social cognition doesn't automatically result in better behavior, however. Other aspects of children's experiences, such as the values they are taught and how socialization processes have been used by their parents, influence whether they use their cognitive abilities in prosocial or antisocial ways.

Genetic and biological factors also influence the child's behavior, which in turn influences the behavior of the adults with whom she interacts. For example, it is likely to be more difficult or complicated to teach a child when Down's syndrome affects her intelligence or a sensory impairment limits her ability to communicate. Some researchers (e.g., Lytton, 1990) believe that biological influences on behavior are very extensive even in the general population, although biology and environment are so intertwined that it's difficult to separate the effects of each (Dodge, 1990; Wahler, 1990).

One influence on a child's behavior that is at least partly determined by biology is temperament. Jerome Kagan of Harvard University has spent a good deal of the last two decades studying consistent temperament differences among children and the stability of these traits over time. He has been partic-

FIGURE 12-8
Although children are alike in many ways, each has individual characteristics—appearance, level of cognitive development, personality, temperament—that influence how she responds to the world and how others respond to her. Individual behavioral differences are apparent even in this small group of girls singing and playing a game in the schoolyard. How each one acts in this situation is influenced by both her inborn traits and her attachment and socialization histories.

ularly interested in shyness—inhibited responses to unfamiliar events—which he has found to be quite stable. For example, an infant who cries, stiffens her muscles, and arches her back in response to an unfamiliar stimulus at 4 months is likely to be shy in her second year (e.g., Kagan & Snidman, 1991).

Kagan believes that temperament may be influenced by two biochemical factors: (1) the concentration of at least one neurotransmitter (a chemical that carries impulses from one nerve cell to the next) in parts of the brain that control crying and motor activity and (2) the density of neurotransmitter receptors on each nerve cell. These factors, which are partially determined by genetics, would explain individual differences in both negative temperament beginning at birth and in exploratory behavior later on. Of course, individual history is a factor too; a child who is rejected by her parents may be anxious and introverted regardless of her genetic makeup (Kagan & Snidman, 1991).

Earlier researchers also noted characteristics of temperament that remained stable over the course of the neonatal period. Alexander Thomas and Stella Chess (1977) identified newborns as "easy," "difficult," and "slow to warm up" according to seven positive and two negative characteristics. They also pointed out that the infant's temperament has an effect on the parents' responses and choice of socialization techniques.

Even earlier studies reported correlations between particular inherited characteristics and specific patterns of behavior (Sheldon, Hartle & McDermott, 1949; Glueck & Glueck, 1950), such as a muscular body build and aggressive behavior. Again, however, this association is no doubt due to the combined effect of biology and socialization. A very large, very active, and very determined baby boy, for example, might induce his large, active, and equally determined parents to play with him roughly and discipline him firmly. As with so many other aspects of child development, no single system completely determines a child's behavior.

AGGRESSION: HOW IT'S LEARNED, HOW IT'S CONTROLLED

"I'm rubber,
You're glue,
Whatever you say bounces off me
And sticks to you."

"Sticks and stones
Will break my bones,
But names will never hurt me."

In the child's timeless response to insults and name calling, we see the movement from physical aggression to verbal aggression that occurs late in the preschool years. Physical aggression peaks in most children when they're 2 or 3 years old and then begins to decline. Verbal aggression continues well into the school years and beyond. Preschoolers still tend to respond to verbal insults with hitting, but by the time they're in elementary school, they're much more likely to respond with words (Parke & Slaby, 1983). Toddlers and young preschoolers use more **instrumental aggression**—aggression intended to gain some object or privilege (Hartup, 1974)—and older preschoolers and school-age children rely on their rapidly growing verbal skills to get what they want as well as to insult and hurt.

FIGURE 12-9
A very young child tries out biting, probably just to see what will happen. Aggressive impulses seem to be innate in human beings, but how they're expressed and controlled are learned behaviors. If the other child cries and the teacher intervenes, this boy will be less likely to try the experiment again.

How do children come to be aggressive? Is it an inborn trait, or do children learn it? There's no doubt that biology plays some role in aggressiveness. Some children seem to be born with stronger emotions, more volatile personalities, or less ability to control their impulses, all of which might make them more difficult to socialize than other children (see Lytton, 1990). But a great deal of aggressive behavior is learned, and it's learned according to some of the same principles we've been discussing—reinforcement, punishment, and observation of aggressive models. In this section we discuss the processes by which children learn aggressive behavior and some of the ways adults can help them control it. In the next section, we discuss more of the ways that adults help children learn prosocial behavior.

Reinforcement, Punishment, and Aggression

Dolores is playing with her dolls in the living room near her little sister, Isabella. Isabella is using a small wooden mallet to play a toy xylophone. Dolores stops playing to listen to the sounds her sister is making. Then she reaches over and grabs hold of the mallet. Isabella, surprised, resists, gripping the mallet more firmly and scrunching up her face in anger. But Dolores persists. She pushes Isabella with her free hand and pulls harder on the mallet. Isabella releases her grip on the toy, and Dolores starts playing her sister's xylophone.

REINFORCEMENT. Dolores succeeded in taking away her sister's toy by force, and her success this time is likely to reinforce her aggressive tactic. The extent to which children are reinforced—or punished—for aggression influences whether they learn to be aggressive or nonaggressive.

In addition to material rewards, such as possession of a toy, aggression can yield **intrinsic reinforcement**—nonmaterial changes in the child's environment. For example, with just a little aggression, children can make other children cry and move away, objects fly across the room and shatter, and adults come running. Aggression can quickly produce a little excitement in an otherwise boring environment (Roedell, Slaby & Robinson, 1977). The child feels a sense of power and becomes the center of attention, even though it's negative attention.

Aggression sometimes increases when children are initially gathered into a group, apparently because their aggression is reinforced. In a study of preschool children's free play, one researcher found that 80 percent of children's aggressive actions were rewarded by victims' giving up objects or leaving the field (Patterson, Litman & Bricker, 1967). Because they were successful, the aggressors were encouraged to aggress again. Children who weren't aggressive at the beginning of the year became more aggressive if they were frequent victims. Apparently they imitated aggression to defend themselves, and then they found that it worked when they wanted to get objects themselves. The only children who didn't become more aggressive were those who failed in their first attempts at defensive aggression.

Studies like this underscore exactly how reinforcement increases behavior— if a behavior works, it will increase. Teachers have to be particularly alert in the first weeks of a nursery or kindergarten school year to situations in which aggression is used to obtain objects. If the few children who initiate these tactics when they enter school aren't prevented from using them, the tactics will be adopted by other children. Teachers should do their best to make sure aggressive practices—grabbing toys, pushing ahead, taking someone else's turn, and so on—don't work. If teachers have more than one of each item, and if equipment is available that several children can use at the same time, the number of occasions in which children are inclined to use aggressive tactics will be reduced.

Positive reinforcement—getting a desired reward—is not the only kind of reinforcement for aggressive behavior. Negative reinforcement—removal of an aversive (undesired) stimulus—also plays a very important role. Studies of especially aggressive children have found that parents who don't attend to their child's misbehavior or don't stop it immediately are teaching him that if he is sufficiently assertive and aggressive, he can put an end to his parents' demands for good behavior (Patterson & Reid, 1984; Youngblade & Belsky, 1990). In these cases, the child's aggression is rewarded, sometimes by positive and sometimes by negative reinforcement.

PUNISHMENT. Adults often punish children for aggressive behavior, but punishment is the least effective strategy for helping children become less aggressive, especially if it's the only or the primary strategy used. As explained earlier, physical punishment models aggression and can lead to anger, resentment, and increased noncompliance. Severe physical punishment is actually associated with very high levels of aggression in children, perhaps because of the combined effects of modeling and resentment. But if a child's aggressive behavior continues after parents and teachers have tried such tactics as induction and reinforcing good behavior, they may need to use punishment in the form of time out from positive reinforcement.

Although time out can be an effective procedure for controlling aggression, it has to be used wisely. Like any other form of punishment, it should not be used for a first infraction, when the child might not have known that some behavior was wrong or how he could have behaved in a more appropriate way. Redirection and induction should be given a chance first. If the adult is satisfied that the child can't be excused on the basis of naivete or ignorance, then time out might be appropriate.

Even here, the punishment must be reasonable. If a teacher, for example, denies a misbehaving child the opportunity to participate in a special activity that had been planned for the class later in the day, the child no longer has any incentive to behave well for the rest of the day. In addition the child might become so frustrated and resentful about losing the privilege that he acts even more aggressively.

To avoid these situations, teachers should explain any contingencies that are associated with special activities—or even with routine activities. Adults should also keep in mind that denial of privileges or participation works best when it's related to a specific offense. For example, if a child is harassing a classmate during free time, it makes more sense to restrict the child's privileges by confining him to an isolated area of the classroom for a few minutes than to tell him he can't go on a scheduled trip to the park later in the day. If a child misbehaves at the park, then it makes sense to decide that there will be no trip to the park the next day.

It's also a good idea to use the minimum removal of privileges, the minimum response cost, necessary to end the misbehavior (Roedell, Slaby & Robinson, 1977). The teacher makes the point that the child must stop behaving inappropriately toward another child by removing him from the free play interaction for a few minutes. A longer period of time out may not be needed to get the child to stop this behavior. Minimum response cost may work better than more severe punishment because the child's anger and frustration are minimized. With his self-esteem intact, his emotions under control, and his feelings for the adult still positive instead of hostile, the child is able to learn from the experience and may even identify with the adult's positive standards (Lepper, 1973).

Observational Learning and Aggression

There's no question that children learn aggression by observing it in others (Bandura & Walters, 1963). Even when an aggressive model isn't reinforced, children may learn the aggressive response and use it when they think it may lead to reinforcement. Obviously these facts have important implications for how children learn aggression from family members and friends as well as from movies and TV. In this section we examine how these processes influence aggressive behavior in children.

THE FAMILY AS A MODEL OF AGGRESSIVE BEHAVIOR. Most parents use physical punishment to discipline their children. This type of parenting gives children impressive models of aggressive behavior. Many parents also model verbal aggression, telling their children they're stupid or saying things like, "I'm going to kill you if you don't start listening to me."

Children also witness violence between their parents. In a national survey taken some 15 years ago, about 4 percent of the respondents—1.8 million couples—stated that one or more episodes of physical violence, such as hitting, beating, or threatening with a weapon, had occurred between them over the course of the previous year (Straus, Gelles & Steinmetz, 1980). If milder forms of aggression, such as pushing, slapping, or throwing an object, are included, the percentage jumps to about 12 percent, or 5.4 million couples. Obviously huge numbers of children have the opportunity to witness violence between their parents. The horrifying extent of family violence is seen in the fact that, according to FBI statistics, nearly one-fifth of all murders are committed by family members and almost one-third of all female homicide victims are killed by their husbands or boyfriends (U.S. Department of Justice, 1984, cited in Emery, 1989).

Even when parents don't model aggression, children often learn aggressive behavior from their brothers and sisters. Aggression between siblings is the most common kind of aggression in families (Straus, Gelles & Steinmetz, 1980). Older siblings are usually the aggressors, but younger siblings quickly learn from them (Dunn & Kendrick, 1982; Parke & Slaby, 1983).

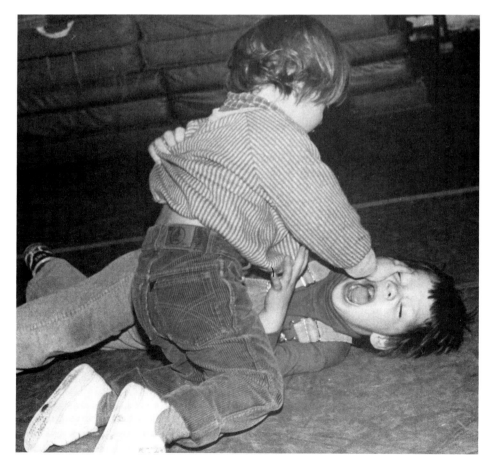

FIGURE 12-10
All siblings fight, but families differ in their tolerance of aggression. Some parents would find this level of violence acceptable, but many wouldn't. Children who are allowed to be aggressive at home bring their aggressive behavior to preschool with them, where they have to learn other ways of interacting.

TELEVISION AS A SOURCE OF AGGRESSIVE MODELS. The ever-present television set is another powerful source of aggressive models in the family. It's common knowledge that children watch a lot of TV, but the statistics are still startling. Virtually every household in the United States has at least one television (Nielson Television Index, 1981). Many parents regulate the number of hours their children are allowed to watch it (Huston et al., 1983), but many more place no restrictions whatsoever on TV viewing (Lyle & Hoffman, 1972). When households have cable TV, the amount of viewing appears to increase even further (Kerkman et al., 1983).

Children begin to watch TV systematically at about $2\frac{1}{2}$ years (Schramm, Lyle & Parker, 1961). Between the ages of 2 and 5, they watch anywhere from 13 to 27 hours per week, or 2 to 4 hours per day (Anderson et al., 1985; Huston et al., 1990). Some studies have shown that TV viewing peaks during the kindergarten year and then declines during the school years (Calvert & Wright, 1982). Other studies have reported that viewing continually increases during the school years and peaks in early adolescence (Liebert, 1986). Whatever the precise number of hours children spend in front of the television, we know that they watch it a lot. By the time the average American child is 18 years old, she has spent more time watching television than in any other activity except sleep (Liebert, 1986; Huston et al., 1990).

Violence on television has been studied extensively. Correlational studies show that children of all ages who see more violence on TV tend to behave more aggressively, and experimental studies give us conclusive evidence that viewing TV violence increases aggression in the viewer. In one ambitious study of cause-and-effect (Freidrich & Stein, 1973), researchers divided nursery school children into three groups and showed them television programs of three different types: aggressive cartoons, such as "Batman" and "Superman"; prosocial programs, such as "Mr. Roger's Neighborhood"; and neutral programs, such as nature films. Each group watched a 20-minute program of a particular type every day for four weeks. Researchers collected baseline data on children's interactions during free play before the study began and observed the children's behavior every day during the study.

After four weeks they found that among the children who were initially above average in aggression, those who saw the violent TV shows showed more aggression than those who watched the other programs. All the children who saw the violent films showed less self-control in waiting for materials or adult attention, regardless of their initial level of aggression. And these same children had more difficulty obeying.

Children have even been observed to increase aggression after watching only one violent TV show (Ellis & Sekyra, 1972). Children who watched a violent sequence from the TV series "The Untouchables" were more willing to do things they believed were hurting other children than children who watched an athletic competition (Liebert & Baron, 1972). Overall the evidence is conclusive: Watching violence on TV is causally related to aggression.

LONG-TERM EFFECTS OF WATCHING TV VIOLENCE. The effects of viewing TV violence appear to be deep and long-lasting. Children seem to become desensitized to violence and accept it more willingly. In one experimental study researchers showed one group of third- and fourth-grade children a violent cowboy movie and another group a nonviolent film (Drabman & Thomas, 1974). They then asked the children to observe a group of younger children and to seek adult help if the children began to fight. The group who had seen the cowboy movie were less likely to summon help when the children fought.

Another study reported correlations between high TV use and desensitization to violence (Cline, Croft & Courrier, 1972). Researchers tested groups of 5- and 12-year-old boys for their emotional reactivity, measured by their pulse rate and other physiological signs of arousal, while they were watching a violent film. Boys of both ages who were high users of TV had milder physical reactions to the violence than boys who didn't watch much TV. They seemed to have grown accustomed, in both mind and body, to observing violence without much reaction.

With violence being accepted and promoted so enthusiastically in our society, how can parents and teachers help children control their aggressive impulses? One of the best approaches to discouraging aggression is to teach and encourage prosocial behavior. This is the area of socialization we discuss next.

PROSOCIAL BEHAVIOR

Prosocial behavior is behavior that benefits others rather than, or in addition to, oneself; it includes helping, sharing, comforting, and cooperating. Children may have an inborn inclination to be helpful, nurturing, consoling—and some children definitely show more of these characteristics than others—but most prosocial behavior, like most aggressive behavior, is learned. And many of the same socialization processes are at work—reinforcement, verbal instruction, observational learning, and practice. A child's level of cognitive development also plays an important part. In this section we discuss how parents and teachers can support children in this aspect of their development.

Reinforcement, Punishment, and Prosocial Behavior

When adults notice and praise children's prosocial efforts, children are motivated to act that way again in the future. Smiles, approving looks, and simple comments like "Good job!" can be just as reinforcing to children as elaborate rewards. Adults often overlook children's positive behavior, perhaps because it seems like normal courtesy to them, at the same time that they're quick to criticize misbehavior. If they get in the habit of expressing their appreciation of children's thoughtfulness, helpfulness, and other prosocial attempts when they occur, they'll increase the likelihood that those behaviors will occur again. One parent occasionally said to her 3-year-old, "Thank you for saying thank you!"

Teachers can also build opportunities for helping into the structure of their classroom day. For example, children can help prepare and serve the snack for the class, with different children counting out cups and napkins, making juice, and distributing crackers each day. Children enjoy this kind of responsibility, and the teacher has the chance to comment on how well they're working together.

Punishment is not an effective way to teach children prosocial behavior, for all the same reasons that it's ineffective in discouraging aggression. There's usually a way to support sharing and cooperating without resorting to punishment. Consider the following example:

FIGURE 12-11
Preschools can structure their programs to include many socialization opportunities. This little girl has asked another child to pour her some milk, and she thanks him when he complies. The teacher can reinforce their actions by complimenting them on a job well done.

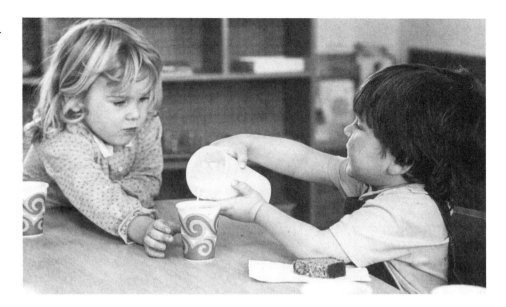

One day during the first week of nursery school, Emily was sitting at a table drawing with crayons. Karen sat down nearby and pulled a piece of paper toward herself. Then she reached over to get a crayon from the box Emily was using.

"No, they're mine!" Emily snapped, grabbing them away. "You can't have any!"

"But I want to draw," Karen protested.

The teacher approached. "Emily," she said, "could Karen use the red crayon while you're using the blue one? Then you could both draw."

"Well, okay," Emily slowly replied. She pushed the crayons toward Karen. After a few moments, she looked over at Karen and said, "What are you going to draw?"

Now imagine that instead of suggesting a way to share the crayons, the teacher took the crayons away from Emily, saying, "Those crayons belong to the whole class. If you can't share them, you can't use them at all!" It's easy to see that Emily would learn very little about prosocial behavior from this harsh lesson.

Verbalization and Prosocial Behavior

If, after Emily shared the crayons, the teacher made positive comments to her about her behavior, she would teach the prosocial behavior even more effectively. "You really are a good sharer," she might say. "You know just how to make sure you and Karen both have fun." As we saw earlier, attributing positive characteristics to a child (positive character attribution) can make the child want to live up to the image in the future (Grusec, 1991).

Another technique parents and teachers use to increase prosocial behavior is **empathy training** (Grusec, 1991). Prosocial behavior can be expected to increase when children are made aware of the effects of their behavior on the feelings and welfare of others (Hoffman, 1982). The teacher might say, for example, "Emily shared the crayons with Karen, so Karen had a chance to

RESEARCH FOCUS

How Children Learn to Help Others

Many people have wondered what is the best way to teach children to help others. One group of researchers set up a study with preschoolers to find out (Yarrow, Scott & Waxler, 1973). They began by collecting baseline data on the children's helping behavior. Children were tested individually to see how they responded to pictures of animals, adults, and children in distress. For example, one picture showed a child being hit on the head by a swing. The child was asked "What's happening in this picture?" and "If you were there and saw that happening, what would you do?" Real-life incidents of distress also occurred during the pretesting session. For example, the tester knocked a vase of flowers to the floor, and a kitten tangled in yarn was brought into the room. The child's responses to the pictures and incidents were recorded and rated in terms of helping behavior.

In the next phase of the experiment, an adult interacted with groups of eight to ten children in a playroom for half an hour a day for two weeks. Half the groups interacted with a nurturing adult who offered help, gave attention and praise, and was friendly and sympathetic. The other half interacted with an adult who was not nurturing, didn't give attention, and criticized achievements.

Next the adult who interacted with the children modeled prosocial behavior either symbolically or symbolically and in real life. The symbolic situation involved a diorama (a small box depicting a situation), in which a toy was helped—for example, a toy monkey was helped to reach some bananas. The real-life situation involved people in the room. For example, a person might enter the room and bump her head; the adult model would comfort her and ask her if she would like to sit down.

In summary, the experiment involved four sets of conditions:

1. Nurturant adult behavior paired with symbolic modeling
   (The friendly adult showed the diorama.)

2. Nonnurturant adult behavior paired with symbolic modeling
   (The unfriendly adult showed the diorama.)

3. Nurturant adult behavior paired with symbolic and real-life modeling
   (The friendly adult showed the diorama and helped the person in the room.)

4. Nonnurturant adult behavior paired with symbolic and real-life modeling
   (The unfriendly adult showed the diorama and helped the person in the room.)

During posttesting—the period when changes in behavior are observed—the children were allowed to play with the diorama and were also taken to a nearby house to visit a mother and baby. During the visit, several "accidents" occurred, such as toys falling out of the baby's crib. The children's helping behavior was recorded in both the symbolic situation with the diorama and the real-life situation with the baby's toys.

It turned out that only the children who interacted with the nurturant adult and who saw helping behavior modeled in both the diorama and the real-life incident increased their helping behavior in the real-life situation with the baby. This indicates that nurturant adults are more effective models than nonnurturant adults, but that nurturance alone isn't enough. Children have to actually see adults helping others in real situations to become helpful themselves. When helping is modeled symbolically, children seem to learn only the principle of helping, not the idea that they can do it too.

A study with kindergarten children turned up similar results (Staub, 1971). In this study, individual children played games with the experimenter, who was nurturant with some children—warm and friendly, smiling often, and praising the child's skill at the games—and non-nurturant with others—

color too. Everyone in the classroom is happier when more children are able to play."

Even though we did see earlier that exhortations to share or help were effective in eliciting prosocial behavior in children (Smith et al., 1983), exhortations to share—simply telling children to do it—aren't very effective in getting children to share when they are out of the range of watchful adults (Elliott & Vasta, 1970). Exhortation is more effective when it is combined with induction about exactly why a person is in need and exactly how a child's helping can contribute positively to the other person's welfare.

Observational Learning and Prosocial Behavior

Verbal instruction, especially of the inductive type, is effective in helping children learn prosocial behavior, but seeing prosocial behavior modeled is even more effective. Some kinds of models and modeling situations, however, are more effective than others. An elaborate study undertaken with preschoolers

task oriented and unfriendly. After they played for a while, the experimenter excused himself and said he had to do one of two things: check on a child in the next room, or respond to a child's crying in the next room, which the child playing games could hear. This was the distress modeling situation.

When the experimenter returned, he explained that the child had fallen but that he had helped her up and she was all right. Then he said he had to go do some work but that the child could continue playing. He also told the child that more crayons could be found in the next room.

After he left, the child heard a crash from the next room followed by the sound of crying. This was the posttesting situation. Children who went to the next room to try to help the crying child saw the tape recorder and were told by the experimenter that he wanted to see how children felt when they heard another child cry. Children who didn't offer direct help, including those who described the incident to the experimenter when he returned, were told that someone else had helped the crying child and that she was fine.

Results indicated that children who saw the adult demonstrate helping behavior by going to the assistance of the "crying child" were more helpful than children who thought he was just checking on another child. In addition, children with whom the adult had been nurturant were much more likely to offer active help rather than just telling the adult about the crying. Even children in the nurturant group who hadn't seen helping modeled were more likely to go to the crying child's aid than were children in the nonnurturant group.

The experimenters suggest that being nurtured gives children the confidence to try to do something in new situations, even if they don't know what to do. Fear of disapproval for doing the wrong thing inhibits children who haven't been nurtured. This experiment underscores the importance of living up to the values we verbalize to children. If we protect, help, and comfort them, and if they see us helping others, they'll learn to help and care for the people in their lives.

showed that adults who are warm and nurturant are the best models. It also showed that seeing helping modeled in real-life situations is more effective than seeing it depicted in fictional situations, such as books, films, or puppet plays (Yarrow, Scott & Waxler, 1973).

A study of kindergarten children showed that the level of nurturance of the adult model is a critical factor in how actively helpful a child is (Staub, 1971). It seems that if the adult is warm and accepting, the child will attempt to help in a situation even if he doesn't know exactly what to do. If an adult is distant and unfriendly, the child is more hesitant, apparently because he's afraid his efforts will be criticized. Both these studies are discussed in detail in Research Focus—How Children Learn to Help Others.

Sharing is another prosocial behavior that's influenced by modeling. One study found that children shared significantly more after they saw a film in which a boy shared his candy with someone who didn't have any (Elliott & Vasta, 1970). Even more sharing occurred among children who saw the film and who then saw the boy rewarded with a toy and heard why he was being

rewarded. In other words, the research showed that the highest level of pro-social behavior resulted from observational learning combined with reinforcement and verbalization.

Although studies show that helping and sharing are both influenced by modeling, sharing is not influenced by the nurturance of the model the way helping is. In fact the more nurturant the relationship with the model, the less likely a child sometimes is to share. This phenomenon is usually explained by pointing to the difference between sharing and helping. Sharing requires some sacrifice on the part of the child. He has to give up part of something he has, and naturally he doesn't want to do this. If he doesn't do the socially accepted thing, the adult model may express disapproval of him. But if he has a warm, accepting relationship with the adult, he may not feel he needs to fear the adult's disapproval. Therefore, he doesn't feel compelled to share.

FIGURE 12-12
Helping and sharing are two forms of prosocial behavior that adults encourage children to learn. A preschooler comforts and helps her brother (left) because she understands his feelings of unhappiness and empathizes with him. She probably has seen her parents behave in a similar way, both with her brother and with her. The girls working together on a project (right) are cooperating and sharing the crayons and stickers. Sharing is often harder for children to learn, perhaps because it involves giving up part of something they have.

Helping is a slightly different matter. Helping often involves empathy—the understanding of someone else's feelings. When we see or hear someone else's distress, we remember what we felt like in similar situations and we feel distress too. Helping or comforting the other person relieves our own feelings of pain or sadness, and thus it's in our own interest to help. A child often doesn't know what to do to help someone in distress, and he may worry that he'll do the wrong thing. But if he has a nurturant relationship with the adult model, he doesn't fear that the adult will ridicule or disapprove of his attempts. He will show the initiative Erikson sees as important to develop at this stage, initiative without fear of making a mistake (Grusec & Skubinski, 1970; Staub, 1971, 1975).

If this explanation is correct, nurturance has the same general effect on children in both helping and sharing situations: It encourages them to act in their own best interest without fear of consequences. The difference is that helping is usually in the child's own interest; sharing is not.

How should parents and teachers act, then? If they're nurturant, children learn to help others in distress, but they don't learn to share. Luckily, the conditions in the experiments were a little different from real life. The children in the studies never expected to see the experimenters again, and they could act just as they wished at the moment (Baumrind, 1972). But in their own lives, children have long-term relationships with adults who have definite expectations of them and whose approval is important to them. Parents and teachers show by their consistent encouragement of sharing that this is a behavior they expect children to learn.

LEARNING SELF-CONTROL

Eli, Sam, and Rebecca were trudging along the darkened street in their Halloween costumes behind their dads. It was late and they were cold and tired. The giddy excitement of dressing up and going trick-or-treating was gone, but the pleasure of eating all that candy drove them on toward home.

"Can I eat a piece of my candy, Daddy?" piped up Rebecca.

"No, not now, Becca," Mike replied. "Wait till we get home."

"Just one piece?" she wailed.

He turned around and looked at her. "You know we talked about this before. Your mom and I want to look at all your candy before you eat any. And we want to make sure you don't eat too much tonight. You'll get a stomachache." He turned back and continued his conversation with Sam and Eli's dad.

When they got to their door, Rebecca and Mike said good night to their neighbors. Looking down at his daughter in the porch light, Mike saw that she had chocolate smeared across her face.

"Hey," he said, squatting down in front of her. "I told you not to eat any candy until we got home."

Rebecca looked down at the ground. "I'm sorry, Daddy," she said. "I just couldn't wait. I had to eat one piece."

Rebecca couldn't resist the temptation of eating her Halloween candy, and her dad was disappointed that she couldn't. Developing self-control of all kinds is an important part of the socialization process. When we help young children learn self-control, we give them a stronger foundation for self-control later. With their greater freedom, older children often encounter formidable temptations, including alcohol and drugs. How can the socialization processes we've been discussing be used to support self-control?

Verbal Instruction and Self-Control

Rebecca's dad could have helped her if he'd suggested she think about something else on the way home. "Don't think about the candy or it'll be harder not to eat any," he might have said. "Why don't you see how many jack-o-lanterns you can count? Or we could sing one of your Halloween songs." Distractions and diversions help children control their impulses. In one study children were told they would receive a large reward later if they could forego a

FIGURE 12-13
''You know you can't have a cookie before dinner!'' Self-control is difficult to learn, especially when temptations are visible. This mother could help her daughter resist her impulses by putting the cookie tin out of sight and by diverting her attention, perhaps to a book or game or to a task that would speed up the dinner preparations.

smaller reward immediately (Mischel & Ebbesen, 1970). Children did everything from covering their eyes to making up games with their hands and feet to avoid taking the smaller reward. In another study children were helped to delay taking rewards like pretzel sticks and marshmallows by being told to think about them as little brown logs and white cotton balls or clouds (Mischel & Baker, 1975).

Other researchers gave children a repetitive task to work on to win attractive rewards (Patterson & Mischel, 1976). They created a temptation dilemma for the children by placing a "Mr. Clown Box" in the same room. The clown made noises and friendly comments and lit up to show toys within the box. Children who paid attention to the clown instead of doing the task would lose out on rewards later.

Researchers gave the children two different self-instructional plans to help them resist the temptation to watch the clown. One was a temptation inhibition plan, in which the child's attention was directed away from the clown. The other was a task-facilitation plan, in which the child's attention was directed toward the task. The temptation inhibition plan was more effective in helping the child resist the temptation.

All these studies show that various strategies, ranging from putting the temptation out of sight to thinking about something besides the temptation's desirable characteristics (for example, thinking about candy as rocks), can help children resist temptations. Research has also shown that younger children don't know that these strategies might work (Glucksberg, Krauss & Higgins, 1975; Patterson, 1982). An adult can help preschoolers by stressing the consequences their actions will have (Meichenbaum & Turk, 1976), by consistently modeling resistance, and by helping them think through strategies for dealing with temptations when adult support is needed.

Self-Control in the Long Term

Although many studies have looked at children's self-control as a function of such socialization techniques as modeling, reinforcement, and verbal instruction, other studies have focused on the relationship between self-control and attachment. Correlational studies of the kind described in Chapter 8 have shown that children who were securely attached as infants are especially persistent in working on difficult or frustrating tasks, another aspect of self-control. In one such study (Arends, 1984, cited in Sroufe, 1990), 3-year-olds with secure attachment histories clearly remained on-task more than did anxiously attached preschoolers. They kept "expecting well" in the face of what was actually an impossible task (a "barrier box").

Although some children consistently show more self-control than others, adults should be aware that self-control is strongly influenced by situations. Adults often manage children's environment to minimize the temptations in it. Parents keep cookies and candy out of sight until they want children to have some. Teachers closely monitor students during exams. These are wise practices, because even adults are apt to yield when social controls and external sanctions are absent. We should "discard any simplistic notion that a person's internal moral standards persist unchanged through life without environmental support," writes one observer, "and accept the fact that internalized standards are vulnerable to external pressure and temptations" (Hoffman, 1984, p. 307). This is not to say that we should give up on supporting internal controls. Rather we should realize that *both* internal and external controls have a role to play when children—or adults—face difficult situations.

A SUMMARY STUDY: SOCIAL-EMOTIONAL COMPETENCE IN PRESCHOOLERS

A recent study has provided an interesting summary of some of the socialization processes we've been considering. The researchers hypothesized that children who show prosocial and nonaggressive social behavior, assertiveness, and a lack of sadness in preschool have a previous history of positive socialization with their mothers (Denham, Renwick & Holt, 1991). To test their hypothesis, they observed and rated the interactions in mother-child pairs as they performed a variety of play/teaching tasks.

The researchers thought that positive social and emotional functioning would be associated with a mother who (1) focuses her child on the task (using such methods as good verbal instruction, positive reinforcement, and modeling), (2) supports the child's attempts at both autonomy and mastery (using positive attribution and reinforcement), and (3) shows positive emotional responsiveness rather than anger. The observers rated these three groups of variables along with the preschooler's corresponding orientation to the task, autonomy, and positive emotion while doing the task.

Their findings confirmed their hypothesis: The mother's task orientation, allowance of autonomy, and positive emotion predicted the preschooler's social-emotional competence, as rated by her teacher. The researchers also found that it was generally the mothers who "led" interaction and "whose interactional characteristics uniquely predicted children's peer competence" (p. 247). They also found specific relationships between mother and child characteristics. The mother's task orientation—her pleasant structuring of the session—buffered the child from appearing sad in the preschool classroom. The mother's support of autonomy predicted assertiveness and contributed to the child's positive social behavior in the classroom. Positive maternal emotion predicted assertiveness in the child, and maternal anger predicted nonassertiveness. Overall, we see that the socialization processes of instruction, reinforcement, and modeling, in combination with emotional attachment, help make a preschooler prosocial, nonaggressive, assertive, and happy.

This study and others like it are important not only because they give us information about what early influences shape the behavior of the preschooler but also because they point out how the aggressive and prosocial skills learned during the preschool years shape the child's later interactions. These skills are precisely the ones that will determine the kind of environment the child will help create for herself in the future.

This view, with its focus on reciprocally interacting systems, is supported by both social learning and attachment theorists. The social learning theorist proposes that appropriate child care in infancy produces social skills in children that are further reinforced by later positive interactions with parents, teachers, and peers. The attachment theorist suggests that sociable attachment behaviors learned in infancy later evoke positive responses from others, confirming the preschooler's internal working models of herself and others as good and lovable. Similarly, both theorists suggest long-term—though not irreversible—reciprocal effects when early experience goes wrong. Children then learn social skills and internal working models that later evoke negative responses from others, reinforcing bad behavior and confirming their models

FIGURE 12-14
Early experiences in which a
child learns that she is good
and lovable provide the basis
for positive social and emotional functioning. Through her
nurturance, interest, and
encouragement, this mother is
helping her daughter become
a happy, competent person.

of themselves as unlovable. Social learning and attachment theorists both
emphasize the importance of early childhood experiences in shaping children
who in turn produce environments that help them remain the kind of social
and emotional beings they already are. Early behaviors tend to maintain themselves, unless there is a major change in the significant figures in a child's life.

OVERVIEW

Most young preschoolers are interested in other
children and eager to play with them, but they
don't have much of a sense of how to make things
work. They may grab toys from other children, or
they may try to hoard all the blocks or play dough.
They may bring a new or special toy from home to
show at preschool and then not be able to let anyone else play with it. They may destroy someone
else's toy, or they may take it home without asking.
Sharing, helping, playing together amicably, settling disputes with words, and controlling
impulses to do what they know they shouldn't are

some of the behaviors children learn in the course of being socialized by attentive parents during the preschool years. By the end of this important and busy social period, they'll have a grasp of many of the skills they'll need to handle the increasingly complex social situations of middle childhood and adolescence. At age 6, they aren't yet completely "civilized," but they're well beyond their comparatively primitive social gestures of just a few years earlier.

CHAPTER REVIEW

SOCIALIZATION PROCESSES

- Currently favored methods of socialization are based largely on both learning and social learning theory.
- The three main socialization processes are verbal instruction, reinforcement, punishment, and extinction; and observational learning.
- The effect of the socialization process depends on the child's attachment relationship with his parents, his level of cognitive development, and his temperament.
- The effects of divorce depend on the family conflict involved, the child's age, and the time or stage of adjustment after the divorce. The effects are generally most disruptive when conflict related to the divorce is great, the divorce is recent, and the child is a preschooler.
- In verbal instruction children are told what behaviors are desirable. Verbal instruction can also be used for attributing positive characteristics to children when they're behaving well.
- Exhortation is a type of verbal communication in which adults tell children what they want them to do, either using power assertion or induction. Verbal instruction combined with reinforcement and modeling is more effective than verbal instruction alone in motivating children to behave in a desired way.
- Reinforcement occurs when a response increases the likelihood that a child will respond the same way again in the same or a similar situation. Socialization is fostered when children receive positive reinforcement for their desirable behaviors.
- Punishment decreases the likelihood that a child will respond the same way again. Some punishments add stimuli to the environment (such as a spanking); others remove stimuli from the environment (such as time out), a process also known as response cost.

- Extinction involves arranging the environment so the child receives no reinforcement at all for his behavior.
- Reinforcement of behavior incompatible with misbehavior is generally considered the best learning method for socializing children. Extinction is difficult to use, since it's not always possible to ignore a child's misbehavior. Punishment has many disadvantages.
- Physical punishment can reduce a child's initiative and drive; make him timid and fearful; restrict him to a few limited responses in difficult social situations; and create hostility between him and the punishing adult.
- The most serious problem with physical punishment is that it can lead to child abuse.
- Physical punishment models aggressive behavior. A positive correlation exists between aggression in children and the use of physical punishment by the parent.
- The most effective way to discipline children is to use induction—reasoning about how their behavior affects others and how they can change it in positive ways.
- In observational learning, children observe how adults act and then imitate their actions. When an adult demonstrates a behavior, we say the adult is modeling that behavior. Children are more likely to imitate a model who is nurturant and helpful and whom the child perceives to be like himself.
- Children's behavior is influenced by their level of social cognition, the values they've been taught, the socialization methods their parents have used, and genetic and biological factors, including temperament. No single factor explains how a child behaves.

AGGRESSION: HOW IT'S LEARNED, HOW IT'S CONTROLLED

- Toddlers and young preschoolers tend to use more physical aggression than older preschoolers and school-age children, who tend to use more verbal aggression; the younger groups use more instrumental aggression, which is implemented to obtain a desired object or privilege.

- Some children seem to be more volatile and to have poorer impulse control than others, but most aggression is learned.
- Children are reinforced for aggression when their aggressive behavior gets them what they want. Aggression sometimes increases when children are brought together in a group for the first time.
- Inattentive parents of very aggressive children tend to reward aggressive behaviors by giving up their demands.
- Severe physical punishment is associated with very high levels of aggression in children, probably due to the combined effects of modeling and hostility.
- Time out can be an effective punishment, but it has to be used appropriately and moderately to minimize the child's loss of self-esteem.
- Much aggressive behavior is learned through obser-

vation. Aggression observed in the family includes physical punishment, verbal abuse, violence between spouses, and violence among siblings.
- Correlational studies reveal that all children, regardless of age, level of intelligence, or socioeconomic status, act more aggressively after they watch very violent TV programs. Experimental studies show that watching violent TV shows is causally related to children's aggression.
- Preschoolers don't have the cognitive ability to understand violence on TV or its consequences, nor can they distinguish between real and nonreal events depicted on TV.
- In the long run, children who watch a lot of violence on TV seem to become desensitized to it and accept aggressive behavior.

PROSOCIAL BEHAVIOR

- One of the best ways to discourage aggression is to model prosocial behavior—behavior that benefits others besides oneself, such as helping, sharing, comforting, and cooperating.
- Reinforcement promotes prosocial behavior by recognizing it and making the child want to attempt it again. Punishment of antisocial behavior is not an effective way to teach prosocial behavior.
- Verbal reinforcement of prosocial behavior helps children understand why their behavior was desirable.
- Children also learn prosocial behavior by observation

and imitation. Effective models are warm and nurturing and demonstrate prosocial behavior in real-life situations.
- Nurturant models make children more likely to help others but less likely to share with others, apparently because in each case, the child feels free to act in her own best interest. Adults have to make it clear that sharing is necessary and expected in many situations.
- Studies have shown that the best way to teach prosocial behavior is through a combination of modeling, reinforcement, and verbalization.

LEARNING SELF-CONTROL

- Learning to exercise self-control is important, especially in adolescence and adulthood, when people face potentially dangerous temptations.
- Adults can help children use diversions and distractions to control their impulses. They can guide the children's thoughts, redirect their actions, or remove the temptation from view.
- Adults can help children by explaining the consequences of their behaviors and by working out strat-

egies of resistance with them. The more internal control a child has acquired from responsive parenting, the more likely he is to be able to resist a temptation when external controls are absent.
- Both attachment theory and social learning theory propose that early experience helps produce children who create experiences that maintain their internal working models and patterns of social behavior.

KEY TERMS

socialization
acute stage of adjustment
    to divorce
transitional stage of
    adjustment to divorce
postdivorce stage of
    adjustment

joint custody
positive attribution
exhortation
reinforcement
punishment
response cost

time out
extinction
aversive stimulus
induction
observational learning
identification

modeling
social cognition
instrumental aggression
intrinsic reinforcement
prosocial behavior
empathy training

SUGGESTIONS FOR FURTHER READING

Eisenberg, N., & Mussen, P. (1989). *The roots of prosocial behavior in children.* New York: Cambridge University Press.
This little book summarizes research on the influences of parents, peers, culture, biology, personal characteristics, situational determinants, and the media on prosocial behavior in children.

Emery, R. (1989). Family violence. *American Psychologist, 44,* 321–328.
This article places child abuse in the context of family violence in general, discussing the development of violence between family members and what to do about it.

Grusec, J. E., & Lytton, H. (1988). *Social development: History, theory, and research.* New York: Springer-Verlag.
This paperback book was written to be used as a text in courses on social development. It has good chapters on socialization and the family, and on the development of self-control and the problem of aggression.

Kagan, J., & Snidman, N. (1991). Temperamental factors in human development. *American Psychologist, 46,* 856–862.
This brief summary describes the stability of children's dispositions to approach or to avoid unfamiliar events, and it explains individual differences in these temperamental characteristics.

Murray, J. P., & Salomon, G. (Eds.) (1984). *The future of children's television.* Boys Town, NB: Boys Town Center.
This book discusses some of the positive potentials of television and some ways in which these potentials might be achieved. Provides a good range of discussion and is fairly easy to read.

Williams, T. M. (Ed.) (1986). *The impact of television: A natural experiment in three communities.* New York: Academic Press.
This book is a report of a field study that probed the effects of the introduction of television. Very interesting reading.

MILESTONES IN PRESCHOOL DEVELOPMENT

AGE	PHYSICAL	COGNITIVE	LANGUAGE	SOCIAL-EMOTIONAL
3 yrs.	Demonstrates true run, with both feet leaving ground Walks upstairs alternating feet Walks downstairs using marked-time climbing Can take most clothes off	Begins to demonstrate pre-operational thinking Knows conventional counting words up to 5 Can solve nesting cup problem by reversing two cups or by insertion	Understands *in, on,* and *under* Speaks in more complete sentences Distinguishes graphics that are writing versus graphics that are pictures Begins to overgeneralize rules for creating verb tenses and plurals	May begin preschool Uses physical aggression more than verbal aggression
3 yrs. 6 mos.	Can hop a few steps on preferred foot Can button large buttons Can put easier clothes on	Can't easily distinguish reality from fantasy Can count five objects before making a partitioning error	Might use syllable hypothesis to create written words Rereads favorite storybooks using picture-governed strategies Often uses scribble-writing	Has difficulty generating alternatives in a conflict situation Will learn aggressive behavior rapidly if these means succeed
4 yrs.	Appears thinner due to longer trunk Can walk a curved line Walks downstairs alternating feet Can gallop Can cut straight line with scissors	Can make a row of objects equal to another row by matching one to one Puts shorter and longer sticks together in piles but can't create a series	Creates questions and negative sentences using correct word arrangement Might create "mock" letters	Watches, on average, 2 to 4 hours of TV per day
4 yrs. 6 mos.	May begin to hold writing tool in finger grip Leans forward more when jumping from a height Can button smaller buttons	Knows conventional counting words up to 15 Is better able to distinguish reality from fantasy	Often reverses letters when writing Understands *beside, between, front,* and *back* Doesn't notice or grasp print conventions	
5 yrs.	Can stop and change direction quickly when running Can hop 8 to 10 steps on one foot	Selects own view in three-mountain task Can create a series through trial and error Creates classes of objects based on a single defining attribute	Understands passive sentences May begin to use invented spellings	Is still poor at self-control; success depends on removal of temptation or diversion by others
5 yrs. 6 mos.	Can connect a zipper on a coat May be able to tie shoes	Can count 20 objects without making a partitioning error	May begin to make print-governed reading attempts with favorite books	Uses more verbal aggression

PRESCHOOL CHILDREN

Serena Cortez was looking for a preschool. Her son had turned 3 in February, and now, in May, he was making headway on toilet training. Serena was expecting another child in the fall, and she wanted a regular, reliable place to take Brian a few mornings a week. Today, she had two appointments, one at the Humpty Dumpty Nursery School, a pre-school for 3-, 4-, and 5-year-olds, the other at Fair Oaks School, a school that started with nursery and went through the eighth grade. Serena had gotten both names from the phone book.

At Humpty Dumpty, she met a young woman leading a group of children in some songs and games in the play yard. "Touch your knees, touch your toes, touch your shoulders, touch your nose," she sang, as the children bent and stretched to find the right part of their anatomy to touch. She invited Brian to join them while Serena went inside to meet Mrs. Wells, the director of the school.

Inside, Serena found the children sitting on the floor playing with blocks and wooden puzzles. Mrs. Wells was working with one child at a table, helping her finish a fabric-covered eyeglasses case.

"These are Mother's Day gifts," she explained to Serena. "I'm working on them individually with the children, so the other children have to play quietly. Usually at this time, I would be reading them a story or helping them do an art project at the tables. You can see the Easter pictures we did last week up on the wall."

When she had finished the project for the day, Mrs. Wells gathered the children together on the floor in front of an easel with a large pad on it. Serena sat down on a pillow with Brian on her lap. Mrs. Wells pointed to a colored square on the pad and said, "Now, what color is this?"

"Orange," called out Brian, "I think it's orange!"

"No, it's not orange," Mrs. Wells said. "Anyone else?"

"Red?"

"No, not red. We did this last week. Doesn't anyone know?"

"Blue? Yellow?"

"Yes, it's yellow. Thank you, Megan."

The lesson went on, and Serena began to feel this school wasn't for her. She wasn't sure what she wanted for Brian, but she didn't think he would be able to sit quietly and answer questions for very long. He was too active and too eager to follow his own interests.

After leaving the Humpty Dumpty Nursery School, Serena drove straight to Fair Oaks. Here, she again found children playing in the yard. A teacher sat on a nearby picnic table watching them. One girl was pounding nails into a log with a hammer, some other children were digging with shovels, some were climbing in trees, some were playing in a play house, some were in the sandbox with the hose running. Inside, Serena found more activities—children painting at easels, dressed up in gowns and high heels, petting a rabbit. At a table, a teacher was helping some children use a food mill to make applesauce for the snack.

"We get them all together for just one activity," one of the teachers explained to Serena. "At 10 o'clock we have juice and a story. That's all they can tolerate at this age. After one story, the children who want to go back to playing can go outside, and children who want to hear a second story can stay. Snack time lasts about 20 to 30 minutes. The rest of the morning they can choose to do whatever they want, either the activity we have for them here at the table—today it was making applesauce—or whatever they create themselves. One day a week we take them to the library, and several times a month we take them on nature walks around the school and the neighborhood."

Serena had to search for Brian after she finished observing the classroom. When she found him at the top of the slide looking completely at home, she realized that this kind of school was going to suit them both.

Serena encountered just two of the many kinds of programs available for preschoolers in this country. Programs vary tremendously in such characteristics as the structure of the day, the content of the curriculum, and the role of the teachers, depending on the theoretical orientation of those who run the programs and the needs of the families and children for whom they're designed. They also vary in cost and method of funding or payment, so that not all programs are available to all families.

In this chapter we discuss the characteristics of these programs and some of the major issues associated with preschool education today. We then treat the assessment and testing of preschoolers, a hotly debated topic right now. How children are tested and evaluated is having profound effects on the very nature of early education in this country. Finally, as in Knowledge in Action: Infants and Toddlers, we discuss living with preschool children—how to make sure they're healthy; how to keep them safe; and how to support their play with toys, books, and games. Together, these topics round out our overall picture of applied knowledge about preschool development.

EDUCATION AND CARE PROGRAMS FOR PRESCHOOL CHILDREN

In 1965 13 percent of all 3- and 4-year-olds in the United States were enrolled in preschool programs. In 1987 the figure had soared to 40 percent (Hymes, 1988). Who are the children who participate in these programs? How do par-

FIGURE 1
These preschoolers have very different experiences than young children did a generation ago. Today, almost half the children in the United States between 3 and 5 years of age participate in organized child care programs.

ents manage to pay for the programs? And what are the programs themselves like? These are some of the questions we address in this section.

Who Are the Children in Preschool? Who Pays for Preschool?

Although many children attend preschool, many more children from economically advantaged families are enrolled in preschool than children from disadvantaged families. In 1987, for example, 67 percent of the children whose family incomes were over $35,000 attended preschool, compared with only 33 percent of those whose incomes were under $10,000 (Children's Defense Fund, 1987). Some publicly funded programs have been introduced to reach children from poorer families who otherwise wouldn't attend preschool. A variety of other programs serve children with special needs, regardless of income level.

PROGRAMS FOR CHILDREN WITH DISABILITIES. One population particularly in need of early educational opportunities consists of children with disabilities. In 1976 Congress passed the Education for All Handicapped Children Act (renamed the Individuals with Disabilities Education Act in 1990), a bill that provided funds to help states pay for the education of all children aged 3 to 18. Under the act, many different programs have been offered to children with different disabling conditions, including hearing and sight impairment, mental retardation, and various kinds of language delays.

Many of these programs resemble preschool programs for ordinary children (described below), but they're adapted to the needs of the children they serve. A major adaptation is the ratio of adults to children. Children with disabilities often need more physical help with routine activities such as eating, dressing, and toileting, and they often need individualized interaction to support language development and social skills. Rather than two teachers for 20 children,

FIGURE 2
Project Head Start attempts to provide an enriched preschool environment for children from economically disadvantaged families. These children are learning about nutrition in a teacher-directed meal-preparation activity in their Head Start class and getting a healthy meal too.

which is considered minimally acceptable in ordinary preschools, these programs may have one teacher for every 6 children, or even one teacher for every 3 children.

Other adaptations include the use of alternative communication systems, such as sign language or Braille, and specially designed equipment and materials for children with motor impairments, such as puzzle pieces with knobs and riding toys with straps or arm pedals. Trained staff know how to position children and provide therapy that helps the children use the motor abilities they do have.

PROGRAMS FOR CHILDREN FROM ECONOMICALLY DISADVANTAGED FAMILIES. Another population in need of early educational opportunities consists of children from economically disadvantaged families. Many of these children attend Project Head Start, the largest of the federally sponsored programs. In 1987 451,000 preschoolers attended Head Start programs, but this was only 16 percent of the 2.5 million children who were estimated to be eligible on the basis of income (Children's Defense Fund, 1987). The government simply hasn't appropriated enough money to fund the programs needed to include all the eligible children. The Human Services Reauthorization Act of 1990 increased the funding of Head Start, and full funding for all eligible 3- to 5-year-olds is to be achieved by 1994 (NAEYC, 1990).

Other kinds of funding for preschools exist as well. When working parents fall below certain income guidelines, some states provide subsidies for full-day preschool programs for their children. Or when parents are enrolled in certain state and federal job-training programs, money often is available for day care for their children. Federal legislation (Child Care and Development Block Grant) passed in 1990 will provide additional funding to the states for child care for low income or welfare-dependent families (NAEYC, 1991).

Employers sometimes provide day care support for employees. This support can take the form of an on-site day care center, a subsidy that helps parents pay for day care, or information and referral services that help parents locate day care resources. The federal tax code also allows deductions for child care costs.

With costs ranging from $4,000 to $10,000 per child per year, day care is out of the reach of many families. As the number of mothers in the work force continues to grow, day care services and their funding are sure to remain major issues for discussion.

Characteristics of Preschool Programs and Issues in Preschool Education

TEACHER-DIRECTED VERSUS CHILD-DIRECTED PROGRAMS. The preschools Serena visited represented two different approaches to education and care for 3-, 4-, and 5-year-olds. The Humpty Dumpty Nursery School tended to take a **teacher-directed** approach, with teachers giving the children lessons with specific content for most of the day. Programs with this orientation attempt to teach skills like counting to 10, naming alphabet letters and colors, and recognizing geometric shapes through recitation, repetition, and drill. The Fair Oaks School, on the other hand, tended to take a **child-directed** approach, with children playing freely for most of the day in such activities as block building, water play, and story reading. In programs like this, very little, if any, specific content is presented, and specific skills are not isolated or taught directly by the teachers.

Had Serena looked further, she might have encountered a third kind of program, one in which the day was divided into separate, alternating periods of teacher-directed and child-directed activities. Ideal programs are often judged to be those in which neither extreme dominates and balance is achieved in an integrated way, rather than by dividing the day into different segments. The day is filled with well-planned but child-appropriate activities around which both teachers and children interact. (For a description of such activities for 4- and 5-year-olds, see Research Focus—Developmentally Appropriate Practices in Programs for 4- and 5-Year-Olds.)

FIGURE 3
In a teacher-directed preschool program, children participate in organized activities with specific educational aims (left). By sitting in a circle for a meeting or game, these children of the Jemez, New Mexico, Pueblo are learning to listen, cooperate with the group, wait for a turn, and take direction from the teacher. In a child-directed program, children choose what they want to do from a variety of possible activities (right). The children feeding and observing the class parakeet are learning to take the initiative, make their own decisions, and cooperate with playmates. Parents make decisions about programs on the basis of their personal beliefs and values, their child's needs, and simply what's available in the community.

RESEARCH FOCUS

Developmentally Appropriate Practices in Programs for 4- and 5-Year-Olds

As we've seen, preschool children don't think the same way older children do. It's not surprising, then, that the kind of programming that educators prepare for school-age children is often inappropriate for very young children. In response to concerns about educational practices and goals, the National Association for the Education of Young Children (NAEYC), the largest professional organization concerned with early education, developed a position statement on appropriate practices for 4- and 5-year-olds (NAEYC, 1986). The following excerpts are taken directly from that statement.

Component	APPROPRIATE Practice	INAPPROPRIATE Practice
Curriculum goals	• Experiences are provided that meet children's needs and stimulate learning in all developmental areas—physical, social, emotional, and intellectual. • Each child is viewed as a unique person with an individual pattern and timing of growth and development. The curriculum and adults' interaction are responsive to individual differences in ability and interests. Different levels of ability, development, and learning styles are expected, accepted, and used to design appropriate activities. • Interactions and activities are designed to develop children's self-esteem and positive feelings toward learning.	• Experiences are narrowly focused on the child's intellectual development without recognition that all areas of a child's development are interrelated. • Children are evaluated only against a predetermined measure, such as a standardized group norm or adult standard of behavior. All are expected to perform the same tasks and achieve the same narrowly defined, easily measured skills. • Children's worth is measured by how well they conform to rigid expectations and perform on standardized tests.
Teaching strategies	• Teachers prepare the environment for children to learn through active exploration and interaction with adults, other children, and materials. • Children select many of their own activities from among a variety of learning areas the teacher prepares, including dramatic play, blocks, science, math, games and puzzles, books, recordings, art, and music. • Children are expected to be physically and mentally active. Children choose from among activities the teacher has set up or the children spontaneously initiate. • Children work individually or in small, informal groups most of the time. • Children are provided concrete learning activities with materials and people relevant to their own life experiences. • Teachers move among groups and individuals to facilitate children's involvement with materials and activities by asking questions, offering suggestions, or adding more complex materials or ideas to a situation. • Teachers accept that there is often more than one right answer. Teachers recognize that children learn from self-directed problem solving and experimentation.	• Teachers use highly structured, teacher-directed lessons almost exclusively. • The teacher directs all the activity, deciding what children will do and when. The teacher does most of the activity for the children, such as cutting shapes or performing steps in an experiment. • Children are expected to sit down, watch, be quiet, and listen or do paper-and-pencil tasks for inappropriately long periods of time. A major portion of time is spent passively sitting, listening, and waiting. • Large group, teacher-directed instruction is used most of the time. • Workbooks, ditto sheets, flashcards, and other similarly structured abstract materials dominate the curriculum. • Teachers dominate the environment by talking to the whole group most of the time and telling children what to do. • Children are expected to respond correctly with one right answer. Rote memorization and drill are emphasized.
Guidance of socio-emotional development	• Teachers facilitate the development of self-control in children by using positive guidance techniques such as modeling and encouraging expected behavior, redirecting children to a more acceptable activity, and setting clear limits. Teachers' expectations match and respect children's developing capabilities. • Children are provided many opportunities to develop social skills such as cooperating, helping, negotiating, and talking with the person	• Teachers spend a great deal of time enforcing rules, punishing unacceptable behavior, demeaning children who misbehave, making children sit and be quiet, or refereeing disagreements. • Children work individually at desks or tables most of the time or listen to teacher directions in the total group. Teachers intervene to

Component	APPROPRIATE Practice	INAPPROPRIATE Practice
	involved to solve interpersonal problems. Teachers facilitate the development of positive social skills at all times.	resolve disputes or enforce classroom rules and schedules.
Language development and literacy	• Children are provided many opportunities to see how reading and writing are useful before they are instructed in letter names, sounds, and word identification. Basic skills develop when they are meaningful to children. An abundance of these types of activities is provided to develop language and literacy through meaningful experience: listening to and reading stories and poems; taking field trips; dictating stories; seeing classroom charts and other print in use; participating in dramatic play and other experiences requiring communication; talking informally with other children and adults; and experimenting with writing by drawing, copying, and inventing their own spelling.	• Reading and writing instruction stresses isolated skill development, such as recognizing single letters, reciting the alphabet, singing the alphabet song, coloring within predefined lines, or being instructed in correct formation of letters on a printed line.
Cognitive development	• Children develop understanding of concepts about themselves, others, and the world around them through observation, interacting with people and real objects, and seeking solutions to concrete problems. Learnings about math, science, social studies, health, and other content areas are all integrated through meaningful activities such as those when children build with blocks; measure sand, water, or ingredients for cooking; observe changes in the environment; work with wood and tools; sort objects for a purpose; explore animals, plants, water, wheels, and gears; sing and listen to music from various cultures; and draw, paint, and work with clay. Routines are followed that help children keep themselves healthy and safe.	• Instruction stresses isolated skill development through memorization and rote, such as counting, circling an item on a worksheet, memorizing facts, watching demonstrations, drilling with flashcards, or looking at maps. Children's cognitive development is seen as fragmented in content areas such as math, science, or social studies, and times are set aside to concentrate on each area.
Physical development	• Children have daily opportunities to use large muscles, including running, jumping, and balancing. Outdoor activity is planned daily so children can develop large muscle skills, learn about outdoor environments, and express themselves freely and loudly. • Children have daily opportunities to develop small muscle skills through play activities such as pegboards, puzzles, painting, cutting, and other similar activities.	• Opportunity for large muscle activity is limited. Outdoor time is limited because it is viewed as interfering with instructional time or, if provided, is viewed as recess (a way to get children to use up excess energy), rather than an integral part of children's learning environment. • Small motor activity is limited to writing with pencils, or coloring predrawn forms, or similar structured lessons.
Aesthetic development	• Children have daily opportunities for aesthetic expression and appreciation through art and music. Children experiment and enjoy various forms of music. A variety of art media are available for creative expression, such as easel and finger painting and clay.	• Art and music are provided only when time permits. Art consists of coloring predrawn forms, copying an adult-made model of a product, or following other adult-prescribed directions.
Motivation	• Children's natural curiosity and desire to make sense of their world are used to motivate them to become involved in learning activities.	• Children are required to participate in all activities to obtain the teacher's approval, to obtain extrinsic rewards like stickers or privileges or to avoid punishment.

SOURCE: National Association for the Education of Young Children.

FIGURE 4
If every child could have the kind of individual attention and affirmation this boy is getting from his Head Start teacher, very few children would fail. But limited financial and human resources mean that the teacher-child ratio in most preschool programs is more like 10:1.

WHICH APPROACH IS BETTER? Because preschool programs like Project Head Start were begun specifically to improve later school achievement among children from economically disadvantaged families, many people have followed the progress and achievement of these children and formed opinions about what and how preschool children should be taught. Overall, opinion is divided on which approach—teacher-directed or child-directed—is superior. Research results have also been mixed. For example, some studies have shown that boys enrolled in nondidactic (noninstructional, or child-directed) preschool programs did better in sixth and eighth grades than boys who had been enrolled in didactic (teacher-directed) preschools. Girls enrolled in didactic programs did better in math but not in reading in sixth and eighth grades (Miller & Bizzell, 1983).

Other studies comparing didactic and nondidactic programs showed little difference in long-term academic achievement but significant differences in social outcomes. Juvenile delinquency rates, for example, were lower for children who had been in nondidactic programs (Schweinhart, Weikart & Larner, 1986). Many preschool programs, including Project Head Start, have not been able to show many long-term effects on achievement scores, but high-quality programs, most of them nondidactic, have demonstrated effectiveness in reducing retention in the same grade in elementary school, placement in special education classes, teenage pregnancy, high school dropout rates, and welfare dependence (Zigler, 1985; Schweinhart, Weikart & Larner, 1986).

OBSTACLES TO DEVELOPING THE MOST APPROPRIATE PRESCHOOL PROGRAMS. The dilemma in developing preschool programs may be that although young children *can* learn a great many academic skills—in mathematics, reading, and writing, for example—they require a personalized, interactive context and the opportunity to use the skills they acquire if they are to stay interested and truly understand what they're taught (Schickedanz et al., 1990). It's the difference between teaching children to read numbers by rote from flashcards and helping them learn numbers by playing a game like Chutes and Ladders or setting the tables for snack. In the former, the skill is isolated and drilled; in the latter, the skill is embedded in a meaningful situation where its usefulness can be appreciated.

The challenge in the years ahead will be to devise meaningful ways to embed academic skills in child-directed activities and daily routines at preschools, especially for children from economically disadvantaged families. At the same time, preschool teachers will need to learn styles of interaction that maintain child-initiated activities and extend children's learning. (For examples, see Schickedanz, 1986, and Kamii, 1985). (For a discussion of a population with unique educational needs, see Special Education Focus—Young Gifted Children.)

ASSESSING THE PRESCHOOL CHILD

In March, Ellen Bernstein took her son to her neighborhood elementary school to register for the kindergarten class that would start the following September. There, a staff member took Andrew into a testing room and screened him for entrance to kindergarten. When they were finished, the staff member told Ellen that Andrew would need to be tested further. "He doesn't seem to have some of the readiness skills he'll need in kindergarten," she explained. "You can schedule an appointment for another test right over there."

Ellen was surprised. Andrew seemed to her to be a bright child. He could think problems through quite well for his age, and he could remember things that had happened to him in the past in minute detail. He had memorized several of his favorite storybooks and could "read" them without missing a word. Lately, he'd been asking his parents what specific words said, and he could read many signs on the street and in stores.

As Ellen waited to schedule the appointment, she thought further about Andrew's abilities. He knew the names of the dinosaurs and which were carnivores and which

FIGURE 5
Fine motor control is still precarious for kindergartners, and patience has its limits. Drastic action may sometimes be required to deal with the frustration.

SPECIAL EDUCATION FOCUS

Young Gifted Children*

At the age of 3, Zachary spent hours experimenting with the various types of equipment on the science table at his pre-school. Time after time, he observed the ball rolling through the elaborate structure of tubes and tunnels. He tried to understand what was happening and why. He used his problem-solving skills in social situations, too. When Darrel stumbled into Zachary's elaborate car and track setup in the block corner, Zachary simply moved the setup out of Darrel's way. Then he helped Darrel begin his own car and track setup nearby.

Four-year-old Margaret sat on a couch in her nursery school listening intently to a prerecorded story on headphones. She held a book in her lap, and her eyes followed the words on the page as she listened. Later, she read the book to a friend. Margaret could make up a story by herself and write it down with very little unconventional spelling. When she saw another child struggling to copy a letter from the chart on the wall, she helped him, saying, "You make a capital A like this."

On the first day of school, Miles bounded into the first-grade classroom reporting that he had a telescope at home to watch the stars and that he and his mom kept track of the birds that visited their bird feeder. Tests revealed that Miles had already mastered the first-grade curriculum. His teacher modified the classroom program for him and allowed him to work independently at his own level. During the year, Miles wrote and illustrated a book about birds in the area, set up a bird-feeding station outside the classroom window, and made presentations about his interests to his classmates. He occasionally tutored some of his classmates, often led small group activities, and enjoyed the rough-and-tumble play on the playground, just as the other 6-year-olds did.

WHAT ARE GIFTED CHILDREN LIKE?

Zachary, Margaret, and Miles have many of the characteristics of gifted children. These children often have large vocabular-

*Written by Dr. Carol Story, Johnson State College, Johnson, VT.

Enrichment is often the best way to support and challenge gifted children

ies and long attention spans; they're sometimes early readers; they exhibit curiosity; they attend to detail; and they have good memories. They often have many mature, in-depth interests, a strong sense of right and wrong, and highly developed imaginations that allow them to create stories and songs. They may be unusually sensitive to changes in their environments, have a heightened awarenss of their own uniqueness, and make mental connections between the past and the future. Gifted children are also sensitive to other children's feelings and needs, and they're often effective problem solvers in both social and academic situations.

Two different formal definitions of giftedness in young children are often recognized:

• Gifted children are those youngsters possessing intellectual ability, scholastic aptitude, creativity, leadership, talent

were herbivores. When they played board games together, he could read the dice and count out the correct number of spaces. He also knew many basic sums. Ellen shook her head and made the appointment.

Later, she talked to a neighbor whose child was a kindergartner that year. "They think Andrew might not be ready for kindergarten, Terry," she told him. "I'm not sure why. What does Jennifer do in kindergarten anyway?"

"Jennifer brings home a lot of papers she's done," Terry told her. "They practice writing numbers and the letters of the alphabet. They do some simple addition problems, and they have papers about the sounds the different letters make. That's the kind of thing they seem to be doing."

"Oh," said Ellen. "I didn't realize kindergarten was so—so formal and academic. I thought it was more a social experience, where kids learned to be together and like school. Andrew is just beginning to write his name. He can't really hold a pencil the right way yet, so it's hard for him to write."

"Maybe that was the problem," suggested Terry.

in the visual and performing arts, and/or psychomotor ability (Marland, 1972).

- Gifted children are those who apply above-average ability, creativity, and task commitment to a special area of interest (Renzulli, 1978).

HOW ARE GIFTED CHILDREN IDENTIFIED?
Parents and teachers who think a young child is gifted can confirm their judgment by observations and rating scales. A checklist for parents is the Things My Child Likes to Do Checklist (Delisle, 1979). A commonly used observational scale for teachers is the Renzulli-Smith Early Childhood Checklist (Renzulli & Smith, 1981). Teachers are also instructed to note which children direct activities or are followed by other children, which ones exhibit the characteristics listed previously, and which children rank at high levels on developmental scales (Cohen & Stern, 1983; Beaty, 1986).

Sometimes, children demonstrate their giftedness by producing a tangible product, such as a book they've written or a block structure they've made. Other times, giftedness is recognized through intelligence or creativity tests. The most widely used tests for identifying gifted children are the Stanford-Binet Intelligence Test and the Wechsler Intelligence Scale for Children-III. Creativity measures include the Torrance Test of Thinking Creatively in Action and Movement (Torrance, 1981) and the Wallach and Kogan Creative Battery (Wallach & Kogan, 1965). Parents and teachers have to use these and other tests of creativity with caution because questions have been raised about their validity. Experts recommend that adults use a variety of tests, along with observation, to identify gifted children.

HOW SHOULD YOUNG GIFTED CHILDREN BE EDUCATED?
When children have been identified as gifted, parents and teachers can help them develop their individual potential in various ways. One of the more common ways is grade accel-eration—the child enters second grade immediately after kindergarten, for example. This option is appropriate only when a child is emotionally and socially mature enough to cope well with older classmates. When a child is socially immature, part-time acceleration is sometimes a good compromise. The child participates with the older students for certain parts of the day, perhaps for math or science instruction, and spends the rest of the day with children the same age. Grade acceleration is rarely an option for a gifted preschooler, because most school districts require that children entering kindergarten be a certain age. Only after a child has entered kindergarten will some school districts begin to consider advanced placement.

Besides grade acceleration and part-time grade acceleration, a third way to meet the needs of gifted children is enrichment. Here, the teacher individualizes the program, broadening and deepening the content of the curriculum, to support the child's special skills and interests and provide intellectual stimulation. Miles's teacher, for example, provided an enrichment program. Because classroom teachers often don't have the time or resources to develop such programs, some school districts provide consultants the teachers can call on for assistance in designing enrichment programs. This resource is rare in school systems, however, and practically nonexistent in preschools, which are almost never part of public school districts.

In many cases, teachers and parents have to work together to provide stimulation and challenges for a young gifted child. Very often it's the parents, especially during the preschool years, who provide the child with an enriched environment. Activities outside of school can include music lessons, special courses at museums, and heavy use of libraries and other community resources. Within the family, the gifted child and his parents can explore books, games, and activities together; attend plays and concerts; travel and sight-see; learn about other peoples and cultures; and adopt an open and curious attitude toward the world, enabling the child to perceive it as a source of endless interest.

"Maybe. They did ask him to write his name. But, you know, there are so many things he can do. It doesn't seem fair to keep him out of school another year just because he can't sit and write the way some of the other kids can."

"But it might be hard on him," Terry said. "If they make the kids sit and write, and he can't do it very well, he could start to think there's something wrong with him, or he might start to hate school."

"That's true, but it does seem unfair. He's really eager to learn, and he wants to be with other children. Why can't they teach him how to hold a pencil correctly? They used to do things like that. Now it seems they want the children to know how to do everything before they even get to school!"

Ellen had come face to face with some of the issues related to the use of tests with very young children. These assessment and screening tools are controversial—and widely used. Since many of them tap knowledge and skills thought to be related to academic functioning, they're often used to assess preschoolers for kindergarten and kindergartners for first grade. Others, including Piagetian tasks, are used in research studies to determine the correlates of various behaviors or the effectiveness of various treatments. Before discussing the concerns many people have about these tests, let's briefly examine some of the most widely used assessment instruments.

Assessment Instruments Used with Preschoolers

Three of the most common tests for preschoolers are the Metropolitan Readiness Tests, the Concepts about Print Test, and the Caldwell Preschool Inventory. A fourth category of test is the Piagetian tasks. Each of these yields information about a different aspect of children's intelligence and is used for a somewhat different purpose.

THE METROPOLITAN READINESS TESTS. The Metropolitan Readiness Tests (Nurss & McGauvran, 1986) are used to assess children's cognitive understandings and knowledge. There are two levels of tests, one simpler and given at the beginning and middle of the kindergarten year, the other more complex and given at the end of kindergarten or the beginning of first grade. Each test is divided into several subtests. Sample items from some of the subtests are shown in Figure 6.

Level 1 assesses children's knowledge in the areas of: auditory memory, rhyming, letter recognition, visual matching, school language and listening, and quantitative language.

The subtests in level 2 are similar but more complex. They assess understanding of beginning consonants, sound-letter correspondence, visual matching, finding patterns, school language, listening, quantitative concepts, and quantitative operations.

THE CONCEPTS ABOUT PRINT TEST. The Concepts about Print Test, also known as the Sand Test, was developed in 1976 for use with kindergarten children and children entering first grade (Clay, 1976). The only material required is a picture book entitled *Sand*. The tester reads the book to the child and asks questions about it. From the child's answers, the tester can tell if the child knows the front of the book from the back; that the reader reads print rather than pictures; that print is scanned from left to right and from top to bottom; how to match a spoken word with a printed word; the difference between a letter and a word; and that print is incorrect when it is inverted. As we saw in Chapter 11, these are some of the understandings about print that seem to be related to good reading achievement in later school years.

THE CALDWELL PRESCHOOL INVENTORY. The Preschool Inventory (Caldwell, 1970) is used with individual children between the ages of 3 and 6 to assess the effectiveness of educational programs like Project Head Start. Children are tested on three basic kinds of abilities: (1) concept activation ("Copy a circle," "Count to five."); (2) personal-social responsiveness ("What is your name?" "Show me your neck."); and (3) vocabulary ("What color is this crayon?").

THE PIAGETIAN TASKS. Piagetian tasks are often used to assess children's intellectual development. For example, a child may be administered the conservation

FIGURE 6
Sample items from the Metropolitan Readiness Test, Level 1.

AUDITORY MEMORY

A. Now put your finger on the little black BIRD. Close your eyes. Don't
peek! Listen. CHAIR CUP. Open your eyes. Mark the right box.

B. Now put your finger on the little black MOON. Close your eyes.
Remember not to peek. As soon as I say the words, open your eyes and
mark. Don't wait for me to tell you to open your eyes. Listen. SPOON
BALL STAR.

RHYMING

A. Put your finger by the top row. The pictures are MILK, LEAF, TIE,
BIKE. Listen to the word I say: LIKE. Mark the one that rhymes with
LIKE, the one that rhymes with LIKE.

LETTER RECOGNITION

A. Put your finger on the little black SPOON at the beginning of the top
row. Look at the letters in this row. Mark the S . . . the S.

VISUAL MATCHING

B. Put your finger on the little black CUP. Look at what is in the red box.
Then mark the box that has in it just what is in the red box.

[red box]

*SOURCE: Nurss, J. R. & McGauvran, M. E. (1986). Metropolitan Readiness Assessment Program (5th ed.).
Orlando, FL: Harcourt Brace Jovanovich, The Psychological Corporation.*

of number task we described in Chapter 10. Required materials are simply a number of discrete objects, such as pennies or checkers. Piagetian tasks are always administered to individual children. In groups, children tend to copy what others are doing. Besides, the Piagetian researcher is just as interested in *why* a child does something as in *what* the child does, so individual discussions have to take place.

Issues in Assessing Preschoolers

Now that we've examined some of the common tests, let's return to the issues raised by Ellen Bernstein's experience. She thought Andrew was a bright child, and she wondered if the problems detected by the tests were important ones. This touches on the issue of **validity**—the question of whether a test measures what it says it does and can predict later performance as it claims. Ellen also wondered about the kindergarten curriculum and why it wasn't what it used to be. She wondered too about what the role of kindergarten was, if children were expected to come to school already knowing what she thought they were supposed to teach.

   Ellen may not have known it, but testing itself is the force that often shapes school curricula and policies about entrance to kindergarten. Whether this should be so is one of the most controversial issues in early education today. We turn now to a discussion of this and related issues.

VALIDITY. The younger the child, the more serious is the problem of test validity. Young children are often unfamiliar with testing formats, don't always relate well to strangers in charge of testing, and grow and change rapidly. Their performance on tests also reflects factors other than their intellectual abilities, such as their experiences at home. For example, one child might do poorly on tests at the beginning of kindergarten because she's never been exposed to the

FIGURE 7
What should children learn in kindergarten? Practicing the alphabet will help these children perform well on tests at the end of the year, but if their program focuses only on academic skills, they will miss out on important early experiences. Kindergartners also need time to explore, discover, use their imaginations, and play with other children.

information being tested before, and another child might do poorly because she has learning difficulties. The tests don't distinguish between these two conditions, but the children's long-term outcomes are likely to be very different. The child without exposure is likely to progress quickly, and the child with learning difficulties is likely to have to struggle. Tests given only a year later may yield radically different results than the tests given at the start of kindergarten.

All these factors threaten the validity of testing done to predict future classroom performance. Readiness tests currently used with preschool and kindergarten children don't predict much better than chance. This means the decisions that schools make about entrance to kindergarten and first grade on the basis of tests are about as accurate as decisions they would make by flipping a coin (Peck, McCaig & Sapp, 1988).

THE INFLUENCE OF TESTING ON THE EARLY CHILDHOOD CURRICULUM. With a strong emphasis on basic skills and test scores in the elementary grades these days, many early childhood programs have started to focus almost exclusively on teaching the information and skills that are contained in readiness and achievement test items. In other words, tests are determining the curriculum, and exploratory activities and play are being squeezed out.

As we discussed in Chapter 11, many experts think that young children need experiences that are broadly based, content rich, interesting, and likely to involve thinking and problem solving. Experiences provided in programs that are "test driven" are unlikely to have these characteristics. A recent report recommended that schools' early childhood classrooms—preschool through third grade—be under the direction of an early childhood coordinator rather than the elementary school curriculum director. This would protect the youngest children from the wave of testing that has swept the schools. Although testing and accountability may be appropriate for older elementary and high school students, the narrow curriculum and high pressure associated with such practices are not appropriate for younger children, in the opinion of the National Early Education Task Force of the National Association of State Boards of Education. Using didactic methods to teach abstract material is an educational approach unsuitable to the needs and abilities of preschool children (Shultz, 1988).

Andrew, for example, knew quite a lot about alphabet letters, number facts, and counting, but his poor fine-motor skills prevented him from expressing his knowledge in ways required and accepted by the school curriculum. Teachers free to do so could easily devise many experiences for Andrew that would enable him to thrive in kindergarten. Later, when his fine motor skills caught up with his intellectual abilities—perhaps in first grade—he could begin to do more written work. But the teachers in his school were probably under pressure to produce good written test scores in their classes. They wanted to make sure that all the children would be able to perform well on the tests before they were admitted to kindergarten. This is the narrowing of curriculum approaches and content in the service of testing that worries many experts.

WHAT SHOULD THE SCHOOL'S MISSION BE? One of the most controversial aspects of testing is the use of test results to delay a child's entry into kindergarten. If a child doesn't do well on readiness tests, the school may recommend that the

FIGURE 8
Some kindergartens use workbooks and pencil-and-paper activities to teach math and language skills (top). Others use manipulatives and hands-on experiences (right). Evidence indicates that kindergartners, like younger children, gain deeper understandings and better problem-solving skills from hands-on experiences.

child be kept out of school for an additional year. Critics say that instead of doing this, schools should individualize their programs more and adjust their curricula to meet the needs of a wider range of children. But schools are under pressure to display good scores on achievement tests, and their "first line of defense" is to exclude children from kindergarten who don't appear to have a good start on mastering skills that show up on tests. The result is that children who could benefit from school are kept out for a longer period of time.

In many parts of the country during the mid- to late 1980s, school districts changed their age requirements for entrance to kindergarten so that children would be older when they started school. Districts that previously required children to be 5 years old by January 1 moved the date up to December 1 or even September 1. In a related trend, some parents, especially those who could afford an additional year of preschool, were voluntarily delaying their child's entry into kindergarten to give him (the child is more often a boy) the maturity to handle the academic material. Again, critics fault schools for both of these trends, charging that the heavy reliance on test scores is fueling narrow academic goals, unnecessary competitiveness and tension among children and parents, and inappropriate pressure on very young children. Like the issue of funding for preschool programs, the issue of testing is likely to be debated for years to come.

LIVING WITH THE PRESCHOOL CHILD

"Get down off the couch, right now! Running and jumping aren't safe in the living room! Go out in the yard if you want to play like that!"

Sentiments like this are familiar to anyone who lives with or cares for preschoolers. They possess boundless energy and the agility and mobility to use it. Their parents and teachers have their hands full trying to keep them healthy, safe, and happily engaged in constructive activities. These are the topics we turn to next.

Ensuring the Health of the Preschooler

Two general areas of preschoolers' health—the communicable health problems parents and teachers may see and the eating and sleeping patterns young children are likely to have—deserve discussion.

COMMUNICABLE HEALTH PROBLEMS. Illness in the preschooler is fairly frequent but usually not very serious. The highest incidence of illness in childhood occurs during the preschool years, perhaps because this is the age when many children first interact frequently with other children in groups, and also perhaps because children interact very directly at this age. They play together closely, share toys, and often sneeze and cough without covering their mouths and noses. Any contagious diseases are quickly passed on to other children.

Three very contagious and somewhat troublesome health problems commonly seen in preschoolers are head lice, ear infections, and chicken pox. Although they're very different in some ways, all are caused by an outside agent, so we discuss them together here.

Head lice are tiny, wingless insects. The female lays eggs, known as nits, on the shaft of the hair near the scalp. When the eggs hatch, the lice that emerge quickly burrow into the scalp to get a meal of blood from their host, leaving a toxin as they feed that causes intense itching. Special shampoos must be used to kill the lice and the nits. Nits then have to be removed from the hair with a fine-toothed comb provided with the shampoo. Hats, clothing, bedding, and all other items that might have come in contact with the lice have to be washed in very hot water or sealed in a plastic bag for two weeks. Lice need blood to survive, so they die inside the plastic bag. Insecticidal sprays are available for furniture and car upholstery, which can't be washed or sealed.

Because lice don't have wings, they're passed from one child to another by direct contact. Items like pillows, combs and brushes, and dress-up hats are all potential sources of infection in preschool classrooms. Teachers can suspect head lice if they see children scratching their heads frequently. Many schools and teachers conduct regular "head checks" to keep infestations from getting established.

Infections of the middle ear—known as **otitis media** to medical personnel—are another common problem in the preschool years. Young children are susceptible to these infections because of the anatomy of their faces. The **Eustachian tubes**, which connect the middle ear to the throat, are in a nearly horizontal position during early childhood because the lower face develops later than the upper face. Fluid accumulates in the middle ear when the child has a cold, it doesn't drain into the throat as it does in older children and adults. Trapped fluid provides a perfect medium for bacterial growth, and this can lead to recurring ear infections. As the lower face grows during the school-age years, the tubes assume a more vertical position and fluid drains more easily. Consequently, school-age children get many fewer ear infections than preschoolers.

Sometimes, ear infections occur so frequently that the middle ear is almost never clear of fluid. If a child has chronic ear infections, despite careful treatment with antibiotics, surgeons will sometimes insert tiny tubes into the eardrum to allow fluid to escape through the ear canal.

Ear infections not only make children feel miserable but also can impair hearing. Good hearing is especially important in early childhood when language is developing, so hearing problems at this time are serious and can have long-term consequences. Many studies have shown a relationship between a history of middle-ear infections and language delays (Teele, Klein & Rosner, 1984), although more recently, studies have indicated that this relationship is not as close as was once thought (Roberts et al., 1986).

Chicken pox is a common viral disease among preschool children. It has a characteristic rash, which starts out as clusters of tiny blisters that soon change into whitish pus-filled pimples, which in turn break and become crusty scabs. Usually the worst symptom for children is the intense itchiness of the rash. Parents can help relieve some of the itching with baking soda baths.

Chicken pox is very contagious, and once it breaks out in a classroom, most children will get it. Luckily, it's rarely serious, except when a child's immune system is already impaired by some other disease, such as leukemia. Complications of chicken pox can include bacterial infection of the skin lesions and brain or kidney inflammation. Because of its danger in these few cases, and because children have to miss seven to ten days of school (the time it takes the lesions to scab over), some people have promoted work on a chicken pox vaccine (**varicella vaccine**). An experimental vaccine has been developed and tested in pilot studies but is not yet available for general use (Takahashi, 1986; Brunell et al., 1988).

EATING AND SLEEPING HABITS. Problems in eating and sleeping patterns can affect preschoolers' short- and long-term well-being and can cause quite a lot of anxiety among adults as well. Eating patterns are often a source of concern to parents and other caregivers. Adults worry about both the small amount of food preschoolers seem to eat and their dislike for certain foods, especially those that adults consider nutritious.

FIGURE 9
When appetites are small, parents should be sure to offer healthy snacks rather than candy bars or bags of chips. Apples are a good choice for preschoolers because they're nutritious, naturally sweet, and easy to handle.

Like toddlers, preschoolers have periods of relatively slow growth when their appetites are small. The only sensible approach when children aren't eating much is to limit nonnutritious snacks and then let their appetites be their guide. Adults can influence children's food preferences in several ways. Contrary to popular belief and practice, forcing or bribing a child to eat something she dislikes is not a good way to change her food preferences. Research has shown that children's rating of a disliked food drops even lower when they are bribed to eat it with a desired food, and the desired food's rating rises. Thus forcing children to eat vegetables to get some dessert apparently teaches them only to like vegetables less and dessert more (Olson, 1986; Olvera-Ezzell, Power & Cousins, 1990).

One of the most effective ways to increase the number of foods that preschoolers like is to expose them to the food and to people who eat it. For example, when children who initially prefer one vegetable to another eat with children who have the opposite preference, they change their preference within days to match that of the other children. They still prefer it even weeks later (Olson, 1986). Eating with adults who like a food they dislike also increases their interest in the food, although not as much as another child's preference does. The more frequent the exposure, the more likely it is that the child will taste the food and learn to like it.

Preschoolers' sleep habits also cause adults concern. Parents and other caregivers often worry about the amount of sleep a child gets, when a child should stop taking naps, how to get children to go to bed and to sleep, and what to do when a child wakes up crying in the middle of the night. How widespread is behavior that adults consider to be problematical?

In one study of preschoolers' sleep-related behavior at home, researchers found that bedtime routines, such as hearing stories, using the toilet, and getting a drink of water, took more than 30 minutes in over half the children. Most of the children took a comfort object, like a stuffed animal or a doll, to bed with them. Almost all the children took at least 30 minutes to fall asleep. Some children had night lights, and the percentage of children who needed them increased between the ages of 2 and 4, before beginning to decline at age 5. Many children called to their parents for an additional kiss or drink of water after being put to bed, and almost all went through periods when they cried or called out during the night (Beltramini & Hertzig, 1983).

A second study investigated bedtime problems in children ranging in age from 15 months to 4 years. Problems included nighttime waking (defined as crying and demanding adult attention) and bedtime struggle (defined as protest and active struggle over going to bed and taking more than an hour for bedtime routines and getting to sleep) (Kataria, Swanson & Trevathon, 1987). At the beginning of this 3-year study, 42 percent of the children had sleep problems; at the end of the study, 38 percent had sleep problems. Sleep disturbances were often associated with some upset in the child's life, such as a change in routines, an illness or accident, or a family move.

These studies and others indicate that sleep-related behaviors that cause adults concern are actually quite common among preschoolers. They resist going to bed, call for a drink or a kiss after they're in bed, take a long time to fall asleep, and wake up and cry in the middle of the night, at least occasionally. What steps can adults take to make the difficult transition to sleep easier for children? Bedtime and naptime routines seem to help. A specific set of events leading up to bedtime—using the toilet, brushing the teeth, having a story read, getting a comfort object, and kissing and hugging—can help manage and prevent problem behavior, both at home and at day care centers. Dimming the lights and putting on some quiet music can also help.

Ensuring the Safety of the Preschooler

Most of the safety precautions described in Knowledge in Action: Infants and Toddlers continue to apply during the preschool years. Children still can't be

FIGURE 10
Preschool schedules can sometimes cause sleep problems. Children require less sleep as they get older, and an afternoon nap can make it hard for an older preschooler to fall asleep at night. If this child is still awake in 15 minutes or so, he may be able to get up and play quietly while his friends finish their nap.

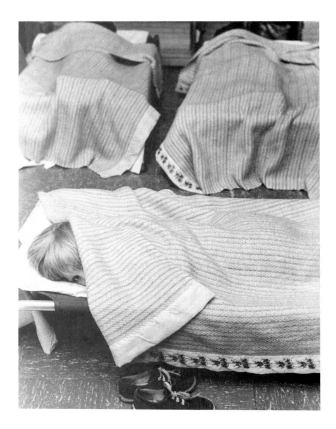

trusted to keep nonedible objects out of their mouths, to leave electrical outlets alone, or to adjust a water faucet to a safe temperature. In fact, preschoolers' greater motor ability and curiosity make them even more likely to get into trouble. Two hazards of early childhood, though of very diferent types, are lead poisoning and sexual abuse.

LEAD POISONING. Lead poisoning is a major hazard of early childhood. When lead enters the body, even in low concentrations, it can result in impaired mental functioning and overactivity. At high levels, it can make children very sick and even cause death.

Children ingest lead in several ways. Water can be contaminated by lead pipes or lead soldering on pipes. Some factory workers carry lead dust home on their clothing; it can mix with regular household dust and be ingested by children when they mouth toys and household objects.

But by far the most common source of lead is lead-based paint, which was used in houses before World War II. Some paints were as much as 50 percent lead. When lead-based paint crumbles, young children can pick up chips and eat them, or the paint chips can be crushed underfoot and combine with household dust, to be inhaled or ingested. When older homes are renovated, the lead-containing airborne dust can be hazardous (Landrigan, 1981). Ironically, the deleading of older houses has sometimes actually created problems of air-borne lead particles, because safe procedures haven't always been followed (Williams, 1989).

In some Northeastern states, laws have been passed prohibiting the sale of houses or the rental of apartments to families with children under 6 years of age if the interior paint is found to contain lead. Day care centers also have to pass inspection to ensure that their spaces are lead free. Despite these measures, lead poisoning is a serious and common problem among young children, especially those who live in older, dilapidated buildings in urban areas. It is estimated that 3 to 4 million children aged 5 and under have blood levels of lead at a toxic level (Bellinger et al., 1991).

CHILD SEXUAL ABUSE. Preschoolers as well as both younger and older children are vulnerable to sexual abuse, which is a sexual act imposed on a minor. Because of their authority and power over children, adults and older adolescents are able to coerce the child into sexual activity with relative ease. Sexually abusive acts range from exposure to adult nudity and overly intimate hugs and kisses to overt sexual intercourse. One consistently traumatic form of sexual abuse is incest, which is defined by law as a sexual encounter (usually intercourse) between people prohibited from marrying each other, such as a child and a parent, grandparent, uncle, aunt, or sibling (Sgroi, Blick & Porter, 1982).

Although sexual abuse has undoubtedly always existed, its incidence has been consistently underestimated. When Sigmund Freud first began using his talking cure, many of his female patients reported traumatic incestuous acts by their fathers. But when Freud reported this finding to his colleagues, he was repudiated; he subsequently attributed these reports to his patients' imaginations (Bowlby, 1988). Today sexual abuse still goes unrecognized and unreported in many cases. Surveys of adult women in the United States, Canada, and Great Britain indicate that at least 15 percent experienced unwanted sexual contact before they were 16 or 17 years old (Bagley & King, 1990).

Adults living and working with children need be aware of the indicators of sexual abuse. They should never ignore or dismiss a child's report of sexual assault. They should also be alert to behavioral indications of abuse, such as sophisticated or unusual sexual behavior or knowledge or very resistant behavior in circumstances that may suggest sexuality to the child, such as a medical examination. Physical symptoms, such as bleeding or bruises in the genital or anal area, bloody underclothing, or pain in the genital area, are another indication of abuse.

With the rediscovery since the late 1960s of the extent of child abuse (see Safety Focus—Child Abuse and Neglect in Knowledge in Action: Infants and Toddlers), attention has focused on the long-term effects of various kinds of abuse. People who have been abused may subsequently mistrust themselves and others, have low self-esteem, lack social skills, experience a sense of helplessness, and have problems identifying and talking about feelings, especially anger, guilt, and depression (Porter, Blick & Sgroi, 1982; Leehan & Wilson, 1985). Physical abuse often leads to aggression toward others; sexual abuse is more likely to produce maladaptive sexual behavior. Both forms of abuse produce lowered self-esteem (Briere & Runtz, 1990). The precise effects depend on the nature of the abuse (including age when it occurred, relationship to the offender, duration, threats, and so on) and the buffering effects of the family and other systems, including treatment (Harter, Alexander & Neimeyer, 1988).

Some schools and communities have developed programs to teach preschoolers "personal safety skills" to help them avoid sexual abuse (Wurtele et al., 1991; Gilbert et al., 1989; Krivacska, 1990), although not all such programs are successful at this age. In one successful three-day program using modeling, rehearsal, praise, and feedback, parents effectively taught children something about protecting themselves from sexual abuse, such as that "secret touches" are wrong. Preschoolers were also taught to say no to sexual solicitation, leave the offender, and tell a resource person. It appears that preschoolers are able to learn these personal safety skills without becoming unduly upset, fearful, or confused about abuse.

Supporting Preschoolers' Play

Preschoolers have many interests and budding skills, and a tremendous range of toys and play items can be provided to support them. Active play is far preferable to TV watching for preschoolers. For a discussion of the current state of TV programming, see Public Policy Focus—Improving Children's Television.

TOYS REQUIRING LARGE MOTOR SKILLS. Swing sets, climbing structures, tricycles, and wagons give preschoolers a chance to use their large muscles. Large building blocks do too, because children have to lift them, carry them, and bend over to put them in place. Younger preschoolers enjoy throwing and catching balls, and older preschoolers can use a low basketball hoop and a plastic baseball and bat. They also enjoy kicking a soccer ball around.

Wide open space is well used by preschoolers, who run, jump, gallop, and roll around on the ground. In winter they like to help shovel snow with a child-sized shovel, and in fall they can rake leaves with a small rake. In spring and summer they like to fill watering cans and carry them to plants. Water and sand are all-time favorites of preschoolers, who will spend hours playing with pails, molds, sifters, scoops, funnels, and other sand and water toys.

FIGURE 11
Art activities for preschoolers should allow for both expansive creativity and messiness. Particularly appropriate for their level of fine motor development are finger painting and painting with sponges or large brushes.

TOYS REQUIRING SMALL MOTOR SKILLS. Children gain much greater skill with their hands during the preschool years, and they enjoy drawing and writing with markers, crayons, paint, and paper. They can also learn to use scissors now, especially if they practice on thin strips of paper that require just one snip to cut through.

Jigsaw puzzles, small construction toys, beads for stringing, simple sewing cards, play dough, and clay all give preschoolers practice with their fine motor skills. Doll clothes also require skilled use of the hands, and Velcro fastenings make them easier than ever to manipulate.

MATERIALS THAT SUPPORT PRETEND PLAY. Pretend play is often the preschooler's favorite kind of play. Dress-up clothes of all kinds help support pretend play, as do baby dolls, stuffed animals, and small dolls or figures. Props help too—dishes, doll clothes, doll carriages and furniture, small kitchen appliances, empty food cartons, a cash register, shopping carts, and doctor's equipment can all be used.

FIGURE 12
Items destined for the thrift shop should be rerouted to the preschooler's toy box or the nursery school dress-up area. Old hats, shoes, and clothes are all children need for hours of pretend play.

PUBLIC POLICY FOCUS

Improving Children's Television

Children's television programming has been an area of intense struggle over the years. Public policymakers have tried to get broadcasters to reduce TV violence, to increase the number of children's shows, especially educational ones, and to limit commercials on children's shows. Broadcasters and advertisers, driven by financial pressures and goals, have resisted most of these efforts.

CONCERNS ABOUT VIOLENCE
Television sets were common in American homes for little more than a decade when concern arose about the amount of violence depicted on TV. In 1960 the National Commission on the Causes and Prevention of Violence issued a report stating that violence on TV was a factor affecting children's aggressive behavior. The report rated television shows for violence and recommended that programs be rated on an annual basis. Over the years, the violence rating indicated that shows were becoming more violent.

During the 1960s and 1970s, the focus of most research on children's television was violence. As we have seen elsewhere in this book, many studies established correlations (but not causal relationships) between the viewing of filmed violence and aggressive behavior. Many people were concerned not only that there were so many violent episodes in cartoons but also that children were watching violent shows intended for adults. Pressure was applied to legislators to take steps to regulate TV to control televised violence, but these efforts failed. Television stations asserted that programming decisions were matters of internal policy, and some lawmakers felt that regulation would violate the stations' First Amendment rights of freedom of speech.

CONCERNS ABOUT PROGRAMMING AND ADVERTISING

The Birth of Public Television
The Federal Communications Commission (FCC) in 1960 officially recognized children as a segment of the public needing

special attention from TV broadcasters. Programming for children got a tremendous boost when the Corporation for Public Broadcasting was founded as a result of a 1967 Carnegie Commission Study. This study called for the creation of a federally funded network of public and educational television stations that would air more and better children's programs. The Public Broadcasting System (PBS) is the network within this system that carries such acclaimed shows as "Mr. Roger's Neighborhood" and "Sesame Street."

Action for Children's Television: Efforts to Limit Advertising
Special interest groups continued to put pressure on the commercial stations as well. In 1970 a grassroots group called Action for Children's Television (ACT) lobbied the FCC to require all stations to provide certain minimal programming for children every day. ACT also proposed that advertising be abolished during children's programs. As a result, the FCC issued their 1974 Children's Television Report and Policy Statement. This was a nonbinding ruling, establishing guidelines for broadcasters to follow in children's programming. Among other things it instructed TV stations to use "separators" between children's shows and commercials (to help children perceive that a commercial isn't part of the show) and to stop using characters from children's shows to push products (a practice known as "host selling"). As we've seen, even school-age children lack the cognitive skills to process accurately the messages sent out by advertisers.

Although the FCC made it clear that stations would be evaluated for their compliance with this ruling at license-renewal time, broadcasters ignored many of the guidelines. In 1976 ACT succeeded in getting a different agency, the Federal Trade Commission (FTC), to consider children a special population with respect to advertising. The FTC proposed a ban on television advertising directed toward children under 8 years of age. The proposal met with so much resistance that the

BOOKS AND BOARD GAMES. Preschoolers love to hear stories, and they also like to look at picture books and attempt to reread them themselves. Many books are available today with cassette tapes, so children can listen to stories even when adults are busy. There are even some excellent television shows that feature the lively reading and discussion of stories and books.

There has been an explosion of new books for children and children's bookstores since the early 1980s. Before that time, libraries bought 90 percent of all children's books sold. By the mid-1980s, parents were buying so many books for their children that the proportion of books purchased by libraries had fallen to 60 percent. Preschoolers can also choose from among several children's magazines, such as *Sesame Street Magazine* and *Your Big Backyard*. They feature stories, games, activities, cartoons, and instructions for making things.

Children begin to enjoy board games during the preschool years. They can learn to play simple games in which cards are drawn or an arrow is spun on a wheel to indicate how many spaces the players move, such as Candyland, Candyland Bingo, Chutes and Ladders, and Hi-Ho Cherry-O. To play these

FTC abandoned its efforts to encourage regulation of TV commercials directed at children (Hymes, 1982).

Efforts to Improve Children's Shows:
The Children's Television Education Act
More recently, efforts to develop a policy for children's television have focused on improving the educational value of shows. In 1984, Rep. Timothy Wirth of Colorado introduced the Children's Television Education Act of 1983 in the House of Representatives. This bill called for TV stations to provide a minimum of one hour of children's programming every weekday. The bill died in 1984.

Rep. Wirth, along with cosponsor Senator Frank Lautenberg, reintroduced the bill in 1985. Under the revised act, broadcasters' licenses would not be renewed if they failed to provide minimal children's programming every day. The bill also called for the FCC to investigate the effects of children's programs produced solely to promote toys or other products—the so-called "program-length commercials." These shows now take up a large part of the air time reserved for children's programs. This bill died in 1986.

Finally, in 1990, two laws were passed regarding children's television. One, The Children's Television Act of 1990, puts a limit on the number of commercials that can be aired during children's programs. During the week, the limit is 12 minutes per hour; on weekends, the limit is 10.5 minutes per hour. In addition, when stations apply for renewal of their broadcast licenses, they must provide information about how they address children's educational and informational needs. Finally, the act created a National Endowment for Children's Educational Television (NAEYC, 1991).

The second law is The Children's Television Violence Act. It makes broadcasters exempt from antitrust laws, which had been invoked after the National Association of Broadcasters developed a self-regulating code in 1980 to limit violence on TV and encouraged all broadcasters to adopt it (NAEYC, 1991). This law was needed because any agreement among competing broadcasters is generally seen as an illegal attempt to form a "trust" or association to control competition.

WHAT SHOULD ADULTS DO?
In addition to supporting public policy regarding televison for children, parents and other caregivers have to control children's TV viewing (Murray & Lonnborg, undated). Adults who are concerned about what children are watching on TV can take the following steps:

- Limit the amount of time children spend watching TV. Active play is preferable to TV watching for children of all ages. Children who don't watch much TV have been found to be more creative, social, activity oriented, and successful in school than children who watch a lot of TV. Experts recommend that adults limit preschoolers to no more than one hour a day and school-age children to no more than two hours a day.
- Screen the programs children watch, and don't allow them to watch shows that contain a lot of violence. Make adult shows off-limits, including news broadcasts, situation comedies, game and talk shows, and many documentaries. Preschoolers can't comprehend most adult programming and often find it upsetting or frightening.
- Watch television with children and explain what is "real" and what is "pretend."
- Encourage children to watch educational programs and shows with a prosocial message.
- Support citizens' groups working for public policies that will improve children's television.
- Substitute high-quality videotapes for television programming.

games, children need only be able to count to ten, match colors, or have some other basic skill, although they may need adult supervision to help them count correctly and take turns. Preschoolers' games are games of chance. As we saw in Chapter 10, they won't have the cognitive skills to play games of strategy, such as Checkers or MasterMind, until they're well into their school years.

OVERVIEW

Preschoolers are active, curious, talkative, and ready for social interactions with peers. These qualities make preschool an appropriate and valuable experience for them. At the same time, children between the ages of 3 and 6 have unique characteristics and needs that make it difficult to design truly effective preschool educational programs. Their cognitive limitations, social inexperience, relatively brief attention span, and urge to use their large muscles in active play mean that schoollike situations will create more problems than they solve. Preschoolers learn best in hands-on situations where they can explore freely, initiate their own activities, and interact on a one-to-one basis with an adult—characteristics that are difficult indeed to incorporate into programs on a large-scale basis. Knowledge and research help adults design educational programs and structure living environments for the enhancement of preschoolers' growth in all domains, but public policies have to be established that support these efforts.

KNOWLEDGE IN ACTION REVIEW

EDUCATION AND CARE PROGRAMS FOR PRESCHOOL CHILDREN

- The preschool population is diverse, but special programs exist to provide educational, social, and emotional experiences to groups who otherwise wouldn't be able to take advantage of preschool.
- Preschool programs adapted to children with disabilities are provided under the Education for All Handicapped Children Act of 1975.
- Several federal, state, and city programs have been established for children from economically disadvantaged households, although funding always falls short of need. Some states subsidize preschool for working parents, and some companies provide day care facilities for their employees. Affordable day care will be a major issue of the 1990s.
- The best preschool programs are judged to be those that offer a balance of teacher-directed activities and child-directed activities throughout the day. Highly interactive educational programs for preschoolers require a very high ratio of teachers to children, perhaps one teacher for every three or four children.

- Preschoolers thrive with individualized adult interaction, hands-on experience, positive feedback, and opportunities to engage in activities that require large motor skills. All this should take place in a safe, nurturing, well-organized environment.
- Gifted children have above-average intellectual ability, creativity, or a demonstrated talent in a particular area. They need educational tasks that challenge and stimulate them. At the preschool level, these activities are most often provided by the parents.
- Children learn a lot from child-directed activities, but they don't learn specific academic skills from them. These are the very activities needed by children from economically disadvantaged families if they are to succeed later on in school. Creative teaching and reduced group size may help solve these problems in the 1990s.

ASSESSING THE PRESCHOOL CHILD

- Preschool children are sometimes tested to assess their intellectual skills, their developmental level, and their readiness for academic tasks.
- These tests are controversial. Their validity is questionable, since most of them don't predict future academic success any better than chance. Their use also narrows the preschool curriculum and squeezes out

more creative, exploratory, and child-initiated activities, which are considered essential to intellectual growth.
- One result of the wave of testing is that less mature children are being kept out of kindergarten rather than given the individualized attention that would support their overall development.

LIVING WITH THE PRESCHOOL CHILD

- Preschoolers get sick fairly often, mainly because of their close contact with other children. They're at risk for getting head lice, developing ear infections, and contracting chicken pox, all of which are more annoying than causes for concern.
- Preschoolers can be picky eaters and should be given nutritious meals and snacks. Coercion and bribery

aren't effective ways to get children to eat food they don't like, but exposing them to people who like other foods does help them expand their diet.
- Sleep behaviors that adults consider problems are actually common among preschoolers. Bedtime and naptime routines are often helpful, as are the understanding and patience of parents and caregivers.

- Lead poisoning is a serious environmental danger for children, and homes and day care centers should be inspected to ensure that the walls aren't covered with lead-based paint.
- Sexual abuse is frequently an extremely damaging experience for children, producing long-term emotional and sexual difficulties. It seems to be possible to teach preschoolers how to protect themselves from sexual abuse without unduly upsetting them.
- Preschoolers enjoy pretend play, outdoor play, toys and activities that require fine motor skills, books, and simple board games.
- Active play is preferable to television for children. Efforts over the years to improve the quality of children's television met with success in 1990 when two laws affecting children's television were passed. Concerns focus on violence, advertising, and the quality of the programming. Responsibility for monitoring and controlling TV viewing falls on the parents.

KEY TERMS

teacher-directed education
child-directed education
validity
head lice

otitis media
Eustachian tubes
chicken pox
varicella vaccine

SUGGESTIONS FOR FURTHER READING

Bagley, C., & King, K. (1990). *Child sexual abuse: The search for healing.* New York: Tavistock/Routledge.
This scholarly and readable book describes the incidence and psychotherapy of child survivors of sexual abuse.

Bass, E., & Davis, L. (1988). *The courage to heal: A guide for women survivors of child sexual abuse.* New York: Harper & Row.
This wonderful book talks about recovery after recognizing the effects of being sexually abused as a child. The stories of 15 survivors highlight particular aspects of the healing process.

Cahan, E. D. (1989). *Past caring: A history of U.S. preschool care and education for the poor, 1820–1965.* New York: Columbia University, School of Public Health, National Center for Children in Poverty.
This short, readable paperback provides a historical sketch of the preschool and day care programs that have been provided to economically disadvantaged children in the United States, since before the Civil War.

Gunzenhauser, N., & Caldwell, B. M. (Eds.). (1986). *Group care for young children.* Skillman, NJ: Johnson & Johnson.
This short paperback contains many interesting chapters, including ones on the child care needs of single and low-income parents, on the opportunities for parent education in child care, on child care and public policy, and on corporate support for child care.

Kagan, S. L., & Zigler, E. F. (1987). *Early schooling: The national debate.* New Haven, CT: Yale University Press.
This book discusses the current trend of public schools providing programs for 4-year-olds. Issues such as the appropriate content and methods to use with preschools are discussed.

National Association for the Education of Young Children. (1986). *Developmentally appropriate practice in early childhood programs serving children from birth through age 8.* Washington, D.C.: NAEYC.
This booklet contains a set of standards for quality early childhood programs.

SCHOOL-AGE CHILDREN

The years between 6 and 12 are in many ways the most tranquil of childhood. Freud claimed that these years were a period of psychosexual latency; Erikson saw them as a time for addressing issues of industry and competence; and Piaget noted the 6- or 7-year-old's development of logical abilities. Regardless of theoretical orientation, we can see a certain quiet steadiness in children this age that didn't exist in earlier years. Physically children grow slowly and predictably, developing the strength, coordination, and motor skills that underlie development in many other domains. Socially and emotionally they become less egocentric and more aware of themselves and others, refining a personal style they're coming to call their own. Intellectually they become capable of reasoning in standard ways. As their reasoning abilities become increasingly complex, they assume more conscious directorship of their thoughts and actions. The school years are above all a time of learning, a time when children apply themselves both to mastering schoolwork and to acquiring social skills. Many of their defining experiences now take place at school, and this is why we've chosen to refer to them as *school-age children* in this book.

c h a p t e r 13

PHYSICAL DEVELOPMENT IN SCHOOL-AGE CHILDREN

As Steve Atkinson set up orange cones at the ends of the school playing field, he heard the children in his first P.E. class of the day coming out of their classroom. They were sturdy first graders, filled with enthusiasm.

"Today we're going to play a game of tag," Steve told the children after he led them in some warm-up jumping jacks and torso twists. "We can play either color tag or freeze tag. Which do you want?"

"Color tag!" they all seemed to shout at once.

"Okay, color tag it is."

"Steve, can me and Sharon be the chasers today?" piped up Yolanda, an energetic 6-year-old.

"Let me check my list," Steve replied. "Everyone needs to have a turn . . . yes, that looks okay, Yolanda. Any other questions? No? Okay, look at your clothes to see what colors you're wearing, and then we'll divide into two sides."

When the class was ready, Yolanda and Sharon stood whispering in the middle of the field for a moment and then turned and called out "RED!" From opposite ends of the field, children started running directly for the other side, and the two girls tagged as many as they could. One unlucky boy discovered he had red on his sneakers after everyone else was behind the lines and had to make a dash for the other side by himself. Yolanda quickly tagged him.

Sharon and Yolanda conferred again and this time called out "YELLOW!" The field once more became a blur of children running, laughing, and trying to dodge the taggers. Sometimes a child would run wide, out to the edges of the field, but most made straight for the other end of the field. Sharon and Yolanda had no trouble tagging all but two of the children in four rounds, and those two became the next taggers. By the end of the class, when Steve had them walk around the field to cool down, the children were pink-cheeked and tired, ready to return to their classroom.

Steve's next class was a group of third and fourth graders, and he offered them a choice of dodge ball, capture the flag, or elbow tag. They chose elbow tag, a more compli-cated game of tag that they were just becoming able to play. Steve liked elbow tag because it required a combination of quick thinking and maneuvering. After the children had jogged once around the field to warm up, they linked arms at the elbow with a part-ner and spread out over the field. Steve asked Cindy to be the first chaser, and Nathaniel agreed to be the first one chased.

As they started running, Nathaniel was able to keep ahead, but when Cindy started to close in, Nathaniel ran over to a pair of classmates and linked elbows with one of them. The other child in the pair pulled her arm free and ran off, and Cindy now ran after her. But she was starting to get out of breath, and soon she too linked elbows with a classmate. The boy on the other end of that chain became the new chaser.

As the game continued, Steve watched the children running, dodging, and stopping short only to take off in another direction after a different child. Sometimes he marveled

FIGURE 13-1
First graders are typically slen-der and sturdy. Children grow slowly and steadily for most of the school years, but height and weight both start to increase rapidly toward the end of this period.

that they were able to keep track of what was going on as well as they could. They too were ready for a rest by the end of the class.

Steve met his last morning class in the gym. The sixth graders had begun learning some basic basketball skills two years earlier, dribbling first with one hand, then with alternate hands, then dribbling around the body while remaining stationary, and finally dribbling and traveling. Later they practiced dribbling around obstacles, changing directions, and dribbling against an opponent. They'd practiced a series of throwing and shooting skills too.

Just this year they were starting to put together the understanding, coordination, and skills really required to play the game. After warm-ups, Steve had them practice dribbling and shooting lay-up shots, and then they played a short game. As he watched them play, Steve noted that many of them would be joining the school's seventh and eighth grade basketball team the following year. He also noted that many of the skills they were using were built on their first experiences in games like color tag, played not so many years ago.

The school years are a period of steady physical growth and rapid skill acquisition. The first grader turns into the taller, leaner, more muscular child of the later elementary school years, able to begin playing a complex game like basketball. This transformation is supported by a physical education program like Steve's, built around games and physical skill development. As children grow, their increasing strength and motor coordination in turn contribute to good health, a sense of independence, high self-esteem, and appropriate cognitive development.

This chapter covers the typical growth patterns of middle childhood as well as normal and abnormal variations in these patterns. It discusses the causes and effects of the most common abnormal variation, childhood obesity. This is followed by a discussion of motor development, including both the fine and gross motor skills that school-age children acquire. Finally this chapter addresses some of the implications of physical development for sports programs and healthy life-styles.

HOW DO THEY GROW?

Increases in Height and Weight

Growth during the school years slows down from preschool rates. The average 6-year-old weighs about 43 pounds and is about 44 inches tall—almost 4 feet. The average 12-year-old weighs a little over 80 pounds and is about 5 feet tall. If you recall, infants double their birthweight in their first six months. In contrast, it takes the average 6-year-old 12 times that long—six years—to double her 6-year-old weight (Figure 13-1).

By the time children are 6 years old, they're about two-thirds of their adult height. And by the end of middle childhood, boys have reached 80 percent of their adult height, and girls have achieved about 90 percent of theirs (Tanner, 1978a). Weight gain during this period is concentrated more in muscle than in fat, so strength increases considerably. Because boys as a group have more muscle cells than girls as a group, they're stronger during the school years as well as during adolescence (Maccoby, 1980).

FIGURE 13-2
The long and lanky school-age child can run, chase, and dodge with speed and skill. In a quieter moment, this 8-year-old traces out a self-portrait that reflects just how much she has grown in the last few years.

Changes in Body Proportions

Up to now the head has grown more rapidly than the body, but now the growth of the head slows dramatically. If you recall from Chapter 5, the brain achieves about 90 percent of its adult weight by age 5. Brain weight equals adult levels by age 6, although many changes, including **lateralization** (dominance of one hemisphere or the other with respect to specific functions) and **myelination** (growth of a fatty sheath on the outer surface of nerve cells), will continue for several years (Cratty, 1986).

Now the trunk and especially the legs begin to grow more quickly, making the school-age child look quite long and slim. The face changes too, becoming longer and thinner. Just as the head grew more rapidly than the body during the first six years of life, the upper part of the head grew more rapidly than the lower part. Now, the lower face and jaw begin to catch up. The cheeks slim down and the face elongates. The eustachian tubes connecting the middle ear to the throat begin to assume a more vertical position, as explained in Knowledge in Action: Preschool Children. Because fluids can drain out of the ear, and children tend to have fewer ear infections, the tiny plastic tubes that some preschoolers need in their ears to prevent ear infections are rarely needed by children over 7 or 8 years old.

The Eruption of Permanent Teeth

Losing the first baby tooth is a rite of passage into middle childhood. A few children lose one or two teeth soon after their fifth birthday, but it's more commonly a 6-year-old phenomenon. First- and second-grade classrooms are usually full of "toothless grins." The process of tooth loss continues over the entire course of middle childhood. By about age 11 or 12, all permanent teeth have erupted except for two sets of molars.

Care of the permanent teeth is especially important, since they'll last for life. Thumb and finger sucking should stop by the time the permanent teeth have come in, or **malocclusion** (improper alignment) may result. If a child doesn't give up this habit, parents may want to consider special counseling. Even without thumb or finger sucking, some children will have overbites and other misalignments of their teeth and will need braces later to correct these problems.

FIGURE 13-3
Wiggly teeth are a frequent topic of interest among school-age children. Sometimes a friend can't resist feeling it for himself.

Normal Variations in Growth Patterns

THE PREADOLESCENT GROWTH SPURT. Throughout childhood different children grow at different rates. These variations are particularly apparent toward the end of the school-age period, when the **preadolescent growth spurt** occurs (this and other aspects of puberty are discussed in detail in Chapter 17). Some children shoot up and begin to develop sexually by the age of 9 or 10, while others retain their childish proportions longer. The age at which the growth spurt occurs can vary among children by several years, but girls as a group usually experience it a few years before boys.

IMPLICATIONS OF THE GROWTH SPURT. The rapid physical change of the later school-age years is both exciting and frightening to children. When one mother discovered that her sixth-grade daughter was concerned about a topic that began with the letter "D," she hastened to assure her that she and her husband had never even considered divorce, only to have the 11-year-old inform her in exasperation that the topic of interest was "development." Children's concern is heightened by the wide variation in timing of the growth spurt and in onset of puberty. The physical changes of puberty, such as the development of breasts and pubic hair, can affect how children are regarded by their peers (Aro & Taipale, 1987; Dornbusch et al., 1981). If a child develops sooner or later than her peers, she may feel awkward and self-conscious.

Added to this self-consciousness about physical development is a strong desire to belong, to be like others, along with a heightened awareness of other

FIGURE 13-4
Normal variation in the timing of the preadolescent growth spurt means that some girls show evidence of sexual development before their friends do, often at 10 or 11 years of age. Many girls begin to drop out of sports towards the end of the school years, perhaps due partly to feelings of self-consciousness about their bodies. Since participation in physical activities like soccer has benefits throughout life, teachers and parents should encourage girls to stay in sports programs.

people's opinions, which characterizes children's thinking from about fourth or fifth grade on. All these developments can combine to make older school-age children vulnerable to wide fluctuations in self-image and how they feel about themselves. Adults can help by making sure children understand their physical development and emerging sexuality and by providing a supportive environment in which developmental changes are an accepted part of each child's life.

Abnormal Variations in Growth Patterns

Although there is a wide variation in children's growth patterns, some children don't grow normally during the school-age years. Some children fail to grow or grow too slowly; others put on too much weight and become obese during childhood. Both of these conditions are cause for concern.

RETARDED GROWTH. Sometimes, children just don't grow properly. Retarded growth can be caused by either social-environmental factors or by organic (physical) ones. Children whose growth is far below what is typical for their age are known as **failure-to-thrive** children. In infants this syndrome is most often caused by parental neglect. But if conditions in the home don't improve, or if there are intermittent episodes of crisis and stress, failure to thrive can continue throughout childhood (Kempe & Kempe, 1978; Kristiansson & Fallstrom, 1987). Failure-to-thrive children are small for their age, appear undernourished, and may be lethargic or listless. The syndrome is treated by working with the neglectful parents or by placing the child in a foster home where proper care can be provided.

Retarded growth can also be caused by a disturbance of the pituitary gland, which supplies growth hormone to the body. Sometimes the disturbance is due to a lesion (an injury from a disease or trauma) in the gland, which can result from an infectious disease such as meningeal tuberculosis. Radiation treatment for tumors of the middle ear or eye or for leukemia can also disturb hormonal production. When the disturbance in the pituitary gland isn't caused by a lesion, the condition is known as **idiopathic growth retardation**; idiopathic pituitary conditions are inherited as recessive characteristics (Frasier, 1979).

Children with low levels of growth hormone are short for their age and often overweight for their height. Their chests and abdomens tend to be chubby, although their head size may be typical for their age (Frasier, 1979). The best indicator of a problem in growth hormone is an extreme deviation from the norm for the child's age. Children with this problem can be given a synthetic hormone, but physicians have to monitor their growth carefully to control their response to this drug (Cara and Johanson, 1990; Raiti et al., 1987).

CHILDHOOD OBESITY. Obesity is the most common deviation from normal growth found among school-age children. Obesity is defined as weight that exceeds normal weight-for-height or weight-for-age by 20 percent (Neumann, 1977). Estimates of the number of overweight school-age children vary from study to study, but the condition is prevalent and on the rise (Epstein, Wing & Valoski, 1985). During the 15-year period from 1966 through 1980, the proportion of obese boys aged 6 to 11 increased from 18 to 20 percent, and the proportion of obese girls increased from 17 to 25 percent. (For a discussion of

HEALTH FOCUS

Treating Childhood Obesity

The later in childhood a baby or child remains overweight, the greater are the chances that the child will become an obese adult. This fact underlies the urgency of getting early weight problems under control as soon as possible. Of all overweight 6-month-olds, 14 percent will become obese adults. By age 7, the odds have increased to 41 percent. By age 13, the odds stand at about 70 percent (Epstein, Wing & Valoski, 1985).

Furthermore, obese children have some of the same health-risk factors that are common in obese adults, including high blood pressure and elevated total cholesterol levels. Overweight children can be enrolled in weight control treatment programs to help them adopt eating and exercise habits that will carry over into their adult years. The goal of these programs is to minimize health risks and maximize self-esteem and personal satisfaction.

One particularly comprehensive program has been developed by the Child Weight Control Clinic at the University of Pittsburgh School of Medicine (Epstein, Wing & Valoski, 1985). The program has three components: diet, exercise, and behavior modification. The diet component uses a "traffic light" system to manage eating. "Go" foods can be eaten in unlimited amounts; "Caution" foods can be eaten in moderate amounts; and "Stop" foods should be avoided.

The exercise program works on a point system. Different activities are rated according to how many calories they burn. Children are given a point goal for the week, but they can choose the exercises they prefer to reach their goal. The behavior modification component has several parts: (1) information mastery, which includes knowledge about food and diet; (2) self-monitoring, which involves keeping a log of foods eaten; and (3) contracting, which requires parents and children to earn back money paid at the beginning of the program by attending weekly training sessions.

Programs like this one obviously call for considerable commitment and investment of time by both the child and the family. Comparative studies have shown that programs involving the parents are more successful than those involving just the child. But it's important, especially for children approaching adolescence, that the child and parents attend separate training sessions, even though they're enrolled in the same overall program (Brownell, Kelman & Stunkard, 1983). This separation gives the child independence and control and shifts responsibility for weight control to the child, who will increasingly be the one who has to maintain it.

why childhood obesity is particularly worrisome and how it can be treated, see Health Focus—Treating Childhood Obesity.)

What causes some children to be overweight? Surprisingly, overweight children don't always eat more than their normal-weight peers. What often does distinguish the two groups is their different levels of physical activity (Berkowitz et al., 1985). The implication is that children's obesity may be due to lower-than-average energy expenditure rather than higher-than-average calorie intake. Obese children also tend to watch more television than normal-weight children (Dietz & Gortmarker, 1984). This habit not only takes up time that could be spent in physical activities and play but also increases snacking, particularly of calorie-dense, "junk" food (Barcus & McLaughlin, 1978; Dietz, 1986).

Children put on this excess weight during middle childhood at a rate of about 5 pounds per year, which amounts to an excess of about 50 calories per day. A 20-minute bike ride would more than offset that number of calories, and one less snack of chips and a cola drink while watching TV would eliminate even more. It's easy to see that for most children a little prevention, begun early in life, can keep weight gain under control.

Strong evidence exists, however, that obesity has a genetic component (Pollitt, Garza & Leibel, 1984). There is a high correlation between obesity in parents and obesity in children. If their parents are obese, 50 percent of obese infants will become obese adults. If their parents aren't obese, only 20 percent of obese infants will become obese adults (Epstein, Wing & Valoski, 1985). Of course, since all family members share a more or less common environment, the high correlation could be due to learning rather than inheritance or to some combination of the two factors.

Many researchers have attempted to sort out the relative effects of genetics and environment on obesity, and their results indicate that genetics accounts for between 20 and 60 percent of the variance in obesity (Brook, Huntley & Slack, 1975; Rao et al., 1975; Garn & Clark, 1976; Foch & McClearn, 1980). In other words, researchers believe that 20 to 60 percent of the difference in weight between obese groups and normal weight groups can be attributed to *something other than* eating patterns and energy expenditure through physical activity—most likely, genetic inheritance. Even though the researchers don't agree on exactly how large the role of genetics is, they all give it considerable importance.

The good news is that environmental factors also play a large role in determining if a person actually becomes obese. The bad news is that some people may indeed have a natural tendency toward obesity. But with rigorous weight-control measures, even these individuals don't have to become overweight. Good habits of physical activity developed during the school-age years may play an especially important role in lifelong fitness.

MOTOR DEVELOPMENT

Rapid Acquisition of Skills

At the beginning of this chapter we saw that children's physical abilities develop impressively over the course of the school-age years. They can handle greater physical demands thanks to bone and muscle growth, and they gain more reasoned control over their movements, largely as a result of brain development. The third graders showed more precision of movement and coordination than the first graders, and the sixth graders showed even greater maneuverability and skill. All these growing abilities enable school-age children to learn games and sports involving gross motor skills, as well as games, hobbies, and crafts that require fine motor skills. Their favored activities range from football and swimming to origami and models. Many school-age children also begin to learn to play a musical instrument.

FIGURE 13-5
The development of specific motor skills depends on both maturation and experience. All children improve in balance, coordination, agility, and muscular strength as they get older, but they need opportunities for practice to master particular sports. These very young Minnesota children are already accomplished ice skaters.

TABLE 13-1   Pencil Grips Found in Preschool and Young School-Age Children

LEVEL 1 (LEAST MATURE GRIPS)

a. (Fist) Pencil is held against the palm with fingers and thumb wrapped around it.
b. (Pronate) Palm is rotated down; pencil is underneath palm; index finger is stretched out toward point of pencil; thumb is on one side of pencil; middle, ring, and little fingers are wrapped around it.
c. Pencil is held between index finger and thumb with shaft extending upward at the joint; fingers are on one side; thumb is on the other side opposite index finger.
d. Pencil is held with index, middle, and ring fingers on one side; thumb is opposite index finger; little finger is supporting pencil opposite ring finger.
e. Pencil is held with index, middle, and ring fingers on one side; thumb is opposite index finger; little finger is curled away from the pencil and is not supporting it.

LEVEL 2

a. Pencil is held with index and middle fingers on one side; thumb is opposite index finger, ring finger is supporting the pencil opposite middle finger.
b. Pencil is held with index and middle fingers on one side; thumb is opposite index finger, ring finger is curled away from pencil and is not supporting it.

LEVEL 3 (MOST MATURE)

a. Pencil is held with index finger on one side; thumb is crossed over index finger, middle finger is supporting pencil opposite index finger.
b. Pencil is held with index finger on one side; thumb is opposite index finger; middle finger is supporting pencil opposite index finger.

SOURCE: Adapted from K. Carlson and J.L. Cunningham (1990). Effect of pencil diameter on the graphomotor skill of preschoolers. Early Childhood Research Quarterly, 5, 279–293.

FIGURE 13-6
Fine motor skills improve quickly in the early school-age years. This first grader is able to write in a mature way, resting her arm on her desk and controlling the pencil with her fingers.

The ability to control and manipulate a pencil or pen often improves rapidly during the early school-age years as children acquire a mature grip on the writing tool and increased ability to manipulate their fingers (Carlson & Cunningham, 1990; Halverson, 1940). Younger children often use a full-palm or fist grip on a pencil, and they keep their hands and arms up off the tabletop. They move the tool with the muscles of the upper arm rather than with the fingers. Because the distance from the pivot (source of movement) to the tool is so great, their marks are very large. As the movements begin to originate in the wrist rather than the upper arm, children are able to make smaller marks. Writing becomes smaller still when children begin to rest the side of their hand on the tabletop and move the tool with their fingers. With this superior control, they can make finer marks and confine their writing to a smaller and smaller amount of space. (See Table 13-1 for a description of types of grip young children use.)

One of the many drawbacks of including handwriting programs in the kindergarten classroom is that many children don't yet have the fine motor control required for this activity. Writing is better taught in the elementary grades, although some first-graders still will find it difficult. Younger children do like to draw and write, but their enjoyment will be dampened if they have to confine their creations to a restricted area, such as the lines on ruled paper. To see the dramatic change in size and precision that takes place in children's handwriting between the ages of $2\frac{1}{2}$ and $7\frac{1}{2}$, look at the samples in Figure 13-7.

Injuries Associated with Excessive Exercise and Growth Patterns

During the school-age period, many children begin to participate in organized sports, such as swim teams and Little League baseball. Although they have the cognitive and motor skills to play sports, children's bones and muscles are immature and easily injured. Immature bones are softer than the fully ossified bones of teenagers and adults, and they can be deformed from strain or squeezing. Immature muscles can also be easily strained or torn.

Prolonged use of one area of the body or of several specific areas can lead to "overuse" injuries, such as sprains, tendinitis, and stress fractures (small breaks) of bones (Harvey, 1982). It can also lead to accelerated bone growth in an overused area (Stoner, 1978). If these injuries are handled improperly, long-term disability can result. This is why restrictions are placed on the amount of time a child can pitch in a Little League game (Milberg, 1976).

Children actually lose flexibility between 5 and 12 or 13 years of age because bones grow a little faster than muscles. At first, muscles get pulled tighter as bones grow; then muscles catch up (Teitz, 1982). Warm-up exercises are especially important during this period, as understood by Steve Atkinson, the P.E. teacher whose classes were described at the beginning of this chapter. Warming up gets muscles into a flexible state before hard use and helps prevent injuries.

The Importance of Physical Education

A healthy body contributes to healthy growth in every other area of development. Good motor coordination and appropriate body strength support both cognitive and social-emotional development, providing children with positive feelings about themselves. Participation in games and sports can help

(a)

(b)

(c)

(d)

(e)

(f)

FIGURE 13-7
As this child's fine motor control improved, he was able to write his name smaller and smaller. His age at the time of writing the different samples (shown reduced here) was (a) 2 years, 9 months; (b) 3 years, 6 months; (c) 4 years, 4 months; (d) 5 years, 7 months; (e) 6 years, 2 months; (f) 7 years, 7 months. Not until he was well over 7 years old was his writing small enough to fit comfortably on regular lined paper.

children learn individual and group social skills. Overall, physical activity can give children a sense of health, mastery, and general well-being.

Despite the acknowledged benefits of motor skill development and physical activity, however, many schools pay very little attention to their physical education programs. Reading, for example, is often taught for an hour every day, but physical education may be taught only once a week, if at all. In 1980 the U.S. Department of Health and Human Services reported that school physical education programs weren't meeting the goal of establishing school-based pro-

FIGURE 13-8
With adult modeling and encouragement, children learn that physical fitness is an important part of lifelong health. These children are participating in a fitness fair and mile run for kids and parents, sponsored by their school's physical education teachers.

grams made up of activities that go beyond competitive sports. Schools emphasize informal games and relays and short, weekly activity times. According to this report, "inadequate investment is being made in conveying the physical skills needed for active life-styles" (Ross & Gilbert, 1985). This is counterproductive to what we know is necessary for good health.

It follows that schools need to devote more of their resources to basic physical education for the elementary grades, and the public needs to support them. Other adults in children's lives can help them develop motor skills and a love of physical activity by playing games and sports with them and by encouraging them to be active. Instead of watching TV, children can play handball or jump rope on the sidewalk. They can play frisbee in the playground or basketball in the school yard. The whole family can go on a bicycle expedition, a walk around the neighborhood, or a hike in the woods. Experiences like these help children discover the pleasures of using their bodies in active ways and provide a solid foundation for the development of healthy life-styles.

OVERVIEW

It's no accident that we so often see school-age children playing sports. They now have the skills and coordination to learn and enjoy nearly every kind of physical activity. They're taller, slimmer, and stronger than they were during their preschool years, and they like to stretch their growing limbs. Those children who avidly pursue physical activities experience many cognitive, emotional, and social benefits, along with an enhanced sense of well-being. The challenge, increasingly, is to make sure that resources, support, and encouragement are available so that all children can have these experiences.

CHAPTER REVIEW

HOW DO THEY GROW?

- Children grow more slowly during the school-age years than they did as preschoolers. By the age of 6, they've reached almost two-thirds of their adult height.
- Most weight gain is concentrated in the muscles, so children increase in strength. Boys have more muscle cells than girls, which tends to make them stronger.
- The growth of the head slows, and the trunk and the legs grow more rapidly. This growth pattern gives school-age children a long and lean appearance. Facial appearance becomes longer and slimmer as the lower face and jaw begin to come into balance with the upper part of the head.
- Most children start to lose their first teeth at about age 6, and by age 11 or 12, they have all their permanent teeth except for two sets of molars.
- All children grow at their own individual rates. Normal variations are particularly apparent toward the end of the school-age period when the preadolescent growth spurt occurs.

- Some children don't grow properly. Children who grow much more slowly than average are called failure-to-thrive children. If their retarded growth is caused by environmental factors, it can be treated by providing counseling to the parents or placing the child in a foster home. If it's caused by physical factors, it can often be treated medically, by administering growth hormone, for example.
- The most common abnormal growth pattern in school-age children is obesity. Studies have shown that obese children exercise less and watch more television than their normal-weight peers. A correlation exists between obesity in parents and obesity in children, suggesting that this condition may have a genetic basis.
- Obese children may have to take extraordinary steps to keep their weight under control. Programs for obese children often use behavior modification techniques that help them take responsibility for their eating habits.

MOTOR DEVELOPMENT

- School-age children rapidly acquire many gross and fine motor skills, and they use and practice these skills in their sports, games, and activities. As their fine motor skills mature, their handwriting becomes smaller and more precise.
- Certain injuries are associated with excessive exercise during these years, because bones and muscles are still immature. When children overuse one part of their bodies, they can suffer stress fractures and sprains, which can lead to long-term disabilities. For

this reason, knowledgeable adults should supervise children's sports programs.
- Children should be encouraged to participate in physical activities and physical education programs. Physical activity promotes cognitive development, increases physical strength, helps develop better motor coordination, improves self-esteem, and provides opportunities for peer interactions. It would be optimal if schools devoted some part of every day to physical education.

KEY TERMS

lateralization of the brain
myelination
malocclusion
preadolescent growth
   spurt

failure-to-thrive
idiopathic growth
   retardation

SUGGESTIONS FOR FURTHER READING

Cratty, B. J. (1986). *Perceptual and motor development in infants and children* (3d ed.). Englewood Cliffs, NJ: Prentice-Hall.

This classic provides a thorough discussion of physical growth and motor development in language that is highly readable. Chapters on hands, visual perception, and the effects of exercise provide interesting information.

Haywood, K. M. (1986). *Life span motor development.* Champaign, IL: Human Kinetics.

This book is very readable and contains interesting material about the effects of practice on motor skills, the ease with which outstanding athletes can be identified early in life, and the extent to which body build is genetically determined.

Lewis, V. (1987). *Development and handicap.* Palo Alto, CA: Blackwell.

This book includes informative discussions of motor development often associated with certain conditions, such as Down's syndrome, spina bifida, and cerebral palsy.

COGNITIVE DEVELOPMENT IN SCHOOL-AGE CHILDREN

Jason and Chris were sitting at opposite ends of the dining room table with books and papers strewn around them. Chris, a second grader, had done his homework and was setting up a chess game. He was waiting for his older brother, who was in the fifth grade, to finish studying for a science test. As he carefully arranged the pawns for the third time, he said, "Are you almost done, Jason? How much longer will you be?"

"Just a few more minutes," Jason answered. "I have to go over this hard part again. It's about changing Fahrenheit temperatures into Celsius."

"Okay, but hurry up!"

"Did you check your math problems, Chris?" their dad, Jack, asked as he came into the room.

"No, but I know they're all right," he replied. Jack began to glance over Chris's homework. "Better check it, Chris," he said.

"Why? What's wrong?"

"Well, just go across and check them. You'll find the mistakes."

Chris took the paper and began to look it over. "Oh," he said, "here's a mistake." He found two more errors and corrected them all. By the time he'd finished, Jason was done studying. "I'll get up early and go over the definitions again," Jason said. He folded up the list he had written out and marked his place in the book with it. "Okay, Chris, let's play chess! What do you want to be, white or black?"

Children make dramatic gains in cognitive skills during the school-age years. Second graders like Chris can do specific tasks using standard procedures, such as adding and subtracting, but they don't easily think about *how* to approach problems. It doesn't occur to them to organize information, pay special attention to certain details, or review their work. Fifth graders like Jason, on the other hand, have much broader ideas about thinking, learning, and problem-solving strategies. They can organize information, identify more difficult material, plan their time, create memory devices, and review their knowledge. All these abilities are reflections of their increasing cognitive sophistication.

The thinking of school-age children is also more logical than the thinking of preschool children. We saw in Chapter 10 that preschoolers often understand and evaluate situations on the basis of appearance. But by the beginning of the school-age years, and with the emergence of the cognitive stage Piaget called concrete operational, children start to use logic and mental operations to understand situations and think about how things work.

Piaget saw the operations and explanations of the concrete operational child as supporting one another in the structure of this cognitive stage. For example, in considering the conservation of liquid problem (the problem of whether the amount of a liquid changes when it is poured into a container of a different size or shape, as described in Chapter 10), the preoperational child judges solely on the basis of the heights of the liquid in the different containers. But the concrete operational child uses such understandings as **identity, compensation,** and **reversibility** to evaluate the problem. Her initial realization that width may compensate for height (compensation) is supported by her previously overlooked knowledge that no liquid has been added or taken away (identity) and that the initial level of liquid could be restored by reversing the action and returning the liquid to its original container (reversibility). The mutual support of these three explanations allows the child to see beyond the single dimension—the heights of the liquid—which misled her when she was preoperational. Figure 14-1 shows several different kinds of conservation that the concrete operational child comes to understand; note, however, that some appear to be more difficult to grasp than others.

Piaget saw the concrete operational child as using this structure of mutually supporting explanations in problems of classification and seriation as well as conservation. He saw her as able to apply concrete operations to objects that are physically confronting her or with which she is intimately familiar. The school-age child still can't think in abstract terms—that ability is the hallmark of Piaget's formal operational thinking, which he believed was generally not achieved until about 12 or 13 years of age.

Although Piaget's ideas are important in understanding cognitive development during the school-age years, his theory does not address some changes in intellectual performance during these years. These changes include growth in the knowledge base (number of facts known), increased capacity and efficiency of memory and cognitive processing (for example, older children can remember more numerical digits in a series than younger children can), and better selection and execution of strategies for allocating mental effort and solving problems (Kuhn, 1988; Sternberg, 1988). This last skill—the use of overall strategies in attacking familiar problems—is known as metacognitive ability and is perhaps the newest and most important mental ability distinguishing school-age from younger children. It is the skill that made the difference in how Jason and Chris approached their homework.

This chapter addresses several topics in cognitive development. We begin with metacognition, and then we look at variations in cognitive development among school-age children, particularly in intelligence as measured by intelligence tests. We then explore the long-standing controversy about whether

FIGURE 14-1
Piaget found that different types of conservation were mastered at different ages, most of them during the school-age years. Conservation is one of the hallmarks of Piaget's concrete operational stage of cognitive development.

Type of Conservation	Dimension	Change in Physical Appearance	Average Age at Which Invariance Is Grasped
Number	Number of elements in a collection	Rearranging or dislocating elements	6–7
Substance (mass) (continuous quantity)	Amount of a malleable substance (e.g., clay or liquid)	Altering shape	7–8
Length	Length of a line or object	Altering shape or configuration	7–8
Area	Amount of surface covered by a set of plane figures	Rearranging the figures	8–9
Weight	Weight of an object	Altering its shape	9–10
Volume	Volume of an object (in terms of water displacement)	Altering its shape	11–14

intelligence is inherited and remains stable or is influenced by a person's experiences. We also consider the issue of cultural bias in intelligence tests. Finally we look at variations among children in factors other than ability that have an impact on academic success. We consider variations both in values and beliefs about academic achievement and in children's self-perceptions of academic competence. Together these topics give a broad picture of cognitive growth during the school years.

METACOGNITIVE ABILITIES

Metacognition refers to the ability to think about thinking, to play with thoughts, and to monitor and deploy mental effort strategically. When a child plays chess or checkers and thinks through his moves in terms of what moves his opponent may make in response, he's not only thinking—he's thinking about thinking. When a child makes up a joke, or laughs at one, he's playing with thoughts. And when a child decides to study one section of a text more than others, makes a list of definitions, or reviews certain material right before the test, he's deploying mental effort strategically.

Metacognition is one of the important cognitive characteristics that develops during the school-age years. This chapter focuses on the metacognitive abilities that allow children to monitor their own thinking and develop mental strategies to help themselves learn and solve problems. Because the ability to understand jokes and riddles is a specific type of **metalinguistic awareness,** we will discuss this behavior in Chapter 15, Language Development in School-Age Children. And because the ability to think about what someone else is thinking can significantly alter the way that children relate socially to other children and to adults, we consider this behavior in Chapter 16, Social and Emotional Development in School-Age Children.

Monitoring Understanding

"Does this make sense?" "Are these instructions correct?" "Do I have all the information I need to do this assignment?" These are some of the questions a child with metacognitive monitoring ability asks while reading or listening to verbal instructions. When does this ability appear? Several studies have investigated this question.

FIGURE 14-2
School-age children begin to understand chess as a strategy game because they can think about how their opponent may respond to their moves. Somewhat later, they'll be able to consider a greater number of possible responses and the implications of each response. Possibly the most brilliant chess game in the history of the game was played by Bobby Fischer at the age of 13.

In some of the research, children have been asked to read text materials containing inconsistencies and contradictions. In one study, two groups of children—8-year-olds and 11-year-olds—were given material to read in which some sentences didn't correspond with the titles of the passages. For example, in a paragraph entitled "A Trip to the Toy Store," they might read, "She walked down the aisle and selected some rolls of paper towels," a sentence that would make more sense in a paragraph entitled, "A Trip to the Supermarket."

Children from both age groups read more slowly when they encountered sentences that didn't seem to make sense in terms of the title of the piece. But when questioned about the material later, many more 11-year-olds than 8-year-olds talked about the problems they had detected in some of the sentences (Harris et al., 1981).

In another study, children were asked to listen to taped instructions about how to create a block building. Both kindergartners and second graders looked puzzled or replayed the tape at points where it contained insufficient information or unfamiliar words. Yet when the children were asked later about their block buildings or the instructions, which had been taped by another child, the second graders were much more likely than the kindergartners to report problems in the instructions (Flavell et al., 1981).

These and other studies show that although both younger and older children indicate by their behavior when they're having problems with understanding, only the older children can report on the inconsistencies or gaps in the instructions. Some people have suggested that younger children just might not have the verbal skills to express the problems in the messages. This isn't really a very plausible explanation because even kindergartners have a fair amount of verbal ability.

Another, more probable, explanation is that younger children lack the background knowledge and experience to know with assurance when something is wrong in their environment. They're more likely to think that they've gotten mixed up or don't understand. Older children, who are surer about what is found in toy stores and supermarkets, for example, might be more inclined to realize there is a problem with the message or instructions, thinking, "Something's wrong here. What is it?" This focus on the message puts them in a better position to pinpoint and remember a problem in the text when they're asked about it.

Developing Memory Strategies

"How can I remember this?" "What are the important ideas here?" "What points are irrelevant?" The ability to think about information this way, as well as to direct mental effort strategically, is another aspect of metacognitive functioning. We saw that Jason, a fifth grader, had this ability—he was able to identify parts of his book that required special study strategies.

Again, younger children aren't very skillful at tasks as simple as remembering pictures from a collection they've examined. When asked to name them from memory, kindergartners say they're ready, but then they can't recall many of the items. They don't seem to organize the items into categories, make associations between the items and something else that will serve as a

FIGURE 14-3
These second graders have put together an impressive "multi-media" project about chickens, and they're justly proud of it. But if they were asked to give an oral report on their work, either spontaneously or with written cue cards, they would show a limited ability to organize their thoughts. The more knowledge they acquire during the school years, the better able they'll be to understand and organize information.

reminder, or go through practice runs to see if they have in fact memorized the items (Flavell, Beach & Chinsky, 1966). Second graders, on the other hand, tend to use some of these memory strategies, although their strategies aren't as sophisticated as those of older children or adults (Lovett & Flavell, 1990). Of course, the more background information and context a person has for new information, the better able the person is to categorize it and develop associations that will help to prompt recall (Ornstein & Naus, 1978).

Younger children can be taught strategies like rehearsal, and this improves their memory considerably (Belmont & Butterfield, 1977). They can be given mnemonics (memory devices), such as "Roy G Biv" for the colors of the rainbow and "My Very Educated Mother Just Served Us Nine Pizzas" for the names of the planets. Young children show some use of strategies in familiar settings with goals that make sense to them—such as remembering where a toy has been hidden—although even here, their skills are fragile and inconsistent (DeLoache, Cassidy & Brown, 1985).

Overall, preschool children and younger school-age children don't use memory strategies efficiently. And older school-age children don't have the skills of high school and college students. The ability to remember, to store and retrieve material efficiently, is a matter of organizing the material conceptually. Thus, it makes sense that an older child, who has more knowledge and skills to use in developing a system to organize material, would be able to remember things better than a younger child, who knows and understands less.

Monitoring the Organization of Text

Other metacognitive skills important to studying emerge even later during the elementary school years. When asked to identify the portions of a text that were closely related to a specified theme, for example, third graders were unable to determine how relevant a passage was. Fifth graders couldn't distinguish among any of the less relevant passages (which ranged from totally irrelevant to somewhat relevant). Seventh graders could identify passages at the extremes (very relevant and very irrelevant) but couldn't make any finer distinctions. Only the twelfth graders in this study could accurately rank all portions of the text in terms of the four levels of relevance specified (Brown & Smiley, 1977).

Other study skills, such as notetaking, summarizing, and outlining, also require metacognitive abilities. Students must weed out irrelevant information, notice redundancies so they don't note the same thing twice, create categories, and use category markers such as topic sentences and headings. Fifth graders can delete irrelevant and redundant information, but they aren't very good at creating categories or using category markers provided by a text. Seventh and tenth graders are much more skillful at these activities, although poorer students, even at the college level, still have great difficulty with them (Brown & Day, 1983).

Analyzing Relationships

Another area of metacognition involves analogical reasoning—reasoning about analogies, or relationships. An example of an analogy is *bicycle: wheel :: ice skates: blade* (read, "bicycle is to wheel as ice skates are to blade.") That is, a wheel supports a bicycle in moving across a surface in the same way that blades support ice skates. In this analogy, the double colon represents a relationship (that of analogy or sameness) between relationships (those of support).

Now suppose a child is asked to complete the analogy *bicycle: road :: skates:* _____ by selecting a word from among the following: *blade, lake, shoe, rink.* Children younger than 9 or 10 often have difficulty with analogies like this (Piaget et al., 1977, cited in Goswami, 1991). Piaget concluded that only with the onset of formal operational thinking at about 12 could children begin to reason about such relationships between relationships. But more recent research indicates that young children—even 3-, 4-, and 5-year olds—have this ability. In one study researchers read children stories about how specific animals protect themselves from predators by using such defense mechanisms as mimicry and camouflage (Brown & Kane, 1988). The researchers then asked children how other animals could protect themselves from predators. The children applied information from the stories to other kinds of animals in very appropriate ways, indicating that they could see similarities among different animals and the predicaments they encountered.

This study and others suggest that it's not analogical reasoning ability itself that accounts for the better performance of older children on many analogy tasks. Younger children do seem capable of reasoning about relationships. Some of the differences are probably due to the greater general knowledge of the older children. But researchers also think that children become increasingly inclined throughout the school years to reflect on their previous knowledge and to seek out relational similarities to solve new problems. Younger children *can* think this way if they are explicitly asked to do so, if they are given practice and feedback, and if the task is in a familiar context. But they don't actively use this kind of thinking to solve problems, and they don't think about logic in general and how it can be applied to new situations. Reasoning

FIGURE 14-4
Metacognitive abilities become increasingly important as children move through elementary school. To succeed in her gifted math class, this sixth grader has to be able to recognize important information, distinguish it from unimportant material, organize it in such a way that she can remember it, and relate it to other knowledge she already has.

about relationships is not a strategy children typically use to solve problems until the later school years (Goswami, 1991).

The Importance of Metacognitive Abilities and Sternberg's Triarchic Theory of Intelligence

Metacognitive abilities are now acknowledged to have a fundamental place in theories of cognitive functioning that are based on principles of information processing. One of the most comprehensive of these approaches is Robert Sternberg's **triarchic theory of intelligence** (1984, 1990). Sternberg focuses on internal mental processes as a fundamental part of intelligence, particularly the higher-order, metacognitive processes a person uses to perform "executive" mental functions. These metacomponents, as Sternberg calls them, allow a person to plan and carry out an overall plan of intelligent action by selecting and combining other, lower-order processes related to knowledge acquisition and performance. Sternberg identifies such metacomponents as (1) recognizing that a problem exists, (2) choosing the lower-order components to combine to solve the problem, (3) selecting a plan by which to combine the components, (4) allocating resources, and (5) monitoring performance (1990). Sternberg calls this view of intelligence, which focuses on the internal world of the individual, the **componential subtheory of intelligence.**

Sternberg's triarchic theory also addresses a second general area, the interrelationship between the intelligent actor and the environment. Consistent with other systems theories, the theory looks at how the person adapts to, shapes, or selects environments over the long term. An intelligent person is seen as one who learns to function well in her environment (whether it is an urban American classroom or a rural African village), or to modify that environment in such a way that she can function well in it, or to find another environment in which she can function well. Sternberg refers to this view of intelligence, which focuses on the external world, as the **contextual subtheory of intelligence.**

The third general area addressed by Sternberg's theory is the relationship between intelligence and relatively immediate experience, especially how the individual learns to deal with novelty and how she makes newly acquired aspects of information processing "automatic." The theory suggests that metacomponents are crucial in understanding novel events and eventually transforming this knowledge into efficient routines. This view of intelligence, which relates intelligence to both internal and external worlds, is labeled the **experiential subtheory of intelligence.**

Sternberg's theory is consistent with other research about the importance of metacognitive abilities for many learning tasks in school, especially once children begin to have the heavy reading assignments associated with the upper grades of elementary school and beyond. Children can't study effectively if they can't distinguish what's important and focus on it, or if they can't organize material in such a way that they can remember it. To learn efficiently and succeed in school, students have to be aware of what they know, what is important to know, and how to sort through and master material. They must also be able to judge the clarity of both verbal and written communications. If a child recognizes that a spoken message is unclear, she can ask a clarifying question. This often prompts an explanation, which gives her access to better information. If she finds that a written message is unclear, she can consult another source, which also enhances learning. Analogical reasoning also influences a child's ability to learn. If she can see relationships across situations, she can apply previous knowledge and derive general concepts or principles.

It isn't clear how children develop all these metacognitive abilities—the ability to monitor messages, use memory strategies, reason analogically, and use metacomponents. Development probably depends on a combination of factors, including maturation, increased knowledge, observation of others who use these strategies, and explicit instruction and practice.

INTELLIGENCE TESTS

Our discussion of metacognitive abilities highlights the importance of school for children in our society. Going to school—learning, practicing, gaining knowledge and skills, establishing a sense of oneself in relation to other children and to adults—is what children do. And success in school is a potent factor in an individual's future success and happiness. It's no wonder that adults—both teachers and parents—are concerned about how children are doing in school, how children who are having difficulties can be helped, and how educational programs can be improved so children can learn better.

One of the ways adults discover how children who are having difficulties in school can be helped is by testing them. Intelligence tests are frequently administered during elementary school years to estimate children's ability to learn academic skills under standard school conditions. Subtests within the IQ test tap different kinds of thinking and different products of thinking, such as the abilities to define words, discuss objects in terms of similarities and differences, and put puzzles together. The fact that IQ test scores do a good job of predicting school achievement is evidence that they do in fact measure *ability to learn school tasks.*

The first intelligence test was developed by Alfred Binet and Theodore Simon in the early 1900s. They had been asked to devise a way to distinguish Parisian schoolchildren who could be expected to succeed from those who would probably fail. Binet and Simon chose tasks requiring judgment and reasoning and administered them to a large number of children. **Norms**—tables

FIGURE 14-5
Many children take intelligence tests, but the validity of these tests for a broad range of diverse populations is under scrutiny today.

of expected results for each age—were calculated to show the average number of tasks passed by children at different ages. Binet and Simon determined a child's **mental age** (MA) by finding the number of tasks passed by the child and looking at the norms to discover the age of the children who typically passed this number of tasks. For example, a 5-year-old who passed only the number of items typically passed by 3-year-olds was said to have a mental age of 3.

But there is a problem with using only mental age as a measure of the learning ability of children of different chronological ages. A given MA has different meanings for children of differing chronological ages. A 2-year-old, for example, with an MA of 3 years is more intelligent than a 5-year-old with an MA of 3 years. The concept of the **intelligence quotient** (IQ) was introduced to take **chronological age** (CA) into account (Stern, 1912). An IQ was calculated according to the following formula:

$$MA/CA \times 100 = IQ$$

A 5-year-old with an MA of 3 has an IQ of 60:

$$MA(3)/CA(5) \times 100 = 60$$

A 2-year-old with an MA of 3 has an IQ of 150:

$$MA(3)/CA(2) \times 100 = 150$$

A child whose MA and CA are the same has an IQ of 100. A child whose MA is higher than his CA, one who learns faster than average, has an IQ of over 100. Today a psychologist can look up a child's IQ directly by checking his score, representing the total number of items he passed, in the norm table for his age group. The ratio method is no longer used. As you can see from the graph showing the distribution of IQ scores in the population (Figure 14-6), half the people tested have IQs between 90 and 110. Only about 2.5 percent

FIGURE 14-6
The normal statistical distribution of IQs, showing percentages of the population expected to fall in each IQ range. (Due to rounding, the total is more than 100 percent.) About half the population have IQs close to the average, which is 100.

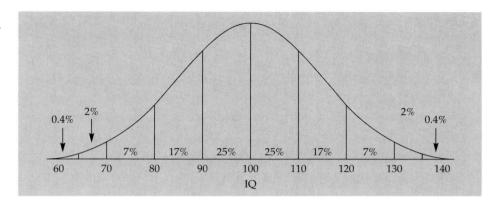

of the population have IQs above 130, and an additional 2.5 have IQs below 70. An IQ lower than 70 is said to fall in the mentally retarded range. (For a discussion of this topic, see Special Education Focus—Mental Retardation.)

There are several controversial issues involved in testing children for intelligence, including the possibility of built-in cultural bias and the problem of "teaching to the test." We will discuss the latter issue, as well as the testing instruments commonly used in schools today, in Knowledge in Action: School-Age Children. Here we discuss the more theoretical issue of the relative contributions of nature and nurture to intelligence. This theoretical issue addresses the question of whether children come into the world with their intellectual abilities established or whether their intelligence is something that grows and develops, or languishes and withers, with their experiences in the world. We will address the issue of cultural bias later in this chapter.

Intelligence: Fixed at Birth or Influenced by Environment?

We've all heard people refer to someone's IQ as a fixed number, even if the person hasn't had an IQ test in years. Is IQ stable over long periods of time, even over a whole lifetime? Does performance on an IQ test indicate a potential for intellectual functioning that remains constant? This has been the traditional view of intelligence. According to this view, intelligence is determined primarily by genetics. A child who receives a score of 90 on an IQ test at age 7 should receive a score of 90 again at 10, regardless of whether her environment has changed.

Obviously, experience influences whether a child will get any single item correct on an intelligence test, since children learn new words, acquire more information, and develop more sophisticated ways of thinking as they get older. But according to the fixed, genetic view of intelligence, a child's *capacity* to learn is unchangeable. A child may pass more items at age 10 than at age 7 because she's had more experiences, but a child who inherited more intelligence would be expected to learn more from experience in those three years than a child who inherited less. Her IQ at 10 would still be the same in relation to her peers as it was when she was 7.

The fixed, genetic view of intelligence has been challenged and fiercely debated for many years. What are the contributions of nature and nurture to intelligence? Can the two ever be separated? To get some answers to these

SPECIAL EDUCATION FOCUS

Mental Retardation

In 1975 Public Law 94-142, the Individuals with Disabilities Education Act, called for children with handicapping conditions to be educated in the "least restrictive environment," which means they should be placed with nonhandicapped children as much as possible. As a result, many children with mild and moderate mental retardation today are members of regular classrooms in public schools. The practice of placing children with disabilities in the same classroom as children without disabilities is called **mainstreaming.** Retarded children are taught within the classroom or out of it, as needed, for varying portions of the day. Teachers with a retarded child in their classroom have to develop a special plan to provide the best education to both the retarded child and the rest of the children in the class.

What is mental retardation? According to the American Association on Mental Deficiency (AAMD), mental retardation is defined as "significantly subaverage general intellectual functioning resulting in or associated with impairments in adaptive behavior and manifested during the developmental period" (Grossman, 1983). Let's consider what all of this means.

"Subaverage general intellectual functioning" is defined as a score of less than 70 on one or more of the individually administered standardized tests of intelligence. "Adaptive behavior" refers to the self-help and social skills needed to get along in everyday life. Problems in adaptive behavior are harder to identify than an IQ below 70, because a person is likely to function better in some environments than others. Usually, observation of the person's behavior, along with some clinical judgment made by a professional health worker, is used to identify impaired adaptive behavior. There are some standardized tests too, however. One of the best known is the Vineland Adaptive Behavior Scales, which outlines the communication, daily-living, and socialization skills that should develop at given ages. For example, at ages 6 and 7, the items on the scale are "uses spoon, fork, and knife competently," "initiates telephone calls to others," and "prints own first and last name" (Sparrow, Balla & Cicchetti, 1984).

"Manifested during the developmental period" means that the delays in intelligence and adaptive behavior occur before the person is 18 years old. If impairments take place after 18, the diagnosis is "dementia," an actual loss of previous intellectual abilities for some biological reason (American Psychiatric Association, 1987).

Degrees of Retardation

Most of us recognize and are familiar with mildly retarded people—for example, some individuals with Down's syndrome may be seen working in the community. More severely retarded people, on the other hand, usually live in special homes and institutions. Four categories of retardation are recognized: mild, moderate, severe, and profound. Each category is defined by a specific IQ range (Baumeister, 1987). In **mild mental retardation,** the category with the largest number of individuals, IQ scores range from 50 to 70. Mildly retarded children often aren't recognized until they've done poorly in elementary school and have been referred for testing.

In **moderate mental retardation**, IQ scores range from 35 to 49. This group makes up about 12 percent of the retarded population. **Severe mental retardation** is defined by IQ scores ranging from 20 to 34, and individuals with **profound mental retardation** have scores below 20.

When dealing with children in school, we encounter different labels. In many states, the term "learning disabilities" is applied to conditions in which the difficulty seems to be in a specific area of learning rather than in intelligence per se (Baumeister, 1987). The special education category of **educable mentally retarded** corresponds roughly with mild mental retardation. The special education category **trainable mentally retarded** corresponds to moderate and severe mental retardation.

The special education terminology refers to programs for the retarded, not strictly to IQ levels. Educable mentally retarded children are taught fundamental academic skills they'll need to function independently as adults. Most trainable mentally retarded children, on the other hand, are considered unlikely to progress beyond the second-grade level in academics. Their curriculum emphasizes vocational, self-help, and social skills.

Causes of Retardation

What agents or conditions are responsible for these different levels of mental retardation? Sometimes, the problem is genetic or chromosomal. Down's syndrome (a disease caused by a chromosomal abnormality) is one of the most common inherited conditions that causes mental retardation. At other times, when a child is born retarded, the condition may have been caused by a disease, such as syphilis, or a drug, such as alcohol. Mental retardation can be caused during childhood

---

questions, many researchers have compared the IQs of people who are related to each other biologically but have been raised in different environments. Some of those studies are considered next.

STUDIES OF IQ AND KINSHIP. In one classic type of study, researchers compared identical twins who had been brought up in different environments (Newman, Freeman & Holzinger, 1937; Shields, 1962). Since identical twins have the same genetic make-up, this kind of study was thought to reveal whether intelligence is determined more by genetic inheritance or by environmental conditions.

Terminology and Levels of Mental Retardation in Two Major Classification Schemes	IQ	Classification Scheme	
		American Association on Mental Deficiency	American Educators
	100		
	90		
	80		Dull normal
	70		
	60	Mild	Educable
	50		
	40	Moderate	Trainable
	30	Severe	
	20		Custodial or Dependent
		Profound	

SOURCES: Grossman, H. (Ed.). (1983). Classification in mental retardation. *Washington, DC: American Association on Mental Deficiency.*
Smith, R. (1971). An introduction to mental retardation. *New York: McGraw-Hill.*

by injury, such as a blow to the head in an auto accident, or by disease, such as meningitis or encephalitis. Children can also become mentally retarded from ingesting toxic substances like lead.

Sometimes, children are mentally retarded because they've been neglected by their parents and haven't received enough cognitive stimulation. As we've mentioned in several other contexts, mental development is correlated with parental responsiveness and involvement and with the availability of play materials in the home (Yarrow, Rubenstein & Pedersen, 1971; Ainsworth & Bell, 1973; White & Watts, 1973; Bradley, Caldwell & Rock, 1988). A fairly high percentage of mild retardation is associated with deprived environments, which tend to occur more frequently in the homes of economically disadvantaged families. Lower socioeconomic status is also associated with greater environmental hazards, poor medical care, and malnutrition, all of which can contribute to impaired mental functioning as well (Brockman & Ricciuti, 1971; Winick, 1976).

Different environments and backgrounds can also produce different approaches to problem solving, which can then lead to different performances on intelligence tests. Children with these different approaches may score lower on IQ tests when they don't actually have any mental impairment (Baumeister, 1987; Miller-Jones, 1989). Because socioeconomic status is correlated with race, a large percentage of individuals judged to be mildly mentally retarded are from racial minorities (Grossman, 1983). It seems clear that some of these judgments may be made on the basis of *different* mental functioning rather than impaired mental functioning. This possibility was at the heart of a California Federal District Court decision that banned the use of IQ scores as a basis for placing children in special education classes (Larry P. V. Riles, 1974). The judge declared that the intelligence tests used were **culturally biased**—constructed and evaluated in such a way that they reflect the specific approach to problem solving found in the dominant, white, middle-class culture.

The results have been interpreted to mean that genetic inheritance is the stronger determinant. Identical twins reared apart, for example, have been found to be closer in intelligence than fraternal twins reared together.

But these results have been challenged. Critics point out that adopted children aren't assigned to new families at random. If parents give up a twin, they often place the baby with a relative or a family similar to their own in important ways, such as socioeconomic level. Agencies, too, try to place babies in homes that are similar to one another. Even though they're reared apart, then, these twins might have been raised in similar environments (Kamin, 1974;

Schwartz & Schwartz, 1974). If adopted children are assigned to similar environments rather than assigned randomly to families, these findings can't be generalized to the whole population. The narrower the range of environments, the greater the apparent effect of heredity on the outcome.

A variation of this kind of study involves comparing the intelligence of adopted children to the intelligence of both their biological and their adoptive parents. In one study, babies of mothers with IQs in the 80s who were placed in good foster homes before they were 6 months old were found to have IQs of about 110 (Skodak & Skeels, 1949). The researchers claimed that the differences between the IQs of the mothers and those of the babies indicate that environment plays an important role in determining intelligence.

This study has also been criticized. For one thing, children don't inherit their parents' characteristics to the same extent that their parents have them. Instead, they differ from their parents in the direction of the mean (average) of the population. For example, if a parent has a very high IQ, the child's IQ is expected to be somewhat less high, and if the parent has a very low IQ, the child's IQ is expected to be somewhat less low. This statistical phenomenon is referred to as **regression toward the mean.** In the study just described, part of the difference in IQ between the children and their biological parents could be explained by this phenomenon (Jensen, 1973).

FIGURE 14-7
Will the mental abilities of these children be closer to those of their biological parents or their adoptive mother? Although researchers have been eager to study adopted children, the results of their studies are complicated by other factors, such as nonrandom placement of children in adoptive homes and the statistical phenomenon known as regression toward the mean.

Another criticism of this study is that the children were selected for adoption on the basis of their good health. In addition, there was a probationary period during which the adoptive parents could reject any child they thought was intellectually impaired. The children actually adopted may have been the ones who were most capable intellectually to begin with. Their higher IQs may have been a result of genetic factors rather than, or in addition to, improved environmental conditions.

Studies of biologically related individuals raised in different environments have been used to estimate statistically the degree to which variations in the IQs of these individuals are due to genetic variations in the general population. The statistic used is known as **heritability,** which may vary between 0 and 1.0. A heritability of .75 would be a very strong genetic influence, and a heritability of .25 would be an important but relatively weak influence.

As in other studies, computing heritability from kinship studies is subject to the criticism that kin are assigned to environments that are likely to be similar in important ways rather than to environments reflecting the broad range to which the general population is exposed. Nevertheless, recent estimates suggest the heritability index for IQ is *on the average* about .50, a moderate genetic influence (Plomin, 1986; 1989). The remaining variation in IQ in the population is thought to be largely due to the effect of experience or environment.

Kinship studies have not yet settled the issue of how much heredity and environment contribute to variations in IQ in the general population. And they certainly have not addressed questions about the source of any *individual's* handicap or the possible benefits of intervention programs (Weinberg, 1989). The question of how specific handicaps or benefits occur will not be answered until the question of how genetics and environment interact to produce high or low IQs is precisely understood (Anastasi, 1958).

STUDIES OF CHANGED ENVIRONMENTAL CONDITIONS. Other researchers have taken a somewhat different approach to the nature-nurture question, one that involves altering children's environment intentionally to see how intelligence is affected. We saw in Chapter 5 that some research has been done in which stimulation was added to babies' environments to see if it would speed up their physical development. In one early study in which children were given colorful objects to look at, they were found to begin reaching and grasping earlier than normal (White, 1971). Similar research has been done to determine if adding stimulation to the environment affects children's intelligence.

In a classic study of intellectual change, two young girls living in an orphanage were transferred by chance to a home for retarded children when they were about 18 months old (Skeels, 1966). There they were cared for by the older girls on the ward. The girls took great interest in the babies and showered them with attention they hadn't received at the crowded, unstimulating orphanage. After a few months, the two children, who had previously been thought to be retarded, showed amazing alertness.

As a result of this development, a research study was undertaken in which 13 more 18-month-old children were transferred from the ward to the home for retarded children. A control group remained in the orphanage. After two years, the children who had been transferred showed an average increase in IQ of about 28 points, and the children who remained behind showed a decline of about the same amount. Because the transferred children no longer showed signs of being retarded, 11 of them were adopted.

A follow-up study of the two groups was done when they had reached adulthood. All 13 of those who had been transferred were self-supporting adults, and many held good jobs. Most had received a high school education. Those who had remained in the orphanage didn't fare nearly as well. Several were still in institutions, and those who weren't held unskilled jobs. Most had completed only a few years of school. Data from this study provide some evidence that the environment can affect intellectual functioning.

Of course, not even the strongest advocates of the genetic position deny that intelligence is affected by environmental factors. The controversy is over the relative importance of the two domains and whether their effects can be understood separately. Systems theorists in particular think that nature and nurture interact in complex ways to affect development. Many believe that it is almost impossible to untangle the effects of one from the other. Still, disagreement about the relative effects of nature versus nurture flourishes today, and one of the reasons for the continuing controversy is that different groups have different tested IQs, a topic we turn to text.

Group Differences in Tested Intelligence

Different groups tend to have different IQs, and these differences are associated with race and with social class, which is defined by income, education, and occupation. Middle-class children have higher IQs as a group than poor children, and black children have IQs that average about 15 points lower than those of white children (Jensen, 1969). (Although some of Jensen's conclusions have been found highly problematic, as mentioned earlier in this book, these data have been judged to be valid.) People have asked the same question about group IQs as they have about individual IQs—are differences due to genetic inheritance or environmental factors?

Research has cast doubt on genetic explanations of group differences in IQ (Scarr & Weinberg, 1978; Weinberg, 1989). In two studies of adoption, one involving white adolescents, the other involving black children adopted into white homes, the results suggest that differences are not genetically based. Black children raised in white middle-class families have an average IQ of 110, about 15 points higher than the IQs of black children raised by their own parents. The average IQ score of both black and white adopted children (110) was higher than the average IQ of their biological parents, which was estimated on the basis of their educational level to be about 100. But adopted children didn't score as high as the biological children of adoptive parents (116.7) or as the adoptive parents themselves (119). The researchers concluded that individual differences within a group from similar environments, such as middle-class white children, may be largely genetic in origin, and that group differences are due largely to differences in environment.

Cultural Bias in Intelligence Tests

What is it about the environment that affects how groups score on IQ tests? Since the 1960s many people have suggested that standard intelligence tests reflect the values and interests of white middle-class culture so strongly that

FIGURE 14-8
Although mainstream culture white children as a group score higher on IQ tests than other groups, these results don't necessarily mean that they are more intelligent. If intelligence tests measured the cognitive skills acquired in the course of growing up in a traditional Native American community, this Navaho girl would probably score higher than her white mainstream culture counterparts.

they contain an inherent bias against individuals from other backgrounds. The subjects covered, the experiences assumed by the questions, the format of the test, the notion of sitting down and taking a test, and the testing situation itself, all imply an approach to problem solving and a view of intelligence that aren't necessarily shared by other cultures. In fact, some people are now suggesting that there are several different kinds of intelligence and that current IQ tests measure only one of them. Gardner (1983), for example, has proposed that intelligence can be linguistic, logical-mathematical, spatial, musical, bodily-kinesthetic, or personal in nature and that different people can have varying amounts of each kind.

Differences in measured intelligence, then, can result from differences in culture. Tests standardized on one cultural group are likely to yield biased results when used with other groups. Experts believe IQ tests might not indicate children's total mental capacity or the level at which they're truly capable of functioning if they are members of minority groups (Miller-Jones, 1989). Since cultural diversity is increasing in the United States, intelligence testing is likely to remain a hotly debated issue in education throughout the 1990s.

ACADEMIC MOTIVATION AND SUCCESS IN SCHOOL

"I know he can do better, and that's why I've asked you to come in," the sixth-grade teacher explained to Gregory's parents. *"An F in math doesn't reflect his real ability at all. As you know, his IQ is very high. Gregory's problem is motivation."*

"We're aware there's a problem," Gregory's father replied. *"It's been getting worse for a few years now, since about third grade. He has a lot of interests—outdoor sports, playing the drums, collecting baseball cards—but he doesn't seem to care about books or school very much. We just don't know how to motivate him to hit the books."*

Conversations like this are difficult for parents and teachers alike. The complex phenomenon of motivation may be harder to define and understand than intelligence, but it's just as important to a child's ultimate success or failure in school. Gregory, for example, had a high IQ, indicating that he had the ability to get above-average grades in math. But for some reason, he wasn't directing his abilities toward the goal of mastering the mathematics required for his grade. Gregory apparently lacked motivation to achieve academically; that is, he did not apply the effort required to achieve in school.

Theories of learning and motivation tend to agree that the effort a student shows depends primarily on two factors: (1) the value of a particular goal to the student and (2) his expectation that he can succeed in achieving the goal. Students who don't make the effort required to learn in elementary school are thought either not to value school achievement or not to expect to be able to learn. When a child appears to be underachieving, a psychologist will test him to discover if he is mentally retarded or has a specific learning disability that interferes with his academic performance. If the child is found to be able, the psychologist can try either to increase the value of academic achievement to the child, such as by giving parents a daily report, or to increase the child's **perceived competence**—his feelings of self-efficacy—by such means as providing counseling to a child who is depressed or who believes he is ineffective. Ideally, of course, it is parents and teachers who teach children to value academic achievement and help them learn that with appropriate effort they can be both competent and effective academically. We consider next how this is done.

Achievement Goals and Academic Values

The first factor in academic motivation is the presence of achievement goals and academic values. For many years, psychologists have studied a "need to achieve" (McClelland et al., 1976) and found it to vary significantly from person to person. If the school psychologist measured Gregory's achievement

FIGURE 14-9
When parents stress achievement goals, children are more likely to have a "need to achieve." The parents of these children clearly expect them to excel and have provided the means for them to do so.

motivation in the way it has traditionally been measured, she would use an assessment instrument in which the person being tested is asked to create stories about pictures. A picture might show two men, identified as "inventors," working on a machine in a shop, for example; or a young boy and a violin; or a boy sitting at a desk with an open book in front of him. The person looks at the pictures and then answers the following questions about each one (McClelland et al., 1976, p. 98):

1. What is happening? Who are the people?
2. What were the circumstances leading up to the situation in the picture?
3. What are the characters thinking? What do they want?
4. What will happen? What will be done?

The tester judges the stories in terms of achievement goals—concern about success in competition with a standard of excellence. Subjects who refer to achievement goals frequently receive high achievement motivation ratings. Subjects who rarely refer to such goals receive low ratings.

Subjects who show a high need for achievement on this test are thought to come from environments that stress excelling and accomplishing goals, usually including academic goals. When parents view education in particular as important and engage in intellectual activities such as reading books at home, children often behave similarly, demonstrating high achievement (Bradley, Caldwell & Rock, 1988). When parents value other, nonacademic activities more highly, children are less likely to value education and academic achievement.

An interesting example of the impact of parental values on achievement motivation involves girls and math. Research has shown that mothers stress achievement in math for boys but not for girls (Baker & Entwisle, 1986) and that girls don't base their developing academic self-image on math performance, while boys do (Entwisle et al., 1988). In other words, girls can still think of themselves as good students even if they don't do well in math, while boys find it more difficult to think of themselves as good students if they do poorly in math. Apparently parental values about boys' and girls' performance in math influence whether children think math is an area in which they should try to perform well.

The math case is a specific instance of the more general case of the role that parental demands play in achievement motivation and achievement. High-achieving children often have parents who are demanding and critical, evaluate their children's performance, and apply some pressure. They also offer praise, get emotionally involved in their children's performance, and provide facilitative help (help that makes a task easier for the child to do or understand) rather than intrusive help (help that takes away from the child's enjoyment of the subject) (Rosen & D'Andrade, 1975).

Parental pressure and demands are effective, however, only when the expectations are reasonable and the child perceives herself to be competent. When parental expectations are unrealistic, when the parent's help is dominating and intrusive, or when the child doesn't believe herself to be competent, the child's effort and her achievement will be lowered (Dweck & Elliot, 1983).

Perceived Competence

The second factor in academic motivation is perceived competence in schoolwork—the child's subjective view of her academic abilities. Perceived competence is often thought to be determined by the child's history of past academic achievement. But even among children with the same academic

FIGURE 14-10
The boy asking the question may believe himself to be less competent at schoolwork than his classmate, even if they have comparable abilities. Perceived competence is a key ingredient in academic motivation, effort, and success.

achievement record, some children perceive themselves to be highly competent academically and others perceive themselves to be not as competent (Phillips, 1987). This self-perception plays a role independent of ability in determining academic effort. Some high-ability children have an "illusion of incompetence": They think they can't do something when they actually can (Langer, 1979; Phillips & Zimmerman, 1990). Because of this belief, they aren't as persistent on academic tasks as they might be, and their achievement suffers. Children with high perceived competence tend to be high achievers; children who see themselves as helpless tend to be low achievers (Carr, Borkowski & Maxwell, 1991; Okra & Paris, 1987).

There are at least three ways in which perceived competence influences effort (Bandura, 1989; 1990). By definition, high perceived competence increases the expectation that effort will be rewarded, which alone leads to greater effort. High perceived competence also reduces anxiety by lowering fear of failure in situations in which the child believes she has some control. When a child believes she has control, she is less likely to experience both the immediate effects of anxiety, such as distracting thoughts about possible negative outcomes, and the effects of chronic stress, such as exhaustion and depression. These states interfere with concentration and performance (Ciaranello, 1988). Finally, children who perceive themselves as competent plan their efforts in detail and rehearse them cognitively—that is, they develop and use metacognitive skills—because they believe such efforts will be rewarded with success.

Children's beliefs about their academic success and failure become more differentiated and effective with age (Skinner, 1990). At the beginning of their school careers, at about 7 or 8 years of age, children tend to distinguish only two sets of factors to account for their successes and failures. One set consists of "unknown" or "hard to tell" causes ("I don't know what happened"); the other set consists of effort; ability; other people, such as teachers; and luck, all of which they feel they can control through effort. At 9 and 10 years, children tend to use one of three sets of factors—unknown causes, internal causes (effort and ability), or external causes (others and luck). At 11 and 12, children tend to believe that academic performance is determined by one of four independent factors—effort, ability, external causes, or unknown causes. At this age, the tendency to attribute success and failure to external causes is an especially good predictor of poor grades in school (Skinner, 1990; Fincham, Hokoda & Saners, 1989).

The Socialization of Perceived Competence

Why is it that some children perceive themselves to be competent at schoolwork and others do not? Like differences among individuals in other aspects of personality, these variations are influenced by the socialization processes described in Chapter 12. These include direct verbal instruction and persuasion, observational learning, and past experiences of success and failure, all mediated in part by the effects of cognitive development and such biological factors as temperament.

As we have repeatedly emphasized, responsive caregiving in early childhood is extremely important for the development of initiative and feelings of

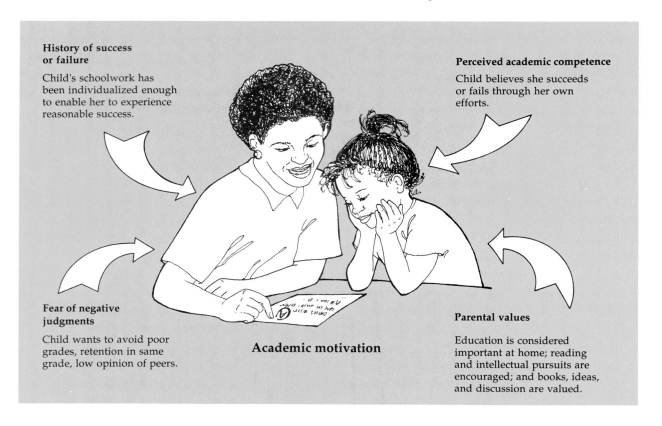

History of success
or failure

Child's schoolwork has
been individualized enough
to enable her to experience
reasonable success.

Perceived academic competence

Child believes she succeeds
or fails through her own
efforts.

Fear of negative
judgments

Child wants to avoid poor
grades, retention in same
grade, low opinion of peers.

Academic motivation

Parental values

Education is considered
important at home; reading
and intellectual pursuits are
encouraged; and books, ideas,
and discussion are valued.

FIGURE 14-11
Factors influencing academic
motivation. In the case
described here, all the factors
support high academic motivation. If conditions are different—for example, if reading,
schoolwork, and academic
success are not especially
important to a child's family—
the child is less likely to be
motivated to achieve in
school.

self-efficacy in the infant and toddler. As the child grows, feelings of self-efficacy in the particular realm of academics become increasingly important for
perceived school competence and effort (Bandura, 1990). Perceived academic
competence is enhanced when the child applies effort and then succeeds at
academic tasks; when he observes others similar to himself being successful
in school; and when his inner experience doesn't suggest failure—that is,
when he doesn't experience feelings of anxiety or depression. Other extremely
important influences on children's perceived competence are the instruction
and persuasive power of parents and teachers. We turn to a more detailed look
at these influences next.

PARENTAL BELIEFS AND EXPECTATIONS. A child's perceived competence is strongly
influenced by her parents' beliefs about her intellectual abilities. In one study,
third graders' views of their academic competence were related more to their
parents' beliefs about their abilities than to their actual record of achievement
in the early elementary grades (Phillips, 1987). Parents' beliefs about the difficulty of school tasks are important too. If the parents of one academically
successful child view school tasks as easy and the parents of another academically successful child view school tasks as difficult, the two children can view
their competence quite differently despite their similar performances (Parsons,
Adler & Kaczala, 1982).

Parents' beliefs about tasks and their child's abilities can be particularly
powerful when the child initially meets with a little failure at a task. Children

FIGURE 14-12
When families and schools expect success, it can make a surprising difference in children's achievement. The important confidence-building message is, ''We know you can do it.''

who perceive themselves to be competent and who judge tasks to be relatively easy are more likely to keep on trying when something turns out to be more difficult than they expected. Children with the opposite perceptions and beliefs may give up without really trying. Many children who persist will probably eventually succeed, and their original perceptions will be confirmed. Children who give up, in contrast, fail at the task, and their original perceptions are confirmed too. Over time, children who consistently avoid challenging tasks become less competent in reality, because they withdraw themselves from situations and experiences in which they could learn.

The effect of parental beliefs on both academic effort and academic achievement may be particularly apparent in the case of girls' math achievement. Girls consistently perceive their academic competence to be lower than boys' in math, even though their records of achievement in elementary school equal or surpass those of boys (Frieze et al., 1978; Dweck, Goetz & Strauss, 1980; Dweck & Licht, 1980). Girls' perceptions that they're less competent than they actually are could be due to different judgments about task difficulty. They could view math as being harder than boys do, for example, which would make their expectation of success lower, despite equal ability. Or girls could be socialized differently about math, perhaps by parental beliefs that girls aren't as good at math as boys. This combination of beliefs, some about the tasks and some about their own abilities, could reduce girls' perceived competence on math tasks and thus contribute to their lower achievement by the time they get to high school.

TEACHER BELIEFS AND EXPECTATIONS. Children are also influenced by the expectations communicated to them by their teachers. High teacher expectations are associated with higher levels of achievement (Purkey & Smith, 1983), and different attributions for success and failure seem to be associated with different patterns of achievement. For example, research has shown that teachers respond differently to failure in boys and girls. When boys fail, teachers tend to attribute their poor performance to a lack of neatness, failure to follow directions, and other nonintellectual aspects of their work. When girls fail, teachers tend to attribute it to their intelligence or ability. One researcher found that teachers attributed boys' failure to motivation problems eight times more often than they did girls' failure (Dweck, 1978). Teachers seem to give boys

FIGURE 14-13
Teachers respond favorably to children they perceive as interested in learning. Children thus contribute to their own learning environments.

the message, "You can do anything, if you'll just try." They seem more often to tell girls, "Well, you can't be good in everything."

These different teacher reactions to boys and girls might account for sex differences in attributions about success and failure. Boys as a group are more likely to attribute success to ability and failure to lack of effort. Girls, on the other hand, tend to attribute success to effort and failure to lack of ability. As a result, girls are likely to respond to failure by decreasing their efforts and their perception of their own competence. Boys who fail, on the other hand, are more likely to believe that if they increase their efforts, they will succeed (Dweck, 1978).

As we have seen in several other contexts, children's behavior depends on complex interactions among many systems, and academic achievement is no exception. From the interaction of the child's biological system with the socializing techniques used by his parents comes a child who in turn actively helps to create his own learning environment in school. In other words, the child himself plays a part in eliciting certain responses from teachers. An example of this is the finding that teacher perceptions of motivation to learn are influenced strongly by a child's restraint-related behavior, a pattern of behavior that includes a positive attitude toward authority and responsibility. Teachers perceive restraint-related behavior as evidence of motivation to learn and respond more favorably to students who display it. Thus teachers do not perceive as motivated to learn students with high interest in learning but low levels of restraint-related behavior and often make fewer attempts to engage them. Conversely, teachers often do perceive as motivated to learn students with high levels of restraint-related behavior but little interest in learning and make more attempts to engage them. Regardless of students' actual, initial motivation to learn, teacher perceptions of students' motivation is highly related to classroom performance (Wentzel et al., 1990). In the long run, this can increase the motivation of an initially poorly motivated student and lower the motivation of an initially highly motivated student.

As this example illustrates, students do indeed create their own environments, consistent with developmental systems theory (Sternberg, 1990; Bandura, 1990). When a child's restraint-related behavior motivates a teacher to expect and reward achievement, or conversely, when a student who does not value academic achievement ignores the teacher and looks for attention primarily from other underachieving students, the child is choosing an environment that maintains and develops precisely the values and personality characteristics that led to the initial choice. The challenge for adults is to encourage children like Gregory to choose environments that help them "hit the books" rather than environments that further encourage aimless pursuits. For a discussion of how American students compare with students in other societies in academic motivation and achievement, see Research Focus—Culture and Academic Performance.

Obviously, these factors other than ability that influence achievement will continue to be of great interest to researchers, parents, and teachers. Their importance should not be underestimated. Without academic values or with misperceptions about competencies, students with considerable ability will not apply themselves and will do poorly in school. Conversely, highly motivated students, even without great gifts, can learn effectively. It is crucial that we understand how to minimize the first situation and maximize the second.

RESEARCH FOCUS

Culture and Academic Performance

Are children in other countries more competent in basic academic skills than American children? If so, why? These questions and others like them have been addressed recently by Harold Stevenson and his colleagues in research conducted in the United States, China, Japan, and Taiwan. Their findings suggest that discrepancies in academic achievements are related to variations in academic values in the different cultures, as well as in expectancies that effort will bring success in school. As with gender, culture-specific academic values and expectations are strikingly apparent in their relationship to achievement in mathematics.

Stevenson and his colleagues (1990b) looked at math proficiency in Chicago (Cook County, Illinois) and Beijing (China) in first and fifth grades. They found that in both a 20-minute group-administered test of computation and a two-session individually administered test of math questions, only 1 to 2 percent of Chinese children scored below the mean of their American counterparts. That is, roughly 98 of 100 Beijing children were above average in terms of Chicago data in both first and fifth grades. The performances of children from the two cities showed large average differences on essentially all of the problems, not just on difficult items. Examples of test items and results for Beijing and Chicago appear in the table.

Stevenson also questioned children's parents and teachers about their attitudes toward academics. He found differences between cultures in parent and teacher academic values and in expectancies of children's academic efficacy. For example, the grades in math required to satisfy Beijing parents were much higher than those that satisfied parents from Chicago. As a result, 89 percent of Chicago children thought their parents were pleased with their math performance, but only 55 percent of Beijing children thought so.

Similarly, teacher values and standards for math were higher in Beijing than Chicago. Some American fifth grade teachers were never observed to be teaching math. American teachers as a whole professed little fondness for math and only modest skill in it.

If mathematics is deemphasized in American schools, do American children excel in other subjects? Several studies indicate that the answer is no. One exemplary study, again conducted by Stevenson and colleagues, investigated the reading skills of first and fifth grade students in Minneapolis-St. Paul, Sendai (Japan), and Taipei (Taiwan). All the students were from similar socioeconomic backgrounds. The Minneapolis-St. Paul metropolitan area tends to have native-born, English-speaking, middle-income families; Sendai is a traditional Japanese city with an economic standing similar to that of Minneapolis; and Taipei is the largest city in Taiwan. In the study the Taiwanese and Japanese children outperformed their American peers in reading skills, though not to the extent that they did in math (Stevenson et al., 1990a).

A number of cultural differences can be identified that have obvious relevance to these variations in academic excellence. One is the length of the school year—174 days in Minneapolis, 230 in Taipei, and 243 in Sendai. Another is the extent to which a standardized curriculum is presented to all children. In both Taiwan and Japan a national curriculum with a relatively strong math component is specified by the ministries of education. In the United States, on the other hand, the curriculum for each grade is determined by local school boards or even left to individual teachers, who may only crudely coordinate their curriculum with the curricula to which any given child has been exposed in previous years.

American parents were again found to have the lowest academic standards of the countries compared and to provide the least support and help for homework. And although no major differences were found in the innate general cognitive ability of the children in the three cultures, American mothers believed innate ability to be significantly more important than did Taiwanese or Japanese mothers in determining how well children do in school. On seven different questions about the importance of effort versus ability, mothers in Taipei and Sendai were found to view effort as more important than American mothers did. Taiwanese and Japanese children were found to have similar beliefs. In sum, then, the higher academic achievement of students in both Taipei and Sendai was found to be related to prevailing cultural practices—greater exposure to subject matter, higher academic standards or values, and greater expectancies that effort will be rewarded.

Does it follow that adults should maximize academic demands on all children? Here the picture becomes more complex. Pressures felt by many American children may actually be higher than those experienced by Chinese and Japanese children, although the origin of such pressures may be unrelated to school (Stevenson et al., 1990a). The American teachers suggested that children in their classrooms had so many personal and family problems that they had difficulty functioning well at school. Three to four times as many Minneapolis teachers complained of problems motivating children and maintaining control of the classroom as did teachers in Taipei or Sendai. Some American parents believe that increasing academic pressure would have negative effects on students, and Stevenson indicates that there may be some basis for these concerns. For children who lack ability, for those whose basic needs are not being met, and for those who believe that academic achievement will not lead to a better life, an increase in academic pressure may not be effective. Concern about the needs of these children in the classroom may cause teachers to lower academic standards for all American children.

Examples of Items from Individual Tests (Percent Correct)

	BEIJING	CHICAGO
First grade:		
There were 15 bunnies. 9 hopped away. How many bunnies were left? (Word problems)	95.8	30.1
Chris has 26 toy cars. Mary has 19. How many do they have in all? (Word problems)	84.7	13.1
Suppose you are a teacher and you want to make up some questions. What kind of word problem would you make up using these numbers: 5 + 2 = (Mathematical operations)	89.8	43.2
The child was asked to draw a circle around one-half of a group of stars arranged randomly in two lines. (Number concepts)	44.9	10.7
An X was marked midway on a line whose endpoints were 0 and 10. The child was asked to estimate the number for X. (Estimation)	57.6	15.8
Fifth grade:		
The teacher gave 3 sheets of paper to each of 9 people. There are still 2 sheets of paper left. How many sheets of paper did the teacher have when he began? (Word problems)	91.6	43.4
A stamp collecting club has 24 members. Five-sixths of the members collect only foreign stamps. How many collect only foreign stamps? (Word problems)	58.8	8.9
Ten cans of pop cost $1.50 at one store. I can get 5 cans for 80 cents at a second store. Where is the pop cheaper? The first or the second store? (Number concepts)	80.7	38.0
Chris and Kim are standing next to each other. It takes Chris 7 steps to get to the door, and it takes Kim 9 steps. Who takes bigger steps? (Measurement)	91.6	55.1

SOURCE: Stevenson, H., et al. (1990b). *Mathematics achievement of children in China and the United States.* Child Development, 61, 1060.

Examples of Items from Group Computation Test (Percent Correct)

	BEIJING	CHICAGO
First grade:		
9 − 1	99.6	51.8
Count 17 dots	96.5	78.3
5 + 4	99.6	77.2
19 + 45	27.2	6.5
Fifth grade:		
__ − 34 = 32	96.1	29.4
13 ÷ 13 =	99.8	70.2
³⁄₈ + ²⁄₈	55.1	38.6
.08 × 10	78.7	20.5

OVERVIEW

School is the defining experience of middle childhood; going to school is what children do. Here, in the elementary years, they gain basic skills in reading, writing, and math, and they begin to learn about science, music, art, geography, social studies, and the environment. Their new abilities to understand, remember, and acquire knowledge are a function of their steadily developing cognitive skills. Without these skills, they wouldn't be able to organize information, study for tests, or respond to the demands of the elementary school curriculum. And since success in school is such an important factor in children's lives, teachers and parents need to encourage and support their budding intellectual abilities in every way they can.

CHAPTER REVIEW

METACOGNITIVE ABILITIES

- Metacognition—the ability to think about thinking—develops during the school-age years. Children start to be able to mobilize their thoughts, target a problem, and apply their thoughts to a solution.
- The development of metacognitive abilites allows children to monitor their understanding of what they hear or read. Studies have shown that young school-age children show some awareness when they don't understand material, but most children can't articulate the problem until they're 10 or 11 years old.
- As children mature, they develop increasingly sophisticated mental strategies that help them study. Younger children don't have the metacognitive skills to use memory efficiently. The ability to remember is related to knowledge, experience, and concepts that one can use to organize what one has read or learned.
- The emergence of metacognitive abilities makes it possible for children to develop the study skills critical to success in school, but teachers need to help by teaching these skills directly.
- Analogical reasoning is used progressively more frequently during the school years, helping children learn and understand new material.
- Metacognitive abilities are a fundamental part of efficient learning and intelligent behavior during the school years, as highlighted by the role of metacomponents in Sternberg's triarchic theory of intelligence.

INTELLIGENCE TESTS

- The IQ was originally computed as the ratio of a child's mental age to her chronological age. It is generally a good predictor of a child's academic ability.
- A person is considered mentally retarded who has lower than average intellectual functioning and delayed development in the social and self-help skills needed to function in daily life. Most children with mild mental retardation (IQ between 50 and 70) aren't diagnosed until they perform poorly in school. As a result of Public Law 94–142, many children who are mildly retarded are educated in regular classrooms—a practice known as mainstreaming.
- The major controversy associated with intelligence testing over the last 50 years has been whether intelligence is determined genetically or largely influenced by a child's environment. Heredity plays an important role in determining intelligence; environmental factors influence, both positively and negatively, what nature has given the child; and the two interact in ways that we often do not yet understand.
- Different groups test differently on IQ tests; experts believe these differences are due largely to environmental differences. It has also been suggested that IQ tests are to some extent slanted toward the cultural framework of the white middle class.

ACADEMIC MOTIVATION AND SUCCESS IN SCHOOL

- Academic values and perceived competence are important determinants of a child's success in school.
- Parental values—the importance parents place on education, high grades, and intellectual activities like

reading—are a powerful determinant of the value children place on academic achievement.

- Perceived academic competence increases academic effort by increasing the child's expectancy of success, reducing interference caused by anxiety, and increasing the use of mental strategies for solving problems.

- Several factors help to determine a child's perceived academic competence. In addition to the perceived self-efficacy a child attributes to himself generally, which results from responsive child-rearing, he learns to attribute to himself differing degrees of competence in differing areas, including academics.

- Perceived academic competence results from socialization processes similar to those that influence other aspects of the child's personality. His history of success, as well as his observations of those he sees as like himself, interact with biological subsystems to influence perceived competence.

- Children's perceptions of their own competence are also enhanced when parents and teachers show that they believe the children to be competent and easily able to succeed at most tasks.

- Parents and teachers may convey ideas and feelings to girls that contribute to their distorted perceptions about academic ability in general and mathematics in particular. Young girls often believe they're not competent in math, even though their math achievement equals or surpasses that of boys.

- Children's initial values and expectations are often magnified and confirmed with time. Children low in perceived competence can be expected to withdraw from failure experiences and become even less competent in meeting similar challenges. Children whose values are consistent with those valued in school are likely to create environments that motivate success; those whose values are inconsistent with academics are likely to place themselves in environments that motivate behavior inconsistent with academic effort.

- Academic success is associated with certain cultural values. Children perform better on academic achievement tests in societies in which academic achievement is valued, academic success is believed to be the result of effort, and meeting children's basic needs is a high priority.

KEY TERMS

identity
compensation
reversibility
metacognition
metalinguistic awareness
triarchic theory of intelligence
componential subtheory of intelligence

contextual subtheory of intelligence
experiential subtheory of intelligence
norms
mental age
intelligence quotient (IQ)
chronological age

mainstreaming
mild mental retardation
moderate mental retardation
severe mental retardation
profound mental retardation
educable mentally retarded

trainable mentally retarded
culturally biased tests
regression toward the mean
heritability
perceived competence

SUGGESTIONS FOR FURTHER READING

Brody, E. B., & Brody, N. (Eds.). (1976). *Intelligence: Nature, determinants, and consequences.* New York: Academic Press.
  This book includes a thorough discussion of the Arthur Jensen issue. It also provides considerable historical context pertaining to IQ testing.
Gardner, H. (1983). *Frames of mind: The theory of multiple intelligence.* New York: Basic Books.
  In this book, Gardner makes the case for different kinds of intelligence and for different distributions of these among individuals. Provides an intriguing view of intelligence written by a recipient of one of the McArthur Foundation "genius" awards.
Gloeckler, T., & Simpson, C. (1988). *Exceptional students in regular classrooms.* Mountain View, CA: Mayfield.
  A practical text and resource guide to the basic competencies a teacher in the regular classroom requires for instructing students with basic needs.

Sigel, I. E. (1985). *Parental belief systems.* Hillsdale, NJ: Erlbaum.
  This book contains several interesting chapters on the relationship between different parental beliefs and children's behavior.
Sternberg, R. J. (1990). *Metaphors of mind: Conceptions of the nature of intelligence.* New York: Cambridge University Press.
  This comprehensive but readable book reviews theories of intelligence, grouping them by radically different ways of looking at the mind.
Sternberg, R. J., & Kolligian, J. (Eds.). (1990). *Competence considered.* New Haven: Yale University Press.
  The contributors to this book describe what we know of the development of perceived self-efficacy. Bandura's concluding chapter is a particularly efficient summary of this work.

chapter 15

LANGUAGE DEVELOPMENT IN SCHOOL-AGE CHILDREN

"Dad, what does 'ano-,' 'ano-,' let's see . . . 'ano-NY-mous' mean?" called 9-year-old Alex from her room.

"How do you spell it?" her dad responded.

"A-n-o-n-y-m-o-u-s," she answered.

"Anonymous. It means without a name, someone whose name you don't know."

A few minutes later, Alex called out again, "Dad, what does 'cat-a-clysm' mean?"

"A disaster."

"Dad, what about 'in-gen-i-ous'?"

"Here, I'll help you find it in the dictionary."

Alex's dad had made his way to Alex's room with dictionary in hand. As they flipped through pages together to find the "I" section, Alex's dad asked, "What are you reading, anyway?"

"Oh, it's The Voyages of Doctor Doolittle, *by Hugh Lofting. I got it out of the library. It's got a lot of big words in it. I used to skip over words I didn't know, but I'm starting to want to know what they all mean."*

Within just a few years, Alex has progressed from a beginning reader to quite an accomplished one. When she first started reading, she sounded out words, which often yielded only an approximation of the word actually printed. She used her knowledge of words—her oral vocabulary—to transform the approximation into an actual word that made sense in terms of the context of what she was reading. Now she chooses more difficult books, so she often comes across words she doesn't know or hasn't heard pronounced. This is one way she increases her vocabulary.

Alex is even more skilled at oral language than she is at reading. She understands and uses many more words than she did a few years ago, and she speaks in longer sentences. Although she hasn't yet mastered every aspect of oral language, she does have the language to formulate and express fairly complicated ideas about the important things in her life. She can also think about and manipulate language in ways that were previously impossible for her. With this ability, she understands and tells jokes and riddles, one of the language hallmarks of the school-age years.

In this chapter, we describe the advances school-age children make in oral language—using and understanding speech—and in written language—reading and writing. We also discuss some other aspects of language development, such as how children learn a second language. Finally, we look at the development of writing, with special attention to children's early spelling strategies.

ORAL LANGUAGE

Most school-age children speak their language with apparent ease and fluidity, and they delight in the twists of language that make jokes funny. Despite their basic oral competence, however, children this age still have a thing or two to master. For example, they're confused by some complex sentence constructions. In this section, we turn first to a discussion of these typical stumbling blocks and then take a closer look at jokes and riddles.

Understanding Syntax

We saw in Chapter 11 that preschool children are confused about some words (like "promise") because they assume they're used the same way as other words (like "tell"). In a similar way, school-age children are confused by cer-

FIGURE 15-1
Just as learning to communicate verbally is the hallmark of early childhood, learning to read is the outstanding achievement of the early school years. The fascination of beginning to decode print can be seen in this first grader's face.

tain seemingly parallel usages. The critical study of this problem was done by Carol Chomsky (1969). She seated children at a table with a blindfolded doll and asked them, "Is this doll easy to see or hard to see?" If the child answered that the doll was hard to see, Chomsky asked the child to make her easy to see. If the child answered that the doll was easy to see, Chomsky asked the child to make the doll hard to see. Children who answered that the doll was hard to see thought they were being asked if it was hard or easy for *the doll* to see, not if it was hard for *them* to see the doll.

Consider the responses of Lisa, aged 6 years, 5 months (Chomsky, 1969, p. 30):

> Is this doll easy to see or hard to see?
> Hard to see.
> Will you make her easy to see?
> If I can get this untied.
> Will you explain why she was hard to see?
> (To doll) Because you had a blindfold over your eyes.
> And what did you do?
> I took it off.

Lisa's confusion apparently resulted from her attempt to use the same strategy she might use with a sentence like "John is eager to see." In this sentence, it's John who will do the seeing. Children who understood the question, on the other hand, responded like Ann, aged 8 years, 7 months (Chomsky, 1969, p. 31):

> This is Chatty Cathy. Is she easy to see or hard to see?
> Easy.
> Would you make her hard to see?
> So you can't see her at all?
> OK.
> (Places doll under table.)
> Tell what you did.
> I put her under the table.

School-age children also confuse the words "ask" and "tell." Consider the example of Samuel, aged 8 years, 5 months (Chomsky, 1969, p. 57):

> Ask Ellen what to feed the doll.
> Feed her hamburgers.
> All right now, tell Ellen what to feed her.
> Again?
> M-hm.
> Tomato.
> Now I want you to ask Ellen something. I want you to ask her what to feed the doll.
> Feed her this thing, whatever it's called.
> All right. Now listen very carefully, because I don't want you to tell her anything this time. I want you to ask her what to feed the doll. Can you do that?
> Let's see, I don't get it.
> OK, just go ahead, and ask her what to feed the doll.
> Feed her eggs.

Samuel interpreted "tell" correctly, but he interpreted "ask" the same way. In Chomsky's examples, even 9- and 10-year-olds were confused by the words "ask" and "tell."

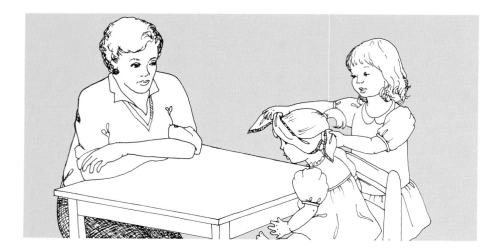

Part of younger children's problem with these constructions is that they still may be relying heavily on context to understand language. They tend to ignore syntax and respond in terms of pragmatic considerations instead—that is, in terms of whether their responses make sense in the situation (Warden, 1986). Sometimes their responses to "ask" and "tell" requests depend on whether they themselves know the answer to the question (Tanz, 1983). If they know the answer, they tend to "tell" rather than "ask." If they don't know the answer, they're more likely to "ask" than to "tell." Sometimes 5- and 6-year-olds seem to understand how these words are used and sometimes they don't, depending on whether they know the answer or not.

Jokes and Riddles

Anyone planning to spend time with school-age children should be prepared to listen to endless jokes and riddles. What is it about middle childhood that makes these language games so popular?

Jokes and riddles are based on ambiguity in the way words are used. It can be ambiguity about how words are pronounced (referred to as **phonologically based ambiguity**), about what words mean (**lexically based ambiguity**), or about how sentences are interpreted (**syntactically based ambiguity**). A child who can't yet think about language at these various levels and who can't make the sophisticated mental comparisons characteristic of Piaget's concrete operational stage won't be able to understand jokes and riddles (McGhee, 1971; 1979).

The ability to pay attention to the form of the language—to the structures used to convey meaning—instead of to the meaning itself is called **metalinguistic awareness.** Children who can tell jokes and riddles have this awareness. They play games with the form of language, trying to get the listener headed down one meaning track instead of another. The punchline reveals the trick meaning:

> "Why did the farmer name his hog Ink?"
> "Because he kept running out of the pen."

FIGURE 15-3
By third grade, children appreciate jokes, riddles, puns, and plays on words. Word play not only tickles their imaginations but gives them a way to handle disconcerting thoughts and feelings. It also provides opportunities for laughing with friends, one of the delights of school-age social life.

This joke is based on lexically based ambiguity: The word "pen" can mean either a writing tool or an enclosed area for animals. Children who tell jokes like this understand that words can have more than one meaning. They exploit this knowledge about language to trick the listener.

The following joke uses phonologically based ambiguity—ambiguity about the sound and pronunciation of words:

> "Knock knock."
> "Who's there?"
> "Duane."
> "Duane who?"
> "Duane the tub . . . I'm dwowning."

Knock-knock jokes are structured to make the listener expect that a person—in this case, "Duane"—is knocking on the door. But "Duane" is a phonological distortion of "drain." The distortion is deliberate, of course, to create an ambiguous situation. In the punchline, the listener finds out that "Duane" actually should have been interpreted as "drain."

In the next joke, it's the structure of the sentence itself—the syntax—that the child exploits:

> "Do you know how long cows should be milked?"
> "How long?"
> "As long as short ones, of course."

In the first question, the word "long" can be interpreted as an adjective modifying cows or as an adverb indicating how long the cows are to be milked. The sentence is ambiguous syntactically, although common sense suggests that we should interpret "long" as an adverb. (The length of a cow is probably not an issue in milking.) The listener interprets "long" as an adverb, only to find out that it's being used as an adjective.

Children's ability to understand the different levels of ambiguity emerges at different times. Children start to understand phonological ambiguity first ("duane the tub"), at age 6 or 7. They understand lexical ambiguity next ("pen"), with appreciation increasing for several years as more and more words are learned. They grasp syntactic ambiguity last, usually not until about 11 or 12 years of age (Shultz & Pilon, 1973), after they've mastered complex syntactic structures like those discussed earlier in this chapter.

Not understanding ambiguity doesn't prevent younger children from trying to tell jokes, however. Even preschoolers master the sentence form of jokes. Here's an attempt at joke telling by a 5-year-old:

> "Why did the radiator leave the room?"
> "I don't know. Why did the radiator leave the room?"
> "Because he was tired of sitting in it!" (followed by
> much laughter on the part of the joke teller)

No ambiguity is created in this joke, and none is resolved in the punchline. But the child knows that when you tell a joke you ask a question, wait for a response (usually, "I don't know"), and then tell the punchline (make an explanatory statement). This kind of practice with the sentence structure and turn-taking aspects of joke telling is very common among 5-year-olds and older 4-year-olds. By the time they get to elementary school, they know how to structure and present jokes to other people. What they still have to figure out during the school-age years is exactly what makes jokes funny. To do this, they must learn more about the phonological, lexical, and syntactic features of language.

Learning a Second Language

If you visited a school in almost any large American city, you would find children whose native tongue is a language other than English. And you would find a tremendous variety of native tongues—Spanish, Chinese, Vietnamese, Tagalog, and many others. The population of American public schools is changing once again, as it's changed in the past. And once again children are being asked to learn English to succeed in the American educational system and, presumably, in the mainstream of American life. How are all these children taught English?

TWO APPROACHES TO TEACHING A SECOND LANGUAGE. There are two main approaches to teaching children English (or any second language) in school. In one method, called Teaching English as a Second Language (TESL), children are taught in English-only classrooms. This approach is known as **immersion** in the new language. The school usually doesn't provide instruction in any subjects in languages other than English. TESL programs are often found in schools with multilingual populations, perhaps eight or ten different first languages. In most cases, it wouldn't be practical or even possible to teach in all those languages.

The second approach is to establish a bilingual program. Children are given instruction in the new language, but they're taught classroom subjects (math, reading, social studies, and so on) in their native language until they become proficient in the second language. These *transition bilingual* programs prepare children to enter classrooms where only the second language is used. Bilingual programs recognize that it's difficult for children to learn subject matter when they don't understand the language in which it's taught. This approach helps

FIGURE 15-4
Because the United States is experiencing a tremendous wave of immigration, there are currently many non-English-speaking students in American schools. Educators are divided on whether the immersion method or the bilingual approach is the more effective way to teach English to these students. Like other new arrivals, this Asian boy has to figure out what his teacher explains to him in English as well as what his classmates say to him in various American dialects.

prevent those children from falling behind in schoolwork while they're learning the new language.

Controversy exists over which is the better approach to teaching English in American schools. Some people think that having the native language available makes it harder for children to learn English—they have less need and motivation to become proficient in it. These people also point to schools as the avenue by which millions of immigrants learned English in the past and became assimilated into American life. They think immersion programs like TESL are the best methods of teaching a second language.

Others think that children should be able to maintain their native language (and culture) on an equal level with their new language, and they favor the bilingual approach. They think a bilingual or multilingual culture offers greater variety and depth to a society, prevents cultural arrogance, and helps children from diverse backgrounds maintain their cultural integrity and self-esteem. Many proponents of this view think there should be more than one "official" language in the United States.

These differences of opinion are likely to increase in the years ahead as the make-up of the American people continues to change and as schools come to serve an increasing number of non-English-speaking children. But aside from the political and cultural aspects of this debate, what are the educational merits of the different approaches to teaching a second language? How do people actually learn a second language?

HOW IS A SECOND LANGUAGE ACQUIRED? Three theories have been proposed to account for the process of learning a new language (McNamara, 1976, p. 46):

1. The child acquires the second language in exactly the same way an infant acquires it as a first language. In other words, learning a second language is **identical** in **process** to learning the same language as a first language.

2. The child uses the structures from her first language to form structures in the second language. This process assumes that there is **interference** between the first and second languages, since different languages have different ways of saying things (different grammars).
3. The child formulates **unique grammatical structures**, using neither the structures of her first language nor the typical developmental structures of the new language.

To study the acquisition of a second language, a researcher must find people who have mastered a first language and are beginning to learn a second. The researcher also has to be familiar with the syntax of both languages and understand the typical sequence of development that children go through in learning each language as a first language. For example, if you recall from Chapter 11, English-speaking children's first questions ("Where it is?") and negative statements ("No go out") are constructed differently from those of older speakers. These first utterances undergo several predictable changes before the standard patterns appear.

The researcher compares the developmental patterns of the person learning the second language with the typical developmental patterns of native speakers of each of the two languages. Let's say that the speaker's native language is French and the language being acquired is English. If the patterns match those of a child learning English as a first language, the evidence supports the identical process model. If the patterns match patterns and structures in French, then the evidence supports the interference model.

Most research has supported the identical process model of second language learning. For example, in one study, two Norwegian children learning English as a second language formed questions with "Wh" words the same

FIGURE 15-5
When interest is high, language and cultural differences don't stand in children's way. These children in the playground of a public school in East Harlem aren't hindered in their play even though they speak a variety of dialects and languages.

way children learning English as a first language do, even though this wasn't how they formed questions in their native Norwegian (Raven, 1974). They said, "What she is doing?" just as English-speaking toddlers do, rather than "What is she doing?"

Even when children have mastered a language whose structure could be applied to English, they don't use what they already know. This is also true when children's first language doesn't resemble English—they don't apply the structures of their own language but pass through the same stages as a child learning English as a first language. Not until children are age 10 or 12 and have well-developed metalinguistic and cognitive abilities do they begin to apply the structures of their native language when learning a second language.

THE SOCIAL CONTEXT OF SECOND LANGUAGE LEARNING. Evidence from studies of second language learning indicates that the immersion approach is the preferable one. It appears that people learn a second language most quickly when they spend a lot of time communicating with native speakers in a natural way. One implication of this finding is that children learning a new language should get involved with children who know the language. One researcher asked children who were learning a new language how they managed to "count themselves in" (Fillmore, 1976, cited in McLaughlin, 1978, pp. 108–110). Following are some of their strategies:

- Join a group and act as if you understand what's going on, even if you don't. (A social strategy)
- Assume that people's statements are directly relevant to the situation at hand or to what they or you are experiencing. Metastrategy: Guess! (A cognitive strategy)
- Give the impression—with a few well-chosen words—that you can speak the language (for example, say "Look" or "Wait a minute"). (A social strategy)
- Give the impression that you understand, and start talking. (A cognitive strategy)
- Look for recurring structures in the formulas you know. (A cognitive strategy)
- Work on the big things first; save the details for later. (A cognitive strategy)

The process these children described is remarkably similar to the one children go through when they learn a first language. They use situations to figure out meanings, and then they use meanings to figure out the language. People who speak the language—friends in the case of children learning a second language, parents in the case of infants acquiring a first language—help them by trying to understand what they're saying. The skilled speakers also simplify their own statements and use gestures and facial expressions to communicate their meanings.

OTHER FACTORS AFFECTING THE ACQUISITION OF A SECOND LANGUAGE. The immersion method works well in natural situations, and it also works in some classroom situations. The method has been successful in Canadian schools, for example, when English-speaking students are placed in French-speaking classrooms. The native English speakers are able to keep up with their schoolwork while learning the second language (Lambert, Just & Segalowitz, 1970). But in American classrooms, non-English-speaking children often don't do very well if they're not given help in learning English (Pflaum, 1986).

Why the different outcomes in these two situations? There are several possible reasons. First, the children in the French immersion programs were middle-class children who had good adult models of bilingualism, enriched preschool backgrounds, and parents who wanted them to learn French. Their native language, English, was not considered less prestigious in Canadian society than the language they were learning. In other words, their acquisition of a second language was strongly supported in many other areas of their lives.

In contrast, many of the non-English-speaking children in American schools come from lower socioeconomic-status families who haven't been able to provide preschool experiences. These children's lower achievement could be caused as much by their lack of early schoollike experiences as by their language immersion experience. Furthermore, in the United States many people find that their native tongue is considered less prestigious than English. Finally, non-English-speaking children in the United States often have few adult bilingual models to copy or look up to for encouragement or inspiration (Pflaum, 1986).

The solutions to some of these problems obviously go beyond the choice of a method for teaching English in schools. Some combination of immersion and bilingual methods may be the best approach to helping non-English-speaking children get their bearings in American classrooms.

American Dialects

Children whose first language isn't English aren't the only ones who have trouble understanding and making themselves understood in American classrooms. Children also speak different dialects of English. **Dialects** are variations within a language. They may be different in pronunciation, in syntax, or in the meaning given to some words. Everyone speaks a dialect, of course—the majority dialect is just one of several variations within a language.

The most common—or the most recognized—dialect in the United States is one associated with ethnicity (as opposed to geographical region or some other distinguishing factor). It's known as Black English Vernacular (BEV), but it's not, of course, spoken by everyone who is black. The grammar of BEV and standard English (SE) are quite similar—they're forms of the same language, after all—but there are some differences. In BEV, for example, the verbs *come* and *say* aren't marked for past tense. A person might use, "He say," rather than, "He said." Auxiliary verbs may also be dropped, resulting in, "What you mean?" rather than "What do you mean?" And "s" may be left off possessives, resulting in sentences like, "This is Susan sweater."

Of course, SE also uses some verbs to express both present and past tense ("I **put** the bat down yesterday." "I **put** the water on the stove every morning.") and some nouns to indicate both singular and plural ("deer," "sheep"). As one language expert has pointed out, "the particular nouns and verbs that work this way are simply a slightly different set in each dialect" (Lindfors, 1987, p. 400).

There are also phonological (pronunciation) differences between SE and various dialects, and these can make it hard for teachers to understand children's speech. In addition, some early spelling inventions can result from these pronunciation differences (Kligman & Cronnell, 1974). For example, a child who says "pack" instead of "park" will probably spell it "pak." A child who pronounces "idea" as "idear" is likely to spell it with an "r" at the end. These are just a few examples of the many dialect-related pronunciation differences that can affect children's spelling (Goodman et al., 1987). Of course, many words in English aren't spelled the way they sound anyway, which makes all children prone to spelling errors when they first learn to write, as we see in the next section.

Some of the same social and political issues involved in the teaching of English as a second language apply to the teaching of SE to children who speak other dialects, particularly BEV. Both are legitimate languages with their own rules and complexities. As a language, one is neither better nor worse than the other. But different dialects do have different social currency. Standard English is the accepted language of schools, businesses, and government in the United States. Children who know SE will have more choices and options than children who don't know it. If children can acquire SE in a way that doesn't threaten their positive feelings about their own dialect, it's to their advantage to do so.

WRITTEN LANGUAGE: LITERACY DEVELOPMENT

In first grade, Will kept a "story journal." This was a book in which he could write stories and draw pictures to illustrate them, or draw pictures to illustrate stories the teacher told the class. Will often asked his teacher to spell words for him because he didn't know how to write them. Sometimes she wrote down in his book what he said. Other times she pronounced the words slowly, emphasizing the sounds within them, and helped Will think about which letters might be used to code them. Often, these two approaches showed up in the same writing sample. Following are some of the entries from his journal:

> November 14. Tatterhood. This is the castle room where the big Christmas tree is and this is one of the trolls.
>
> January 9. Sno Wit and Ros Rd (Snow White and Rose Red). This is the hows in sprigtim (This is the house in springtime). The first vines from the red rose are starting to bloom.
>
> March 4. The Emperor's New Clothes. This is the emperor sitting in his bedroom. And this is the prim ministr looking at the cloth that the crooks are not reale makeng (And this is the prime minister looking at the cloth that the crooks are not really making).

In second grade, Will kept another journal. This one was a log of personal entries—a kind of diary. By now, Will had had a lot of experience sounding out words, although he knew this didn't always produce correct spellings. He also had learned to read in first grade, and his interest in reading for fun gave him the opportunity to see how many words are spelled.

But Will didn't really worry about spelling, because he knew he could correct it later if he wanted to publish something for the class library. He just wanted to get his thoughts down. His journal was for himself and no one else, unless he wanted to show it to someone. The following are some entries he was willing to share:

FIGURE 15-6
Keeping a journal of stories and pictures is an appropriate literacy activity for first graders. These girls are gaining important reading and writing skills and solidifying their understanding of the connection between oral and written language.

October 3. Tomareoe I em going to Morgan's huos. After I go to Morgan's huos then the nex day Ryan will cyom ovr. I kant wat.

December 15. Last Toosdy my tooth fell owt. I got a korter fore it. Yestrdy we wedt ies skating. I liek ies skating.

March 26. I got a crikit. It is a fymale. I hop it has babies.

March 29. Yestrday my criket askapt. It was in the bathroom right wen I cam in. I coght it wen I saw it. I em glad it was in the bathroom at the same time I was.

It looked like Will's writing had deteriorated from his first-grade level, but that was because he was more on his own now. His phonetic spelling is a good reminder of how many unusual spellings there are in English. By third grade, Will's spelling had improved a bit:

September 15. The day before scool started I came back from High Lake. It is a tarifck plaes to go on vacation. I plaed pewe golf. I colekted rocks. I plaed shufllboard. I liked it alott.

October 25. Fore Halloween I am going to be a ninja. Marcus is going trick or treting with me. I cant wate.

April 20. I had a grate Eastre! I woke up and saw a big Eastre basket. I had a milk chocklat bunny, a chickin filled with marshmelo and other candy.

By fourth grade, Will's spelling was becoming much more standard, and his ideas about writing had changed quite a lot too:

November 5. It was Thursday September 17, 3987. The battle raged on. "We got some reinforcements, but still it looks bad" (said Capitan Feragon).

"Boss, they are launching an attack on the base." "I wonder why the aliens want to fight. I sent a squad of 5 to get some energy." They were having better luck than we were . . .

May 23. I was walking down the path to my secret club, then I tripped on a big rock. I was so mad I kicked it 2 feet away from me and under it fownd a tresure map and a golden medaliun. I ran home. When I got there I was almost completely out of breth. I ran upstairs like who knows what! I quickly unrolled the map and looked for a name on the map. The name was Sir Fransis Fake. "What a name!" I said . . .

By now, Will had learned many words from all the literacy activities he engaged in both in and out of school. Although quite a few spellings still eluded him, his continuing exposure to books and other written material in the years ahead would help him master the intricacies of written English. (The development of other writing skills is discussed in Chapter 19.)

Reading and writing are intimately connected. The improvement in Will's writing from first to fourth grade is due in large part to the reading he's done. The books and stories his parents and teachers read to him also gave him important literacy experiences. Reading is considered the most critical skill children acquire in the early school years.

As you might expect with anything considered so important, there is debate over the best way to teach reading. In this section we discuss some of the thinking on reading instruction, summing up what is currently known about this topic. We then discuss the development of writing, with special attention to children's unusual spelling strategies.

Learning to Read

Learning to read is a complex process, one that involves the integrated use of many different skills. In Chapter 11, we discussed some of the preliminary components of reading that are often acquired by preschoolers. These included the understanding that reading involves getting meaning from print, the knowledge that letters of the alphabet represent phonemes (single speech sounds), and the ability to recognize letters of the alphabet. Many children, but not all of them, bring these understandings to their first-grade reading instruction. How do they get from this level of emergent literacy to a level we would call "beginning reader"?

TWO APPROACHES TO TEACHING READING. Some teachers typically teach reading using a **skills approach**. They focus on teaching "word attack" skills that children can use to "get to meaning." Once children can sound out or recognize printed words, they're able to read and understand the text. Other teachers use a **whole language approach** to teaching reading. They focus on the meaning of a text and rely on children's thinking ability to abstract and arrive at word attack skills.

Before the whole language view became popular in recent years, the "great debate" about teaching reading in American schools centered on two different skills approaches. One, called the **phonics approach**, is a synthetic (meaning "building" or "putting together") approach that emphasizes knowledge of letter-sound correspondences. Children start with letters and combine them to

FIGURE 15-7
Although children become literate partly by being in a print-rich environment, they also need instruction and practice in specific reading skills.

build words. The second, called the **"look-say" approach**, is an analytic approach that starts with whole words and expects that children will eventually begin to think about them in terms of their parts—letters and sounds.

THE BASIS OF THE WHOLE LANGUAGE APPROACH. The difference between both of the skills approaches and the whole language approach is that the whole language approach emphasizes language at a level higher than that of individual words. It also focuses on cueing systems other than the visual-graphic (letter-sound knowledge). According to this view, children use three cueing systems when they read. For one, they predict the parts of speech—nouns, verbs, and so on—that are likely to come next on the basis of their knowledge of oral language. Only certain kinds of words will fit grammatically at various points in a sentence. These cues about syntax are known as **syntactic cues**. For another, they predict words that will make sense in the context of what they're reading. They will realize that a man flew off in a plane, for example, not in a plant. Cues about context are known as **semantic cues**. Finally, readers use visual-graphic information—letter-sound correspondences—but not as the only, or even the most important, source of cues about the passage they're reading, according to advocates of the whole language approach (Newman, 1985).

RESEARCH FOCUS

Dyslexia: When Children Can't Read

"I thought I must have been absent the day the other kids learned how to read."

So spoke a child whose inability to read caused him embarrassment and confusion before he was finally diagnosed as dyslexic. His reaction is typical of children (and adults) who have trouble doing what they see others doing so easily—getting meaning from print. Although they appear normal in every other way, these people are unable to learn to read (or have extreme difficulty learning to read). **Dyslexia** is a generic term that simply refers to this difficulty in individuals who don't have any other condition (such as mental retardation) that would account for the problem. Dyslexia is not uncommon, but it's difficult to say exactly how many children suffer from it because poor reading can be caused by so many other factors.

WHAT CAUSES DYSLEXIA?

Over the years, many hypotheses have been proposed to explain dyslexia. Neuropsychiatrist Samuel Torry Orton suggested that it was caused by vision problems. He had noticed that dyslexics often see letters and words as their mirror images—for example, "b" for "d" or "was" for "saw." He also observed that dyslexics often reversed letters and words in their writing. (As you recall, letter reversals are normal in children's writing during the emergent literacy stage.) Other experts identified visual-motor or motor problems as the cause of dyslexia (Metzger & Werner, 1984; Regcher & Kaplan, 1988). They hypothesized that improper visual tracking or scanning or some other visual problems were the culprits.

Current research is pointing not to visual deficits but to language processing as the primary problem in dyslexia. Re-

searchers have found that children with dyslexia often have trouble segmenting words phonemically, discriminating among words, and remembering words on the basis of their phonological (sound) characteristics. These children have much more difficulty using letter sounds to decode words than normal readers do. They also have more difficulty distinguishing between grammatical and ungrammatical sentences, understanding sentences read to them, and naming letters, words, and colors (Vellutino, 1987).

HOW CAN DYSLEXICS BE HELPED?

In the past, many remedial treatments were based on the visual-motor theories of dyslexia and involved visual and perceptual training techniques (Metzger & Werner, 1984). Not surprisingly, given current research, these early techniques were not very successful.

Today, the focus is much more on direct tutoring of reading skills. Even though dyslexics are particularly weak in phonics, experts don't recommend stressing this area alone (Vellutino, 1987). Instead, they recommend that remedial reading programs take a holistic approach and emphasize all the cueing systems used in reading—syntactic, semantic, and visual-graphic. As we've seen, learning to read involves much more than just knowing letter-sound correspondences and being able to segment words phonemically, even though these are important. It also involves developing vocabulary, learning words in meaningful contexts, becoming familiar with print conventions, and so on. Dyslexic children need plentiful opportunities both to develop oral language skills and to learn more specific reading skills. With direct tutoring and extra effort, they usually *can* learn to read.

Although skills approaches to reading have their merits, they traditionally tended to focus too narrowly and for too long on isolated phonics skills, without providing children with authentic reading and writing tasks from which to learn or in which to apply them. The whole language approach is more comprehensive and engages children in actual reading and writing *while* they are acquiring basic decoding skills, not after a long initial period of skills instruction. However, some proponents of the whole language approach have tended to underplay the need for some explicit skills instruction, perhaps because early reports suggested that home literacy learning occurred naturally, given a print-rich environment. More recent study of these environments, however, indicates that parent interaction and instruction are involved in home literacy learning, although the instruction lacks the contrived and rigid characteristics of much school-based learning (Hiebert, 1991; Schickedanz, et al., 1990). Many experts now agree that a balance between explicit skills instruction and experience in authentic reading and writing tasks offers the best approach to beginning reading (Adams, 1990).

Learning to Write

Like reading, writing begins during the preschool years. As described in Chapter 11, preschoolers delight in scribble writing, and they expend great efforts on creating shopping lists, stories, and letters to grandma. Many of them understand that writing is a pencil-and-paper version of spoken language. They also start to understand some print conventions, such as that print is read from left to right and from top to bottom. As much as they learn between the ages of 3 and 6, however, the development of writing only begins in that period. The ability to express ideas and thoughts in writing continues to develop throughout the elementary school years and beyond.

THE LETTER-NAME SPELLING STRATEGY. One of the first ideas that is often solidified in first grade, if not earlier, is that spoken words are represented on paper by mapping their sounds to alphabet letters. This insight (again, as described in Chapter 11) assumes the ability to think about speech at the phonemic level— the level of individual speech sounds, as opposed to the level of syllables or words. Once children know the names of letters and can segment words into phonemes, they can begin to create words by using a **letter-name spelling strategy.** Because the names of letters include at least one sound that the letter makes—if you say the letter A, you hear the long A sound—children can begin to spell words by using their knowledge of letter names.

Words spelled by using this simple strategy are pretty unusual looking, of course. We saw some examples of it in Will's journal—words like "wat" ("wait"), "ovr," "wen," and "hop" ("hope"). Children's early spellings are invented, created according to their own rules.

TABLE 15-1   Examples of Children's Invented Spellings

Words Created Using a Letter-name Strategy	Words Created by Substituting the Nearest Tense Vowel for a Lax Vowel	Words Created by Focusing on the Affrication in T and D Followed by R
Kit (kite)	Fes (fish)	Chran (train)
Da (day)	Pan (pen)	Chra (tray)
Mi (my)	Mas (mess)	Chri (try)
Kat (Kate)	Git (got)	Griv (drive)
Tabl (table)	Biks (box)	Gri (dry)
Hare (cherry)		
Hrh (church)		
Lade (lady)		
Babe (baby)		
Fas (face)		
Tigr (tiger)		

Sometimes the letter-name strategy leads to an especially unusual spelling. For example, a child might write "chicken" as HIKN. At first glance, you might assume the child was just sloppy and forgot the "c" at the beginning of the word. But actually, the child figured this spelling out carefully by going through the letters until she came to one that contained the "ch" sound—the letter "h." Table 15-1 provides examples of typical spellings based on a letter-name strategy.

SPELLING WORDS WITH SHORT VOWELS. Other unusual spellings are the result of even more amazing detective work. Like the distinctive features of written alphabet letters (described in Chapter 11), the phonetic features of sounds overlap. Even though sounds differ in one or more feature—which is why we can perceive them as different sounds—they also share some features. When children are trying to decide how to represent a short vowel, they simply search the phonetic features of the long vowels until they get to the letter whose name "says" that sound. The letter they come up with is often an incorrect one that shares phonetic features with the right one (Read, 1975).

For example, a child might write "then" as THIN. The short e in "then" has some phonetic features in common with both long i and long e. It shares a similar shape of the vocal track—the position of the tongue in relation to the roof of the mouth—with long i. It shares place of articulation—the specific spot in the vocal track where the sound is formed—with long e. Apparently, young children experience shape of the vocal track as a more dominant feature than place of articulation. This is why they first represent short e with i. To see for yourself, form the short e and long i in your mouth, and observe the similarities and differences. Table 15–1 includes more examples of word spelling based on this strategy.

SPELLING WORDS WITH OTHER PHONETIC FEATURES. Another phonetic feature sometimes trips up children. Some sounds are **affricated**—spoken with a release of air. The sound associated with the letters "ch" and the soft sound of the

FIGURE 15-9
Third graders have sufficient
literacy skills to do a library
project. They can read well
enough to research a topic,
and they can write well
enough to put together a
report. But it always makes life
easier to do a joint project
with a buddy.

letter "g" are examples of affricated sounds. Some letters are affricated in some contexts but not in others. The letters "d" and "t" fall into this category. They're usually not affricated, as in "dog" and "toy," for example, but when they're followed by "r," as in "drain" and "train," they are affricated.

Our language writes these sounds as "d" and "t" regardless of whether they're affricated. But children notice the affrication of "d" and "t" when they're followed by "r" and think they aren't sounds that should be represented by the letters "d" and "t." They focus on the affrication as the dominant feature and associate the sounds with other affricated sounds. Consequently, to represent an affricated "d" they choose "g," and to represent an affricated "t" they choose "ch." The result is "train" written as CHRAN and "trouble" written as DRBL. Table 15–1 includes more examples.

As children see more and more words spelled in the standard way, in books, on signs, on word-study lists, and so on, they gradually learn which phonetic features are attended to for the sake of spelling and which ones are ignored. They also learn the whole set of sounds each letter of the alphabet can represent and the "tricks of the trade" in spelling English words, such as the function of silent e. Like Will, they progress from strict phonetic transcription of sounds they hear in words to more sophisticated conventional spelling over the course of middle childhood (Treiman, 1985).

FIGURE 15-10
With years of spelling lessons and experience encountering words in books, children gradually learn the many unusual word spellings that characterize the English language. This fourth grader probably knows how to spell such difficult words as *achieve, freight, knight,* and *gnat.*

OVERVIEW

Children enter first grade with a firm grasp of oral language and, in many cases, some important understandings about written language as well. Over the course of the next several years, they typically master all the basics of grammar and syntax and become fluent readers and competent writers. Thanks to their developing metalinguistic awareness, they delight in jokes, riddles, and games with words and language—the hallmark of the school-age years. By the time children leave elementary school, their language development is virtually complete. In the years ahead, their remaining tasks will include expanding their vocabulary, tackling increasingly sophisticated books, and refining their writing skills.

CHAPTER REVIEW

ORAL LANGUAGE

- Young school-age children have mastered the rudiments of language, but they're still confused by certain words and usages, such as "ask" and "tell." They often rely less on syntax than on whether they know an answer or think a particular answer makes sense. Even at 9 and 10 years, children still confuse some words.
- School-age children love jokes and riddles because they've just begun to understand the ambiguous use of words, the heart of verbal humor. The ambiguity can be based on similar-sounding words, words with similar meanings, or sentences that can be understood in different ways. Understandings of these different types of ambiguity develop at different ages.
- The ability to notice deep linguistic structures rather than the meaning of words is known as metalinguistic awareness. Preschool children learn the form of jokes, but they don't have the metalinguistic understanding to know what makes jokes funny.
- American public schools have traditionally been filled with children of different backgrounds who learned to speak English in the classroom. Today, we are again experiencing a rise in diversity in school populations.
- The two main approaches to teaching English to non-native speakers are Teaching English as a Second Language (TESL) and bilingual programs. The TESL program is based on immersion of the students in the new language. In the bilingual approach, children are taught English, but they learn classroom subjects in their native language until they become somewhat proficient in English. There is debate over which of these approaches is preferable.
- There are three theories about how children learn a second language: They learn it the same way native speakers learn it as toddlers (the identical process theory); they use structures from their own native tongue (the interference theory); or they devise new grammatical structures as they learn (the unique grammatical structure theory). Most research supports the identical process model of learning a second language.
- Children learn a second language most quickly when they spend time playing and communicating with other children who speak the language. There is a definite socioemotional component that influences children's attitudes toward learning a second language.
- Dialects are variations in pronunciation, syntax, or word meanings within a language. The most common dialect in the United States is Black English Vernacular, which differs from standard English in several ways. Teachers need to help children learn the most accepted dialect at the same time that they convey respect for the children's first dialect.

WRITTEN LANGUAGE: LITERACY DEVELOPMENT

- Reading and writing are intimately connected. Reading is considered the most important skill children learn in the early school years.
- There are two main approaches to teaching reading: the skills approach—either phonics or look-say—and the whole language approach.
- The whole language approach, which relies on several cueing systems rather than focusing on isolated skills, is currently a popular method of teaching reading. When combined with some explicit phonics instruction, it is effective.

- When children first learn to write, they use a letter-name spelling strategy, relying on letters to "say" their names. Early writing looks unusual but can be deciphered phonetically. Invented spellings give way to conventional ones during the school years.

KEY TERMS

phonologically based
    ambiguity
lexically based ambiguity
syntactically based
    ambiguity
metalinguistic awareness

immersion
identical process theory
interference theory
unique grammatical
    structure theory
dialect

skills approach
whole language approach
phonics approach
"look-say" approach
syntactic cues
semantic cues

dyslexia
letter-name spelling
    strategy
affricated

SUGGESTIONS FOR FURTHER READING

Bissex, G. (1980). *GNYS AT WRK: A child learns to write and read.* Cambridge, MA: Harvard University Press.
This book presents a case study of the author's son from age 5 to age 9. It chronicles his writing and reading development. Very interesting reading!

Geller, L. G. (1985). *Word play and language learning for children.* Urbana, IL: National Council of Teachers of English.
This book provides a thorough discussion of children's use of jokes and riddles.

Goodman, K. S., Smith, E. B., Meredith, R., & Goodman, Y. (1987). *Language and thinking in school: A whole-language curriculum.* (3d ed.). New York: Richard C. Owen.
This undergraduate text provides useful information about the theoretical basis of the whole language approach to the teaching of reading and writing. It also provides useful guidance for teachers who want to implement a whole language program.

McLaughlin, B. (1984). *Second-language acquisition in childhood.* (Vol. 1). Hillsdale, NJ: Lawrence Erlbaum.
This book provides a good overview of second language acquisition. Chapters cover different second language acquisition situations, such as simultaneous acquisition of two languages and successive acquisition of two languages.

Read, C. (1975). *Children's categorization of speech sounds in English.* Urbana, IL: National Council of Teachers of English.
This is the classic source in which young children's inventive spellings are analyzed. Provides vital information for understanding this child behavior.

SOCIAL AND EMOTIONAL DEVELOPMENT IN SCHOOL-AGE CHILDREN

A group of fourth graders were huddled together at one end of a table in the lunchroom, talking in hushed tones. They looked for all the world like conspirators hatching a plot—which is exactly what they were doing.

"Look, we've got to have enough time to get the streamers tacked onto the wall, the balloons blown up and hung from the windows, the cupcakes on her desk, and 'Happy birthday, Mrs. Townsend' written on the blackboard," said Paul. "That'll take maybe ten minutes. But how do we get her out of the classroom for that long?" He looked around the circle of intent faces. "Any ideas?"

"How about if we get Mr. Steinberg to call her on the intercom to come to the office to get a message?" suggested Amy.

"No, that won't work," Paul responded. "She always sends one of us to the office to get messages."

"I know!" said David. "We'll have someone fake getting hurt on the playground and have to go to the nurse's office. Then the nurse can call Mrs. Townsend to come see if it's okay for the kid to come back to class. Then on the way back to the classroom, the kid could faint, and Mrs. Townsend would . . . "

"That doesn't make any sense," interrupted Gina. "The nurse always decides if you can come back to the classroom. Teachers don't decide that. And anyway, Mrs. Townsend would realize something was funny if the nurse asked her to come down."

"Let's tell her we met her husband out front with their baby, and he wants her to come out because he can't make the baby stop crying!" exclaimed Leroy.

"She'd never fall for that!" Paul scoffed. "That's ridiculous!"

"Then you think of something!" retorted Leroy. And they all fell silent for a few minutes . . . waiting for the next idea to surface.

It's not easy to figure out how to give someone a surprise birthday party. The remarkable thing is that these fourth graders were able to think about it at all—to invent ruses and then imagine how Mrs. Townsend might react to them. Younger children would be completely incapable of thinking this way. The ability to put oneself in someone else's place and anticipate what that person is likely to think, feel, or do—known as **social role-taking ability**—is one of the hallmarks of the social and emotional development of the school-age child.

In this chapter, we discuss the growth of this new awareness, which gives school-age children more social sophistication than they had just a few years earlier. They're also developing better social skills and becoming much more interested in friendship and acceptance by the group. Unfortunately, some children aren't successful at making friends or interacting with a group, and their experience of rejection is a matter of serious concern. Children's popularity, or lack of it, is the second topic covered in this chapter, along with some strategies for teaching unpopular children how to get themselves included in the group.

We also examine the development of moral reasoning in school-age children. Finally we look at cognitive and personality differences between boys and girls, and we consider why these sex differences exist. Social and emotional development is broad and complex during the school years, and this chapter suggests some of the richness of children's experience.

SOCIAL ROLE-TAKING ABILITY

We could see the ability to understand the feelings, thoughts, and intentions of another in Paul, Gina, and the other fourth graders who were trying to plan a surprise birthday party for their teacher. The social role-taking ability they demonstrated is just one part of **social cognition**—the child's growing understanding of a broad range of social and interpersonal events. This understanding gradually increases during middle childhood, the period from 6 to 10 years of age (Shantz, 1975).

Social role-taking ability involves judging what cognitive and emotional processes other people are going through. It leads children to a greater understanding of others as well as of themselves, since they can now think of themselves from the point of view of others. This ability consists of several different, but interacting, components—understanding emotions, understanding intentions, and understanding thinking. In this section we consider how children develop in relation to each of these dimensions.

Understanding Other People's Emotions

Children make great advances in understanding emotions during middle childhood. We've seen that as infants, they were able to discriminate emotions by reading people's happy or angry faces, and between 2 and 3 years, they began to label and talk about emotions. Between ages 4 and 7, children start to match appropriate emotional responses to specific situations (Barden et al., 1980; Borke, 1971). But at this age they still lack sophisticated understandings about emotions. They don't know, for example, that two different emotions can be felt simultaneously about the same situation. They also don't understand that a situation can elicit different emotions from different people. These are some of the understandings they acquire during the school-age period.

UNDERSTANDING SIMULTANEOUS EMOTIONS. Experiences of emotions can be simple and straightforward, or they can be complex and difficult. Consider this situation:

The Golden Eagles soccer team coach was awarding his players their plaques at the end-of-season pizza party. He was surrounded by noisy, excited 7- and 8-year-olds. After he handed out the last plaque, he uncovered a large trophy still to be awarded. The two best players on the team fixed their eyes on the trophy eagerly. "The trophy this year," announced the coach, "is for team spirit. It goes to the player who did the most for the whole team. He was always enthusiastic at practices and games, and he gave tremendous support to all the other players—Jasper!"

"Jasper! Why does he get the trophy?" wailed the team star.

"Yeah—he didn't score any goals," cried his rival, as parents exchanged exasperated looks and applauded loudly to drown out their voices.

Jasper jumped up to receive his trophy with a broad smile on his face. Later, when his parents asked him how he felt at that moment, he said, "I felt happy that I got it."

"But didn't you feel mad when Max said that you didn't deserve it, that the trophy should go to the player who made the most goals?"

"No, not really."

That night, Jasper's parents discussed his good-natured approach to life. "He takes things so well," his dad said. "I would have been furious if my teammates said I didn't deserve the trophy. But not Jasper. He just felt happy that he'd gotten it."

When Jasper's dad placed himself in his son's situation, he readily admitted that he would feel "mixed emotions"—happy about winning the trophy but mad about the comments made by the others when it was awarded. But Jasper didn't seem to experience conflicting emotions. He felt happy about winning the trophy, and that was it. This is typical of children's "all or none" reactions. They seem to feel all sad, all happy, or all angry, but not more than one of these emotions at the same time. An adult, in contrast, might feel more than one emotion about the same event—happiness and sadness about a child's going away to school, for example, or anger and sadness about a deliberately set fire.

Two researchers have developed a model for thinking about how children progress in their ability to experience and talk about simultaneous emotions (Harter & Buddin, 1987). They proposed the notions of **targets**—the object, person, or situation at which an emotion is directed—and of **valence**—the positive or negative nature of the emotion. They hypothesized that it might be easier for children to experience two positive emotions directed toward the same target simultaneously than a positive and a negative emotion toward the same target.

The study they did confirmed this hypothesis. They found that children aged 4 to 6 weren't able to put feelings together simultaneously at all. Sometimes they denied that two feelings could be experienced at the same time, or they sequenced two feelings ("First I'd feel excited; then I'd feel happy."). These children do have concepts for separate emotions, but they can't differentiate and integrate them at the same time. They sequence them instead.

Children aged 6 to 8 acknowledged that they experienced two emotions at the same time, but they included only same-valence emotions directed toward the same target ("I felt happy and excited about getting an A on my spelling test."). But they had difficulty feeling two different positive emotions about

FIGURE 16-1
The thrill of a merry-go-round gives two boys unmixed joy. Children's emotional experiences are direct and intense, partly because they don't have the internal buffer adults have. As they become more sophisticated emotionally, children learn to distinguish different feelings more clearly and to handle their emotions in a greater variety of ways.

two different targets ("I felt happy about my new board games and very excited about the tickets to the baseball game.")

Children aged 8 to 9 said they could experience two same-valence emotions directed toward different targets at the same time ("I'd feel happy about the spelling test and excited about the class picnic"), but they couldn't imagine being able to feel two different-valence emotions—one positive, one negative—at the same time. One child said, "I couldn't feel happy and frightened at the same time; I would have to be two people at once!" (Harter & Buddin, 1987, pp. 392–393).

Ten-year-olds said they experienced two different-valence emotions at the same time, but only when they were directed at two different targets ("I was scared in the theatre watching the movie, but I was happy that I had popcorn to eat."). Their range of emotions was larger than ever, but they couldn't bring a positive and a negative emotion to a single target at the same time ("The movie made me feel happy and scared.").

Not until they were 11 or 12 years old did children say they could feel opposite emotions toward the same target at the same time ("I was happy that I was going to overnight camp, but I was scared about staying in a new place.").

This study shows that children become more sophisticated about how they understand and experience their emotions as they develop. The study also suggests that out of a mass of undifferentiated positive and negative emotions, children gradually distinguish and form concepts of different, distinct feelings. An older child or adult might have distinguished and named a variety of feelings evoked by the situation Jasper found himself in—pride, pleasure, excitement, embarrassment, anger, humiliation. Jasper mentioned only that he felt "happy." As he develops, his understanding of his emotions will become more refined and sophisticated.

UNDERSTANDING SITUATIONS. An important part of understanding how other people are feeling involves understanding situations and the feelings they typically evoke in people. Not being invited to a friend's party would make most people feel hurt, for example, and winning a prize in a contest would make most people feel excited. But other situations are more equivocal (ambiguous) than these—some people might feel good about them, others might feel bad.

Young children often don't recognize that some situations are more equivocal than others. One group of researchers set out to discover how children of different ages thought people would feel about a variety of situations (Gnepp, McKee & Domanic, 1987). Would they realize that some situations are quite clear but that others aren't so clear? The researchers presented kindergartners and first, second, and third graders with a series of equivocal situations (for example, "child gets an egg salad sandwich for lunch" or "child is approached by a small dog while playing") and unequivocal situations (for example, "all the lights go off when child is playing alone" or "child drops and breaks favorite toy") (Gnepp, McKee & Domanic, 1987, p. 116).

The children were asked to tell how a "story child" (a hypothetical child) would feel about the situation. After stating an emotion they believed the story child would feel, children were asked to explain why they thought the child would feel that way. The researchers wondered if children would respond to an equivocal situation by attributing a wider range of emotional reactions to the child pictured in the situation than they would for unequivocal situations. This would indicate that they realized that the equivocal situation is more likely to evoke different emotions from different people. They found that children did respond this way. They also found that older children recognized equivocal situations more clearly than younger ones, suggesting that as children get older, they develop more sophisticated knowledge about the emotions that different situations can elicit.

Children also gave different kinds of explanations for their choices of emotion for the equivocal situations than they did for the unequivocal ones. In the equivocal situations, children explained why the story child felt the way she did by referring to her supposed interpretation of the event ("She would be happy about an egg salad sandwich, because she knows that eggs are good for her."). This indicates that they realized that people's responses to a situation might vary, depending on how they viewed or interpreted the event. Of course, we can't know for sure how a person will feel about a particular situation, even an unequivocal one, unless we know the meaning of that situation to the person. One common ambiguous situation is that in which a person expresses displaced aggression, being harsh with one person because she is angry at another. The man who kicks the cat because his boss yelled at him and the child who hits her younger sister because she's angry at her mother are both expressing displaced aggression. Situations like this are particularly difficult for 5-year-olds to understand; by 9 years, they're having less trouble. Children improve at understanding displaced aggression when they become more aware of the discrepancies that can exist between feelings and the expression of those feelings (Miller & DeMarie-Dreblow, 1990).

FIGURE 16-2
Playing alone while other children are playing together nearby is a situation that would make most children feel sad. In general, young school-age children understand this type of situation. Other, more complicated situations require a level of understanding that isn't attained until age 10 or 11.

As children develop, their understandings of all these factors become more refined. They realize that people can have mixed emotions, that some situations are more ambiguous than others, and that people can have reasons for their actions that aren't apparent on the surface. In many ways, children become more "emotionally literate" as they move through middle childhood.

Understanding Other People's Intentions

"Mom, Kelly broke the lid of my treasure box!"

"I didn't mean to! I didn't know it was under the paper when I leaned on the table!"

"It's all cracked! You broke it, and I'm gonna break something of yours to pay you back!"

Parents and teachers are sometimes surprised when children don't recognize and respond differently when something happens accidentally. Children don't seem to notice or care how or why an event occurred; they care only about the event itself and its consequences. Adults, in contrast, understand that unfortunate events, such as breaking something or hurting someone, can occur under a variety of circumstances. They base their responses in part on the intentions of the person responsible for the event, on whether it was deliberate or accidental. Why don't children respond this way?

One problem is that the discrimination between "deliberate" and "accidental" is difficult for children to make. Most adults judge intentions by people's

FIGURE 16-3
It's very hard for children to distinguish deliberate actions from accidental ones. If another child says "I'm sorry" and offers comfort and support, as this boy is doing, a child who has been hurt is more likely to respond appropriately.

facial expressions and verbalizations. An angry expression accompanied by a sarcastic statement would lead most adults to conclude that the speaker's intentions were hostile. A surprised or sad expression accompanied by the statement, "I'm sorry—I was only trying to help," would lead most adults to assume a prosocial intention.

Children younger than age 6 or 7 aren't very skillful at detecting intentions in situations where damage occurs. In one study, kindergartners and second and fourth graders were shown videotaped vignettes of a child destroying an object (Dodge, Murphy & Buchsbaum, 1984). The vignettes showed intentions ranging from hostile to accidental to "innocent bystander." Researchers clearly showed that the younger the children were, the more difficulty they had in identifying and discriminating intentions.

This study emphasizes the necessity of helping young children understand situations that are even slightly ambiguous. Adults can point out people's expressions to children to encourage them to look for intention cues: "Look at how sad Kelly's face looks. She feels bad about breaking the lid of your box." They can also teach children to take the words "I'm sorry" as a cue that something was an accident and calls for a different response. In this case, though, adults need to be certain that the apology is genuine, rather than a response that the child has picked up as a way to "get off the hook."

If young children have a hard time understanding intention when it's clearly stated, they're completely in the dark when someone deliberately tries to mislead them. This means they're virtually defenseless against the claims of television advertising. Even sixth graders aren't very skillful at taking intentions into account when judging the information given about products in television commercials (Ross et al., 1981). They take the information at face value without allowing for the fact that the advertiser may be trying to deceive them. Even though children begin to be able to detect intention at about 6 years, and their abilities improve throughout the school years, detecting deception is very difficult even for 11- and 12-year-olds.

Understanding Other People's Thinking

Chairs were arranged in the middle of the classroom to make a train, and children were busy getting dressed up to go on a trip. Alice was behind the ticket counter selling tickets marked "New York," "New Jersey," "Maine," "Canada," and "Florida." As the first customer approached the ticket counter, Alice asked, "Where are you going?"

"To my grandma's house," replied Natalie.

Alice looked at the teacher as if to say, "What do I do now?" She knew she didn't have any tickets that said that. The teacher suggested she ask Natalie where her grandma lived.

"Where's she live?" Alice inquired.

"Next door to Mrs. McKinney," answered Natalie.

Alice again looked at the teacher in bewilderment.

"Ask what city her grandma lives in, or what state."

"What city does she live in?" Alice asked.

"I don't know," came the reply.

Finally, the teacher intervened. "Natalie, when you go on a trip to see your grandma, your mom tells me that you're going to New Jersey. Is that where you want to go on the train today?"

"Uh-huh."

"Give this lady one ticket to New Jersey," the teacher told Alice, who then searched through the pile of tickets to find an appropriate ticket.

A third aspect of social role-taking ability, besides understanding other people's emotions and intentions, is understanding their thinking and what they know. The incident just described, which took place in a preschool classroom, illustrates how limited the 4- or 5-year-old's ability is in this area. Natalie couldn't understand what Alice didn't know, and Alice couldn't understand what Natalie didn't know. But during the school-age years, children develop the ability to think about other people's knowledge and thinking. Note the example of the fourth graders we saw at the beginning of the chapter, who were able to generate several different ruses for getting Mrs. Townsend out of the classroom and then to evaluate them from her point of view.

Children's ability to think about other people's thinking and their own thinking has been studied in a variety of ways. Some researchers have asked children to play strategy games, which by their very nature require children to think about the other person's thinking.

FIGURE 16-4
''He may think I'll make this move, so I'll make a different one instead . . .'' When children begin to think about what others may be thinking, they become more skilled at playing strategy games and also become capable of greater self-awareness and greater understanding of others.

Other researchers have asked children to give directions for constructing a design to a second child whose view of the design is blocked (Krauss & Glucksberg, 1969). Still other researchers have presented dilemmas to children involving social role-taking ability and asked them to think about other people's thinking. A classic study involved a dilemma involving a girl named Holly (Selman, 1976):

> Holly is an 8-year-old girl who likes to climb trees. She is the best tree climber in the neighborhood. One day while climbing down from a tall tree, she falls off the bottom branch but does not hurt herself. Her father sees her fall. He is upset and asks her to promise not to climb trees any more. Holly promises.
>
> Later that day, Holly and her friends meet Shawn. Shawn's kitten is caught up in a tree and can't get down. Something has to be done right away, or the kitten may fall. Holly is the only one who climbs trees well enough to reach the kitten and get down, but she remembers her promise to her father.

After hearing the dilemma, children are asked several questions, including, "What does Holly think her father will do if he finds out she climbed the tree?" On the basis of this type of study, Selman and his colleagues concluded that children's ability to think about other people's thinking evolves through five stages:

Stage 0 (ages 4 to 6)—**egocentric role taking.** At the beginning of this stage, children are unaware of differences in points of view. They think there's only one point of view, the one held by them—and by everyone else. A child at this stage typically answers the question about Holly's father by saying, "He will feel happy because he likes kittens." By the end of this stage, children begin to realize that people's views can differ.

Stage 1 (ages 6 to 8)—**social-information role taking.** The child understands that people interpret situations differently but thinks the source
of these different views is different information. The child doesn't realize
that people can have different views about the same information. The
child isn't really taking the role of another person except in the limited
sense of thinking about what the other person doesn't know. "If he didn't
know why she climbed the tree, he would be angry," the child says about
Holly's father. "But if Holly told him why she did it, he would realize
that she had a good reason." The child doesn't realize that even if he
knew why Holly climbed the tree, her father might still be angry—
because of his view of the situation.

Stage 2 (ages 9 and 10)—**self-reflective role taking.** Children know that
people think about their thoughts and feelings. Their developing metacognitive abilities allow them to think about their own thinking or about
another person's thinking about them, but they can't consider both people's thinking simultaneously. They may say that Holly's father won't be
angry: "Holly knows that her father will understand why she climbed
the tree, so she knows that he won't want to punish her at all." Or they
may say that Holly's father *will* be angry because he knows that she
understands his concern about her climbing trees.

Stage 3 (ages 10 to 12)—**mutual role taking.** Children can now consider
their point of view and another point of view simultaneously, as a dis-
interested third party. The child can speculate about what people are
thinking about other people's thoughts. "Let's see," the child might say
about Holly, "Holly wanted to get the kitten because she liked kittens,
but she knew that she wasn't supposed to climb trees. Holly's father
knew that Holly had been told not to climb trees, but he couldn't have
known beforehand about this situation. He'd probably punish her anyway, just to enforce his rule."

Stage 4 (ages 12 to 15 and older)—**social and conventional system role
taking.** The child appreciates the view of the "generalized other"—the
social system—and uses it to help understand the view of a particular
person. The perspective of the social group is now taken into account.
"Holly's father would probably get angry and punish her," the child
might say, "because that's what fathers must do if they want their children to obey." If the child has moved beyond a conventional view of
morality (see the discussion of Kohlberg later in this chapter), the child
might say, "You'd really have to know Holly's father to know if he would
get angry. Some fathers would get angry; others wouldn't."

Recently researchers have looked carefully at how a child learns that the
target individual asked about (for example, Holly's father) can come to a different conclusion about information than the child (Dixon & Moore, 1990).
They think it's partly a matter of the child's coming to understand the different
values that people can have. The researchers even found that children seem
to focus on different values (Stage 2) *before* they focus on different information
(Stage 1). These researchers do agree, however, that Selman's higher stages
involve considering both perspectives simultaneously (Stages 3 and up), while
the lower stages (1 and 2) involve simply distinguishing perspectives and considering them one at a time. In that respect the order of stages proposed by
Selman held up.

All the studies of children's social role-taking ability showed that older children are better able than younger children to think about what other people think, know, or understand. But even adults sometimes get confused in social situations, projecting their own thoughts and feelings onto others. The gradual development of social role-taking ability is a measure both of growing emotional and cognitive maturity and of the help children receive in understanding the inner thought processes of other people.

Social Role-Taking Ability and Social Behavior

You might expect that as children develop higher levels of social role-taking ability, their social behavior will improve. Some studies have shown this to be true (Buckley, Siegel & Ness, 1979), but others haven't (Eisenberg-Berg, 1979; Strayer, 1980).

There really isn't any reason for a relationship between awareness and positive social actions to exist, however. A child's ability to understand emotions, detect intentions, and think about what another person is thinking doesn't automatically lead to good social behavior. The ability to see the world through another's eyes may lead a child to act on the other's behalf, "but this ability may also be used to one's own advantage at another's expense" (Smith et al., 1983, p. 121). Children's motivations and values—their ideas of what a "good person" would do and their motivation to live up to those standards—determine how they will use their awareness. (See the discussion of moral development later in this chapter.) Although their understanding improves during middle childhood, whether they become more prosocial depends on factors other than social role-taking ability, including their temperamental predispositions and the socialization techniques their parents have used.

SOCIAL SKILLS AND POPULARITY

By the time children are in elementary school, they usually have a social "style" that characterizes how they act with their peers, who become increasingly important during this period. Middle childhood is a time of friendships and wide-ranging peer interactions that offer opportunities for affection, learning, and just plain fun. But some children don't have the experience of friendship during these years. Some children are unpopular, disliked by others, for a variety of reasons. This situation shouldn't be taken lightly. Not having friends in childhood is correlated with poor achievement in school (Roff, Sells & Golden, 1972; Green, Beck & Forehand, 1980), a higher likelihood of disliking and dropping out of school (Ladd, 1990), juvenile delinquency (Roff, Sells & Golden, 1972), and bad conduct discharges from the military (Roff, 1961).

Although these correlational data do not prove that lack of early friendships causes poor achievement later, the strength and number of negative correlations have led researchers to study popularity and to try to remedy individual cases of peer rejection. When children have negative interaction patterns, it's important to help them learn social skills before they gain a reputation among their peers for fulfilling such roles as bully or victim (as described in Chapter 8). Peer rejection because of a reputation for patterns of behavior like aggression and avoidance may limit future chances for change. A bully may drive away all but those aggressive classmates who encourage further aggression,

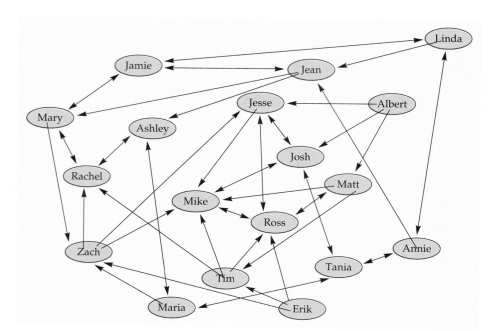

FIGURE 16-5
A sociogram can be con-
structed from children's
responses to questions about
which classmates they like the
best or want to sit near.
Researchers can then determine which children are popular—those whose names
come up most often—and
which children may need
some help with their social
skills.

and a victim may be victimized by such large groups of children that it's hard
to fight back successfully, leading him to avoid other children altogether. In
ways like these, rejection by peers may intensify the social interaction patterns
that caused the child to be rejected in the first place.

When researchers measure popularity, or social status, they use sociometric
techniques such as interviews and questionnaires. Usually children are asked
to name or list the classmates they like the most and the least. From their
answers, researchers can determine which children are liked by many children
(these children have **popular status**), which ones are disliked by many children (**unpopular status**), which ones are neither liked nor disliked by many
children (**neglected status**), and which ones are both liked and disliked by
other children (**controversial status**) (Asher & Dodge, 1986). Researchers have
used a variety of observations and experiments to try to see how children get
their status.

Popularity and Social Behavior

FRIENDLINESS. Popular children tend to be friendly, outgoing, agreeable, cooperative, enthusiastic, and helpful (Hartup, 1983; Patterson, Kupersmidt &
Griesler, 1990). Unpopular or rejected children may also be outgoing and initiate a lot of social interactions, but their overtures tend to be aggressive and
disruptive (Dodge, Coie, Pettit & Price, 1990). For example, a preschool child
may snatch a toy, run a short distance away, look back at the victim, and smile.
The child may be making a bid to play, but the outcome of such harassing
tactics is usually rejection.

GROUP ENTRY STRATEGIES. In addition to exhibiting positive and friendly social
behavior, popular children approach the entry of an ongoing play group in

different ways than unpopular children do. The age-old problem of getting included in play has been the subject of a variety of studies. In one study researchers organized second and third graders into "host" children, who were engaged in play with the researcher, and "entry" children, who were asked to enter the play (Putallaz & Gottman, 1981). The sociometric status of all the children had been determined previously.

Unpopular children tried to enter the group by asking more questions than popular children did, by talking more about themselves, and by disagreeing more. Popular children, in contrast, didn't interrupt the ongoing play or draw attention to themselves. Also, when popular children disagreed with another child about something, they tended to state a general rule and provide an alternative action the playmate could take. "You're not supposed to pick a card from that pile," they might say, "You're supposed to draw from his hand." Unpopular children tended to state their objections in personal ways, such as "No!" or "Don't do that!", and they suggested no alternative.

A study of kindergartners turned up similar findings (Dodge et al., 1983). These researchers categorized children's peer-group entry strategies as follows: wait and hover; attention getting (but not aversive); group-oriented statements; questions; self-referent statements; and disruption (aversive).

FIGURE 16-6
Researchers have found that one of the most successful group entry strategies is mimicking the peer group. Although the girl on the right doesn't have a partner right now, she's demonstrating that she understands the group activity and would be able to fit in if the opportunity arose. Since she doesn't appear aggressive or disruptive, her chances of being included may be quite good.

They found that group-oriented statements were used more by popular children than by rejected or neglected children. Disruptive tactics, on the other hand, were used more—in fact, ten times more—by rejected children. Waiting and hovering was the tactic of choice for neglected children. Although entry into the group was fairly difficult for all children—that is, it typically required several bids—the tactics used by popular children were the most successful, and popular children were allowed to join the group more frequently than rejected or neglected children.

In studies with older children, the same researchers identified other successful strategies, which they labeled "mimicking the peer group" (Dodge et

al., 1983) and "nonverbal synchrony with the group's activity," or gradually merging with the group (Dodge et al., 1987). The most successful sequence of tactics consisted of waiting and hovering, mimicking the peer group, and making group-oriented statements. Perhaps waiting and hovering gives the child time to size up the situation. Mimicking the group's behavior may signal to the group that the child would be able to join in the play. And making group-oriented statements may let them know that the child would not take over the play situation, which would be disruptive.

Joining rather than disrupting ongoing play is one of a number of specific social skills that appear to be an important ingredient in children's social status. It has been demonstrated that children who haven't yet learned these skills but are motivated to learn them can be helped by direct training. A successful social skills training technique involves an adult coach who role-plays social interactions with the child, coaches her in appropriate skills, and provides feedback about her performance. One exemplary training program (Oden & Asher, 1977) taught skills such as those related to social participation (getting involved and paying attention), cooperation (sharing and taking turns), communication (listening and talking appropriately), and social validation (looking at the other person and giving support). Another taught asking positive questions, offering useful suggestions, and offering supportive statements (Ladd, 1981). These are but a few of the many specific social skills that have been taught directly (Goldstein, 1980).

Although there is evidence that children who have been coached may become more popular as a result, such extensive training is a luxury beyond the capacity of most school systems. Often it initially falls to the classroom teacher to try to help these children. Activities that require cooperation may help facilitate peer relations (Johnson & Johnson, 1974), and pairing unpopular children with popular children for activities can improve the unpopular children's status, at least temporarily (Chennault, 1967). But children whose behavior is inappropriate and disruptive and who are rejected by their peers need more help than this, help for both themselves and their families. For a discussion of antisocial behavior in school-age children, see Special Education Focus—Does Early Antisocial Behavior Fade Away?

OTHER FACTORS ASSOCIATED WITH POPULARITY. Early attachment history is related to a child's social style and social and emotional development, as we saw in Chapter 8. Recent research with school-age children is consistent with that reported for infants in showing that supportive experiences within the family contribute greatly to social interactions with peers. One study found that boys rejected by their peers experience poorer family monitoring, poorer discipline, and more family stress than average boys (Dishion, 1990). These factors are believed to cause antisocial behavior and academic problems, which in turn cause rejection by peers.

Another study focused on interaction between parents of boys who are "more-liked" by their peers versus parents of "less-liked" boys with their own as well as other boys (Austin & Lindauer, 1990). Parents of less-liked boys were found to have more intensive, controlling, and intrusive interactions with all boys, while parents of more-liked boys had more extensive interactions that allowed them to praise and encourage children more. These findings emphasize the importance of supportive interactions and appropriate discipline and are consistent with reports that peer-rejected children, especially those who are aggressive, have particularly unsupportive relationships with their fathers (Patterson, Kupersmidt & Griesler, 1990).

Parental support and responsiveness are also associated with another factor that contributes to social success—the child's belief that he controls social outcomes. This belief in turn helps him overcome rejections and persist toward social goals (Lepore et al., 1989). That is, just as perceived academic self-efficacy is associated with increased effort in the academic realm, perceived social self-efficacy, initially related to parental attachment, is associated with persistent effort in the social realm. Like the securely attached 3-year-olds who persisted at Ahrend's (1984) "barrier box" (see Chapter 12), children who have secure social attachments subsequently perceive themselves as socially competent, and this perception of self-efficacy encourages them to persist until they have established satisfying social relationships in school and elsewhere (Sroufe, 1990). And perhaps equally important is the fact that current warm family relationships dampen the effect of social rejection generally. For example, children who have experienced rejection by one or more peers are protected against adjustment difficulties by warm relationships with their mothers (Patterson, Cohn & Kao, 1989).

Physical attractiveness is also correlated with popularity (Lerner & Lerner, 1977; Cavior & Dokecki, 1973), although the cause of this relationship is not entirely clear. A common explanation is that attractive children may draw more people into social interaction in infancy by virtue of their "cuteness." Greater social experience would give them more practice in reading social cues and coordinating their behavior with that of others. Positive social responses might lead them to smile more and make more friendly gestures, which are also associated with greater popularity. Attractive children would have a long history of positive interactions by the time they entered school.

MORAL DEVELOPMENT

Moral development is a complex process that involves both cognitive and emotional growth. Several different researchers and theorists have proposed ways of thinking about children's moral development; we discuss three of them here.

Piaget's Study of Moral Reasoning

"WHICH CHILD IS NAUGHTIER?" To investigate children's moral reasoning, Piaget presented them with a pair of stories and asked them which child was "naughtier" (Piaget, 1965 p. 122):

A. A little boy who is called John is in his room. He is called to dinner. He goes into the dining room. But behind the door there was a chair, and on the chair there was a tray with twelve cups on it. John couldn't have known that there was all this behind the door. He goes in, the door knocks against the tray, bang go the twelve cups, and they all get broken!

B. Once there was a little boy whose name was Henry. One day when his mother was out he tried to get some jam out of the cupboard. He climbed up onto a

SPECIAL EDUCATION FOCUS

Does Early Antisocial Behavior Fade Away?

Do children who are disruptive, aggressive, or destructive gradually become as cooperative and productive as their classmates? Unfortunately, no. Research indicates that early aggression and antisocial behavior are very good predictors of later social problems. These include juvenile delinquency (Roff, 1961; Farrington & West, 1971; Venezia, 1971; Loeber, 1982), lowered adult achievement, and marital instability (Caspi, Bem & Elder, 1987). Apparently, it's the rare child who "outgrows" severe behavioral problems without some kind of help (Loeber et al., 1989).

In one longitudinal study, researchers identified early classroom behaviors that were associated with later delinquency and school misconduct. These behaviors included the following (Spivack, Marcus & Swift, 1986, p. 128):

- Annoying social behavior, such as poking and excessive talking and noisemaking in the classroom

- A tendency to rush into things without listening, reflecting impatience and a need to move ahead constantly without looking back or learning from experience

- Negative and defiant behavior toward the teacher

- Self-centered verbalization, such as interruptions, irrelevant remarks, and unexamined personal thoughts

These early behaviors seem to set in motion maladaptive social interactions that continue to snowball. Children without the social skills to get off to a good start in interactions with other children are rejected and excluded. Being left out deprives them of the experience and practice they need to develop the social skills they lack (Lieberman, 1977; Krantz, 1982; Dodge, Murphy & Buchsbaum, 1984).

Some experts suggest that children whose behavior is extremely antisocial in the early grades may have been "temperamentally difficult" from early infancy. But we saw in our discussion of attachment in Chapter 8 that temperament alone isn't a very good predictor of later difficulties. Trouble usually develops only when the parents of a "difficult" child

can't adapt to the child. This problem of the "match" between child temperament and parenting style may be at the root of some patterns of maladaptive classroom behavior (Spivack, Marcus & Swift, 1986).

The first line of defense against the development of severe antisocial tendencies in children, then, is to facilitate attachment between infants and their parents. For children who miss out on this preventive step and arrive at preschool as aggressive and antisocial young children, therapeutic nursery schools can help. When antisocial children get to elementary school without having received any treatment, it's up to their teachers to help them break out of a vicious cycle. It is extremely important to be sure aggressive behavior is not rewarded (Perry, Williard & Perry, 1990). Teachers can also try coaching children in social skills, as described in this chapter (Oden & Asher, 1977; Ladd, 1981). They may also try teaching the children social-cognitive problem solving (Spivack & Shure, 1982). This involves helping children think of other ways to behave in conflict situations and thinking through the consequences of different actions.

Teachers with an antisocial child in the classroom experience tremendous stress coping with the child's behavior, and they need to be able to talk to someone knowledgeable about this situation. Extremely skillful management of the child is necessary for an extended period of time. Appropriate treatment involves firmness without hostility, consistency without rigidity, and support for developing social and cognitive skills that will help the child learn to regulate his own behavior (Spivack, Marcus & Swift, 1986, p.130). Unfortunately, few teachers have the time, energy, or training necessary to change the behavior of severely antisocial children. They need additional resources in the school and community, including counseling for the child's family, to help problem children in any real way. As difficult as it is to provide for this kind of treatment, it's crucial to the child's future development. Early antisocial behavior doesn't simply fade away; it often simply gets worse.

The antisocial child is a constant source of tension and disruption in the classroom. He may turn every situation into an occasion for malicious behavior. Often, outside help is needed to help the child learn better ways of interacting.

◄ **FIGURE 16-7**
"Which child is naughtier?" 5-year-olds judged the two cases by how many cups were broken; 10-year-olds judged them by the boys' intentions. By questioning children of different ages about their beliefs, Piaget arrived at a timetable of moral development. He suggested that an important shift in moral reasoning occurs at 11 or 12, when children begin to think less in terms of God-given absolutes and more in terms of agreement and reciprocity among equals.

chair and stretched out his arm. But the jam was too high up and he couldn't reach it and have any. But while he was trying to get it he knocked over a cup. The cup fell and broke.

Most adults wouldn't blame John for breaking the 12 cups. After all, he was called to dinner, and he didn't know the cups were behind the door. Henry, on the other hand, was doing something he wasn't supposed to be doing. Even though he broke only one cup, his intentions weren't very good.

Piaget found that children under 6 years of age judged John to be naughtier because he broke more cups. They based their judgment on the amount of damage done, not on the boys' intentions. Piaget's theory is consistent with recent research in which 3- to 5-year-olds were asked to describe things they thought were "bad" (Tisak & Block, 1990). Most of the events they mentioned involved negative consequences to others, such as physical harm and property damage. Piaget found that by middle childhood, children were beginning to take intentions into account and to base their judgments on them. These children thought Henry was naughtier in the moral dilemma described above.

CHILDREN'S MORAL JUDGMENTS ABOUT LYING AND STEALING. Young children use similar criteria to judge lying. They judge the seriousness of a lie not by whether the child who told it intended to deceive but by how much the lie varies from the truth. A 6-year-old said one person was worse because what he said "could never happen." A character who said he saw a dog as big as a cow was judged worse by a 7-year-old because "there's no such thing." By the age of 10, children judged the severity of a lie not in terms of its truth value but in terms of intention to deceive.

Perception of stealing follows a similiar pattern. Younger children judge the seriousness of stealing by the amount stolen, not by its purpose. When Piaget presented them with the case of a boy who stole a roll to give to a hungry friend and a girl who stole a ribbon for herself, 6-year-olds said the boy's theft was worse "because rolls cost more." But a 9-year-old said, "The little girl was worse. The little girl took the ribbon for herself. The little boy took the roll, but to give it to his friend who had no dinner" (Piaget, 1965).

THE SHIFT IN MORAL REASONING. Piaget found that between ages 5 and 10, children's reasoning moves from objective judgments—based on physical results or damage—to subjective judgments—based on intentions and other psychological considerations (Piaget, 1965; Lickona, 1976). He referred to objective judgments as **moral realism.** The shift away from moral realism could be due to several factors. As we've seen, young children can't detect intentions very well. They often mistake accidents for hostile acts. It could be that they *are* considering intentions in making their moral judgments, but they're not very good at distinguishing deliberate acts from unintentional ones. In the case of John and Henry, they might not have recognized that John didn't mean to break the cups.

There may also be a cognitive-language aspect to the shift in moral reasoning. Young children may be able to identify false assertions that are unintentional (such as when a person is told something untrue and passes it on, believing that it's true), yet they still consider them lies (Wimmer, Gruber & Perner, 1984). To these children, "lying" means making assertions that aren't true. As children get older, their ability to detect intentions may not improve as much as their understanding that "lying" includes *both* making a false statement *and* intending to deceive.

The socialization processes that parents and teachers have used may also influence children's development in moral reasoning. Children need to learn that intentions do make a difference in whether something is right or wrong, but very often their own intentions aren't valued. It's the rare child who hasn't protested, "I didn't mean to do it!" and yet still been punished.

Kohlberg's Study of Moral Reasoning

Lawrence Kohlberg's work on moral reasoning is based on the work of Piaget, but it goes further. Piaget felt that children are capable of mature moral reasoning by the age of 11 or 12 when they routinely take intentions into account. In contrast, Kohlberg attempted to differentiate additional stages of moral development during adulthood, when, he believed, higher levels of moral reasoning could be reached.

THE CASE OF HEINZ. Kohlberg approached moral reasoning in terms of people's relationship to society's rules. Like Piaget, he posed moral dilemmas to gain insight into reasoning. One dilemma he used is that of Heinz, a man who was faced with the choice of stealing medicine or letting his wife die (Kohlberg, 1969, p. 379):

> In Europe, a woman was near death from cancer. One drug might save her, a form of radium that a druggist in the same town had recently discovered. The druggist was charging $2,000, ten times what the drug cost him to make. The sick woman's husband, Heinz, went to everyone he knew to borrow the money, but he could only get together about half of what it cost. He told the druggist that his wife was dying and asked him to sell it cheaper or let him pay later. But the druggist said no. The husband got desperate and broke into the man's store to steal the drug for his wife. Should the man have done that? Why?

KOHLBERG'S LEVELS OF MORAL DEVELOPMENT. On the basis of responses to situations like this, Kohlberg identified three levels of moral development, with two stages at each level. At Level I, which he labeled *preconventional*, people make moral decisions on the basis of self-interest, either to avoid punishment or to gain rewards (see Reasons for Doing Right, in Table 16-1). Both of the following responses to the Heinz dilemma are considered Level I responses (Kohlberg, 1969, p. 381):

> Pro: If you let your wife die, you will get in trouble. You'll be blamed for not spending the money to save her and there'll be an investigation of you and the druggist for your wife's death.

> Con: You shouldn't steal the drug because you'll be caught and sent to jail if you do. If you do get away, your conscience would bother you thinking how the police would catch up with you at any minute.

At Level II, the *conventional* level, people have chosen to conform to the standards expected of them by society. They're guided by a concern for the general good and a desire to maintain social order. At Level III, labeled *postconventional*, people define their values in terms of principles, whether philosophical, religious, or personal in some other way. They're guided by concerns that transcend the maintenance of social order.

According to Kohlberg, the levels and stages are hierarchical—a person moves forward through them one by one, and no stage can be skipped. Research hasn't consistently supported this claim (Rest, 1983; Hoffman, 1984). There's also some philosophical debate about whether a "universal principle of justice" really exists, as Kohlberg claims. Carol Gilligan, for example, has argued that Kohlberg ignored the social context of moral behavior. According to Gilligan, women are socialized *not* to base decisions on personal, self-chosen principles but to consider the consequences of moral decisions for others (Gilligan, 1977; 1982). Other critics have argued that Kohlberg's scheme stresses the individual versus the group (Hogan, 1975; Wallach & Wallach, 1983).

Younger children (under age 10) are incapable of reasoning at Kohlberg's highest level. Children between 10 and 12 years old may be in Stage 2, 3, or 4, but they're rarely in Stage 5. Not until adolescence are children able to rea-

TABLE 16-1 Kohlberg's Moral Stages

	CONTENT OF STAGE		
Level and Stage	*What Is Right*	*Reasons for Doing Right*	*Social Perspective of Stage*
Level I—Preconventional Stage 1—Heteronomous morality	To avoid breaking rules backed by punishment, obedience for its own sake, and avoiding physical damage to persons and property.	Avoidance of punishment, and the superior power of authorities.	*Egocentric point of view.* Doesn't consider the interests of others or recognize that they differ from the actor's; doesn't relate two points of view. Actions are considered physically rather than in terms of psychological interests of others. Confusion of authority's perspective with one's own.
Stage 2—Individualism, instrumental purpose, and exchange	Following rules only when it is to someone's immediate interest; acting to meet one's own interests and needs and letting others do the same. Right is also what's fair, what's an equal exchange, a deal, an agreement.	To serve one's own needs or interests in a world where you have to recognize that other people have their interests, too.	*Concrete individualistic perspective.* Aware that everybody has his own interest to pursue and these conflict, so that right is relative (in the concrete individualistic sense).
Level II—Conventional Stage 3—Mutual interpersonal expectations, relationships, and interpersonal conformity	Living up to what is expected by people close to you or what people generally expect of people in your role as son, brother, friend, etc. "Being good" is important and means having good motives, showing concern about others. It also means keeping mutual relationships, such as trust, loyalty, respect, and gratitude.	The need to be a good person in your own eyes and those of others. Your caring for others. Belief in the Golden Rule. Desire to maintain rules and authority that support stereotypical good behavior.	*Perspective of the individual in relationships with other individuals.* Aware of shared feelings, agreements, and expectations that take primacy over individual interests. Relates points of view through the concrete Golden Rule, putting yourself in the other guy's shoes. Does not yet consider generalized system perspective.
Stage 4—Social system and conscience	Fulfilling the actual duties to which you have agreed. Laws are to be upheld except in extreme cases where they conflict with other fixed social duties. Right is also contributing to society, the group, or institution.	To keep the institution going as a whole, to avoid the breakdown in the system "if everyone did it," or the imperative of conscience to meet one's defined obligations. (Easily confused with Stage 3 belief in rules and authority.)	*Differentiates societal point of view from interpersonal agreement or motive.* Takes the point of view of the system that defines roles and rules. Considers individual relations in terms of place in the system.

son at the highest stages. But this doesn't mean that all adolescents—or all adults, for that matter—will reach the highest stages. The stage a person actually reaches depends on several factors, including exposure to moral reasoning and values more advanced than theirs, in interactions with supportive family members, peers, and others (Walker & Taylor, 1991). Such exposure can challenge children to think about their moral beliefs. It also exposes children to the morals of their family and other important adults.

Moral Reasoning and Moral Behavior

Many people have been interested in these and other studies of moral reasoning as a way of understanding children's behavior. We've all seen children behave in appallingly selfish, disrespectful, or unkind ways, and we know that

TABLE 16-1   (continued)

	CONTENT OF STAGE		
Level and Stage	*What Is Right*	*Reasons for Doing Right*	*Social Perspective of Stage*
Level III—Postconventional, or principled Stage 5—Social contract or utility and individual rights	Being aware that people hold a variety of values and opinions, that most values and rules are relative to your group. These relative rules should usually be upheld, however, in the interest of impartiality and because they are the social contract. Some nonrelative values and rights like *life* and *liberty*, however, must be upheld in any society and regardless of majority opinion.	A sense of obligation to law because of one's social contract to make and abide by laws for the welfare of all and for the protection of all people's rights. A feeling of contractual commitment, freely entered upon, to family, friendship, trust, and work obligations. Concern that laws and duties be based on rational calculation of overall utility, "the greatest good for the greatest number."	*Prior-to-society perspective.* Perspective of a rational individual aware of values and rights prior to social attachments and contracts. Integrates perspectives by formal mechanisms of agreement, contract, objective impartiality, and due process. Considers moral and legal points of view, recognizes that they sometimes conflict and finds it difficult to integrate them.
Stage 6—Universal ethical principles	Following self-chosen ethical principles. Particular laws or social agreements are usually valid because they rest on such principles. When laws violate these principles, one acts in accordance with the principle. Principles are universal principles of justice: the equality of human rights and respect for the dignity of human beings as individual persons.	The belief as a rational person in the validity of universal moral principles, and a sense of personal commitment to them.	*Perspective of a moral point of view* from which social arrangements derive. Perspective is that of any rational individual recognizing the nature of morality or the fact that persons are ends in themselves and must be treated as such.

SOURCE: *Kohlberg, L. (1976). Moral stages and moralization. In T. Lickona (Ed.),* Moral development and behavior: Theory, research, and social issues *(pp. 34–35). New York: Holt, Rinehart & Winston. Reprinted with permission.*

most of them try out lying and cheating. Do these behaviors decrease as children's moral reasoning ability grows? Unfortunately, the relationship between moral reasoning and social behavior has been neglected (Shantz, 1975). The studies we do have indicate a consistent relationship between level of moral reasoning and behavior, although not a perfect one (Hoffman, 1984).

As with social role-taking ability and social behavior, however, we shouldn't expect a perfect relationship between moral reasoning and specific moral behaviors, especially since none of the theories predicts such a relationship. A moral reason can be used to justify a number of different behaviors, and people may disagree about the morality of each behavior.

When a moral dilemma exists—a situation in which choices relating to morality have to be made—factors other than simple moral reasoning must come into play if a person is to perform a particular moral act. This is espe-

FIGURE 16-8
In Kohlberg's scheme, people who have attained the postconventional level of moral reasoning define their values in terms of deeply felt moral or philosophical principles. If these principles are violated by current laws, people at postconventional level act in terms of the principles, perhaps trying to change the law.

cially true when the "immoral" choice is a "selfish" one, bringing personal pleasure or gain. Two important factors that help children make moral choices are social control and self-control (Bandura, 1991).

Social control means that the situation is one in which there are social rewards for making the moral choice and social sanctions for making the immoral choice, or transgressing. Social controls are often not a simple matter of societal standards. As we saw in the discussion of social skills and popularity, children tend to select environments that support their previously held values. In the case of morality, this means they tend to associate with children who have similar moral values, and in doing so they choose social support for their own standards of self-evaluation (Bandura, 1991).

The second factor, self-control, has to do with the child's inner feelings of satisfaction and self-respect when she acts morally and dissatisfaction and guilt when she doesn't. Children who are high in self-control are more likely to behave consistently with the dictates of their moral reasoning. One theorist suggests that for these children, moral principles have been linked to strong feelings of empathy for others and have thus become "hot cognitions," in his terminology (Hoffman, 1991). When a child with this kind of history recognizes a situation as one involving moral principles, she considers alternative actions and their consequences at the same time that she empathizes with any victims in the situation. Morality and empathy are paired because moral principles inherently involve fairness, caring for others, and concern for the general welfare. Repeated pairing of the two leads the child to show fervent feelings in relation to the moral principle themselves. Children prone to strong feelings of empathy can thus be expected to behave most consistently with moral principles. For them, empathy and morality work together to support self-control, which in turn leads to feelings of satisfaction and self-respect. As suggested in Chapter 8, children with the strongest feelings of empathy with others are those with secure attachment histories (Sroufe, 1983, 1990).

In addition to variations in social controls and self-control, there are also variations in perceptions of whether a situation is one in which moral principles apply. A number of processes can lead children to believe that neither social controls nor self-control need be activated in particular situations (Bandura, 1991). One of these processes involves misconstruing immoral conduct as moral. For example, a child may believe an act of violence is necessary to defend herself or her society (using reasoning like that of Kohlberg's Stage 4), when in fact violence is not necessary. Another process involves transforming a deplorable act into an acceptable one by comparing it to other deplorable acts that adults failed to punish. Not understanding consequences and blaming the victim are other processes that undercut the expectation that moral reasoning or moral controls should apply. And, of course, not seeing oneself as a responsible, causal agent—believing that one is "just carrying out orders" and has no choice but to obey—has repeatedly provided the rationale for reprehensible acts by gangs both large and small.

Moral behavior, then, is determined by more than moral reasoning as described in cognitive-developmental theories like Piaget's and Kohlberg's. It is also influenced by varying expectations about whether moral rewards and punishments will be applied, varying levels and processes of self-control, and varying perceptions of situations (Bandura, 1991).

Although lower levels of moral reasoning are roughly associated with higher levels of some kinds of antisocial behavior, such as juvenile delinquency (Nelson, Smith & Dodd, 1990), even adults with advanced levels of moral reasoning at times fail to do what they think is right. Still, higher levels of moral reasoning are an important ingredient in moral behavior. When adults fail, they often feel guilty and experience cognitive dissonance—a conflict between what they've done and what they think of themselves. In order for a person's morality-related actions to elicit the strongest emotions and the deepest anxieties, being moral should be central to the person's identity (Blasi 1984; Davidson & Youniss, 1991). We discuss this topic further in Chapter 20, along with considerations of what parents can do to encourage children and teenagers to apply moral controls.

SEX DIFFERENCES AND SEX-ROLE DEVELOPMENT

Margo burst into the house in tears after school one day, and her mother rushed into the room to see what was wrong.

"The boys say I can't play football with them any more," Margo sobbed. "They say they don't want to hang around with anyone who plays with Barbie dolls. Just because today I wanted to play Barbies at lunchtime with Becky and Sarah, they went off without me after school. When I caught up with them, they said if I was going to play girl things, I couldn't play with them. It's not fair! I can run faster and throw a ball farther than almost any of them! It's just not fair!"

FIGURE 16-9
Very few physical, cognitive, or personality differences exist between boys and girls in middle childhood. When both sexes are given opportunities to practice and play sports, they develop comparable skills.

Margo has run headlong into sex-role stereotyping, the notion that people have to be confined to certain activities depending on whether they're male or female. We encounter these ideas every day in our society, but is there any basis for them in fact? Are there important differences in behavior between males and females? And if so, in what ways are they cultural or biological, learned or innate?

Every culture makes assumptions about the activities, abilities, social positions, and other characteristics that are appropriate for women and men. These learned characteristics together comprise **sex roles** in that culture (Angrist, 1969; Block, 1973). But there are biological bases for the differences in behavior, too. Here we look first at differences in cognitive ability and personality between boys and girls. Then we discuss sex-role development—how and why girls and boys develop different patterns of behavior.

Sex Differences

Sex differences are average differences between boys and girls or between men and women. If we determined the average weight and height for men and women, for example, we would find that the means differ: Men are taller and heavier, on average, than women. This doesn't mean that we can't find a woman who is taller and heavier than a given man, because some women will be above average and some men will be below average. What it means is that the averages for the sexes line up this way. In addition to sex differences in physical characteristics, there are sex differences in cognitive abilities and personality. We note these below, along with some cautions about their interpretation.

COGNITIVE ABILITIES. There are no significant differences between girls and boys in overall IQ or on tasks requiring reasoning, logic, or verbal creativity. But some cognitive differences do exist, and these become accentuated in adolescence and adulthood. Girls have slightly better verbal skills during infancy and toddlerhood and again after adolescence begins. Boys take the lead in mathematics and spatial abilities, but again, not until adulthood. There is no general pattern of superiority: Girls are better at verbal analytical tasks, and boys are better at mathematical and spatial tasks. Since most of these differences emerge in adulthood, girls and boys in middle childhood show very few differences in cognitive abilities (see Table 16-2 for a summary of these differences and similarities).

PERSONALITY CHARACTERISTICS. Contrary to popular opinion, girls are not more sociable, nurturant, timid, fearful, or anxious than boys, nor are they less persistent on tasks or less achievement oriented than boys. Girls think just as well of themselves as boys do, although boys and girls (and men and women) apparently think well of themselves for different reasons.

Girls *are* less aggressive than boys. When they're in groups, they're less active than boys, although this wasn't true in infancy. When they're alone, girls and boys are equally active. Girls seem to have a lower expectation of success than boys, especially on novel intellectual tasks. And they feel less in control of what happens to them (see Table 16-3 for a summary of differences and similarities in personality).

INTERPRETING SEX-DIFFERENCE DATA. A few words of caution are in order about interpreting data that reveal cognitive and personality differences between

TABLE 16-2   **Differences and Similarities in Cognitive Abilities between Boys and Girls**

Differences	Similarities
1. Girls have better verbal abilities between birth and age 3 and after the age of 11 or 12. They vocalize more and talk earlier. During middle childhood, boys and girls have similar verbal abilities.	1. Boys and girls do equally well in reasoning and logic as measured by tasks resembling those used by Piaget.
2. Boys are better in mathematical tasks but not until adolescence.	2. Boys and girls do equally well on tasks involving non-verbal creativity.
3. Boys have better spatial abilities, but again, the differences do not emerge decisively until adolescence.	3. Boys and girls have the same group IQs.
4. Girls have fewer problems than boys with reading.	
5. Girls get better grades in school than boys of all ages.	
6. Boys do better than girls on analytic tasks involving mathematical or spatial abilities.	
7. Girls do better than boys on verbal analytic tasks such as making different words from a set of letters.	

SOURCES: Bee, H. (1978). Overview: Sex differences. In H. Bee (Ed.), Social issues in developmental psychology. New York: Harper & Row; Black, B. (1989). Interactive pretense: Social and symbolic skills in preschool play groups. Merrill-Palmer Quarterly, 35, 379–397. Brooks-Gunn, J., (1979). Matthews, W. S. (1979). He and she: How children develop their sex-role identity. Englewood Cliffs, NJ: Prentice-Hall; Maccoby, E. E., & Jacklin, C. N. (1974). The psychology of sex differences. Stanford, CA: Stanford University Press; Pearson & Ferguson (1989). Gender differences in patterns of spatial ability, environmental cognition, and math and English achievement in late adolescence. Adolescence, 24, 421–431. Tavris, C., & Offir, C. (1977). The longest war: Sex differences in perspective. New York: Harcourt Brace Jovanovich.

TABLE 16-3   Differences and Similarities in Personality between Boys and Girls

Differences	Similarities
1. Boys are more aggressive than girls of all ages. 2. Boys cry somewhat more than girls between the ages of 1 and 6, especially when frustrated, as when they are separated from their mothers. 3. Boys show more anger and upset behavior than girls between the ages of 1 and 6, but it's uncertain whether they differ when they are older. 4. Girls between 1 and 6 comply with demands from adults more readily than boys, but boys appear to be more susceptible to peer pressure, even in adulthood. 5. Boys appear to be more peer oriented than girls at all ages and spend more time with groups of peers than girls do. Girls tend to spend their time with one or two best friends. 6. Girls *report* more fear and anxiety than boys do, and teachers *report* that girls are more timid and anxious than boys. 7. Boys between the ages of 1 and 12 may be more active than girls, but the data are inconclusive. When boys are alone, they seem no more active than girls, but when they're with a group of boys, they're apparently more active. During infancy, girls and boys have the same level of activity. 8. Boys are judged to be tougher and more dominant between the ages of 1 and 12. In adulthood men appear to be more dominant than women, but in some situations the reverse may be true. 9. Girls have lower expectancies for success than boys, but the differences are not consistently apparent until adolescence and adulthood.	1. Boys and girls appear to be equally sensitive to people and social stimuli. For example, as infants they attend equally to faces and objects. (Studies yield mixed results on this issue, but consistent differences have not been found.) 2. Boys and girls show the same degree of empathy or altruistic behavior, such as helping someone in distress. 3. The data on the nurturant behavior of boys and girls in the United States reveal no differences. A review of cross-cultural studies does indicate that girls are more nurturant than boys. When communities are analyzed separately, however, there were often no differences; when there were, it was sometimes found that boys were more helpful than girls (in Okinawa, for example). Cross-cultural data in general show that girls are more often assigned responsibility for younger siblings than boys. Studies of communities in the United States, in which girls are not assigned this task, indicate that boys and girls do not differ in nurturant behavior. 4. Girls and boys appear to be equally fearful, timid, and anxious when actual *behavior* is observed. However, if you recall, girls report more feelings of fear and anxiety. 5. Girls and boys tend to be equally motivated to achieve in neutral situations. Boys seem to be aroused to achieve by competition to a greater extent than girls. 6. Girls and boys seem to be equal in self-esteem during childhood, but they seem to feel positively about themselves for different reasons. Girls and women seem to think positively about themselves for their social skills, but boys and men seem to think positively of themselves for more individual traits such as ambition or dominance. 7. Girls and boys are equally persistent in most tasks.

SOURCES: *Bee, H. (1978). Overview: Sex differences. In H. Bee (Ed.),* Social issues in developmental psychology. *New York: Harper & Row; Brooks-Gunn, J. & Matthews, W. S. (1979).* He and she: How children develop their sex-role identity. *Englewood Cliffs, NJ: Prentice-Hall; Maccoby, E. E., & Jacklin, C. N. (1974).* The psychology of sex differences. *Stanford, CA: Stanford University Press; Tavris, C., & Offir, C. (1977).* The longest war: Sex differences in perspective. *New York: Harcourt Brace Jovanovich; Ruble, D. N. (1984). Sex-role development. In M. H. Bornstein & M. E. Lamb (Eds.),* Developmental psychology: An advanced text. *Hillsdale, NJ: Lawrence Erlbaum.*

boys and girls. First, studies that demonstrate sex differences are more likely to be published than studies that don't, because differences are considered more newsworthy. Problems of sampling and generalizability may make the published data even more distorted. If you recall from Chapter 1, researchers have to be extremely careful about getting representative samples of children in their studies, and they have to make sure their results are generalizable to the rest of the population.

They also have to make clear what age children they're talking about when they find sex differences. As mentioned previously, some differences appear during toddlerhood, disappear during middle childhood, and reappear in adolescence and adulthood. If researchers don't specify the age of the children exhibiting sex differences they've found, differences might appear to be more pervasive than they really are. A difference found between 3-year-olds, for example, might also be construed to exist between 8-year-olds.

Definitions create other problems. If we define sociability as making friends or seeking out the company of others, we can conclude that boys are more sociable (Baumrind & Block, 1967; Whiting and Edwards, 1973). But if we define sociability as depicting people in drawings or enjoying the company of a few best friends rather than a large group of peers, we can conclude that girls are more sociable (Goodenough, 1957; Waldrop, cited in Maccoby & Jacklin, 1974). The specific definition a researcher chooses can determine what differences the study demonstrates. And if we compare studies that have used different definitions, we find that the differences cancel each other out. On the basis of the studies just cited, for example, we can't really say whether boys or girls are more sociable.

A serious problem in interpreting the results of sex differences studies is that group differences for boys and girls are typically very small. This means that many individual boys and girls don't fit neatly into group patterns. For example, the average performance for girls in math falls below the average performance for boys. But some girls are well above average in math and thus perform better than most boys. Similarly, some boys are well above average in verbal ability and perform better than most girls. Many boys and girls are both above and below average in different skills for their gender group. The danger in talking about small differences—and these differences are very small—is that we start to assume that individual boys and girls will closely match the overall pattern for their gender group. These assumptions are what produce **sex-role stereotypes.**

Explaining Sex Differences

Boys and girls are more similar than they are different, especially in middle childhood. But the small differences that do exist have been well documented. The question is: Are these differences inborn, or are they learned through experience?

BIOLOGY AND SEX DIFFERENCES. Both spatial ability and aggression are more dominant in males than in females, and as a result, they are often explained in terms of biology. Some people have hypothesized, for example, that spatial ability may be a sex-linked recessive trait. If you recall from Chapter 3, girls (with their XX chromosomes) inherit an X chromosome from each parent, and boys (with XY chromosomes) inherit their one X chromosome from their mother. If the gene for spatial ability is carried on the X chromosome and is recessive, it could be overridden in girls by a dominant gene inherited from their fathers. Because boys receive only one X chromosome, any recessive gene carried on it can be expressed. (This model is illustrated in Table 16-4.) Thus, boys would have a better chance of inheriting good spatial abilities.

To explain aggression, researchers have pointed to the male sex hormone testosterone as a possible factor. During the sixth week of gestation, the testes begin to produce male sex hormones known as androgens. These hormones trigger the physical development of the male genitals. If the hormones aren't released, the fetus won't develop male genitals even though it has the typical XY male chromosome. Androgens may also act on the hypothalamus in the brain during puberty, triggering the emergence of male sexual behavior (Levine, 1966; Phoenix, Goy & Resko, 1978).

TABLE 16-4   Possible Patterns for Spatial Genes in Males and Females

FEMALES		
Chromosomes		Consequences
X^1	X^2	
s	s	good spatial ability
s	S	carrier for good spatial ability but performs poorly
S	s	carrier for good spatial ability but performs poorly
S	S	poor spatial ability

This model predicts that one out of four females will inherit good spatial ability

MALES		
Chromosomes		Consequences
X	Y	
s	—	good spatial ability
S	—	poor spatial ability

This model predicts that one out of two males will inherit good spatial ability

SOURCE: From The longest war: Sex differences in perspective *by Carol Tavris and Carole Offir, © 1977 by Harcourt Brace Jovanovich, Inc. Reprinted by permission of the publisher.*

Evidence for a link between male sex hormones and aggression comes from several sources. Animal studies have shown that female monkeys given testosterone before they were born engage in more aggressive play than untreated females (Young, Goy & Phoenix, 1964). Female animals given testosterone in infancy engage in more fighting (Edwards, 1969; Joslyn, 1971).

In humans, prenatal accidents sometimes result in masculinized females, individuals with XX chromosomes but with male genitals. Even when these children's genitalia were corrected surgically, their mothers reported that they continued to display masculine behavior. They enjoyed outdoor play, thought of themselves as "tomboys," and didn't like to play with dolls (Erhardt & Baker, 1974). Since the male genitals would have produced testosterone during prenatal development, these girls would have had higher levels of the hormone in their bodies. Additionally, testosterone levels in boys have been found to be related to their aggressive behavior and attitudes (Olweus et al., 1980), and some evidence exists for a relationship between high testosterone levels and criminal behavior in males (Parke & Slaby, 1983).

This evidence is suggestive, but it isn't conclusive. The strongest evidence comes from animal studies, but hormones may not have the same powerful effect in humans that they have in animals, as we saw in the bonding and attachment studies described in Chapter 8. In the studies of masculinized girls, we must take into account the fact that their parents knew of their condition. They may have tolerated more aggressive behavior in these girls, thinking it appropriate because of their developmental histories. Their behavior may have been more a result of how they were socialized than of their biological development.

All in all, we can't really know for sure to what extent aggression, spatial abilities, or any other aspect of sex-role behavior is determined by biology. The alternative explanation for sex differences is socialization.

SOCIALIZATION AND SEX DIFFERENCES. If sex differences aren't innate—and the evidence is shaky, as we've shown—then they must be learned during the socialization process. This learning is explained differently by different theories. Social learning theory explanations call on the principles of reinforcement, punishment, and modeling. Cognitive explanations refer to the child's growing cognitive abilities and the concepts of gender identity and gender constancy (see Research Focus—The Development of Gender Identity).

Whatever theory we believe, we can easily see that boys and girls are treated differently. Research studying North American children has supported these everyday observations. Fathers play more with their sons than they do with their daughters (Lamb, 1977; Weinraub & Frankel, 1977; Austin & Braeger, 1990), and they play with them in more physical ways. Boys under 2 years of age are already provided with more sports equipment, tools, and large and small vehicles than girls, who have more dolls, toys representing fictional characters, and child's furniture (Pomerleau et al., 1990). Girls of this age also wear more pink clothes and have more pink pacifiers and jewelry. Toddler boys are punished more than girls, and they misbehave more as well (Minton, Kagan & Levine, 1971). Toddler boys play alone at home more than girls (Smith & Doglish, 1977). In the early elementary grades, teachers expect boys to be more active and unruly than girls (Minuchin & Shapiro, 1983). At home,

◄ **FIGURE 16-10**
Testosterone or socialization? Although animal studies reveal a relationship between aggression and male hormones, human behavior is much more complicated than animal behavior. This boy's aggressiveness may result as much from environmental factors, such as his parents' socialization methods and the models he sees in his family, school, community, and society, as from any biological influences.

RESEARCH FOCUS

The Development of Gender Identity

"When I'm growed up, I'll have a baby too," said 3-year-old Jacob, patting his mother's stomach. She looked at him blankly for a few moments before responding.

"No, Jacob," she finally said. "You're a boy."

"I know," he answered.

"Well . . . boys don't have babies," his mother went on slowly. "Men can be daddies, but only women can be mommies."

"I know. But when I grow up to be a woman, I'll have a baby."

Jacob's mother needn't be alarmed. Jacob knows he's a boy, but he doesn't know he'll always be a boy, and this is typical of children's understanding at this age. By age 2½ most children have **gender identity,** meaning they label themselves correctly as a boy or a girl (Slaby & Frey, 1975), but they don't yet have **gender constancy,** which is the understanding that they will always be the sex they are now. Cut your hair, change your clothes, act a little differently, and you can change your sex, too, according to a 3-year-old. The solid understanding that these criteria aren't what determine gender is not attained by most children until the age of 6 or 7 (Huston, 1983).

Lawrence Kohlberg, whose work on moral development is discussed in this chapter, based a theory of sex-role development on cognitive changes that occur as children get older. Because children think they can change gender up until the school years, they don't pay close attention to adult mod-

eling of sex-typed behavior during the preschool years, and they don't model it systematically themselves. But as gender constancy emerges at about age 7, children begin to act increasingly like adults who are the same sex they are. They tend to conform rigidly to their ideas of appropriate behavior for their sex during middle childhood. Later, as they start to observe exceptions to the general rule that men and women behave differently and begin to be able to think about what might be (in adolescence), they moderate their views (Huston, 1983).

Parents and teachers who have made an effort to teach children that "boys and girls can do all the same things" may despair as they see school-age children adopting narrowly stereotyped roles and behaviors. Unless adults can somehow change the world in such a way that males and females don't model sex-typed behavior, children's advancing cognitive abilities will propel them inevitably to make these sex-typed distinctions. But just as inevitably, exceptions and even more advanced thinking will gradually make their mark, and this is where adults can make a difference. By exposing children to nonstereotypical sex-role behavior, they provide models and images that clearly broaden perspectives (Bigler & Liben, 1990). Children's sex-role attitudes are also affected by the traditionalism of the opposite-sex parent and the amount of time that parent spends with the child (Nelson & Keith, 1990). As children's cognitive abilities continue to advance in adolescence, they are able to attain a greater degree of flexibility in their views of human potential.

"Nonstereotypical role models, such as female police officers and male elementary school teachers, open up the wide range of possible human experiences to children."

elementary school-age boys are given more freedom from parental supervision than girls (Newson & Newson, 1978).

Boys and girls in American society are not the only ones to be treated differently. Cross-cultural studies show that parents in many other societies tend to pay more attention to boys than to girls; to expect more achievement, self-reliance, and autonomy from boys; and to be gentler and more sociable with girls (Bronstein, 1984; Zern, 1984). Within American society, however, there may be some variation in parental treatment of boys and girls depending on social class and racial group. Sex-typing, particularly of girls, tends to be stronger in working-class families than in middle-class families (McBroom, 1981). And some evidence indicates that African American parents make fewer gender-related distinctions between their sons and daughters, with the result that African American females are socialized more toward employment and economic responsibility than white females are (Smith, 1982; Binion, 1990). In spite of these variations, however, boys and girls in our society are generally treated differently.

How can being treated differently lead to different behavior? First, more experience with rough-and-tumble play could make boys more familiar and comfortable with the kinds of behavior used in physical aggression. Second, boys' toys are oriented more toward war and fighting than girls' toys, and boys' toys support aggressive play. When children use aggressive toys, they're more likely to be aggressive with each other (Berkowitz & LePage, 1967). Third, since toddler boys play alone more at home, their behavior may come under less scrutiny than that of girls. There are more opportunities for girls' behavior to be shaped into more socialized forms.

At school, teachers' expectations of boys may account for the fact that they praise boys more, give them more help, accept their comments more readily, and permit them to dominate classroom discussions (Sadaker & Sadaker, 1985). Teachers may feel that girls are already better behaved and need less praise and help. They may also think they're better able to wait for their turn and listen to others.

Direct reinforcement and punishment are supported by what children see modeled around them in real life, as summed up in the following excerpt (Huston, 1983, pp. 420–421):

> The average child sees women cooking, cleaning, and sewing; working in "female" jobs such as clerical, secretarial, sales, teaching, nursing; choosing to dance, sew, or play bridge for recreation; and achieving in artistic or literary areas more often than in science and engineering. That same child sees men mowing the lawn, washing the car, or doing household repairs; working in "male" occupations; choosing team sports, fishing and achieving in math, science, and technical areas more often than in poetry or art. In school, the teachers of young children are women; the teachers of older students and the administrators with power are usually men. Peers and siblings pursue sex-stereotyped activities, games, and interests more often than they engage in cross-sex activity.

The mass media also provide opportunities for children to observe sex-typed behavior. Virtually every study of the content of television shows has found that females are underrepresented and that roles and behavior are stereotyped (Huston, 1983). Toy commercials show boys and girls playing with completely different toys, and the ads themselves are made differently: "high levels of inanimate action, frequent changes to new scenes, rapid cuts, sound effects, and loud lively music typify boys' ads. Moderate levels of action, few scene

FIGURE 16-11
Mom's encouragement sends a powerful message to this little girl about getting her nails done. In our society, girls learn at an early age that appearance and behavior are important concerns for them. Girls are praised for being pretty, nice, or good, while boys are approved for being strong, competent, or smart. Socialization seems to account for most of the behavior differences we see between the sexes.

changes, fades, dissolves, and soft tinkly music typify girls' ads (Leary, Huston & Wright, 1983, p. 1).

Children's books also provide sex-stereotyped versions of life. One study analyzed the male and female characters and images in books that had received awards and honors for excellence. Although the number of male characters in books published between 1981 and 1985 had dropped from the number found in the 1976 to 1981 books (Dougherty & Engel, 1986), the numbers still didn't match the equal proportions found in 1951 to 1955 books. And in books that kindergarten and primary-grade teachers read to children in the classroom, the main character is male over 70 percent of the time (Smith, Greenlaw & Scott, 1987).

Females are typically presented as more dependent than males, as revealed in a study of themes in over 100 recently published fiction books (White, 1986). Females are more likely to receive help, and males are more likely to give it: "The girls and women in children's fiction do seem to reflect the cultural stereotype of the helpless female, the perennial damsel in distress in need of male protection" (White, 1986, p. 255).

Children can hardly help but get the message: Males and females act differently, are treated differently, and have different kinds of lives. Biological differences that do exist are sure to be exaggerated by the subtle and not-so-subtle messages that bombard children from their earliest days of life.

OVERVIEW

Children acquire important social understandings during the school years, largely as a result of their growing ability to put themselves in someone else's shoes. This social role-taking ability allows them to become aware of other people's thoughts, feelings, and intentions, which in turn contributes to their developing moral sense. At the same time, school-age children are becoming more self-aware and more concerned about what others think of them. Friends become increasingly important, as children seek ways to define themselves in relation to others. The pattern of social interaction children establish during the school years often endures and becomes part of their adaptation to life.

CHAPTER REVIEW

SOCIAL ROLE-TAKING ABILITY

- During the school years, children's social role-taking ability—the ability to judge what others are thinking and feeling—improves dramatically. This ability—just one aspect of social cognition—gives them greater personal insight and better understanding of others.
- Social role-taking ability has three components: understanding other people's emotions, understanding other people's intentions, and understanding other people's thinking.
- As they mature, children begin to understand how ambiguous and complex emotional responses can be. Young children typically have "all or none" emotional reactions. Later they become able to make subtler distinctions between emotions and to be aware when they're experiencing conflicting emotions at the same time.

- They also come to realize that the same situation can evoke different emotional responses in different people and that people may react differently because of personal histories and interpretations.
- Toward the end of middle childhood, children begin to discriminate between "accidental" and "deliberate" intentions, and they learn they should respond accordingly. Even older children have difficulty detecting intentions when they're being deliberately deceived.
- School-age children gradually become able to realize that other people can have points of view and opinions other than theirs. Children need help from adults to understand the inner thought processes of others.
- The development of social role-taking skills isn't necessarily associated with improved social behavior.

SOCIAL SKILLS AND POPULARITY

- Children's social status is an important predictor of later behavior. Unpopular children tend to achieve less in school and have more problems later in life.
- Popular children tend to be friendly and outgoing in positive ways. Their strategies for entering an ongoing play situation are noticeably different from those of unpopular children.
- Coaching a child in social skills and adapting coaching techniques to classroom use can be effective methods of changing a child's social status.

- Other factors that correlate with children's popularity include family interaction patterns, perceived social self-efficacy, and physical appearance.
- Children who are antisocial, disruptive, and destructive in elementary school need help to change their patterns of interaction before their behavior gets worse.

MORAL DEVELOPMENT

- Moral development is a complex process that involves both cognitive and emotional growth.

- Young children judge the seriousness of stealing by the amount stolen and the seriousness of lying by how much the lie varies from the truth. They don't take intentions or other factors into account.

- Piaget found that between ages 5 and 10, children shift from objective judgments, based on physical results, to subjective judgments, based on intentions and other psychological considerations. He felt that by age 11 or 12, children shift away from moral realism and become capable of mature moral reasoning.
- Piaget suggested that children's understanding of the rules of games reflects their evolving sense of how "right" and "wrong" are established.
- Kohlberg suggested that the growth of moral reasoning is reflected in three levels of moral development.

Children don't reach the highest level until adolescence, but not all adolescents (nor all adults) reach this level. Research hasn't consistently supported Kohlberg's claims.

- A relationship does exist between moral development and social behavior, but even as adults, our behavior may not always meet our moral standards. Behavior is more likely to be consistent with the moral standard if social control and self-control are strong and if the situation is seen as one in which these moral controls should be activated. Responsive parenting encourages empathy and self-control.

SEX DIFFERENCES AND SEX-ROLE DEVELOPMENT

- Sex roles are cultural assumptions about abilities, activities, social positions, and other characteristics appropriate to men and women. Sex differences are average differences between the sexes in physical characteristics, cognitive abilities, and personality.
- There are no significant differences between girls and boys in intelligence or reasoning ability. Some cognitive differences and some personality differences do exist, but differences are small and there is no overall pattern of superiority.
- The danger in focusing on small differences between boys and girls is that all children will be expected to fit into sex-role stereotypes.

- Researchers have investigated two characteristics of boys—their greater aggressiveness and their better spatial abilities—to see if they could link them to genetic or hormonal factors. But research has been unable to demonstrate the role played by biology in these characteristics in humans.
- Boys and girls are treated differently by parents and teachers and represented differently in books and television programs. In their daily life, children observe women and men performing tasks traditionally associated with one sex or the other. Socialization may well account for most of the sex-typed behavior we see in children.

KEY TERMS

social role-taking ability	self-reflective role taking	controversial status
social cognition	mutual role taking	moral realism
targets	social and conventional	sex roles
valence	system role taking	sex differences
egocentric role taking	popular status	sex-role stereotypes
social-information role	unpopular status	gender identity
taking	neglected status	gender constancy

SUGGESTIONS FOR FURTHER READING

AAUW Educational Foundation and The Wellesley College Center for Research on Women (1992). *How Schools Shortchange Girls*. Washington, D.C.: AAUW Educational Foundation and National Education Association.

A synthesis of the available research on girls in school, this report makes clear that gender bias in the American school system deprives girls of equal educational treatment. Emphasizing the social and economic consequences of this situation, it includes strategies for change and suggestions for a new educational policy.

Asher, S., & Coie, J. (1990). *Peer rejection in childhood*. New York: Cambridge University Press.

This book is designed to integrate existing knowledge about why some children are not accepted by peers, what the consequences of peer rejection are, and how rejected children can be helped.

Archer, J., & Lloyd, B. (1982). *Sex and gender*. New York: Cambridge University Press.

A very thorough treatment of the sex and gender issue, including chapters on physical sex differences, aggression and power, socialization, and possible changes in sex roles in the future.

Bornstein, M. H., and Lamb, M. E. (Eds.) (1988). *Developmental psychology: An advanced textbook* (2d ed.). Hillsdale, NJ: Lawrence Erlbaum.

This book has good chapters on moral development and sex-role development. Written at a higher level than the Grusec and Lytton book cited below.

Coles, R. (1986). *The moral life of children*. Boston: Atlantic Monthly Press.

This book, written by the noted psychiatrist, contains many examples of moral thinking evident in children.

Grusec, J. E., & Lytton, H. (1988). *Social development*. New York: Springer-Verlag.

This book contains thorough chapters on moral development and sex-role development. For the student who wants a readable yet extensive briefing on these topics.

Kozol, J. (1992). *Savage Inequalities: Children in America's Schools*. New York: Crown.

A penetrating examination of social and economic class inequalities in American schools. The author shows that social policy in public schooling has been turned back in recent years, particularly in urban schools.

MILESTONES IN SCHOOL-AGE DEVELOPMENT

AGE	PHYSICAL	COGNITIVE	LANGUAGE	SOCIAL-EMOTIONAL
6 yrs.	Has 90% of adult size brain Reaches about two-thirds of adult height Begins to lose baby teeth Moves a writing or drawing tool with the fingers while the side of the hand rests on the table top Can skip Can tie a bow	Begins to demonstrate concrete operational thinking Demonstrates conservation of number on Piaget's conservation tasks Can create series operationally rather than by trial and error	Might use a letter-name spelling strategy, thus creating many invented spellings Appreciates jokes and riddles based on phonological ambiguity	Feels one way only about a situation Has some difficulty detecting intentions accurately in situations where damage occurs Demonstrates Kohlberg's preconventional moral thinking
7 yrs.	Is able to make small, controlled marks with pencils or pens due to more refined finger dexterity Has longer face Continues to lose baby teeth	Begins to use some rehearsal strategies as an aid to memory Becomes much better able to play strategy games May demonstrate conservation of mass and length	Appreciates jokes and riddles based on lexical ambiguity Might have begun to read using a print-governed approach, but coordination of cueing systems might be imbalanced	May express two emotions about one situation, but these will be same valence Demonstrates Kohlberg's conventional thinking Understands gender constancy
8 yrs.	Plays jacks and other games requiring considerable fine motor skill and good reaction time Jumps rope skillfully Throws and bats a ball more skillfully	Still has great difficulty judging if a passage is relevant to a specific theme May demonstrate conservation of area	Begins to sort out some of the more difficult syntactic difficulties, such as "ask" and "tell" Might be able to integrate all cueing systems for smooth reading Becomes more conventional speller	May express two same-valence emotions about different targets at the same time Understands that people may interpret situation differently but thinks this is due to different information
9 yrs.	Enjoys hobbies requiring high levels of fine motor skill (sewing, weaving, model building)	May demonstrate conservation of weight	Interprets "ask" and "tell" correctly	Can think about own thinking or another person's thinking but not both at the same time.
10 yrs.	May begin to menstruate	Begins to make better judgments about relevance of a text Begins to delete unimportant information when summarizing	Becomes more sophisticated conventional speller	Can take own view and view of another as if a disinterested third party
11 yrs.	May begin preadolescent growth spurt if female	May demonstrate conservation of volume	Begins to appreciate jokes and riddles based on syntactic ambiguity	Still has trouble detecting deception Spends more time with friends
12 yrs.	Has reached about 80 percent of adult height if male, 90 percent if female Has all permanent teeth except for two sets of molars Plays ball more skillfully due to improved reaction time Probably has begun to menstruate	Shows much greater skill in summarizing and outlining May begin to demonstrate formal operational thinking		May begin to demonstrate Kohlberg's postconventional moral thinking

SCHOOL-AGE CHILDREN

"Mom, what's a mammal?" asked Amber one night at bedtime. She was poring over her sister's latest issue of National Geographic World.

"A mammal? Let's see, that's an animal who gives birth to live babies, rather than laying eggs, and who nurses the babies with milk from mammary glands, like breasts," replied her mother, Suzanne, as she settled down to read a storybook.

Amber pondered this for a moment and then announced, "When I grow up, I'll be a mammal."

"No, you're already a mammal," her mother answered with a smile, thinking about how her definition had led Amber to this conclusion. Then, as she considered how to clarify it, she thought about the changes she'd seen in her daughter in the last few months. She was used to Amber's being a child who spent hours drawing, pretending, and playing fantasy games. Now, halfway through first grade, Amber was surprising her parents every day with her sophisticated new interests and questions about the world. In the recent past she had wanted to know why the moon was out during the day, what the difference was between a digital clock and a regular clock, whether it was possible to touch a rainbow, how the microwave oven cooked food, whether she lived in New York or the United States or both, and how to spell countless words. She brought home crystals she had made in science class, practiced making up her own mazes and dot-to-dot pictures, and on more than one occasion sent her parents to the encyclopedia to answer her questions. Suzanne sometimes wondered what had happened to her dreamy little girl.

"Mammal is the name of a big group of animals that includes human beings," she finally said as Amber settled down on her lap clutching the magazine. "Cats and dogs are mammals, and cows and horses, but not birds or fish, because they lay eggs and don't nurse their babies. So people are all mammals, whether they're mothers or not. Want to read this article about them, or do you want to read a story?"

FIGURE 1
Formal schooling places cognitive, emotional, social, and physical demands on young children. Even first graders, like these girls working in their school computer lab, are expected to have reached certain levels of development.

"The article," answered Amber. Suzanne put the storybook aside with some regret, but as she observed her daughter's enthusiasm about the magazine, she became caught up in it herself—and in the exciting, seemingly sudden, transformation in Amber's intellectual interests.

At age 6½, Amber is in the process of becoming "rational." This dramatic cognitive change makes it possible for children to begin to learn and understand things in a completely new way. By about 6 or 7 years of age, children are beginning to think more logically about the world around them; they have insights into the notions of conservation, seriation, and classification; they can make fine distinctions between reality and fantasy; and they're becoming more aware of their own and others' thoughts and feelings.

Not coincidentally, "formal" schooling—formal in the sense that it is mandated by law and is characterized by direct instruction—begins when children are about 6 or 7. Every part of the elementary school curriculum assumes that children have basic cognitive understandings about space, time, number, and classification. Cognitive skills are necessary for such tasks as reading a map; realizing how a category, such as mammal, and a specific case, such as cow, are related; telling time; and playing a musical instrument, to name just a few.

Development in other domains also helps children handle the demands of elementary school. Emotionally they are increasingly able to function as individuals separate from their parents, outside the family, in a world of teachers and peers. Their growing awareness of what others may be thinking and feeling helps them navigate their way through social interactions with other children. And underlying all these changes is the physical growth and development that enable children to spend a day at school, play sports or visit friends in the afternoon, and get their homework done at night.

In this chapter we address some of the topics that concern the parents and teachers of these active, curious school-age children. The first is after-school care for children whose parents work. Thousands upon thousands of "latch-key" children now go home to an empty house after school and take care of themselves until a parent gets home. Families and communities have tried a variety of approaches to this situation, which is becoming more pressing as more parents join the work force. As in other knowledge in action sections, we also consider how children are assessed at this age, and we conclude with a discussion of living with the school-age child.

AFTER-SCHOOL CARE FOR SCHOOL-AGE CHILDREN

"I'm home, Elliott!" Martha called out as she shoved open the front door with her atta-ché case in one hand and a bag of groceries in the other. But instead of the greeting she expected, she heard alarmed voices in the next room.

"Your mom's home!"

"Oh no!"

Walking into the family room, Martha saw a strange sight. Elliott, her 10-year-old son, was squeezing out a dripping towel, and Norm, his 11-year-old friend from next door, was mopping up water from the floor. The aquarium was half empty, and the gold-fish were darting back and forth at the far end of the tank.

"What happened?" Martha asked.

"Well, see, Norm had this idea . . ."

"But it was you who threw the marble that hit the aquarium . . ."

"But it was your idea to play bombardier . . ."

"You were throwing marbles?" Martha asked.

"Yeah. We each had a pile of them and we were seeing . . ."

"You were throwing marbles in the house?"

"Yeah. We were seeing how hard we could throw them at the couch and one of them hit the fish tank."

"Is there glass in the fish tank?"

"No, I don't think so . . . well, just a little. See, it's just this little hole. The water stopped coming out after it got below the hole . . ."

Martha took off her coat and looked more closely at the damage.

"Well, let's get the fish out of there. I'm afraid you guys are going to have to buy a new aquarium. And Norm, I'm going to think about whether you can come over again after school when I'm not here."

"Okay."

"Whatever made you play a game like that? You know you're not supposed to throw anything in the house."

"Well, Mom, we're not supposed to throw balls in the house. You never said not to throw marbles in the house."

"Use your head, Elliott. Was this a good idea?"

"But I didn't know before that a marble could break an aquarium."

"Still, never throw anything in the house," Martha answered. "Now let's clean all of this up."

In her mind, Martha was wondering how many more times she would come home to a new, unexpected disaster. It seemed as if she couldn't keep ahead of her son's inven-tiveness. She knew he needed more supervision, and she desperately wished she could be at home after school or that there was some place for him to go. But so far, their com-munity offered nothing in the way of after-school recreation or care programs. Martha resolved to put some more effort into finding or creating a solution to her family's after-school problem.

Even at age 10 or 11, children don't have the judgment and experience to know what the consequences of all their actions may be. What to do about this after-school period of two to three hours every day is a matter of tremendous concern for parents, teachers, and communities.

The Need for After-School Care

The gap between the time children finish school and the time working parents get home from their jobs is a consequence of the school schedule, which usually runs from about 8 A.M. to about 3 P.M. This schedule has been shaped by several forces, including the historical need for rural children to help with farm chores, the need for children to have a day that's not so long that they get exhausted, the need for teachers to have planning and paper-grading time, and the need for schools to control their operating costs.

This isn't the first time that after-school care has been a problem. The theme of the 1943 American Association of School Administrators convention was "door key" children—children who wore a house key around their necks because they went home after school to an empty house. These were children whose mothers worked in defense-related jobs and whose fathers were away in the war (Stroman & Duff, 1982). By 1947, there had been a return to prewar "normalcy"—less than one mother in five was still working outside the home.

Today, however, child care patterns are being shaped not by a specific historical event but by long-term economic and social trends. No one expects the patterns of previous years, in which mothers were at home when children got out of school, to reappear. In 1986 more than three out of five mothers were working outside the home (Bailey, 1986). By 1990, nearly four out of five mothers of school-age children were in the work force. Many of their children are "latchkey" children, who again are wearing keys around their necks to let themselves into their homes after school.

The Effects of Being a Latchkey Child

What are the consequences of being a latchkey child? Surprisingly few studies have been done to investigate this question, and the research that is available provides somewhat mixed findings. Several studies have found that urban children in first through sixth grades who were left alone after school feel afraid and lonely (Long & Long, 1982; Zill, 1983). They're afraid of noises, the dark, and intruders, and they report that they're bored.

Studies of suburban and rural children, on the other hand, haven't found the same patterns, although these studies didn't include children younger than fourth grade (Rodman, Pratto & Nelson, 1985; Galambos & Garbarino, 1983). These children might not have felt afraid because they were older or because their environments were relatively safer.

One study turned up an important relationship between child-rearing practices and susceptibility to peer pressure on the part of children—in this case, fifth, sixth, eighth, and ninth graders—who were left unsupervised after school (Steinberg, 1986). The study made use of three broad categories of child-rearing techniques and styles identified in earlier research by Diana Baumrind and labeled **permissive, authoritarian,** and **authoritative** (Baumrind & Block, 1967). (For a discussion of Baumrind's work, see Research Focus—How Can Parents Raise Competent Children?) Researchers found that the authoritative

RESEARCH FOCUS

How Can Parents Raise Competent Children?

Most parents would probably agree that their goal is to raise children who will someday be competent, independent, and able to succeed on their own in the world. But how to achieve this goal is a question on which there's considerably less agreement. Some parents believe they should be kind and understanding and make few demands. Others believe they should be tough, stern, and aloof. Still others think they should demonstrate firm expectations but be willing to explain their stands. Is there an approach to parenting that leads more reliably than other approaches to competent and self-sufficient children? If so, what is it?

Psychologist Diana Baumrind investigated many parent-child relationships (1972) and identified three broad patterns or styles of parenting, which she labeled *authoritarian, authoritative,* and *permissive.* Parents identified as authoritarian have set expectations for children's conduct, which often come from absolute standards, such as religious teachings. These parents demand obedience from their children, and they use forceful means to get it. Children aren't permitted to question rules and regulations, nor do parents attempt to explain them. Authoritarian parents might be described as rigid.

Parents identified as authoritative also have firm expectations, but they explain rules and discuss situations with their children. These parents acknowledge the child's interests and point of view but don't hesitate to enforce adult standards when the child and adult views are in conflict. They use both

force—power—and reason to ensure that the child complies with adult expectations. Their expectations, however, aren't established according to absolute standards set primarily by some higher authority.

Parents identified as permissive accept the child's behavior and wishes. They don't insist that the child conform to adult standards. When there is a difference of opinion between adult and child, the adult attempts to reason with the child but doesn't use power to force the child to comply.

In her study, Baumrind found that the most competent children were raised by authoritative parents. These children were both more responsible and more independent than children raised by either authoritarian or permissive parents. Baumrind emphasized that authoritative parenting isn't merely a compromise position between two extremes. As she put it, authoritative parents "reflect a synthesis and balancing of strongly opposing forces of tradition and innovation, divergence and convergence, accommodation and assimilation, cooperation and autonomous expression, tolerance and principled intractability" (1972, p. 257). This kind of flexible parenting, characterized by firm standards and the use of reason, seems to provide children with the kind of discipline and socialization that serves them well as they grow into adults. This process, as well as Baumrind's more recent research, is described in more detail in Chapter 20.

FIGURE 2
As the number of two-career and single-parent families increases, so does the number of children who let themselves into their homes after school with their own keys. What they do with their unsupervised time depends to a large degree on the child-rearing techniques their parents have used. A child with a variety of hobbies, interests, and skills, such as this boy practicing Japanese lettering, may have better ideas to draw on when faced with unfilled hours.

FIGURE 3
After-school programs provide a safe place for children to play, snack, and socialize. Activities typically include drawing and painting, playing games or sports, watching television or movies, and relaxing with friends.

style of parenting was associated with less susceptibility to peer pressure. In other words, parents who have brought their children up by reasoning with them and using induction, by listening and compromising, when appropriate, while at the same time setting limits, have children who are less likely to get into trouble when they're on their own after school. Parents who are either dictatorial (the authoritarian style) or lax about discipline (the permissive style) have children who are more likely to get into trouble.

The more removed from supervision the children in this study were, the more important was their child-rearing history. Some parents make specific plans with their children about what they will do after school, check with them after school by telephone, and know exactly where they'll be, even though the children are not directly supervised. This parental knowledge is known as **distal supervision**. When even distal supervision was lacking, the effects of authoritative parenting showed up the most in different children's after-school choices and behaviors. Authoritative parenting has been shown to be the most effective style for helping children internalize their parents' norms and standards for behavior, so it's not surprising that it would help children resist peer pressure.

Aside from these studies, there has been little research on the effects of being a latchkey child, either in the short or the long term. Future research will have to tell us whether latchkey children are gaining important skills, developing feelings of responsibility and self-reliance, and using their time constructively or wasting time, feeling neglected, afraid, and resentful, and becoming more open to undesirable activities.

After-School Programs and Services

What can parents, schools, and communities do to improve the child care situation for school-age children? Some communities have developed after-school programs in the public schools. In many schools in the Boston area, for example, after-school programs use school building space. The programs are funded by tuition payments, governed by parent boards, and operated with professional staff. In other communities, children go to a day care or child care center for an after-school program, sometimes by bus. In still other communities, there are various kinds of recreational programs to keep children active and supervised after school.

Hotline services are another approach to helping children cope with after-school time. Children can call to report problems, to get help with homework, or just to talk. A service called "PhoneFriend" is an example of a successful hotline set up for school-age children (Guerney & Moore, 1983). The "PhoneFriend" program was developed by the American Association of University Women on a college campus in Pennsylvania, and the first "Phone-Friend" program operated there, beginning in 1982. Since that time more than 1,000 other sites have used the training materials developed by the Pennsylvania program to start their own programs (Peterson, 1990). In "Phonefriend" programs, volunteers are trained in listening and action skills, and they can instruct children in areas such as first aid, power failures, lost items, problems with pets, and general problem solving. In one large-scale study of a "PhoneFriend" service operated in the Midwest (Peterson, 1990), researchers found that calls were made mostly by children between the ages of 5 and 12, and that within this age span 7- to 10-year-olds made the most calls. A content analysis of 4,827 calls revealed that most calls were about some physical problem, such as lost shoes, a sick pet, or an appliance that wouldn't work. For the youngest children (5- to 7-year-olds), physical problem calls outnumbered emotional/social problem calls by 2 to 1. For 8-year-olds, physical problems outnumbered emotional/social problem calls by only about 10 percent; calls from children over 8 divided about evenly between physical problems and emotional/social problems. Girls called more often than boys (61.04 percent compared to 38.96 percent), but when boys called, the content of their calls was similar to girls'. For a summary of all calls, see Box 1, Content of Calls to an After-School Hotline.

A program operated by the Reston Children's Center in Fairfax, Virginia, demonstrates another creative solution to the after-school child care problem. Known as the "Senior Satellite Program," it's designed for the oldest children associated with the center, the 11- to 13-year-olds. This program is based at the center, but it allows children to spend their time outside the center. Children check in after school, and then they might spend some time in the center, at home, or with friends. The center develops contracts between children and their parents that specify how after-school time is to be spent (McKnight & Shelsby, 1984).

BOX 1   Content of Calls to an After-School Hotline

Content of Call	Number of Children Making This Type of Call	Content of Call	Number of Children Making This Type of Call
I. *Individual Physical Problem Situations*	1807	7. Falls	1
A. Domestic Emergency	995	8. Blisters/breaking	5
1. Spills/stains (e.g., paint on shirt, Kool-Aid on rug)	609	9. Foreign object (peanut in nose)	2
		10. Splinter	4
2. Broken glass (window, cut, etc.)	69	11. Something in eye	2
3. Dropped/broken/scratched family property (stereo pulled off shelf, computer dropped, record scratched)	166	12. Crushing injury (finger in door)	1
		13. Illness: indigestion/headache/etc.	3
		14. Animal bites, scratches	33
4. Toy broken (bike flat tire, doll's head off)	14	15. Miscellaneous injury/illness	6
5. Lost own property (left shoes at lake)	39	D. Request for information	196
6. Lost other property (playing with Mom's contacts, lost one; took money of father's, lost it)	19	1. How to operate an appliance (turn on water)	14
		2. How to discuss an issue with parent (ask for a puppy)	22
7. Water damage/leakage	24	3. How to deal with stranger (in the abstract, no stranger is actually present)	9
8. Something in house, shouldn't be (wasp, mouse, raccoon)	10	4. Sexual information	14
9. Electrical appliance doesn't work/power failure	21	5. What to do during a tornado or thunderstorm watch	1
10. Miscellaneous emergencies	22	6. About food (how to cook, where to find)	28
B. Animal Emergency	204	7. Request for nonemergency phone numbers (library dial-a-story)	36
1. Pet threw up/pet soiled in house	90		
2. Pet got out of cage in house (bird, hamster)	7	8. Miscellaneous	52
3. Pet got out of house (dog, cat)	12	E. Strangers	60
4. Pet lost for some time, can't find	16	1. Phone calls	15
5. Pet ill (not sick at stomach #1 above)/choked/had kittens (need a vet)	18	2. At door	33
		3. Other locations (followed me from school)	11
6. Animal injury—very mild (soap in dog's eye)	9	4. Miscellaneous	1
7. Animal injury—major (hit by car, shot with gun)	16	F. School	195
		1. Asks for academic help (e.g., "What is a verb?" "How do you spell 'conversation'?")	62
8. Pet fighting	1		
9. Pet damaged or destroyed property	22	2. Lacks book, paper, pencil needed for schoolwork	58
10. Miscellaneous emergencies	13	3. Miscellaneous	75
C. Injury/Illness	156		
1. Cuts (hands, face, arms)	44	II. *Emotional/Social*	1193
2. Burns	11	A. Emotional Expression (not directly involving another living person)	675
3. Lost tooth	2		
4. Bump/bruise	14		
5. Insect bites/stings	19	1. Bored	389
6. Sprains	3		

SOURCE: Adapted from L. Peterson (1990). PhoneFriend. A developmental description of needs expressed by child callers to a community telephone support system for children. Journal of Applied Developmental Psychology, 11 *(1), 105–122.*

ASSESSMENT OF THE SCHOOL-AGE CHILD

In Chapter 14 we discussed intelligence tests for school-age children and some of the issues associated with their use. Here, we discuss some of the specific assessment instruments that are commonly used with children this age as well as an issue of growing concern—teaching to the test.

BOX 1 Content of Calls to an After-School Hotline

Content of Call	Number of Children Making This Type of Call	Content of Call	Number of Children Making This Type of Call
2. Lonely	86	4. Social behavior (I worry about being a tattletale)	15
3. Scared	105	5. Best friend moves away or goes on vacation	3
4. Hungry	22		
5. Homesick	1	6. Asks permission of PhoneFriend about doing something	16
6. Mad/complain (too much homework, not fair)	26		
7. Grief reactions—pets	4	7. Miscellaneous	22
8. Grief reactions—people	14	E. Boy/Girl Friends—Romantic	47
9. Sad/depression	22	1. Shyness	1
10. Concern about making a decision that does not involve another person	1	2. Parent objects to relationship	1
		3. To go steady or not	4
B. Parent Problems	53	4. To have intercourse or not	7
1. Lack of time with parent	4	5. Homosexuality	1
2. Name calling by parent	2	6. Miscellaneous	33
3. Unfair discipline not involving another sibling	12	F. Babysitter	8
4. Promise breaking	2	G. Teacher	8
5. Fighting—verbal	4	H. Other Familiar Adults	4
6. Fighting—physical	4	*III. Conversation*	1081
7. Parent drinking	1	A. Sharing	167
8. Sexual harassment by parent	1	1. Jokes	21
9. Divorce-related issues	1	2. Story (child retelling story on library dial-a-story)	26
10. Miscellaneous	6		
C. Sibling	164	3. Experience (fun I had on the weekend)	85
1. Sibling did damage/made a mess	14	B. "Just to Talk/Chat"	639
2. Sibling spilled, wet pants, etc.	5	C. Curious about PhoneFriend	191
3. Other information regarding babysitting younger sibling (how to rock to sleep, change a diaper)	49	D. Talk to Television Spokesperson	30
		E. Request to Speak with Specific Person (e.g., talked to Linda before, child asks for her mom, who is a PhoneFriend Volunteer)	48
4. Fighting—verbal	24		
5. Fighting—physical	19		
6. Sibling gets child in trouble with parent	3	*IV. No Go*	485
7. Sibling injured/ill	6	A. Hang-up—Crank	163
8. Sibling won't leave me alone/bothering me	19	B. Prank—No Content (giggles, etc.)	42
9. Sibling won't let me play/do what I want	5	C. Wrong Number/Friend Gave It as Their Number	48
10. Sibling took caller's property, snack, etc.	3	D. Prank—Made-Up Story	187
11. Miscellaneous	17	E. Heavy Breathing	11
		F. Obscene	34
D. Friends—Platonic	230	*V. Call Back*	110
1. Cruel treatment by peers (boys hold their nose when I go by, rock throwing)	97	*VI. Referral to Other Agency (e.g., 911—emergency dispatch)*	7
2. Argument with friend	70		
3. Rivalry between friends (I asked two people to sleep over, and Mom says I can only have one)	7	*VII. No Data Listed by Volunteer*	129

Intelligence Tests

Children having academic problems are often individually given an intelligence test by a psychologist to try to estimate learning ability and recommend special educational help where required. Probably the best-known individually administered intelligence test is the **Stanford Binet Intelligence Scale—**

Fourth Edition. The first edition of this test was developed at Stanford University as a modification of the original Binet and Simon test. The fourth edition is designed for examinees from preschool age through adulthood, and it bears little resemblance to the original test. The fourth edition contains subtests relating to such abilities as logical reasoning, perceptual-motor coordination, and language skills.

The most commonly used individually administered test is the **Wechsler Intelligence Scale for Children—Third Edition,** often called the *WISC-III* (Wechsler, 1991). This test, used with children between the ages of 6 and 16, is divided into verbal and performance sections, and each of these sections has six or seven subtests. A child receives three scores on this test, including a verbal IQ, a performance IQ, and a full-scale IQ, which is based on the first two scores.

The verbal part of the WISC-III tests children on information, arithmetic, vocabulary, comprehension, digit span, and the ability to distinguish similarities; the performance part tests them on picture completion, coding, picture arrangement, block design, object assembly, symbol search, and the ability to work mazes. For an example of the kind of questions that appear on the WISC-III, see Box 2.

Achievement Tests

Unlike intelligence tests, which measure general abilities, achievement tests measure knowledge, information, and skills in specific areas such as math, science, or reading. They're usually administered to determine whether an individual child, or a group of children, has attained a grade-appropriate level of knowledge and competence.

One frequently used set of achievement tests is the Iowa Tests of Basic Skills, which provides an achievement test for each grade level from first through ninth grades (Hieronymous & Hoover, 1986). The various tests measure fundamental skills in the areas of reading, spelling, vocabulary, language use, work-study, math, social studies, science, writing, and listening.

Issues in Testing: Teaching to the Test

Standardized tests that measure high-level skills and complex problem-solving abilities are relatively difficult to devise. It's easier to write multiple-choice test items that measure knowledge of facts. When a panel of psychologists analyzed the items on one standardized test, they judged 70 percent of the questions to require memorization of facts, 15 percent to require comprehension, 12 percent to require analytical thinking, and 3 percent to require evaluations (Bowman & Peng, 1972). Most tests just don't test abilities such as drawing inferences, analyzing, or making judgments (Aiken, 1982).

Unfortunately, the level at which subject matter is tested is likely to be the level at which it's taught. The result is that teaching often goes just as far as the test and no farther. As one observer has concluded, "Efficient tests tend to drive out less efficient tests, leaving many important abilities untested—and untaught" (Frederiksen, 1984). But tests of high-level skills can be constructed. More attention to the construction of such tests will be required in the United

BOX 2 **Paraphrased Wechsler-like Questions**

GENERAL INFORMATION

1. How many wings does a bird have?
2. How many nickels make a dime?
3. What is steam made of?
4. What is pepper?

GENERAL COMPREHENSION

1. What should you do if you see a man forget his hat when he leaves his seat in a restaurant?
2. Why do some people save sales receipts?
3. Why is copper often used in electrical wires?

ARITHMETIC

1. Sue had two pieces of candy and Joe gave her four more. How many pieces of candy did Sue have all together?
2. Three children divided 18 pennies equally among themselves. How many pennies did each child receive?
3. If two pencils cost 15¢, what will be the cost of a dozen pencils?

SIMILARITIES

1. In what way are a lion and a tiger alike?
2. In what way are a saw and a hammer alike?
3. In what way are an hour and a week alike?
4. In what way are a circle and a triangle alike?

VOCABULARY

This test consists simply of asking, "What is a _____?" or "What does _____ mean?" The words cover a wide range of difficulty or familiarity.

PERFORMANCE TESTS

In addition to verbal tasks of the kinds illustrated above, there are a number of performance tasks involving the use of blocks, cutout figures, paper and pencil puzzles, and so on.

SOURCE: Paraphrased questions printed by permission of The Psychological Corporation, 757 Third Avenue, New York, NY.

States as the demand grows for a national curriculum and a common, national test of academic achievement.

LIVING WITH THE SCHOOL-AGE CHILD

As in the previous stages of childhood, adults who live and work with school-age children have certain practical concerns, which we discuss next.

Ensuring the Health of the School-Age Child

Middle childhood is a time of relatively robust energy and good health. Most children have been immunized against the childhood diseases that used to punctuate children's lives—mumps, measles, whooping cough, diphtheria, and polio. And because so many children attend day care and preschool, many of them have had chicken pox before they get to elementary school.

The main illnesses that school-age children have to contend with are virus-based colds accompanied by sore throat, cough, and fever; virus-based influenza; and bacterial-based strep throat with sore throat and fever. Children who are basically healthy and whose illnesses are properly tended with rest, fluids, and nutritious food usually don't have much trouble getting through colds and flu. Physicians usually control strep throat with antibiotics to keep it from

HEALTH FOCUS

Children and AIDS

Even very young children are falling victim to Acquired Immune Deficiency Syndrome, or AIDS. There is currently no cure for this disease, and it invariably leads to death. AIDS is caused by the human immunodeficiency virus (HIV), which destroys the immune system and is transmitted through sexual contact or through contact with the blood of infected individuals. Although no cases are known to have occurred through any other kind of contact, the virus has been found in human saliva, which raises questions about transmittal through biting. A larger concern about biting is that of blood in saliva from possibly undetected sores in the mouth.

As of November 1988, 1230 cases of AIDS had been confirmed in children aged 12 and younger. The number of cases has grown rapidly; in November 1986, only 383 cases were confirmed (APA Task Force on Pediatric AIDS, 1989). Children contract AIDS in three main ways—prenatally, from their mothers (79 percent of all children's cases were contracted this way); from blood transfusions, as during surgery (13 percent); and from blood components used to treat blood coagulation disorders such as hemophilia (5 percent) (Siebert, 1987). Prenatal infection is expected to be the major source of children's cases in the future, since more women of childbearing age are becoming infected from intravenous drug use or from sexual contact with infected intravenous drug users. Infection from blood supplies has decreased dramatically as blood-screening tests have improved.

Concern arises when a child who is HIV-infected enrolls in day care, preschool, or school. Parents worry that their child will catch the virus from the infected child, and teachers worry that they too might become infected. All of the available evidence indicates that AIDS is not contracted through casual, everyday contact, and there have been no known cases of AIDS transmitted in schools or day care centers (Massachusetts Department of Public Health, 1985). On the basis of this fact, the Centers for Disease Control recommend that children who are HIV positive not be barred from school (Cooper, Pelton & LeMay, 1988). This recommendation has also been endorsed by the U.S. Department of Education (Massachusetts Department of Public Health, 1985).

Under certain conditions, however, children who are HIV positive should not be placed in the regular day care, preschool, or elementary classroom. If the child has a tendency to bite, for example, or if there are open sores that can't be covered, the child shouldn't be in a regular classroom. HIV-infected children under 3 years of age shouldn't be in group settings. At this age, children tend to drool and bite, and they aren't toilet trained (Cooper, Pelton & LeMay, 1988). The departments of public health in most states have developed specific policies about school attendance by children with AIDS. School districts can obtain information from these departments or from state departments of education or day care licensing agencies.

turning into a more serious respiratory infection or rheumatic fever. An occasional child will get tonsillitis—tonsils that become abscessed and susceptible to repeated infections—and will have to have a tonsillectomy. One very serious problem on the rise among children is discussed in Health Focus—Children and AIDS.

Because children are usually so healthy at this age, adults can turn their attention to helping them develop healthy life-styles. Schools often teach the principles of good nutrition, and parents can talk about healthy foods with their children quite naturally when making lunches or snacks. Both schools and parents can help children develop skills in games and sports and learn to love physical activity. If children are overweight, adults can help them learn how to keep their weight under control, as discussed in Chapter 13. They can also teach them about the dangers of smoking, drinking, and taking drugs. But because of children's increased awareness of the world around them at this age and the different choices people make, probably the strongest and most valuable lesson adults can give them is the example of their own healthy life-style.

Ensuring the Safety of the School-Age Child

Another concern adults have is making sure school-age children are safe. Accidents are the leading cause of death at this age (Christopherson, 1989). Although children now have more knowledge and skills than they did as tod-

FIGURE 4
Once children are at school and spending time with friends, adults can't control their eating habits as much as they could when they were younger. Information about food and diet can help children eat properly. Class cooking projects are a good hands-on way to teach children the basics of nutrition.

dlers or preschoolers, they also have certain other internal and external pressures to contend with. For one, school-age children care very much about being accepted by peers. When they were younger, they may have been more interested in "doing what Mom said." Now, they may be led into danger by their overwhelming desire to be part of the group.

Because they're more competent, school-age children also have more independence and autonomy from adult supervision. But this very independence means that they don't have the same access to adult judgment and planning as they did when they were younger and more dependent (Zuckerman & Duby, 1985). And even 12-year-olds simply don't have the experience or judgment to cope with every situation that comes up. But adults can take some steps to keep children safe even when they can't be with them.

BICYCLE ACCIDENTS. Many children die every year in bicycle accidents, most of which (95 percent) involve a collision between a bike and a car. Of all children, those between the ages of 10 and 14 have the highest rate of bicycle fatalities, followed by those between the ages of 5 and 9. Boys are three-and-a-half times more likely to die in a bicycle accident than are girls (Friede et al., 1985).

Serious injuries and deaths almost always involve head injuries. The obvious conclusion is that if children wear well-fitted, specially designed helmets,

FIGURE 5
Safety equipment is essential in many children's activities, including bicycling, skate boarding, and roller blading. Knee pads, elbow pads, and gloves protect children from scrapes and bruises; helmets protect them from injuries that are potentially much more serious.

they will be protected at least somewhat from this danger. Although no controlled studies have been done to determine exactly how effective helmets are in preventing head injuries, it seems probable that they do help (Friede et al., 1985). Less than 2 percent of elementary school children wear bicycle helmets (Weiss, 1986), probably in part because of their cost, which ranges from $30 to $70. But many parents consider this an inexpensive investment when measured against their child's safety and their own peace of mind.

Children can also be taught safe bicycle-riding procedures, such as riding with traffic rather than against it. Accidents in which children were riding toward oncoming traffic account for 5 percent of bicycle fatalities and 20 percent of nonfatal accidents (Friede et al., 1985). Additionally, bicycle accidents can be reduced when communities enforce traffic laws. In Minnesota, where some communities issue citations and require violators to attend a "bike violator's seminar," accidents have been reduced by between 30 and 100 percent (Friede et al., 1985). Communities can also make biking safer by establishing bike paths and building speed bumps, both of which are effective in reducing collisions between bicycles and cars.

PEDESTRIAN ACCIDENTS. Another kind of accident common among children is being hit by a car while on foot. About 2,000 children are killed each year by cars, and many more are injured (Guyer, Talbot & Pless, 1985). Usually the children involved in this kind of accident are between ages 5 and 9, are hit during daylight hours, and are struck when they dart out into the street or play near driveways (rather than at busy intersections) (Rivara, Reay & Bergman, 1989; Stevenson & Stevenson, 1990).

How to protect children from this kind of accident is a matter of some debate. Some experts think children should be taught safety rules and then allowed to negotiate streets by themselves. Others argue that even school-age children can't be taught to be careful enough. These experts say that 6- and 7-year-olds can't understand or follow rules necessary for crossing safely at intersections and that even 9-year-olds sometimes forget to look behind them before crossing a street (Rivara, Reay & Bergman, 1989).

Adults probably should begin to teach children safe pedestrian rules early in the school years but not allow them to cross streets alone until they're 9 or 10 years old. Even at this age, children should be shown the safest way home from school and taught to cross busy streets where a crossing guard is available. Parents also need to lobby for appropriate speed limits on streets near their schools and homes.

EYE INJURIES. A final area in which adults can help keep children safer is protection of the eyes. The importance of good eyesight to everyday living makes the prevention of eye injuries especially important. Most eye injuries in children occur between the ages of 6 and 14 (Grin, Nelson & Jeffers, 1987), many more of them in boys than in girls. The highest percentage of these injuries occur during a sports activity (16 percent), closely followed by incidents involving sticks or branches (9 percent) and BB guns (8 percent). They also occur when a child is struck in the eye by a thrown object, such as a rock or a snowball, or jabbed in the eye with a pen or pencil. In sports, the highest rate of injury occurs in baseball (when the child is hit in the eye with the ball while batting) and in tennis, followed by soccer, basketball, and hockey.

FIGURE 6
School-age children are creative, dexterous, and often very talented. The right art materials have given this girl the opportunity not just to express herself but to experience the satisfaction of having completed an impressive painting.

Most sports-related injuries can be prevented, according to the National Society to Prevent Blindness, if some safety guidelines are followed. They recommend that children wear safety helmets with face protectors for baseball, face masks for hockey, and eye guards for other sports. Children whose eyesight is already impaired should wear safety goggles for all sports and not participate in certain sports, such as boxing.

Eye injuries from air-powered guns (BB guns) could be reduced if children weren't allowed to use them, and seven states have laws prohibiting their use by individuals under age 18 (Grin, Nelson & Jeffers, 1987). Adults can help prevent other injuries by teaching children how to keep their eyes and their friends' eyes safe—by not throwing objects, by not playing with sticks and branches, and by using pens and pencils properly.

Supporting the School-Age Child's Play

WHAT DO THEY LIKE TO PLAY? Now that so much has been said about these first through sixth graders, we can ask what *they* might consider the most important question of all—what do they like to play? Playing is still an integral part of their lives, as it was when they were toddlers and preschoolers, although they've added many interests and activities. They enjoy active games and board games, jokes and riddles, and physical activities like bike riding and ball playing. They like sports, reading, movies, theater productions, television, concerts, and hobbies. Their newly emerging ability to classify makes collecting (stamps, coins, rocks, insects, baseball cards) an activity they can understand and enjoy.

School-age children typically prefer playing with other children to playing alone. And they can usually play in harmony for long periods of time without constant adult guidance or intervention. When they're together, younger school-age children are often given to bursts of giggling and silliness. When adults ask, "What's so funny?" they only laugh harder.

Younger school-age children still love sociodramatic play. They play school and "house" and go off on long fantasy adventures. They play with dolls, stuffed animals, and toy figures. Although fantasy play tends to decrease after the age of 8, it is still very prevalent in young school-age children (Wall, Pickert & Gibson, 1989).

TOYS AND PLAYTHINGS. Because of their advancing physical and cognitive skills, school-age children enjoy toys and games that are beyond the abilities and understanding of younger children. Playthings that support a child's large motor skills might include a baseball bat, ball, and glove; skis; a basketball and hoop; a soccer ball; roller skates; ice skates; a frisbee; a bicycle; a scooter; and a jump rope.

To support fine motor development, parents might provide marbles, jacks, yo-yos, model and craft kits, and drawing and construction material, such as markers, paints, paper, scissors, scotch tape, and glue. Particularly appropriate for school-age children's level of cognitive development are cameras, calculators, microscopes, binoculars, magnets, and materials for hobbies. Because of their new understanding of the world and their intense interest in it, school-age children can be delightful companions on expeditions to natural history museums, hikes and camping trips, and almost any other outing of mutual interest.

GAMES, BOOKS, AND MAGAZINES. As we saw in Chapter 14, school-age children are able to play strategy games because they can think about what other people are thinking. They're now capable of winning against the very adults who taught them the games just a few years earlier. Games they enjoy include checkers, chess, Chinese checkers, Othello, Risk, Scrabble, MasterMind, Battleship, Stratego, Boggle, and FourSight—all games that involve "second guessing" an opponent.

Most children become completely fluent readers during middle childhood. They enjoy selecting their own books and reading them independently. A children's librarian can help them or their parents with ideas about interesting or appropriate books to read. Many children's magazines are published too; Table 1 lists some of them.

VIDEO GAMES. A whole new kind of activity opened up to school-age children in the 1980s with the advent of video games. Millions of parents brought these

FIGURE 7
School-age children like swimming not because it's good exercise but because it's so much fun. If parents make sure they're safe in the water and use sunscreen, swimming is an outstanding activity for school-age children.

games home from the toy or electronics store and hooked them up to their TV sets, and many others allowed their children to play video games at the arcades that seemed to spring up overnight in communities all over the country. After watching their children play these games—eyes glued intently to the video screen or body hunched over a game machine in a noisy arcade—many parents wondered how positive an experience they were having.

Although long-term studies haven't been done, some experts believe that playing video games is an activity that needs to be controlled, if not eliminated. It involves children in an indoor, nonphysical activity, sometimes for

TABLE 1 Magazines for School-Age Children

TITLE	AGES	CONTENT
Child Life	7–9	Health, safety, nutrition
Children's Digest	8–10	Health, safety, nutrition
Cobblestone	8–14	History
Creative Kids	6–14	Stories, poems, art, and music submitted by children
Cricket	6–12	Short stories, poems
Faces	8–14	History
Highlights for Children	2–12	Stories, poems, learning activities
Jack and Jill	6–8	Health, safety, nutrition
National Geographic World	8–13	General interest
Odyssey	8–14	Astronomy and space science
Owl	8–14	Environmental education
Penny Power	8–14	Consumer education
Ranger Rick	6–12	Nature study
Stone Soup	6–13	Stories, poems, and art submitted by children
Contact	8–14	Science and technology

SOURCE: Adapted from Children's Magazine List. (1987). Glassboro, NJ: Glassboro State College, Educational Press Association of America.

hours on end, usually with very little interaction with other children or adults. Some children get bored fairly quickly, but for others it's a "behavioral addiction" they can't control without adult help. These children show apparently compulsive involvement in the games and a lack of interest in other activities (Griffiths, 1991). The content of many video games is violent, and some of it is sexist and racist as well.

Once exposed to video games, however, many school-age children are interested in trying them, for the challenge of beating the game if nothing else. Some parents believe in strictly limiting the hours a child can play per day; others allow unlimited playing so the child will tire of it sooner. Some refuse to buy video games; others would rather have their child playing at home than spending time in the less desirable arcade environment. Whatever parents decide to do, they'll want to keep a close eye on both the content of the games and their child's behavior during and after playing.

OVERVIEW

School-age children are increasingly able to take care of themselves. They have rational understandings of how the world works; they can read, write, and express themselves; they're starting to get a grasp on social interactions; and they're physically strong and healthy. Yet they still have limitations and need responsible adult supervision in many situations. This is why after-school care is important even for 11- and 12-year-olds. It also accounts for the high rate of accidents among school-age children. Adults who live and work with children this age have to find a balance between keeping them safe and allowing them the independence they need to continue maturing.

KNOWLEDGE IN ACTION REVIEW

AFTER-SCHOOL CARE FOR SCHOOL-AGE CHILDREN

- As long-term economic trends propel more and more parents into the work force, after-school care for their school-age children becomes an important concern.
- Studies indicate that children who have been raised by parents using the authoritative style of parenting, as opposed to the authoritarian or permissive style,

are better able to resist peer pressure when left unsupervised after school. The long-term effects of being a latchkey child are still unknown.

- Some schools and communities have after-school programs for school-age children, and other communities have hotlines for children at home alone after school.

ASSESSMENT OF THE SCHOOL-AGE CHILD

- The intelligence tests most commonly administered to school-age children are the Stanford Binet Intelligence Scale—Fourth Edition, the Wechsler Intelligence Scale for Children—Third Edition (both individually administered tests).

- An important issue is "teaching to the test." Some experts claim that the emphasis on tests and test scores has reduced school curricula to test items.

LIVING WITH THE SCHOOL-AGE CHILD

- School-age children tend to be healthy and active. Adults can help them develop and maintain healthy life-styles by teaching them about nutrition and encouraging them to participate in sports and other physical activities.
- AIDS is a problem of growing proportions among children, who most often contract it prenatally. Currently the Centers for Disease Control recommend that children with AIDS attend school unless they have a tendency to bite, have open sores, or are under 3 years of age.
- Accidents are the leading cause of death among school-age children. Adults can enforce a variety of

measures to keep children safe when they're riding bicycles or skateboards or crossing streets. Adults can also teach children not to endanger their eyes and can make sure their eyes are protected during sports.

- School-age children enjoy a variety of games, activities, and sports. They prefer playing with other children to playing alone. They're skilled readers and enjoy picking out their own books. Adults can support their reading with frequent visits to the library and with magazine subscriptions.
- Parents may want to monitor their children's television viewing and the amount of time they spend playing video games.

KEY TERMS

permissive parenting
　　style
authoritarian parenting
　　style
authoritative parenting
　　style
distal supervision

Stanford-Binet Intelligence Scale—Fourth
　　Edition
Wechsler Intelligence
　　Scale for Children—
　　Third Edition (WISC-
　　III)

SUGGESTIONS FOR FURTHER READING

Baroody, A. (1987). *Children's mathematical thinking.* New York: Teachers College Press.

This readable book discusses the development of mathematical concepts in children during the preschool and elementary school years. It also provides interesting discussions of the shift from "informal" mathematics to the formal mathematics required in school.

Klein, E. (Ed.). (1985). *Children and computers. New directions in child development.* San Francisco: Jossey-Bass.

Computers are being used in many elementary school classrooms. This book provides some data on the effects that computer use might have on children's problem-solving strategies, their knowledge about change and motion, and their story editing. Interesting reading for computer enthusiasts.

Martin, A. (1988). Screening, early intervention, and remediation: Obscuring children's potential. *Harvard Educational Review, 58*(4), 488–501.

This account, written from an elementary teacher's perspective, points out some of the limits of testing. She contrasts both the information provided by formal evaluations with that provided by teacher observation and the recommendations made by outside specialists with those provided by teaching colleagues.

Shepard, L. A., & Smith, M. L. (1988). Escalating academic demand in kindergarten: Counterproductive policies. *Elementary School Journal, 89,* 135–145.

This article focuses primarily on the problems resulting from the use of formal tests to screen for, and make retention decisions about, kindergarten, but it discusses wider issues of test use as well. It also discusses the effects of extensive test use, including "teaching to the test."

GLOSSARY

accommodation With respect to the human eye, refers to the ability of the lens to adjust to objects at different distances. With respect to Piaget's theory, refers to the process of change in mental structures.

acuity The resolving power of the eye—its ability to see closely spaced, thin lines versus widely spaced, broad lines, for example.

acute stage of adjustment to divorce The initial two years following a divorce, during which children are likely to show the most disruption in their behavior.

affrication A feature of speech that is characterized by the slow release of air.

amenorrhea Absence of menstruation that can occur for a number of reasons, including a severe reduction in body fat due to anorexia nervosa or extremely high levels of physical activity.

American College Testing Program The publisher of the ACT test, which is used extensively as part of college application packages.

amniocentesis Analysis of amniotic fluid to determine the presence of various chromosomal and chemical abnormalities in the fetus.

anoxia Oxygen deprivation.

anxious/ambivalent attachment A pattern of mother-child relationship marked by a mixture of approach and withdrawal behavior on the part of the child upon reunion with the mother after separation.

anxious/avoidant attachment A pattern of mother-child relationship marked by avoidance of the mother by the child during play and upon reunion after separation.

Apgar scale An assessment instrument used to assess infants' physiological functioning at birth.

apnea A period during which breathing stops.

assimilation A process basic to Piaget's theory of intellectual development that involves the taking in of new information by current mental structures.

attachment The emotional tie between infants and their caregivers, usually their parents.

authoritarian parenting style Parenting behavior marked by high levels of adult control and references to absolute authority as a result of parental status or religious doctrine.

authoritative parenting style Parenting behavior marked by firm parental control accompanied by reasoning about the basis for expectations.

aversive stimulus A stimulus that someone finds repulsive and tries to avoid.

axons The part of a nerve cell that carries impulses away from its own cell toward another.

babbling Early vocalization consisting of consonant-vowel combinations.

Babinski reflex A reflex present in young infants characterized by fanning of the toes when the outer edge of the sole is stroked.

baseline data The data collected in a research study before a treatment is introduced to assess natural or typical conditions.

behavior modification A specific behavioral technique that utilizes reinforcement systematically to change behavior.

behavioral states The varying patterns of sleep and wakefulness found in infants.

behaviorism A theoretical orientation that emphasizes external influences on behavior and direct observation of behavior in research.

biased sampling Subjects included in a study who are not representative of the population of interest as a whole.

bilirubin A by-product of red blood cell destruction that is excreted from the body.

binocular fixation The ability to use both eyes in a coordinated fashion when looking at objects.

blind study A study in which the researchers have no knowledge about which subjects have certain characteristics of interest.

bonding Refers to the initial emotional tie that some researchers and theorists believe mothers have toward their newborn infants.

book babble A type of expressive jargon that has the intonation patterns of reading rather than conversation.

Brain Stem Evoked Response A test used to detect an infant's ability to hear. It uses electrodes to measure brain reaction to sound.

Brazelton Neonatal Behavioral Assessment Scale An assessment designed to measure young infants' reflexive and adaptive behavior.

center of gravity The point in the body around which the weight is distributed evenly.

centering According to Piaget, the tendency of preschool children to focus on one dimension of a relationship at a time instead of coordinating two dimensions.

cephalocaudal trend The pattern of physical and motor development that proceeds from the head to the tail.

cesarean birth Delivery of an infant through an incision in the mother's abdominal and uterine walls.

chicken pox A common childhood disease caused by a virus and characterized by itchy skin lesions.

child-directed educational approach Educational programs in which children's interests and choices are taken into account.

chorionic villus sampling A biopsy procedure in which tissue from the chorion is extracted for analysis to determine the presence or absence of chromosomal abnormalities in the fetus.

chromosomes The strands of DNA inside the nucleus of the cell that contain the genes.

chronological age Age measured from the birthdate.

class inclusion The concept of hierarchical classes necessary to understand complex classification schemes.

classical conditioning The pairing of a stimulus with another stimulus that reliably produces a response, such that the second stimulus itself begins to elicit the response.

clique A closely knit peer group based on specific interests such as music, sports, or physical appearance.

closed method Refers to observational studies in which specific data-collection techniques are used to enable researchers to collect more reliable data.

cohort A group of subjects who share the same history of experience.

cohort effects Differences among age groups that are due to historical events rather than to developmental differences.

colostrum The substance excreted from the breast before the milk begins to flow.

compensation A specific kind of reasoning about spatial rearrangement of objects of mass in which the child logically multiplies one dimension (e.g., height) with another (e.g., width) to account for differences in appearance from a standard.

componential subtheory of intelligence One of the three views of intelligence in Sternberg's triarchic theory of intelligence, the componential theory focuses on internal mental processes such as knowledge acquisition components, performance components, and metacomponents.

concepts Ideas about general sets of characteristics that apply across many individual cases.

concrete operational thinking Thinking characterized by logic about events observed.

conditioned response The response elicited by the conditioned stimulus that was originally elicited by the unconditioned stimulus.

conditioned stimulus The stimulus paired with the unconditioned stimulus in classical conditioning, such that it elicits the response initially elicited by the unconditioned stimulus.

conservation The ability to realize that changes in spatial arrangement of objects or liquids, for example, do not change their number or amount.

consolability The ease with which an upset baby can be quieted.

construct validity The soundness with which a measure measures the theoretical variable, or construct, it is supposed to assess. Construct validity is not easily observed; it is usually expressed as the extent of correlation between the measure and other measures thought to be associated with the construct of interest.

context bound A characteristic of early language comprehension in which word meaning is heavily dependent on clues in the situation.

contextual subtheory of intelligence One of the three views of intelligence in Sternberg's triarchic theory of intelligence, the contextual subtheory focuses on how the individual adapts to, shapes, or selects environments over the long term.

control group A subject group in an experimental research study that is excluded from the treatment but is like the treatment group in every other way.

controversial status Sociometric rating in which a child receives many like and dislike elections by peers who are asked to list children who fall within these two categories.

conversational babble A type of expressive jargon that has the intonational patterns of conversation.

coordination errors A type of error made by young children when they count objects, such that their verbal tags aren't coordinated with the objects they are counting.

correlational study A study in which variables of interest are observed to see the extent to which they vary together in lawful ways. The variables are usually studied in naturally occurring groups of subjects instead of subjects who have been randomly assigned to treatment groups.

Crib-O-Gram A procedure used to measure auditory response directly by assessing brain waves.

critical period The specific time frame during which specific behaviors are thought to develop.

cross-sectional design A research design that uses groups of subjects of different ages to determine differences due to development.

crowd A term sometimes applied to a relatively large

group of teenagers whose interests and backgrounds may be somewhat more varied than those of a clique.

crowning During the birthing process, the first showing of the infant's head outside the birth canal.

culturally biased tests Tests that contain a predominance of items that are more consistent with the experiences of some cultural groups than with others.

decentration The trend in cognitive development that allows children to see things from points of view other than their own. In pretend play, decentration is shown when children remove themselves from the center of the action.

decontextualization The trend in pretend play that involves object substitution.

decontextualized language Language that is not dependent on immediate physical or social cues.

deferred imitation Imitation separated in time from the observance of the behavior.

dependent variable The behavior observed by a researcher to see if changes occur as a result of changes made in the independent variable.

developmental systems approach A framework or theory that assumes a reciprocal interaction among all levels of the hierarchy of living systems as these interactions go on over time.

dialect Slight variations within a language.

distal supervision A characteristic of school-age child care programs in which children call or check in but are allowed to leave the program premises to engage in activities or go home.

distinctive features The variations in lines that can be combined in a number of ways to create different alphabet letters.

Down's syndrome A collection of physical and mental difficulties caused by the inheritance of an extra twenty-first chromosome.

drive reduction Refers to satiation of sex, hunger, and thirst, for example.

ductus arteriosus Route of fetal blood circulation that circumvents the lungs.

dyad A pair, as in mother and child.

dyslexia Extreme difficulty learning to read, which is most often caused by problems with language processing.

ectopic pregnancy A pregnancy in which the embryo develops outside the womb, most typically in the fallopian tube.

educable mentally retarded Retardation within a very moderate range such that the person can learn academic skills to a certain level with the help of special education.

ego A term used by Freud to refer to that part of the personality that experiences the external world and seeks to satisfy the id in ways that are not punished.

ego identity A concept of self in relation to society, especially as this relates to commitment to occupation, sexuality, religion, and politics. Similar to psychosocial identity.

ego psychoanalytic The point of view of relatively recent theorists who identify with the psychoanalytic tradition but emphasize the ego and a course of ego development that is independent of the id and its instincts.

egocentric role taking The description used by Selman to refer to an individual's assumption that different views of the same situation are due to differences in information about the situation.

embryoblast The part of the ball of cells, forming soon after fertilization, that will become the embryo itself.

emergent literacy Refers to the forms of written language behavior that precede conventional forms. For example, young children read their storybooks using picture-governed, rather than print-governed, strategies.

empathy The ability to understand how others feel.

empathy training Verbally instructing children about the effects of their behavior on the feelings and welfare of others.

empirical Related to data or experience rather than to theory.

encopresis Inability to control bowel function, often due to distension of musculature of the anus.

endogenous smile Grimace of face resembling a smile that is caused by internal factors.

enuresis Failure to control the bladder at night.

environmental print Print found on such things as road signs, store fronts, and food containers.

epigenic Refers to development in which structures change in form rather than simply increasing in size.

equilibration A Piagetian notion that the individual tries to keep assimilation and accommodation in balance.

ethology The study of animal behavior.

Eustachian tube Small tube that connects the middle ear to the throat.

exhortation Verbal appeals for prosocial behavior.

exosystem In Bronfenbrenner's ecological model, the system or settings that do not immediately affect the child, but influence the child indirectly, such as a parent's job or the local school board.

experiential subtheory of intelligence One of the three views of intelligence in Sternberg's triarchic theory of intelligence, the experiential subtheory focuses on the relationship between intelligence and relatively immediate experience, especially how the individual learns to deal with novelty and how she makes newly acquired aspects of information processing automatic or routine.

experimental study   A research study in which subjects are randomly assigned to treatment groups.

expressive jargon   A type of talk in which nonsense words are used with realistic-sounding intonation patterns.

external validity   Refers to the extent to which conclusions drawn in one study can be generalized to individuals not included in the study.

extinction   In behavioral theory, refers to the reduction of a behavior due to lack of response to it.

face validity   The extent to which a measure appears (on its face) to measure accurately what it is supposed to assess.

failure-to-thrive   Terminology that refers to infants who fail to grow normally.

fallopian tubes   Tubes connecting the ovaries to the uterus, through which the egg passes and in which fertilization takes place.

family process variables   Characteristics of families having to do with relationships rather than demographics.

fetal alcohol syndrome   A pattern of characteristics acquired prenatally from harmful levels of maternal alcohol consumption, which may include mental retardation, lower-than-average birth weight, microcephaly, and unusual facial features.

fontanelles   Soft spots on the top of a baby's head that will close as the skull grows and fuses.

formal operational thinking   Piaget's highest level of intellectual development in which deductive, if-then reasoning becomes possible.

fraternal twins   Twins who aren't identical genetically because they originated from two different eggs.

fused visual image   One visual image instead of two; fusion of visual images may not be present until about four months of age.

gag reflex   Involuntary movement elicited when the back of the throat is pushed by something.

gender constancy   The realization that sex does not change with alterations in hairstyle or clothing.

gender identity   The categorization of oneself as a boy or a girl.

genes   The basic units of inheritance in all living things.

germ cells   Cells involved in reproduction—sperm in the male and ova in the female.

gestation   Prenatal development.

glial cells   Cells surrounding nerve cells in the brain that serve a supportive, nutritive function, such as the production of myelin.

glycogen   The form in which starch is stored in the body before being converted to sugar and metabolized.

gonads   Sex organs that create sperm and ova.

grasping reflex   The involuntary movement resulting in the curling of toes or fingers when the sole of the foot or the palm of the hand is stroked or pressed.

growth spurt   A rapid increase in growth such as that which occurs during pubescence.

habituation   The decrement in response that follows repeated presentation of a stimulus.

head lice   Small parasites that infect the head and cause itching.

heritability   A statistical estimate of the degree to which a characteristic of biologically related individuals is due to genetic variations in the population.

hidden or invisible displacement   A technique for hiding an object during the administration of the Piagetian object permanence task in which the object hidden is first placed inside a container.

hierarchical inclusion   The embedding of subordinate classes within superordinate classes within a classification framework.

hierarchical systems   All systems included in an arrangement in which systems are included in a larger system, which is in turn an element of a larger system, and so on.

holophrase   A word-word utterance that carries the meaning of a whole statement.

hyaline membrane disease   A condition in which the lungs do not work properly due to the absence of surfactant—common among infants born prematurely.

hyperbilirubinemia   A condition in which too much bilirubin is present in the bloodstream.

hypothermia   A condition in which the body temperature dips below normal.

id   The term coined by Freud to refer to that part of personality driven by inherited and unconscious instincts.

identical process theory   Refers to a theory of second language acquisition in which it is assumed the child learns the second language in the same way a child would for whom it is a first language.

identical twins   Twins resulting from division of the same zygote.

identification   A term from Freudian theory that refers to the aligning of behavior and values with another person, usually a child with an adult.

identity, identity argument   The justification given for a judgment of conservation that mentions that nothing has been added or taken away from the original amount or number.

identity achievement   The end result of the searching and decision-making process that begins in adolescence and continues into young adulthood through which individuals select a vocation, decide how they fit into a peer group, and choose what kind of person they want to be.

identity diffusion   An absence of commitment to important decisions about one's identity, including occupation, sexuality, religion, and politics.

identity foreclosure   A premature ending of the search for identity by making decisions without first exploring and thinking through many different options.

identity moratorium   A temporary stopping of the search for identity, sometimes due to the desire to avoid going through the conflicts associated with making major decisions.

idiopathic growth retardation   Growth retardation that is caused by hormonal problems rather than other disease or lesions.

imitation   The copying of another's behavior.

immersion   An approach to second language learning in which the learner is placed in close contact with native speakers and is expected to pick up the language without special instruction.

immunoglobulins   Proteins that are responsible for the body's resistance to specific diseases.

imprinting   An innate tendency to follow or attach to the first moving object seen during a critical early developmental period.

independent variable   The variable in an experimental study that is changed to see if it has an effect on other variables.

induction   Used by Hoffman to refer to a particular socialization procedure in which the child is helped to see the effects of his behavior on others.

information-processing view of intellectual development   A view that contrasts with Piaget's and that stresses increases in memory and rules learned from experience rather than qualitative differences captured by the notion of stages.

informed consent   Consent given for participation in a research study after receiving detailed information about the study's procedures and possible detrimental effects.

instinct   According to Freud, the mental representation of body states and needs.

instrumental aggression   Aggressive acts committed for the purpose of obtaining some reward.

instrumental conditioning   Conditioning that results from the use of rewards and punishments following a behavior.

integration of play   Complex combining of themes in pretend play.

intelligence quotient   A score computed by considering a person's chronological age in relation to his or her mental age as determined on an intelligence test.

interference theory   Refers to a theory of second language acquisition in which the child is assumed to use knowledge of his or her first language when learning a second language.

internal validity   Refers to characteristics of the design of a research study that determine whether the researcher can infer correlation or causation, for example.

internal working model   According to attachment theory, the child's model of self or of attachment figure(s)

initially acquired in the first years of life—a model that is or becomes largely unconscious and contributes to the child's behavior.

intrinsic motivation   Motivation that comes from within the person rather than from external rewards.

intrinsic reinforcement   Reinforcement that comes from the individual's own pleasure following a behavior rather than from praise or tokens provided by others.

intuitive   Behavior based on what seems or feels right rather than on well thought-out logic.

irreversibility   The inability of young children to play back an action in their heads to recreate an original position of objects, for example.

joint custody   Parental rights (custody) shared equally by mother and father.

kernicterus   Staining of the brain with bilirubin.

Kuder General Interest Survey, Form E   An instrument used to measure an individual's aptitude for various occupations.

lanugo   The covering of hair typical on newborn infants.

lateralization of the brain   The specialization of functions on one side of the brain over the other.

letter-name spelling strategy   Exploitation of the sound information found within letter names to create unconventional spellings.

lexically based ambiguity   Language ambiguity caused by double meanings for some words and by words that are pronounced the same even though they are spelled differently.

libido   Another name for sex drive.

locomotor skills   Motor skills that involve movement of the legs and feet.

longitudinal design   A research design used in developmental research in which the same group of children is studied over a period of time.

"look-say" approach to teaching reading   A teaching method that relies primarily on the teaching of sight words rather than decoding skills.

macrosystem   In Bronfenbrenner's ecological model, the broadest system influencing the child, that is, consistencies in the culture or subculture.

mainstreaming   The placement of children with special needs in classrooms with children who are not disabled.

malocclusion   Misalignment of the teeth that often is corrected by wearing braces.

marked-time climbing   The procedure of climbing in which both feet are placed on each step before one foot is placed on the next step.

maturation   Physical changes attributed to genetic control.

meiosis   Reproduction of germ cells, in which the number of chromosomes is reduced by half.

mental age   The child's level of functioning as measured by an IQ test.

metalinguistic awareness   A specific aspect of metacognition that refers to awareness of the structure and form of language.

microsystem In Bronfenbrenner's ecological model, the system experienced directly by the child, that is, family and immediate school environment.

mild mental retardation A measured IQ between 50 and 70.

mitosis Division of a body cell into two cells, each genetically identical to the original cell.

mock letters Marks used by young children to write. These marks contain features of conventional letters, but in combinations other than those that define actual alphabet letters.

modeling Term used by social learning theorists to refer to demonstrations of behavior that can be observed and repeated by others.

moderate mental retardation Measured IQ within the range of 34 to 50.

molded A characteristic of an infant's head that results from the skull being squeezed together as it passes through the birth canal.

moral realism The term used by Piaget to refer to the young child's tendency to confuse physical damage and intention in making moral judgments.

Moro reflex Movement caused by a sudden dropping back of the head or by loud noises.

morpheme The smallest unit of meaning in a language.

morphological rules Rules that govern how words can be changed to alter their meaning. Changes in verb tenses, for example, are morphological changes.

multischeme combinations Complex pretend play in which a variety of actions pertaining to a play theme are combined.

mutual role taking Term used by Selman to refer to the ability to stand back and think about your own thinking and another's thinking, all at the same time.

myelin The fatty substance that coats the outer surface of neurons and makes impulses travel efficiently.

myelination The process whereby a fatty sheath is formed on the outside of neurons.

nature-nurture controversy The debate about whether genetic inheritance or environment exerts the most influence over development.

negative reinforcer Something withdrawn from the environment following a behavior, which has the effect of increasing the frequency of that behavior in the future.

negatively correlated The relationship between two variables when an increase in one is associated with a decrease in the other.

neglected status A sociometric rating in which a child receives few like or dislike nominations from peers.

neonate An infant under one month of age.

neonatal period The period from birth up to one month

after birth.

Neurological Examination of the Full-Term Newborn Infant Assessment instrument developed by Pretchel to determine the neurological integrity of the newborn.

neurological ripening Refers to maturation of the nervous system controlled by genes.

neurons The type of cells found in the brain.

norm Age-related expectations for behavior that are established by determining when half of the children of a given age can perform the behavior.

object permanence Refers to knowing that objects out of sight still exist.

observational learning Learning by watching others.

ontogenetic Having to do with the evolution and biological development of the individual organism, often contrasted with phylogenetic, which has to do with the development of the race.

operant conditioning Changes in behavior brought about by the responses that follow specific behaviors.

operational A description of Piaget's third level of intellectual thinking in which logic—thinking processes— overrules perception.

orthography A writing system for representing an oral language.

ossification The process of mineral deposition in bones.

otitis-media Infection of the middle ear.

overextend What children do with words when they apply them outside the boundaries of accepted meaning.

overgeneralize The application of a rule of language, or of a word meaning, beyond the accepted range.

oviduct Tube connecting each ovary to the uterus, through which the egg passes and in which fertilization takes place.

palmar grasp Reflex in which the fingers fold inward toward the palm of the hand when the palm is stroked or pushed.

partitioning error A counting error that results from failure to distinguish objects that already have been counted from those still needing to be counted.

perceived competence Perceived self-efficacy.

perinatal Referring to the time period immediately after birth.

period of the embryo The time period from implantation to the eighth prenatal week.

period of the fetus The time period from the eighth prenatal week to birth.

period of the ovum The prenatal period from conception until implantation.

permissive parenting Parenting behavior marked by few expectations for and little control of child behavior.

perseveration error A mistake babies make in Piaget's Stage 4 in the course of acquiring object permanence, found when they look for a toy under the screen where the toy first disappeared even after seeing it disappear under a second screen.

phoneme The smallest unit of sound in a language.

phonemic awareness The child's conscious awareness of the individual sounds within words.

phonemic segmentation Separating the individual speech sounds within words.

phonics approach to teaching reading Teaching technique that stresses decoding skills versus sight words or prediction strategies.

phonologically based ambiguity Language ambiguity based on how things sound.

phototherapy A procedure used to reduce bilirubin in the blood of newborn infants.

pincer grasp Grasp formed by juxtaposing the thumb and forefinger.

popular status Sociometric rating in which a child receives many like nominations from peers.

positive attribution To indicate verbally to an individual the particular positive characteristics that belong to her—a socialization process that can encourage her to see herself in similar positive ways.

positively correlated The relationship between two variables when an increase in one is associated with an increase in the other or when a decrease in one is associated with a decrease in the other.

positive reinforcer Something that is added to the environment after a behavior is exhibited, which results in an increase in the behavior.

postdivorce stage of adjustment This is the final of three stages of response to a divorce in which new patterns of family living have been established in the family.

preadolescent growth spurt Rapid increase in growth, particularly in height, that occurs just prior to puberty.

predictable text Text that has a high level of rhyming words or repeated phrases, which make it easy to remember.

predictive validity The soundness with which a measure predicts later manifestations of the behavior of interest, usually expressed as the extent of correlation between the predictor measure and a measure of the later behavior of interest.

prehension Grasping with hands.

prelinguistic Refers to vocal behavior prior to the stage when real words are used.

prenatal Prior to birth.

prenatal development Development that occurs prior to birth.

preoperational thinking Piaget's second level of intellectual development, during which thinking is dominated by perception rather than logic.

preprogrammed Refers to neurological structures that are thought to be innate.

pretense Pretend play.

pretesting Data collection on variables of interest prior to a treatment.

primary rewards Things that satisfy primary drives, such as hunger or sex.

primary sex characteristics Bodily changes that are vital to preparing for reproduction versus the accompanying changes such as growth of pubic and facial hair.

profound mental retardation Extreme deficits in mental ability—measured IQ below 35.

projective space An aspect of space having to do with the point of view or the vantage point from which something is seen.

prosocial behavior Positive social behavior such as helping and sharing.

protowords Short strings of consonant-vowel combinations that sound like words.

proximodistal trend The development of muscular control that proceeds from the center of the body to the extremities, such as the hands.

pseudoimitation Repetition of a behavior that is already in the child's repertoire.

psychosocial identity A concept of self in relation to society, especially as this relates to commitment to occupation, sexuality, religion, and politics. Similar to ego identity.

pubescence The period prior to puberty—sexual maturity—marked by rapid growth and other physical changes.

punishment In operant theory, the process of decreasing the probability of a behavior by following it with a stimulus or with the removal of a stimulus.

reaction time The time it takes for the individual to process an event and make some response, such as swinging a bat at a pitched ball.

readiness Usually means a certain level of development assumed to be achieved by maturation of the nervous system.

reading readiness An outdated term that was once used to refer to levels of development thought necessary before children could learn about written language.

realist Someone who believes that knowledge is absolute and determined fully by the nature of the real world.

receptive speech The language a person can understand.

recessive Refers to a specific kind of gene whose trait is not expressed unless it is paired with a second gene of the same type.

reciprocal interaction The influence of one system on a second system, which contributes to an effect of the second on the first.

reflexes Involuntary movements elicited by specific stimuli.

regression toward the mean A statistical term that means extremes or exceptions tend not to be maintained.

reinforcement In operant conditioning, the process of increasing the probability of a behavior by following it with a stimulus or with the removal of a stimulus.

relativist Someone who believes that knowledge is relative, or related to the mind of the particular observer.

reliable Consistent or stable across different measurements of the behavior of interest, usually expressed as the extent of correlation between repeated measurements of the behavior of interest or the extent of correlation between the measurements of different observers.

representational thinking The ability to think using symbols rather than having to think through sensorimotor actions.

research bias The influence on a study's results that comes from the researcher's views, not from the data.

response cost Refers to punishment using the removal of rewards.

reversals Letters written in mirror image or upside-down, which are frequently characteristic of the writing of preschool and young elementary-age children.

reversibility The characteristic of thinking that allows one to replay an action in his or her mind.

risk factor Some characteristic of a group that increases its members' chances of having developmental problems.

rooting reflex The movement involving turning of the head and searching with the mouth, following stroking of the cheek.

sample A relatively small number of people who are chosen as representative of a larger population.

scheme Term used by Piaget to refer to an organized pattern of behavior.

Scholastic Aptitude Tests A commonly used college entrance examination developed by the College Entrance Examination Board.

School and College Ability Tests The publisher of the SAT tests, which are frequently used as part of the application package for college admissions.

scope of a theory The range of areas and issues addressed by a theory.

scribble writing Wavy lines or tight bunches of lines that capture the linear nature of print but lack specific alphabet letters.

secondary rewards Something that is present when a primary reinforcer satisfies a primary need, such that in time it, too, becomes a reinforcer.

secondary sex characteristics Physical changes that are not directly related to reproductive capacity.

secular growth trend The trend toward increases in height with each succeeding generation.

secure attachment The pattern of behaviors thought to characterize the optimal relationship between adult and child.

self-efficacy belief The belief that one is effective in, or capable of, controlling the events that affect one's life; same as perceived self-efficacy.

self-reflective role taking Selman's description of his Stage 2 in which children can think about their own thoughts or another's thoughts, but not simultaneously.

semantic cues used in reading Reliance on the meaning of words to predict and monitor one's reading.

sensorimotor period Piaget's first period of intellectual development, which lasts from birth up to about 24 months of age.

separation distress Upset state resulting when an infant's primary caregiver leaves.

sequential design A research design that combines the study of different age groups and the same age groups over a period of time to determine developmental differences.

seriation The ability to place items in order according to size.

severe mental retardation A term used in educational circles to refer to profound retardation.

sex differences Differences in personality, cognition, and social behavior that have been found to be related to gender.

sex-linked characteristics Inherited characteristics due to genes carried on the X or Y chromosome.

sex-role stereotypes Specific social behavior and statuses assigned and assumed on the basis of gender.

sex roles Sets of social and occupational behaviors commonly found more often in members of one sex than in members of the opposite sex.

sexually transmitted diseases (STDs) Diseases transmitted through sexual intercourse or other sexual behavior.

shaping The technique of using rewards to gradually develop a desired behavior.

shared meaning An understanding between toddlers about the social game they're playing.

single-scheme combinations A type of pretend play in which the child confines actions to a single idea, such as feeding a baby.

size constancy Seeing an object's real size as unchanging in spite of changes in the size of the image on the retina as the distance of the object varies.

skills approach to the teaching of reading Any of the approaches that focus on identifying words specifically versus relying on context or language to predict.

small-for-date baby A baby who is full term but who, for nutritional or other reasons, hasn't attained a normal birth weight.

social cognition Thinking about social phenomena.

social games Repetitive actions involving two children or an adult and child.

social information role taking Selman's stage in which

children realize that they see a situation differently than someone else but assume the different views are due to differing information.

social learning theory A branch of behavioral theory that stresses observational learning.

social referencing The use of adult facial expressions by infants to make judgments about the safety of new situations or people.

social role-taking ability The ability to think about what another person is thinking or to understand what another person is feeling.

social smile Smile elicited by social stimuli.

socialization The processes by which children learn to behave according to social expectations and standards.

sociodramatic play A type of pretend play involving several children who adopt different roles.

somatic cells All cells in the body except those involved in reproduction.

sphincters Circular muscles that control the opening of the bladder and anus, for example.

Stanford-Binet Intelligence Scale One of the most frequently used, individually administered, standard intelligence tests for children.

stranger anxiety Distress shown by infants, beginning around 6 months of age, around unfamiliar adults.

Strong-Campbell Interest Inventory A measurement tool that is commonly used to determine an individual's likes and dislikes as they might relate to different occupations.

sucking reflex The expression-suction motion that is elicited in an infant when the roof of the mouth is stroked or pressed.

superego The part of the personality thought by Freud to serve as the conscience to control impulses of the id.

suprasegmental features of language Features having to do with intonation and stress.

surfactant Substance in the lungs that prevents collapse after a breath is exhaled, the absence of which creates problems in premature infants.

syllabic hypothesis A hypothesis entertained by young children when they write words by using one mark for every "beat," or syllable, contained within a word.

symbolic representation Thinking by manipulating ideas or images in one's head.

syntactic cues used in reading Cues that come from the reader's knowledge of the grammar of his or her language.

syntactically based ambiguity Language ambiguity derived from the different ways a sentence can be interpreted.

syntax Refers to the basic rules in a language that govern the grammatical organization of sentences.

system Groups of elements that have similar rules for relating to other elements within that system—rules that differ from the rules for relating to entities outside that system.

tags Term used to refer to number words used in counting.

tagging errors Among the first counting errors made by preschoolers in which unconventional labels (e.g., a, b, c) are used, or conventional tags (labels) are used in nonstandard order (e.g., one, two, five, ten)

target The term used to indicate the thing, person, or situation that elicits a feeling from an individual.

teacher-directed education An approach in which children are given little leeway to make decisions or follow their interests.

telegraphic speech A characteristic of toddler speech that refers to the presence of only those words necessary for getting the message across.

teratogens Chemicals or other agents, such as irradiation, that cause defects in the developing fetus.

theme Refers to the content of a play episode—what the playing is about.

theory Sets of hypotheses used to explain phenomena.

time out A form of punishment in which the individual is removed from situations in which rewards prevail.

tonic neck reflex A reflex exhibited in infants in which the leg and arm on the side of the body the head faces are extended, while the leg and arm on the other side are flexed.

tonus Muscle tension.

tracking An educational term that refers to the practice of placing students of similar achievement and ability levels together for instruction.

trainable mentally retarded A description used by educators to refer to moderately retarded individuals.

transitional stage of adjustment to divorce The middle period between the first adjustment to the divorce and a later period of settling into new patterns of family relationships.

triarchic theory of intelligence Robert Sternberg's theory of human intelligence, a theory made up of componential, contextual, and experiential subtheories.

trophoblast That part of the developing mass of cells formed from the zygote that will become the tissues that support a developing fetus.

ultrasound Sound waves moving so fast that they can't be heard. The sound waves that are transformed into images to visualize a baby in utero.

unconditioned response A response that naturally follows a specific stimulus.

unconditioned stimulus A stimulus that naturally leads to a given response.

underextend What children do when they don't apply a word as broadly as the word's meaning actually allows.

unique grammatical structures theory A theory of second language acquisition in which it is assumed that the learner doesn't apply knowledge from his first language and doesn't approach it the way a first language learner would either.

unpopular status   A sociometric category for individuals who receive many dislike nominations from peers—they are rejected by peers.

valence   Used by researchers who study emotions to refer to positive or negative emotions.

validity   The extent to which instruments measure what they are intended to measure.

variable   Something that is changed or changes to take on a different value or form.

varicella vaccine   A vaccine developed to prevent the viral infection known as chicken pox.

vernix caseosa   The greasy white covering common on newborns that lubricates their skin and protects them from infection.

Wechsler Adult Intelligence Scale—Revised   The most widely used, individually administered intelligence test used with individuals 17 years and older in the United States.

Wechsler Intelligence Scale for Children   A well-known intelligence test.

whole language approach to the teaching of reading   An approach that stresses the use of context and language knowledge more than decoding strategies that focus on individual words.

zygote   The cell that results when an ovum is fertilized by a sperm.

REFERENCES

AAUW Educational Foundation and the Wellesley College Center for Research on Women (1992). *How schools shortchange girls*. Washington, DC: AAUW Educational Foundation and National Education Association.

Abbey, A., Oliansky, D., Stilianos, K., Hohlstein, L. A., & Kaczynski, R. (1990). Substance abuse prevention for second graders: Are they too young to benefit? *Journal of Applied Developmental Psychology, 11*, 149–162.

Acredolo, L. P. (1978). Development of spatial orientation in infancy. *Developmental Psychology, 14*, 224–234.

Adams, M. J. (1990). *Beginning to read: Thinking and learning about print*. Cambridge: MIT Press.

Adelson, J. (1975). The development of ideology in adolescence. In S. E. Dragastin & G. H. Elder (Eds.), *Adolescence in the life cycle*. Washington, DC: Hemisphere.

Adler, N. E., Kegeles, S. M., Irwin, C. E., & Wibbelsman, C. (1990). Adolescent contraceptive behavior: An assessment of decision processes. *Journal of Pediatrics, 116*, 463–471.

Ahrend, R. (1984). *Preschoolers' competence in a barrier situation: Patterns of adaptation and their precursors in infancy*. Doctoral dissertation. University of Minnesota.

Aiken, L. R. (1982). Writing multiple-choice items to measure higher-order educational objectives. *Educational and Psychological Measurement, 42*, 803–806.

———. (1985). Review of ACT Assessment Program. In J. V. Mitchell (Ed.), *The ninth mental measurement yearbook*. Lincoln, NB: University of Nebraska Press.

Ainsworth, M. D. S., & Bell, S. M. (1973). Mother-infant interaction and the development of competence. In K. Connolly & J. Bruner (Eds.), *The growth of competence*. New York: Academic Press.

Ainsworth, M. D. S., Blehar, M. D., Waters, E., & Wall, S. (1978). *Patterns of attachment*. Hillsdale, NJ: Lawrence Erlbaum.

Akhtar, N., Dunham, F., & Dunham, P. J. (1991). Directive interactions and early vocabulary development: The role of joint attentional focus. *Journal of Child Language, 18*, 41–49.

Aleksandrowicz, M. K., & Aleksandrowicz, D. R. (1974). Obstetrical pain-relieving drugs as predictors of infant behavior variability. *Child Development, 45*, 935–958.

Als, H. (1977). The newborn communicates. *Journal of Communication, 27*(2), 66–73.

AMA Council on Scientific Affairs. (1981). Marijuana: Its health hazards and therapeutic potentials. *Journal of the American Medical Association, 246*, 1823–1877.

American College Testing Program. (1984). *Counselor's handbook*. Iowa City, IA: American College Testing Program.

American Psychiatric Association. (1987). *Diagnostics and statistical manual of mental disorders*. (3d ed. rev'd). Washington, DC.

Ames, L. B. (1937). The sequential patterning of prone progression in the human infant. *Genetic Psychology Monographs, 19*, 409–460.

Ammerman, R. T., & Hersen, M. (1990). *Children at risk: An evaluation of factors contributing to child abuse and neglect*. New York: Plenum Press.

Anatasi, A. (1958). Heredity, environment, and the question "How?" *Psychological Review, 65*, 197–208.

Anbar, A. (1986). Reading acquisition of preschool children without systematic instruction. *Reading Research Quarterly, 1* (1), 69–84.

Anderson, D. R., Field, D. E., Collins, P. A., Lorch, E. P., & Nathan, J. C. (1985). Estimates of young children's time with television: A methodological comparison of parent reports with time-lapse video home observation. *Child Development, 56*, 1345–1357.

Angrist, S. S. (1969). The study of sex roles. *Journal of Social Issues, 25*, 215–232.

Anisfeld, E. (1982). The onset of social smiling in preterm and full-term infants from two ethnic backgrounds. *Infant Behavior and Development, 5*, 387–395.

Anisfeld, E., Casper, V., Nozyce, M., & Cunningham, N. (1990). *Child Development, 61*(5), 1617–1627.

APA Task Force on Pediatric AIDS. (1989). Pediatric AIDS and human immunodeficiency virus infection: Psychological issues. *American Psychologist, 44*(2), 258–264.

Apgar, V. (1953). Proposal for a new method of evaluating the newborn infant. *Anesthesia and Analgesia, 52*, 260–267.

Apgar, V., Holaday, D., James, L., Neisbrot, I., & Berrien, C. (1958). Evaluation of the newborn infant: Second report. *Journal of the American Medical Association, 168*, 1985–1988.

Appel, M., & Campos, J. J. (1977). Binocular disparity as a discriminable stimulus parameter for young infants. *Journal of Experimental Child Psychology, 23*, 47–56.

Applebee, A. N., Langer, J. A., & Mullis, V. S. (1986). *The writing report card: Writing achievement in American schools*. Princeton, NJ: Educational Testing Service.

Archer, J., & Lloyd, B. (1982). *Sex and gender*. New York: Cambridge University Press.

Archer, J., & Lopata, A. (1979). Marijuana revisited. *Personnel and Guidance Journal, 51*, 244–250.

Ariagno, R. L. (1984). Evaluation and management of infantile apnea. *Pediatric Annals, 13* (3), 210–211.

Arnett, J. (1990). Contraceptive use, sensation seeking, and adolescent egocentrism. *Journal of Youth and Adolescence, 19*(2), 171–180.

Aro, H., & Taipale, V. (1987). The impact of timing of puberty on psychosomatic symptoms among fourteen-to-sixteen-year-old Finnish girls. *Child Development, 58*(1), 261–268.

Asher, S. R., & Coie, J. (1990). *Peer rejection in childhood.* New York: Cambridge University Press.

Asher, S. R., & Dodge, K. A. (1986). Identifying children who are rejected by their peers. *Developmental Psychology, 22*(4), 444–449.

Astington, J. W., Harris, P. L., & Olson, D. (Eds.). (1988). *Developing theories of mind.* New York: Cambridge University Press.

Attel, I., & Brooks-Gunn, J. (1988). Development of eating problems in adolescent girls: A longitudinal study. *Developmental Psychology, 25*(1), 70–79.

Austin, A., Berghow, A., & Lindauer, S. L. (1990). Parent-child conversation of more-liked and less-liked children. *Journal of Genetic Psychology, 15*, 5–27.

Austin, A., & Braeger, T. J. (1990). Gendered differences in parents' encouragement of sibling interaction: Implications for the construction of a personal premise system. *First Language, 10*, 181–197.

Bagley, C., & King, K. (1990). *Child sexual abuse: The search for healing.* New York: Tavistock/Routledge.

Bailey, S. L., & Hubbard, R. L. (1991). Developmental changes in peer factors and the influence on marijuana initiation among secondary school students. *Journal of Youth and Adolesence, 20*(3), 339–360.

Bailey, S. M. (Ed.). (1986). When school is out and nobody's home. *Research Report* (Wellesley College Center for Research on Women, Wellesley, MA), 5(2), 1.

Bailey, W. J. (1985). Ten smoking education programs for schools. *Journal of School Health, 55*(1), 33–34.

Baillargeon, R. (1987). Letter to the Editor. *Cognition, 26*, 189–190.

Baillargeon, R., Spelke, E. S., & Wasserman, S. (1985). Object permanence in five-month-old infants. *Cognition, 20*, 191–208.

Baker, D. P. & Entwisle, D. R. (1986). The influence of mothers on the academic expectations of young children: A longitudinal study of how gender differences arise. *Social Forces, 65*, 670–694.

Baldwin, S. E., & Baranoski, M. V. (1990). Family interactions and sex education in the home. *Adolescence, 25*, 573–582.

Ball, E. W., & Blachman, B. A. (1991). Does phoneme awareness training in kindergarten make a difference in early word recognition and developmental spelling? *Reading Research Quarterly, 26*(1), 49–66.

Bamford, F. N., Bannister, R. P., Benjamin, C. M., Hillier, V. F., Ward, B. S., & Moore, W. M. O. (1990). Sleep in the first year of life. *Developmental Medicine and Child Neurology, 32*, 718–724.

Bandura, A. (1973). *Aggression: A social learning analysis.* Englewood Cliffs, NJ: Prentice-Hall.

———. (1977). *Social learning theory.* Englewood Cliffs, NJ: Prentice-Hall.

———. (1986). *Social foundations of thought and action: A social cognitive theory.* Englewood Cliffs, NJ: Prentice-Hall.

———. (1989). Human agency in social cognitive theory. *American Psychologist, 44*, 1175–1184.

———. (1991). Social cognitive theory of moral thought and action. In W. Kurtines & J. Gewirtz (Eds.), *Handbook of moral behavior and development: Vol. 1. Theory.* (45–104). Hillsdale, NJ: Lawrence Erlbaum Associates.

Bandura, A., & Walters, R. (1963). *Social learning and personality development.* New York: Holt, Reinhart & Winston.

Banks, M. S. (1980). The development of early infancy. *Child Development, 51*, 646–666.

Banks, M. S., & Salapatek, P. (1976). Contrast sensitivity function of the infant visual system. *Vision Research, 16*, 867–869.

———. (1983). Infant visual perception. In P. Mussen (Ed.), *Handbook of child psychology: Vol. 2. Infancy and developmental psychobiology* (4th ed., pp. 435–571). New York: Wiley.

Barabas, G., & Taft, L. T. (1986). The early signs and differential diagnosis of cerebral palsy. *Pediatric Annals, 15*(3), 203–214.

Barcus, E. F., & McLaughlin, L. (1978). *Food advertising on children's television: An analysis of appeals and nutritional content.* Newtonville, MA: Action of Children's Television.

Barden, R. C., Zelko, F. A., Duncan, S. W., & Masters, J. C. (1980). Children's consensual knowledge about the experiential determinants of emotion. *Journal of Personality and Social Psychology, 39*, 968–976.

Barnes, F., & Hassid, P. (1985, Fall). Bradley/Lamaze. *Childbirth Educator,* Special Issue, 40–47.

Baroody, A. (1987). *Children's mathematical thinking.* New York: Teachers College Press.

Barr, R. G., McMullan, S. J., Heinz, S., Leduc, D. G., Yaremko, J., Barfield, R., Francoeur, E., & Hunziker, U. A. (1991). *Pediatrics, 87*(5), 623–630.

Bass, E., & Davis, L. (1988). *The courage to heal: A guide for women survivors of child sexual abuse.* New York: Harper & Row.

Bates, E. (1979). *The emergence of symbols.* New York: Academic Press.

Batten, S., Hirschman, J., & Thomas, D. (1990). Impact of the special supplemental food program on infants. *The Journal of Pediatrics, 117*(2), S101–S109.

Baumeister, A. A. (1987). Mental retardation. *American Psychologist, 42*(8), 796–800.

Baumrind, D. (1971). Current patterns of parental authority. *Developmental Psychology Monographs, 4*(1), 72.

———. (1972). Socialization and instrumental competence in young children. In W. W. Hartup (Ed.), *The young child: Reviews of research* (Vol. 2, pp. 202–274). Washington, DC: The National Association for the Education of Young Children.

———. (1984). Rearing competent children. In W. Damon (Ed.), *Child development today and tomorrow.* San Francisco: Jossey-Bass.

———. (1991). The influence of parenting style on adolescent competence and substance use. *Journal of Early Adolescence, 11*(1), 56–95.

Baumrind, D., & Block, A. E. (1967). Socialization and practices associated with dimensions of competence in pre-school boys and girls. *Child Development, 38,* 291–329.

Bayley, N. (1969). *Bayley scales of infant development: Manual.* New York: The Psychological Corporation.

Beaty, J. J. (1986). *Observing the development of the young child.* Columbus, OH: Merrill.

Beck, A. T., Rush, A. J., Shaw, B., & Emery, G. (1979). *Cognitive therapy of depression.* New York: The Guilford Press.

Bee, H. (1978). Overview: Sex differences. In H. Bee (Ed.), *Social issues in developmental psychology* (2d ed.). New York: Harper & Row.

Bell, D. C., & Bell, L. G. (1983). Parental validation and support in the development of adolescent daughters. In H. D. Grotevant and C. R. Cooper (Eds.), *Adolescent development in the family.* San Francisco: Jossey-Bass.

Bell, T. W. (1971). Stimulus control of parent or caretaker behavior by offspring. *Developmental Psychology, 4,* 63–72.

Bellinger, D., Sioman, J., Leviton, A., Rabinowitz, M., Needleman, H. L., & Waternaux, C. (1991). Low-level lead exposure and children's cognitive function in the preschool years. *Pediatrics, 87*(2), 219–226.

Belmont, J. M., & Butterfield, E. C. (1977). Learning strategies as determinants of memory deficiencies. *Cognitive Psychology, 2,* 411–420.

Belsky, J. (1980). Child maltreatment: An ecological integration. *American Psychologist, 35,* 320–335.

———. (1984). The determinants of parenting: A process model. *Child Development, 55,* 83–96.

———. (1988). The effects of infant day care, reconsidered. *Early Childhood Research Quarterly, 3*(3), 235–272.

Belsky, J., & Nezworski, T. (Eds.) (1988). *Clinical implications of attachment.* Hillsdale, NJ: Lawrence Erlbaum Associates.

Belsky, J., & Vondra, J. (1989). Lessons from child abuse: The determinants of parenting. In D. Cicchetti & V. Carlson (Eds.), *Child maltreatment: Theory and research on the causes and consequences of child abuse and neglect.* New York: Cambridge University Press.

Beltramini, A. V., & Hertzig, M. E. (1983). Sleep and bedtime behavior in preschool-aged children. *Pediatrics, 71*(2), 153–158.

Bennett, W. J. (1987a). *James Madison High School.* Pueblo, CO: U. S. Government Printing Office.

———. (1987b). *What works? Schools without drugs.* Washington, DC: U. S. Department of Education.

Berger, M. J., & Goldstein, D. P. (1980). Impaired reproductive performance in DES-exposed women. *Obstetrics and Gynecology, 55,* 25–27.

Berkowitz, L., & LePage, A. (1967). Weapons as aggression—eliciting stimuli. *Journal of Personality and Social Psychology, 1,* 202–207.

Berkowitz, R. L., Agras, W. St., Korner, A. F., Kraemer, H. C., & Zeanah, C. H. (1985). Physical activity and adiposity: A longitudinal study from birth to childhood. *Journal of Pediatrics, 106*(5), 734–738.

Berryman, C., & Schneider, D. (1982). *Patterns of work experience among high school students: Educational implications.* Paper presented at the Annual Meeting of the National Council for the Social Studies, Boston, MA.

Berzonsky, M. (1988). Self-theorists, identity status, and social cognition. In D. Lapsley & F. C. Power (Eds.), *Self, ego, and identity: Integrative approaches* (pp. 243–262). New York: Springer-Verlag.

Bever, T. G. (1970). The cognitive basis for linguistic structures. In J. R. Hayes (Ed.), *Cognition and the development of language.* New York: Wiley.

Bigler, R., & Liben, L. (1990). The role of attitudes and interventions in gender-schematic processing. *Child Development, 61,* 1440–1452.

Binet, A., & Simon, T. (1905). Methodes nouvelles pour le diagnostic du niveau intellectual des anormous [New methods for diagnosing children's intellectual development]. *L'Année Psychologique, 11,* 191–244.

Binion, V. (1990). Psychological androgeny: A black female perspective. *Sex Roles, 22,* 487–507.

Black, B. (1989). Interactive pretense: Social and symbolic skills in preschool play groups. *Merrill-Palmer Quarterly, 35,* 379–397.

Blasi, A. (1988). Identity and the development of the self. In D. Lapsley & F. C. Power (Eds.), *Self, ego and identity: Integrative approaches.* NY: Springer-Verlag.

———. (1984). Moral identity: It's role in moral functioning. In W. Kurtines & J. Gewirtz (Eds.), *Morality, moral behavior, and moral development.* New York: Wiley.

Blass, E. M., Ganchrow, J. R., & Steiner, J. E. (1984). Classical conditioning in newborn humans 2–48 hours of age. *Infant Behavior and Development, 7,* 223–235.

Blehar, M. C. (1974). Anxious attachment and defensive reactions associated with day care. *Child Development, 45,* 683–692.

Block, J. H. (1973). Conceptions of sex role: Some cross-cultural and longitudinal perspectives. *American Psychologist, 28,* 512–576.

Bloom, B. S. (1984). Changing infant mortality: The need to spend more while getting less. *Pediatrics, 73*(6), 862–865.

Bloom, L., Lightbown, P., & Hood, L. (1975). Imitation in language development. *Monographs of the Society for Research in Child Development, 40* (Serial No. 160).

Blume, J. (1970). *Are you there God? It's me, Margaret* (p. 100). New York: Bradbury Press.

Blumenthal, S. J., & Kupfer, D. J. (1988). Overview of early detection and treatment strategies for suicidal behavior in young people. *Journal of Youth and Adolescence, 17*(1), 1–17.

Bodner, B., Benjamin, A., McLean, F. H., & Usher, R. H. (1986). Has use of cesarean section reduced the risks of delivery in the preterm breech presentation? *American Journal of Obstetrics and Gynecology, 154*(2), 244–249.

Bohlin, G., Hagekull, B., Germer, M., Anderson, K., & Lindberg, L. (1989). Avoidant and resistant reunion behaviors as predicted by maternal interactive behavior and infant temperament. *Infant Behavior and Development, 12,* 105–117.

Bonica, J. J. (1967). *Principles and practices of obstetric analgesia and anesthesia.* (Vol. 1). Philadelphia: Davis.

Borke, H. (1971). Interpersonal perception of young children:

Egocentrism or empathy? *Developmental Psychology, 5,* 263–269.

Bornstein, M. H. (1989). Information processing (habituation) in infancy and stability in cognitive development. *Human Development, 32,* 129–136.

Bornstein, M. H., & Lamb, M. E. (Eds.) (1988). *Developmental psychology: An advanced textbook* (2d ed.). Hillsdale, NJ: Lawrence Erlbaum.

Bornstein, M., & Sigman, M. (1986). Continuity in mental development from infancy. *Child Development, 57*(2), 251–274.

Bower, T. G. R. (1974). *Development in infancy.* San Francisco: W. H. Freeman.

———. (1977). *A primer of infant development.* San Francisco: W. H. Freeman.

Bowlby, J. (1969b). *Attachment and loss: Vol. 1, Attachment.* London: Hogarth.

———. (1988). *A secure base: Parent-child attachment and healthy human development.* New York: Basic Books.

Bowman, C. M., & Peng, S. S. (1972). *A preliminary investigation of recent advanced psychology tests in the GRE program—an application of a cognitive classification system.* Unpublished ETS report, Princeton, NJ.

Brackbill, Y., Kane, J., Manniello, R. L., & Abramson, D. (1974). Obstetric premedication and infant outcome. *American Journal of Obstetrics and Gynecology, 118,* 377–384.

Bradley, R. H., Caldwell, B. M., & Rock, S. L. (1988). Home environment and school performance: A ten-year follow-up and examination of three models of environmental action. *Child Development, 59*(1), 852–867.

Brainerd, C. J. (1978). *Piaget's theory of intelligence.* Englewood Cliffs, NJ: Prentice–Hall.

Branigan, G., & Stokes, W. (1976). Introduction: A sketch of language development. *Journal of Education, 158,* 4–11.

Brazelton, T. B. (1961). Psychophysiologic reactions in the neonate. *The Journal of Pediatrics, 58,* 513–518.

———. (1969). *Infants and mothers.* New York: Delacorte/Seymour Lawrence.

———. (1970). Effects of prenatal drugs on the behavior of the neonate. *American Journal of Psychiatry, 126,* 95–100.

———. (1973a). *Neonatal assessment scale.* Philadelphia: J. B. Lippincott.

———. (1973b). *Neonatal behavioral assessment scale.* London: Heinemann.

———. (1984). *Neonatal behavioral assessment scale* (2d ed.). Philadelphia: J. B. Lippincott.

Brazy, J. E. (1988). Effects of crying on cerebral blood volume and cytochrome aa3. *Journal of Pediatrics, 112*(3), 457–461.

Brehm, S. S. (1981). Oppositional behavior in children: A reactance theory approach. In S. S. Brehm, S. M. Kassin, & F. X. Gibbons (Eds.), *Developmental social psychology theory* (pp. 96–121). New York: Oxford University Press.

Brennan, W. M., Ames, E. W., & Moore, R. W. (1966). Age differences in infants' attention to patterns of different complexities. *Science, 151,* 354–356.

Brenner, J., & Mueller, E. (1982). Shared meaning in boy toddlers' peer relations. *Child Development, 53*(2), 380–391.

Bretherton, I. (1984). Representing the social world in symbolic play: Reality and fantasy. In I. Bretherton (Ed.), *Symbolic play* (pp. 3–41). New York: Academic Press.

Bretherton, I., Fritz, J., Zahn-Waxler, C., & Ridgeway, D. (1986). Learning to talk about emotions: A functionalist perspective. *Child Development, 57,* 529–548.

Briere, J., & Runtz, M. (1990). Differential adult symptomatology associated with three types of child abuse histories. *Child Abuse and Neglect, 14,* 357–364.

Briggs, C., & Elkind, D. (1977). Characteristics of early readers. *Perceptual and Motor Skills, 44,* 1231–1237.

Brigitte, J. (1980). *Birth in four cultures.* Montreal, Canada: Eden Press.

Brittain, C. (1963). Adolescent choice and parent-peer cross-pressures. *American Sociological Review, 28,* 385–391.

Brockman, L. M., Ricciuti, H. N. (1971). Severe protein-calorie malnutrition and cognitive development in infancy and early childhood. *Developmental Psychology, 4,* 312–319.

Brody, E. B., & Brody, N. (Eds.) (1976). *Intelligence: Nature, determinants, and consequences.* New York: Academic Press.

Bronfenbrenner, U. (1977). Toward an experimental ecology of human development. *American Psychologist, 32,* 513–531.

———. (1979). *The ecology of human development: Experiments by nature and design.* Cambridge: Harvard University Press.

———. (1989). Ecological systems theory. In R. Vasta (Ed.), *Annals of child development. Vol. 6.* London: Kingsley.

Bronson, G. (1990a). The accurate calibration of infant's scanning records. *Journal of Experimental Child Psychology, 49,* 79–100.

———. (1990b). Changes in infants' visual scanning across the 2- to 14-week period. *Journal of Experimental Child Psychology, 49,* 101–125.

Bronson, W. (1981). *Toddlers' behaviors with agemates: Issues of interaction, cognition and affect.* Norwood, NJ: Ablex.

Bronstein, P. (1984). Differences in mothers' and fathers' behaviors toward children: A cross-cultural comparison. *Developmental Psychology, 20*(6), 995–1003.

Brook, C. G. B., Huntley, R. M. C., & Slack, J. (1975). Influences of heredity and environments in determination of skinfold thickness in children. *British Medical Journal, 2,* 719–721.

Brookhart, J., & Hock, E. (1976). The effects of experimental context and experiential background on infants' behavior toward their mothers and a stranger. *Child Development, 47,* 333–340.

Brookmeyer, R. (1991). Reconstruction and future trends of the AIDS epidemic in the United States. *Science, 253,* 37–41.

Brooks-Gunn, J., Boyer, C. B., & Hein, K. (1988). Preventing HIV infection and AIDS in children and adolescents:

Behavioral research and intervention strategies. *American Psychologist, 43*(11), 958–964.

Brooks-Gunn, J., & Furstenberg, F. F. (1989). Adolescent sexual behavior. *American Psychologist, 4*(2), 249–257.

Brown, A. L., & Day, J. D. (1983). Macrorules for summarizing texts: The development of expertise. *Journal of Verbal Learning and Verbal Behavior, 22,* 1–14.

Brown, A. L., & Smiley, S. S. (1977). Rating the importance of structural units of prose passages: A problem of metacognitive development. *Child Development, 48,* 1–8; 1088–1096.

———. (1978). The development of strategies for studying texts. *Child Development, 49,* 1076–1088.

Brown, J. V., & Bateman, R. (1978). Relationships of human mothers with their infants during the first year of life: Effects of prematurity. In R. W. Bell & W. P. Smotherman (Eds.), *Maternal influences and early behavior.* Holliswood, NY: Spectrum.

Brown, L. K., DiClemente, R. J., & Reynolds, L. A. (1991). Commentary: HIV prevention for adolescents: Utility of the health belief model. *AIDS Education and Prevention, 3*(1), 50–59.

Brown, R. (1973). *A first language.* Cambridge, MA: Harvard University Press.

Brown, R., Cazden, C. B., & Bellugi, U. (1969). The child's grammar from I to III. *Minnesota Symposium on Child Psychology. Vol. 2.* Minneapolis: University of Minnesota Press.

Brown, R., & Fraser, C. (1964). The acquisition of syntax. In U. Bellugi & R. Brown (Eds.), The Acquisition of Language. *Monographs of the Society for Research in Child Development, 29,* 43–79.

Brown, R., & Hanlon, C. (1970). Derivational complexity and order of acquisition in child speech. In J. R. Hayes (Ed.), *Cognition and the development of language.* New York: Wiley.

Brown, A., & Kane, M. (1988). Preschool children can learn to transfer: Learning to learn and learning by example. *Cognitive Psychology, 20,* 493–523.

Brown, R. H. (1980). Marital discord and divorce. In S. B. Friedman & R. A. Hockelman (Eds.), *Behavioral pediatrics: Psychosocial aspects of child health care* (pp. 255–258). New York: McGraw-Hill.

Brown, W. A. (1979). *Psychological care during pregnancy and the postpartum period.* New York: Raven.

Brownell, K. D., Kelman, J. H., & Stunkard, A. J. (1983). Treatment of obese children with and without their mothers. Changes in weight and blood pressure. *Pediatrics, 71,* 515–523.

Brunell, P. A., Novelli, V. M., Lipton, S. V., & Pollock, B. (1988). Combined vaccine against measles, mumps, rubella, and varicella. *Pediatrics, 81*(6), 779–789.

Buchanan, C. M. (1991). Pubertal status in early-adolescent girls: Relations to moods, energy, and restlessness. *Journal of Early Adolescence, 11*(2), 185–200.

Buckley, N., Siegel, L. S., & Ness, S. (1979). Egocentrism, empathy, and altruistic behavior in young children. *Developmental Psychology, 15,* 329–330.

Bumpers, D. (1984). Securing the blessings of liberty for posterity: Preventive health care for children. *American Psychologist, 39*(8), 896–900.

Buss, A., & Plomin, R. (1987). Commentary. In H. Goldsmith, A. Buss, R. Plomin, M. Rothbart, A. Thomas, S. Chess, R. Hinde, & R. McCall (Eds.), Roundtable: What is temperament? Four approaches. *Child Development, 58,* 505–529.

Butarescu, G. F. (1978). *Perinatal nursing: Vol. 1. Reproductive health.* New York: Wiley.

Butler, D. (1979). *Cushla and her books.* Boston: The Horn Book.

Butler, R. A. (1953). Discrimination learning by rhesus monkeys to visual exploration motivation. *Journal of Comparative Physiological Psychology, 46,* 95–98.

Caesareans up. (1987, November 3). *San Jose Mercury News,* pp. 1, 16A.

Cahan, E. D. (1989). *Past caring: A history of U. S. preschool care and education for the poor, 1820–1965.* New York: Columbia University, National Center for Children in Poverty.

Caldwell, B. M. (1970). *Preschool inventory.* Princeton, NJ: Educational Testing Service.

———. (1984). What is quality child care? *Young Children, 39*(3), 3–8.

Calvert, S. L., & Wright, J. C. (1982). *Relation of age, sex, and SES to children's patterns of home television viewing.* Paper presented at the Biennial Meeting of the Southwestern Society for the Research in Human Development, Galveston, TX.

Campbell, A. V. (1984). Ethical issues in prenatal diagnosis. *British Medical Journal, 288,* 1633–1634.

Campos, J. J., Barret, K. C., Lamb, M. E., Goldsmith, H. H., & Stenberg, C. (1983). Socioemotional development. In Paul H. Mussen (Ed.), *Handbook of child psychology* (4th ed.). New York: Wiley.

Campos, J. J., Hiatt, S., Ramsay, D., Henderson, C., & Svejda, M. (1978). The emergence of fear on the visual cliff. In M. Lewis & L. Rosenblum (Eds.), *The development of affect,* (pp. 149–182). New York: Plenum Press.

Caplan, F. (1978). *The first 12 months of life.* New York: Bantam.

Cara, J. F., & Johanson, A. J. (1990). Growth hormone for short stature not due to classic growth hormone deficiency. *Pediatric Clinics of North America, 37*(6), 1229–1254.

Carlson, K., & Cunningham, J. L. (1990). Effect of pencil diameter on the graphomotor skill of preschoolers. *Early Childhood Research Quarterly, 5*(2), 279–293.

Carlson, V., Barnett, D., Cicchetti, D., & Braunwald, K. (1989). Disorganized/disoriented attachment relationships in maltreated infants. *Developmental Psychology, 25*(4), 525–531.

Carlsson, S. G., Fagerberg, H., Horneman, G., Hwange, C. P., Larsson, K., Rodgab, M., Schaller, J., Danielsson, B., &

Gundewall, C. (1978). Effects of amount of contact between mother and child on the mother's nursing behavior. *Developmental Psychology, 11*, 143–150.

Carr, M., Borkowski, J. G., & Maxwell, S. E. (1991). Motivational components of underachievement. *Developmental Psychology, 27*(1), 108–118.

Carter, A. (1975). The transformation of sensorimotor morphemes into words: A case study of the development of "more" and "mine." *Journal of Child Language, 2*, 233–250.

Cashore, W. J., & Stern, L. (1982). Neonatal hyperbilirubinemia. *Pediatric Clinics of North America, 29*(5), 1191–1203.

Caspi, A., Bem, D. J., & Elder, G. H. (1987). Moving against the world: Life-course patterns of explosive children. *Developmental Psychology, 23*(2), 308–313.

Cavior, N., & Dokecki, P. R. (1973). Physical attractiveness, perceived attitude similarity, and academic achievement as contributors to interpersonal attractiveness among adolescents. *Developmental Psychology, 9*, 44–54.

Cazden, C. (1972). Language development and the preschool environment. In C. Cazden (Ed.), *Language in early childhood education*. Washington, DC: National Association for the Education of Young Children.

———. (1987, October). *The dangerous myths of decontextualization and autonomous texts*. Paper presented at the Twelfth Annual Boston University Conference on Language Development, Boston. (11).

Centers for Disease Control (1992). *HIV/AIDS surveillance report*. Atlanta, GA: CDC.

Cernoch, J., & Porter, R. H. (1985). Recognition of maternal axillary odors by infants. *Child Development, 56*(6), 1593–1598.

Chandler, M. (1987). The Othello effect: Essay on the emergence and eclipse of skeptical doubt. *Human Development, 30*, 137–159.

———. (1988). Doubt and developing theories of mind. In J. Astington, P. Harris, & D. Olson (Eds.), *Developing theories of mind*. Cambridge: Cambridge University Press.

Chandler, M., Boyes, M., & Ball, C. (1990). Relativism and stations of epistemic doubt. *Journal of Experimental Child Psychology, 50*, 370–395.

Charner, I., & Fraser, B. (1988). *Youth and work: What we know, what we don't know, what we need to know*. Washington, DC: Institute for Educational Leadership.

Chasnoff, I. J., & Griffith, D. R. (1989). Cocaine exposed infants: Two year follow-up. *Pediatric Research, 25*, 249.

Chasnoff, I. J., Landress, H. J., & Barrett, M. E. (1990). The prevalence of illicit drug or alcohol use during pregnancy and discrepancies in mandatory reporting in Pinellas County, Florida. *The New England Journal of Medicine, 322*(17), 1202–1206.

Chayen, S. (1978). An assessment of the hazards of amniocentesis. *British Journal of Obstetrics and Gynecology, 85*, 2–5.

Chennault, M. (1967). Improving the social acceptance of unpopular educable mentally retarded pupils in special classes. *American Journal of Mental Deficiency, 72*, 455–458.

Cherlin, A. J., Furstenberg, F. F., Chase-Lansdale, P. L., Kiernan, K. E., Robins, P. K., Morrison, D. R., & Teitler, J. O. (1991). Longitudinal studies of effects of divorce on children in Great Britain and the United States. *Science, 252*, 1386–1389.

Children's Defense Fund. (1987). *A children's defense budget*. Washington, DC: The Children's Defense Fund.

Children's Magazine List. (1987). Glassboro, NJ: Glassboro State College, Educational Press Association of America.

Chomsky, N. (1959). A review of *Verbal behavior*, by B. F. Skinner. *Language, 35*, 26–58.

———. (1969). *The acquisition of syntax in children from 5 to 10*. Cambridge, MA: MIT Press.

———. (1965). *Aspects of the theory of syntax*. Cambridge, MA: MIT Press.

Christophersen, E. R. (1989). Injury control. *American Psychologist, 44*(2), 237–241.

Ciaranello, R. (1988). Neurochemical aspects of stress. In N. Garmezy & M. Rutter (Eds.), *Stress, coping, and development in children*. Baltimore: Johns Hopkins University Press.

Clark, E. (1978). Non-linguistic strategies and the acquisition of word meaning. In L. Bloom (Ed.), *Readings in language development*. New York: Wiley.

———. (1983). Meanings and concepts. In J. Flavell & E. Markman (Eds.), *Handbook of child psychology, Vol. III* (pp. 787–840). New York: Wiley.

Clark, M. M. (1976). *Young fluent readers*. London: Heinemann Educational Books.

Clark, M., Hager, M., & Gosnell, M. (1986, May). A breakthrough against CF? *Newsweek*, p. 69.

Clarke, C. A. (1968). The prevention of rhesus babies. *Scientific American, 219*, 46–65.

Clarke-Stewart, A., & Fein, G. (1983). Early childhood programs. In M. M. Haith & J. J. Campos (Eds.), P. H. Mussen (Series Ed.), *Handbook of child psychology: Vol. 2. Infancy and developmental psychobiology*. New York: Wiley.

Clarke-Stewart, K. A., Vanderstoep, L. P., & Killian, G. A. (1979). Analysis and relocation of mother-child relations at two years of age. *Child Development, 50*, 777–793.

Clay, M. M. (1976). *The early detection of reading difficulties: A diagnostic survey*. Aukland, New Zealand: Heinemann.

———. (1983). Getting a theory of writing. In B. M. Kroll & G. Wells (Eds.), *Explorations in the development of writing*. (pp. 259–284) New York: John Wiley & Sons.

———. (1987). *Writing begins at home*. Portsmouth, NH: Heinemann Educational Books.

Cline, V. B., Croft, R. G., & Courrier, S. (1972). The desensitization of children to television violence. *Proceedings of the American Psychological Association, 80*, 99–100.

Clyman, R. B., Emde, R. N., Kempe, J. E., & Harmon, R. J. (1986). Social referencing and social looking among twelve-month-old infants. In T. B. Brazelton & M. W. Yogeman (Eds.), *Affective development in infancy* (pp. 75–94). Norwood, NJ: Ablex.

Cohen, D. H., & Stern, V. (1983). *Observing and recording the behavior of young children*. New York: Teachers College Press.

Cohen, F. L. (1984). *Clinical genetics in nursing practice.* Philadelphia: Lippincott.

Cohen, L., & Gelber, E. (1975). Infant visual memory. In L. B. Cohen & P. Salapatek (Eds.), *Infant perception: From sensation to cognition* (Vol. 1). New York: Academic Press.

Cohen, L. B., & Strauss, M. S. (1979). Concept acquisition in the human infant. *Child Development, 50,* 419–424.

Cohen, S. E., & Parmelee, A. H. (1983). Prediction of five-year Stanford-Binet scores in preterm infants. *Child Development, 54,* 1242–1253.

———. (1988). Antecedents of school problems in children born prematurely. *Journal of Pediatric Psychology, 13*(4), 493–508.

Coles, R. (1986). *The moral life of children.* Boston: Atlantic Monthly Press.

Coles, R. & Stokes, G. (1985). *Sex and the American Teen-ager.* New York: Harper & Row.

Collias, N. E. (1956). The analysis of socialization in sheep and goats. *Ecology, 37,* 228–239.

Collis, G. M. (1977). Visual co-orientation and maternal speech. In H. R. Schaffer (Ed.), *Studies in mother-infant interaction.* London: Academic Press.

Collis, G. M., & Schaffer, H. R. (1975). Synchronization of visual attention in mother-infant pairs. *Journal of Child Psychology and Psychiatry, 16,* 315–320.

Committee on Adolescence. (1989). Care of adolescent parents and their children. *Pediatrics, 83*(1), 138–140.

Committee on Communication (1989). Impact of rock lyrics on music videos on children and youth. *Pediatrics, 83*(2), 314–315.

Committee on Sports Medicine. (1989). Anabolic steroids and the adolescent athlete. *Pediatrics, 83*(1), 127–128.

Committee on Substance Abuse (1990). Drug-exposed infants. *Pediatrics, 86,* 639–642.

Conger, J. J., & Petersen, A. C. (1984). *Adolescence and youth.* New York: Harper & Row.

Congressional Budget Office (1987). *Educational achievement: Explanations and implications of recent trends.* Washington, DC: U. S. Government Printing Office.

Connell, D. K. & Meyer, R. G. (1991). Adolescence suicidal behavior and popular self-report instruments of depression, social desirability, and anxiety. *Adolescence, 26*(101), 113–119.

Connell, J. P., & Goldsmith, H. H. (1982). A structural modeling approach to the study of attachment and strange situation behaviors. In R. J. Emde & R. J. Harmon (Eds.), *The development of attachment and affiliative systems.* New York: Plenum.

Conway, E., & Brackbill, Y. (1970). Delivery medication and infant outcome: An empirical study. *Monographs of the Society for Research in Child Development, 35,* 24–34.

Cooley, M. L., & Unger, D. G. (1991). The role of family support in determining developmental outcomes in children of term mothers. *Child Psychiatry and Human Development, 21,* 217–234.

Coon, H., Fulker, D. W., DeFries, J. C., & Plomin, R. (1990). Home environment and cognitive ability of 7-year-old children in the Colorado Adoption Project: Genetic and environmental etiologies. *Developmental Psychology, 26,* 459–468.

Cooper, E. R., Pelton, S. I., & LeMay, M. (1988). Acquired immunodeficiency syndrome: A new population of children at risk. *Pediatric Clinics of North America, 35*(6), 1365–1387.

Crall, J. J. (1986). Promotion of oral health and prevention of common pediatric dental problems. *Pediatric Clinics of North America, 33*(4), 887–898.

Cratty, B. J. (1986). *Perceptual and motor development in infants and children.* (3d ed.) Englewood Cliffs, NJ: Prentice-Hall.

Crikelair, G. F., & Dhaliwal, A. S. (1976). The cause and prevention of electrical burns of the mouth in children. *Plastic and Reconstructive Surgery, 58,* 206–209.

Crisp, A. H., Palmer, R. L., & Kalucy, R. S. (1976). How common is anorexia nervosa? A prevalence study. *British Journal of Psychiatry, 27,* 1030–1035.

Crittenden, P., & Ainsworth, M. D. S. (1989). Child maltreatment and attachment theory. In D. Circhetti & V. Carlson (Eds.), *Child maltreatment: Theory and research on the causes and consequences of child abuse and neglect* (pp. 432–463). New York: Cambridge University Press.

Crnic, K. A., Ragozin, A. S., Greenberg, M. T., Robinson, M. M., & Basham, R. B. (1983). Social interaction and developmental competence of preterm and full-term infants during the first year of life. *Child Development, 54,* 1199–1210.

Crockenberg, S. B. (1981). Infant irritability, mother responsiveness and social support influences on the security of infant-mother attachment. *Child Development, 52,* 856–865.

———. (1985). Toddlers' reactions to maternal anger. *Merrill-Palmer Quarterly, 31*(4), 361–373.

Cruttenden, A. (1970). A phonetic study of babbling. *British Journal of Disorders in Communication, 5,* 110–118.

Csikszentmihalyi, M., & Larson, R. (1984). *Being adolescent.* New York: Basic Books.

Cunningham, A. S., Jellifee, D. B., & Jelliffee, E. F. P. (1991). Breast-feeding and health in the 1980s: A global epidemiological review. *The Journal of Pediatrics, 118*(5), 659–665.

Daniel, J. (1989, March 14). Fatal attraction: Steroids—The athlete's drug. *The Tab,* pp. 40–41.

Dargassies, S. (1966). Neurological maturation of the premature infant of 28 to 41 weeks' gestation age. In F. Faulkner (Ed.), *Human development.* London: W. B. Saunders.

Darwin, C. (1859). *The origin of species.* London: Murray.

Davidson, P., & Youniss, J. (1991). In W. Kirtines & J. Gewirtz (Eds.), *Handbook of moral behavior and development: Vol. 1. Theory.* Hillsdale, NJ: Lawrence Erlbaum Associates, Publishers.

Dawe, H. C. (1934). An analysis of two hundred quarrels of preschool children. *Child Development, 5,* 139–157.

Dawson, D. A. (1986). The effects of sex education on adolescent behavior. *Family Planning Perspectives, 18,* 162.

Delattre, E. (1990, November). *Ethics and urban gang tyranny: Betrayal of our children.* Paper presented at the Olin Public Lecture Series, Boston University, Boston, MA.

Delisle, J. (1979). Things my child likes to do. In R. S. Renzulli, S. M. Reis, & L. H. Smith (Eds.), *The revolving door identification model.* Mansfield Center, CT: Creative Learning Press.

DeLoache, J. S., Cassidy, D. J., & Brown, A. L. (1985). Precursors of mnemonic strategies in very young children. *Child Development, 56*(1), 125–137.

DeLoache, J. S., Sugarman, S., & Brown, A. L. (1985). The development of error correction strategies in young children's manipulative play. *Child Development, 56*(4), 928–939.

Demetras, M. J., Post, K. N., & Snow, C. E. (1986). Feedback to first language learners: The role of repetitions and clarification questions. *Journal of Child Language, 13*, 275–292.

Denham, S., Renwick, S., & Holt, R. (1991). Working and playing together: Prediction of preschool social-emotional competence from mother-child interaction. *Child Development, 62*(2), 242–249.

Dennis, W. (1960). Causes of retardation among institutional children: Iran. *Journal of Genetic Psychology, 96*, 47–59.

Desmond, M. M., Franklin, R. R., Vallbona, C., Hilt, R. H., Plumb, R., Arnold, H., & Watts, J. (1963). The clinical behavior of the newly born I. *Journal of Pediatrics, 12*, 307–325.

Desor, J. A., Maller, O., & Andrews, K. (1975). Ingestive responses of human newborns to salty, sour, and bitter stimuli. *Journal of Comparative and Physiological Psychology, 89*, 966–970.

deVilliers, J., & deVilliers, P. (1973). Development of the use of word order in comprehension. *Journal of Psycholinguistic Research, 2*, 331–341.

Dewey, J., & Bentley, A. F. (1949). *Knowing and the known.* Boston: Beacon.

Dickinson, D. (1989). Effects of a shared reading program on one Head Start language and literacy environment. In J. B. Allen & J. M. Mason (Eds.), *Risk makers, risk takers, risk breakers* (pp. 125–153). Portsmouth, NH: Heinemann Educational Books.

Dickinsin, D. & Snow, C. (1987, May). *Oral language correlates of reading behavior.* Paper presented at the Thirty-Second Annual Meeting of the International Reading Association, Anaheim, CA.

Dickinson, D. K. (1984). First impressions: Children's knowledge of words gained from a single exposure. *Applied Psycholinguistics, 5*, 359–373.

DiClemente, R. J., Forrest, K. A., Mickler, S., & Principal Site Investigators (1990). College students' knowledge and attitudes about AIDS and changes in HIV-preventive behaviors. *AIDS Education and Prevention, 2*(3), 201–212.

Dietz, W. H. (1986). Prevention of childhood obesity. *Pediatric Clinics of North America, 33*(4), 823–833.

Dishion, T. (1990). The family ecology of boys' peer relations in middle childhood. *Child Development, 61*, 874–892.

Dix, T., Ruble, D., & Zambarabo, R. (1989). Mothers' implicit theories of discipline: Child effects, parent effects, and the attribution process. *Child Development, 60*, 1373–1391.

Dixon, J. A., & Moore, C. F. (1990). The development of perspective-taking: Understanding differences in information and weighing. *Child Development, 61*, 1502–1513.

Dobbing, J. (1984). Infant nutrition and later achievement. *Nutrition Reviews, 42*(1), 1–7.

———. (Ed.). (1987). *Early nutrition and later achievement.* London: Academic Press.

Dodge, K. A. (1990). Nature versus nurture in childhood conduct disorder: It is time to ask a different question. *Developmental Psychology, 26*(5), 698–701.

Dodge, K. A., Coie, J., Pettit, G., & Price, J. (1990). Peer status and aggression in boys' groups: Developmental and contextual analysis. *Child Development, 61*, 1289–1309.

Dodge, K. A., Murphy, R. R., & Buchsbaum, K. (1984). The assessment of intention-cue detection skills in children: Implications for developmental psychopathology. *Child Development, 55*, 163–173.

Dodge, K. A., Petit, G. S., McCloskey, C. L., & Brown, M. M. (1987). Social competence in children. *Monographs of the Society for Research in Child Development, 51* (2, Serial No. 213).

Doleys, D. M., & Dolce, J. J. (1982). Toilet training and enuresis. *Pediatric Clinics of North America, 29*(2), 297–312.

Donaldson, M. (1978). *Children's minds.* New York: Norton.

Dorfman, S. F. (1983). Deaths from ectopic pregnancy, United States, 1979–1980. *Obstetrics and Gynecology, 62*(3), 334–338.

Dornbusch, S. M., Carlsmith, J. M., Gross, R. T., Martin, J. A., Jennings, D., Rosenberg, A., & Duke, P. (1981). Sexual development, age and dating: A comparison of biological and social influences upon one set of behaviors. *Child Development, 52*(1), 179–185.

Dorris, M. (1989). *The broken cord.* New York: Harper & Row.

Dougherty, W. H., & Engel, R. E. (1986). An 80s look at sex equality in Caldecott winners and honor books. *The Reading Teacher, 40*(4), 394–398.

Downs, M. P. (1978, Fall). That a child may hear. *Deafness Research Foundation Receiver.*

Downs, W. R., & Rose, S. R. (1991). The relationship of adolescent peer groups to the incidence of psychosocial problems. *Adolescence, 26*(102), 377–386.

Doyle, A. (1975). Infant development in day care. *Developmental Psychology, 11*, 655–656.

Drabman, R. S., & Thomas, M. H. (1974). Does media violence increase children's toleration of real-life aggression? *Developmental Psychology, 10*, 3–13.

Drillien, C. M., Thomson, A. J. M., & Burgayne, K. (1980). Low birthweight children at early school age: A longitudinal study. *Developmental Medicine and Child Neurology, 22*, 26–47.

Duncan, P. D., Ritter, P. L., Dornbusch, S. M., Gross, R. T., & Carlsmith, J. M. (1985). The effects of pubertal timing on body image, school behavior, and deviance. *Journal of Youth and Adolescence, 14*, 227–235.

Dunn, J., & Kendrick, C. (1982). *Siblings*. Cambridge, MA: Harvard University Press.

Dunn, M. S., Shennan, A. T., Zayack, D., & Possmayer, F. (1991). Bovine surfactant replacement therapy in neonates of less than 30 weeks' gestation: A randomized controlled trial of prophylaxis versus treatment. *Pediatrics, 87*(3), 377–386.

Durkin, D. (1966). *Children who read early*. New York: Teachers College Press.

Dweck, C. S. (1978). Achievement. In M. E. Lamb (Ed.), *Social and personality development* (pp. 114–130). New York: Holt, Rinehart & Winston.

Dweck, C. S., & Elliot, E. S. (1983). Achievement motivation. In Paul H. Mussen (Series Ed.), *Handbook of child psychology* (4th ed.). E. Mavis Hetherington (Ed.), *Vol. 4: Socialization, personality, and social development* (pp. 643-692). New York: Wiley.

Dweck, C. S., Goetz, T. E., & Strauss, N. L. (1980). Sex differences in learned helplessness: IV. An experimental and naturalistic study of failure generalization and its mediators. *Journal of Personality and Social Psychology, 38,* 441–452.

Dweck, C. S., & Licht, B. G. (1980). Learned helplessness and intellectual achievement. In J. Garber and M. Seligman (Eds.), *Human helplessness: Theory and applications*. New York: Academic Press.

Early Childhood Education Commission (1986). *Take a giant step: Final report of the early childhood commission*. New York: Office of the Mayor.

Eckerman, C., Whatley, J., & Kutz, S. (1975). Growth of social play with peers during the second year of life. *Developmental Psychology, 11,* 42–49.

Educational Testing Service. (1979). *School and college ability tests II and III*. Monterey, CA: CTB/McGraw-Hill.

Edwards, D. A. (1969). Early androgen stimulation and aggressive behavior in male and female mice. *Physiology and Behavior, 4,* 333–338.

Edwards, P. (1989). Supporting lower SES mothers' attempts to provide scaffolding for book reading. In J. B. Allen & J. M. Mason (Eds.), *Risk makers, risk takers, and risk breakers* (pp. 222–250). Portsmouth, NH: Heinemann Educational Books.

Egan, M. C. (1977). Federal nutrition support programs for children. *Pediatric Clinics of North America, 24,* 229–239.

Ehrenberg, M. F., Cox, D. N., & Koopman, R. F. (1991). The relationship between self-efficacy and depression in adolescents. *Adolescence, 26*(102), 361–374.

Eilers, R., Wilson, W., & Moore, J. (1977). Developmental changes in speech discrimination. *Journal of Speech and Hearing Research, 20,* 766–780.

Eimas, P. D. (1974). Auditory and linguistic processing of cues for place of articulation by infants. *Perception and Psychophysics, 16,* 513–521.

Eimas, P. D., Sikqueland, D. R., Jusczyk, P., & Vigorito, J. (1971). Speech perception in infants. *Science, 171,* 303–306.

Eisenberg, N., & Mussen, P. (1989). *The roots of prosocial behavior in children*. New York: Cambridge University Press.

Eisenberg-Berg, N. (1979). Development of children's prosocial judgment. *Developmental Psychology, 15,* 128–137.

Elbers, L., & Ton, J. (1985). Playpen monologues: The interplay of words and babbles in the first-words period. *Journal of Child Language, 12,* 551–565.

Elder, G. H. (1963). Parental power legitimation and its effects on the adolescent. *Sociometry, 26,* 50–65.

Elkind, D. (1976). *Child development and education: A Piagetian perspective*. New York: Oxford University Press.

Elliot, R., & Vasta, R. (1970). The modeling of sharing: Effects associated with vicarious reinforcement, symbolization, age and generalization. *Journal of Experimental Child Psychology, 10,* 8–15.

Ellis, G. T., & Sekyra, F. (1972). The effect of aggressive cartoons on the behavior of first grade children. *Journal of Psychology, 81,* 37–43.

Elstner, C. L., Carey, J. C., Livingston, G., Moeschler, J., & Lubinsky, M. (1984). Further delineation of the 10p deletion syndrome. *Pediatrics, 73*(5), 670–675.

Emde, R. N., Gaensbauer, T. J., & Harmon, R. J. (1976). Emotional expression in infancy: A behavioral study. *Psychological Issues, A Monograph Series, 10*(7,37). New York: International Press.

Emery, R. E. (1989). Family violence. *American Psychologist, 44*(2), 321–328.

Emery, R. E., Hetherington, E. M., & DiLalla, L. F. (1984). *Divorce, children, and social policy*. In H. W. Stevenson & A. E. Siegel (Eds.), *Child development research and social policy* (Vol. 1, pp. 189–266). Chicago: University of Chicago Press. Press.

Empey, L. T. (1975). Delinquency theory and research. In R. Grinder (Ed.), *Studies in adolescence* (pp. 475–490). New York: Macmillan.

Engstrom, G. (1971). *The significance of the young child's motor development*. Washington, DC: The National Association for the Education of Young Children.

Entwisle, D. R., Alexander, K. L., Pallas, A. M., & Cadigan, D. (1988). The emergent academic self-image of first graders: Its response to social structure. *Child Development, 58*(5), 1190–1206.

Epstein, L. H., Wing, R. R., & Valoski, A. (1985). Childhood obesity. *Pediatric Clinics of North America, 32*(2), 363–379.

Erhardt, A. A., & Baker, S. W. (1974). Fetal androgens, human central nervous system differentiation, and behavior sex differences. In R. C. Friedman, R. M. Richart, and R. L. Vandewiele (Eds.), *Sex differences in behavior*. New York: Wiley.

Erikson, E. H. (1950). *Childhood and society*. New York: Norton.

———. (1963). *Childhood and society*. New York: Norton.

———. (1968a). *Identity: Youth and crisis*. NY: Norton.

———. (1968b). Psychosocial identity. In *International Encyclopedia of Social Sciences* (pp. 61–65). New York: Crowell-Collier.

Erickson, J. (1984). Drug use: The family connection. *Family Learning, 1*(1), 100.

Erikson, P. S., Gennser, G., Lofgran, O., & Nilsson, K. (1983). Acute effects of maternal smoking on fetal breathing and movements. *Obstetrics and Gynecology, 61*(3), 367–372.

Eron, L. D., Walder, L. L., Huesmann, L. R., & Lefkowitz, M. M. (1974). The convergence of laboratory and field studies of the development of aggression. In J. De Wit & W. W. Hartup (Eds.), *Determinants and origins of aggressive behavior* (pp. 347–380). The Hague: Mouton.

Fagot, B. I., & Kavanagh, K. (1990). The prediction of anti-social behavior from avoidant attachment classification. *Child Development, 61*(2), 864–873.

Fantz, R. L. (1963). Pattern vision in newborn infants. *Science, 140,* 296–297.

Fantz, R. L., Ordy, J. M., & Udelf, M. S. (1962). Maturation of patterns of vision in infants during the first six months. *Journal of Comparative and Physiological Psychology, 55,* 907–917.

Farrington, D. P., & West, D. J. (1971). A comparison between early delinquents and young aggressives. *British Journal of Criminology, 11,* 341–358.

Farrior, E. S., & Ruwe, C. H. (1987). Women, Infants, and Children Program prenatal participation and dietary intakes. *Nutrition Research, 7,* 451–459.

Federman, E. J., & Yang, R. K. (1976). A critique of obstetrical pain-relieving drugs as predictors of infant behavior variability. *Child Development, 47,* 294–296.

Fein, G. (1975). A transformational analysis of pretending. *Developmental Psychology, 11*(3), 291–296.

———. (1981). Pretend play in childhood: An integrative review. *Child Development, 52,* 1095–1118.

———.(1984). The self-building potential of make-believe play, or "I got a fish, all by myself." In T. D. Yawkey & A. D. Pellegrini (Eds.), *Child's play: Developmental and applied* (pp. 125–142). Hillsdale, NJ: Lawrence Erlbaum.

Fein, G., Johnson, D., Kosson, N., Stork, L., & Wasserman, L. (1975). Sex stereotypes and preferences in the toy choices of 20-month-old boys and girls. *Developmental Psychology, 11*(4), 527–528.

Fein, G., & Rivkin, M. (Eds.). (1986). *The young child at play: Reviews of research* (Vol. 4). Washington, DC: National Association for the Education of Young Children.

Feinman, S., & Lewis, M. (1983). Social referencing at ten months: A second-order effect on infants' responses to strangers. *Child Development, 54*(4), 878–887.

Fenson, L. (1984). Developmental trends for action and speech in pretend play. In I. Bretherton (Ed.), *Symbolic play,* (pp. 249–270). New York: Academic Press.

Fenson, L., & Ramsay, D. S. (1980). Decentration and integration of the child's play in the second year. *Child Development, 51,* 171–178.

Fernald, A. (1984). The perceptual and affective salience of mothers' speech to infants. In L. Feagans, C. Garvey, & R. Golinkoff (Eds.), *The origins and growth of communication.* Norwood, NJ: Ablex.

———. (1985). Four-month-old infants prefer to listen to motherese. *Infant Behavior and Development, 8,* 181–195.

———. (1989). Intonation and communicative intent in mothers' speech to infants: Is the melody the message? *Child Development, 60*(6), 1497–1510.

Fernald, A., & Mazzie, C. (1991). Prosody and focus in speech to infants and adults. *Developmental Psychology, 27,* 209–271.

Ferreiro, E. (1986). The interplay between information and assimilation in beginning literacy. In W. Teale and E. Sulzby (Eds.), *Emergent literacy.* Norwood, NJ: Ablex.

Ferreiro, E., & Teberosky, A. (1979). *Literacy before schooling.* Portsmouth, NH: Heinemann Educational Books.

Ferris, T. (1988). *Coming of age in the Milky Way.* New York: Morrow.

Field, T., Demsey, J., & Shuman, H. H. (1983). Five-year fol-low-up of preterm respiratory distress syndrome and post-term postmaturity syndrome infants. In T. Field & A. Sostek (Eds.), *Infants born at risk: Physiological, perceptual, and cognitive processes* (pp. 317–335). New York: Grune & Stratton.

Field, T., Healy, B., & LeBlanc, W. P. (1989). Sharing and syn-chrony of behavior states and heart rate in non-depressed versus depressed mother-infant interactions. *Infant Behavior and Development, 12,* 357–376.

Fillmore, L. W. (1976). *The second time around: Cognitive and social strategies in second language acquisition.* Doctoral Dissertation. Stanford University, Stanford, CA.

Fincham, F., Hokoda, A., & Sanders, R. (1989). Learned help-lessness, test anxiety, and academic achievement: A lon-gitudinal analysis. *Child Development, 60*(1), 138–145.

Finkelhor, D., Hotaling, G., Lewis, I., & Smith, C. (1990). Sex-ual abuse in a national survey of adult men and women: Prevalence, characteristics, and risk factors. *Child Abuse and Neglect, 14,* 19–28.

Finkelstein, N. W., & Ramey, C. T. (1977). Learning to control the environment in infancy. *Child Development, 48,* 608–619.

Flavell, J. H., Beach, D. H., & Chinsky, J. M. (1966). Sponta-neous verbal rehearsal in memory tasks as a function of age. *Child Development, 37,* 283–299.

Flavell, J. H., Everett, B. A., Croft, K., & Flavell, E. (1981). Young children's knowledge about visual perception: Further evidence of Level 1–Level 2 distinctions. *Developmental Psychology, 17,* 99–103.

Flavell, J. H., Green, F. L., & Flavell, E. R. (1986). Develop-ment of knowledge about the appearance-reality distinc-tion. *Monographs of the Society for Research in Child Devel-opment, 51*(1, Serial No. 212).

Flavell, J. H., Shipstead, S. G., & Croft, K. (1978). Young chil-dren's knowledge about visual perception: Hiding objects from others. *Child Development, 49,* 1208–1211.

Foch, T. T., & McClearn, G. E. (1980). Genetics, body weight and obesity. In A. J. Stunkard (Ed.), *Obesity.* Philadelphia: Saunders.

Fox, R., Aslin, R. N., Shea, S. L., & Dumais, S. T. (1980). Ste-reopsis in human infants. *Science, 207,* 323–324.

Fraiberg, S. (1975). Intervention in infancy: A program for

blind infants. In B. Z. Friedlander, G. M. Steritt, & G. E. Kirk (Eds.), *Exceptional infant* (Vol. 1). New York: Brunner/Mazel.

Frank, D., Zuckerman, B., Reece, H., Amaro, H., Hingson, R., Fried, L., Cabral, H., Levenson, S., Kayne, H., Vinci, R., Bauchnmer, H., & Parker, S. (1988). Cocaine use during pregnancy: Prevalence and correlates. *Pediatrics, 82,* 888–895.

Frasier, S. D. (1979). Growth disorders in children. *Pediatric Clinics of North America, 26,* 1–12.

Fredericks, B. C., & Kendrick, A. S. (1985). Health and safety—A special look at day care for sick children. *Child Care News, 12*(3), 4–5.

Frederiksen, N. (1984). The real test bias. *American Psychologist, 39*(3), 193–202.

Frenkel, L. D. (1986). Pertussis immunization. *Pediatric Annals, 15*(6), 452–454.

Freud, S. (1925). Instincts and their vicissitudes. In S. Freud, *Collected papers* (Vol. 4). London: Institutes for Psychoanalysis & Hogarth Press.

Freund, L. S., Baker, L., & Sonnenschein, S. (1990). Developmental changes in strategic approaches to classification. *Journal of Experimental Child Psychology, 49,* 343–362.

Friede, A. M., Carey, V., Azzara, M. A., Gallagher, S. S., & Guyer, B. (1985). The epidemiology of injuries to bicycle riders. *Pediatric Clinics of North America, 32*(1), 141–151.

Friedman, S. C., Jacobs, B. S., & Wertmann, A. W. (1981). Preterms of low medical risk: Spontaneous behaviors and soothability at expected date of birth. *Infant Behavior and Development, 5*(1), 3–10.

Friedrich, L. K., & Stein, A. H. (1973). Aggressive and prosocial television programs and the natural behavior of preschool children. *Monographs of the Society for Research in Child Development, 38*(151).

Frieze, I. H., Fisher, J., Hanusa, G., McHugh, M. D., & Valle, V. A. (1978). Attributions of the causes of success and failure as internal and external barriers to achievement in women. In J. Sherman & F. Denmark (Eds.), *Psychology of women: Future directions of research.* New York: Psychological Dimensions.

Friman, P. C. (1986). A preventive context for enuresis. *Pediatric Clinics of North America, 33*(4), 871–885.

Frisch, J. L. (1977). Sex stereotypes in adult-infant play. *Child Development, 48,* 1671–1675.

Frodi, A. M., & Lamb, M. E. (1978). Fathers' and mothers' responses to the face and cries of normal and premature infants. *Developmental Psychology, 14*(5), 490–498.

Furrow, D., & Nelson, K. (1986). A further look at the motherese hypothesis: A reply to Gleitman, Newport, and Gleitman. *Journal of Child Language, 13,* 163–176.

Furstenberg, F. F., Brooks-Gunn, J. I., & Morgan, S. P. (1987). *Adolescent mothers in later life.* New York: Cambridge University Press.

Fuson, K. (1988). *Children's counting and concepts of number.* New York: Springer-Verlag.

Gaensbauer, T. J., & Harmon, R. J. (1982). Attachment behavior in abused/neglected and premature infants. In R. N. Emde & R. J. Harmon (Eds.), *The development of attachment and affiliative systems* (pp. 263–279). New York: Plenum Press.

Galambos, N. L., & Garbarino, J. (1983). Identifying the missing link in the study of latchkey children. *Children Today, 12*(4), 2–4.

Gallatin, J. E. (1975). *Adolescence and individuality.* New York: Harper & Row.

Galler, J. (1987). The interaction of nutrition and the environment in behavioral development. In J. Dobbing (Ed.), *Early nutrition and later achievement,* (pp. 125–207).

Garcia, C., & Rosenfeld, D. L. (1977). *Human fertility: The regulation of reproduction.* Philadelphia: F. A. Davis.

Gardner, H. (1983). *Frames of mind: The theory of multiple intelligences.* New York: Basic Books.

Garn, S. M. (1966). Body size and its implications. In L. W. Hoffman & M. L. Hoffman (Eds.), *Review of child development research* (Vol. 2). New York: Russell Sage Foundation.

Garn, S. M., & Clark, D. C. (1976). Trends in fatness and the origins of obesity. *Pediatrics, 57,* 443–456.

Garner, R. (1987). *Metacognition and reading comprehension.* Norwood, NJ: Ablex.

Garrett, W., & Robinson, D. E. (1970). *Ultrasound in clinical obstetrics.* Springfield, IL: Charles C. Thomas.

Garvey, C. (1977). *Play.* Cambridge, MA: Harvard University Press.

Gathercole, V. C. (1985). More and more and more about more. *Journal of Experimental Child Psychology, 40,* 73–104.

Gedda, L. (1961). *Twins in history and science.* Springfield, IL: Charles C. Thomas.

Geller, L. G. (1985). *Word play and language learning for children.* Urbana, IL: National Council of Teachers of English.

Gelman, R., & Gallistel, C. R. (1978). *The child's understanding of number.* Cambridge, MA: Harvard University Press.

Gelman, R., & Meck, E. (1983). Preschoolers' counting: Principles before skill. *Cognition, 13,* 343–359.

General Mills, Inc. (1979). *Family health in an era of stress: The General Mills American family report.* Minneapolis, MN: General Mills.

George, C., & Main, M. (1981). Social interactions of young abused children: Approach, avoidance, aggression. In E. M. Hetherington & R. D. Parke (Eds.), *Contemporary readings in child psychology* (2d ed.). New York: McGraw-Hill.

Gesell, A., & Thompson, H. (1929). Learning and growth in identical infant twins: An experimental study of the method of co-twin control. *Genetic Psychology Monographs, 6,* 1–124.

Gibson, E. (1969). *Principles of perceptual learning and development.* Englewood Cliffs, NJ: Prentice-Hall.

Gibson, E. J., & Walk, R. (1960). The "visual cliff." *Scientific American, 202,* 64–72.

Gil, D. G. (1970). *Violence against children: Physical child abuse in the United States.* Cambridge, MA: Harvard University Press.

Gilbert, N., Berrick, J., LeProhn, N., & Nyman, N. (1989). *Pro-

tecting young children from sexual abuse: Does preschool training work? Lexington, MA: Lexington Books.

Gilligan, C. (1977). In a different voice: Women's conceptions of the self and of morality. *Harvard Educational Review, 47,* 481–517.

———. (1982). *In a different voice: Psychological theory and women's development.* Cambridge, MA: Harvard University Press.

Ginsberg, G. P., & Kilbourne, B. K. (1988). Emergence of vocal alternation in mother-infant interchanges. *Journal of Child Language, 15,* 221–235.

Ginsburg, H. P., & Opper, S. (1988). *Piaget's theory of intellectual development* (3d ed.). Englewood Cliffs, NJ: Prentice-Hall.

Gleason, J. (1967). Do children imitate? *Proceedings of the international conference on oral education of the deaf.* Vol. 11, 1441–1448.

Glucksberg, S., Krauss, R. M., & Higgins, E. T. (1975). The development of referential communication skills. In F. D. Horowitz (Ed.), *Reviews of child development research* (Vol. 4). Chicago: University of Chicago Press.

Glueck, S., & Glueck, F. (1950). *Criminal careers.* New York: Knopf.

Gnepp, J., McKee, E., & Domanic, J. A. (1987). Children's use of situational information to infer emotion: Understanding emotionally equivocal situations. *Developmental Psychology, 22*(1), 114–123.

Godwin, A., & Schrag, L. (1988). *Setting up for infant care: Guidelines for centers and family day care homes.* Washington, DC: National Association for the Education of Young Children.

Goldberg, S. (1982). Some biological aspects of early parent-infant interaction. In S. Moore & C. Cooper (Eds.), *The young child: Reviews of research* (Vol. 3, pp. 35–36). Washington, DC: National Association for the Education of Young Children.

———. (1983). Parent-infant bonding: Another look. *Child Development, 54*(6), 1355–1382.

Goldberg, S., & Devitto, B. (1983). *Born too soon: Preterm birth and early development.* San Francisco: W. H. Freeman.

Goldfield, B. A., & Snow, C. D. (1984). Reading books with children: The mechanics of parental influence on children's reading achievement. In J. Flood (Ed.), *Understanding reading comprehension* (pp. 231–256). Newark, DE: International Reading Association.

Goldin-Meadow, S., Seligman, M., & Gelman, R. (1976). Language in the two-year-old. *Cognition, 4,* 189–202.

Goldman, A. S., & Smith, C. W. (1973). Host resistance factors in human milk. *Journal of Pediatrics, 82,* 1082.

Goldstein, H., Sprafkin, R., Gershaw, V., & Klein, P. (1980). *Skillstreaming the adolescent.* Champaign, IL: Research Press.

Golinkoff, R. M. (1986). 'I beg your pardon?': The preverbal negotiation of failed messages. *Journal of Child Language, 13,* 455–476.

Golinkoff, R. M., & Hirsh-Pasek, K. (1990). Let the mute speak: What infants can tell us about language acquisition. *Merrill-Palmer Quarterly, 36*(1), 67–91.

Gonzales-Mena, J., & Eyer, D. (1989). *Infants, toddlers, and caregiving.* Mountain View, CA: Mayfield.

Goodenough, E. (1957). Interest in persons as an aspect of sex differences in the early years. *Genetic Psychology Monographs, 55,* 287–323.

Goodfield, J. (1981). *An imagined world.* New York: Harper & Row.

Goodlad, J. (1984). *A place called school: Prospects for the future.* New York: McGraw-Hill.

Goodman, K. S., Smith, E. G., Meredith, R., & Goodman, Y. M. (1987). *Language and thinking go to school* (3d ed.). New York: Richard C. Owen.

Gopnik, A., & Astington, J. W. (1988). Children's understanding of representational change and its relation to the understanding of false belief and the appearance reality distinction. *Child Development, 59*(1), 26–37.

Gopnik, A., & Graf, P. (1988). Knowing how you know: Young children's ability to identify and remember the sources of their beliefs. *Child Development, 59*(5), 1366–1371.

Gorbman, A., Dickhoff, W. W., Vigna, S. R., Clark, N. B., & Ralph, C. L. (1983). *Comparative endocrinology.* New York: Wiley.

Gordon, I. (1990). *Baby learning through baby play.* New York: St. Martin's Press, 1980.

Goswami, U. (1991). Analogical reasoning: What develops? A review of research and theory. *Child Development, 62*(1), 1–22.

Gottfried, A., & Brown, C. (Eds.) (1986). *Play interactions: The contribution of play materials and parental involvement to children's development.* Salisbury, NC: Lexington Press.

Gottfriend, A., & Gaiter, J. (Eds.) (1985). *Infant stress under intensive care.* Baltimore: University Park Press.

Gottlieb, G. (1991). Experiential canalization of behavioral development: Theory. *Developmental Psychology, 27*(1), 4–13.

Gowers, S. G., Crisp, A. H., Joughin, N., & Bhat, A. (1991). Premenarcheal anorexia nervosa. *Journal of Child Psychology and Psychiatry, 32*(3), 515–524.

Granrud, C. (1987). Size constancy in newborn human infants. *Investigative Ophthalmology and Visual Science, 28* (Supplement) 5.

Grant, L. M., & Demetriou, E. (1988). Adolescent sexuality. *Pediatric Clinics of North America, 35*(6), 1271–1289.

Grantham-McGregor, S., Schofield, W., & Powell, C. (1987). Development of severely malnourished children who received psychosocial stimulation: Six-year follow-up. *Pediatrics, 79,* 247–254.

Granucci, P. (1986). *A case study of one child's literacy development from 24 to 36 months.* Unpublished doctoral dissertation, Boston University.

Green, A. H., Gaines, R. W., & Sandgrund, A. (1974). Child abuse: Pathological syndrome of family interaction. *American Journal of Psychiatry, 131,* 882–886.

Green, J. A., Gustafson, G. E., & West, M. J. (1980). Effects of infant development on mother-infant interactions. *Child Development, 51*, 199–207.

Green, K. D., Beck, S. J., & Forehand, R. (1980). Validity of teacher nomination of child behavior problems. *Journal of Abnormal Child Psychology, 8*(3), 397–404.

Greenburg, M., Pelliteri, O., & Barton, J. (1957). Frequency of defects in infants whose mothers had rubella during pregnancy. *Journal of the American Medical Association, 165*, 675–678.

Greenough, W. T., Black, J. E., & Wallace, C. S. (1987). Experience and brain development. *Child Development, 58*(3), 539–559.

Greenough, W. T., & Juraska, J. M. (1979). Experience-individual changes in brain fine structure: Their behavioral implications. In M. E. Hahn, F. Jensen, & B. C. Dudek (Eds.), *Development and evolution of brain size* (pp. 296–320). San Diego, CA: Academic Press.

Greensher, J., & Mofenson, H. C. (1985). Injuries at play. *Pediatric Clinics of North America, 32*(1), 127–139.

Greenwood, S. G. (1979). Warning: Cigarette smoking is dangerous to reproductive health. *Family Planning Perspectives, 11*(3), 168–172.

Greer, S., Bauchner, H., & Zuckerman, B. (1989). The Denver Developmental Screening Test: How good is its predictive validity? *Developmental Medicine and Child Neurology, 31*, 774–781.

Grether, J. K., & Schulman, J. (1989). Sudden infant death syndrome and birth weight. *The Journal of Pediatrics, 114*(4), 561–567.

Griffiths, M. (1991). Amusement machine playing in childhood and adolescence: A comparative analysis of video games and fruit machines. *Journal of Adolescence, 14*, 53–73.

Grin, T. R., Nelson, L. B., & Jeffers, J. B. (1987). Eye injuries in childhood. *Pediatrics, 80*(1), 13–17.

Grogaard, J., Lindstrom, D., Parker, R., Culley, B., & Stahlman, M. (1990). Increased survival rates in very low birthweight infants (1500 grams or less): No association with increased incidence of handicaps. *The Journal of Pediatrics, 117*, 139–146.

Gross, R. T., & Duke, P. M. (1980). The effect of early versus late physical maturation in adolescent behavior. *Pediatric Clinics of North America, 27*, 71–77.

Grossman, H. J. (Ed.). (1983). *Classification in mental retardation* (8th ed.). Washington, DC: American Association on Mental Deficiency.

Grubb, W. N., & Lazerson, M. (1982). *Broken promises.* New York: Basic Books.

Grusec, J. E. (1990). Socializing concern for others in the home. *Developmental Psychology, 27*(2), 338–342.

Grusec, J. E., & Skubinski, S. (1970). Model nurturance, demand characteristics of the modeling experiment, and altruism. *Journal of Personality and Social Psychology, 14*, 352–359.

Grusec, J. E., & Lytton, H. (1988). *Social development.* New York: Springer-Verlag.

Guerney, L., & Moore, L. (1983). Phone Friend: A prevention-oriented service for latchkey children. *Children Today, 12*(4), 5–10.

Guntheroth, W. G., Lohmann, R., & Spiers, P. S. (1990). Risk of sudden infant death syndrome in subsequent siblings. *The Journal of Pediatrics, 116*(4), 520–524.

Gunzenhauser, N. E., & Caldwell, B. M. (Eds.) (1986). *Group care for young children. Pediatric Round Table: 12.* Skillman, NJ: Johnson & Johnson.

Gustafson, G. E. (1984). Effects of the ability to locomote on infants' social and exploratory behaviors: An experimental study. *Developmental Psychology, 20*(3), 397–405.

Guttmacher, A. F. (1973). *Pregnancy, birth and family planning.* New York: New American Library.

Guyer, B., Talbot, A. M., & Pless, I. B. (1985). Pedestrian injuries to children and youth. *Pediatric Clinics of North America, 32*(1), 163–174.

Haaf, R. F., & Bell, R. Q. (1967). A facial dimension in visual discrimination by human infants. *Child Development, 38*, 893–899.

Hainline, L., Harris, C., & Krinsky, S. (1990). Variability of refixations in infants. *Infant Behavior and Development, 13*, 321–342.

Haith, M. M., Bergman, T., & Moore, M. J. (1977). Eye contact and face scanning in early infancy. *Science, 198*, 853–855.

Hales, D. J., Lozoff, B., Sosa, R., & Kennel, J. H. (1977). Defining the limits of the maternal sensitive period. *Developmental Medicine and Child Neurology, 19*, 454–461.

Hallman, M., & Gluck, L. (1982). Respiratory distress syndrome—update 1982. *Pediatric Clinics of North America, 29*(5), 1057–1075.

Halmi, K. A., Casper, R. C., Eckert, E. D., Goldberg, S. C., & Davis, J. M. (1979). Unique features associated with age of onset of anorexia nervosa. *Psychiatric Research, 1*, 209–215.

Halmi, K. A., & Falk, J. R. (1981). Common psychological changes in anorexia nervosa. *International Journal of Eating Disorders, 1*, 16–27.

Halverson, H. M. (1940). Motor development. In A. Gesell (Ed.), *The first five years of life: A guide to the study of the preschool child* (pp. 65–107). New York: Harper.

Hann, D. M. (1989). A systems conceptualization of the quality of mother–infant interactions. *Infant Behavior and Development, 12*, 251–263.

Harlow, H. F. (1958). The nature of love. *American Psychologist, 13*, 673–685.

Harris, P. L. (1983). Infant cognition. In P. H. Mussen (Ed.), *Handbook of child psychology* (4th ed.): Vol. 2. *Infancy and developmental psychobiology.* New York: Wiley.

Harris, P., Kruithof, A., Terwogt, M. M., & Visser, P. (1981). Children's detection and awareness of textual anomaly. *Journal of Experimental Child Psychology, 31*, 212–230.

Harter, S. (1988). The construction and conservation of the self: James and Cooley revisited. In D. Lapsley & F. C. Power (Eds.), *Self, ego, and identity: Integrative approaches* (pp. 43–70). New York: Springer–Verlag.

———. (1990). Causes, correlates and the functional role of global self-worth: A life-span perspective. In R. Sternberg & J. Kolligian (Eds.), *Competence considered* (pp. 67–97). New Haven: Yale University Press.

Harter, S., Alexander, P., & Neimeyer, R. (1988). Long-term effects of incestuous child abuse in college women. Social adjustment, social cognition, and family characteristics. *Journal of Consulting and Clinical Psychology, 56* (1), 5–8.

Harter, S., & Buddin, B. J. (1987). Children's understanding of the simultaneity of two emotions: A five-stage developmental acquisition sequence. *Developmental Psychology, 22*(3), 388–399.

Hartup, W. W. (1974). Aggression in childhood: Developmental perspectives. *American Psychologist, 29,* 336–341.

———. (1983). Peer relations. In P. H. Mussen (Ed.), *Handbook of child psychology* (4th ed.) (Vol. III). New York: Wiley.

Harvey, J. H. (1982). Overuse syndromes in young athletes. *Pediatric Clinics of North America, 29*(6), 1369–1381.

Haviland, J. (1982). Sex-related pragmatics in infants. *Journal of Communication, 27,* 80–84.

Hawdon, J. M., Key, E., Kolvin, I., & Fundudis, T. (1990). Born too small—is outcome still affected? *Developmental Medicine and Child Neurology, 32,* 943–953.

Hayes, C. D. (Ed.). (1987). *Risking the future: Adolescent sexuality, pregnancy, and childbearing* (Vol. 1). Washington, DC: National Academy Press.

Haynes, H., White, B. W., & Held, R. (1965). Visual accommodation in human infants. *Science, 148,* 528–530.

Haywood, K. M. (1986). *Life span motor development.* Champaign, IL: Human Kinetics.

Heath, S. B. (1983). *Way with words: Language, life, and work in communities and classrooms.* New York: Cambridge University Press.

Heath, S. B., & Thomas, C. (1984). The achievement of preschool literacy for mother and child. In H. Goelman, A. Obserg, & F. Smith (Eds.), *Awakening to literacy* (pp. 51–72). Portsmouth, NH: Heinemann Educational Books.

Held, R., & Hein, A. (1963). Movement-produced stimulation in the development of visually guided behavior. *Journal of Comparative and Physiological Psychology, 56,* 822–876.

Helfer, R. (1978). *Childhood comes first: A crash course in childhood for adults.* East Lansing, MI: Ray E. Helfer.

Herbst, A. L., Scully, R. E., & Robboy, S. J. (1975). Problems in the examination of DES-exposed females. *Obstetrics and Gynecology, 46,* 353–355.

Herman, P. A., Anderson, R. C., Pearson, P. D., & Nagy, W. E. (1987). Incidental acquisition of word meanings from expositions with varied text features. *Reading Research Quarterly, 22*(3), 263–284.

Herrman, H. J., & Roberts, M. W. (1987). Preventive dental care: The role of the pediatrician. *Pediatrics, 80*(1), 107–110.

Hersher, L., Moore, A. U., & Richmond, R. B. (1958). Effects of modified maternal care in the sheep and goat. *Science, 128,* 1342–1343.

Hiatt, S., Campos, J., & Emde, R. M. (1979). Facial patterning and infant emotional expressions: Happiness, surprise, and fear. *Child Development, 50,* 1020–1035.

Hiebert, E. H. (1991). Research directions: The development of word-level strategies in authentic literacy tasks. *Language Arts, 68,* 234–240.

Hieronymous, A., & Hoover, H. (1980). *Iowa Tests of Basic Skills, Form H.* Chicago: Riverside Publishing Company.

Hill, J. P., & Holmbeck, G. (1986). Attachment and autonomy during adolescence. In G. Whitehurst (Ed.), *Annals of child development* (Vol. 3). Greenwich, CT: Jai Press.

Hill, J. P., Holmbeck, G. N., Marlow, L., Green, T. M., & Lynch, M. E. (1985). Menarchal status and parent-child relations in families of seventh-grade girls. *Journal of Youth and Adolescence, 14,* 301–316.

Hirschman, R., & Katkin, E. S. (1974). Psychophysiological functioning, arousal, attention, and learning during the first year of life. In H. W. Reese (Ed.), *Advances in child development and behavior.* (Vol. 7). New York: Academic Press.

Hirshberg, L., & Svejda, M. (1990). When infants look to their parents: Infants' social referencing of mothers compared to fathers. *Child Development, 61,* 1175–1186.

Ho, M. W. (1984). Environment and heredity in development and evolution. In M. W. Ho & P. T. Saunders (Eds.), *Beyond neo-Darwinism: An introduction to the new evolutionary paradigm.* San Diego, CA: Academic Press.

Hofferth, S. L. (1987). The effects of programs and policies on adolescent pregnancy and childbearing. In S. L. Hofferth and C. B. Hayes (Eds.), *Risking the future: Adolescent sexuality, pregnancy, and childbearing* (Vol. 2, pp. 207–263). Washington, DC: National Academy Press.

Hoffman, M. (1982). Development of prosocial motivation: Empathy and guilt. In N. Eisenberg (Ed.), *The development of prosocial behavior* (pp. 281–313). San Diego, CA: Academic Press.

———. (1991). Empathy, social cognition, and moral action. In W. Kurtines and J. Gewirtz (Eds.), *Handbook of moral behavior and development: Vol. 1 Theory.* Hillsdale, NJ: Lawrence Erlbaum Associates.

———. (1988). Moral development. In M. H. Bornstein and M. E. Lamb (Eds.), *Developmental psychology: An advanced textbook.* 2d ed. Hillsdale, NJ: Lawrence Erlbaum.

Hofsten, C. von. (1982). Eye-hand coordination in newborns. *Developmental Psychology, 18,* 450–461.

Hogan, R. (1975). Theoretical egocentrism and the problem of compliance. *American Psychologist, 30,* 533–540.

Hogge, W. A., Schonberg, S. A., & Golbus, M. S. (1986). Chorionic villus sampling: Experience of the first 1000 cases. *American Journal of Obstetrics and Gynecology, 154*(6), 1249–1252.

Hunt, J. McV. (1965). Intrinsic motivation and its role in psychological development. *Nebraska Symposium on Motivation, 13,* 189–282.

Hunziker, U. A., & Barr, R. G. (1986). Increased carrying reduces infant crying: A randomized controlled trial. *Pediatrics, 77*(5), 641–647.

Hurwitz, E., Gunn, W., Pinsky, P., & Schonberger, L. (1991). Risk of respiratory illness associated with day-care attendance: A nationwide study. *Pediatrics, 87*, 62–69.

Huston, A. C., & Wright, J. C. (1983). Children's processing of television: The informative functions of formal features. In J. Bryant & D. R. Anderson (Eds.), *Children's understanding of television: Research on attention and comprehension.* New York: Academic Press.

Huston, A. C., Wright, J. C., Kerkham, D., Seigle, J., Rice, M., & Bremer, M. (1983). *Family environment and television use by preschool children.* Paper presented at the Biennial Meeting of the Society for Research in Child Development, Detroit, MI.

Huszti, H., & Chitwood, D. (1989). Prevention of pediatric and adolescent AIDS. In J. Seibert & R. Olson (Eds.), *Children, adolescents and AIDS.* Lincoln: University of Nebraska Press.

Huttenlocher, J., & Presson, C. B. (1973). Mental rotation and the perspective problem. *Cognitive Psychology, 4*, 277–299.

Huttenlocker, J., Haight, W., Bryk, A., Seltzer, M., & Lyons, T. (1991). Early vocabulary growth: Relation to language input and gender. *Developmental Psychology, 27*(2), 236–248.

Hymes, J. (1982). *Early childhood education. The year in review: A look at 1981.* Carmel, CA: Hacienda Press.

———. (1988). *Early childhood education. The year in review: A look at 1987.* Carmel, CA: Hacienda Press.

———. (1989). Early childhood education, the year in review: A look at 1988. Washington, DC: National Association for the Education of Young Children.

Ingalls, A. J., & Salerno, M. C. (1975). *Maternal and child health nursing.* St. Louis: C. V. Mosby.

Inhelder, B., & Piaget, J. (1958). *The growth of logical thinking from childhood to adolescence.* New York: Basic Books.

———. (1969). *The early growth of logic in the child.* (E. A. Lunzer & D. Papert, Trans.) New York: Norton.

Institute of Medicine (1985). *Preventing low birthweight: Summary.* Washington, DC: National Academy Press.

Irwin, C. E. (1989). Risk-taking behaviors in the adolescent patient: Are they impulsive? *Pediatric Annals, 18*(2), 122–133.

Isabella, R. A., & Belsky, J. (1991). Interactional synchrony and the origins of infant-mother attachment: A replication study. *Child Development, 62*(2), 373–384.

Itons-Peterson, M. J., & Reddel, M. (1984). What do people ask about the neonate? *Developmental Psychology, 20*(3), 358–359.

Izard, C. (1982). *Measuring emotions in infants and children.* New York: Cambridge University Press.

Izard, C. D., & Dougherty, L. (1982). Two complementary systems for measuring facial expressions in infants and children. In C. E. Izard (Ed.), *Measuring emotions in infants and children.* New York: Cambridge University Press.

Jackson, A. W., & Hornbeck, D. W. (1989). Educating young adolescents: Why we must restructure middle grade schools. *American Psychologist, 44*(5), 831–836.

Jackson, D. A. (1990). *Close relationships and the five personality factors: Construct validation of a measure of intimacy maturity.* Doctoral dissertation, Boston University.

Jacobs, B. W., & Isaacs, S. (1986). Pre-pubertal anorexia nervosa: A retrospective controlled study. *Journal of Child Psychiatry, 27*, 237–250.

Jacobson, J. L., Fein, G. G., Jacobson, S. W., & Schwartz, P. M. (1984). Factors and clusters for the Brazelton Scale: An investigation of the dimensions of neonatal behavior. *Developmental Psychology, 20*(3), 339–353.

Jacobvitz, D., & Sroufe, L. A. (1987). The early caregiver-child relationship and attention-deficit disorder with hyperactivity in kindergarten: A prospective study. *Child Development, 58*(6), 1488–1495.

James, W. (1920). *Letters.* Vol. 1. Boston: Atlantic Monthly Press.

Janofsky, M. (1989, March 6). Coach's drug use shaped philosophy. *The New York Times*, p. C7.

Jensen, A. (1969). How much can we boost IQ and scholastic achievement? *Harvard Educational Review, 39*, 1–123.

———. (1973). *Educability and group differences.* New York: Harper & Row.

———. (1974). Cumulative deficit: A testable hypothesis? *Developmental Psychology, 10*, 996–1019.

———. (1977). Cumulative deficit in IQ of blacks in the rural south. *Developmental Psychology, 13*, 184–191.

Jensen, R., & Moore, S. G. (1977). The effect of attribute statements on cooperativeness and competitiveness in school-aged boys. *Child Development, 48*, 305–307.

Johnson, C., Lewis, C., Love, S., Lewis, L., & Stucky, M. (1984). Incidence and correlates of bulimic behavior in a female high school population. *Journal of Youth and Adolescence, 15*(1), 15–26.

Johnson, D. W., & Johnson, R. T. (1974). Instructional structure: Cooperative, competitive and individualistic. *Reviews of Educational Research, 44*, 213–240.

Johnson, H. R., Mykre, S. A., Ruvalcaba, R. H. A., Thuline, H. C., & Kelley, V. C. (1970). Effects of testosterone on body image and behavior in Klinefelter's syndrome: A pilot study. *Developmental Medicine and Child Neurology, 12*, 454–460.

Johnson, K. (1988). *Teens and AIDS: Opportunities for prevention.* Washington, DC: Children's Defense Fund.

Johnson, M. D. (1990). Anabolic steroid use in adolescent athletes. *Pediatric Clinics of North America, 37*(5), 1111–1123.

Johnston, F. E., Low, S. M., deBaessa, Y., & MacVean, R. B. (1987). Interaction of nutritional and socioeconomic status as determinants of cognitive development in disadvantaged urban Guatemalan children. *American Journal of Physical Anthropology, 73*, 501–506.

Johnston, J. R., & Slobin, D. I. (1979). The development of locative expressions in English, Italian, Serbo-Croatian, and Turkish. *Journal of Child Language, 16,* 532–547.

Jolios, V. (1934). Inherited changes produced by heat treatment in *Dresophilia Melanogaster. Genetics, 16,* 476–494.

Jones, E. (1986). *Teenage pregnancy in industrialized countries.* New Haven, CT: Yale University Press.

Jones, H. C., & Lovinger, P. W. (1985). *The marijuana question.* New York: Dodd, Mead.

Jones, H. F. (1949). Adolescence in our society. In Anniversary Papers of the Community Service Society of New York: *The family in a democratic society* (pp. 70–82). New York: Columbia University Press.

Jones, W. M. (1977). The impact on society of youths who drop out or who are undereducated. *Educational Leadership, 34,* 413–416.

Joos, S. K., Pollitt, E., Mueleer, W. H., & Albright, D. L. (1983). The Bacon Chow study: Maternal nutritional supplementation and infant behavioral development. *Child Development, 54,* 669–676.

Joshi, N. P., & Scott, M. (1988). Drug use, depression, and adolescents. *Pediatric Clinics of North America, 35*(6), 1349–1364.

Joslyn, W. D. (1971). Androgen-induced social dominance in infant female rhesus monkeys. *Journal of Child Psychology and Psychiatry, 84,* 35–44.

Jurgen, H., Wimmer, H., & Perner, J. (1986). Ignorance versus false belief: A developmental lag in attribution of epistemic states. *Child Development, 57*(3) 567–582.

Kagan, J., Kearsley, R. B., & Zelazo, P. R. (1978). *Infancy: Its place in human development.* Cambridge, MA: Harvard University Press.

Kagan, J., & Snidman, N. (1991). Temperamental factors in human development. *American Psychologist, 46*(8), 856–862.

Kagan, S. L., & Zigler, E. E. (1987). *Early schooling: The national debate.* New Haven, CT: Yale University Press.

Kahler, K. S. (1989, February 26). The growing traffic in illegal steroids. *The Boston Sunday Globe,* p. 78.

Kamhi, A. G. (1986). The elusive first word: The importance of the naming insight for the development of referential speech. *Journal of Child Language, 13,* 155–161.

Kamii, C. (1982). *Number in preschool and kindergarten.* Washington, DC: National Association for the Education of Young Children.

———. (1985). *Young children reinvent arithmetic.* New York: Teachers College Press.

Kamin, L. J. (1974). *The Science and Politics of IQ.* Potomac, MD: Lawrence Erlbaum.

———. (1978). A positive interpretation of apparent "cumulative deficit." *Developmental Psychology, 14,* 195–196.

Kaplan, E. L., & Kaplan, G. A. (1970). The prelinguistic child. In J. Eliot (Ed.), *Human development and cognitive processes* (pp. 358–381). New York: Holt, Rinehart & Winston.

Kappas, A., Drummond, G. S., Manola, T., Petmezoki, S., & Valaes, T. (1988). Sn-protoporphyrin use in management of hyperbilirubinemia in term newborns with direct Coombs-Positive ABO incompatibility. *Pediatrics, 81*(4), 485–497.

Karen, R. (1990). Becoming attached. *The Atlantic Monthly,* February, 1990, 35–70.

Karniol, R. (1989). The role of manual manipulative stages in the infant's acquisition of perceived control over objects. *Developmental Review, 9,* 205–233.

Kataria, S., Swanson, M. S., & Trevathon, G. E. (1987). Persistence of sleep disturbances in preschool children. *Journal of Pediatrics, 110*(4), 642–646.

Katchadourian, H. A. (1977). *The biology of adolescence.* New York: W. H. Freeman.

Katz, L., & Hamilton, J. R. (1974). Fat absorption in infants of low birth weight less than 1,300 gm. *Journal of Pediatrics, 85,* 6081.

Kaufman, J., & Zigler, E. (1989). The intergenerational transmission of child abuse. In D. Cicchetti & V. Carlson (Eds.), *Child maltreatment: Theory and research on the causes and consequences of child abuse and neglect* (pp. 129–152). New York: Cambridge University Press.

Kaye, K. (1982a). *The mental and social life of babies.* Chicago: The University of Chicago Press.

———. (1982b). Organism, apprentice, and person. In E. Z. Tronick (Ed.), *Social interchange in infancy: Affect, cognition, and communication.* Baltimore: University Park Press.

Kaye, K., & Charney, R. (1980). How mothers maintain "dialogue" with two-year-olds. In D. Oldson (Ed.), *The social foundations of language and thought.* New York: Norton.

Kazdin, A. E. (1987). Treatment of antisocial behavior in children: Current status and future directions. *Psychological Bulletin, 102,* 187–203.

Keating, D. (1980). Thinking processes in adolescence. In J. Adelson (Ed.), *Handbook of adolescent psychology.* New York: Wiley.

Kegeles, S., Adler, N., and Irwin, D. (1988). Sexually active adolescents and condoms: Changes over one year in knowledge, attitudes and use. *American Journal of Public Health, 78*(4), 460–461.

Kelley, B., & Gilman, J. (1983). Follow-up of 373 children born after second trimester amniocentesis. *Pediatric Nursing, 9*(2), 95–97.

Kelly, C., & Goodwin, G. C. (1983). Adolescents' perception of three styles of parental control. *Adolescence, 18*(71), 567–571.

Kelly, D. H., & Shannon, D. C. (1982). Sudden infant death syndrome and near sudden death syndrome: A review of the literature, 1964–1982. *Pediatric Clinics of North America, 29*(5), 1241–1261.

Kemler-Nelson, D. G., Hirsh-Paseck, K., Jusczyk, S. W., & Cassidy, K. W. (1989). How the prosodic cues in motherese might assist language learning. *Journal of Child Language, 16,* 55–58.

Kempe, C. H. , Silverman, F. N., Steele, B. F., Droegemueller, W., & Silver, H. K. (1962). The battered child syndrome. *Journal of the American Medical Association, 181,* 4–11.

Kempe, R. S., & Kempe, C. H. (1978). *Child abuse.* Cambridge, MA: Harvard University Press.

Kerkay, J., Zsako, S., & Kaplan, A. (1971). Immunoelectrophoretic serum patterns associated with mothers of children affected with the G_1-trisomy syndrome (Down's syndrome). *American Journal of Mental Deficiency, 75,* 729–732.

Kerkman, D., Wrigh, J. C., Huston, A. C., Rice, M., & Bremer, M. (1983). *Preschoolers who get cable TV: Family patterns, media orientations, and media use.* Paper presented at the Biennial Meeting of the Society for Research in Child Development, Detroit, MI.

Kimmel, D. C., & Weiner, I. B. (1985). *Adolescence: A developmental transition.* Hillsdale, NJ: Lawrence Erlbaum.

Klaus, M. H., & Fannaroff, A. A. (1973). *Care of the high-risk neonate.* Philadelphia: W. B. Saunders.

Klaus, M. H., Jerazauld, R., Kreger, N. C., McAlpine, W., Steffa, M., & Kennell, J. H. (1972). Maternal attachment importance of the first post-partum days. *New England Journal of Medicine, 286,* 460–463.

Klaus, M. H., & Kennell, J. H. (1976). *Maternal-infant bonding.* St. Louis: Mosby.

Klein, E. (Ed.) (1985). *Children and computers. New directions in child development.* San Francisco: Jossey-Bass.

Kligman, D., & Cronnell, B. (1974). *Black English and spelling.* ERIC ED 108 234. Washington, DC: U. S. Government Printing Office.

Kline, M., Tschann, J. M., Johnston, J. R., & Wallerstein, J. S. (1989). Children's adjustment in joint and sole physical custody families. *Developmental Psychology, 25*(3), 430–436.

Klinnert, M. (1981). *The regulation of infant behavior by maternal facial expression.* Unpublished doctoral dissertation, University of Denver, Denver, CO.

Kogon, D. P., Oulton, M., Gray, J. H., Liston, R. M., Luther, E. R., Peddle, L. J., & Young, D. C. (1986). Amniotic fluid phosphatdylglycerol and phosphyatidylcholine phosphorus as predictors of fetal lung maturity. *American Journal of Obstetrics and Gynecology, 154*(2), 226–230.

Kohlberg, L. (1969). Stage and sequence: The cognitive developmental approach to socialization. In D. A. Goslin (Ed.), *Handbook of socialization theory and research* (pp. 347–480). Chicago: Rand McNally.

———. (1976). Moral stages and moralization. In T. Lickona (Ed.), *Moral development and behavior: Theory, research, and social issues* (pp. 219–249). New York: Holt, Rinehart & Winston.

Kohnstamm, G., Bates, J., & Rothbart, M. (1989). *Temperament in childhood.* New York: John Wiley & Sons.

Konner, M. (1982). Biological aspects of the mother-infant bond. In R. N. Emde & R. J. Harmon (Eds.), *The development of attachment and affiliative systems* (pp. 137–159; 237–259). New York: Plenum Press.

Kopp, C. B., & Krakow, J. B. (1983). The developmentalist and the study of biological risk: A view of the past with an eye toward the future. *Child Development, 54,* 1086–1108.

Korner, A. (1971). Individual differences at birth: Duplications for early experience and later development. *American Journal of Orthopsychiatry, 41,* 608–610.

Korner, A., & Grobstein, R. (1966). Visual alertness as related to soothing in neonates: Implications for maternal stimulation and early deprivation. *Child Development, 37,* 867–876.

Korner, A., & Thoman, E. B. (1972). The relative efficacy of contact and vestibular–proprioceptive stimulation on soothing neonates. *Child Development, 43,* 443–453.

Kozol, J. (1992). *Savage inequalities: Children in American's Schools.* New York: Crown.

Krantz, M. (1982). Sociometric awareness, social participation, and perceived popularity in preschool children. *Child Development, 53,* 376–379.

Kratcoski, P. E., & Kratcoski, J. E. (1975). Changing patterns in the delinquent activities of boys and girls: A self-reported delinquency analysis. *Adolescence, 37,* 53–91.

Krauss, R. M., & Glucksberg, S. (1969). The development of communication: Competence as a function of age. *Child Development, 42,* 255–266.

Kreutter, K. J., Gewirtz, H., Davenny, J. E., & Love, C. (1991). Drug and alcohol prevention project for sixth graders: First-year findings. *Adolescence, 26*(102), 287–293.

Kristiansson, B., & Fallstrom, S. P. (1987). Growth at the age of 4 years subsequent to early failure to thrive. *Child Abuse and Neglect, 11,* 35–40.

Krivacska, J. (1990). *Designing child sexual abuse prevention programs: Current approaches and a proposal for the prevention, reduction, and identification of sexual misuse.* Springfield, IL: Charles C. Thomas.

Kroger, J. (1985). Separation-individuation and ego identity status in New Zealand university students. *Journal of Youth and Adolescence, 14,* 133–147.

Kron, R. E., Stern, M., & Goddard, K. E. (1966). Newborn sucking behavior affected by obstetrics sedation. *Pediatrics, 37,* 1012–1016.

Krongrad, E., & O'Neill, L. (1986). Near miss sudden infant death syndrome episodes? A clinical and electrocardiographic correlation. *Pediatrics, 77*(6), 811–815.

Kuder, G. F. (1975). *General interest survey (form E) manual.* Chicago: Science Research Associates.

Kuhn, D. (1988). Cognitive development. In M. H. Bernstein & M. E. Lamb (Eds.), *Developmental psychology:* An advanced textbook. 2d ed. (pp. 205–260). Hillsdale, NJ: Lawrence Erlbaum.

———. (1989a). Children and adults as intuitive scientists. *Psychological Review, 96*(4), 674–689.

———. (1989b). Making cognitive development research relevant to education. In W. Damon (Ed.), *Child development today and tomorrow* (pp. 261–287). San Francisco: Jossey-Bass.

Kulberg, A. (1986). Substance abuse: Clinical identification and management. *Pediatrics Toxicology, 33*(2), 325–361.

Kurzweil, S. (1988). Recognition of mother from multisensory interactions in early infancy. *Infant Behavior and Development, 11,* 235–243.

Laboratory of Comparative Human Cognition. (1983). Culture and cognitive development. In P. Mussen (Ed.), *Handbook of child psychology: Vol. 1. History, theory, and methods.* New York: Wiley.

Ladd, G. E. (1981). Effectiveness of a social learning method for enhancing children's social interaction and peer acceptance. *Child Development, 52,* 171–178.

Ladd, G. (1990). Having friends, keeping friends, making friends, and being liked by peers in the classroom: Predictors of children's early school adjustment? *Child Development, 61,* 1081–1100.

Lamb, M. E., (1977). The development of parental preference in the first two years of life. *Sex Roles, 3,* 495–497.

———. (1982). Parent–infant interaction, attachment, and socioemotional development in infancy. In R. M. Emde & R. J. Harmon (Eds.), *The development of attachment and affiliative systems* (pp. 195–211). New York: Plenum Press.

Lambert, W. E., Just, M. N., & Segalowitz, N. (1970). Some cognitive consequences of following the curricula of the early school grades in a foreign language. In J. A. Alatis (Ed.), *Twenty-first annual round table: Bilingualism and language contact.* Washington, DC: Georgetown University Press.

Landrigan, P. (1981, December). *Report of the 84th Ross Conference on Pediatric Research.*

Lane, D., and Stratford, B. (1985). *Current approaches to Down's syndrome.* New York: Praeger.

Langer, E. J. (1979). The illusion of incompetence. In L. C. Perlmutter & R. A. Monty (Eds.), *Choice and perceived control* (pp. 301–313). Hillsdale, NJ: Lawrence Erlbaum.

Largo, R. H., Graf, S., Kundu, S., Hunziker, U., & Molinari, L. (1990). Predicting developmental outcome at school age from infant tests of normal, at-risk and retarded infants. *Developmental Medicine and Child Neurology, 32,* 30–45.

Lartz, M. N., & Mason, J. M. (1988). Jamie: One child's journey from oral to written language. *Early Childhood Research Quarterly, 3*(2), 193–208.

Lasch, C. (1977). *Haven in a heartless land.* New York: Basic Books.

Lavine, L. (1977). Differentiation of letterlike forms in pre-reading children. *Developmental Psychology, 13*(2), 89–94.

Leary, A., Huston, A. C., & Wright, J. C. (1983, April). *The influence of television production features with masculine and feminine connotations on children's comprehension and play.* Paper presented at the biennial meeting of the Society for Research in Child Development, Detroit, MI.

Lee, D. (1986). *Language, children and society: An introduction to linguistics and language development.* New York: New York University Press.

Leehan, J., & Wilson, L. (1985). *Grown-up abused children.* Springfield, IL: Charles C. Thomas.

Lefkowitz, M. M. (1981). Smoking during pregnancy: Long-term effects on offspring. *Developmental Psychology, 17*(2), 192–194.

Leflore, L. (1988). Delinquent youths and family. *Adolescence, 23,* 629–647.

Leifer, A. D., Leiderman, P. H., Barnett, C. R., & Williams, J. A. (1972). Effects of mother-infant separation on maternal attachment behavior. *Child Development, 43,* 1203–1218.

Lemish, D., & Rice, M. L. (1986). Television as a talking picture book: A prop for language acquisition. *Journal of Child Language, 13,* 254–274.

Lenz, W. (1966). Malformations caused by drugs in pregnancy. *American Journal of Diseases of Children, 112,* 99–106.

Leonard, C. H., Clyman, R. I., Piecuch, R. E., Juster, R. P., Ballard, R. A., & Behle, M. B. (1990). Effect of medical and social risk factors on outcome of prematurity and very low birthweight. *The Journal of Pediatrics, 116*(4), 620–626.

Lepore, S., Kiely, M., Bempechat, J., & London, P. (1989). Children's perceptions of social ability. Social cognitions and behavioral outcomes in the face of social rejection. *Child Study Journal, 19,* 254–271.

Lepper, M. (1973). Dissonance, self-perception, and honesty in children. *Journal of Personality and Social Psychology, 13,* 495–507.

Lerner, R. M. (1978). Nature, nurture and dynamic interactionism. *Human Development, 21,* 1–20.

———. (1991). Changing organism–context relations as the basic process of development: A developmental contextual perspective. *Developmental Psychology, 17*(1), 27–32.

———. (1986). *Concepts and theories of human development.* (2d ed.). New York: Random House.

Lester, D. (1988). Youth suicide: A cross-cultural perspective. *Adolescence, 23*(92), 955–966.

———. (1991). Social correlates of youth suicide rates in the United States. *Adolescence, 26*(101), 55–58.

Levenstein, P. (1977). The mother–child home program. In M. C. Day & R. Parker (Eds.), *The preschooler in action: Exploring early childhood programs* (2d ed.) (pp. 28–49). Boston: Allyn and Bacon.

Levine, S. (1966). Sex differences in the brain. *Scientific American, 214,* 84–90.

Lewis, C., & Osborne, A. (1990). Three-year-olds' problems with false belief: Conceptual deficit or linguistic artifact? *Child Development, 61,* 1514–1519.

Lewis, V. (1987). *Development and handicap.* Palo Alto, CA: Blackwell.

Liberman, I., Shankweiler, D., Fischer, F. W., & Carter, B. (1974). Explicit syllable and phoneme segmentation in the young child. *Journal of Experimental Child Psychology, 18,* 201–212.

Lickona, T. (1976). Research on Piaget's theory of moral development. In T. Lickona (Ed.), *Moral development and behavior: Theory, research, and social issues* (pp. 219–240). New York: Holt, Rinehart & Winston.

Lieberman, A. F. (1977). Preschoolers' competence with a peer: Relations with attachment and peer experience. *Child Development, 48,* 1277–1287.

Lieberman, A. F., Weston, D. R., and Pawl, J. H. (1991). Preventive intervention and outcome with anxiously attached dyads. *Child Development, 62,* 199–209.

Liebert, R. M. (1986). Effects of television on children and adolescents. *Journal of Development and Behavioral Pediatrics, 7*(1): 43–48.

Liebert, R. M., & Baron, R. A. (1972). Some immediate effects of televised violence on children's behavior. *Developmental Psychology, 6*, 469–475.

Lilienfield, A. M. (1969). *Epidemiology of mongolism*. Baltimore: Johns Hopkins Press.

Lindfors, J. W. (1987). *Children's language and learning* (2d ed.). Englewood Cliffs: Prentice-Hall.

Linn, M. C. (1983). Content, context, and process in reasoning. *Journal of Early Adolescence, 3*, 63–82.

Lipsitt, L. P. (1977). Taste in human neonates: Its effect on sucking and heart rates. In J. M. Weiffenbach (Ed.), *Taste and development: The genesis of sweet preference*. Washington, DC: U.S. Government Printing Office.

Lipsitt, L. P., Engen, T., & Kaye, H. (1963). Developmental changes in the olfactory threshold of the neonate. *Child Development, 34*, 371–376.

Lipsitt, L. P., & Levy, N. (1959). Electrotactual threshold in the neonate. *Child Development, 30*, 547–554.

Little, B. B., Snell, L. M., Klein, V. R., & Gilstrap, L. C. (1989). Cocaine abuse during pregnancy: Maternal and fetal indications. *Obstetrics and Gynecology, 73*(2), 157–160.

Loban, W. (1975). *Language development: Kindergarten through grade twelve*. Urbana, IL: National Council of Teachers of English.

Loeber, R. (1982). The stability of antisocial and delinquent child behavior: A review. *Child Development, 53*, 1431–1446.

Loeber, R., Tremblay, R., Gagnon, R., & Charlesbois, P. (1989). Continuity and desistance in disruptive boys' early fighting at school. *Development and Psychopathology, 1*, 39–50.

Long, T. J., & Long, L. (1982). *Latchkey children: The child's view of self care*. Resources in Education, (ERIC Document Reproduction Service No. ED 211 119).

Long, W., Thompson, T., Sundell, H., Schumacher, R., Volberg, F., Guthrie, R., & American Exosurf Neonatal Study Group (1991). Effects of two rescue doses of a synthetic surfactant on mortality rate and survival without bronchopulmonary dysplasia in 700 1350-gram infants with respiratory distress syndrome. *Journal of Pediatrics, 118*(4), 595–605.

Lovett, S., & Flavell, J. (1990). Understanding and remembering: Children's knowledge about the differential effects of strategy and task variables on comprehension and memorization. *Child Development, 61*(6), 1842–1859.

Lowrey, G. H. (1978). *Growth and development of children* (7th Ed.). Chicago: Year Book.

Lowry, D. T., & Towles, D. (1989). Soap opera portrayals of sex, contraception, and sexually transmitted diseases. *Journal of Communication, 39*(2), 76–83.

Lubchenco, L. O., Delivotia-Papodopoulos, M., & Searle, D. (1972). Long-term follow-up studies of prematurely born infants II. Influences of birth weight and gestational age on sequelae. *Journal of Pediatrics, 80*, 509–512.

Lucey, J. F., & Dangman, B. (1984). A reexamination of the role of oxygen in retrolental fibroplasia. *Pediatrics, 73*(1), 82–95.

Lyle, J., & Hoffman, H. (1972). Children's use of television and other media. *Television in everyday life: Patterns of use*. Washington, DC: U.S. Government Printing Office.

Lytton, H. (1990). Child and parent effects in boys' conduct disorders. *Developmental Psychology, 26*(5), 683–697.

Maccoby, E. E. (1980). *Social development: Psychological growth and the parent-child relationship*. New York: Harcourt Brace Jovanovich.

Maccoby, E. E., & Jacklin, C. N. (1974). *The psychology of sex differences*. Stanford, CA: Stanford University Press.

Maddi, S. R. (1976). *Personality theories*. Homewood, IL: Dorsey.

Magnuson, D. (1988). *Individual developmental from an interactional perspective: A longitudinal perspective*. Hillside, NJ: Erlbaum.

Magnusson, D., Stattin, H., & Allen, V. L. (1985). Biological maturation and social development: A longitudinal study of some adjustment processes from mid-adolescence to adulthood. *Journal of Youth and Adolescence, 14*, 267–283.

Maier, H. (1987). *Three theories of child development* (3d ed.). New York: Harper & Row.

Maier, S., Seligman, M., & Solomon, R. (1969). Pavlovian fear conditioning and learned helplessness. In B. A. Campbell & R. M. Church (Eds.), *Punishment and aversive behavior*. New York: Appleton-Century-Crofts.

Main, M. (1981). Avoidance in the service of attachment: A working paper. In K. L. Immelmenn, G. W. Barlow, L. Petrinovitch, & M. Main (Eds.), *Behavioral development*. Cambridge, England: Cambridge University Press.

Mandler, J. M., Bauer, P. J., & McDonough, L. (1991). Separating the sheep from the goats: Differentiating global categories. *Cognitive Psychology, 23*(2), 263–298.

Mann, L., & Boyce, S. (1982). Fundamental frequency and discourse structure. *Language & Speech, 25*, 341–383.

Marcia, J. E. (1980). Identity in adolescence. In J. Adelson (Ed.), *Handbook of adolescent psychology* (pp. 159–187). New York: Wiley.

———. (1988). Common processes underlying ego identity, cognitive/moral development, and individuation. In D. Lapsky and F. C. Power (Eds.), *Self, ego, and identity: Integrative approaches* (pp. 211–225). New York: Springer-Verlag.

Marek, E. (1989, April). The lives of teenage mothers. *Harper's Magazine*, pp. 59–64.

Marks, A. (1980). Adolescent suicide: Epidemiologic study of recent trends. In F. A. Oski & J. N. Stockman (Eds.), *1980 yearbook of pediatrics*. Chicago: Yearbook.

Marland, S. P. (1972). Education of the gifted and talented. *Report to the Congress of the United States by the United States Commissioner of Education and background papers submitted to the United States Office of Education*. Washington, DC: U.S. Government Printing Office.

Marold, D. (1987). *Correlates of suicidal ideation among young adolescents*. Unpublished doctoral dissertation. University of Denver.

Marsiglio, W., & Mott, F. L. (1986). The impact of sex education on sexual activity, contraceptive use and premarital pregnancy among American teenagers. *Family Planning Perspectives, 17*, 132.

Marston, A. R., Jacobs, D. F., Singer, R. D., Widaman, K. F., & Little, J. D. (1988). Adolescents who apparently are invulnerable to drug, alcohol, and nicotine use. *Adolescence, 23*(9), 593–598.

Martin, A. (1988). Screening, early intervention, and remediation: Obscuring children's potential. *Harvard Educational Review, 58*(4), 488–501.

Martin, A. D., Simpson, J. L., Rosinky, B. J., & Elias, S. (1986). Chorionic villus sampling in continuous pregnancies. *American Journal of Obstetrics and Gynecology, 154*(6), 1353–1362.

Martinez, F. D. (1991). Sudden infant death syndrome and small airway occlusions: Facts and a hypothesis. *Pediatrics, 87*(2), 190–198.

Marwich, C., & Simmons, D. (1984). Medical news: Changing childhood disease patterns linked with day-care boom. *Journal of the American Medical Association, 251*, 1245–1251.

Marx, G. F. (1961). Placental transfer and drugs used in anesthesia. *Anesthesiology, 22*, 294.

Mason, J. (1980). When do children begin to read? An exploration of four-year-old children's letter and word reading competencies. *Reading Research Quarterly, 15*, 203–227.

Massachusetts Department of Public Health, Public Health Fact Sheet: AIDS. (1985, November).

Matas, L., Arend, R. A., & Sroufe, L. A. (1978). Continuity of adaptation in the second year: The relationship between quality of attachment and later competence. *Child Development, 49*, 547–556.

Matthews, W. (1979). *He and she: How children develop their sex–role identity.* Englewood Cliffs, NJ: Prentice-Hall.

McAllister, A. L., Perry, C. & Maccoby, N. (1979). Adolescent smoking: Onset and prevention. *Pediatrics, 63*(4), 650–658.

McBroom, W. H. (1981). Parental relationships, socioeconomic status, and sex role expectations. *Sex Roles, 7*, 1027–1033.

McClelland, D. C., Atkinson, I. W., Clark, R. A., & Lowell, E. L. (1976). *The achievement motive.* New York: Halsted Press.

McCormick, C. E., & Mason, J. M. (1989). Fostering reading for Head Start children with little books. In J. B. Allen & J. M. Mason (Eds.), *Risk makers, risk takers, risk breakers* (pp. 154–177). Portsmouth, NH: Heinemann Educational Books.

McCormick, M., Gortmaker, S., & Sobol, A. (1990). Very low birthweight children. Behavior problems and school difficulty in a national sample. *The Journal of Pediatrics, 117*, 687–693.

McCune-Nicolich, L. (1981). Toward symbolic functioning: Structure of early pretend games and potential parallels with language. *Child Development, 52*, 785–797.

McCune-Nicolich, L., & Fenson, L. (1984). Methodological issues in studying early pretend play. In T. Yowkey &

T. Pellegrini (Eds.), *Child's play.* Hillsdale, NJ: Lawrence Erlbaum.

McGhee, P. E. (1971). Cognitive development and children's comprehension of humor. *Child Development, 42*, 123–138.

———. (1979). *Humor: Its origin and development.* San Francisco: W. H. Freeman.

McGowan, R. W., Jarmon, B. O., & Peterson, D. M. (1974). Effects of a competitive endurance training program on self-concept and peer approval. *Journal of Psychology, 86*, 57–60.

McKnight, J., & Shelsby, B. (1984). Checking in: An alternative for latchkey kids. *Children Today, 13*(3), 23–25.

McLaughlin, B. (1978). *Second language acquisition in childhood.* New York: Wiley.

———. (1984). *Second language acquisition in childhood* (Vol. 1). Hillsdale, NJ: Lawrence Erlbaum.

McLaughlin, E., & Crawford, J. D. (1985). Burns. *Pediatric Clinics of North America, 32*, 61–75.

McNeill, D. (1966). Developmental psycholinguistics. In F. Smith & G. A. Miller (Eds.), *The genesis of language: A psycholinguistic approach* (pp. 15–84). Cambridge, MA: MIT Press.

Meehan, A. M. (1984). A meta-analysis of sex differences in formal operational thought. *Child Development, 55*, 1110–1124.

Meichenbaum, D., & Turk, D. (1976). The cognitive-behavioral management of anxiety, anger, and pain. In P. O. Davison (Ed.), *The behavioral management of anxiety, depression, and pain.* New York: Brunner/Mazel.

Melton, G. (1988). Adolescents and prevention of AIDS. *Professional psychology: Research and practice, 19*(4), 403–408.

Mennuti, M. T., DiGaetano, A., McDonnell, A., Cohen, A. W., & Liston, R. M. (1983). Fetal-maternal bleeding associated with genetic amniocentesis: Read time versus static ultrasound. *Obstetrics and Gynecology, 62*(1), 26–30.

Menyuk, P. (1969). *Language and maturation.* Cambridge, MA: MIT Press.

———. (1977). *Language and maturation.* Cambridge, MA: MIT Press.

Merritt, A., & Valdes-Dapena, M. (1984). SIDS research update. *Pediatric Annals, 13*(3), 193–207.

Merritt, T. A., Hallman, M., Berry, C., Pohjovouri, M., Edwards, D. K., Jaaskelainan, J., Grafe, M. R., Vaucher, Y., Wozniak, P., Heldt, G., & Rapola, J. (1991). Randomized, placebo-controlled trial of human surfactant given at birth versus rescue administration in very low birth-weight infants with lung immaturity. *Journal of Pediatrics, 118*(4), 581–594.

Mestayan, G., & Varga, R. (1960). Chemical thermoregulation of full-term and premature newborn infants. *Journal of Pediatrics, 56*, 623–629.

Metzger, R. L., & Werner, D. B. (1984). Use of visual training for reading disabilities: A review. *Pediatrics, 73*(6), 824–829.

Meyer, R. E. (1989). Who can say no to illicit drug use? *Archives of General Psychiatry, 46*(2), 189–190.

Michelsson, K., Rinne, A., & Paajanen, S. (1990). Crying,

feeding and sleeping patterns in 1 to 12-month-old infants. *Child: Care, Health, and Development, 16,* 99–11.

Milberg, A. (1976). *Street games.* New York: McGraw-Hill.

Millar, W. S. (1974). Conditioning and learning in early infancy. In B. Foss (Ed.), *New perspectives in child development.* Harmondsworth, England: Penguin.

Miller, G. A., Galanter, E. H., and Pribram, K. H. (1960). *Plan and the structure of behavior.* New York: Holt, Rinehart and Winston.

Miller, J. G. (1971). The nature of living systems. *Behavioral Science, 16,* 277–301.

Miller, L. G., & Bizzell, R. P. (1983). Long-term effects of four preschool programs: 6th, 7th, and 8th grades. *Child Development, 54,* 725–741.

Miller, M. (1987, November 23). Drug use: Down but not in the ghetto. *Newsweek, 110,* 33.

Miller, M. A., & Brooten, D. A. (1977). *The childbearing family: A nursing perspective.* Boston: Little, Brown.

Miller, P., & DeMaire-Dreblow, D. (1990). Social-cognitive correlates of children's understanding of displaced aggression. *Journal of Experimental Child Psychology, 49,* 488–504.

Miller, R. E., & Rosenstein, D. J. (1982). Children's dental health: Overview for the physician. *Pediatric Clinics of North America, 29*(3), 429–438.

Miller, R. L., Brickman, P., & Bolen, D. (1975). Attribution versus persuasion as a means for modifying behavior. *Journal of Personality and Social Psychology, 21*(3), 430–441.

Miller, S., & Garvey, D. (1984). Mother-baby role play: Its origins in social support. In I. Bretherton (Ed.), *Symbolic play: The development of social understanding* (pp. 101–130). New York: Academic Press.

Miller-Jones, D. (1989). Culture and testing. *American Psychologist, 44*(2), 360–366.

Millstein, S. G. (1989). Adolescent health. *American Psychologist, 44*(5), 837–842.

Mineka, S., Gunnar, M., & Champoux, M. (1986). Control and early socioemotional development: Infant Rhesus monkeys reared in controllable versus uncontrollable environments. *Child Development, 57,* 1241–1256.

Minton, C., Kagan, J., & Levine, J. A. (1971). Maternal control and obedience in the two-year-old. *Child Development, 42,* 1873–1894.

Minuchin, P. P., & Shapiro, E. K. (1983). The school as a context for social development. In P. H. Mussen (Ed.), *Handbook of child psychology* (4th ed., Vol. 4). New York: Wiley.

Mischel, W. (1976). *Introduction to personality.* New York: Holt, Rinehart & Winston.

Mischel, W., & Baker, N. (1975). Cognitive transformation of reward objects through instructions. *Journal of Personality and Social Psychology, 31,* 254–261.

Mischel, W., & Ebbesen, E. (1970). Attention in delay of gratification. *Journal of Personality and Social Psychology, 16,* 329–337.

Mizukami, K., Kobayashi, N., Ishii, T., & Iwata, H. (1990). First selective attachment begins in early infancy: A study using telethermography. *Infant Behavior and Development,* 13, 257–271.

Moerk, E. L. (1989). The LAD was a lday and the tasks were ill-defined. *Developmental Review, 9,* 21–57.

Mofenson, H. C., & Caraccio, T. R. (1987). *Pediatric Annals, 16*(1), 864–874.

Moffit, A. R. (1971). Consonant cue perception by twenty- to twenty-four-week-old infants. *Child Development, 42,* 717–731.

Morishima, H. O., Daniel, S. S., Finster, M., Poppers, P. J., & James, L. S. (1966). Transmission of mepivocaine hydrochloride (carbocaine) across the human placenta. *Anesthesiology, 27,* 147–154.

Morphett, M. V., & Washburne, C. (1931). When should children begin to read? *Elementary School Journal, 31,* 496–503.

Morrow, L. M. (1988). Young children's responses to one-to-one story readings in school settings. *Reading Research Quarterly, 23*(1), 89–107.

Moses, L. J., & Flavell, J. H. (1990). Inferring false beliefs from actions and reactions. *Child Development, 61,* 929–945.

Moses, N., Mansour-Max, B., & Lifshitz, F. (1989). Fear of obesity among adolescent girls. *Pediatrics, 83*(3), 393–398.

Moskowitz, B. A. (1978). The acquisition of language. *Scientific American, 239,* 92–108.

Mueller, E., Bleir, M., Krakow, J., Hegedus, K., & Cournoyer, P. (1977). The development of peer verbal interaction among two-year-old boys. *Child Development, 48,* 284–287.

Muir, D., & Field, J. (1979). Newborn infants orient to sounds. *Child Development, 50,* 431–436.

Mullis, I., Owen, E., & Phillips, G. (1990). *America's challenge: Accelerating academic achievement: A summary of findings from 20 years of NAEP.* Princeton, NJ: Educational Testing Service.

Muma, J. R. (1986). *Language acquisition: A functionalistic perspective.* Austin, TX: Pro-Ed.

Murphy, C. M., & Messer, D. J. (1977). Mothers, infants, and pointing: A study of gesture. In H. R. Schaffer (Ed.), *Studies in mother-infant interaction.* London: Academic Press.

Murray, A., Dolby, R. M., Nation, R. L., & Thomas, D. B. (1981). Effects of epidural anesthesia on newborns and their mothers. *Child Development, 52,* 71–82.

Murray, A. D. (1988). Newborn auditory brain stem evoked response (ABRs): Prenatal and contemporary correlates. *Child Development, 59*(3), 571–588.

Murray, A. D., Johnson, J., & Peters, J. (1990). Fine-tuning of utterance length to preverbal infants: Effects on later language development. *Journal of Child Language, 17,* 511–525.

Murray, J. P., & Lonnborg, B. (undated). *Children and television.* Boys Town, NB: The Boys Town Center.

Murray, J. P., & Salomon, G. (Eds.) (1984). *The future of children's television.* Boys Town, NB: The Boys Town Center.

Murstein, B. L., Chalpin, M. J., Heard, K. V., & Vyse, S. A. (1989). Sexual behavior, drugs, and relationship patterns on a college campus over thirteen years. *Adolescence, 24,* 125–139.

Musick, J. S., Clark, R., & Cohler, B. (1981). The Mothers' Project: A program for mentally ill mothers of young children. In B. Weissbourd & J. Musick, (Eds.), *Infants: Their social environments.* Washington, DC: National Association for the Education of Young Children.

Naeye, R. (1983). Maternal age, obstetric complications, and the outcome of pregnancy. *Obstetrics and Gynecology, 61*(2), 210–216.

Naeye, R. L., Blanc, W., & Paul, C. (1973). Effects of maternal nutrition on the human fetus. *Pediatrics, 52,* 494–503.

National Association for the Education of Young Children. (1986). Position statement on developmentally appropriate practice in programs for 4- and 5-year-olds. *Young Children, 41,* 20–29.

National Association for the Education of Young Children (1990). Washington update. *Young Children, 46*(1), 61.

National Association for the Education of Young Children (1991). Public Policy Report: 101st Congress: The children's congress. *Young Children, 46*(2), 78–81.

National March of Dimes. (1973).

Needham, J. (1959). *A history of embryology.* New York: Abelard-Schuman.

Neimark, E. D. (1981). Confounding with cognitive style factors: An artifact explanation for the apparent nonuniversal incidence of formal operations. In I. Sigel, D. Brodzinsky, & R. Golnikoff (Eds.), *New directions in Piagetian research and theory.* Hillsdale, NJ: Lawrence Erlbaum.

Nelson, C., & Keith, J. (1990). Comparison of female and male early adolescent sex-role attitude and behavior development. *Adolescence, 25,* 183–204.

Nelson, K. (1973). Structure and strategy in learning to talk. *Monographs of the Society for Research in Child Development, 38.*

Nelson, K. E., & Nelson, K. (1978). Cognitive pendulums and the linguistic realization. In K. E. Nelson (Ed.), *Children's language* (Vol. 1). New York: Gardner Press.

Neuman, S. B. (1988). The displacement effect: Assessing the relation between television viewing and reading performance. *Reading Research Quarterly, 23*(4), 414–440.

Neumann, C. G. (1977). Obesity in pediatric practice: Obesity in the preschool and school-age child. *Pediatric Clinics of North America, 24,* 117–122.

Newberger, C. M. (1980). The cognitive structure of parenthood: Designing a descriptive measure. In *New directions in child development* (Vol. 7) (pp. 45–67). San Francisco: Jossey-Bass.

Newcomb, M. D., & Bentler, P. M. (1989). Substance use and abuse among children and teenagers. *American Psychologist, 44*(2), 242–248.

Newell, A., Shaw, J. C., & Simon, H. A. (1958). Elements of a theory of human problem solving. *Psychological Review, 65,* 151–166.

Newman, H. H., Freeman, F. N., & Holzinger, K. J. (1937). *Twins: A study of heredity and environment.* Chicago: University of Chicago Press.

Newman, J. M. (1985). Insights from recent reading and writing research and their implications for developing whole language curriculum. In J. M. Newman (Ed.), *Whole language: Theory and use.* Portsmouth, NH. Heinemann Educational Books.

Newport, E. L., Gleitman, H. J., & Gleitman, L. R. (1977). Mother, I'd rather do it myself: Some effects and noneffects of maternal speech style. In C. E. Snow & C. A. Ferguson (Eds.), *Talking to children: Language input and acquisition.* Cambridge, England: Cambridge University Press.

Newson, J., & Newson, E. (1978). *Seven years old in the home environment.* London: Penguin.

Nezworski, T., Tolan, W., & Belsky, J. (1988). Intervention in insecure infant attachment. In J. Belsky, & T. Nezworski (Eds.), *Clinical implications of attachment.* Hillsdale, NJ: Lawrence Erlbaum Associates.

Nicholas, S. W., Sondheimer, D. L., Willoughby, A. D., Yaffe, S. J., & Katz, S. L. (1989). Human immunodeficiency virus infection in childhood, adolescence, and pregnancy: A status report and national research agenda. *Pediatrics, 83*(2), 293–308.

Nicolich, L. (1977). Beyond sensorimotor intelligence: Assessment of symbolic maturity through analysis of pretend play. *Merrill-Palmer Quarterly, 23,* 89–99.

Nielsen, G., Collins, S., Meisel, J., Lowry, M., Eng, M., & Johnson, D. (1975). An intervention program for atypical infants. In B. Z. Friedlander, G. M. Sterritt, & G. E. Kirk (Eds.), *Exceptional infant: Assessment and intervention.* (Vol. 3). New York: Brunner/Mazel.

Nielson Television Index. (1982). *Child and teenage television viewing (special release).* New York: Nielson Television Index.

Ninio, A., & Bruner, J. (1978). The achievement and antecedents of labelling. *Journal of Child Language, 5,* 1–15.

Nissen, H. W. (1930). A study of exploratory behavior in the white rat by means of the obstruction method. *Journal of Genetic Psychology, 37,* 361–376.

Norbert, R., & Morgan, K. A. (1991). Assessing differences in chemically dependent adolescent males using the child behavior checklist. *Adolescence, 26*(101), 183–194.

Nowinski, J. (1990). *Substance abuse in adolescents and young adults: A guide to treatment.* New York: W. W. Norton.

Nuland, S. B. (1988). *Doctors: The biography of medicine.* New York: Knopf.

Nurss, J. R., & McGauvran, M. E. (1986). Metropolitan Readiness Assessment Program (5th ed.). Orlando, FL: Harcourt Brace Jovanovich.

Oakes, J. (1985). *Keeping track: How schools structure inequality.* New Haven, CT: Yale University Press.

Oden, S., & Asher, S. R. (1977). Coaching children in social skills for friendship making. *Child Development, 48,* 495–506.

O'Driscoll, K., & Foley, M. (1983). Correlation of decrease in perinatal mortality and increase in cesarean section rates. *Obstetrics and Gynecology, 61*(1), 1–5.

Okra, E. R., & Paris, S. G. (1987). Patterns of motivation and reading skills in underachieving children. In S. J. Ceci (Ed.), *Handbook of cognitive, social, and neuropsychological aspects of learning disabilities* (Vol. 2) (pp. 115–146). Hillsdale, NJ: Erlbaum.

Oliver, J. E., & Taylor, A. (1971). Five generations of ill-treated children in one family pedigree. *The British Journal of Psychiatry, 119,* 473–480.

Olsen, J. A., Jensen, L. C., & Greaves, P. M. (1991). Adolescent sexuality and public policy. *Adolescence, 26*(102), 417–430.

Olson, R. (Ed.). (1986). The manipulation of children's eating preferences. *Nutrition Reviews, 44*(10), 327–328.

Olvera-Ezzell, N., Power, T. G., & Cousins, J. H. (1990). Maternal socialization of children's eating habits: Strategies used by obese Mexican-American mothers. *Child Development, 61*(2), 395–400.

Olweus, D., Mattsson, A., Schalling, D., & Low, H. (1980). Testosterone, aggression, physical and personality dimensions in normal adolescent males. *Psychosomatic Medicine, 42,* 253–269.

Ornstein, P. A., & Naus, M. J. (1978). Rehearsal processes in children's memory. In P. A. Ornstein (Ed.), *Memory development in children.* Hillsdale, NJ: Lawrence Erlbaum.

Oster, G., & Caro, J. (1990). *Understanding and treating depressed adolescents and their families.* New York: John Wiley & Sons.

Padina, R., & Schnele, J. (1983). Psychosocial correlates of alcohol and drug use of adolescent students and adolescents in treatment. *Journal of Studies on Alcohol, 44*(6), 950–973.

Pai, A. C. (1974). *Foundations of genetics.* New York: McGraw-Hill.

Paneth, N. (1986). Etiologic factors in cerebral palsy. *Pediatric Annals, 15*(3), 191–201.

Papousek, H. (1967). Experimental studies of appetitional behavior in human newborns and infants. In H. Stevenson, E. Hess, & H. Rheingold (Eds.), *Early behavior: Comparative and developmental approaches.* New York: Wiley.

Papousek, H., & Bernstein, P. (1969). The functioning of conditioning stimulation in human neonates and infants. In A. Ambrose (Ed.), *Stimulation in early infancy.* New York: Academic Press.

Paratore, J. (1991). *An investigation of an intergenerational approach to literacy.* Boston University Intergenerational Literacy Project. School of Education, Boston University.

Pardeck, J. T. (1991). A multiple regression analysis of family factors affecting the potential for alcoholism in college students. *Adolescence, 26*(102), 341–347.

Parke, R. D., & Lewis, N. G. (1981). The family in context: A multilevel interactional analysis of child abuse. In R. W. Henderson (Ed.), *Parent-child interaction: Theory, research, and prospects* (pp. 169–204). New York: Academic Press.

Parke, R. D., & Slaby, R. G. (1983). The development of aggression. In P. H. Mussen (Ed.), *Handbook of child psychology* (Vol. 4). New York: Wiley.

Parke, R. D., & Suomi, S. J. (1980). Adult male-infant relationships: Human and nonprimate evidence. In K. L. Immelmann, G. Barlow, M. Main, & L. Petrinovitch (Eds.), *Behavioral development: The Bielefeld interdisciplinary project.* New York: Cambridge University Press.

Parsons, J. E., Adler, T. F., & Kaczala, C. M. (1982). Socialization of achievement attitudes and beliefs: Parental influences. *Child Development, 53*(2), 310–321.

Parten, M. (1932). Social play among preschool children. *Journal of Abnormal and Social Psychology, 27,* 243–269.

Partol, S. (1980). *The correlates of parental awareness.* Doctoral dissertation, Graduate School of Education, Boston University.

Pastor, D. L. (1981). The quality of mother–infant attachment and its relationship to toddler's initial sociability with peers. *Developmental Psychology, 17,* 326–338.

Patterson, C. (1982). Self-control and self-regulation in childhood. In T. Field & A. Huston-Stein (Eds.), *Review of human development.* New York: Wiley.

Patterson, C., Cohn, D., & Kao, B. (1989). Maternal warmth as a protective factor against risks associated with peer rejection among children. *Developmental and Psychopathology, 1,* 21–38.

Patterson, C., Kupersmidt, J., & Griesler, P. (1990). Children's perceptions of self and of relationships with others as a function of sociometric status. *Child Development, 6,* 1335–1349.

Patterson, C., & Mischel, W. (1976). Effects of temptation-inhibiting and task-facilitating plans on self-control. *Journal of Personality and Social Psychology, 33,* 209–217.

Patterson, G. L., Litman, R. A., & Bricker, W. (1967). Assertive behavior in children: A step toward a theory of aggression. *Monographs of the Society for the Research in Child Development, 32,* 1–43.

Patterson, G. R., DeBaryshe, B. D., & Ramsey, E. (1989). A developmental perspective on antisocial behavior. *American Psychologist, 44*(2), 329–335.

Patterson, G. R., & Reid, J. B. (1984). Social interaction processes within the family: The study of moment-by-moment family transactions in which human social development is embedded. *Journal of Applied Developmental Psychology, 5,* 237–262.

Pearson, J., & Ferguson, L. (1989). Gender differences in patterns of spatial ability, environmental cognition, and math and English achievement in late adolescence. *Adolescence, 24,* 421–431.

Peck, J. T., McCaig, G., & Sapp, M. E. (1988). *Kindergarten policies: What is best for children?* Washington, DC: National Association for the Education of Young Children.

Peck, R. F., & Havighurst, R. (1960). *The psychology of character development.* New York: Wiley.

Perkins, R. P., Nakashima, I. I., Mullin, M., Dubansky, L. S., & Chin, M. L. (1978). Intensive care in adolescent pregnancy. *Obstetrics and Gynecology, 52*(2), 179–188.

Perlstein, P. H., Hersh, C., Glueck, C. J., & Sutherland, J. M. (1974). Adaptation to cold in the first three days of life. *Pediatrics, 54,* 411.

Perry, D., Williard, J., & Perry, L. (1990). Peers' perceptions of the consequences that victimized children provide aggressors. *Child Development, 61,* 1310–1325.

Peskin, J. (1980). Female performance and Inhelder's and Piaget's tests of formal operations. *Genetic Psychology Monographs, 101,* 245–256.

Peterson, A. C. (1979). Can puberty come any earlier? *Psychology Today, 12,* 45.

Peterson, A. C., & Taylor, B. (1980). The biological approach to adolescence: Biological change and psychological adaptation. In J. Adelson (Ed.), *Handbook of adolescent psychology* (pp. 117–155). New York: Wiley.

Peterson, L. (1990). PhoneFriend: A developmental description of needs expressed by child callers to a community telephone support system for children. *Journal of Applied Developmental Psychology, 11*(1), 105–122.

Pfeiffer, S. I., & Aylward, G. P. (1990). Outcome for preschoolers of very low birthweight: Sociocultural and environmental influences. *Perceptual and Motor Skills, 10,* 1367–1378.

Pflaum, S. W. (1986). *The development of language and literacy in young children* (3d ed.). Columbus, OH: Charles E. Merrill.

Phillips, C. (1974). Neonatal heat loss in heated cribs versus mothers' arms. *Child and Family, 4,* 307–314.

Phillips, D. A. (1987). Socialization of perceived academic competence among highly competent children. *Child Development, 58,* 1308–1320.

Phillips, D. S., & Zimmerman, M. (1990). The developmental course of perceived competence. In R. J. Sternberg & J. Kolligian (Eds.), *Competence considered*. New Haven: Yale University Press.

Phinney, J. S., Feshbach, N. D. & Farver, J. (1986). Preschool children's response to peer crying. *Early Childhood Research Quarterly, 1*(3), 189–206.

Phoenix, C. H., Goy, R. W., & Resko, J. A. (1978). Psychosexual differentiation as a function of androgenic stimulation. In H. Bee (Ed.), *Social issues in developmental psychology* (2d ed.). New York: Harper & Row.

Piaget, J. (1952). *The origins of intelligence in children* (M. Cook, Trans.). New York: International Universities Press.

———. (1954). *The construction of reality in the child* (M. Cook, Trans.). New York: Ballantine Books.

———. (1963). *The origins of intelligence in children* (M. Cook, Trans.). New York: Norton. (Original work published 1936).

———. (1965). *The moral judgment of the child* (M. Gabain, Trans.). New York: Free Press. (Original work published 1932).

———. (1967). *The child's conception of space* (F. T. Langdon & J. L. Lunger, Trans.). New York: Norton.

———. (1969). *The child's conception of the world*. (J. Tomlinson & A. Tomlinson, Trans.). Totowa, NJ: Littlefield, Adams.

Piaget, J., & Inhelder, B. (1967). *The child's conception of space*. (F. J. Langdon & J. L. Lunger, Trans.). New York: Norton. (Original work published 1948.)

Piaget, J., Montangero, J., & Billeter, J. (1977). Les correlats. In J. Piaget (Ed.), *L'abstraction reflechissante* (pp. 115–129). Paris: Presses Universitaires de France.

Ploman, L., & Persson, B. (1957). On the transfer of barbiturates to the human fetus and their accumulation in some of its vital organs. *Journal of Obstetrics and Gynaecology of the British Empire, 64,* 706–711.

Plomin, R. (1989). Environment and genes: Determinants of behavior. *American Psychologist, 44*(2), 105–111.

Plomin, R., & Dunn, J., (Eds.) (1986). *The study of temperament*. Hillsdale, NJ: Lawrence Erlbaum.

Plummer, G. (1952). Anomalies occurring in children exposed in utero to the atomic bomb in Hiroshima. *Pediatrics, 10,* 687.

Pollitt, E., Garza, C., & Leibel, R. L. (1984). Nutrition and public policy. In H. W. Stevenson & A. E. Siegel (Eds.), *Child development research and social policy* (pp. 421–470). Chicago: University of Chicago Press.

Pollock, L. (1987). *A lasting relationship: Parents and children over three centuries*. London: University Press of New England.

Pomerleau, A., Bolduc, D., Malcuit, G., & Cossette, L. (1990). Pink or blue: Environmental gender stereotypes in the first two years of life. *Sex Roles, 22,* 359–367.

Porter, F. S., Blick, L. C., & Sgroi, S. (1982). Treatment of the sexually abused child. In S. Sgroi (Ed.), *Handbook of clinical intervention in child sexual abuse*. Lexington, MA: Lexington Books.

Power, T. G., & Parke, R. D. (1982). Play as a context for early learning. In L. M. Laosa & I. E. Sigel (Eds.), *Families as Learning Environments for Children* (pp. 147–178). New York: Plenum Press.

Powers, S. I., Hauser, S. T., & Kilner, L. A. (1989). Adolescent mental health. *American Psychologist, 44*(2), 200–208.

Prawat, R. S., Anderson, A. L. H., & Hapkeiwicz, W. (1989). Are dolls real? Developmental changes in the child's definition of reality. *Journal of Genetic Psychology, 150*(4), 359–374.

Prechtl, H. F. R. (1982). Assessment methods for the newborn infant, a critical evaluation. In P. Stratton (Ed.), *Psychobiology of the human newborn* (pp. 21–52). New York: Wiley.

Prechtl, H. F. R., & Beintema, D. J. (1964). *The neurological examination of the full-term newborn infant: Clinics in developmental medicine*, No. 12. London: Heinemann.

Prechtl, H. F. R., & O'Brien, M. J. (1982). Behavioral states of the full-term newborn: The emergence of a concept. In P. Stratton (Ed.), *Psychobiology of the human newborn* (pp. 53–73). New York: Wiley.

Purkey, S. C., & Smith, M. S. (1983). Effective schools: A review. *The Elementary School Journal, 83*(4), 427–452.

Putallaz, M., & Gottman, J. M. (1981). An interactional model of children's entry into peer groups. *Child Development, 52,* 986–994.

Pyle, R., Mitchell, J., Eckert, E., Halverson, P., Neumann, P., & Goff, G. (1983). The incidence of bulimia in freshman college students. *International Journal of Eating Disorders, 2,* 75–85.

Radke-Yarrow, M., Zahn-Waxler, C., & Chapman, M. (1983). Children's prosocial dispositions and behavior. In P. H. Mussen (Ed.), *Handbook of child psychology*, (Vol. 4, 4th ed.). New York: Wiley.

Raiti, S., Kaplan, S. L., Vliet, V., & Moore, W. V. (1987). Short-term treatment of short stature and subnormal growth rate with human growth hormone. *Journal of Pediatrics, 110*(3), 357–361.

Ralph, N., & Morgan, K. (1991). Assessing differences in

chemically dependent adolescent males using the *Child Behavior Checklist. Adolescence, 26*(101), 183–194.

Ramey, C. T., & Finkelstein, N. W. (1978). Contingent stimulation and infant competence. *Journal of Pediatric Psychology, 3*, 89–96.

Randt, R. D. (1985). Ball-catching proficiency among 4-, 6-, and 8-year-old girls. In J. E. Clark & J. H. Humprey (Eds.), *Motor development: Current selected research* (Vol. 1). Princeton, N.J: Princeton Book.

Rappaport, L., & Levine, M. (1986). The prevention of constipation and encopresis: A developmental model and approach. *Pediatric Clinics of North America, 33*(4), 859–869.

Rauh, V., Wasserman, G., & Brunelli, S. (1990). Determinants of maternal child-rearing attitudes. *American Academy of Child and Adolescent Psychiatry, 26*, 375–381.

Raven, R. (1974). The development of Wh-questions in 1st and 2nd language learners. In J. C. Richards (Ed.), Thought and Language/Language and Reading. *Harvard Educational Review*, (Reprint Series No. 14), 150–179.

Read, C. (1975). *Children's categorization of speech sounds in English.* Urbana, IL: National Council of Teachers of English.

Reece, E. A., Assimakopoulos, E., Zheng, X., Hagay, Z., & Hobbins, J. (1990). The safety of obstetric ultrasonography. Concern for the fetus. *Obstetrics and Gynecology, 76*, 139–146.

Reese, H. W., & Lipsitt, L. P. (1970). *Experimental child psychology.* New York: Academic Press.

Regcher, S. M., & Kaplan, S. B. (1988). Reading disability with motor problems. *Pediatrics, 82*(2), 204–210.

Reichelderfer, T. E., Overbach, A., & Greensher, J. (1979). Unsafe playgrounds. *Pediatrics, 64*, 962–963.

Reilly, A., & Stark, R. (Eds.) (1980). The communication game. In *Pediatric Round Table: 4.* New York: Johnson & Johnson.

Renzulli, J. S. (1978). What makes giftedness? Re-examining a definition. *Phi Delta Kappan, 60*, 180–184.

Renzulli, J. S., & Smith, L. H. (1981). The early childhood checklist. In J. S. Renzulli, S. M. Reis, & L. H. Smith (Eds.), *The revolving door identification model.* Mansfield Center, CT: Creative Learning Press.

Rest, J. R. (1983). Morality. In P. H. Mussen (Ed.), *Handbook of child psychology: Vol. 3. Cognitive development.* New York: Wiley.

Reynolds, F. (1990). *Guiding young children: A child-centered approach.* Mountain View, CA: Mayfield.

Rhodes, L. (1981). I can read! Predictable books as resources for reading and writing instruction. *The Reading Teacher, 34*, 511–518.

Ricard, R. J., & Snow, C. E. (1990). Language use in and out of context. *Journal of Applied Developmental Psychology, 11*(3), 251–266.

Richards, M. P., & Bernal, J. F. (1972). An observational study of mother-infant interactions. In N. B. Jones (Ed.), *Ethological studies of child behavior.* London: Cambridge University Press.

Ricks, M. H. (1985). The social transmission of parental behavior: Attachment across generations. In I. Bretherton & E. Waters (Eds.), Growing points of attachment theory and research. *Monographs of the Society for Research in Child Development, 50*(1–2).

Rivara, F. P., Reay, D. T., & Bergman, A. B. (1989). Analysis of fatal pedestrian injuries in King County, WA, and prospects of prevention. *Public Health Reports, 104*(3), 293–297.

Roberts, E. J., & Gagnon, J. (1978). *Family life and sexual learning: Vol. 1. Summary Report.* Cambridge, MA: Population Education.

Roberts, J. E., Sanyal, M. A., Burchinal, M. R., Collier, A. M., Ramey, C. T., & Henderson, F. W. (1986). Otitis media in early childhood and its relationship to later verbal and academic performance. *Pediatrics, 78*(3), 423–430.

Roberts, W., & Strayer, J. (1987). Parents' responses to the emotional distress of their children: Relations with children's competence. *Developmental Psychology, 23*(3), 415–422.

Robertson, L. S. (1985). Motor vehicles. *Pediatric Clinics of North America, 32*(1), 87–94.

Robson, K. S. (1967). The role of eye-to-eye contact in maternal-infant attachment. *Journal of Child Psychology and Psychiatry and Allied Disciplines, 8*, 13–25.

Rochat, P. (1989). Object manipulation and exploration in 2- to 5-month-old infants. *Developmental Psychology, 25*(6), 871–884.

Rode, S. S., Chang, P. N., Fisch, P. O., & Sroufe, L. A. (1981). Attachment patterns of infants separated from birth. *Developmental Psychology, 17*, 188–191.

Rodman, H., Pratto, D. J., & Nelson, R. S. (1985). Child care arrangements and children's functioning: A comparison of self-care and adult-care children. *Developmental Psychology, 21*, 413–418.

Roedell, W. C., Slaby, R. C., & Robinson, H. B. (1977). *Social development in young children.* Belmont, CA: Wadsworth.

Roff, M. (1961). Childhood social interactions and young adult bad conduct. *Journal of Abnormal and Social Psychology, 63*, 333–337.

Roff, M., Sells, S. B., & Golden, M. M. (1972). *Social adjustment and personality development in children.* Minneapolis: University of Minnesota Press.

Rondal, J. A. (1985). *Adult-child interaction and the process of language acquisition.* New York: Praeger.

Rorty, R. (1981). Nineteenth century idealism and twentieth century textmakers. *Monist, 64*, 155–174.

Rose, S. A., & Blank, M. (1974). The potency of context in children's cognition: An illustration through conservation. *Child Development, 45*, 499–502.

Rosen, B. C. & D'Andrade, R. (1975). The psychosocial origins of achievement motivation. In U. Bronfenbrenner & M. H. Mahoney (Eds.), *Influences on human development* (2d ed.) (pp. 438–450). Hinsdale, IL: Dryden Press.

Rosen, J., & Dickinson, J. (1990). Vaginal birth after Cesarean: A meta-analysis of indicators for success. *Obstetrics and Gynecology, 76*, 865–869.

Rosenblatt, J. S. (1969). The basis of synchrony in the behavioral interaction between the mother and her offspring in the laboratory rat. In B. M. Foss (Ed.), *Determinants of infant behavior* (Vol. 3). London: Methuen.

Rosenblith, J. F., & Sims-Knight, J. E. (1985). *In the beginning: Development in the first two years.* Belmont, CA: Wadsworth.

Rosenzweig, M. R. (1984). Experience, memory, and the brain. *American Psychologist, 39*(4), 365–376.

Rosett, H. L., Weiner, L., Lee, A., Zuckerman, B., Dooling, E., & Oppenheimer, E. (1983). Patterns of alcohol consumption and fetal development. *Obstetrics and Gynecology, 61*(5), 539–546.

Ross, G., Lipper, E., & Auld, P. (1990). Social competence and behavior problems in premature children at school-age. *Pediatrics, 86*, 391–397.

Ross, J. G., & Gilbert, G. G. (1985). The national children and youth fitness study: A summary of findings. *Journal of Physical Education, Recreation and Dance, 56*(1), 3–8; 45–50.

Ross, R. P., Campbell, T., Huston-Stein, A., & Wright, J. C. (1981). Nutritional misinformation of children: A developmental and experimental analysis of the effects of televised food commercials. *Journal of Applied Developmental Psychology, 1*, 329–347.

Rotter, J. G., Liverant, B., & Crowne, D. P. (1961). The growth and extinction of expectancies in chance controlled and skilled tests. *Journal of Psychology, 52*, 161–177.

Rovee-Collier, C. K., Early, C., & Stafford, S. (1989). Ontogeny of early event memory. III. Attentional determinants of retrieval at 2 and 3 months. *Infant Behavior and Development, 12*, 147–161.

Rovee-Collier, C. K., & Lipsitt, L. P. (1982). Learning, adaptation and memory in the newborn. In P. Stratton (Ed.), *Psychobiology of the human newborn* (pp. 147–190). New York: Wiley.

Rovet, J., & Netley, C. (1983). The triple X chromosome syndrome in childhood: Recent empirical findings. *Child Development, 54*(4), 831–845.

Rubenstein, J., & Howes, C. (1976). The effects of peers on toddler interaction with mother and toys. *Child Development, 47*, 597–605.

Rubin, K., Fein, G., & Vandenberg, B. (1983). Play. In P. Mussen (Ed.), *Handbook of child psychology* (Vol. 4) (4th ed.). New York: Wiley.

Rubin, J. Z., Provenzano, F. J., & Luria, Z. (1974). The eyes of the beholder: Parents' views on sex of newborns. *American Journal of Orthopsychiatry, 44*, 512–519.

Rubin, Z. (1970). Measurement of romantic love. *Journal of Personality and Social Psychology, 16*, 265–273.

Ruble, D. N. (1984). Sex-role development. In M. H. Bornstein & M. E. Lamb (Eds.), *Developmental psychology: An advanced text.* Hillsdale, NJ: Lawrence Erlbaum.

Rutter, M. (1981). Socioemotional consequences of day care for preschool children. *American Journal of Orthopsychiatry, 51*, 4–28.

Sachs, J., & Truswell, L. (1978). Comprehension of two-word constructions by children in the one-word stage. *Child Language, 5*, 17–24.

Sadaker, M., & Sadaker, D. (1985). Sexism in the schoolroom

of the '80s. *Psychology Today, 19*(3), 54–56.

Salapatek, P. (1968). Visual scanning of geometric figures by the human newborn. *Journal of Comparative and Physiological Psychology, 66*, 247–258.

———. (1975). Pattern perception in early infancy. In L. B. Cohen & P. Salapatek (Eds.), *Infant perception: From sensation to cognition: Vol. 1. Basic visual processes.* New York: Academic Press.

Saltus, R. (1987, July 20). Tests can foretell genetic destiny. *Boston Globe*, p. 47.

Saltz, R. (1979). Children's interpretation of proverbs. *Language Arts, 56*, 508–514.

Saltzman, L. (1973). Adolescence: Epoch or disease. *Adolescence, 8*, 247–256.

Sameroff, A. J. (1972). Learning and adaptation in infancy. In H. W. Reese (Ed.), *Advances in child development and behavior* (Vol. 7). New York: Academic Press.

———. (1981). Longitudinal studies of preterm infants: A review of Chapters 17–20. *Developmental Psychology*, 387–394.

———. (1983). Developmental systems: contexts and evolution. In P. M. Mussen (Series ed.) & Wm. Kessen (Ed.), *Handbook of child psychology: Vol. 1, History, theory and methods* (4th ed.) (pp. 237–294). New York: Wiley.

Sarvela, P., & McClendon, E. J. (1983). Correlates of early adolescent peer and personal substance use in rural northern Michigan. *Journal of Youth and Adolescence, 12*(4), 319–332.

Sawyers, J., & Rogers, C. (1988). *Helping young children develop through play.* Washington, DC: National Association for the Education of Young Children.

Saxe, G. B., Guberman, S. R., & Gerhart, M. (1987). Social processes in early number development. *Monographs of the Society for Research in Child Development, 52*(2, Serial No. 216).

Scafidi, F., Field, T., Schanberg, S., Bauer, C., Tucci, K., Roberts, J., Morrow, C., & Kuhn, C. (1990). *Massage stimulates growth in preterm infants: A replication. Infant Behavior and Development, 13*, 167–188.

Scaife, M., & Bruner, J. S. (1975). The capacity for joint visual attention in the infant. *Nature, 253*, 265–266.

Scarr, S., & Weinberg, R. A. (1978). Attitudes, interests and IQ. *Human Nature, 1*, 29–36.

Schaefer, E. (1989). Dimensions of mother-infant interaction: Measurement, stability, and predictive validity. *Infant Behavior and Development, 12*, 379–393.

Schaeffer, B., Eggleston, V. H., & Scott, J. L. (1974). Number development in young children. *Cognitive Psychology, 6*, 357–379.

Schaffer, H. R., & Emerson, P. E. (1964). The development of social attachments in infancy. *Monographs of the Society for Research in Child Development, 29* (Serial No. 94).

Schaie, K. W. (1965). A general model for the study of developmental problems. *Psychological Bulletin, 64*, 92–107.

Schauble, L. (1990). Belief revision in children: The role of prior knowledge and strategies for generating evidence. *Journal of Experimental Child Psychology, 49*, 31–57.

Schickedanz, D. (1976). *Effects of an intervention in childrearing on Uzgiris-Hunt scale performance.* Paper presented at the Annual Meeting of the New Hampshire Speech and Hearing Association, Portsmouth, NH.

Schickedanz, J. (1990). *Adam's righting revolutions: A case study of one child's writing development from one to seven.* Portsmouth, NH: Heinemann Educational Books.

———. (1986). *More than the ABCs: The early stages of reading and writing.* Washington, DC: National Association for the Education of Young Children.

———. (1989). The place of specific skills in preschool and kindergarten. In D. S. Strickland & L. M. Morrow (Eds.), *Emerging literacy.* Newark, DE: International Reading Association.

———. (1990). Preschoolers and academics: Some thoughts. *Young Children, 46*(1), 4–14.

Schickedanz, J., & Sullivan, M. (1984). Mom, what does U-F-F spell? *Language Arts, 61*(1) 7–17.

Schinke, S., Gilchrist, L., & Small, R. (1979). Preventing unwanted adolescent pregnancy: A cognitive behavioral approach. *American Journal of Orthopsychiatry, 49,* 81–88.

Schleifer, M. J. (1987). Toothbrush adaptations. *Exceptional Parents, 17*(5), 22–24.

Schlesinger, I. M. (1974). Relational concepts and underlying language. In R. Schiefelbusch & L. Lloyd (Eds.), *Language perception: Acquisition, retardation and intervention.* Baltimore: University Park Press.

Schneider, P. E., & Peterson, J. (1982). Oral habits: Considerations in management. *Pediatric Clinics of North America, 29*(3), 653–668.

Schneirla, T. (1957). The concept of development in comparative psychology. In D. Harris (Ed.), *The concept of development.* Minneapolis: University of Minnesota Press.

Schneirla, T. C., Rosenblatt, J. S., & Tobach, E. (1963). Maternal behavior in the cat. In H. L. Rheingold (Ed.), *Maternal behaviour in mammals* (pp. 122–168). New York: Wiley.

Schramm, W., Lyle, J., & Parker, E. B. (1961). *Television in the lives of our children.* Stanford, CA: Stanford University Press.

Schwartz, M., & Schwartz, J. (1974). Evidence against a genetical component to performance on IQ tests. *Nature, 248,* 84–85.

Schwartz, P. (1983). Length of day-care attendance and attachment behavior in eighteen-month-old infants. *Child Development, 54,* 1073–1078.

Schwartz, R. C., Barrett, M. J., & Saba, G. (1985). Family therapy for bulimia. In D. M. Garner & P. Garfinkel (Eds.), *Handbook of psychotherapy for anorexia nervosa and bulimia.* New York: Guilford Press.

Schweinhart, I. J., Weikart, D. P., & Larner, M. B. (1986). Consequences of three preschool curriculum models through age 15. *Early Childhood Research Quarterly, 1,* 15–45.

Seeds, J. W., & Cefalo, R. C. (1983). Techniques of early sonographic diagnosis of bilateral cleft lip and palate. *Obstetrics and Gynecology, 62*(Suppl.3), 2S–7S.

Seibert, J., & Olson, R. (1989). *Children, adolescents and AIDS.* Lincoln: University of Nebraska Press.

Seidman, D., Ever-Hadani, P., & Gale, R. (1990). Effect of maternal smoking and age on congenital anomalies. *Obstetrics and Gynecology, 76,* 1046–1050.

Select Committee on Hunger, U.S. House of Representatives. (1988, October). *Strategies for expanding the special supplemental food program for women, infants, and children (WIC) participation: A survey of WIC directors.* Washington, DC: U. S. Government Printing Office.

Selman, R. (1976). Social–cognitive understanding: A guide to educational and clinical practice. In T. Lickona (Ed.), *Moral development and behavior: Theory, research, and social issues* (pp. 219–240). New York: Holt, Rinehart & Winston.

Sgroi, S. (1982). *Handbook of clinical intervention in child sexual abuse.* Lexington, MA: Lexington Books.

Sgroi, S., Porter, F. & Blick, L. (1982). Validation of child sexual abuse. In S. Sgroi (Ed.), *Handbook of clinical intervention in child sexual abuse* (pp. 39–80). Lexington, MA: Lexington Books.

Shannon, M., Lacouture, P. G., Roa, J., & Woolf, A. (1989). Cocaine exposure among children seen at a pediatric hospital. *Pediatrics, 83*(3), 337–342.

Shantz, C. U. (1975). The development of social cognition. In E. M. Hetherington (Ed.), *Reviews of Child Development Research* (Vol. 5, pp. 257–323). Chicago: University of Chicago Press.

Share, D. J., Jorm, A. E., Maclean, R., & Matthews, R. (1984). Sources of individual differences in reading achievement. *Journal of Educational Psychology, 76,* 466–477.

Shaw, F., Zelnick, M., & Kanter, J. F. (1975). Unprotected intercourse among unwed teenagers. *Family Planning Perspectives, 7,* 39.

Sheldon, W. H., Hartle, E. M., & McDermott, E. (1949). *Varieties of delinquent youth.* New York: Harper & Row.

Shelton, P. G., Ferratti, G. H., & Dent, M. (1982). Maintaining oral health. *Pediatric Clinics of North America, 29*(3), 653–668.

Shepard, L. A., & Smith, M. L. (1988). Escalating academic demand in kindergarten: Counterproductive policies. *Elementary School Journal, 89,* 135–145.

Sherman, B. L., & Dominick, J. P. (1986, Winter). Violence and sex in music videos, TV, and rock n' roll. *Journal of Communication,* pp. 79–93.

Sherman, T. (1985). Categorization of skills in infants. *Child Development, 56,* 1561–1573.

Shields, J. (1962). *Monozygotic twins.* London: Oxford University Press.

Shirley, M. M. (1933). *The first two years: A study of twenty-five babies* (Vol. II). Minneapolis: University of Minnesota Press.

Showalter, E. (1985). *The female malady: Women, madness, and English culture, 1830–1980.* New York: Penguin Books.

Shultz, T. (1988). Right from the start: Report of the National Association of State Boards of Education. National Early Education Task Force. Alexandria, VA: NASBE.

Shultz, T. R., & Pilon, R. (1973). Development of the ability to detect linguistic ambiguity. *Child Development, 44,* 728–733.

Siebert, J. M. (1987). AIDS FACTS: A profile of the growing problem. *APA Division 37 Newsletter, 10*(1), 1;7.

Siegel, I. E., Brodzinsky, D. M., & Golinkoff, R. M. (Eds.) (1981). *New directions in Piagetian theory and practice.* Hillsdale, NJ: Lawrence Erlbaum.

Siegel, L. (1983). The prediction of possible learning disabilities in preterm and full-term children. In T. Field & A. Sostek (Eds.), *Infants born at risk: Physiological, perceptual, and cognitive processes* (pp. 295–315). New York: Grune & Stratton.

Siegel, M., Fuerst, H., & Guinee, V. (1971). Rubella epidemicity and embryopathy. *American Journal of Diseases of Children, 121,* 469–473.

Siegler, R. S. (1976). Three aspects of cognitive development. *Cognitive Psychology, 8,* 481–520.

———. (1978). The origins of scientific reasoning. In R. S. Siegler (Ed.), *Children's thinking: What develops?* Hillsdale, NJ: Lawrence Erlbaum.

———. (1983). Information processing approaches to development. In P. H. Mussen (Ed.), *Handbook of child psychology: Vol. 1. History, theory, and methods.* New York: Wiley.

———. (1986). *Children's thinking.* Englewood Cliffs, NJ: Prentice-Hall.

Siegler, R. S., & Liebert, R. M. (1975). Acquisition of formal scientific reasoning by 10- and 13-year-olds: Designing a factorial experiment. *Developmental Psychology, 11,* 401–402.

Sigel, I. E. (1985). *Parental belief systems.* Hillsdale, NJ: Erlbaum.

Sigman, M., Newmann, C., Janse, A. A. J., & Bwibo, N. (1989). Cognitive abilities of Kenyan children in relation to nutrition, family characteristics, and education. *Child Development, 60*(6), 1463–1473.

Silvio, K. (1984). SIDS and apnea monitoring: A parent's view. *Pediatric Annals,13*(3), 229–231.

Simmons, R. G., & Blyth, D. A. (1987). *Moving into adolescence: The impact of pubertal change in school context.* New York: A. de Gruyter.

Simons, R. L., Whitbeck, L. B., Conger, R. D., & Chyi-In, W. (1991). Intergenerational transmission of harsh parenting. *Developmental Psychology, 27,* 159–171.

Sinclair, C. (1973). *Movement of the young child: Ages two to six.* Columbus, OH: Merrill.

Sinclair, J. C. (1975). The effect of the thermal environment on neonatal mortality and morbidity. In K. Adamson & H. A. Fox (Eds.), *Preventability of perinatal injury.* New York: A. R. Liss.

Singal, D. (1991, November). The other crisis in American education. *The Atlantic Monthly,* 59–74.

Siqueland, E. R., & Lipsitt, L P. (1966). Conditioned head-turning in human newborns. *Journal of Experimental Child Psychology, 3,* 356–376.

Skeels, H. M. (1966). Adult status of children with contrasting early life experiences. *Monographs of the Society for Research in Child Development, 31* (Serial No. 105).

Skinner, E. (1990). Age differences in the dimensions of perceived control during middle childhood: Implications for developmental conceptualizations and research. *Child Development, 61*(6), 1882–1890.

Skodak, M., & Skeels, H. M. (1949). A final follow-up study of one hundred adopted children. *Journal of Genetic Psychology, 75,* 86–125.

Skurnick, J. H., Johnson, R. L., Quinona, M. A., Foster, J. D., & Louria, D. B. (1991). New Jersey high school students' knowledge, attitudes, and behavior regarding AIDS. *AIDS Education and Prevention, 3*(1), 21–30.

Slaby, R. G., & Frey, R. S. (1975). Development of gender constancy and selective attention to same-sex models. *Child Development, 46,* 849–856.

Slade, A. (1987). Quality of attachment and early symbolic play. *Developmental Psychology, 23*(1), 78–85.

Slater, A. M., & Findlay, J. M. (1975). Binocular fixation in the newborn baby. *Journal of Experimental Child Psychology, 20,* 248–273.

Slater, A. M., Mattock, A., & Brown, E. (1990). Size constancy at birth: Newborn infants' responses to retinal and real size. *Journal of Experimental Child Psychology, 49,* 314–322.

Slater, L., & Brewer, M. F. (1984). Home versus hospital phototherapy for term infants with hyperbilirubinemia. *Pediatrics, 73*(4), 515–519.

Slobin, D. I. (1982). Universal and particular in the acquisition of language. In E. Wanner & L. R. Gleitman (Eds.), *Language acquisition: The state of the art.* Cambridge, England: Cambridge University Press.

Smith, C., & Lloyd, B. (1978). Maternal behavior and perceived sex of infant: Revisited. *Child Development, 49,* 1263–1265.

Smith, C. L., Leinbach, M. D., Stewart, B. J., & Blackwell, J. M. (1983). Affective perspective-taking, exhortation, and children's prosocial behavior. In D. L. Bridgeman (Ed.), *The nature of prosocial development* (pp. 113–134). New York: Academic Press.

Smith, D. P. (1986). Common day-care diseases: Patterns and prevention. *Pediatric Nursing, 12*(3), 175–179.

Smith, E. J. (1982). The black female adolescent: A review of the educational, career, and psychological literature. *Psychology of Women Quarterly, 6*(3), 261–288.

Smith, J. (1984). Psychosocial aspects of infantile apnea and home monitoring. *Pediatric Annals, 13,* 219–224.

Smith, N. J., Greenlaw, M. J., & Scott, C. J. (1987). Making the literate environment equitable. *The Reading Teacher, 40*(4), 400–407.

Smith, P. K., & Doglish, L. (1977). Sex differences in parent and infant behavior in the home. *Child Development, 48,* 1250–1254.

Smithe, R. (1971). *An introduction to mental retardation.* New York: McGraw–Hill.

Snow, C. E., & Ninio, A. (1986). The contribution of reading books with children to their linguistic and cognitive development. In W. Teale & E. Sulzby (Eds.), *Emergent literacy: Reading and writing.* Norwood, NJ: Ablex.

Snyder, L., Schonfeld, M., & Offerman, E. (1945). The Rh factor and feeble-mindedness. *Journal of Heredity, 36,* 9–10.

Sorensen, R. C. (1973). *Adolescent sexuality in contemporary*

America. New York: World.

Sostek, A., Smith, Y. F., Katz, K. S., & Grant, E. G. (1987). Developmental outcomes of preterm infants with intraventricular hemorrhage at one and two years of age. *Child Development, 58*(3), 779–786.

Sparrow, S. S., Balla, D. A., & Cicchetti, D. V. (1984). *Vineland Adoptive Behavior Scales.* (A revision of the *Vineland Social Maturity Scale* by E. A. Doll.) Circle Pines, MN: American Guidance Service.

Spieker, S., & Booth, C. (1988). Maternal antecedents of attachment quality. In J. Belsky & T. Nezworski (Eds.), *Clinical implications of attachment* (pp. 95–135). Hillsdale, NJ: L. Erlbaum Associates.

Spirito, A., Stark, L., Fristad, M., Hart, K., & Owens-Stively, J. (1989). Adolescent suicide attempters hospitalized on a pediatric unit. In S. Chess, A. Thomas & M. E. Hertzig (Eds.), *Annual progress in child psychiatry and child development.* New York: Brunner/Mazel.

Spivack, G., & Shure, M. B. (1982). Cognition of social adjustment: Interpersonal cognitive problem-solving thinking. In B. B. Lahey & A. E. Kazden (Eds.), *Advances in child psychology* (pp. 323–372). New York: Plenum Press.

Spivack, R., Marcus, J., & Swift, M. (1986). Early classroom behaviors and later misconduct. *Developmental Psychology, 22*(11), 124–131.

Spivak, H., Prothrow-Stith, D., & Hausman, A. J. (1988). Dying is no accident. *Pediatric Clinics of North America, 35*(6), 1339–1347.

Sprinthall, N. A., & Collins, W. A. (1984). *Adolescent Psychology* (pp. 116–117). Reading, MA: Addison-Wesley.

Sroufe, L. A. (1981, October). *Infant caregiver attachment and patterns of adaptation in preschool: The roots of maladaptation and competence.* Paper presented at the Minnesota Symposium.

———. (1982). Attachment and the roots of competence. In H. E. Fitzgerald & T. H. Carr (Eds.), *Human development: Annual editions.* Guildford, CA: Dushkin.

———. (1983). Infant-caregiver attachment and patterns of adaptation in preschool: The roots of maladaptation and competence. In M. Perlmutter (Ed.), *Minnesota symposium in child psychology* (Vol. 16, pp. 41–83). Hillsdale, NJ: Lawrence Erlbaum.

———. (1988). The role of infant-caregiver attachment in development. In J. Belsky & T. Nezworksi (Eds.), *Clinical implications of attachment.* Hillsdale, NJ: Lawrence Erlbaum Associates.

———. (1990). An organizational perspective on the self. In D. Cicchetti & M. Beeghly (Eds.), *The self in transition: Infancy to childhood* (pp. 281–308). Chicago: The University of Chicago Press.

Stark, E. (1986). Young, innocent, and pregnant. *Psychology Today, 20*(10), 28–35.

Starr, R., Onbowitz, H., & Bush, B. (1990). The epidemiology of child maltreatment. In R. Ammerman & M. Herson (Eds.), *Children at risk: An evaluation of factors contributing to child abuse and neglect.* New York: Plenum Press.

Staub, E. (1971). A child in distress: The influence of nurturance and modeling on children's attempts to help. *Developmental Psychology, 5,* 124–132.

———. (1975). *The development of prosocial behavior in children.* Morristown, NJ: General Learning Press.

———. (1979). *Positive social behavior and morality.* (Vol. 2). New York: Academic Press.

Stein, L. Ozdamar, O., Kraus, N., & Paton, J. (1983). Follow-up of infants screened by auditory brainstem response in the neonatal intensive care unit. *Journal of Pediatrics, 103*(3), 447–453.

Steinberg, L. (1986). Latchkey children and susceptibility to peer pressure: An ecological analysis. *Developmental Psychology, 22,* 433–439.

Steinberg, L., & Silverberg, S. B. (1986). The vicissitudes of autonomy in early adolescence. *Child Development, 57*(4), 841–851.

Stenberg, C., Campos, J., & Emde, R. (1983). The facial expression of anger in seven-month-old infants. *Child Development, 54,* 178–184.

Stern, D. (1977). *The first relationship: Infant and mother.* Cambridge, MA: Harvard University Press.

Stern, G. (1973). *Principles of human genetics* (3d ed.). San Francisco: W. H. Freeman.

Stern, W. (1912). *The psychological methods of testing intelligence* (G. M. Whipple, Trans.). Baltimore: Warwick & York.

Sternberg, R. J. (1984). Toward a triarchic theory of human intelligence. *Behavioral and Brain Sciences, 7*(2), 269–316.

———. (1985). *Beyond IQ: A triarchic theory of human intelligence.* New York: Cambridge University Press.

———. (1988). Intellectual development: Psychometric and information-processing approach. In M. Bornstein & M. Lamb (Eds.), *Developmental psychology: An advanced textbook.* Hillsdale, NJ: Lawrence Erlbaum Associates.

———. (1990). *Metaphors of mind: Conceptions of the nature of intelligence.* New York: Cambridge University Press.

Sternberg, R. J., & Kolligian, J. (Eds.). (1990). *Competence considered.* New Haven: Yale University Press.

Stevenson, H., Chen, C., Lee, S., & Fuligni, A. (1991). Schooling, culture and cognitive development. In L. Okagaki & R. Sternberg (Eds.), *Directors of development: Influences on the development of children's thinking.* Hillsdale, NJ: Lawrence Erlbaum Associates.

Stevenson, H., and Shin-ying, L., in collaboration with Chen, C., Stigler, J., Hsu, C., and Kitamura, S. (1990a). Contexts of achievement: A study of American, Chinese, and Japanese children. With Commentary by G. Hatans; and a Reply by H. Stevenson and S. Lee. *Monographs of the Society for Research in Child Development, 55* (1–2, Serial No. 221).

Stevenson, H., Shin-ying, L., Chuansheng, C., Lummis, M., Stigler, J., Fan, C., and Fang, G. (1990b). Mathematics achievement of children in China and the United States. *Child Development, 61,* 1053–1066.

Stevenson, M. F., & Stevenson, J. J. (1990). Safe care/Safe play: Child care as a site for injury prevention. *Children Today, 19,* 17–32.

Stoner, L. J. (1978). Selecting physical activities for the young child, with an understanding of bone growth and development. *Reviews of Research for Practitioners and Parents, 1,* 32–42.

Stratton, P. (1982). Rhythmic functions in the newborn. In P. Stratton (Ed.), *Psychobiology of the human newborn* (pp. 119–145). New York: Wiley.

Straus, M. A., Gelles, R., & Steinmetz, S. (1980). *Behind closed doors.* New York: Doubleday.

Strayer, F. F. (1980). Social ecology of the preschool peer group. In W. A. Collins (Ed.), *Development of cognition, affect, and social relations: Minnesota Symposium in Child Development* (Vol. 3). Hillsdale, NJ: Lawrence Erlbaum.

Streeter, L. (1976). Language perception of 2-month-old infants shows effects of both innate mechanisms and experience. *Nature, 259,* 39–41.

Streissguth, A. P. (1979). Fetal alcohol syndrome. *Women and Health, 4,* 223–238.

Streissguth, A. P., Barr, H. M., & Martin, D. C. (1983). Maternal alcohol use and neonatal habituation assessed with the Brazelton Scale. *Child Development, 54,* 1109–1118.

Streissguth, A. P., Barr, H. M., Sampson, P. D., Darby, B. L., & Martin, D. C. (1989). IQ at age 4 in relation to maternal alcohol use and smoking during pregnancy. *Developmental Psychology, 25*(1), 3–11.

Strohner, H., & Nelson, K. E. (1974). The young child's development of sentence comprehension: Influence of event probability, nonverbal context, syntactic form, and strategies. *Child Development, 45,* 567–576.

Stroman, S. H., & Duff, R. E. (1982). The latchkey child: Whose responsibility? *Childhood Education, 59,* 76–79.

Strong, E. K., & Campbell, D. P. (1981). *Manual for the Strong-Campbell interest inventory* (3d ed.). Stanford, CA: Stanford University Press.

Sulzby, E. (1985). Children's emergent reading of favorite storybooks: A developmental study. *Reading Research Quarterly, 20*(4), 458–481.

———. (1991). Assessment of emergent literacy: Storybook reading. *The Reading Teacher, 44*(7), 498–500.

Sun, S. W., & Lull, J. (1986, Winter). The adolescent audience for music videos and why they watch. *Journal of Communication,* pp. 115–125.

Sunberg, N. D., Tyler, L. E., & Taplin, J. R. (1973). *Clinical psychology: Expanding horizons.* Englewood Cliffs, NJ: Prentice-Hall.

Sussman, E. J., Nottelmann, E. D., Inhoff-Germain, G. E., Dorn, L. D., Cutler, G. B., Jr., Loriaux, D. L., & Chrousos, G. P. (1985). The relation of development and social-emotional behavior in young adolescents. *Journal of Youth and Adolescence, 14,* 245–264.

Svejda, M. J., Pannabecker, B. J., & Emde, R. N. (1982). Parent-to-infant attachment: A critique of the early "bonding" model. In R. M. Emde & R. J. Harmon (Eds.), *The development of attachment and affiliative systems.* New York: Plenum Press.

Takahashi, M. (1986). Clinical overview of varicella vaccine.

Development and early studies. *Pediatrics,* (Special Suppl.), 736–741.

Tanner, J. M. (1970). Physical growth. In P. H. Mussen (Ed.), *Carmichael's Manual of Child Psychology* (Vol. 1, 3d ed.). New York: Wiley.

———. (1978a). *Education and physical growth* (2d ed.). New York: International Universities Press.

———. (1978b). *Fetus into man: Physical growth from conception to maturity.* Cambridge, MA: Harvard University Press.

———. (1981). Growth and maturation during adolescence. *Nutrition Review, 39,* 43–55.

Tanz, C. (1983). Asking children to ask: An experimental investigation of the pragmatics of relayed questions. *Journal of Child Language; 10,* 187–194.

Tarby, T. J., & Volpe, J. J. (1982). Intraventricular hemorrhage in the premature infant. *Pediatric Clinics of North America, 29*(5),1077–1104.

Taub, H. B., Goldstein, K. M., & Caputo, D. V. (1977). Indices of neonatal prematurity as discriminators of development in middle childhood. *Child Development, 48,* 797–805.

Taylor, I. (1981). Writing systems and reading. In G. E. Mackinnon & T. G. Waller (Eds.), *Reading research: Advances in theory and practice* (Vol. 2). New York: Academic Press.

Teale, W. (1986). Home background and young children's literacy development. In W. Teale & E. Sulzby (Eds.), *Emergent literacy.* Norwood, NJ: Ablex.

Teale, W., & Sulzby, E. (1986). Emergent literacy as a perspective for examining how young children become writers and readers. In W. Teale and E. Sulzby (Eds.), *Emergent literacy.* Norwood, NJ: Ablex.

Tecle, D. W., Klein, J. O., & Rosner, B. A. (1984). Otitis media with effusion during the first three years of life and development of speech and language. *Pediatrics, 74*(2), 282–287.

Teitz, C. C. (1982). Sports medicine concerns in dance and gymnastics. *Pediatric Clinics of North America, 29*(6), 1399–1421.

Terman, L. M. (1916). *The measurement of intelligence.* Boston: Houghton Mifflin.

Thomas, A. T., & Chess, S. (1977). *Foundations of physiological psychology.* New York: Harper & Row.

Thompson, R. (1988). The effects of infant day care through the prism of attachment theory: A critical appraisal. *Early Childhood Research Quarterly, 3*(3), 273–282.

Thompson, R. F. (1967). *Foundations of physiological psychology.* New York: Harper & Row.

Thorlindsson, T., & Vilhjalmsson, R. (1991). Factors related to cigarette smoking and alcohol use among adolescents. *Adolescence, 26*(102), 399–417.

Tisak, M., & Block, J. (1990). Preschool children's evolving conceptions of badness: A longitudinal study. *Early Education and Development, 1,* 300–307.

Trautman, P. D., & Shaffer, D. (1989). Pediatric management of suicidal behavior. *Pediatric Annals, 18*(2), 134–143.

Trehub, S. (1973). Infants' sensitivity to vowel and tonal contrasts. *Developmental Psychology, 9,* 91–96.

Trehub, S. E., Bull, D., & Thorpe, L. (1984). Infants' perception of melodies. The role of melodic contour. *Child Development, 55,* 821–830.

Trehub, S. E., & Endman, M. W., & Thorpe, L. A. (1990). Infants' perception of timbre: Classification of complex tones by spectral structure. *Journal of Experimental Child Psychology, 49,* 300–313.

Trehub, S. E., & Rabinovitch, M. S. (1972). Auditory-linguistic sensitivity in early infancy. *Developmental Psychology, 6,* 74–77.

Treiman, R. (1985). Phonemic awareness and spelling: Children's judgments do not always agree with adults'. *Journal of Experimental Child Psychology, 39,* 182–201.

Trickett, P. K., & Kuczynski, L. (1986). Children's misbehavior and parental discipline strategies in abusive and nonabusive families. *Developmental Psychology, 8,* 240–260.

Troy, M., & Sroufe, L. A. (1987). Victimization among preschoolers: Role of attachment relationship history. *Journal of the American Academy of Child and Adolescent Psychiatry, 26*(2), 166–172.

Turner, R. R. (1984). How big is the drug problem? *Family Learning, 1*(3), 6–7.

Ullman, L., & Krasner, L. (1969). *Psychological approach to abnormal behavior.* Englewood Cliffs, NJ: Prentice–Hall.

Ungerer, J. A., Zelazo, P. R., Kearsley, R. B., & O'Leary, K. (1981). Developmental changes in the representation of objects in symbolic play from 18–35 months of age. *Child Development, 52,* 186–195.

U. S. Department of Education. (1986). *What works: Research about teaching and learning.* Washington, DC: U. S. Department of Education.

U. S. Department of Health and Human Services, Centers for Disease Control (1992). *AIDS Prevention Guide for Parents and Other Adults Concerned about Youth.* Atlanta, GA: Centers for Disease Control.

U. S. Department of Justice, Federal Bureau of Investigation (1984). *Uniform crime reports for 1983.* Washington: U. S. Government Printing Office.

U. S. Public Health Service. (1983). Promoting Health/Preventing disease. Public Health Service implementation plans for attaining the objectives for the nation. *Public Health Reports* (Suppl), p. 3.

Uzgiris, I. C. (1973). Patterns of cognitive development in infancy. *The Merrill-Palmer Quarterly, 19,* 181–204.

———. (1989). Infants in relation: Performers, pupils and partners. In W. Damon (Ed.), *Child development today and tomorrow.* San Francisco: Jossey-Bass.

Uzgiris, I., & Hunt, J. McV. (1975). *Assessment in infancy: Ordinal scales of psychological development.* Urbana, IL: University of Illinois Press.

Van den Boom, D. (1989). Neonatal irritability and the development of attachment. In G. Kohnstamm, J. Bates, & M. Rothbart (Eds.), *Temperament in childhood.* New York: John Wiley & Sons.

Van Thorne, D., & Vogel, F. (1985). The presence of bulimia in high school females. *Adolescence, 20,* 45–51.

Vaughn, B., Engeland, B., Sroufe, L. A., & Waters, E. (1979). Individual differences in infant-mother attachment at twelve and eighteen months: Stability and change in families under stress. *Child Development, 50,* 971–975.

Vaughn, B., Gove, F. L., & Egeland, B. (1980). The relationship between out-of-home care and the quality of infant-mother attachment in an economically disadvantaged population. *Child Development, 51,* 971–975.

Vellutino, F. R. (1987). Dyslexia. *Scientific American, 256*(3), 34–41.

Venezia, P. A. (1971). Delinquency prediction: A critique and suggestion. *Journal of Research in Crime and Delinquency, 8,* 108–117.

Verhulst, F. C., Van Der Lee, J. H., Akkerhuis, G. E., Sanders-Woudstra, J. A. R., Timmer, F. C., & Donkhorst, I. D. (1985). The prevalence of nocturnal enuresis: Do DSM III criteria need to be changed? A brief research report. *Journal of Child Psychology, 26*(6), 989–993.

Wahler, R. G. (1990). Who is driving the interactions? A commentary on "Child and Parent Effects in Boys' Conduct Disorders." *Developmental Psychology, 26*(5), 702–704.

Walden, T. A., & Baxter, A. (1989). The effect of context and age on social referencing. *Child Development, 60*(6), 1511–1518.

Walden, T. A., & Ogden, T. A. (1988). The development of social referencing. *Child Development, 59,* 1230–1240.

Walker, L., & Taylor, J. (1991). Family interactions and the development of moral reasoning. *Child Development, 62*(2), 264–283.

Wall, S. M., Pickert, S. M., & Givson, W. B. (1989). Fantasy play in 5- and 6-year-old children. *The Journal of Psychology, 123*(3), 245–256.

Wallach, M. A., & Kogan, N. (1965). *Modes of thinking in young children.* New York: Holt, Rinehart & Winston.

Wallach, M. A., & Wallach, L. (1983). *Psychology's sanction for selfishness: The error of egoism in theory and therapy.* San Francisco: W. H. Freeman.

Walters, J. (1975). Birth defects and adolescent pregnancies. *Journal of Home Economics, 67,* 23–27.

Warden, D. (1986). Notes and discussion: How to tell if children can ask. *Journal of Child Language, 13,* 421–428.

Wasserman, R. L., & Ginsburg, C. M. (1985). Caustic substance injuries. *Journal of Pediatrics, 107*(2), 169–174.

Waterman, H. (Ed.) (1985). *Identity in adolescence: Processes and contexts.* New Directions in Child Development, No. 30. San Francisco: Jossey-Bass.

Waters, E., & Deane, K. E. (1982). Infant-mother attachment: Theories, models, recent data, and some tasks for comparative developmental analysis. In L. W. Hoffman, R. Gandelman, & H. R. Schiffman (Eds.), *Parenting: Its causes and consequences.* Hillsdale, NJ: Lawrence Erlbaum.

Watson, M. W., & Fischer, K. W. (1977). A developmental sequence of agent use in late infancy. *Child Development, 48,* 483–494.

Watt, J. (1990). Interaction, intervention, and development in small-for-gestation-age infants. *Infant Behavior and Development, 13*, 273–286.

Webster's New World Dictionary. (1983). New York: World.

Wechsler, D. (1974). *Manual for the Wechsler intelligence scale for children—Revised*. New York: Psychological Corporation.

———. (1981). *Wechsler Adult Intelligence Scale—Revised*. New York: Psychological Corporation.

———. (1991). *Wechsler Intelligence Scale for Children* (3d ed.). San Antonio, TX: Psychological Corporation.

Wehren, A., DeLisi, R., & Arnold, M. (1981). The development of noun definitions. *Journal of Child Language, 8*, 165–175.

Weinberg, R. A. (1989). Intelligence and IQ. *American Psychologist, 44*(2), 98–104.

Weinraub, M., & Frankel, J. (1977). Sex differences in parent–infant interactions during free play, departure, and separation. *Child Development, 48*, 1240–1249.

Weiss, B. D. (1986). Bicycle helmet use by children. *Pediatrics, 77*(5), 677–679.

Weitzman, M., & Adair, R. (1988). Divorce and children. *Pediatric Clinics of North America, 35*(6), 1313–1323.

Wellman, H. M. (1990). *The child's theory of mind*. Cambridge, MA: The MIT Press.

Wells, G. (1985). Preschool literacy-related activities and success in school. In D. R. Olson, N. Torrance, & A. Hildyard (Eds.), *Literacy, language, and learning: The nature and consequences of reading and writing* (pp. 229–255). Cambridge, England: Cambridge University Press.

———. (1986). *The meaning makers*. Portsmouth, NH: Heinemann Educational Books.

Wennberg, R., Woodrum, D., & Hodson, A. (1973). The perinate. In D. Smith and E. Bierman (Eds.), *The biologic ages of man*. Philadelphia: W. B. Saunders.

Wentzel, K. R., Weinberger, D. A., Ford, M. E., & Feldman, S. S. (1990). Academic achievement in preadolescence: The role of motivational, affective, and self-regulatory processes. *Journal of Applied Developmental Psychology, 11*(2), 179–193.

Werner, H., & Kaplan, B. (1952). The acquisition of word meanings: A developmental study. *Monographs of the Society for Research in Child Development, 15*(1, Serial No. 51).

West, K. L. (1981). Assessment and treatment of disturbed adolescents and their families: A clinical research perspective. In M. Lasky (Ed.), *Major psychopathology and the family*. New York: Grune & Stratton.

Wexler, K. (1982). On extensional learnability. *Cognition, 11*(1), 89–95.

White, B. L. (1971). *Human-infants: Experience and psychological development*. Englewood Cliffs, NJ: Prentice-Hall.

White, B. L., & Watts, J. C. (1973). *Experience and environment: Major influences on the development of the young child*. Englewood Cliffs, NJ: Prentice-Hall.

White, H. (1986). Damsels in distress: Dependency themes in fiction for children and adolescents. *Adolescence, 21*, 251–256.

White, R. W. (1959). Motivation reconsidered: The concept of competence. *Psychological Review, 66*, 297–333.

Whiting, H. T. (1969). *Acquiring ball skills: A psychological interpretation*. London: Prentice-Hall.

Wilcox, B. M. (1969). Visual preferences of human infants for representation of the human face. *Journal of Experimental Child Psychology, 7*, 10–20.

Will, J. A., Self, P. A., & Datan, N. (1976). Maternal behavior and perceived sex of infant. *American Journal of Orthopsychiatry, 46*(1), 135–139.

Williams, A. L., Uren, E. C., & Bretherton, L. (1984). Respiratory viruses and sudden infant death. *British Medical Journal, 288*, 1491–1493.

Williams, G. (1989). Lead paint alert. *Practical Homeowner, 4*(5), 24–26.

Williams, H. (1983). *Perceptual and motor development*. Englewood Cliffs, N.J: Prentice-Hall.

Williams, T. M. (Ed.) (1986). *The impact of television: A natural experiment in three communities*. New York: Academic Press.

Wimmer, H., Gruber, S., & Perner, J. (1984). Young children's conceptions of lying: Lexical realism—moral subjectivism. *Journal of Experimental Child Psychology, 37*, 1–30.

Winick, M. (1974). Childhood obesity. *Nutrition Today, 9*, 6–12.

———. (1976). *Malnutrition and brain development*. New York: Oxford University Press.

Winick, M., Meyer, K. K., & Harris, A. C. (1975). Malnutrition and environmental enrichment by early adoption. *Science, 190*, 1173–1175.

Winitz, H., & Irwin, O. (1958). Syllabic and phonetic structure of infants' early words. *Journal of Speech and Hearing Research, 1*, 250–256.

Wirtz, P. (1987). *Intense employment while in high school*. Washington, DC: George Washington University Graduate Institute for Policy Education and Research Working Paper.

Wittgenstein, L. (1963). *Philosophical investigations*. Oxford: Blackwell.

Wolff, P. (1965). The development of attention in young infants. *Annals of the New York Academy of Sciences, 118*, 815–830.

———. (1966). The causes, controls, and organizations of behavior in the newborn. *Psychological Issues, 5*, 1–105.

———. (1969). The natural history of crying and other vocalizations in early infancy. In B. Foss (Ed.), *Determinants of infant behavior* (Vol. 4). London: Methuen.

Wolff, P. H. (1969). Observations of the early development of smiling. In B. M. Foss (Ed.), *Determinants of infant behavior* (Vol. II). London: Methuen.

Woolley, J. D., & Wellman, H. M. (1990). Young children's understanding of realities, nonrealities, and appearances. *Child Development, 61*, 946–961.

Wright, H. F. (1960). Observational child study. In P. H. Mussen (Ed.), *Handbook of research methods in child development*. New York: Wiley.

Wurtele, S., Currier, L., Gillispie, E., & Franklin, C. (1991). The efficiency of a parent-implemented program for teaching preschoolers personal safety skills. *Behavior Therapy, 22,* 69–83.

Wynne, E. A. (1979). Facts about the character of young Americans. *Character, 1,* 1–7.

Yaden, D. B., Smolkin, L. B., & Conlon, A. (1989). Preschoolers' questions about pictures, print convention, and story text during reading aloud at home. *Reading Research Quarterly, 24*(2), 188–214.

Yarrow, L. J., Rubenstein, J. L., & Pedersen, F. A. (1971, April). *Dimensions of early stimulation: Differential effects on infant development.* Paper presented at the Biennial Meeting of the Society for Research in Child Development, Minneapolis, MN.

———. (1975). *Infant and Environment: Early Cognitive and Motivational Development.* New York: Wiley.

Yarrow, M. R., Scott, P. M., & Waxler, C. Z. (1973). Learning concern for others. *Developmental Psychology, 8,* 240–260.

Yonnger, B. (1985). The segmentation of items into categories by 10-month-old infants. *Child Development, 56*(6), 1574–1583.

Yopp, H. K. (1988). The validity and reliability of phonmeic awareness tests. *Reading Research Quarterly, 23*(2), 159–177.

Young, W. C., Goy, R. W., & Phoenix, C. H. (1964). Hormones and sexual behavior. *Science, 143,* 212–218.

Youngblade, L., & Belsky, J. (1990). Social and emotional consequences of child maltreatment. In R. Hammerman & M. Hersen (Eds.), *Children at risk: An evaluation of factors contributing to child abuse and neglect.* New York: Plennum Press.

Youniss, J., & Smoller, J. (1985). *Adolescents' relations with mothers, fathers, and friends.* Chicago: University of Chicago Press.

Zakin, D. F., Blyth, D. A., & Simmons, R. G. (1984). Physical attractiveness as a mediator of the impact of early pubertal changes for girls. *Journal of Youth and Adolescence, 13,* 439–450.

Zani, B. (1991). Male and female patterns in the discovery of sexuality during adolescence. *Journal of Adolescence, 14,* 163–178.

Zern, D. S. (1984). Relationships among selected child-rearing variables in a cross-cultural sample of 110 societies. *Developmental Psychology, 20*(4), 683–690.

Zeskind, P. S., & Ramey, C. T. (1978). Fetal malnutrition: An experimental study of its consequences on infant development in two caregiving environments. *Child Development, 49,* 1155–1162.

Zigler, E. (1985). Assessing Head Start at 20: An invited commentary. *American Journal of Orthopsychiatry, 55*(4), 603–609.

Zill, N. (1983). *American children: Happy, healthy and insecure.* New York: Doubleday/Anchor Press.

Zimmerman, D. R. (1973). *Rh: The intimate history of a disease and its conquest.* New York: Macmillan.

Zucker, P. (1986). Interview with our new president. *American Anorexia/Bulimia Association, Inc., Newsletter, 9*(2), 3–4.

Zuckerman, B. S., & Dubey, J. C. (1985). Developmental approach to injury prevention. *Pediatric Clinics of North America, 32*(1), 17–29.

Zuckerman, B. S., Frank, D. A., Hingson, R., Amaro, H., Levenson, S. M., Kayne, H., Parker, S., Vinci, R., Aboagye, K., Fried, L. E., Cabral, H., Timperi, R., & Bauchner, H. (1989). Effects of maternal marijuana and cocaine use on fetal growth. *The New England Journal of Medicine, 320*(12), 762–768.

Zuckerman, B. S., & Hingson, R. (1986). Alcohol consumption during pregnancy: A critical review. *Developmental Medicine and Child Neurology, 28,* 649–661.

Zussman, R. (1980). Situational determinants of parental behavior. *Child Development, 51,* 792–800.

AUTHOR INDEX

NOTE: Dates in parentheses refer to multiple author studies.

SUBJECT INDEX

NOTE: Page numbers in *italics* refer to illustrations separated from accompanying text.

Preschoolers *(continued)*
 prosocial behavior by, 382, 383, 390–96
 reaction time improvement in, 314
 self-control in, 396–98
 seriation tasks and, 324–27
 sleep habits of, 423–24
 social/emotional development in, 369–404
 socialization of, 370, 371–84
 summary of changes in, 297
 theory of mind of, 332–37
 thinking about thinking by, 335–36
 TV watching by, 389
Preschools
 adult-child ratios in, 412
 aggression control in, 385–86
 appropriate practices for, 410–11
 differences in, 405–6
 funding alternatives for, 408–9
 prosocial behavior learning in, 390, 391
 socialization in, 372, 374
 teacher- vs. child-directed programs, 405–6, 409
Pretend play, 192–205
 appearance/reality distinction and, 336–37
 developmental stages of, 204, 205
 peer interaction in, 257
 by preschoolers, 427
 by school-age children, 555
Pretend vs. real. *See* Appearance vs. reality
Pretense. *See* Pretend play
Pretesting, 22
Primary rewards, in classical conditioning, 56
Primary sex characteristics, 569, 570, 571
Privileges, denial of,
 for aggression control, 387
 appropriate use of, 381
Probability tasks, 590
Problem solving
 infant attachment and, 252
 information-processing approach to, 594–96
 in sensorimotor stage, 188–93
Productive speech, 210
Progesterone, production of, 569
Project Head Start, 408, 412
Projection, *51*
Projective concept, writing and, 362
Prosocial behavior
 defined, 390
 development of, 253–55
 modeling of, 382
 by preschoolers, 382, 383, 390–96
 social cognition and, 383
Protowords, 211
Proverbs, age and response to, 606–7
Proximodistal development, 165
Pseudoimitation, 194–95, 199
Psychoanalytical theory, 49–52
 on attachment, 231–32
 research orientation and, 67
Psychological problems
 suicide and, 644–46
Psychosexual vs. psychosocial theory, 53
Puberty
 impact of, 440, 561, 563–65
 onset of, 440
 timing of, 571–79

Pubescence, 565
Pubescent growth spurt, 565–67
Public Broadcasting System (PBS), 428
Punishment
 aggression and, 386–90
 defined, 376
 physical, disadvantages of, 378–81, 386–90
 prosocial behavior and, 390–91
 response costs, 376
 sex differences in, 531–33
 sex-typing by, 531–33
 socialization by, 376, 378–81
Push toys, 292

Quinine, as teratogen, 104

Race, IQ tests and, 463
Rational-altruistic parenting, 641
Rationality, in school-age children, 540–41
RDS (Respiratory distress syndrome), 139
Reaction formation, *51*
Reaction time, development of, 314
Readiness, in maturational theory, 48
Readiness tests
 curriculum influenced by, 424–25
 for kindergarten, 416
 validity of, 418–19
Reading
 achievement tests, 548
 in adolescence, 606–7, 666, 667
 children's storybook, 364
 emergent, 350. *See also* Emergent literacy
 language development and, *214*, 215, 218–20
 look-say approach to, 494
 phonics approach to, 493
 skills approach to, 493
 Verbal Interaction Stimulus Materials, 271
 whole language approaches to, 493, 494–95
 writing and, 491–92
Reading problems, approaches to, 493–94
Reading Rainbow, 428, 666
Realist approach to knowledge, 600
Receptive speech, 210
Recessive genes. *See* Genes
Redirection, for aggression control, 387
Reflexes, 127
 neonatal assessment tools, 143, 144
 of neonates, *126*, 127–29
 in sensorimotor stage, 188, 199
Reflexive behavior, of neonates, *126*, 127–29
Regression toward the mean, in IQ, 464
Reinforcement
 aggression and, 385–86
 attachment and, 232, 234
 in behaviorism, 57
 with classical conditioning, 56
 defined, 375
 intrinsic, 386
 in language development, 221, 223–25
 modeling and, 382

positive vs. negative, 57–58
 for prosocial behavior, 390–91
 sex-typing by, 531–33
 socialization by, 375–76
 as toilet training approach, 287
Relational concepts, 332
Relativist approach to knowledge, 600
Relevance, ability to determine, 456–57, 612
Reliability, 18
Renzulli-Smith Early Childhood Checklist, 415
Repetition, in toddler social games, 256–57
Representation, symbolic, 199, 205
Representational thinking, emergence of, 198
Representative sample, 20–22
 longitudinal study and, 31
Repression, as defense mechanism, *51*
Reproduction
 cell division and conception, 76–77, 77–78
 multiple births, 79–80
 sex determination, 77–78
Research
 See also Theory
 as critical thinking, 14
 major methods of, 24–30. *See also* Methodology
 sex difference studies, 527–29
Researcher bias, 20
Respiration, in neonates, 124
Respiratory problems, as prematurity risk, 139–40
Response cost, 376
 minimizing, 387
Responsibility
 adolescent sexuality and, 629
 parenting style and, 543
"Restricted affect," attachment and, 241
Retarded growth, in school-age children, 441. *See also* Developmental delays; Mental retardation
Retrolental fibroplasia (RLF) blindness, 140
Reversals, in early writing, 359
Reversibility, conservation of number by, 320, 452
Rewards, in classical conditioning, 56
Rh incompatibility, 99
 neonatal jaundice and, 125
Rhyming, preschool test of, 416, 417
Riddles, by school-age children, 482, 484–86
Risk-taking behavior, accidental death and, 664–665
Rites of passage, 564, *565*
RLF (retrolental fibroplasia) blindness, 140
Role confusion, ego identity vs., 622–23
Role-taking, stages of, 511–12. *See also* Social role-taking ability
Roller skating, skills development in, 307
Rooming-in, 96, 98
Rooting reflex, *126*, 127, *128*
Rotter, Julian, as social learning theorist, 58
Rubella (German measles), prenatal problems from, 102, *104*, 105
Running skills development, 303–5, 308